SOCIAL WORK PRACTICE

THEORIES AND SKILLS

Vimala Pillari

Dominican University

Allyn and Bacon
Boston   London   Toronto   Sydney   Tokyo   Singapore

Series Editor, Social Work and Family Therapy: Patricia Quinlin
Editor-in-Chief, Social Sciences: Karen Hanson
Series Editorial Assistant: Annemarie Kennedy
Editorial-Production Service: Omegatype Typography, Inc.
Composition and Prepress Buyer: Linda Cox
Manufacturing Buyer: Suzanne Lareau
Cover Administrator: Linda Knowles
Electronic Composition: Omegatype Typography, Inc.

Library of Congress Cataloging-in-Publication Data

Pillari, Vimala.
    Social work practice : theories and skills / Vimala Pillari.
       p.   cm.
    Includes bibliographical references and index.
    ISBN 0-205-26486-7
      1. Social service.   2. Social case work.   I. Title.
    HV40 .P54 2002
    361.3'2—dc21   2001018901

Printed in the United States of America

10 9 8 7 6 5 4 3 2 1   06 05 04 03 02 01

Dedicated to Kapil,
a prince and a gentleman

CONTENTS

PART TWO   THE CONTEXT OF HELPING   97

CHAPTER **5** INFLUENCE OF ENVIRONMENTS ON GENERALIST PRACTICE   97

CHAPTER **6** GENERALIST PRACTITIONER ROLES   117

CHAPTER 7 THE CLIENT   149

CHAPTER **8** COMMUNICATION AND INTERVIEWING   175

CHAPTER **9** THE PROFESSIONAL RELATIONSHIP   219

PART THREE THE PROCESS OF HELPING   251

CHAPTER 10 THE ENGAGEMENT PROCESS   251

CHAPTER **11** ASSESSMENT 286

CHAPTER 12 PLANNING 324

CHAPTER **13** INTERVENTION   337

CHAPTER 14 EVALUATION   379

CHAPTER **15** TERMINATION   400

PREFACE

The book is divided into three parts for easy understanding of generalist social work practice. Part One of *Social Work Practice* presents generic material that all social work students need to understand in order to become effective generalists. Chapter 1 presents the purpose and goals of social work practice within the *ecosystems perspective*. This conceptual framework gives students an opportunity to view diverse clients from a broad holistic perspective. Inherent in this perspective is the concept of strengthening and empowering clients. Clients of diverse racial and ethnic groups as well as gender issues are presented with appropriate examples in order to help students view differences with sensitivity and understanding. Chapter 2 interprets the values and ethics of the profession and the ethical dilemmas that beginning practitioners may face with clients. This chapter also provides diverse client examples. Chapter 3 highlights the knowledge base of social work practice with an emphasis on critical thinking. Chapter 4 discusses the functions of social work, the basic skills of helping, and accountability. Thus Part One prepares the students with a conceptual framework, values, knowledge, and skills to begin their role as a generalist practitioner.

Part Two deals with the basic working knowledge and understanding of environments, roles, and communication that a student needs to understand and apply as a generalist. Chapter 5 includes understanding how both physical and social environments affect and influence people, and vice versa. Generalist practitioners need to have an awareness of environments in order to be effective in their different roles. Chapter 6 presents the different roles of the generalist—from counselor to advocate—as well as other issues and special concerns of a beginning practitioner. Chapter 7 illustrates the rights of clients. It also explores their different roles and some of the factors that affect the emotional, social, and physical behaviors of diverse clients. Chapter 8 discusses communication patterns, cultural and gender factors in communication, the interviewing process, and how these relate to the skills of helping. Chapter 9 emphasizes the importance of a professional relationship and factors that could affect such a relationship.

Part Three highlights the specific skills of helping different size systems such as individuals, families, groups, communities, and organizations in the generalist problem-solving process. Chapter 10 deals with the engagement phase in the helping process. Identifying problems through the process of exploration and moving toward negotiation with diverse clients is highlighted. Chapter 11 discusses the nature, content, and process of assessment, including the skills required to make an assessment. Factors that cause problems in making an assessment are presented. Chapter 12 focuses on the planning stage of the helping process, followed by Chapter 13 which comprehensively discusses the different types of intervention that are used with different client systems. Chapter 14 deals with the purpose and methods of evaluation. Chapter 15 concludes the text with a discussion of termination and its purpose and functions. Termination with different size systems and diverse clients is highlighted.

The terms *client, clients, clientele,* and *clients from different sized systems* have been used interchangeably throughout the book. Similarly, the terms *generalist, worker,* and *practitioner* are all used to refer to the social work professional. A number of diverse cases are presented in the book. At times, the client is an individual; at other times the client is a family, a group, an organization, or a community.

Finally an instructor's workbook will accompany the text book. The purpose of the workbook is to make classroom teaching exciting, thoughtful, interesting, and rewarding.

ACKNOWLEDGMENTS

It is with pleasure that I thank some colleagues and students who were an integral part of this book's development. My special thanks to Dr. Issac Alcabes for his unwaivering support and constructive criticism, to Margaret Manzella for her comments from a practitioner's perspective, and to a number of students, especially Laura Woodruff and Gloria Jensen, whose comments were valuable. Special thanks also to Judy Fifer for her guidance; to Alyssa Pratt, who was always there to support the process; and to Pat Quinlin and Karen Hanson, all from Allyn and Bacon.

I would also like to thank the following reviewers: Stephen Anderson, University of Oklahoma; Fred Avant, Stephen F. Austin State University; L. Rene Bergeron, University of New Hampshire; Jan Black, California State University—Long Beach; Ellie Brubaker, Miami University; Valerie Chang, Indiana University Purdue University Indianapolis; Barbara Coats, University of Illinois, Chicago; Valire Carr Copeland, University of Pittsburgh; Jeanette R. Davidson, Columbia University; Sally Goren, University of Illinois, Chicago; Judith I. Gray, Ball State University; Patricia Ann Guillory, Southern University at New Orleans; Lloyd Hawes, University of South Dakota; John Kayser, University of Denver; Robert C. Kersting, Westfield State College; Emma Quartaro, Seton Hall University; Glenda Dewberry Rooney, Augsburg College; Santos Torres, California State University; Francisco Villaruel, Michigan State University; and Joseph Walsh, Virginia Commonwealth University; Jan Wrenn, Andrews University.

GENERAL PERSPECTIVES ON HELPING

1

GENERAL PERSPECTIVES

Angela is standing at a bus stop in busy New York City. She is grieving over the loss of her husband who disappeared three months ago. Angela, the mother of three children, desperately looks for work, but does not find any. She uses up her savings to pay rent and take care of basic necessities. Within a month she runs out of money. The landlord of her apartment building is kind enough to let her stay for an extra month. Friends also help her as much as they can, but the few friends she has are not able to help for long. Angela is far away from her hometown in Oregon. At the end of the month, her landlord makes her vacate the apartment. Forced to the streets, Angela looks for any type of food to feed her hungry children, even from garbage cans. Angela and her children are joining the throngs of the new homeless.

Social workers are constantly made aware of the plight of the homeless, one of the most difficult human issues that confronts their profession. Social work started as charity giving, but through the years it developed a new sophistication battling old and new issues in society and working within the framework of persons-in-environment.

Another case illustrates the multifaceted aspects of homelessness and the complexity of social problems that fall within the broad context of social work. A frail woman walks the streets of New York, making her way between parked cars, helplessly jostled by busy people as they rush past her. Like a walking musty closet, the "bag lady" has adorned her thin body with all the clothes she can wear. She grumbles as she adjusts her bag. She is desperately hungry for she has not eaten in two days; another homeless person beat her to the garbage cans. She discreetly asks a woman for some money, but the woman frowns at her and disappears into the crowd. The old lady has walked for hours and is now growing faint. Hunger pangs torture her. With great determination she walks toward a crowded restaurant. A man pushes past her to get a taxi; she loses her balance and falls to the ground. The impact is severe and she finds herself unable to get up from the crowded sidewalk. Everything turns hazy and dark as she closes her weary eyes.

The plight of the homeless is well publicized, but how much accurate information do we have on their numbers and condition? According to the U.S. Bureau of Census (1993) there were 178,828 homeless people in 11,000 shelters and 49,793 on the streets: 228,621 total on a given day. Other more current estimates put the total number at a million or more (Ginsberg, 1995, pp. 348–349; Slester & Miller, 1993, p. 135). The prevalent discrepancies in counts of the homeless hinge mostly on whether the count is of people homeless on one given day or people who were homeless any time in the past twelve months. Undercounts also appear because some of the homeless are "doubling up" for a night (sleeping on a friend's or relative's floor), or "hotbedding" (sleeping in shifts in the same beds), or are otherwise hard to find. A 1987 report (Rossi, Wright, Fisher, & Willis, 1987) on

the homeless confirms that they do not fit into a single mold. Some suffer from extreme poverty, high levels of mental and/or physical disability, and severe social isolation. Many suffer problems with health, drug abuse, and alcoholism. Some come from mental hospitals—the mentally ill abandoned by society in the name of deinstitutionalization. Others are the sudden and new poor who, with the loss of jobs, could not maintain their middle-class lifestyle. And then there are runaways—perhaps young men who wish to return home but are not welcome, or young women who fear their return home due to severe home conflicts. The picture is broad and often obscured by the number and complexity of homeless individuals' needs.

Homelessness is not a new problem. Over a century ago, Leo Tolstoy tried to puzzle out a plan to rid Moscow of the poor and the homeless. The famous Russian novelist and aristocrat found out that "of all the people I noted down, I really helped none. I did not find any unfortunates who could be made fortunate by a mere gift of money." Today, we face this frustrating problem halfway around the world in modern urbanized America— the richest land in the world. It is a blessing that at least some of us have stopped blaming the victim as we watch more communities experiment with homeless-aid programs.

How do these programs work? Some of them attempt to instill discipline and propriety in the homeless. These attempts could be of value if the programs offered genuine rehabilitative opportunities. However, as frequently happens to the poor and needy, some shelter operators provide austere accommodations and few social services. They believe homeless families, many headed by single mothers on welfare, will stay forever if shelters are too comfortable. Tragically, recent studies in New York City show the so-called bed-of-nails policy has backfired. Statistics indicate that despite their poor facilities these spartan shelters tend to attract the homeless for months and sometimes years on end.

Nowhere is the tragic lack of rehabilitative opportunities more evident than in New York City's infamous welfare hotels, which have a single case-worker for every sixty homeless families. Jean Chappell's tragic story is typical. She and her five young children were evicted in 1985 after she left her husband. Since then, she has shuttled in and out of shelters, ending up in 1986 at the Brookyln Arms Hotel, where she contracted pneumonia. Subsequently, she lost her job.

At this hotel, she and her young children quickly found out that they were more likely to encounter a detective looking for a drug dealer than a social worker. Jean's crowded, roach-infested room made self-sufficiency difficult. The walls of her room were so thin that sleep and conversations were constantly interrupted by sounds from the surrounding rooms. After a meal of canned food, the family was forced to washed dishes in the bathtub because there was no kitchen. For Jean, and thousands of other shelter residents who live on government assistance, the system does little more than prolong their homelessness. Ironically, the cost of shelter in these welfare hotels is greatly inflated and much higher than most people pay for adequate housing.

Today there are more attempts to make aid programs work by assisting the about-to-become homeless where they live. By helping to rebuild their support networks and stretch the safety net where the homeless live, communities are making attempts to prevent shelters from becoming revolving doors for the homeless and, most importantly, to preserve low-cost housing (Whitman, 1988).

Like the problem of homelessness, there are other social problems that are diverse and complex. Social workers are as capable as other professionals of damaging their clients if they are not well prepared to handle such problems as AIDS, teenage pregnancies, teenage school shootings and killings, and preteen and teen gang problems. Thus, it becomes the responsibility of all social workers to prepare themselves through professional education to give clients the highest quality of service possible.

MEANING OF SOCIAL WORK

In its basic form, social work practice can be described as a process wherein people with problems and unmet needs engage with social workers in receiving help that results in change (Sheafor, Horejsi, & Sheafor, 2000). This type of change includes individual change, as well as changes in families, groups, communities, and social organizations.

Numerous definitions of social work exist. For now, we will look at two. A widely accepted, classic definition of social work was put forth by Werner Boehm (1958):

> Social work seeks to enhance the social functioning of individuals, singularly and in groups, by activities focused upon their social relationships which constitute interaction between individuals and their environments. These activities can be grouped into three functions: restoration of impaired capacity, provision of individual and social resources, and prevention of social dysfunction. (p. 18)

The National Association of Social Workers (NASW, 1973), which is the professional social work organization, defines social work as "a professional activity of helping individuals, groups, and communities to enhance or restore their capacity for social functioning and to create societal conditions that are favorable to their goals" (pp. 4–5).

Based on these different definitions, social work has three major purposes:

1. To promote the problem-solving, coping, and developmental capacities of people
2. To enhance the effective and humane operation of the systems that provide people with resources and services
3. To help link people with systems that provide them with resources, services, and opportunities (Baer & Federico, 1978)

Figure 1.1 graphically depicts the major purposes of social work.

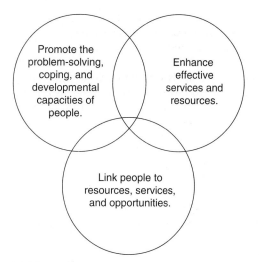

FIGURE 1.1   **Major Purposes of Social Work**

GENERALIST PRACTICE

As the profession of social work takes on new challenges, it also is evolving to suit the needs and purposes of present-day conditions. Today we view social work practice in generalist terms. As Mattaini (1993) notes, generalist social work is an organic whole and not simply an aggregation of distinct roles. Although social workers have to take on different roles, they recognize the coherence and flow among activities they perform as social workers as they work to address clients' needs. Performing different functions requires somewhat different skills, although we can use many skills at multiple levels. Finally, the generalist goal is to achieve a professional identity as a social worker who does what is necessary, in collaboration with clients, to address problems regardless of systemic level.

Thus attempts to develop a unified profession that addressed the society's need for practitioners able to work with a wide variety of issues led to generalist practice. A generalist practitioner may be asked to help a homeless family, a battered partner, an alcoholic parent, a lonely and sick elder, a group of people struggling with self-esteem issues,

a community that is overwhelmed with drug problems, or an agency that is falling apart due to lack of funding as it struggles to amend its rules and policies to conform to modified federal rules.

Generalist practice provides an integrated and multilevel approach to meeting the purposes and goals of social work. Generalist practitioners acknowledge the interplay of personal and collective issues prompting them to work with a variety of human systems including individuals, families, groups, communities, and organizations in order to create change that maximizes constructive human functioning. This means that generalist social workers work directly with client systems at all levels connecting clients to available resources, intervening with organizations to enhance the responsiveness of resource systems, advocating appropriate social policies to ensure equitable distribution of resources, and researching all aspects of social work (Miley, O'Melia, & DuBois, 1998). The multitude of levels and settings in which generalist social work practice occurs are shown in Figure 1.2.

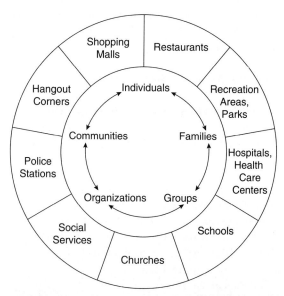

FIGURE 1.2   **Generalist Social Work Practice**

The Council on Social Work Education describes generalist social work practice in its Curriculum Policy Statement (1994) for the bachelor's degree in social work (B5.7) and the master's degree in social work (M5.7). According to the council, generalist practice is the application of an eclectic knowledge base, professional values, and a wide range of skills to target systems of any size in order to bring about change within the context of four primary processes:

1. Generalist practice involves working effectively within an organizational structure and doing so under supervision.
2. It requires that the social worker assume a number of professional roles.
3. The generalist has to apply critical thinking skills to the planned change process.
4. Generalist practice emphasizes empowerment of the client system.

Generalist social work practice can involve many types of problems, it is essential that social workers be well-prepared to address different kinds of issues and problems. In the following pages we will look at some of the problems that people face in different settings.

PEOPLE AND PROBLEMS

In addition to homelessness, there are many types of problems with which social workers deal that vary in size and magnitude. Let us look at a few diverse cases.

Alice, a fourteen-year-old girl, runs away from home because she is unhappy with her home situation. She is picked up by the State Police and sent back home. Alice and her parents are required to see a social worker to resolve their problems as mandated by the court.

Five-year-old Andy is caught stealing money from another child and is referred to the school social worker who invites the parents to be part of the process of helping Andy.

Alicia and Robert are receiving help from a private practitioner because of marital conflicts that range from financial issues to Robert's unfaithfulness.

The worker who heads an alcoholic treatment group helps group members become supportive of each other. Jessica, a member in this group, has an alcoholic father and is married to a man who is an alcoholic. In the group setting, discussion and self-revelation help Jessica to process her problems with the support of similar people, which helps her to understand that she is not alone.

A new three-generation refugee family comes for help to an agency in order to cope better with confusing cultural differences and to make use of available community resources.

A private welfare organization that has overspent its funding needs help in planning, raising funds, and proper utilization of its resources.

A generalist practitioner should be well prepared to address many different and difficult situations. In generalist practice we can help people in practically any setting including family health, justice, education, and work. In generalist practice, as Johnson (1995) indicates, the "social worker assesses the situation with the client and decides which system is the appropriate *unit of attention* or focus of work for the change effort" (p. 1, emphasis added).

Generalist social work practice focuses on the interface between systems with equal emphasis on the goals of social justice, humanizing systems, and improving the well-being of people. The initial level of generalist practice consists of five elements:

1. The generic foundation
2. A multilevel problem-solving methodology
3. A multiple theoretical orientation
4. A knowledge, value, and skill base that is transferable between and among diverse contexts and locations
5. An open assessment unconstricted by any particular theoretical approach (Schatz, Jenkins, & Shaefor, 1990, p. 223)

As Landon (1995) notes, there is an eclectic choice of theory with multimethod and multilevel approaches to offering help. How systems such as individuals, families, groups, communities, and organizations can be helped depends on how knowledge will be presented to social work students who should get a broad perspective of people and problems. The ecosystems perspective serves this purpose well and therefore will be used as a conceptual framework for this book.

In a clear analysis of the ecological systems theory in social work, Siporin (1980) indicates, that the ecosystems theory has enabled us to gain a broader perspective and a holistic and dynamic understanding of people and their sociocultural–physical milieu.

Also, the ecosystems perspective has been utilized as a superstructure that enables the combined and integrative use of different types of theories for different kinds of system functions (Siporin, 1985). The ecosystems perspective is a metatheory that offers social work practitioners and clinicians a way of thinking about and assessing the relatedness of people and their environments.

Using the ecosystems framework this book will present a general problem-solving method of intervening with different types of clients such as individuals, families, groups, communities, and organizations. Problem solving entails the four important concepts of values, knowledge, skills, and accountability. The target of change can be any size system and the stages of helping generally involve the influence of environments; diverse worker and client roles; communication and interviewing; the meaning and utilization of professional relationships; and step-by-step stages of helping different client groups. The latter includes how to engage clients in diverse settings, how to make an assessment, and how to plan, intervene, evaluate, and terminate.

Thus, as generalists, social workers learn a wide array of skills to prepare themselves to work with people who have personal problems as well as to work with broad issues that affect the community at large. What follows is a foundation for understanding the broad and all-encompassing ecosystems perspective as a conceptual framework.

ECOSYSTEMS PERSPECTIVE— THE CONCEPTUAL FRAMEWORK

Social work, by both traditional and practice definitions, is the profession that provides the formal knowledge, theoretical concepts, specific functional skills, and essential social values used to implement society's mandate to provide safe, effective, and constructive social services to individuals (micro level), families and groups (mezzo level), organizations and communities (macro level) that enhances social functioning and improves quality of life. However, everyone cannot be an expert on every aspect of helping. Armed in a broad sense with the knowledge of people and environments, a social worker is equipped with the basics to think and act as an effective practitioner. Social work cases are seldom narrowly defined, so the field of practice is open to an array of interventions (Meyer, 1983; Meyer & Mattaini, 1995). Thus, a social work professional needs training and expertise in a wide range of areas to handle life problems effectively.

The ecosystems perspective provides the social worker the synthesis that is required to work with different clientele and this framework is wedded to the person–environment "fit." To begin, it is important to understand the meaning of a system. A system is a set of elements that forms an orderly interrelated and functional whole. A system can contain any type of things as long as these things have some relationship to each other. For instance, a family is a system where members are related to each other and perform different functional roles. Other examples of systems include a social services department where different areas are connected, a large public corporation and a newly formed group. Depending on the situation, the major focus of attention may be on an individual, a family, a group, a community, an organization or some combination of these.

The ecosystems perspective, which is a combination of ecology and general systems theory, was developed to arrange, integrate, and systematize knowledge about the interrelationships of people with each other and with their environments. First, let us look at ecology, which deals with the study of complex reciprocal and adaptive transactions among organisms and their environments. Ecological awareness and congruence with one's world has theoretical underpinnings in ancient Eastern ideas in which all events and processes are interwoven, mutually influencing, and endlessly moving in a dynamic flow. Thus time itself is not linear and directional but is experienced as cycles of returning events and recurring patterns and relationships (Germain & Gitterman, 1996). Similarly, general systems theory was designed to specify the processes of transactions within and among systems.

How systems change and survive depends on their adaptability. Boulding (1978) describes this process by using the term *niche* to refer to the immediate environment: "Niches continually change. They may shrink or they may expand, and if they shrink too much, species that are well adapted to a particular niche will become extinct as the niche shrinks to zero" (p. 111).

Thus, the basic model for ecological thinking as identified by biologists refers to the adaptability of organisms and environment. In a social work example, Chauncey and his wife, Rachael, live in a home where all their basic needs are satisfied. This is the niche that nourishes their emotional and physical well-being. However, one day their home accidentally burns down and the couple is not able to recover a single item from the remains. For a long period of time, though they receive help which allows them to survive, they are disoriented, unhappy, and unable to function at their best because their immediate, familiar, comfortable environment—their niche—has been destroyed.

Ecologists are also interested in the linkages among systems and how change in one system may affect other organisms connected to the system. To describe the ecological processes, Handler (1970), a biologist, identified three major variables:

1. The arrangement and distribution of organisms in relation to time and space
2. The way in which energy flows
3. The roles of the organisms involved (p. 456)

These variables as they apply to social work will be discussed further, for they will play a major role in the assessment and intervention stages of diverse activities in which the social worker and the clientele participate (Greif & Lynch, 1983). The ecological setting becomes the natural milieu for the social worker to define and view the problem in a broad perspective. This perspective also offers the possibility of a field-wide framework applicable in all situations.

The social worker who thinks in ecological terms understands the need to assess the environment of a problem or issue, taking into consideration the indirect and direct influences on the client system in terms of ecological variables. These variables may range from intimate human relationships and helping organizations to the political atmosphere. For instance, the homeless New York woman mentioned earlier did not seem to have any intimate personal relationships; she wandered the streets and lived off the contents of garbage bins. In spite of the odds against her, she survived because the environment could provide her the basic goods for survival. However, when the economy of the city worsened and there were more homeless people on the streets looking for food, she faced a harsher environment. When she fainted on the busy street, helping professionals such as police and nurses had to be involved. If too many homeless people died or fainted on crowded roads, this would also affect the political climate and something drastic would have to be done. This problem would affect the terrain of the city and, in many ways, the country as well.

The terrain expands to include different systems as problems expand, illuminating the interrelatedness between people and environments. At times this relatedness is narrow in focus; for example, when family members deal with intimate issues. With intimate personal problems the family is the chief terrain, but the occupational and other significant terrains may be involved as well. At other times this relatedness expands, such as with a drug-infested community that needs massive cleanup operations involving individuals and community organizations working together.

Germain expanded on some of the variables that need to be considered by the ecologically trained social worker. In terms similar to Handler's, Germain wrote specifically about the ecological variables of time (1976) and space (1978), and the manner in which they impact the client. The way clients organize, use, and respond to time and the effects of spatial arrangements on the individual, family, or group also impact clients.

Because some ordering of multiple, transacting ecological variables is necessary, the ecosystems perspective combines ecology and general systems theory. General systems theory helps in the ordering and organizing of data, such as the structural relatedness of abstract concepts and propositions (Greif & Lynch, 1983). As Janchill (1969) points out "system theory is not itself a body of knowledge; it is a way of thinking and analysis that accommodates knowledge from many sciences" (p. 77).

The historical roots of general systems theory reach back to the 1920s and are attributed to the work of biologist Ludwig Von Bertalantfy. Von Bertalantfy (1967) observed that a system is a "set of elements standing in interaction" (p. 115). These elements exist in both open and closed systems. The fundamental difference between the two systems is the transaction with the environment. A closed system in the social work arena could be a family services agency that does not receive new ideas, clients, or funding from which it can draw energy. If this state of affairs were to continue, the agency would stagnate and eventually close. As Greif and Lynch (1983) indicate, there are six basic concepts in general systems theory that are applicable to open systems. Besides these, there are twelve principles that explain a system's internal operations as well as its relationship with the external environment. The basic concepts that refer to open systems are boundaries, structure, hierarchy, transactionality, frame of reference, and time.

(See Figure 1.3) The section that follows explains these terms; a case study then illustrates the basic concepts.

BOUNDARIES   A system has its own spatial or dynamic boundaries and, in some form, is separate from the rest of the environment. The system has its own identity. Some systems have boundaries that are more permeable than others. A system is called open or closed depending on boundary permeability, that is, how information and energy flow.

STRUCTURE OF A SYSTEM   Structure refers to the set of elements within a system's boundaries and the enduring patterns that are present in the relationship of these elements. While energy exchange takes place, the system continues to maintain a sameness with its structural characteristics. For instance, relationships between students and teachers exhibit the enduring pattern of educational authority of the teacher over the student based on knowledge.

HIERARCHY   A hierarchical relationship exists within systems that are nested within other systems and also have subsystems within themselves. For instance, a family is a small system embedded in a community, which is a large system. The family must follow the broad rules of the community and the society, an even larger system. The family system has subsystems within it, such as the mother–father subsystem, the sibling subsystem, and the parent–child and children subsystem. In a family system, children living at home follow the rules and regulations set by parents. Older siblings have more power than the younger ones in the family. Thus subsystems also have hierarchical rules and regulations that they follow.

TRANSACTIONALITY   To understand the influence of the multiple elements inherent in every situation, we need to look at the case in transactional terms to comprehend the influences that literally cross over the system (individual, family, group,

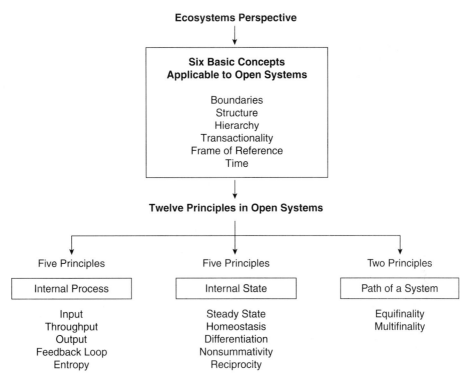

FIGURE 1.3   **Ecosystems Perspective—Overview**

organization, or community). A transaction suggests multidimensional interactions and influences all in interplay with each other (Germain & Gitterman, 1996). This transaction takes place not only with other systems but also within the hierarchy of subsystems. For example, a father who is angry with his boss, and brings that anger home, has a ripple effect on different family members.

FRAME OF REFERENCE   Frame of reference informs the observer of what is being studied—a family, a person, an institution, or a community. This concept is needed to establish the nature of the system.

TIME   Every system exists within a time dimension that consists of a past, a present, and a future. Depending on how a system is involved with other systems, the future is viewed in terms of the system's potential.

These six concepts define any living system in a manner that differentiates it from other systems.

Sixteen-year-old Tina has four brothers. She has her own *boundaries* that make her different from others. Tina's family has boundaries as well, which make it a discrete system from other family systems. There are boundaries between parents and children that set rules of behavior in the family. The *structure* of this family includes all people in the family system and how they interact with each other; the interactions between family members can be warm and open, or they can be distant and indifferent, or a combination of two at different times, depending on life circumstances of the family. The hierarchial position in the family refers to the varying roles and status that individual members have in the family. *Hierarchy* means that family members are ranked in terms of age, position, and status in the family. For instance, Tina is the oldest child and has more power than her youngest sister, three-year-old Sheila. The parents are in control of the children and are at a higher level hierarchically. Some members have more power than others with reference to certain family issues. For instance, a seventeen-year-old has more outside privileges than his three-year-old sister. This relationship also affects the hierarchical system. The *transactions* that take place in this family happen in different ways. Each family member interacts with another and with people outside of the family such as neighbors in the community and coworkers at a job, and so forth. All these transactions affect and are affected by the different types of relationships that people have with each other. The *frame of reference* indicates to the observer that the unit of attention or area of interest is the family rather than any single family member. All families exist in *time*. Thus each family has its own past, present, and future made up of landmarks, dates, and transitional situations. The manner in which the family responds to its present determines how it will respond to the future.

In addition to these basic concepts, the first five principles in general systems theory are related to *internal processes*. They explain the manner in which interactions take place between different subsystems. They are input, throughput, output, feedback loop and entropy. Following an explanation of these terms, a case study illustrates the use of the different principles.

Input is the way a system takes energy, matter, and information from the outside environment. *Throughput* means that once input is accepted into the system, this input is acted on, transformed, coded, and used for the functioning of the system. *Output* is the response of the system. Output has a direct effect on the environment and acts as both input to other systems and as input to the original system through the feedback loops. *Feedback loops* consist of positive information that acts to maintain a system's equilibrium or negative feedback which disrupts the system, promoting change (Von Bertalantfy, 1967). Thus *positive feedback* says that a system is fol-

lowing a steady course to its goals, whereas *negative feedback* says that the system needs correction because it has deviated from its course. In real life, both positive and negative feedback are necessary to bring about growth and change.

Entropy occurs when a system begins to deviate too far from its course and does not experience any corrections. If a system has no energy input from the outside and no exchange, it will wind down and run out of its own energy (Von Bertalantfy, 1967). An example of the entropic process is found in a community during a hurricane warning. The community stores up enough food for a week or more, rather than going to look for food during or immediately after a hurricane. The community system tries to maximize the input–output ratio, or in this case, to store and use food sparingly, so that the community members have enough energy to maintain themselves. In other words, their eating habits are in tune with outside circumstances to guard against the system's depletion of energy. If a serious hurricane were to devastate the area, the successful storage and use of food would provide the community available energy to result in healthy maintenance of the system. This scenario represents *negative entropy* and counteracts entropy.

The Adams family is always on the move, because the father is transferred frequently in his job. Their last move was from a small town in Virginia to Los Angeles, California. The Adams family needs sufficient information, or input, to fit into the new community. The manner in which this information is processed—called throughput—depends on the clarity of the information and the types of support that are available for the Adams family in the neighborhood. The family members process information uniquely, based on their own historical and cultural upbringing in a small town. After a period of four months, Mr. Adams loses his job when his company lays off a number of employees due to financial difficulties. Caught in a strange environment with very little money and separated from family and friends, Mrs. Adams starts to panic. Mr. Adams goes out every day looking unsuccessfully for a job and brings feedback to his family that paints a terrible picture of the outside world. The children have made friends with the neighbors and bring back a different kind of feedback. Based on the internal processing of these mixed experiences, individual family members may feel and behave differently in their transactions with the outside world (output).

Negative feedback—a correction in perception—might operate so that Mr. Adams would be less depressed in his job hunting and Mrs. Adams more cautious in the manner in which she spends money. The children, functioning mostly in their own world of friends, are having a good time. Some of these friends are drug users, but it has not affected the family at the moment. To the extent that the father, mother, and children remain connected to their personally defined external environments and bring back to the family their impressions and experiences, which in the long run affect each of them, the family system will remain open in a state of negative entropy. If this family were to withdraw and bring in no new experiences, it would suffer entropy and wind down. When a family starts to disintegrate due to money or drug problems, it is still in a state of entropy.

The internal state of a system is also determined by five principles. They are steady state, homeostasis, differentiation, nonsummativity and reciprocity. A case illustration that incorporates these terms follows explanations of the terms.

With input of energy and a continual growth process that includes throughput and feedback, the system maintains itself in a *steady state*. The system uses the energy to maintain itself while helping to adapt to inconsistencies in the environment.

Homeostasis, which is also called balance, and equilibrium are also used to define the maintenance of a system at a recognizable level. In order to maintain homeostasis, the system needs the ability to negotiate successfully with the environment for sustenance. For instance, when the mother in a traditionally structured family is an alcoholic, a dysfunctional life pattern emerges in which the father and children have adjusted in terms of housework division. The father cooks, cleans, and sends the children to school; when the children return home, they watch television and eat cookies to satisfy their hunger until the father comes home and cooks dinner. The mother is seen as not being available to the family. This has become an accepted way of life and the family is in

a state of homeostasis. Perhaps when the children reach adolescence there may be attempts to rebalance the family with the mother getting help for her alcoholism, which in turn would affect the homeostasis of the family.

Differentiation is the tendency of a system to increase in order and complexity over time (Von Bertalantfy, 1967). For example, growing older normally indicates acquisition of more knowledge and life experiences; thus people become highly differentiated.

Nonsummativity is the result of increased differentiation (Keeney, 1979). This concept asserts that data collected from isolated parts of a system cannot be added up to represent the whole system. For example, when a university increases its size from 5,000 students to 25,000 students, the central administration has to decentralize administrative authority for the institution to be effective as a whole because of the varied functions of the new and recently expanded departments.

Reciprocity is the process of interrelatedness of elements. When change occurs in one part of the system, it affects the whole system. For example, when one family member has a life transition such as the loss of a job or a pregnancy, the whole family is affected.

The principles that explain the internal processes of a system can be observed in the Adams family. Because the family is in a new environment and the father has lost his job, the family is experiencing considerable stress. This situation affects the equilibrium or homeostasis of the family.

Let's look at fourteen-year-old Rowena Adams. Her parents recently found drugs hidden under her bed. Rowena has started to experiment with drugs so she can be part of her peer crowd in Los Angeles. The rural, Christian, patriarchal family background produces a unique kind of a cultural response to drug use. Rowena is told that she will go to hell for using drugs and is punished severely, losing all privileges for a month. When she rebels as a reaction to her punishment, this upsets the family's homeostasis or equilibrium for a few days. However, because this family is very traditional, the essential paternal hierarchy is maintained and the family, through its traditional balancing efforts, persists in a steady state.

As different external events are assimilated by the family members, the emerging qualities of differentiation appear. After two months, Mr. Adams finds a job that helps him make new social contacts as well as build up his self-esteem. The children develop acceptable new interests outside the home. The children also seek and adopt new ways of behavior and seek new social experiences compatible with the family's values.

The differentiation process further individualizes each family member's behavior. The father has become outgoing, the mother is learning to feel more comfortable in her new surroundings, and the children are rapidly adapting to a new and different culture from the one they were used to in the hills of rural Virginia. The quality of the increasing differentiation of the Adams family is non-summative. We cannot add one family member's experience to another to explain family behavior. However, the principle of reciprocity shows that even with individual growth and changes in different family members, they are still a family because they are structurally and systemically related, interacting, and growing because they change in their responses to each other. As Mr. Adams becomes more outgoing with the passage of time, Mrs. Adams, who is close to her family in West Virginia, becomes more "tied" to her Southern ways. Rowena follows her father and becomes more acculturated to Los Angeles, whereas another child follows the mother's lead and continues to be traditionally Southern in her ways. The point is that all these behavior patterns have reciprocal consequences for all the family members.

The last two principles that affect a system—equifinality and multifinality—deal with the path or trajectory of a system. *Equifinality* suggests that a system can reach the same final state from a variety of different paths and different initial conditions. A rich or poor person, irrespective of where he or she is born, is influenced in innumerable ways by different personal and environmental factors, but moves toward the same goal of going to college and becoming more educated.

Multifinality says that similar conditions may lead to dissimilar ends. This is the converse of equifinality and indicates that diverse final states can be reached from the same starting conditions. For example, there are three sons in a family whose parents rear them to value hard work and education. However, each one of the adult children turn out differently. One child becomes a lawyer, another a traveling salesman, and the youngest becomes a drug dealer. Although they are from the same family with similar role models, each one picks a different path to reach his goals in life.

If the Adams family, transplanted from rural Virginia to Los Angeles, had sought or been referred for social work help, the goal would probably have been to help the family maintain its structure as a family and a steady state over time. A practitioner utilizing the principle of equifinality might have helped the family review a whole range of options to reach the goal of reestablished family balance. The different ways of achieving this might have included any of the following activities. The mother might visit her children in school so that she could be exposed to other parents and understand the differences between a rural and an urban school system. The father's competence in living could be utilized to help his wife adjust and adapt. The children, who are more outgoing and have healthier relationships, including no drug use, outside of the home could be helped not to feel guilty about abandoning their mother. Family treatment could help to sort out the issues and mixed communications that are causing the family's balance to be upset. In this situation, equifinality would be operative because all of the interventions are derived from different locations in the system. Given the reciprocity that is present among different family members, each could contribute to the agreed-upon goal of improved family balance.

Multifinality could occur if, for instance, Rowena became pregnant out of wedlock. This event would upset the family in many ways. Because the family was originally culturally bound, rurally and religiously, it would be easy for the father to blame himself for accepting and becoming part of the urban culture. The mother, in turn, might withdraw and attempt to close the family to outside influences. The younger children might perceive their environment as threatening and refuse to go to school. These multiple ripple effects could, if attention were not paid to them, drive the family toward closure and entropy.

Suppose the Adams family sought upward mobility that could be achieved through a number of ways (equifinality). An event like a promotion at the workplace in which Mr. Adams becomes the executive manager of a large successful computer company gives his children and wife opportunities to fulfill their own dreams. For instance, Mrs. Adams goes back to school to get her master's degree, the youngest child is admitted to a elite private school, and the older children go to different expensive private schools. Thus there are multifinality consequences among family members, all of which would contribute to the goal of upward mobility.

The case studies also indicate how information and energy flow into a system and determine how open or closed a system can be.

The ecosystems perspective, which is utilized as a conceptual framework in this text, gives the social work practitioner the capacity for a better and expanded understanding of the social environment in which all human beings exist. When viewing people as individuals, families, groups, organizations, or communities in their ecological milieu, it is possible to assess their strengths and weaknesses in their own physical, psychological, and social contexts through the type of interactions that take place between people and those environments. Finally, it can safely be said that the ecosystems perspective is unique in that it furnishes a framework for the social worker to use different theories of human behavior and differential practice models without being tied to any specific intervention, skills, method, or knowledge (Meyer, 1983).

In addition to the ecosystems perspective, the practitioner can use the strengths and empowerment perspectives as well, as they fit within the person–environment ecosystems arrangement. Highlighting strengths and working with clients to bring out their potentials and empower them should lead to effective intervention. Many programs highlight empowerment including programs such as the Independent Living Model (Deegan, 1992), self-help groups (Silverman, Segal, & Anello, 1992), the Case Management Model developed by Rapp (Kishardt & Rapp, 1992), the Advocacy/Empowerment Model (Rose, 1992), and the Partnership Model (Shera, 1993).

The empowerment perspective recognizes that belonging to a disempowered group can have personal as well as social costs (Gutierrez, Parsons, & Cox, 1998). Direct and indirect power blocks are the primary social mechanisms that restrict people from access to material resources. Direct power blocks affect people in concrete ways such as inadequate health services for the poor. Indirect power blocks include a lack of resources coupled with social values that support structures of inequality. Indirect power blocks lead to further negative valuation and stigma to members of oppressed groups.

In the empowerment perspective, power is present at three different levels:

1. *Personal*—feeling and perceptions regarding the capacity to influence and resolve one's own problems
2. *Interpersonal*—experiences with others to facilitate problem resolution
3. *Environmental*—assumes that societal institutions can facilitate or thwart self-help efforts (Gutierrez, 1994; Pinderhughes, 1989; Solomon, 1976)

The empowerment practice perspective uses the ecosystems perspective to help generalists understand multilevel interventions (Simon, 1994). For instance, when working with communities important factors that need to be considered include being able to understand and serve a community through facilitation and participation. Whether differences involve race, ethnicity, class, or women's issues, generalist recognize and embrace the conflict that characterizes cross-cultural work. More importantly, the social worker must recognize and build on ways in which specific groups of people have worked effectively with their own communities, build on existing structures, involve community members in leadership roles, and understand and support the need for such communities to have their own separate programs and organizations (Gutierrez & Lewis, 1999).

In order to work effectively with different types of client groups and use appropriate interventions, it is necessary to be a critical thinker. All practitioners should be able to use critical thinking in order to make effective evaluations. Critical thinking will be discussed in greater detail in Chapter 4 in the discussion of knowledge. To help any type of clientele, it is important that we think in clear terms about what we are trying to improve. Critical thinking is a rich concept that has been developed from the work of many people.

A recognized authority on critical thinking, Ennis (1987) has provided the practical definition of critical thinking. According to him, "critical thinking is reasonable, reflective thinking that is focused on deciding what to believe or do" (p. 9). When critical thinking is practical, it helps a person decide what to believe or do on a wide range of questions from personal to effective career decisions.

In order to use critical thinking a person must carefully examine the evidence in a particular situation, including the claims of all those involved, before drawing a conclusion. As Halpern (1996) indicates, the term *critical* describes thinking that emphasizes evaluation of evidence of some kind; for example, evaluating a home situation before deciding whether a child should be removed for negligence or abuse and poor hygiene. However, *critical* is not meant in a negative sense. Kuhn (1993) claims that critical thinking and scientific thinking both involve the coordination of theory and evidence and Lipman (1991) denotes that critical thinking involves a refinement of thinking. A working definition of critical thinking involves the evaluation of evidence relevant to a claim so that a sound conclusion can be drawn. In order to be a critical thinker we must know how to use our reasoning.

A disposition to think critically is the tendency to use critical thinking skills in approaching a situation or question (Bensley, 1998). Throughout this text there will be presentations of case studies in which reasoning skills must be used to understand why a particular way of helping is better than another or whether to believe a person who uses the "revolving door" to constantly receive help. For this purpose one must be disposed to use knowledge and skills. When confronted with a case situation, relevant knowledge should be used to analyze actual person–environment situations.

As the intake worker in a residential treatment center for adolescent sexual offenders, you meet Solomon and his mother who has arrived to admit him into the court-mandated treatment. Thirteen-year-old Solomon has sexually molested his six-year-old sister and his eight-year-old cousin. Solomon has a history of sexual abuse and experienced severe beatings until age nine. His mother, a single parent, attempting to make both ends meet, is struggling with her own feelings of shame, guilt, and powerlessness as she attempts to do the "right thing" by both her children.

Critically analyze the case and decide how to help the mother, the son, and the family as a whole.

SENSITIVE PRACTICE WITH DIVERSE CLIENTS

Social work is one of the professions constantly called upon to work with different types of clients from different socioeconomic backgrounds. Clients differ in age, gender, health, ethnic group, race, education, occupation, sexual preference, physical attractiveness, physical and mental abilities, intellectual and verbal abilities, behavior, and so forth. As we are aware, the United States is becoming increasingly multicultural with a variety of cultures that add to our richness and differences. Furthermore, people live their lives as part of different multicultural entities of all sizes from families to social classes to ethnic and religious groups. A great deal of sensitivity is required to be aware not only of differences in groups, but also that the lives of unique individuals may reveal different levels of biculturalism and acculturation. As Thyer (1994) indicates, it is paradoxical that although a deep awareness of differences sensitizes the generalist, the crux of culturally sensitive practice is to be able to individualize a case without being influenced by categories and labels.

Ethnic and Racially Sensitive Practice

Discrimination and oppression are closely connected to historical racism in our society. Discrimination is based on prejudice, which is an unjustified negative attitude toward an individual based solely on that individual's membership in a group (Worchel, Cooper, & Goethals, 1988). Prejudice is a distorted view that results from preconceived and stereotypical thinking which provides psychological permission to behave in a way that discriminates against differences perceived in others (Hogan-Garcia, 1999). Oppression, as the term implies, is placing restrictions, extreme limitations, and constraints on a group of people or an institution (Barker, 1995). Often stereotypes are based on some attribute or attributes that present an oversimplified view of a group of individuals. Let us look at a few such instances.

An African American millionaire moves into an exclusive white neighborhood. Among other things, he owns horses. When he goes to the stable in the morning, one of the young Anglo men who is working with the horses mistakes him for a stable boy and is filled with aversion when he realizes that the owner is African American. The millionaire constantly faces such situations in the neighborhood as he is mistaken for a waiter, a chauffeur, and so forth. The discrimination and stereotypical thinking present in a number of people in the United States is also evident when a lesbian couple displaying physical affection toward each other in a heterosexual club are verbally harassed or when a woman in her fifties goes to a club where almost all the members are about thirty years of age and rude comments are made to her and about her.

It is clear that people face differential environmental circumstance due to their backgrounds. Although it is practically impossible for social workers as generalists to be aware of all the cultural or differences in people, it is a good idea for social workers to politely and sensitively ask questions about the people with whom they work. It is not only ignorance about other cultures that causes us to offer ineffective services, it is also the attitudes that we carry with us. With a sensitive and positive attitude, it is quite possible to ask questions about behaviors, customs, and traditions that we do not know or understand. A genuine, caring, and sensitive attitude will help generalists create effective working relationships with different types of clients. Working with dif-

ferences is an important aspect of being a generalist and a social worker.

A perspective that will be used throughout this text is called affirmative diversity. Jones (1990) describes affirmative diversity as the affirmation of the fundamental value of human diversity in society, with the belief that enhancing diversity increases rather than diminishes quality. This perspective will be used to strengthen the cultural pluralism perspective of this book. The cultural pluralism perspective places a positive emphasis on cultural distinctness of racial and ethnic groups from the structure, values, norms, and attitudes present in the dominant culture. Within this cultural pluralism perspective, everyone has a culture, a race, a gender, a sexual orientation, physical abilities and disabilities, and a place in the social order. This perspective supports the value of understanding diversity and explicitly focuses on people in their own contexts (Trickett, Watts, & Birman, 1993). Diversity cases will be presented in different chapters of this book.

Disability Sensitive Practice

People with physical and emotional disabilities comprise another group of people who are stereotyped and discriminated against both overtly and covertly. People with disabilities often are portrayed as perpetual children (Mackelprang & Salsgiver, 1999). Included in the stereotyping of the disabled, is the perceptions that they are incompetent. As Mackelprang (1986) reports:

> [In rehabilitation] they really blew it. They told me when to get up, when to go to bed, when and what to eat. They told me when to take my medications and didn't always bother to tell me why I was taking them. I had to go to therapy at 9:00 A.M. It didn't matter that I've always been a late sleeper. They even told me when I could or couldn't take a crap. Then after three months of this, I was told that I was ready to go home and live completely independently. Hell, what a joke. (p. 43)

A constructive way of working with people with disabilities involves combining the strengths and empowerment perspectives under the umbrella of the ecosystems framework of looking at different systems and the environment. This will be presented in different chapters.

Sensitive Practice with Gays and Lesbians

Gochros, Gochros, and Fischer (1986) distinguish several components of sexual identity: *biological sex* relates to genetics and anatomical features that highlight male or female primary and secondary sexual characteristics; *gender identity* involves subjective feelings about being male or female in society, that is, taking on typically masculine and feminine roles and behaviors; and *erotic preference* refers to a person's attraction to same-sex or different-sex partners. Regardless of their erotic preferences, people are likely to embrace a gender identity that is congruent with their biological sex.

In recent times we have seen hate crimes against gays and lesbians based on homophobia, which is a negative irrational fear and emotional reaction to homosexuality that manifests itself in contempt and malice. As Markowitz (1991) notes:

> Ignorance, insensitivity, stereotyped thinking, outright prejudice, discrimination and a host of negative attitudes all can be loosely grouped under the umbrella of homophobia. At its most blatant, homophobia takes the form of outrage against gays-lesbians which enable someone to feel justified in striking out against those they consider traitors to the natural order of human relationships. (pp. 29–31)

Homophobia has complex implications for the delivery of services in the helping process. Generalists should, as Oliver and Brown (1987) point out,

> become aware of themselves, their biases, and their uniqueness if they are to become more accepting of values and lifestyles that differ from their own. Only with such awareness will they feel comfortable being affirmatively active in securing resources for all of their clients, heterosexual, bisexual or homosexual. (p. xii)

Many gays and lesbians go through the process of coming out, which involves recognizing and accepting their homosexual identity and publicly revealing their identity to their nongay family members, friends, and colleagues. When gays and lesbians approach a generalist for help, the generalist should be able to help them sort out their feelings and consider how to deal with the process of coming out. As Booth (1990) explains:

> We must understand that coming to accept one's "difference" with respect to sexual orientation is not an easy process. People will come to us confused about these issues and if we fail to detect the cues, we cannot assist them. We must try to comprehend the difficulties inherent in being a homosexual in a heterosexual society. This involves the perceived need to hide one's partner and one's very identity, for example, as well as learning how to deal with those who are intolerant of these kinds of differences. (pp. 12–13)

Generalists need to view the issues from an ecosystems perspective, keeping the social context of everyday life in mind.

Gender Sensitive Practice

Sexism in society can be described as the belief that one sex is superior to the other based on the deeply ingrained characteristics of sexual inequality rooted in the social order of life (Robertson, 1987). Sexism is generally seen in prejudicial attitudes and discriminatory actions against females, thus giving gender privilege to men. Institutionalized sexism is prevalent in most families as well as in the economic, political, welfare, and religious structures of society (Day, 1989). Sexism has its roots in our male and female role socialization by which sexist attitudes and practices favor men and prefer masculine traits and behavior to feminine traits and behaviors. Our patriarchal society confers authority and power to men and relegates women to a second-class status. The "old boy network" is the place where big business deals often take place. Poor and minority women are especially jeopardized when all women are discriminated against because of their gender (McGoldrick, Garcia-Preto, Hines, & Lee, 1989).

Many women and some men advocated for the Equal Rights Amendment (ERA), which twice failed to pass. This constitutional amendment asked for equal protection under the law against sexual discrimination in a twenty-four-word statement: "Equality of rights under the law shall not be denied or abridged by the United States or by any state on account of sex."

In many ways, sexism limits choices and opportunities for both men and women. The goal in society should not be to create a homogenous society but rather one in which there are choices for both men and women and where social justice prevails. When men and women realize their own potential, it leads to more productivity, togetherness, and a better way of life. Gochros and Ricketts (1986) advocate that sexism is a two-way street: when women are oppressed, so also are men. In that sense, sexism should be redefined in terms of policies, attitudes, beliefs, practices, laws, words, and concepts that deliberately or unintentionally lock people in arbitrarily and rigidly defined roles and behaviors, which lead to devaluing attributes or unequally limiting social, sexual, and economic opportunities on the basis of sex.

Van Den Bergh (1995) uses five concepts to define feminism:

1. **Equality.** This involves equal or identical rights, opportunities, and choices for women. It means simply that men's or women's rights should not be discriminated against with regard to opportunities and choices on the basis of gender.
2. Inherent in feminism are the attitudes and actions of people. Feminism implies that people are viewed from a fair and objective perspective that avoids stereotypes.
3. Feminism involves all aspects of life. That is, a woman has a right to her body, to equal opportunity in the job market, and equal legal and political rights. We need to acknowledge

that our social, legal, and political system is geared toward men and not women.
4. Feminism highlights the need to provide education and advocacy on behalf of women.
5. Feminism involves the appreciation of individual differences. The feminist perspective highlights the concept of empowering women by emphasizing individual strengths and qualities, including women's choices and decisions in their own lives.

In spite of successes in some areas, there has been a feminization of poverty, with women emerging as the "new poor." Thus breaking the cycle of poverty is all the more difficult because of the inherent inequalities present in a social structure that is not favorable to women.

Nadine, in her late thirties with four children, was divorced by her middle-class husband. With the help of a good lawyer, her ex-husband provided minimum support and left town. Nadine's work skills were minimal as she had never really worked outside the home. Her children, ranging in age from two to twelve, were frequently ill, necessitating numerous absences from her new job. Burdened by her role as sole supporter of the children, lack of money, and a low-paying job, Nadine soon found herself in the poverty cycle, a new and frightful experience for her and the children.

In practice with women, social workers need to emphasize a feminist perspective. Van Den Bergh and Cooper (1987) view such practice as a model of activism and sensitivity, growth and change, and challenge and risk. They emphasize that feminist social work practice is an effective means to improve the quality of life by facilitating social change. Further discussion on women's needs and issues will appear in different chapters of the book.

GENERALIST PRACTICE PROCESS

Working as a generalist is not random or chaotic, neither is it a linear process. Certain processes are required in order to help different types of clients.

These processes occur in a rough sequence, although they are recursive, so one often cycles backward to move ahead.

First and foremost, the generalist must be able to engage clients in a genuine fashion, not as a separate process but holistically throughout the helping process. This involves the generalist's knowledge, values, and skills in working with clients as well as understanding the different roles that generalists and clients can take on during the process. Accountability for the type of results incurred is also an important aspect of the helping process. Interviewing and maintaining the professional relationship through effective communication is a necessary aspect of the helping process. Skilled social workers are aware that they must facilitate conditions of empathetic communication, warmth, respect, and authenticity (Meyer and Maittaini, 1995). There has been recognition of the centrality of the helping relationship (Perlman, 1979) for clients at all different levels working with individuals, families, groups, communities, and organizations through engagement, making an assessment, planning, intervention, evaluation, and termination. A generalist who cannot achieve the necessary empathetic relationship will fail with most clients. Because people often are not the best judges of their interpersonal skills, supervised practice in the field and constructive feedback are necessary for ensuring competence.

All of these factors are part of the helping process and are crucial to effective practice. They are discussed in subsequent chapters, and the different phases of the helping process are presented in detail in Part Three.

CHAPTER SUMMARY

Chapter 1 introduces the reader to people and problems by presenting multifaceted problem situations. The need for and meaning of professional social work is presented. The three major purposes of social work are to promote the problem-solving, coping, and developmental capacities of people; to enhance the effectiveness and humane operation of the systems that provide people with resources, services, and opportunities; and to link people to systems that provide them with resources, services, and opportunities.

Generalist practice has become the mode of helping different size systems. As social work practice grew, the ecological perspective and later the ecosystems perspective became widely used.

The ecosystems perspective is used as the conceptual framework in this book because it provides the social worker with the synthesis that is required to work with different clients. The ecosystems perspective is a combination of ecology—the study of complex reciprocal and adaptive transactions among organisms and their environments—and general systems theory. As Janchill (1969) pointed out, "System theory is not itself a body of knowledge; it is a way of thinking and analysis that accommodates knowledge from many sciences" (p. 77).

Six basic concepts in general systems theory are applicable to open systems. They are boundaries, structure, hierarchy, transactionality, frame of reference, and time. In addition to these six concepts, there are twelve principles that explain a system's internal operations as well as its relationship with the external environment. The first five principles explain the manner in which interactions take place between different subsystems; they include input, output, throughput, feedback loop, and entropy. The internal state of a system is also determined by five additional principles: steady state, homeostasis, differentiation, nonsummativity, and reciprocity. The last two principles—equifinality and multifinality—deal with the path or trajectory of a system.

The ecosystems perspective gives the social work practitioner the capacity for a better and expanded understanding of the social environment in which all human beings exist. The ecosystems perspective is also unique because it furnishes a framework for the social worker to use differential practice models without being tied to any specific intervention, skills, methods, or knowledge.

Generalists work with different types of people and therefore need to practice with sensitivity. Diversity requires that social workers will assist clients who come from different socioeconomic groups, races, ethnic groups, and sexual preferences. Discrimination and oppression are closely connected to historical racism in our society. It is important to be sensitive and ask relevant questions to understand and work with diverse clients. People with physical and emotional disabilities are often stereotyped and discriminated against. Gays and lesbians are discriminated against through homophobia, ignorance, insensitivity, stereotyped thinking, and outright prejudice. The need for feminist perspective while working with female clients is important. Feminism involves all aspects of life and includes equality, a view of all people from a fair and objective perspective, and advocacy for women.

Finally, the generalist practice process of helping includes the following stages: engagement, assessment, planning, intervention, evaluation, and termination.

2

VALUES

The purpose of this chapter is to explain the importance of values in generalist social work practice. With reference to individuals, families, groups, organizations, and community practice, this chapter presents the following topics: philosophy and values; values and social structure; how social work values can be operationalized; individual, group, and societal values; ethnic and gender sensitive values; value dilemmas between workers and client; and the general values and principles of social work including respect for the dignity and worth of clients, acceptance of clients, uniqueness and individuality in clients, self-determination in clients, confidentiality, and self-awareness. Individual cases are presented throughout the chapter to delineate the presence, absence, or violation of a value.

PHILOSOPHY

Social work as a profession has a value orientation that gives purpose, meaning, and direction to persons who practice the profession. Social work's

professional values cannot be divorced from societal values, as this profession espouses and champions selected social values. Society, in turn, sanctions and recognizes this helping profession with supportive legislation, funding, and delegation of responsibility. The social work profession also has a Code of Ethics which consists of of principles that define the expectations of its members. The purpose of the code is to safeguard the profession and its reputation and to provide criteria to protect the public from exploitation by practitioners who are incompetent, reckless, and irresponsible in their work (Hepworth & Larsen, 1993).

Nowadays, the social worker is usually viewed as a doer of good, a provider of services, a professional who has an array of skills, and a moral agent of the community. Historically, social work was embedded primarily in a social and moral philosophy of help being "handed down" to the poor. Through the years, the social work profession succeeded in developing a methodology with humanitarian purposes such as viewing all clients as worthy beings with dignity regardless of their issues. The philosophy of social work, which is based on altruistic values of helping people, holds and affirms that even when the institutionalized profession serves more bureaucratic functions, it should continue to maintain its humanitarian philosophy.

Derived from the Greek, *philosophy* in its oldest and broadest sense means "love of wisdom." A philosophy can be described as a set of beliefs and attitudes, ideals, aspirations and goals, values, norms, and ethical precepts or principles. Philosophy requires the full development of our intellectual abilities and positive traits of character; it is a lifelong journey of reflection and action, of open-mindedness, and of purpose and commitment (Chaffee, 1998). Every profession is characterized by its own perspective and set of beliefs, as well as a collective conscience with which these beliefs are used. This attitude is called professional philosophy. It provides a rationale and ideal by which one works and finds meaning in work.

According to Hook (1967), a philosophy is "an affair of values and value judgments (for) . . . the intelligent conduct of human affairs," through which one searches for wisdom and sufficient knowledge to decide about what one should do in life. Social work professionals have philosophical and ethical standards by which they can analyze a reality in conjunction with moral–evaluative measures. The standards created in the profession are called norms and precepts and will be discussed in this chapter.

It is necessary to have a philosophy central to our work with individuals, families, groups, organizations, and communities that embodies the ideals and goals of a profession. A danger in this profession is that social workers become insensitive and judge clients in a harsh manner. When dealing with people day after day, some professionals begin to treat clients as objects; as things to be directed and managed. As one former social worker described, her work with pregnant teens: "I was sick and tired of being the helper . . . I was tired, so I used shortcuts. All I wanted to do was to get rid of them . . . if you've seen one, you've seen them all." It is important for the social worker to listen and respond empathetically according to the specific needs of the person(s) and the situation(s).

In the professional philosophy of social work, social workers ascribe great importance to meeting basic survival needs and self-actualization needs. One basic way to help people move toward the achievement of these needs is through caring and empathetic behavior.

As Mayeroff (1971) voices something all professionals perhaps harbor in themselves, noting eloquently:

> to care for another person, in the most significant sense, to help him grow and actualize himself . . . by helping the other grow I do actualize myself . . . Through caring for certain others, by serving them through caring, a man lives the meaning of his own life. In the sense in which a man can ever be said to be at home in the world, he is home not through dominating or explaining, or appreciating, but through caring and being cared for . . . Caring becomes my way of thanking for what I have received; I thank by caring all the more for my appropriate others and the conditions of their existence. It is, in some ways, like showing appreciation for a gift by using it fully. (p. 30)

How can we ensure that these qualities of nonjudgmental empathy and caring are part of the social work mosaic? At the outset it can be said that social work values of caring and respect can only be taught when the student or trainee is already inclined in this direction. Upon entering the profession, every social work student should strive to make these cardinal values of social work part of his or her attitudes, and should become aware of and nurture these qualities. When professional social workers display these values in their behaviors they are in better positions to handle ethical factors in working with such diverse systems as individuals, groups, organizations, and communities. Values are not just to be read and studied for an exam, for it is mostly through trial and error that beginning practitioners are able to inculcate these values in their work. The practical aspect of caring includes linking clients with resources, while the human relations aspect involves demonstrating concern and respect. All of these values will be discussed in the last section of this chapter. For now, it is sufficient to know that armed with these values, social workers can be important catalysts in helping people and in so doing will see themselves grow as professionals. Students who wish to become social workers will support the values of the social work profession in their careers.

VALUES

Social work practice is guided by a set of values about human beings and how values relate to the situations in which people or social workers find themselves. Values can be described as strong beliefs, which emerge from the way one feels and which guide human actions and behaviors (Johnson & Schwartz, 1997). The values of social work serve as an ethical guide for individual social workers in day-to-day work. An example is the belief that society has an obligation to help every person reach his or her fullest potential. These are assertions not about how the world is and what we know about it, but about how the world should be. Values are not subjected to scientific investigation and must be accepted on faith. Thus when speaking of a value, it may be considered to be right or wrong depending on the particular belief system or ethical code that is being used as a standard.

Although the terms *values* and *ethics* have been used interchangeably, they have slightly different meanings. As Loewenberg and Dolgoff (1992) note, "values are concerned with what is *good and desirable*, while ethics deal with what is *right and correct*" (p. 21). Although professional values are often defined as the core distinguishing characteristics of the social work profession, these values in many ways reflect the larger societal values and express general preference rather than specific directions for action. Though it would be ideal to have widespread consensus among social workers, it is difficult to present values as mono-

lithic. Values are diverse among ethnic, racial, different lifestyle groups and power groups, and so forth. However, developing an awareness of and a flexible attitude about working with people is an important criteria for a social worker.

Before discussing professional values, it is important to recognize that social work values are intricately combined with knowledge and skills and move us toward an effective helping process. One without the other would not lend itself to a productive and constructive helping process as seen in Figure 2.1.

Professional ethics are embedded in our professional values. McGowan (1995) describes professional ethics as guidelines about how members of the profession translate their values into action. In many ways, they provide direction about how people *ought* to act. In other words, professional values are specific, demanding, and potentially controversial. Reamer (1987) comments that social work values focus on "a commitment to human welfare, social justice, and individual dignity" (p. 801). Cournoyer (1991) summarizes the importance of social work ethics in the following manner: "Ethical decision making constitutes the *sine qua non* of professional social work practice.

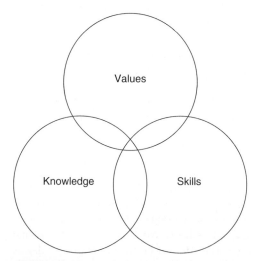

FIGURE 2.1   **Integral Aspects of Social Work Practice**

Ethical responsibilities take precedence over theoretical knowledge, research findings, practice wisdom, agency policies, and of course, the social worker's own personal values, reference, and beliefs" (p. 43). Hepworth and Larsen (1993) note that the values of a profession refer to beliefs, usually strongly held beliefs, about people and the preferred goals for people, the preferred means of achieving these goals, and the necessary and acceptable conditions of life. People are complex, and ethical dilemmas in difficult situations make decisions a tremendously complicated task. Therefore, understanding social values is imperative to being an effective and professional social worker.

The different types of values include ultimate, proximate, and instrumental values. The most abstract values are *ultimate values*, which tend to be most easily agreed upon by large groups of people. Such values include liberty, justice, worth, and dignity of people. *Proximate values* are specific to a desired goal. For example, right to life versus abortion on demand, parents' attitudes about utilizing different disciplining methods with children, or freedom in a classroom with reference to how and what assignments should be given to students. *Instrumental values* specify desired means to reach a goal; they are normally seen as modes of conduct. Confidentiality and self-determination are means of operationalizing the worth and dignity of people and these are instrumental values (Johnson, 1995). Values are a definite aspect of and factor in our social structure and our attitudes.

Mrs. Eva is eighty-five-years-old and has terminal cancer. She is in terrible pain, and having led a satisfying and fulfilling life, she would prefer to die. She is severely depressed and is contemplating suicide. What value issues are suggested by this case? How would you handle it?

Mrs. Pearl was given legal custody of her granddaughter because her daughter, Sharon, became a prostitute and neglected the child. Diane, the eight-year-old girl, lived with her grandmother for three years. Meanwhile, Sharon fell in love, got off the streets, and started living with a fairly well-employed man. Though no longer a prostitute, she still continues to use drugs. At this point in her life

Sharon wants her daughter back. How should this case be handled?

A generalist in a crowded industrial town is working with tenants to organize a rent strike against their landlord who is demanding and receiving rents but neglects making necessary repairs, providing adequate heat and water supplies, and getting rid of rats and roaches in the building. The generalist wonders, however, if he should inform the tenants of the risks of eviction involved in the rent strike. He suspects that if the tenants were fully informed of the risks, they would reconsider their decision to strike, which means that the essential improvements in the apartment building would not be made. What should he do?

All of these vignettes highlight value dilemmas. Social work is not a hard science but a combination of art and science. Therefore, in any given situation, the worker may have to make decisions based on values rather than purely on knowledge. An important question arising in the first case is whether the elderly person has the moral right to take her life.

In the second situation, one must consider values that justified the grandmother's taking the girl away from her mother. Why did Sharon agree to this arrangement? What values support Sharon in reclaiming custody of her daughter at this point? Would claiming her right as a parent be sufficient reason to return the child? Should the fact that she is still on drugs affect the decision? Should the fact that she is living with a man to whom she is not married influence the decision? If this situation occurred in another country, at a different time and place, would the case be handled differently?

In the third case, what are the obligations of the generalist to the tenants? Is it all right to take a risk and hope the landlord will not evict them, or should the tenants be made aware of all the pros and cons?

VALUES AND SOCIAL STRUCTURE

Values in every culture serve as important guides in selecting appropriate behavior. For instance, in the United States the lengthy hospitalization of a person can result in financial problems if the person and family do not have insurance and sick leave coverage. In other countries where such arrangements are mandated, this particular problem is unknown (Lowenberg, 1983). Therefore, identical situations may result in crisis in one society but not in another. In the latter example, institutional arrangements exist to cope with medical conditions and their cost. How a situation is treated in a country depends on the structural or institutional arrangements, which in turn are based on political and cultural features of a country. Different structural arrangements also reveal different value systems. For example, being an unwed mother may be acceptable in one culture whereas in another culture it would be considered scandalous.

Ted became homeless as a result of losing his job. This happened six months after his wife left him for another man. To cope with his wife's infidelity, Ted drank heavily and was hardly ever at his office. When he did go to work, he fought with his colleagues and made mistakes in his accounting. As a result he was fired from the job. Unfortunately, Ted had no savings, and his family, which lived 3,000 miles away, refused to help him financially. Ted was angry and frustrated, but being newly homeless he still had the will to fight for himself. He carries a banner and walks in front of the White House, protesting against homelessness and lack of low-income housing. U.S. values allow him to do this without interference to his individuality and personality. In Communist China, anyone involved in such a protest would probably be thrown in prison or killed. The difference in the value systems is political.

Hamilton (1958), a pioneer in social work, saw the importance of values more than forty years ago. She wrote that each client collectively incorporates the cultural environment of which she or he is a part. Thus "every treatment objective is a value judgment, culturally shaped . . . It is too easy to forget that every treatment goal, just like community planning is influenced by our value system" (p. xi). However, it is important to note that there are obvious value differences be-

tween the United States, Japan, Russia, France, and Chile. In addition to the national values of each country, school, family, and workplace values are part of the societal culture. It would be impossible to think of social work without awareness of the culture in which it is embedded.

An American social worker on a temporary assignment in a traditional Eastern culture may be surprised that arranged marriages are more common and accepted than marriages of choice. In arranged marriages men and women are chosen for each other by their parents. American social workers who do not understand this value premise may intervene inappropriately and be dismissed for not being knowledgeable and culturally sensitive.

Values are adopted and established through the social norms of each society. Social norms may be described as standards, patterns, or models that constitute the rules or directives of behavior, both formal and informal, and expectations held collectively by a culture, group, organization, or society (Barker, 1995). Social norms are regulatory rules, standards, and criteria by which we judge the worth of persons and their behavior. Thus, social norms are developed through our experiences in living in a particular society. A social norm common to many cultures is that one should love and protect members of one's family. Norms provide explanatory reasons for one's behavior and reality. They become social rules that specify what is expected and tolerated, and how and to whom responsibility for events and their consequences are assigned. Social norms provide a variety of socially sanctioned choices to act upon.

What we are discussing is group idealogy, which reflects a distinctive perspective of a group of people. Group idealogy is based on the group's common values, norms, and beliefs. Values, as noted in the earlier examples, are general beliefs that shape people's selection of behavior. Values guide any society's desirable ends and means.

Norms are changing in many countries, for example, today it is easier than in the past for a person to say what he or she overtly thinks of a government. Changing norms, however, may create problems, conflicts, and ambiguities for people. Changing values about sexual behaviors and reproduction create dissonance, conflict, and ambiguity for people. For example, if teenage pregnancy became an accepted aspect of growing up, government and social welfare institutions would no longer consider it to be a serious problem and prevention efforts would not occur. This could result in a population of single-parent families, with marriage becoming outdated and unnecessary, which in turn could lead to tremendous conflicts and ambiguity in family structures. Violating norms also affects the values of a culture. Thus it is necessary to recognize value issues.

Vicky, a single parent, is upset and consults a social worker about the problems she is having with three adolescent sons. Her immediate problem is her sixteen-year-old son, Ronnie, who wants to quit school without regard to future educational needs or employment.

Emily works in a rural public welfare agency, where she becomes aware of a great deal of discrimination. She collects data revealing that the director makes a number of decisions that deny poor migrant workers the public assistance benefits for which they are eligible. Emily realizes that the director is prejudiced against the migrant workers, most of whom are Mexican Americans. Emily believes if she confronts the director with this evidence she will be denied a promotion that is long overdue or perhaps even fired. What should she do?

There are many issues to review in the first case. With reference to obtaining factual knowledge, the social worker should obtain any available information about the single parent, her adolescent sons, and the school. The value issues in this situation include the mother's, the son's, and the social worker's beliefs about school education, itself. The beliefs in U.S. society about the appropriate degree of schooling indicate that one should have at least a high school diploma. Is it necessary for Ronnie to finish school to become successful in life? Another value issue would be whether the social worker feels it is appropriate to discuss the son with his mother in the son's absence. Surely such a session would have consequences, and value judgments

may be formed regarding those consequences. Each of these value issues needs to be dealt with. How should these issues be resolved?

In the second case, though there is a blatant denial of benefits to migrant workers, how can Emily deal with the situation without jeopardizing herself or her values? Is being a whistle-blower an option? Is Emily willing to take risks? Does she have a support network? These are options that she should weigh carefully based on her value system and the work reality.

To deal with these value issues in work, the social worker can use the following typology of components in a social work intervention (Kelman & Warwick, 1978). Such interventions involve efforts to bring about change in the lives of different types of clientele, and the components consist of:

1. The choice of goals and the change efforts in this direction: What clients might choose to do is not merely what they want, but may also be subtly influenced by what the worker sees as desirable. Thus, the worker and a client may view something as a social obligation or desirable and worthy in order to move on and achieve it. The worker's approach to their clients should include an ability to listen attentively and empower them to move towards goals that are appropriate for them. Careful observation and understanding the client's needs and strengths is crucial for effective helping.

Middle-aged Lita, who had spent her adult life taking care of her husband and their three now adult children, was suddenly and dramatically abandoned when her husband without warning told her he wanted a divorce because he was in love with another woman. Lita was devastated. She met with a social worker, who observing her vulnerability, tragedy, and lack of personal resourcefulness, urged Lita to go to college and earn her bachelor's degree. Although Lita was not interested in pursuing higher education, she reluctantly and hesitantly agreed. The worker did not realize for sometime that she was imposing her own values about education and inappropriately urging this client to go to college. The worker found out later that Lita had other plans. She did not wish to pursue education but instead wanted to look for a full-time job.

2. The definition of the target of change: This involves a combination of both empirical (experience) and value issues. These are connected not only to outcomes that can be achieved by seeking to change oneself or others, but also to those whose obligation it is to change (Garvin, 1997). Thus, there is a variation in the advice being given depending upon the value system and experience of the counselor.

Amy, an older student, had many problems in the first month of her social work field placement due to personality clashes with her field supervisor. The student went to see the university counselor (who was a social worker) after being criticized again and again for her lack of knowledge and ability. The counselor looked at Amy as the target of change and urged her to modify her behavior and "fit in"; practical-minded Amy saw the target of change as her field placement.

3. The choice of means used to implement the intervention: The relationship of the means to the end can become a moral issue when a person uses means affecting others negatively to reach a goal. The question then becomes whether this goal would prevent others from reaching their goals.

Nina was the new social worker in a residential agency for emotionally disturbed children. Eleven-year-old Frank, her client, refused to come for the group sessions. Whatever Nina tried led to negative results. Eventually she decided on a plan. She promised him a chocolate every time he attended a session. This reward of a chocolate led Frank to comply with the worker's wishes. Later on, she was replaced by another social worker who refused to give the child chocolates, as he expected her to based on his relationship with his earlier social worker. The new worker criticized this reward as bribery and explained how the group sessions might help him in his behavioral goals. All the other group members enthu-

siastically agreed with her, but Frank was sulky and angry. The new social worker had to work with him on a one-on-one basis before he was willing to return to the group as a productive member.

4. The assessment of the consequences of the intervention: Outcomes of interventions are evaluated by empirical methods and ethical issues. A worker who is trained as a behaviorist may insist that a worker evaluate the outcomes based on how goals were met; whereas, the psychodynamically trained worker may argue that a subjective view of the sense of well-being the client feels is also important. An ethical issue thus arises in that many social workers believe "unanticipated consequences," such as a client's sense of fulfillment, are all side effects and should be considered part of the intervention and be identified and assessed (Garvin & Seabury, 1984). Factors such as development of new behaviors by the client involve self-esteem and affect the sense of wellness, which in turn has effects on the client's immediate relationships. Such factors, therefore, should be viewed as important consequences in interventions and evaluated accordingly.

Gina, a former professor and a full-time mother with three school-age children, meets with a generalist because she is very depressed. She explained that her life seems empty. She misses the classroom and the students after 16 years of staying home and taking care of her family.

Gina's family participates in the next few sessions. The family hears Gina's longing for a teaching position, and her husband and children encourage her to find a professorship. Reluctantly and diffidently, Gina agrees and applies for a teaching position at a nearby university. To her surprise, she is offered the position. Soon after she takes the position, Gina is a changed person. Her depression disappears and her self-esteem soars high. At her final session with the generalist she says in a elated voice, "Making money doing what you love is the best way to live." The professorship helped the client to get rid of her depression, build her self-esteem, and thereby bring more happiness to her family life.

While working with clients, the social work practitioner has to be aware of societal values, group values, and the values of the client as well as his or her own values.

SOCIETAL VALUES, GROUP VALUES, AND INDIVIDUAL VALUES

Values can be further classified as individual, group and societal values. *Societal values* are the broadest. They are highly generalized values, such as honesty, happiness, goodness, and decency, that are upheld by the entire social system. *Group values* are upheld by members of one group, but they may not be significant to another group. A group of religious people may believe in prayer and refuse to tolerate anyone in the group who does not share this belief. Finally, *individual values* are held by one individual but not necessarily held by others.

Seventeen-year-old Della, who comes from a strict, conservative home, refuses to have sex before marriage. Most of her friends see her as odd. Della is not perturbed, for she is aware that her values differ from her peers. Della's individual values also reflect her upbringing, which includes family and group religious values.

Freedom is considered an important societal value in the United States. However, when the question arises of whether young, pregnant, single teenagers should be given the option to decide if they should have their babies, freedom is not considered to be quite as important. Many adults oppose teenagers having options, believing teens are too immature to make such decisions. Pro-choice and pro-life groups have different opinions about abortion in general, based on what they consider to be right. Though both groups of people may believe that life is sacred, they have different goals and different strategies to reach these goals.

Different groups of people in the same society have different values. Parsons (1960) observes that "every subsystem has a value system of its own, which is a differentiated and specialized version of

the general value system" (p. 193). Parsons also describes how group values relate to societal values. Group values usually derive from groups and families and complement societal values. Making money and being successful are generally accepted societal values and are further influenced by gender, age, religion, and ethnic group variations. For a group of studious, hardworking teenagers, success is measured directly in terms of doing well in school; for adults, success is chiefly measured by the amount of money made. Of course, both involve hard work. But even the manner in which money is made may vary from group to group. Some consider people who make money in drug deals to be successful; others see them as criminals.

One young boy of fourteen was dealing drugs and made thousands of dollars every month. When the dangers of his lifestyle were pointed out to him, he retorted that everyone in his neighborhood dealt drugs. The teen added that he did not care if he was caught or shot by law officers as long as he made the money to do what he wanted.

It is evident from this example that differences in group values do not just happen but develop as a result of and in response to differential life experiences, which influence any individual's expectations.

With regard to individual behaviors, it is difficult to analyze values because they can differ from societal and group values and sometimes can even be inconsistent with a person's stated individual values (Lowenberg, 1983). A person may be aware that a particular kind of behavior is not in balance with his or her own value orientation, but undertake the behavior anyway.

Sixteen-year-old Keith did not like to smoke and was aware of smoking's ill effects. Nevertheless, he smoked to "look cool" and be accepted by his peers. When questioned, Keith said he knew smoking was bad for him and admitted he did not like to smoke. Shrugging his shoulders, he added he did it anyway because all his peers did.

Behavior preferences are filtered based on the lifestyle of a person and, as seen in this case example, behaviors can be inconsistent with value systems of an individual.

Twenty-two-year-old Valerie was a devout Catholic who refused to use or allow her husband to use contraceptives. She was already the mother of three children. The couple came in for marital counseling because they were having arguments about birth control, which also brought up financial issues. Though Valerie appeared to understand the family's financial strains, she was adamant about not using any form of contraception. Apparently the partners held different value systems although both saw themselves as good Catholics.

In order to be effective, the social worker has to look at the person–situation configuration. Thus, the worker needs to look at both psychosocial (internal) and environmental (external) factors to understand the values and behaviors of the people with whom they work. To make this process easier and to highlight our professional outlook, the National Association of Social Workers (NASW) developed a *Code of Ethics* that all social work professionals need to follow.

VALUES FOR SENSITIVE PRACTICE WITH ETHNIC, RACIAL, AND OPPRESSED POPULATIONS

The United States is a multicultural society. In terms of ethics, social workers champion social justice and value the democratic process. Changing demographics, cultural pluralism, and variations in lifestyles in the U.S. society magnify the need for social workers to be ethnically sensitive and nonsexist in their professional practice. Social workers of various subcultures practice with people of different ethnic and racial groups, socioeconomic status, cultural backgrounds, ethnic heritage, religious preferences, and sexual orientation. In order to work effectively and with sensitivity to cultural differences, social workers must understand diversity and its implications for social work practice (Anderson, 1990). According to Jenkins (1993) diversity is nurtured through

self-knowledge, multicultural education, and empathy. Whenever possible, social workers must take responsibility for confronting inequalities and social injustice. Social workers should value client strengths and competencies and work in collaboration with clients to develop and implement constructive and creative solutions (Dubois & Miley, 1996).

As Lum (1996) explains, cultural belief is based on rich customs and traditions, along with family and ethnic community values. Cultural belief systems influence the customs and skills of people. In some ethnic communities, the cultural element reinforces positive functioning through family support systems, self-identity and self-esteem, and the ethnic group's philosophy of living.

Ethnicity and race are closely related to culture. *Ethnicity* refers to a distinct group of people who define themselves as distinct because they share a common culture, language, religion, ancestry, and a combination of other characteristics. *Race* refers to physical characteristics and skin color. The term *racism* indicates judgments that people make about others solely on the basis of such superficial physical or social characteristics such as skin color, language differences, and so forth. A *minority group,* as Schaefer (1993) defines it, is a "subordinate group whose members have significantly less control or power over their lives than that held by the members of the dominant or majority group" (p. 6). Schaefer further explains that there are characteristics that represent a minority group. They include physical and cultural characteristics that distinguish them from the dominant group. People experience prejudice and discrimination because of membership in a minority group. Minority group members share a strong sense of solidarity with others in the group, and generally marry within the same group.

U.S. culture has a history of racism and discrimination against different ethnic and racial groups. Hence it is important that social workers be sensitive to the needs of different types of clientele. In order to be sensitive to the needs of clients, social workers have to be aware of the prejudices they grew up with and refrain from similar acts of discrimination. Behaviors that social workers have to avoid include stereotyped explanations of the behavior of persons of specific ethnic or minority groups; offering the same type of help to all clients belonging to a particular population; overlooking and dismissing the importance of cultural and ethnic behaviors, or in extreme cases using it to explain all behaviors; and avoiding or excessively discussing issues of race and culture.

All of these factors can be a burden when clients have to not only deal with their own problem situation, but also with a social worker's subtle, or at times overt, prejudicial comments. In fairness to clients, social workers must strive to learn about their clients' cultures and ethnic backgrounds and also recognize that seldom does one person acquire more than a superficial knowledge of another culture. In every ethnic group, the manner in which culture is assimilated by any single family and its members also depends on other factors such as class, exposure to other culturally different groups, and so forth. Thus each individual in a culture also experiences that culture differently. There will be individual differences and expressions of culture by different clientele from the same ethnic group. Making generalizations and stereotyping different cultures would be negative and would open a door for problems in communication between the worker and clients (Sheafor, Horesji, & Horesji, 1997).

It is important for social workers to be aware of their own weaknesses, strengths, and biases so that they are aware that they are not making inappropriate judgements based on race or ethnicity. As Green (1995) puts it:

> Social workers often emphasize . . . the value of knowing 'where the client is coming from.' But it is equally important that professionals know where they are coming from. (p. 10)

As Sheafor et al., (1997) indicate, acknowledging differences in ethnicity or race may be an acceptable way of giving permission to clients, which might help them to express concern about acceptance or difficulties in communication.

Workers need to be aware that overlooking strengths, misreading nonverbal communication, and misunderstanding family dynamics are fairly common errors in cross-cultural helping. Ethnic behaviors motivated by religion, spirituality, family obligations, and sex roles can be often misunderstood. Social workers may not be able fully to appreciate clients' situations including the contextual and systemic aspects of their lives. Because it is difficult to read cultural contextual situations and nonverbal cues, workers should move slowly in order to reach feelings (Sheafor et al., 1997).

The social worker should be aware that in different cultures authority is viewed differently. In some, the concept of individual rights is overlooked in favor of respect to authority. Generally in Hispanic and some traditional Asian cultures the father is seen as the head of the family; his opinion is sought out and respected and decisions are made accordingly. Also in the Native American cultural nations, certain persons perform the role of the advisor and other family members will wait for their opinion before making decisions.

Workers should not be afraid to ask questions concerning a client's culture, their values, traditions, and customs. If you are sensitive and empathetic, clients from different cultures will take time to explain their way of living and their problems in terms that you can understand as they begin to appreciate your sensitive caring. Revealing your lack of knowledge of their culture and being openminded about learning about it also present your own vulnerability to the clients, and this is a humane way of building a relationship.

These are some important factors that underlie cross-cultural helping. As we proceed into different ways and styles of cross-cultural helping, information that will be useful to you in working with diverse clients and different size systems will be presented.

Another diverse population that has been discriminated against is that of gays and lesbians. As Nancy Humphreys, the president of National Association of Social Workers (NASW) from 1979–1981 so eloquently put it, a social worker needs to have knowledge as well as sensitivity to gay and lesbian issues in order to be an effective helper. Hidalgo, Peterson, and Woodman, (1985) stated:

> First, gays and lesbians who receive social services from social workers are becoming an increasingly large constituent group of the profession. Second, many social workers are gay or lesbian, some out of the closet, but quite a few still choose to hide themselves in order to evade the stigma society attaches to the gay person. Third, and perhaps most importantly, gay and lesbian people represent an oppressed population, the protection of whose rights, as those of all oppressed populations, should be of primary concern to the profession of social work. (p. 167)

Gay men and lesbians constitute approximately 10 percent of the population of the United States. They are represented as clients in different fields of practice and social workers should be aware and work with them accordingly.

Practitioners should examine their own attitudes toward homosexuality. There are two different and opposing ways by which social workers may approach helping homosexuals. At one extreme, practitioners may mistakenly regard homosexuality itself as an overriding problem, regardless of the problem(s) presented by the client. On the other hand, some social workers may dismiss or overlook homosexuality, believing that it has no impact on the helping process. Both views are detrimental to the helping process and to the client. Practitioners need to examine their own level of comfort or discomfort, receptiveness or defensiveness, and reexamine their own knowledge or lack of it concerning the lifestyles of their clientele.

Sexual orientation is central to our personhood. Therefore, social workers should have the capacity to understand and affirm the sexual orientation of their clients. This simply means that in order to be helpful to others, social workers must be honest with themselves about their own motives and vulnerabilities as well as the pertinent issues that could contribute to misunderstandings and inappropriate interventions (Booth, 1990).

Duleny and Kelly (1982) suggest that "the guiding principles for social workers who want to work effectively with gay and lesbian clients are the same principles followed in working with heterosexual clients: accept the client as a total human being, accept his or her sexual orientation, and do not pretend to have all the answers" (p. 180).

Tracy, a college freshman, visited the University Counseling Center to meet with Judy, a social worker. He was hesitant and uncomfortable and observed the worker carefully. Judy sensed his uneasiness and invited him to sit down, then talked generally about how difficult it is to discuss problems. Tracy looked down at his shoes and talked about the members of his family, who are devout Christians. His father is a preacher. Growing up, Tracy faced strict rules and regulations at home. At a later point, Tracy mentioned to Judy that he was gay but his parents did not know. He felt that his father would be upset if he found out about his lifestyle, and Tracy did not know how to tell him or for that matter anyone else at home. At the same time, he was tired of pretending and lying to his parents. Now, that he was away from home, he wondered if this might be the right time for him to let his family know about his sexual orientation. Judy is empathetic and supportive and works with him, specifically discussing the different options that he could use in coming out to his parents.

VALUE DILEMMAS BETWEEN WORKER AND CLIENT

As has been noted, values and ethics are unprovable assumptions or tenets of faith guiding the conduct of social work. Values affect every aspect of a worker's social intervention process in dealing with problems. Thus it is important for social workers to be aware of value dilemmas, as we all come from homes which have inculcated certain kinds of values. Social workers, being human, show various value preferences; therefore, it is important that we be flexible enough to accommodate changing and different value positions on most moral and political issues.

Cindy, a second-year social work student, became upset in her classroom when a professor talked about abortion and the need to look at the client's needs, goals, and lifestyle before attempting to offer help to the client. Cindy complained that her religious beliefs did not permit her to discuss abortion. Then came the ethical dilemma. What would she do if she were faced with a teenager who demanded an abortion? After extensive discussion in the classroom, Cindy reached the conclusion that she would refer this client to another social worker because she might not be able to deal with this issue objectively. Perhaps Cindy's point of view will never change, but it is not unusual for social workers to have their own diverse value positions. However, such differences do not reflect divergence among social workers on the ultimate values that have been delineated earlier. What needs to be understood is that there are many possible means for achieving given ends, and rigid assumptions about preferred means do not stand the test of time.

Value dilemmas may not always sound real in the classroom, but confrontation with value dilemmas happens very early in the world of real practice. Often such dilemmas are the result of conflicts between a social worker's personal and professional values and the value system of the client. Seasoned professionals and students alike experience conflict over problematic situations like child or spousal abuse, incest, rape, and abortion. A social worker will be successful in her or his role by being flexible and open-minded, and by remembering that we all come from different family backgrounds. For example, being kind to others is an accepted family value for one person, but it may have to be inculcated more carefully in others, who were taught to look out for themselves as number one.

It is not unusual for individuals who have personal issues to get into the helping professions as a way of understanding themselves and as a way of helping others. This is not peculiar to social work but is found in psychiatry, counseling, psychology, and other helping professions. This situation might present a value dilemma for the profession itself. Should students with personal issues be weeded out of social work education programs? Here, too, flexibility comes into play because some of these individuals work sincerely at their own issues and become highly effective and productive generalists.

Twenty-seven-year-old Florence, who was an incest victim, became a social worker. She had apparently worked through her own trauma, but continued to have a special interest in incest victims and specialized in working with them. This is not uncommon with helping professions. Often the fact that the worker has had a serious problem and has dealt with it successfully will help him or her be more sensitive and insightful to what a client is going through and be more effective in helping.

It is important that generalists be aware of their own values and how they fit into the profession's values and ethics. Social workers must constantly reevaluate their work and be aware of clients whose values differ from their own, or whose behavior appears offensive to the worker, because of differences in family upbringing.

Social workers, like other people, have different kinds of personalities. Some are vulnerable to responding negatively to certain types of behaviors and not to others.

Sarah generally enjoyed working with various types of clients, but was suddenly repulsed by a client who walked into her office. This client was smelly and behaved in an aggressive and sullen manner. Demanding that Sarah deal with her son immediately, the woman loudly told Sarah she had no time for game playing. She wanted her son to be taken care of and placed in an institution right away for his drug abuse. She banged an angry fist on the table and waited, as Sarah later commented, "for the world to fall at her feet." After Sarah got over her initial discomfort, she handled the client as best as she could. While in supervision, Sarah said she understood the client was overly anxious about her son and had behaved in such a way as to get the quick attention she needed. Later, Sarah was able to accept the fact that this client might always behave in this manner. Social workers should become aware right from the beginning of their professional training that they will encounter all kinds of people as clients.

There are other situations in which a social worker may feel uneasy because the client demonstrates excessively dependent, withdrawn, manipulative, passive, or self-defeating behaviors. If the worker gets caught up in the situations the client creates, the worker has created a dilemma for herself or himself.

It would be very difficult for a worker to live up to the expectations of all clients. A client who is excessively dependent needs to be informed that the worker is not all powerful and cannot provide ready-made solutions. A worker should learn to tolerate silence without feeling uncomfortable when working with a silent and withdrawn client.

Thirteen-year-old Don felt forced by his foster parents to come for clinical sessions. During sessions, Don would sit for the entire fifty-five minutes without uttering a word. At first the social worker was anxious and pushed Don to participate in the session. After receiving no response, the worker finally gave up, thinking Don would not return for help. However, he came back the following week and the next week, so the worker went beyond the verbal aspect and assumed that the client liked coming for the clinical sessions. The awkward silence became comfortable silence. At the beginning of each session the worker would make some comments to Don. He did not reply but obediently walked to a chair and sat down with his head bent. Three weeks later the worker was rewarded when Don looked up with a twinkle in his eye when the worker complimented Don about his punctuality. Every evening he had to walk from his school to the agency and he was always on time. Eventually this led to a constructive working relationship. The worker recognized that "it just took time" for the relationship to become constructive.

It is imperative that social workers respond to withdrawn behaviors with patience and understanding. Rather than closing the case and saying that the outcome was negative, the social worker waited patiently for verbal communication. With managed care today, this might seem a luxury but moving at the client's pace is important. Utilizing the preauthorization attempts to match the need of the client with the appropriate services within a system may be helpful, keeping in mind the cost-containment goals of managed care (Wernet, 1999).

When faced with explosive, manipulative, hostile, and sometimes involuntary clients, it is best that the social worker first explore her or his own feelings in order to handle such clients in an ethical manner. If the worker responds defensively or counterattacks the client, any help will be counter-productive. Also negative behavior on the part of social workers is unlikely to lead to productive sessions, because clients may view the behavior of the workers as similar to the experiences that they have encountered with other people in life situations.

Amanda, a social work student who had a conflictual relationship with her mother, was faced with the dilemma of working with an older woman who happened to look like her mother. When the client started to complain about her problems in getting help from her housing project, Amanda impatiently threw the empowerment perspective out of the window and asked the client to keep quiet and not ramble all the time. This made the client uncomfortable. Because of her discomfort, the client participated unwillingly in the session, only answering questions that Amanda asked of her. Amanda realized her mistake in treating the client like her mother after she made the statement. Amanda asked her supervisor to help her. Because Amanda had sufficient insight to be aware of her own problem, the client was fortunate. Some social workers may overlook their own issues, muddling their clinical sessions and thus causing more problems for their client and themselves.

Another potentially problematic group of clients exhibits self-defeating behaviors. Workers who are uncomfortable with such behaviors have to watch their *own* behaviors carefully so that they do not impose their standards on these clients. However, when the timing is right, the social worker should make it a point to help the clients see their own self-defeating behaviors, perhaps presenting alternative options for them to consider that might strengthen their potentials.

Gladys represented her small community to the state government. But instead of highlighting the strengths of her community that would benefit by having a social welfare services agency in her community she emphasized the problems, downplayed the strengths of the community, and repeatedly mentioned defeats, deficits, and drawbacks of the community people. She did not receive the necessary funds, which were instead offered to a more "deserving community." Gladys had taken on a self-defeating approach with state authorities. This angered the community members. Later, in her sessions with a practitioner she put herself down and highlighted her drawbacks, again displaying her self-defeating behavior.

In all these situations, it is important to understand the culture of the client; that is, the family culture as well as ethnic, class, and religious backgrounds. This is also true when dealing with compliant clients. Is compliance a part of the family or ethnic culture, or is it basically the client's way of communicating? Failure to understand the difference can lead a social worker to make an incorrect assessment.

A young Anglo man from a poor, single-parent family explains why he was compliant—he did not have enough clothes and he was acutely aware of his low-status at his high school:

> I had one pair of jeans, and I wore them every day. I was always afraid of what people thought of me—that this guy doesn't have anything, that he's wearing the same Levis all the time, he's having to work in the cafeteria for his lunch. What's going on? I think that's what made me so shy [and perhaps compliant to authorities as well as to peers]. (Andersen & Collins, 1995, p. 174)

The young man's compliance came from his sense of shame and insecurity that he was not good enough because he did not fit in with his peers in high school.

Value dilemmas are usually faced by two sets of people: social workers and clients. If a client faces a value dilemma about having an abortion, obtaining a divorce, or leaving her job to stay home with her children, it is important that the worker sees this as the client's dilemma. With this recognition, the worker can be objective in offering constructive help, but leave decisions to the client. However, if the worker has strong feelings about morality and feels that the client is doing something immoral, such as being unfaithful to a spouse, it could also become the worker's dilemma. The worker should view a client's situation objectively and nonjudgmentally and deal with it honestly so that it does not stand in the way of helping the client move on in life. Illegal and dangerous behavior such as incest, abuse, and threats to self or others, however, require the worker to report the offense to legal authorities.

In all professions it is necessary to have guidelines for dealing with people and feelings, such as the NASW's *Code of Ethics*. The very nature of such guidelines is to leave room for interpretation in each case. The guidelines help organize one's thinking and approach in the analysis of difficult problems and lend order to the justification of one's conclusions. Sometimes, clear-cut solutions seem beyond reach, particularly when there are difficult ethical dilemmas (Reamer, 1987).

A systematic examination of these dilemmas should be part of classroom discussions as well as in the field where beginning professionals are dealing with clients. Understanding clients' problems and issues objectively also leads to the worker's own professional growth. Such growth continuously improves the quality of social work.

The next section looks at the different professional values and ethical principles that underlie generalist social work practice.

PROFESSIONAL PRACTICE PRINCIPLES

On the basis of the philosophy, the set of value orientations, and the ethical standards emphasized by the NASW, a set of basic professional principles, also called *cardinal values* (Hepworth, Rooney, & Larsen, 1997) has evolved in order to help, guide, and limit the helping actions of social work professionals. This section will present a thorough exposition of the cardinal principles of the social work accompanied by demonstrations of how these values apply to specific clinical situations.

The cardinal principles are based on Judeo-Christian and humanistic moral beliefs that have practical implications connected to the helping process. The Judeo-Christian heritage teaches us to dislike the sin but not the sinner. When a social worker meets with the person who is accused of unacceptable behavior, professional objectives are in place to help the client, as a person in his or her own right, to get the person's cooperation in relation to other family members, and to gather information needed for constructive intervention. It would be difficult, if not impossible, to get the person to participate in the process if she or he is treated with contempt. None of this means that the worker has to accept or convey approval of the behavior in question. As social workers, our job is not to judge; it is to provide a professional service. Before clients can communicate with a worker, they have to feel comfortable, and respected in the worker's presence, only then will the clients be willing to risk accurate information and honest feelings.

Also while working with clients, we are less likely to judge them if we try to understand the reasons for their being "unproductive," "irresponsible," "stupid," "immoral," "cruel," or "delinquent." The temptation to be judgmental about clients becomes less strong as you find that many clients have suffered various forms of deprivation and have been victims of harsh, abusive, rejecting, or exploitative behaviors. Many clients come from situations where they received very little respect and lacked sustained love during critical periods of their development, causing them to view themselves as unworthy people.

Armed with the professional practice principles depicted in Figure 2.2, social workers can develop valuable tools for helping people and, in the process, see themselves grow as professionals. These principles also enable beginning professionals to function in stressful situations with problems that may seem totally insolvable. The

beginning social worker learns to engage in non-defensive as well as nonpunitive contact with clients who are cold, hostile, resistive, rejecting, overly dependent and overly complying, placating, or possibly very frightened.

The basic professional principles of social work initially presented by Gordon Hamilton (1940) and elaborated by Biestek (1957) have been refined and modified according to the current times and adopted in the NASW *Code of Ethics*. They include the following:

Respect for the dignity and worth of a client

Acceptance of the client

Uniqueness and individuality of clients

Client's self-determination

Confidentiality

Worker's self-awareness

By accepting these principles as part of social work standards, the professional makes a public commitment to certain responsibilities and standards and the social worker holds himself or herself publicly accountable for observing and following them. These principles are applicable to individual, family, group, organization, and community situations.

Some practice principles evolve primarily from our value base, others from a knowledge base. The foregoing list focuses on the former. While examining these principles you will be presented with value clarification situations that help you to look at yourself, and in the process become aware of your personal values and the implications of these values for you as a social worker. The purpose of this section is not only to present the principles but also to help you look at yourself and broaden your perspective through expanded thinking.

Respect for the Dignity and Worth of Clients

Respect for the dignity and worth of clients requires that all persons, irrespective of their back-

FIGURE 2.2 **Professional Practice Principles**

ground, age, race, sex, lifestyle, beliefs, socioeconomic status, or behaviors, should be treated as people with dignity. This is based on the assumption that all individuals are worthy beings, including people who display antisocial behavior. Think about people who commit serious crimes including a whole host of offenses such as sex abuse, rape, drug and alcohol abuse, family violence, child abuse, incest, and, at the far end of the scale, murder. How do you feel? Would you be able to work with such people and to treat them as individuals who have dignity and worth?

As Reamer (1987) puts it:

> The concept of dignity implies that human beings have a right to be respected and that social workers should not discriminate among individuals based on considerations such as those related to race, ethnicity, gender, sexual preference, or socioeconomic status. Social workers also generally assume that all people have certain basic needs, such as those related to food, shelter, health care, and mental health—and that all individuals should have equal opportunities to meet these needs. (p. 801)

Respectful communication with others affirms their sense of dignity and worth. Professionally, effective social workers treat people with consideration, respect their uniqueness, appreciate the validity of their point of view, and listen carefully to what they say.

When you read that you should respect the worth and dignity of clients without judging them, it does not mean that you approve of or condone illegal, immoral, or abusive acts and behaviors. Being nonjudgmental in treatment does not mean that you allow clients to avoid responsibility for their behaviors but rather that you help them take ownership and accept responsibility for their behaviors. This type of help comes from a worker who is understanding and has positive intentions to ameliorate difficulties. When social workers blame clients, they are being negative and punitive with no useful purpose.

Maluccio (1979) indicated that "there is a need to shift the focus in social work education

and practice from problems or pathology to strengths, resources, and potentialities in human beings and their environments. If this shift occurs, practitioners would be more likely to view clients as capable of organizing their own lives" (p. 401). This is a positive way of looking at clients, highlighting their strengths rather than their weaknesses, which also focuses on respect for individual dignity. How would you feel if your weaknesses were constantly pointed out to you and your strengths overlooked? This does not mean that we deny our weaknesses or pretend that we do not have problems, but rather that we should examine the manner in which problems are handled. When positives are presented and highlighted in a person's life situation, it is easier for that person to be motivated to address and deal with weaknesses. When clients feel respected, they are more likely to gain self-respect.

Unfortunately, many social workers tend to highlight and focus on clients' weaknesses rather than strengths. As Maluccio (1979) found in his study of social worker and client perceptions of treatment outcomes and client levels of functioning, there are some striking disparities between worker and client perceptions:

> In general, clients presented themselves as proactive, autonomous human beings who are able to enhance their functioning and competence through the use of counseling service along with the resources operant in themselves and their social networks. Workers, on the other hand, tended to view clients as reactive organisms with continuing problems, weakness, and limited potentialities. (p. 399)

Utilizing the strengths perspective within an ecosystems framework is a positive way of looking at clients.

Dignity for a client comes from actively participating in decision making, planning, and action. The clients' sense of worth and dignity is respected and preserved to the extent that they are involved in decisions and actions affecting them (Compton & Galaway, 1994). To assume that a worker knows what is best for a client robs the client of dignity and also runs the risk of what Mathew Dumont (1968) calls the rescue fantasy:

> The most destructive thing in [practice] is a "rescue fantasy" [in the practitioner]: a feeling that the [practitioner] is divinely sent to pull tormented souls from the pit of suffering and adversity and put them back on the road to happiness and glory. A major reason this fantasy is so destructive is that it carries the conviction that the patient will be saved only through and by the [practitioner] . . . When such a conviction is communicated to patients, verbally or otherwise, they have no choice other than to rebel and leave or become even more helpless, dependent, and sick.

Thus, imposing on a client by taking over, even when based on the desire to be helpful, can hurt rather than help the client. Correspondingly, opportunities for the client to participate will be missed unless the worker is willing to maintain expectations—expectations for participation, expectations for engagement in problem-solving activities, and expectations that the problem will be solved (Compton & Galaway, 1994) or that the client will learn better coping and adapting skills to deal with such situations.

As Saleeby (1992) reiterates, Oxley (1966) discussed the importance of client motivation through worker expectations:

> . . . the worker should learn to expect a little bit more than the client expects of himself. Social workers are very well versed in beginning where the client is but perhaps too often tend to stay where the client is. If they instead assume the responsibility for leadership and imparting realistic hope, they may more effectively strengthen a client's ego and help him (her) to reach or to achieve his (her) full potential and assume social responsibility.

Therefore, your expectations permitting and encouraging client participation will move the client to do more himself or herself and as well as strengthen the dignity of the client.

The dignity and worth of the client is further enhanced by helping the client to become accountable. Implicitly this means that clients' dignity is enhanced when they are treated as people who are responsible for their thoughts, decisions, and behaviors. Accountability does not mean imposing consequences. It simply means enhancing the client's dignity as a responsible person. Also, accountability is a two-way street. The client has the right to expect you to be accountable as well.

Sixty-five-year-old Mrs. Sanchez, a Puerto Rican woman, was married to a school teacher who had a mistress in a nearby town. Mrs. Sanchez was very patient and hoped that the affair would end. She commented that most men, sooner or later, have a mistress somewhere and therefore she was tolerant. Mrs. Sanchez's Anglo social worker, Carmel, was flabbergasted. She chided Mrs. Sanchez for being tolerant. Carmel hastily commented that Mrs. Sanchez should get rid of her husband. Half way through her angry comments Carmel realized that she was overstepping her boundaries without understanding Mrs. Sanchez, her problems, and her culture. At this point Carmel backed off and apologized for her impulsive comments.

No person or social institution is infallible. If a social worker has made a mistake or forgotten to do something, or if an agency has not fulfilled its responsibilities, the best thing to do is to admit the error and apologize in a nondefensive manner. An honest admission of fallibility is likely to make social workers more credible in clients' eyes. An admission of imperfection might also make it easier for clients to acknowledge and deal with their issues when confronted by the generalist. As Compton and Galaway (1994) indicate, confrontation in social work arises out of a desire to support the inherent dignity of an individual and help him or her be responsible rather than out of the anger or frustration that a worker may be experiencing.

Also, the manner in which social workers communicate with clients tells them whether they are respected. Therefore, workers have an obligation to constantly review and be aware of what they are communicating verbally and nonverbally about human dignity. People, including clients, build their self-images on the messages they receive from other people about themselves. People who feel good about themselves have a sense of their own strength and capabilities and tend to deal appropriately with their environment (Compton & Galaway, 1994).

Similarly, social workers must be sensitive to the messages they send out. Do we, in the little things that we do, communicate to other people that they are unique and valued? Social workers can show this by respecting their clients' right to privacy, being on time to keep our appointments with clients, offering constructive and realistic compliments whenever possible, accepting setbacks in the helping process as a necessity, and not blaming clients. Also, workers should constantly ask themselves: "What are my actions communicating to the client about my perception of him or her?"

The beginning generalist needs to think through the practice implications and the challenges of maintaining positive values without imposing them on others. Can you divest yourself of possible tendencies to judge people whose behavior may be highly offensive to you? Another important factor is that you, as a worker, must develop the composure and equanimity to not show embarrassment, dismay, shock, or discomfort when people with problems are presenting and discussing value-laden and emotionally charged situations that are associated with socially unacceptable behaviors (Hepworth et al., 1997).

To effectively help a client, you have to respect the client as a person with inherent worth and dignity. In the case studies that follow, how would you respond to the client while he or she asks for help, keeping this principle in mind. Discuss the feelings and attitudes you experienced while reading about these clients.

Edna is an abusive parent who has been referred to you for help. You were abused as a child. How would you deal with Edna's case? Could you respect her as a person? Even if you have worked through your own feelings, life is a process of ups and downs and you experience fairly constant reminders of your own past. If you were at a low point in your own life, could this cause problems for the client? Total honesty and self-awareness is a necessity in such situations.

A young, single, homeless mother has been arrested for stealing food from a restaurant. An investigation proves that she found an access to the kitchen and has habitually taken food for the past three months. How would you handle this case? In conversation with you, she laments that she was afraid of seeing her children starve. She also adds tiredly that she has found out that it is a cruel world. Your family upbringing and background is conservative. You had your mouth washed with soap if you lied or cheated. You despise dishonesty, whatever the circumstances. How would you deal with the client? Would you empathize with her or disagree, be condescending or authoritative? Would you be able to spend the time to reevaluate your values and rethink honesty and people's circumstances? Can you truly respect this client as a person with worth and dignity when you work with her?

Twenty-year-old Elsie comes to you for help. She has just found out that her husband is having an affair. Unfortunately, as she put it, a week ago she found out that she was pregnant and she is in a dilemma. She is extremely hurt and wants a divorce and an abortion. How would you deal with this situation? Your upbringing is such that you approve of neither and you just had a baby three months ago. How would you deal with her problems? What are the options open to you as a social worker?

You are the group worker for perpetrators who have been court-mandated for counseling. Every one of them has sexually abused a child, in most cases, his or her own. You have a five-year-old daughter and are protective of her. Given a choice in your field work, you would not work with this group of people, but you have few options. Think about it and discuss it.

In a general staff meeting at a large county department of human services, the tension was mounting and staff members were arguing about the director's decision, in an effort to cut costs in the agency, to end the practice of generalists sending appointment letters to their clients. These letters were sent to clients who did not have access to a phone; the workers notified clients about a week in advance about the date and time they would be making a home visit. Faced with a tight budget, the director calculated that using secretarial staff for typing and mailing the letters was unnecessary. When the director announced the policy, some of the staff objected and questioned how they were supposed to let clients know they would be paying them a home visit. The social work supervisor confronted the director, saying "You are ignoring the clients' rights. This does not show respect for their worth and dignity. No one can expect to see you without scheduling an appointment ahead of time. Why should clients be treated with less respect?" Other workers joined in the protest. The director, who was concerned about cutting costs and avoiding criticism from the county government, stormed out of the meeting in anger. How would you react to this new information from the director and how would you handle it? If you were the supervisor how would you use your advocacy strategies to reach a compromise between the director and the clients' needs?

Acceptance of the Client

The generalist has to learn to accept clients of all kinds. In the social work field, professionals work with people of different religious, ethnic, racial, and socioeconomic backgrounds and sexual orientation. Beyond this, clients have specific family backgrounds that also influence behavior and lifestyles.

Acceptance involves respecting clients' rights to be themselves and acknowledging their needs and feelings of inadequacy. Carl Rogers (1961) stressed the importance of having "positive regard" and "non-possessive warmth" for clients, irrespective of who they are. This does not mean reassuring the client that everything will turn out all right, or taking over and playing the savior. A lot depends on the amount of effort clients wish to invest in their own situations, and false promises or quick reassurances only lead to credibility gaps in the worker–client relationship.

Beginning and experienced professionals need to understand why they wish to be in the social work profession. They also need to be aware of the way they feel about certain client groups and certain types of behaviors that may trigger negative feelings and strain relationships. These include clients who neglect or abuse vulnerable family members or who have violated major laws or mores of society and show no remorse. How does one deal with such clients? Because it is very important to accept clients while working with them, it is essential that professionals develop

awareness of their reactions to these behaviors and evolve patterns of response to safeguard the helping relationship.

Again, social workers are people. They may be vulnerable to responding negatively to some types of behaviors and not to others. According to Hepworth et al. (1997), some behaviors that pose threats to acceptance and respect by a worker include:

When a client acts extremely helpless and is also excessively dependent.

When a client is verbally aggressive or is completely sullen all the time.

When a client smells excessively.

When a client dresses shabbily in unclean clothes.

When a client is excessively manipulative and exploitative.

When the client reveals passive noncompliant behavior.

One way of learning to accept clients is to work at understanding your own feelings, attitudes and behavior. As you read the cases that follow, ask yourself these questions: What are your feelings and attitudes while reading about the case? Were your feelings the result of the actuality of the given situation, or are they the result of preconceived beliefs about such clients? What would your experiences be with these clients? Would you be comfortable, uneasy, or judgmental? What values do you think would be reflected in your behavior, attitudes, and feelings?

Take your time and analyze each case from your perspective. If you notice biases creeping in, be honest with yourself and question why you feel the way you do. If it is warranted, can you consciously work at changing your behavior? After you have examined your own feelings, attitudes, and behaviors, decide why you will or will not be comfortable with a client. Also bear in mind the principles or cardinal values of social work. Being a social worker implies that you need to work with different and, at times, difficult situations. Are you prepared to do so?

You, a new generalist, are asked to start a self-help group for men suffering from AIDS. You are upset about the new assignment because the whole subject of AIDS makes you very nervous. How would you deal with this situation? Would you take time to read, discuss, and understand AIDS as a disease and as a social problem in order to be empathetic to the victims, or would you avoid the issue and be of minimal help to the AIDS victims. Think it over.

In a clinical session, eighteen-year-old Tracey informs you that she was sexually molested by her father until she was almost fifteen. She is now living in another state with her boyfriend. Her father calls her frequently and is aware that she is receiving help. At one session, she agitatedly says that her father will be visiting her the following week and adds that he wishes to come with her to see you. At that session, he laments to Tracey that he is ashamed and regrets his earlier behavior. How would you react to the father? Would you accept and trust him? Would you take a instant dislike to him? Would you be overly cautious?

You are interviewing a couple. It is obvious that there has been battering in the family. The husband is the abuser. The wife appears to be a frightened and timid person who is very compliant to her husband. How would you feel about this case and why? How would you handle it?

Jon sought help with marital conflicts, but after a short period of time his wife divorced him. Jon complains that he feels helpless and does not have anything to live for. Two weeks after his wife leaves him, you find out that he has been dealing drugs. Responding to your query, he says that he would not have any money without the drug deals. He is also suffering from depression and anxiety. Would you accept him and work with him? Why or why not?

Mandated by the court, a young rapist in a group session complains that he dislikes his mother and therefore all women. He has raped about five young girls. You are a woman and the only social worker in that system. Would you accept the client? How would you deal with this situation?

In the helping process, the social worker's acceptance lowers a client's anxieties, increases self-respect and self-esteem, aids in the client's expression of feelings, builds up trust between the worker and the client, and establishes respect for the worker as a competent practitioner.

Uniqueness and Individuality of Clients

This principle is intertwined with accepting clients as individuals with dignity and self-worth. Uniqueness is a multidimensional concept, and it differentiates one person from another (Pray, 1991). All clients are unique, and social workers should both affirm and highlight the individuality of those whom they serve. Honoring the uniqueness of clients is central to social work. Respecting uniqueness is a clearly defined concept in the NASW *Code of Ethics*, one that is accepted as fundamental to the social work profession. Many social workers claim strict adherence to such a worthy and respectable value stance. However, in their haste to subscribe to something that is obviously positive, social workers often fail to explore what the concept means. Many times they fail to examine how they came to accept the concept as central to their professional value base, and they do not examine how they are actually applying the value in their day to day work experiences (Pray, 1991). Many years ago, Richmond insightfully noted (1917):

> Sometimes a case worker tends to become over absorbed in the individual case, but a [more common] failing of the modern type of worker is that, oppressed by the condition of the mass, he misses a clear conception of the one client's needs. He thinks of him as one of a class. (pp. 96–97)

All people are unique in their physical and mental characteristics. They differ from each other in their physical features, mental endowments, physiological functioning, interests and talents, motivation, goals, values, emotional and behavioral patterns, socioeconomic status, and so forth. All of us need to accept the fact that there will never be two people who are exactly the same in their ways of being and thinking. Problems may appear similar and some situations may be similar, but people are unique and almost always very different from each other. Tillich (1962), a theologian who directed attention to the philosophy of social work, commented on the uniqueness of every person and situation as people's existential nature. Also William Gordon (1969) related that the social work profession does not attempt to move either the environment or the person toward any ideal model but rather attempts to establish linkages between persons and their environments, thus giving the widest possible diversity for both people and environments.

However, problems arise in our society when differences are labeled and stereotyped and when people are viewed as objects and treated alike. People of different races and ethnic groups, irrespective of their differences in terms of religion, educational status, and social class, are often pigeonholed and stereotyped as being the same. The pitfalls of labeling are well documented by sociologists studying deviance from a labeling perspective (Becker, 1963; Platt, 1977; Schur, 1973). Barker (1995) points out that in a labeling theory the hypothesis is that when people are assigned a label, such as paranoid schizophrenia, to indicate some kind of disorder or deviance, others tend to react to the subjects as though they are deviant. The subjects may in turn begin to act in a way that meets the others' expectations in the model of a self-fulfilling prophecy (p. 207). When people, particularly children in their impressionable years, are labeled as unmanageable, stupid, and/or dull, this labeling often leads to other problems. Those who are labeled respond to others based on the label rather than their unique characteristics.

A thirteen-year-old who was labeled as suffering from "conduct disorder," had lived at a residential treatment center for three years. When he misbehaved, his social worker attempted to structure him by reiterating rules he needed to follow. In turn, he teasingly responded to her that he was "crazy" and she should not expect him to behave, because all social workers knew they were working with crazy kids and he was one of them—impressive insight from a so-called disturbed adolescent.

This teenager was attempting to live up to the label that was created for him (Pillari, 1991).

Another case of labeling shows how the poor quality of schools, the attitudes of teachers and coaches, and the antieducation biases of peers has an effect on students. A forty-two-year-old African American man who got a college degree through his athletic scholarship and became a successful professional relates:

> By junior high, you either get identified as an athlete, a thug, or a bookworm. It's very important to be seen as somebody who's capable in some area. And you don't want to be identified as a bookworm. I was very good with books, but I was a kind of covert about it. I was a closet bookworm. But with sports, I was somebody so I worked hard at it. (Messner, p. 174)

Assessment techniques through which individuality can be explored and subsequent categorization or labeling minimized are discussed in Chapter 11.

It is important to acknowledge some of the few advantages in labeling clients with ailments such as mental illness. Labeling that has been reached after a proper diagnosis by a medical professional can help a social work practitioner to work with clients based on the assessment. The practitioner will also have to develop an understanding of prescribed medications and their side effects on clients.

One way of appreciating a person's uniqueness is being able to enter that individual's world in an attempt to understand his or her life experiences, thoughts, feelings, daily stresses, hopes, longings, disappointments, and hurts. By spending time with and learning more about a person, one can gain a full appreciation of the rich and complex individuality and uniqueness of that person. This does not mean that once you understand, you condone. It simply means that you look at that person as an individual with problems in living, a client, who is different from other clients with whom you are working. Your role as a social worker continues to be the same—to help clients work through issues or cope and adapt to those issues, however simple or complex they may be.

Affirming a person's individuality and uniqueness is impossible when practitioners are blind to a client's unique differences because they are influenced by prejudices and stereotypes. Prejudice is the holding of derogatory social attitudes or cognitive beliefs, the expression of negative affect, or the display of hostile or discriminatory behavior towards members of a group based on their membership in that group (Brown, 1995).

A stereotype is an inference drawn from the assignment of a person to a specific category. The word *stereotype* has a curious origin. It actually derives from an aspect of printing process in which a mold is made so as to duplicate patterns or pictures on a page. Lippmann (1922) was a political journalist who first saw the aptness of the term to describe how people use cognitive molds to reproduce images of people or events in their minds—the "pictures in our heads" as he called them (p. 4). A second explanation for the origin of stereotypes is that they derive, however tenuously, from some aspect of social reality. This does not mean any stereotype of a group is in some way objectively "true" in the sense that it accurately describes the group's actual characteristics. Rather, the suggestion is that a group's culturally distinctive behavior patterns or the particular socioeconomic circumstances in which the group finds itself could provide the context in which certain stereotypical perceptions could flourish. This is the "grain of truth" theory of the origin of stereotypes (Allport, 1954; Brewer & Campbell, 1976; Brown, 1995).

Prejudices in our society are directed toward people who are different from us in terms of race, ethnicity, gender, religion, sexual orientation, political preference, and lifestyle. When we get to the root of prejudice, often there is misinformation about a particular group of people, along with limited or inaccurate information. Many times, people have had no interaction with members of the groups toward which they are prejudiced.

One student was very frightened to work with the elderly because Dick was terrified of becoming old. When there was a discussion of the elderly in the first semester class, he stayed away from class. As often happens in such situations, his second-year field placement turned out to be in a geriatric center. As Dick got used to the elderly,

his prejudices diminished; by the end of the year, they had disappeared completely. The student's frequent personal contacts with the elderly had a positive effect. Dick enjoyed his work with the elderly to such a great degree and worked so efficiently and compassionately with them that he was offered a job after he received his degree, and took it.

Often, when people are subjected to actual experiences with a particular group of people, differences—whether they are real or imagined—shrink to insignificance. This is due to the fact that people are more aware of their similarities than differences. Being freed of prejudices makes members of another group look worthwhile and interesting.

Frequently, stereotyped perceptions are directly related to prejudices that usually derive from preconceived opinions about people based on their membership in different groups (Hepworth & Larsen, 1993). Stereotypes about others make it difficult to see the uniqueness and individuality of people. Negative prejudices can lead a worker to unwittingly restrict a client from achieving his or her potential.

Some of the different types of prejudices prevalent in the United States include stereotyped perceptions of racial and ethnic minority groups, women, different lifestyles, the elderly, people with physical and mental disabilities, AIDS victims, and the homeless. Unchecked prejudices lead to discriminatory behavior (see Figure 2.3). Awareness and willingness to work on their prejudices can enable social workers and clients to move more easily into constructive working relationships.

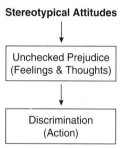

FIGURE 2.3 **Stereotypes**

Although one of the first steps toward working with different people is to be aware of one's own prejudices and biases, it is completely unrealistic to think that all people can get rid of all their prejudices. It is impossible to be totally free of preconceived attitudes, but developing an awareness of and acknowledging biases puts the practitioner in a position to attempt to overcome them.

All of us have varying degrees of prejudice. What is necessary for the practitioner is to expand his or her awareness of prejudices that might limit effective work with different types of clients. In the case studies that follow, note how the situations could be handled with reference to uniqueness and individuality. Keep in mind that in the cases presented the purpose is not to focus on the client but to focus on yourself in terms of your awareness of your own attitudes, behaviors, and, feelings. It may be a good idea to begin a personal journal where you can examine your own values and self-awareness as a beginning professional.

A fifty-year-old woman, Carolyn, sits in front of you. She is having problems disciplining her children who live at home. The children range in age from five to twenty; the oldest is a single parent herself. Recently, Carolyn has been beaten by her oldest child and has a swollen face. As she is communicating with you, you are nearly overcome by her body odor. You also notice that she has on dirty clothes and constantly picks her nose. She wears no makeup. When you talk about the daughter who had beaten her, she laughs. Her laughter appears inappropriate to you. How did you react to the case as you read it? Did you have physical reactions that reflected uneasiness, annoyance, irritation, or repulsion on your part? Why? How would you deal with the situation if you were Carolyn's social worker?

A fourteen-year-old girl, Linda, from a upper middle-class family comes to your agency because she is pregnant. Her parents are career people and her father is well known. She desperately wants an abortion and requests that you give her information about safe clinics. Her friends have suggested that your agency will be able to help, which is true; you frequently make referrals to abortion clinics when there are unwanted pregnancies. How would you handle this case? Linda does not want her parents to know. She has a lot of money to pay you and the agency if you can help her in the abortion. She looks and behaves very differently from any kind of client you have had. What are your initial reactions to her?

A young couple planning to be married soon comes to you for marriage counseling. The man is Caucasian, athletic, and very good-looking with blonde hair and blue eyes. The woman is African American, dark-complexioned, and very good-looking. You are a single Anglo man. Do you have prejudices and stereotypes about people? Are they reflected in your attitudes, body reactions, and feelings? How would you handle this case?

You were brought up to believe that different races were all right but they should not mix. As an adoption worker, you have just learned that a Caucasian couple wants to adopt a black child. How would you respond to this situation?

A lesbian couple walks in for help. Karen is in her forties and Julie is in her thirties. They have recently become lovers and want to pursue a committed relationship. Karen is very resentful of Julie's congenial relationship with her parents, who are accepting of her lifestyle. Karen does not have a good relationship with her parents and is also very possessive of Julie. She will not allow Julie to visit her parents and is very resentful when Julie talks to them. Julie complains that Karen is very possessive, and Karen in turn complains that Julie is insensitive to her feelings and would rather spend more time on the phone with her mother than with her. They wish to work things out. As they see it, everything else is all right in this relationship. What feelings and attitudes did you experience? How would you handle this case?

You are placed in a hospital setting. Your understanding is that you will work with dialysis patients. You are very excited and eager to learn. Due to some sudden changes, you move to the AIDS ward where more help is needed. You are faced with a young, wasted man dying of AIDS. How do you feel? How would you handle the case?

As a student in an ethnicity class, you are asked to speak to each other about yourselves and then participate in a group encounter that highlights differences in people. There are Caucasians, African Americans, Asians, Native Americans, and Hispanics in the class. How would you feel and handle this situation? What reactions have you had to similar people and situations in the past?

Your idea of an agency is influenced by field work experiences in the university system. During your first year, you were placed in two middle-class settings, where you worked well with clients. But due to changed circumstances, in the second-year field practicum you are placed in a public welfare agency with sparse furnishings, working with poor people. The agency workers appear to look down on their clients. How would you deal with your clients? How would you deal with the culture of the agency staff?

It is important to recognize that all of us have some form of prejudice. To say that we are completely without prejudices is, of course, deceiving ourselves. People who are not willing to acknowledge and come to terms with their prejudices will, in the long run, do more harm than good to clients.

Self-Determination in Clients

This principle is based on the fact that self-determination enables clients to reflect their own dignity and uniqueness. It also reflects the fact that we live in a democracy. When people possess inherent dignity, they should be able to choose and make decisions about their own lifestyles, provided they follow the rules of society and do not hurt themselves or others. The NASW *Code of Ethics* (1996) upholds clients' rights to make their own choices. The freedom to choose and decide reflects the principle of self-determination.

Biestek (1957) defined self-determination as the "practical recognition of the right and need of clients to freedom in making their own choices and decisions" (p. 103). As part of self-determination, the client should have the freedom to develop new alternatives in order to expand opportunities for self-determination. Biestek continues that the principle is limited by the client's capacity for informed and constructive decision making within the framework of civil and moral law, and also by the social work agency's functional responsibilities.

Hollis (1967) and Hollis and Wood (1981) describe how self-determination relates to freedom and self-growth. They say that for growth to take place from within there must be freedom—that is, freedom to think, freedom to choose, and freedom from condemnation, freedom from coercion, and freedom to make mistakes as well as to act wisely. Clients should be encouraged to experience and exercise the freedom to direct their own thoughts and behaviors. Clients are often limited by their own stereotypical, patterned behaviors; they do not know what alternatives to choose, simply because they have not been exposed to different options. However, even if there are no options, clients should be encouraged to discuss and acknowledge their frustration, anger, and other emotions.

If a social worker has to act on behalf of clients who have been adjudged legally incompetent, the social worker should safeguard the interests and rights of the clients who cannot or may not be able to self-determine. When another individual has been legally authorized to act on behalf of a client, the social worker should deal with that person, *always* keeping the client's best interests in mind. The social worker should never engage in any action that violates or diminishes the civil or legal rights of clients.

Self-determination implies that the client should be able to make decisions or choices between possible courses of action. Often, self-determination involves a quest for alternatives in order to expand opportunities for self-determination. Helping clients to self-determine may involve assisting them to develop alternatives and resources in a community in new ways or develop different ways of responding to outside or environmental needs. Empowerment-based social work practice creates opportunities for clients to exercise not only choices but their privilege to choose. Involving social services consumers—that is, clients—at all levels of decision making quells potential encroachments on self-determination (Miley, O'Melia, & Dubois, 1998). As Tower (1994) states: "If practitioners align themselves with the interests of consumers, including consumer input and control, the result will be greater self-determination among clients and less ethical discord regarding paternalism within the helping professions" (p. 196).

The extent to which social workers affirm self-determination rests to a large extent on their perception of the helping role. If a social worker views his or her job as providing solutions and takes over and solve clients' issues, they force clients into dependency. This approach demeans clients because it views them as incapable of taking care of themselves. It relegates clients to a position of passive cooperation or passive resistance (Hepworth et al., 1997). If you think your major role is to give advice and find solutions for the client, you could foster excessive dependency, which may prevent clients from affirming their strengths. Such behavior is counterproductive and does not encourage open communication. Doing things for clients that they could do for themselves also denies them opportunities to gain strength and self-respect as they struggle with problems. Fostering excessive dependency also leaves people feeling weaker rather than stronger and does a disservice to clients (Hepworth et al., 1997).

Although social workers subscribe to the rule of self-determination, we also subscribe to enhancing the client's autonomy. But coercion or paternalism infringe upon the autonomy of a client and also deprive a person from exercising choice. As Abramson (1985) indicates, a worker who takes paternalistic action for a client should be obligated to justify such actions and assume responsibility for the same. Situations in which such paternalism is justified occur when a client is a child or is considered mentally incompetent, or when the consequences of an act are far reaching, for example, when a client makes a serious effort to commit suicide.

Self-determination can be constrained in one of two ways. Blockages in the environment may limit opportunities and prevent a person from self-determining; for instance, a social worker cannot help a person get into a housing complex when there is inadequate housing. Unfortunately, there are clients whose range of response is limited by their own stereotyped and patterned behaviors, feelings, and cognition. They lack the ability to self-determine because internal blockages limit their ability to see and use alternative courses of action. Internal blocks include cognitive structures that may prevent clients from considering alternatives to their thinking, behaving, and patterned emotional responses to social situations.

Some clients display learned helplessness. Such clients believe they cannot avoid victimization and, therefore, adopt helplessness as a way of life, which becomes passive dependency. People who are passively dependent often believe that there is nothing they can do to control events. They are unable to make decisions because their self-determination is constrained.

It is crucial to remember that social workers are not engaged in the process of forcing people to change. Unless there is a report indicating that a client cannot seriously self-determine, any work aimed at changing clients' values and behavior should be considered only in light of needs and the life satisfaction and only when the client and the generalist work together (Compton & Galaway, 1994).

According to Compton & Galaway (1989), the principle of self-determination guides the practitioner in three different directions: (1) to consider how values may restrict progress toward the goals desired by the clients; (2) to determine the alternatives and their consequences for achieving the goals; and (3) to consider the needs and rights of others.

Another essential factor to remember is that while the social worker is not the chief person to judge what is best for the client this does not preclude giving advice at certain times. As Charlotte Towle (1945) noted more than fifty years ago, "The social worker's devotion to the idea that every individual has a right to be self-determining does not rule out valid concern with directing people's attention to the most desirable alternative" (p. 25). Workers have an obligation to share their own thinking, but their input should be presented as information and not as an edict to be followed.

While considering the value of self-determination, practitioners ask the following questions laid out by Compton and Galaway (1994):

1. Is the practitioner able to commit clients and self to a quest for alternatives?
2. Is the social worker able to make a special effort to increase clients' opportunities for decision making?
3. Does the social worker have an obligation to offer viewpoints and suggestions to clients while allowing clients to have the ultimate right to make decisions?
4. Does the social worker attempt to change clients' values that are inconsistent with the concept of self-determination and interfere with efforts to attain the goals?
5. Does the practitioner always maintain a distinction between worker and client determination?

Another important point to remember is that client self-determination is based on rules and authority of society, which are closely interrelated. Thus society has a right and duty to intervene in the lives of people under certain circumstances. This role is delegated to social workers by society for reasons of mutual protection and as an alternative to what could be considered more drastic intervention, social punishment, or self-destruction. The social worker's use of authority and coercion is justified when this use is in accordance with statutory provisions universally applied; when this action contributes to a client's maturation, well-being, or safety; and when it helps to build responsibility in clients' minds. When a client wishes to do something wrong, the worker cannot force him or her *not* to do it. But social workers have an obligation to report certain kinds of wrongdoing to appropriate authorities. For example, when a client mentions to you that he had attempted to kill himself once, changed his mind at the last minute, but may again want to end his life, the appropriate authorities, including the police and his immediate family should be informed.

A worker's activities and involvement with a client may be limited by a legal authority such as the courts or the prison system. The courts limit self-determination but for a good cause: to protect the innocent public from clients' activities. Clients who are offenders are required to receive coerced services, thus, their degree of self-determination may hinge largely on the type of services offered and the manner in which they are made available.

The withholding of self-determination may mean temporary interference with a client's liberty, but some people forfeit their right to freedom by violating laws and infringing on the rights of others. These infringements might include criminal acts resulting in incarceration, such as child abuse or neglect, status offenses such as running away from home or habitual truancy, unethical acts, and refusal to secure medical services for minor children and violation of moral laws.

In order to encourage self-determination, workers must help clients view problems realistically, consider solutions and their consequences, and implement change-oriented strategies. Clients should also be helped to learn more about their own strengths and weaknesses, look and move toward opportunities for growth, and deal with obstacles, which are part of change and growth. The case studies that follow explore the principle of self-determination in a variety of circumstances. How would you deal with the notion of self-determination, keeping in mind the best interests and welfare of the client?

Eighty-year-old Leonard is a recipient of public assistance. He is in poor health, and his memory and thinking are also affected. Initially, you were called in on an emergency basis because Leonard had been smoking in bed and set the bed on fire. His apartment is in deplorable condition. He is very forgetful and is incapable of taking care of himself, and may need supervised care in a nursing home. After a discussion about care, Leonard gets angry and opposes the suggestion about moving to a nursing home. On inquiry, you find out that Leonard has five married children living in the area. His children are generally uninvolved but insist that you persuade their father to move into a nursing home. How would you handle this case?

Thirty-year-old Teresa is frustrated and unhappy. After her husband died in a car accident, Teresa managed to feed and clothe her three children because she has held a decent job. But due to an economic crisis in her company, she has been laid off and has no other source of income. Teresa is depressed and in one session with the worker she constantly talks about suicide or getting rid of the children. How would you handle this case situation?

A young woman with mental disabilities living in an institution has been sexually acting out for years. Since age fourteen she has given birth to four children. She is now almost twenty years old, unmarried, and pregnant again. She does not take care of her children, all of whom have been placed in foster homes. Her family has no interest in her or her children. Should she carry this pregnancy to term? Should she be sterilized after delivery? Should she be allowed to carry any pregnancy to term? Should she be sent back home to her family? How would you handle this situation?

In a residential setting for emotionally disturbed children, fifteen-year-old Lisa is pregnant again. She had one baby whom she mistreated, and the child was placed in foster care. Lisa's background shows that she was physically and sexually abused as a child. The consulting psychiatrist says that if Lisa is not allowed to go through her pregnancy she will become depressed. He also notes that her interest in the child may be short-lived as she apparently talks of the unborn child as if it was a plaything for her immediate amusement. You are a married social worker without children as you are infertile, but you love children. How would you counsel Lisa? Why?

Tom and Cynthia have been married for three years. One day in a fit of anger, Tom beat Cynthia after having a very bad day at work. He claimed that Cynthia was inattentive to him when he came home from work and wanted to share his problems with her. Cynthia had been preoccupied with their three-month-old child. That episode took place over a year ago. Since then, Cynthia has been physically abused by him at least a half dozen times. After each incident, however, Tom becomes very remorseful, buys gifts for Cynthia and promises never to beat her. But the pattern continues. Cynthia comes to see the worker because Tom is now threatening to beat their son when he cries or gets in his father's way. Cynthia is afraid that he will beat the child. She says she's become accustomed to Tom beating her, but is afraid for her young son. She has never worked outside the home and feels she has to settle for second best. How would you handle this case?

In conclusion, it can be said that social workers who advocate self-determination based on the

needs of the clients, functions of the agency, and rules of society can foster collaboration, affirm client strengths, activate resources, and expand opportunities (Miley et al., 1998).

Principle of Confidentiality

An important ethical consideration is the nature of the relationship within which the confidences the client shares with the worker are protected. The principle of confidentiality reflects a commitment of trust, without which the therapeutic relationship cannot develop fully. The terms *privileged communication* and *confidentiality* have been used interchangeably to describe this principle, but there is a distinct difference between these two concepts. Privileged communication is a legal concept that deals with the admission of evidence into court (Gothard, 1989). Confidentiality refers to the "laws or rules of professional ethics that regulate the disclosure of information obtained in psychotherapy" (Gothard, p. 65).

There are two types of confidentiality: absolute and relative. Absolute confidentiality refers to the ethical position demanding that the practitioner not break confidentiality under any circumstances. It means that information shared with the therapist should never be discussed or shared with anyone else, either in the form of a written case record or a computerized record. Relative confidentiality, which is more common, refers to the ethical position mandating that the practitioner may break confidentiality under certain circumstances. With relative confidentiality, information can be used for educational purposes and shared both in written and oral forms within an agency and also with others outside the agency under special circumstances (Watkins, 1990).

Confidentiality also means that the personal affairs of clients should never be an item of gossip, either in private or public situations. This consideration is a way of respecting and affirming the worth of clients. Confidentiality is necessary for all purposes—legal, ethical, and practical. In order for clients to share all their issues, they need to trust the worker and be able to talk unreservedly.

The worker has to assure the client, both verbally and nonverbally, that all information is confidential. If there is to be breach of confidentiality, there must be specific legal, ethical, or practical reasons. Otherwise both the worker and the agency should be responsible for safeguarding the client's interests. At times another social worker, other professional, or another agency may want information about a client for relevant purposes. In these situations, it is necessary that the information be provided only with the written, informed consent of the client, releasing the social worker and the agency from liability in revealing this information.

Another reason why confidentiality is critical is that the confidential information clients share with workers could destroy family relationships. This includes information about marital infidelity, illicit activities, emotional abuse when the client was growing up, and the like. Social workers must maintain strict confidentiality when clients confide detrimental information about their family history or information that is shocking. Such information should be held confidential unless it could hurt someone in the future. For example, when a 22-old-woman mentions that she was sexually abused by her father and fears for her four younger sisters who are still living at home, the worker must find out if the younger siblings are being molested and handle the case accordingly. Legal authorities may have to become involved in this case. Similarly, if a woman asking for help states that she had an affair and is HIV positive, however traumatic, the husband must be informed of the same.

An unjustified breach of confidentiality is a violation of justice and is tantamount to a secret being stolen (Biestek, 1957). Clients bring in all kinds of information, humorous, traumatic, and bizarre. It is the social worker's responsibility not to reveal this information inappropriately. In addition to the loss of a client's trust, breach of confidentiality could result in a malpractice suit and loss of the right to practice.

A number of cases involving client–worker privilege of confidentiality have been decided by courts. Two decisions upheld the confidentiality of client communications with social workers and stated that the communication is a privilege just like communications between lawyers and clients or physicians and patients (Schwartz, 1989).

The NASW *Code of Ethics* (1996) specifically addresses confidentiality and privacy applicable to individual relationships:

> In terms of confidentiality and privacy, the social worker should respect the privacy of clients and hold in confidence all information obtained in the course of professional services.
>
> The social worker should *not* share with others confidences revealed by clients, without their consent, unless it is for compelling professional reasons. The social worker should inform the client fully about the limits of confidentiality in a given situation, the purpose for which information is obtained and how it may be used. The social worker should afford clients reasonable access to any official social work records concerning them. When providing clients with access to records, the social worker should take due care to protect the confidences of others contained in those records. The social worker should obtain informed consent of clients before taping, recording, or permitting third-party observation of their activities. When social workers provide counseling services to families, couples, and groups, workers cannot guarantee that all participants will honor all such agreements. (pp. 9–10)

However, the right to confidentiality is not always absolute. For instance, the information on the client is usually typed by clerical staff and information may be shared in staff meetings where other involved professionals, such as the psychiatrist, the supervisor, and the cottage parent, are present. The main purpose of any form of disclosure is to serve the client better or protect others in the client's life. Social workers should maintain confidentiality when information is transmitted to other parties through use of computers, electronic mail, facsimile machines, telephones, telephone answering machines, and other electronic or computer technology.

In some cases, protecting others in the client's life could be a compelling reason to overlook the client's right to confidentiality. In some settings—

for example, child protective services, foster care, probation, parole, and mental health—the worker is required to report on what the client says and does as a basis for decision making. There is mandated reporting of child abuse or neglect in all states. Thus when a little girl is being sexually abused by her father who happens to be the client, it is in the best interests of the child that this information be reported to protect her from a harmful and dangerous situation.

In child abuse and neglect cases a *waiver of privilege,* supported by various state courts, places the child's welfare first. In 1981, in response to the growing concern about child abuse and neglect, the NASW issued *Standards for Social Work Practice in Child Protection.* Among its provisions:

> The Social Worker Shall Comply with Child Abuse and Neglect Reporting Laws and Procedures. It is the responsibility of every social worker to obtain knowledge of the state's child abuse and neglect laws and procedures, and to share the knowledge with employers and colleagues. In addition, whenever it is necessary to report a case of suspected abuse and neglect, the social worker shall collaborate with CPS and, as appropriate, shall explain the report and the CPS procedure to family members. (p. 27)

There are *duty-to-warn laws* in the United States based on *Tarasoff v. The Regents of University of California.* Handed down by the Supreme Court of California in 1976, the decision placed a firm duty on therapists to warn local authorities about a patient who threatened to harm a third party and to warn the potential victim. As Gothard (1990) reports, in the Tarasoff case a female student at the University of California broke off a brief relationship with a male student. The man whom Ms. Tarasoff rejected started going to a psychologist at the university counseling center. At least two months before he actually committed the murder, the male student mentioned to the therapist that he intended to kill his ex-girlfriend. The therapist, with the concurrence of two psychiatrists at the clinic, determined that these threats were real and

reported them to the campus police who were supposed to place the male student in a mental hospital for observation. While in custody, the student convinced the police that he was rational. The police released him with a warning and a promise that he would stay away from Ms. Tarasoff. The student stopped going to the psychologist after this incident and shortly thereafter went to Ms. Tarasoff's residence and killed her. Her parents were not informed of the potential danger to their daughter. They later filed a lawsuit. In that case, the court ruled:

> When a therapist determines, or pursuant to the standards of his profession should determine, that his patient presents a serious danger of violence to another, he incurs an obligation to use reasonable care to protect the intended victim against such danger. The discharge of this duty may require the therapist to take one or more of the various steps, depending upon the nature of the case. Thus it may call for him to warn the intended victim or others likely to apprise the victim of the danger, to notify the police, or to take whatever other steps are reasonably necessary under the circumstances. (p. 340)

Based on this ruling there is a special relationship between the therapist and a potential victim of the therapist's patient. *Tarasoff v. The University of California* places a duty on the therapist to warn the potential victim of the patient's threat of violence (Gothard, 1990).

In the mid-1980s, two variations were added to the Tarasoff duty-to-warn principle. Of special relevance to social workers are the following: (1) social workers have a duty to warn sexual partners of a client's diagnosis of acquired immune deficiency syndrome (AIDS) or a positive test for human immunodeficiency virus (HIV); and (2) the social worker has a duty to warn the loved ones of a client's suicidal propensities (Gothard, 1990).

Confidential information can be used to help prevent serious problems such as a man threatening suicide. If a practitioner does not make appropriate disclosure in potentially damaging situations, the practitioner is liable to civil prosecution for carelessness and negligence.

On the other hand, there are situations in which the case records may be subpoenaed. Because clients and other personnel have access to records, it is important for practitioners to work toward providing maximum confidentiality. Clients must be made aware that their sessions are being recorded or videotaped. It would be unethical to do so without a client's permission or knowledge. Videotapes of clients are useful for training sessions and for understanding moment-to-moment transactions. However, clients must be asked permission and informed of their right to decline. Also their written permission must be obtained before the worker can record or tape them.

One of the biggest problems faced by the beginning practitioner or the self-conscious student is how to ask for permission. In most instances, when the worker explains that a recording will be used for supervision or training purposes, the client wishes to be helpful and does not object. Whether the tape will be erased after discussion or used for other teaching purposes should also be explained. Finally, the worker must explain the procedures involved in audio or video recording before the client is asked to sign the waiver form.

When writing case records, the worker should record no more than what is required by the agency. Case records should be maintained in locked files and only those people who should have access ought to have a key to the files. Normally, social workers, other clinicians, their supervisors, and the required staff are allowed access to these records.

The case studies that follow ask you to consider how you as a social worker would deal with confidentiality issues.

You are working with a group of young adolescent boys in a residential setting. While in group session, a couple of the group members start to laugh about the rules of the agency, because they have used drugs while in this setting. Another boy mentions that some of the boys get together secretly to sexually abuse a boy who behaves like a girl. Another boy talks about wanting to run away

from the agency. The adolescents trust you completely. You have even had dinner with them in their cottage. They enjoy their "casual rap" with you. How would you handle this situation?

A highly qualified physician with an extremely fast-growing practice is in therapy with you. He is divorced from his first wife and has just remarried. The custody of his three children is still unresolved; however, he mentions that the custody hearing will take place shortly. The ex-wife has violated his visitation rights for a year. Your client tells you that if the wife does not bring the children to see him in the court room as promised, he will definitely kill her. He has a plan and talks about it. He appears to be more qualified as a professional than you. What should you do?

A former client of yours comes to you in a panic. She has just reentered the agency system. In tears, she confides that she just found out that her oldest child, Daryl, whom you had also seen in therapy for a period of time, is sexually abusing his eight-year-old stepsister. She says that she is afraid but trusts you, and she does not want anyone to know about the family incest situation. She describes 14-year-old Daryl as having made a mistake about which he is really sorry and upset. The children are living in the house with her at this point. You have worked with this family for a period of fourteen months and recognize certain strengths in the family. How would you discharge your ethical responsibility in this situation and also your legal responsibility? It is obvious that the client does not wish to be reported. How would you handle this situation?

Roxy and Randy are in their late thirties and have been married for over nineteen years. They are Catholics and practice their religion diligently. Randy is a police officer and Roxy stays home and takes care of their six children. They are receiving help from you because they have a number of marital conflicts, which through the years have created a gap and lack of caring between the couple. After a few sessions, you realize that the situation is not so hopeless. Both of them wish to work at their relationship. They do not believe in divorce. At times, Roxy has asked for individual sessions, in which she has vented some of her frustrations in the marriage. After four months of therapy, Randy asks for a separate session. He confides with guilt that he had at least two affairs in the past few years. He has a long discussion about his past and why he did what he did. At the end of the session, he requests that you not repeat this information to his wife because she is not aware of it. She could use it against him or even divorce him. How would you handle this situation?

You are working in a hospital setting where there are AIDS patients. Some of them look healthier than others. You work with all of them and have learned to like and respect them. One of these clients, who is in his early twenties, has deteriorated and is clearly dying of AIDS. He is emaciated and hardly able to get up from his bed. He tells you that he wants to die, and you empathize with him. Two days later you find he has acquired a weapon through a friend and has concealed it in his bed. He tells you he will kill himself. You have seen him change from a bright, fairly healthy person to a helpless, weak, and angry man. How would you react to his statements? Would you experience any conflicting emotions regarding the kind of action to take? Why?

All social workers need to practice based on the principle of confidentiality contained in the NASW *Code of Ethics,* and adhere to the statutory enactments, common law principles, and the policies, regulations, and procedural rules of their employing agencies. Following standard procedures with confidentiality is necessary for creating trusting relationships in which a client can confide in a worker.

Worker Self-Awareness

Because workers in the helping professions constantly have to deal with clients' problems, they have to be aware of their own strengths and weaknesses in terms of moral responsibilities and obligations. Ideally social workers should know and understand the effects of their behavior on others as well as accurately perceive their own actions and feelings. In short, self-awareness helps generalists to sort out personal perspectives and provides insight from which to empathizes with clients' situations. Generalists have to be aware that their attitudes, expectations, professional and personal values, and cultural identities influence their work with different types of clients.

Besides being an important part of working with clients, self-awareness is crucial at every stage of helping. Questions that ask workers to look at

themselves in their own family of origin at different stages of the life cycle represent a beginning step toward self-awareness. Such questions include how workers reacted to separations and transitions during their developmental years. What patterns of behavior were encouraged and nurtured in their own families and what type of behaviors were rejected or punished? Has an understanding of their own patterns of behavior helped them become better professionals? If there were any serious problems in the worker's formative years is the worker aware of them, and better still have these issues been resolved?

Workers must be professional in all their dealings with clients. For example, a worker's short temper and impatient attitude would be considered a weakness, which the worker must control while in a helping session with a client. When the client speaks slowly and deliberately, the worker must control his or her impatience, which has nothing to do with the client's interests. Another worker may feel that a personal strength is his or her ability to reflect warmth. When challenged with a difficult client, the worker who is aware of this strength can use these warm feelings professionally to understand and help a client. Most clients can sense whether people care about them. Workers should also take care not to project their own problems onto the client's life.

Mark, a social worker, went through a bad divorce. His wife took the four children, the house, and the car. Mark was virtually on the streets before moving into an apartment. He carried angry, negative feelings toward his ex and toward women in general. While in private practice during this period, he encouraged and brought about more separations and divorces than he had previously in his career. Though a fairly good practitioner, Mark was still too close to his problems and viewed all his clients' marital conflicts as an opportunity for personal vengeance against women. He managed to set the husbands and wives against each other. Mark was not aware that he was subjectively treating all marital issues as crisis situations. Three years after his divorce, when his private practice was practically wiped out, he finally realized that he had carried his problems over into his clients' lives, but much damage had already been done. For the first time, he was able to reflect and look at himself as he really was: an angry, bitter man who had never reconciled himself to his divorce, which he saw solely as his wife's fault.

A professional who has developed an in-depth awareness of self would be careful not to let his or her personal feelings get in the way of the therapeutic situation. Beginning professionals may not realize how often they project their personal feelings into their cases. At times, biases arising from their own relationships and experiences are carried over to clinical sessions.

Martha, a beginning professional, ardently opposed her eighteen-year-old client's desire to live on her own in an apartment away from her family. Martha's family had ingrained in her that only "bad" girls move out and live by themselves when they are teenagers. Though the circumstances in the client's life were completely different—she had an abusive father and an alcoholic mother—Martha continued to be uneasy about the client's desires to move out.

It is imperative that social workers entering the profession understand that helping others requires you to understand yourself, your feelings, and your own life. Only when we accept our personal impulses, feelings, and limitations are we able to accept differences and negative feelings like hostility, anger, aggression, and pain in others. Without awareness, we may not find it easy to accept others; thus, we should be aware of our internal motivation before we judge others. The worker is of little use to the client if he or she exploits the client out of curiosity, a desire to manage the client's life, or a need to punish or withhold favors.

Learning to help a client means understanding both the client's feelings and the worker's own feelings and life experiences that are different from the client's. Being sensitive to oneself is different from being sensitive to the client. Slowly and steadily, the beginning practitioner has to learn and refine his or her ability to be sensitive to clients' feelings. The worker may not live clients' experiences but should be able to understand and empathize with their pain.

There is no doubt that self-awareness is a central value and ethical principle. For that reason the professional is constantly required to carry on a process of conscious reflection.

Self-knowledge in terms of a professional's preferences, prejudices, and limitations, in addition to self-awareness of weaknesses and strengths, is necessary in order to guide other people's behaviors. Self-awareness and self-knowledge help the worker maintain objectivity, protect the client's integrity, and avoid manipulation or authoritative control of the client. Professionals should conduct themselves in a disciplined, trustworthy manner in order to meet clients' needs. Self-awareness is a prerequisite for self-acceptance and self-criticism. All these factors also lead to the emotional neutrality, impartiality, and empathy necessary for an effective helping relationship (Shulman, 1999).

Social workers, however, are not superhuman. They are not necessarily free from prejudice and intolerance; neither are they immune to the irritating behavior of some clients. To develop a real tolerance for human behavior in all its manifestations involves a natural liking for people. Beyond that, self-awareness helps the worker learn to reduce and set aside personal defenses against self-knowledge (Hamilton, 1951). Social workers do not relinquish their sense of personal or professional values, but instead learn to understand and accept a wide range of emotions, attitudes, and behaviors.

John, a beginning professional and a second-year social work student who was also a Catholic priest, was discussing a case in class. He mentioned that a woman client had stayed with him in therapy for one year, much against his wishes. He recognized that he disliked her and was constantly angry with her because her problems were endless. John was aware that it was not the client's problems that bothered him as much as her personality. She was clingy to the point of irritation. He added: "I am aware that I do not like her for my own personal reasons. She is naggingly persistent, but I also see that this is my weakness and I try very hard to accommodate her and deal with her issues. At times, I get impatient and she senses it, and I have shared with her my frustration in not being able to help her."

John was an honest person who recognized and ac-knowledged his own feelings. However, John was not able to utilize his self-awareness to establish the kind of limits and structure necessary to create a problem-focused treatment relationship. John also acknowledged that his self-awareness was only on the surface, and he had not really worked through his own unresolved conflicts con-cerning women, particularly domineering women. Most of us have trouble with overly dependent and controlling clients and are aware of it. That beginning awareness is the stepping-stone for moving toward and learning effec-tive ways of offering help. It is best to acknowledge our own biases and understand when we do not know how to deal with clients.

Based on the knowledge you have acquired about yourself, examine the following case studies as exercises in further expanding your awareness of your own values and attitudes. All of the cases are designed to help you look at yourself so you can begin to understand your own strengths, weaknesses, and what different situations mean to you. Self-awareness will increase your effective-ness in affirming the self-respect and dignity of clients.

Amy is the family scapegoat. Her mother is the chief scapegoater, followed by Amy's sisters, brothers, and fa-ther. You realize that everything that goes wrong in the family is automatically blamed on Amy. You understand the dynamics of the situation because you were treated the same way as a child. Your natural impulse is to pro-tect Amy and tell off the rest of the family members. Why do they make you angry? How would you handle this situation?

You are a divorced woman who had a long, drawn-out, nasty divorce. You are working through a couple's marital problems. The husband is domineering and will not allow his wife to say anything that resembles independent thinking. You naturally feel like taking sides with the wife and asking the man to get out of the room. Why do you feel this way? How would you deal with the situation?

An older woman enters the clinical sessions, and at-tempts to take charge of the session, asking you, the ther-apist, personal questions in a controlling and domineering manner. You are very uncomfortable. This scenario re-minds you of your childhood days when your mother

controlled you completely. Your natural impulse with this client is to ask her to leave and not come back. You real-ize that this is not professional. Why do you feel this way? How would you deal with this situation?

You are from a wealthy, altruistic family and decided to become a social work professional. You are working in a shelter for the homeless. While talking to a withered, long-bearded, middle-aged man, who smells of liquor, you ask him how he came to be on the streets. He is very talkative and overly friendly with you. He flirts with you seeing you as a naive, inexperienced woman. He laughs, saying that he had four jobs but lost all of them. He prefers his present way of life; however, he adds impishly he would not mind if you took him home and gave him a job. How would you deal with this situation?

Most of the case vignettes presented have dealt with problems currently receiving a great of attention in our society. This chapter has presented the general principles of practice derived from the NASW *Code of Ethics*. These professional princi-ples should be used to nurture ethical integrity and principled behaviors in all professional social workers. It is essential for the professional to make choices with regard to moral and ethical princi-ples in order to assist clients in ways that amelio-rate their life problems.

CHAPTER SUMMARY

Professional social workers place great importance on meeting the basic survival and self-actualization needs of their clients. The values of social work are beliefs about what is desirable or good for a person or society. There are three types of values in social work: ultimate values are abstract; prox-imate values are specific to desired goals; and in-strumental values specify desired means to reach a goal. In every culture, values serve as a guide to se-lecting appropriate behavior. Social norms are reg-ulatory rules, standards, and criteria by which we judge the worth or rightness of people and be-havior. Violating norms also affects the values of the culture. Societal values are highly generalized values such as honesty, happiness, goodness, and decency that are upheld by the entire society. Group values are upheld by members of one group, but they may not be significant to another group. Group values are derived from groups and families and complement societal values. Making money and being successful are generally accepted societal values and are further influenced by gender, age, religion, and ethnic group variations. Individual values are difficult to analyze because they differ from societal and group values; also, a person's actual individual values may be inconsistent with a person's stated individual values.

Social work has developed its own ethics of professional conduct, which are based broadly on large societal values. The National Association of Social Workers (NASW) has developed its own professional social work *Code of Ethics*. The code specifies the conduct and comportment of professional social workers and the social worker's ethical responsibility toward clients, colleagues, employers and employing agencies, the social work profession, and to society.

Value dilemmas are faced by both social workers and clients. If a client faces a dilemma about having an abortion, obtaining a divorce, or leaving her job, the worker should see this as the client's dilemma. But if the client is being unfaithful to her spouse and the worker's values differ from the client's, this could become the worker's dilemma. However, the worker must view these problems objectively and nonjudgmentally.

Ethical standards emphasized by the NASW compromise a set of basic professional principles. Also called cardinal values, these principles have evolved to help guide and limit the helping actions of social work professionals.

The basic principles of social work include the following: respect for the dignity and worth of a client, acceptance of the client, uniqueness and individuality of clients, client self-determination, confidentiality, and worker self-awareness. These principles evolve primarily from a value base. Respect for a client requires that all persons, irrespective of their background, age, gender, lifestyle, beliefs, status in life, and behaviors, are treated as people with dignity. Acceptance of a person is respecting his or her right to be himself or herself and acknowledging his or her needs and feelings. Respect for the uniqueness and individuality of a client involves accepting a person as an individual who has dignity and self-worth. All clients are unique, and social workers should affirm and highlight the individuality of the people whom they serve.

Self-determination of clients reflects the clients' dignity and uniqueness, and includes allowing them to choose and make decisions about their own lifestyles provided that they do not violate the rules of society and do not hurt others. The principle of confidentiality spells out a commitment of trust without which the therapeutic relationship cannot develop fully. There is absolute confidentiality, which refers to the ethical position demanding the generalist not break confidentiality under any circumstances, and relative confidentiality, which refers to the ethical position that a practitioner may have to break confidentiality under certain circumstances. The principle of self-awareness requires that social workers be aware of their own strengths and weaknesses with regard to obligations and responsibilities to clients' problems. In order to help people who are in vulnerable situations, it is important for the professional to make choices about moral and ethical principles.

3

KNOWLEDGE

This chapter is written to help in understanding and assimilating the importance of knowledge. Though this is a theoretical chapter, it provides food for thought in the hope that students will ardently pursue the development of knowledge. There are three reasons for this chapter:

1. To help in understanding the different components of social work knowledge with critical thinking
2. To help in understanding that professionals can also be knowledge builders in the profession
3. To understand that the knowledge base in social work is constantly evolving within the context of social changes

This chapter includes the following subtopics: characteristics of knowledge, critical thinking, knowledge from other fields, liberal arts perspective, propositional and procedural knowledge, selecting and organizing knowledge, theories of behavior, the core knowledge base of social work practice, and contextual knowledge.

WHAT IS KNOWLEDGE?

Social work knowledge is built on a body of information, theories, values, and skills. Historically, this knowledge building did not happen systematically but rather randomly, and in a fragmented manner. This is because social work had to draw its relevant knowledge and theory from related professions and disciplines. At first this integration of knowledge was done irregularly, with a bias toward one area of knowledge more than another; however, through the years this process happened in a more orderly and disciplined manner (Bartlett, 1970).

For all professions, including social work, there is a need to have a sound knowledge base that provides the background for thinking, seeing, knowing, understanding, and doing. There are many ways to discover knowledge—through research, practice, and experiences with clients. Some seekers of truth demand objectivity and distance; others rely on personal and empathetic knowledge. Besides relying on empirical knowledge, others highlight the authenticity of material by "being there" (Geertz, 1988) or through the public and shared consensus that Siporin (1989) calls "practice wisdom."

In order to carry out the values and goals of social work practice effectively, professionals build on a broad base of knowledge and skills. Gordon (1964) defines knowledge as the picture that people have of the world and their place in it. Knowledge consists of ideas, beliefs, thoughts, and other cognitive mental material. Nickerson (1986) defines knowledge as information that decreases uncertainty about how to achieve a certain outcome. For example, we can ask what knowledge will help to solve problems faced by clients, such as child abuse and teenage gangs. Knowledge ranges from a belief that we can know reality with certainty by direct observation (Gambrill, 1997) to the viewpoint that there is never any certainty and we must critically appraise and synthesize information from multiple sources (Kitchener, 1986). Popper (1992) defines knowledge as problematic and tentative guesses about what is true. It is the result of selective pressures from the real world where our guesses come into contact with the environment through a process of trial and error (Munz, 1985). The *New Shorter Oxford English Dictionary* (1993) states that knowledge is

> the fact of knowing a thing, state, person and so forth, leading to familiarity gained through experience. Knowledge is intellectual perception of fact or truth; clear and certain understanding of awareness, especially as opposed to opinion; and theoretical or practical understanding of art, science, industry and so forth. (p. 1503)

Bartlett (1970) indicates that "knowledge propositions refer to verifiable experience and appear in the form of rigorous statements that are made as objective as possible" (p. 63).

Social workers have to develop their own theories and models of practice through commitment to an orderly process of discovery. Knowledge building happens through the utilization of both quantitative and qualitative research methodologies, which is discussed in greater detail in the section on the core knowledge of social work. Also,

when a problem such as child abuse or alcoholism is of profound interest, professionals can study and work with people facing such issues and, after a period of time, conceptualize knowledge about the issue and be ready to contribute to knowledge building. Knowledge is generally built by research methods.

Quantitative research methods require the use of standardized measures so that the varying perspectives and experiences of people can be fitted into a limited number of predetermined response categories to which numbers are assigned. Qualitative research produces findings that are not arrived at by means of statistical analysis or other means of quantification. In qualitative research, we find out what people do, know, think, and feel by observing, interviewing, and analyzing them. Qualitative data permit the researcher to study selected issues in depth and detail and develop a theory (Pillari, 1991). Another more detailed description of qualitative research comes from Sherman and Reid (1994), who say that qualitative research can be defined simply as research that produces descriptive data based on spoken or written words and observable behavior. It can be further defined as procedures for identifying the presence or absence of something, or describing the amount of something in words; this is in contrast to quantitative methods, which involve numerically measuring the degree to which some feature is present. Deciding what to count as a unit of analysis is essentially a qualitative and interpretive issue that requires judgment and choice in the development of themes, categories, classifications, and typologies from data collected in naturalistic situations, rather than performing experiments or using other types of controlled conditions common to quantitative procedures (Sherman & Reid, 1994).

Hartman (1990) points out that the boundaries of the social work profession are wide and deep and encompass a concern about the nature of society, social policies, social justice, and social programs. There is a deep and persistent concern for human associations, communities, neighborhoods, organizations, and families. There is also concern for life stories and the narratives of people we serve, as well as the meaning of these experiences. We cannot say that any one way of knowing is adequate to explore this vast and varied territory. The social work field continues to build its knowledge base, exploring, accumulating, and redefining knowledge from different fields into the social work arena.

CHARACTERISTICS OF KNOWLEDGE

By its very nature, social work knowledge is interdisciplinary, and obtained from other fields, particularly the social and behavioral sciences. As the profession grows and changes, social workers have begun to rely more and more on knowledge that derives from within the social work profession itself (Bartlett, 1970).

Efforts are being made to move the social work profession toward a knowledge base similar to that of the hard sciences such as biology; however, these efforts have been largely unsuccessful. Concern for the complex phenomena represented by humans in their social environment tends to make the nature of social sciences ambiguous and gives a quality of "softness" to its knowledge base (Johnson, 1995).

Reynolds (1975) presents some of the characteristics of knowledge, including *abstractness*, in terms of interdependence of time and space, and *intersubjectivity*. Part of the latter, *explicitness* involves description in necessary detail and with terms that are selected to ensure that the audience agrees on the meaning of concepts. *Rigorousness* (logical vigor) is the use of logical systems that are shared and accepted by relevant scientists to ensure agreement of the predictions and explanations of theory. Although Reynolds discusses empirical techniques, qualitative knowledge that is not empirically bound also contributes to knowledge building in the social work profession.

The sources of knowledge available to the social worker are varied and vast, because social work takes a broad view of the social functioning of people in various situations. A social worker should be able to evaluate the knowledge available (Hollis, 1968). He or she should use judgment in the choice of knowledge to apply to particular situations and keep an open mind as to the tentativeness of the knowledge base and the knowledge about the person-in-environment.

The worker must be able to think systematically, critically, and creatively about theory. Goldstein (1990) stated that social work is far more an art than an applied science. He further stated, "reflectively, creatively, and imaginatively the mind of the practitioner strives to blend and incorporate fragments of theory, information, intuitions, sensations, and other perceptions into what is somewhat ambiguously called 'understanding' " (p. 41). Combining the art of being a social worker and the utilization of knowledge requires critical thinking.

CRITICAL THINKING

As a practitioner it is important to think critically about practice-based questions.

For example, a social worker informs you that Mrs. Johnson recalls being abused as a child by her mother and has been through a great deal of counseling. The social worker suggests to you that you should use both Mrs. Johnson and her now elderly mother in order to help Mrs. Johnson work through her related anger. Utilizing critical thinking, do you believe this is the only way to help this client?

While driving to work you see an advertisement about a residential treatment setting for adolescents which claims "We've been serving young people successfully for the past fifty years." Do you believe what you have read? If not, what type of evidence would you require to be convinced and why?

To be truly competent practitioners, we should carefully consider our beliefs and actions. As Gibbs and Gambrill (1996) indicate, critical thinking involves the use of standards such as clarity, accuracy, relevance, and completeness. Critical thinking also requires evaluating evidence, considering alternative points of view, and being genuinely fair-minded in accurately presenting opposing viewpoints. Being a critical thinker requires making a genuine effort to fairly critique all views—preferred and not preferred. Such practitioners value accuracy over "winning" or social approval.

Paul (1993) lists the following characteristics of critical thinking:

- It is purposeful.
- It is responsive to and guided by intellectual standards such as accuracy, precision, clarity, depth, and breadth.
- It supports the development in the thinker of intellectual traits of humility, integrity, perseverance, empathy, and self-discipline.
- The thinker can identify the *elements of thought* present in thinking about any problem, such that the thinker makes the logical connection between the elements and the problem at hand. Further, the critical thinker will routinely ask the following questions:

  What is the *purpose* of my thinking (goal/objective)?

  What precise *question* (problem) am I trying to answer?

  Within what *point of view* (perspective) am I thinking?

  What *concepts* or ideas are central to my thinking?

  What am I taking for granted, what *assumptions* am I making?

  What *information* am I using (data, facts, observation)?

  How am I *interpreting* that information?

  What *conclusions* am I coming to?

  If I accept the conclusions, what are the *implications*? What would the consequence be if I put my thoughts into action?

For each of the given elements, the thinker must consider standards that shed light on the effectiveness of his or her thinking.

Critical thinking is also a form of self-assessment and self-improvement. There is integrity in the whole concept of critical thinking as it yields a well-reasoned answer to your questions (Paul, 1993).

In social work practice we deal with people as people who have problems. When we help people we need to be *purposeful* and *focused* in our approach in order to be objective, understanding and helpful. Critical thinking should be utilized as a way of analyzing a case as well as a form of self-assessment.

Nineteen-year-old Tina, a single mother with two young children was referred to Child Protective Services (CPS) by her neighbors for neglect of her children. She was agitated, scared, and sobbing when the CPS social worker met her. The two children clung to her and the four-year-old attempted to wipe her mother's tears. To determine if Tina had neglected her children, the practitioner had to ask precise questions to receive answers that would help her make a decision based on information rather than assumptions. In this case, what perspective is the worker using while viewing the client? Is the worker integrating the information, the conclusions, and implications for the family?

The information that the worker received revealed that Tina recently lost a job for being habitually late to work at a factory. Her parents lived in another state and she had no support systems. She had been frantically looking for jobs but swore that she had never deliberately or really neglected her children. Her children were developmentally normal and were outgoing in the worker's presence. Tina appeared extremely upset about leaving her children alone for two days, but added that she had never done this before. The neighbors complained that this was a pattern with her.

The worker has to make a decision about the health and well-being of the children. How can the worker use critical thinking in an integrated manner in order to make an objectively reasoned decision to help the children? In almost all case situations critical thinking is an important aspect of the helping process.

Creativity is closely connected to critical thinking and plays a role in critical thinking. Creativity is required to discover assumptions, alternative explanations, and biases. Thinking styles, attitudes, and strategies associated with creativity are:

- readiness to explore and to change
- attention to problem finding as well as problem solving
- immersion in a task
- restructuring of understanding
- belief that knowing and understanding are products of one's intellectual process
- withholding of judgment
- emphasis on understanding
- thinking in terms of opposites
- valuing complexities, ambiguity, and uncertainty combined with an interest in finding order
- valuing feedback but not deferring to convention and social pressures
- recognizing multiple perspectives on a topic
- deferring closure in the early stages of a creative task

  (based on Green, 1989; Nickerson, Perkins, & Smith, 1985; Weisberg, 1986).

Is critical thinking necessary? Do clients receive better services if social workers utilize critical thinking skills? Research that is both historical and empirical shows that it does matter. The history of the human service professions reveals that caring is not enough to protect people from harmful practices and to ensure that they receive helpful services (Breggin, 1991; Morgan, 1983; Szasz, 1994).

The danger of thinking uncritically is that time and resources may be wasted, or worse that clients may not get the type of help they need (Gibbs & Gambrill, 1996). Examples of ineffective interventions and iatrogenic effects (helper-induced harm) include institutionalizing healthy deaf children wrongly labeled as having emotional problems (Lane, 1991), institutionalizing adolescents for treatment of substance abuse even though there is no evidence that this works (Schwartz, 1989), and negligent medical care in American

hospitals that injures or kills approximately 100,000 people annually (Health Letter, 1992, p. 1). Some interventions are used because they are easier to administer or because they earn money for the provider. But practitioners may also choose ineffective interventions due to faulty reasoning. Fortunately, through appropriate knowledge, skills can be learned that will help make sound decisions.

Social work knowledge and critical thinking help social workers make wise choices in selecting options that, compared with others, are most likely to help clients attain the outcomes they value. As a social worker, it will help to evaluate claims and arguments in order to recognize false assertions that may get in the way of helping clients. Another important aspect of critical thinking is that it sets the beginning stages of the move toward knowledge building in the transitioning from student to practitioner.

KNOWLEDGE FROM OTHER FIELDS

Social work knowledge is borrowed from different fields, and knowledge building in social work started with contributions from diverse fields. However, it is important to remember that knowledge original to social work has also been exported to the knowledge bases of other professions and operationalized in their fields of practice. For instance, in *On Becoming a Person* Carl Rogers (1961) acknowledged that the origins of his thinking on the core conditions of the helping relationship came from his contact with psychiatric social workers and his involvement in social work national organizations, rather than from theories or practices then predominant in academic or clinical psychology. The concept of helping family members as a unit started in social work and was recorded by pioneer thinker Mary Richmond (1917) in her book *Social Diagnosis*. This work took on a new dimension when psychiatrists started to work with families in the 1950s, but so-cial work was not acknowledged for its contribu-tions to helping family members as a group. There are numerous examples in the history of social work in which our practice theories and ap-proaches were rediscovered and popularized by other professions without credit, although bor-rowed knowledge in social work and other pro-fessions has been a two-way street. Borrowing or contributing to other professions should be viewed in a positive and healthy fashion as we move to-wards holism and integration in our fast-moving global economy and culture.

For social workers to be well-rounded profes-sionals, the Council on Social Work Education (CSWE) advocates that students who enter a social work program have a basic general education background at the bachelor's level. This includes knowledge in humanities, communications, nat-ural sciences, social sciences, health education, and physical education. This liberal arts perspective gives students a broad base of knowledge.

Liberal Arts Perspective

Because the sources of social work knowledge are varied and related to a number of other disciplines and because human behavior is extremely com-plex, the social work student needs a strong liberal arts perspective. This perspective consists of knowledge of the social sciences, including sociol-ogy, psychology, anthropology, history, political science, economics, and, more recently, ethology and philosophy. These varied subjects provide ex-planations about human nature and the human condition. Studying natural sciences, such as biol-ogy and ecology, provides tools for scientific think-ing and an understanding of the physical aspects of the human condition. The study of humanities aids in the development of creative and critical thought processes, and provides an understanding of the nature of human behavior through the ex-amination of creative endeavors and the cultures of human society (Johnson, 1995). Exposure to

these areas of study helps the social worker de-velop an expanded capacity for dealing with dif-ferent types of human problems. Thus, the broader the social worker's perspective in liberal arts, the easier it will be to think critically about, under-stand, and work with human beings.

With people's concern for the environment and its effects on coexistence, it is obvious that ecology has started to play an important role in our lives. Today we no longer view ourselves as conquerors of nature but acknowledge that we need to live in harmony with nature with the *person–environment fit* providing the network for understanding and working with people. Environmental knowledge is obtained from subjects such as biology, geog-raphy, and ecology, and efforts are made through the ecosystems perspective to inculcate these dif-ferent types of knowledge systemically into our profession.

Drawing on knowledge from a wide range of subjects, we have a broad base for understanding and working with people and for building new theories.

THEORY SELECTING AND ORGANIZING KNOWLEDGE

The purpose of this discussion on knowledge and theory is to help social workers develop their own theories through commitment to an orderly pro-cess of discovery. Theory building has led social work professionals to rethink and reevaluate the manner in which knowledge from other fields can be utilized. A theory can be described as a combi-nation of concepts and propositions about reality. When social work thinking is blended with a sub-ject from another field, this modified information becomes professional social work knowledge and adds to the theory base.

Goode (1969) describes professional knowl-edge as the product of a profession's common base of practice. The definition of its scientific knowledge base is interrelated with its value system, its practice theory, and its interventive repertoire. Mastering professional knowledge affords the practitioner professional and societal sanction and authority.

Siporin (1975) indicates that the body of knowledge used by social workers is called professional knowledge. Goode (1969) has offered the following criteria to distinguish such knowledge:

1. Professional knowledge is formulated at a theoretical, abstract level and organized into principles.
2. Professional knowledge is applicable to problems of living.
3. Professional knowledge is considered to be potent for problem solving.
4. Professional knowledge is a basis for society's turning over to a profession certain problems for problem solving.
5. Professional knowledge is so recognized by society that disputes over the validity of solutions about problems are turned over to the profession as a final arbiter.
6. Professional knowledge is developed by the profession.
7. Professional knowledge is of such a high order of difficulty that society views the profession as possessing a kind of mystery of knowledge not available to other people.

Baier (1969) indicates that social work knowledge also contains *meliorative knowledge*—the "capacity of things to confer benefits on people, and of improvements in people's lives" (p.74). Social work also has *operational knowledge*, that is, knowledge obtained by the professional social worker that can be applied and tested in different situations (Siporin, 1975).

When knowledge is taken from other fields, it is important that the theories be evaluated in relation to the social work field and fitted into social work theory. In addition to using valuable knowledge from other fields, social workers should also follow an orderly process of discovering or selecting theories solely for social work practice. What is the criteria for selecting and organizing? It is suggested that knowledge be developed carefully and critically based on the functions, values, and skills of social work.

Trader (1977) identified five areas of concern and asked questions that may be used as criteria in borrowing theories to be used in social work practice for knowledge building.

1. *Pathology–Wellness Balance.* Are the basic concepts in the theory based on a sense of wellness or illness? What is the focus of the theory? Does it highlight the illness or the wellness perspective? Does it focus on strengths or deficits in individuals? Are theories of wellness and illness based on the expectations of the dominant culture or do the theories also consider racial, ethnic, gender, age, and class differences?
2. *Practitioner–Client Control Balance.* Does this theory highlight the worker as having more power than the client or is there room in this theory for power to be shared? Who is seen as responsible for bringing about changes in the client? Who carries more responsibility in changing the client's situation, is it the worker or the client? Does this theory view people as dependent, interdependent, or independent? Does this theory allow for shared control and power? How does the practice, using this theory, develop its legitimacy?
3. *Personal–Societal Impact Balance.* Does this theory advocate a specific personal-deficit compared to a societal model? Does this theory take into account historical, social, political, economic, as well as socialization processes in disadvantaged groups of people while dealing with clients? Does this theory provide opportunities for linkages to happen between the personal, social, and environmental aspects of behavior?
4. *Internal–External Change Balance.* Is change synonymous with adjustment? How does the theory emphasize change? Are internal psy-

chic changes highlighted in comparison with changes that occur in social environment? Does the theory imply that the nature of society is primarily punitive rather than supportive? Are changes acceptable only in terms of the dominant societal patterns or do they allow for a variety of patterns? To what degree is change viewed as being synonymous with adjustment?

5. *Rigidity–Flexibility Balance.* Is the theory flexible enough to be creative in its application to people as well as in knowledge building? Does the theory accommodate new knowledge, and are there built-in characteristics for the continual assessment of the utility of the theory?

Social work professionals must develop criteria for selecting and organizing knowledge, as this is a necessity for continued professional growth and the survival of social work. All the theories utilized in social work practice reflect one or more of the concerns mentioned by Trader. For instance if a theory highlights wellness and strengths, how does it impact individuals, people, and society? Does it bring about internal changes in a person and external changes in his or her environment? Finally what is the degree of flexibility available in the theory for it to be creative when utilized with people as well as in knowledge building? A critical and constant evaluation should be made of all theories for their practical application to people and environments.

After any area of knowledge has been selected and organized, it can be made into a theory. A well-constructed theory meets four criteria: fit with studied phenomena, understanding, generality, and control (Glaser & Strauss, 1967; 1978; Strauss & Corbin, 1990). The four central criteria can be explained in the following manner.

1. *Fit.* If a theory is faithful to the everyday reality of the substantive area (for example, the field of family and child welfare) and is also carefully induced from diverse data, then it should fit that substantive area.

2. *Understanding.* Because theory represents reality, it should also be comprehensible and make sense to both the persons and situations being studied and to those practicing in that area.

3. *Generality.* If the data are understandable and interpretations are broad and can be conceptualized, then the theory would have sufficient variation to make it applicable to a variety of contexts related to that phenomenon.

4. *Control.* Lastly, the theory should provide control with regard to action toward that phenomenon. However, all theories do not lead to actions since much is beyond human control.

All theories of social work practice manifest these criteria. Social work practitioners should think critically and constantly evaluate theories that are relevant to the client population they are serving.

THEORIES REGARDING INDIVIDUALS, GROUPS, FAMILIES, ORGANIZATIONS, AND COMMUNITIES

In order to be a generalist practitioner you have to acquire eclectic knowledge. An eclectic knowledge base requires knowledge from different fields that helps us to understand the dynamics of people's situations and determine what skills would work best in those situations. Different types of theories regarding individual, group, and organizational behavior have been integrated into social work knowledge and many theories from other fields have become an integral part of generalist social work practice. In this section, a few of the important theories that influenced and have become an integral part of social work knowledge will be presented. In using theories from different fields of knowledge, the social work practitioner has to critically evaluate which is the best approach for the welfare of a specific client system.

Psychoanalytic Theory

In relation to individuals and families, psychoanalytical theory specifies that human behavior is largely controlled by the unconscious aspect of the mind, which uses basic drives and instincts to reach certain desires. Psychoanalytical thinking was founded by Freud (1923/1974), and by the 1930s Freud and psychoanalysis had become "almost a national mania" (Trattner, 1979, p. 213). In its early years, psychoanalysis seemed to offer social workers everything they needed to know. The Freudian formulation of personality structure consisted of the id, the ego, and the super ego. Freudian thinking emphasized internal forces that acted on the individual, and to social workers seemed to explain failure as the fault of "resistant clients."

Psychoanalysis was viewed as "scientific" and provided a theoretical base. It put forth an understanding of human development as a series of developmental stages and careful examination of the past was used to discern disturbances in development. In psychoanalytical theory, theories of causation provided the guidelines for gathering data from which a diagnosis could be determined. The goals of treatment were usually concerned with the improvement or restoration of social functioning (Allan, 1979). However, psychoanalytic theory was overused with middle-class clients when "talking therapy" became commonplace, which in turn led to the abandonment of poor clients who were not verbally competent enough to present and discuss their problems vividly and work through their issues in verbal discussions. There was also a degree of rigidity in worker and client roles with workers having more control and the concept of illness rather than wellness was emphasized.

Ego Psychology

A more recent development of psychoanalytic thinking, ego psychology focuses on the ego as an important aspect of personality. In terms of adaptation to internal and external reality, the ego and its functions are directly related to the growth of all individuals. As a person develops the ability to cope, his or her skills increase as well. The maturing ego efficiently acquires a progressive sense of reality and a greater ability to invest (cathect) and sustain relationships, to tolerate frustration, to enhance impulsive control, to master cognitive and motor tasks, to increase communicative powers, and to broaden integrative abilities (Henri & Saul, 1971). Heinz Hartmann (1964) discusses the conflict-free ego sphere as the ensemble of functions that at any given time exert their effects outside the region of mental conflicts. Hartman indicates that people are born with a preadaptation to an average expectable environment and are equipped with an innate apparatus for establishing their relationships with their environments.

According to Robert White (1960) the ego begins to master reality even when a child is very young. The child's ego learns to avoid failure or punishment by identifying the situations that are associated with them. White underscores competence as a major driving force in life for all individuals. Having such powers, a person develops a sense of confidence, mastery, and autonomy in overcoming difficult situations and increasingly strengthens his or her coping mechanisms. Ego development is seen both as a maturational and a learning process (Wasserman, 1979).

Another popular theorist was Erik Erikson (1963, 1982) who examined the psychosocial stages of development. Erikson identified eight stages of development during which a person experiences major crises and conflicts. Each conflict has its own time for emerging as dictated by both biological maturation and the social demands that developing persons face at different points in their lives.

Piaget (1950) began to study cognitive development in the 1920s. He defined intelligence as a basic life process that helps an organism to adapt to its surroundings. Piaget stated that the organism learns to function in a manner by which it can cope with the demands of its immediate environment.

The theories of ego psychology are applicable to a large percentage of the population and can be comfortably used with different types of clients. With the person–environment configuration of its knowledge base, ego psychology theories were ideal for social work practitioners to look at clients holistically. Ego psychology can be successfully combined with the underlying social work philosophy of the person–situation configuration in the assessment and intervention of clients.

Social Learning Theory

Another source of knowledge for social workers is social learning theory, particularly its behavioral aspect. This theory represents behavior as evolving through its interactions with the environment. These processes are usually analyzed in terms of gratification, that is, positive reinforcement, as well as pain or punishment called negative reinforcement. Under both those circumstances, the environment also provides a source of stimuli to which the individual responds (based on the theories of the behaviorist) and elicits behaviors in predictable ways.

Individuals who contributed to the development of this theory were Thorndike (1911), Watson (1913, 1925), Skinner (1935), Hull (1943), Tolman (1949), Dollard and Miller (1950), Spence (1956), Bandura (1962), and others. In reality there was no single theory but rather a cluster of theories all more or less resembling each other; at the same time, each of the theories possessed certain distinctive qualities. These theories began as attempts to explain the acquisition and retention of new forms of behavior, with the learning process being given a predominant emphasis. Although innate factors are not ignored, social learning theory is primarily concerned with the process of mediation and internal and external stimulation and responses.

Behaviorists have extended the scope of their attention to include the examination of thought processes and problem solving. The term *cognitive behavior theory* refers to modification of thought processes in therapy as presented by behaviorists (Garvin, 1997). For example, a man who cheats on his wife is helped to understand the pain he is causing her, the manner in which it is af-

fecting his personality, and its consequences for their marriage. The client is helped to use his own reasoning powers to move toward more acceptable behavior in the marriage. In this process behavior modification concepts that enhance a client's self-esteem and rational thought are used to help a client evaluate and modify his behavior.

Perhaps the major contribution of the learning theories is the wealth of information they have provided about young children and adolescents. By observing children, the learning theorists studied how children begin to make friends, become interested in doing well in school, learn to abide by school codes, and so forth (Gewirtz & Pelaez-Nogueras, 1992; Grusec, 1992). Behavioral modification continues to be a helpful way of working with young children as well as the mentally ill and people with mental retardation where the reward and punishment system can be used to reinforce socially acceptable behaviors.

Beside ego psychology and behaviorism, other theories are also important for understanding human behavior.

Role Theory

Role theory includes the ways by which an individual could view expectations while occupying a position in a social system. A role is a "socially expected behavior pattern usually determined by an individual's status in a particular society" (*Webster's Tenth Collegiate Dictionary*, 1996, p. 1015). The expectations of others can create some degree of conflict or ambiguity. For instance, a person who has to play the role of a wife, a mother at home, a student, wage earner, and political activist outside the home can be conflicted at times due to different expectations.

According to role theory, children are sometimes designated by parents and other significant caretakers to play roles like the "smart kid," the "bad kid," and so forth.

Those who have utilized the "role" concept in social work (Peal, 1975; Strean, 1975; Werner, 1967) have emphasized that the definition of roles focuses on social determinants of patterned behaviors of persons in the social position they occupy. Thus, children in families learn roles based on observation and play. Mead (1934) was one of the first writers to focus on the learning of socially relevant roles. She stated that at a young age children learn to take the role of mother, father, brother, sister, and teacher during their play time. As individuals age, they also learn about explicit and implicit roles. *Explicit roles* are conscious and exposed to observation by all participants in communication. *Implicit roles* are those that people play sometimes without conscious awareness. When parents quarrel, a child may be "trained" from a young age to interfere in order to bring about peace in the family, possibly at the risk of getting herself or himself hurt (Pillari, 1991). Even as the child becomes older he or she may automatically continue to be involved in parental conflicts playing the "scapegoat" role in the family and eventually being blamed for everything that goes wrong. At the same time, the child may willingly take blame without a conscious awareness of his or her role. Role theory also discusses deviancy and the different roles that habitual lawbreakers take on. Role conflicts involving ambivalence and confusion are also part of role theory. Role theory is an important and relevant aspect of social work knowledge as it helps practitioners and clients to look at the personal and social behaviors that are required of all roles.

Generalist practitioners work with individuals, families, groups, communities, and organizations. In the ecosystems perspective, these different systems are often interrelated when working with people. Brief descriptions of these different systems as they relate to social work knowledge and practice are presented in the section that follows.

Family Theory

Families are small groups that are a vital concern of generalist social work practice. A vast amount of knowledge has been accumulated and utilized in understanding and working with families. The developmental processes in families and the transactions that maintain family patterns and individual family member's behaviors are part of the knowledge base of generalist social work practice. Family behavior knowledge also includes family communication patterns, as well as the power, role, and status situations in the family and their effect on different family members (Pillari, 1997). It is only since the 1960s and 1970s that family therapy has emerged as a psychotherapeutic speciality (Okun & Rappaport, 1980).

Family therapy, more commonly known in the field as social work with families regards problems and dysfunctions as emanating from the family system rather than from intrapsychic problems of any one family member. Normally, symptoms are viewed as reflections of stress within a larger system. The stress could be related to a developmental or nondevelopmental crisis in the family. Family theory views the individual within the social context in which he or she lives.

Group Theory

Social work knowledge includes theories about groups and group behaviors, families, communities, and individuals. Knowledge of group theory is necessary in order to understand client groups, peer groups, and family groups.

A group is defined as a "collection of people brought together by mutual interests who are capable of consistent and uniform action" (Barker, 1987, p. 66). Group theory utilized in generalist social work practice offers unique opportunities for individuals to grow, learn, and heal. The objectives of different group theories include rehabilitation, habilitation, correction, socialization, prevention, problem solving, and learning social values (Reid, 1991).

The different types of groups include educational groups, growth groups, mutual-sharing groups, task groups, and remedial groups. The aim of group theory is to understand group members in order to help them reach a higher level of functioning.

Communities

Theories regarding communities abound. In practice we need to understand the interplay between the larger system, or communities, and clients.

What is a community? In its broadest sense, the term *community* refers to a number of people with common ties or interests. Generally, they live in the same geographic area, as residents of a certain neighborhood, city, or region. They may share a common religion or ethnic heritage, as do African Americans, Jews, Italians, and Irish (Pillari & Newsome, 1997). At times, it may be necessary to bring about change in a community in order to bring about change in community members. The theoretical knowledge helps professionals understand different types of communities and how they function.

Certain basic factors help define a community for social work purposes. The community is seen as a client. Accordingly, the needs of the community are paramount in order to understand and offer help. These needs are generally identified by problems that affect large numbers of people. In community work the intergroup process utilizes community agencies and resources to ferret out social problems so the resources of the community can be ascertained and tapped (Skidmore et al., 1997). As Fellin (1987) states, the social worker must understand communities as a major element of the social environment. Knowledge about communities is needed for assessing the impact of the environment on the development of individuals in the community. The social worker should know how to locate resources from various communities to which the client relates such as national helping networks. For instance, if a child has been abducted from a parent by his or her former partner, the community resources should be able to use the national network for missing children in order to locate the child.

A worker may not be able to help a community if he or she does not understand the language or culture, has prejudicial notions about a particular community, ignores the clients' lack of economic opportunities, or does anything that violates the community's behavioral norms (Garvin & Seabury, 1997).

Organizations

Most social workers are employed within social welfare organizations. These are formal organizations that are legitimized by the state to deliver social services and benefits to citizens, participate in the control of antisocial behavior on behalf of the state (Austin & Hasenfeld, 1985; Kamerman, 1983) and also promote the public interest or common welfare (Bellah et al., 1985). There are different types of organizations in different communities. They include United Way, community welfare councils, coordinating councils, community information services, and state, national, and international agencies that are established in order to understand social problems and help resolve them. Generally, a formal organization gives substance to a movement. Without a formal organization, activities often take place on a hit-or-miss basis (Skidmore et al., 1997).

Organization also can be described as the *process* of establishing a structure in order to achieve certain goals. In community social work, formulating a structure includes consideration of community needs and resources, as well as the utilization of the resources in order to satisfy the needs (Skidmore et al., 1997).

The practitioner needs to have some knowledge of organizational concepts, which include organizational goals, the structure of an organization, and decision making within the organization. For example, social workers in large organizations needs to learn how to bring about organizational change in order to be more responsive to clients' needs. In addition, the practitioners need tested knowledge about social welfare organizations in order to work with different clientele. Knowledge about social welfare organizations includes understanding agencies, their administrative and supervisory structures, governance procedures, personnel practices, and policies regarding clients that can facilitate good social work practice.

All the theories presented in the preceding pages will be used in the application of the conceptual framework of the ecosystems perspective in learning about how to work with different types of people. Some of the postmodern theories that are becoming useful in helping different client systems include feminist theory, multicultural theory, and the emerging narrative theories of practice.

Feminist Theory

Feminist theory is egalitarian, participatory, and validates each person's life in context (Lewis, 1991). According to Van Den Bergh and Cooper (1987), in utilizing feminist theory: a client's problem should be viewed within a sociopolitical framework. Clients should be offered encouragement to free themselves from traditional gender role bonds. Help should focus on the identification and enhancement of clients' strengths rather than on pathologies. Women should be empowered to receive the type of help they require to control their own lives and balance between their personal and work life should be encouraged. Because other women are viewed as valuable and important in feminist theory, women should reevaluate their relationships with other women, for they may serve as effective resources in helping achieve each other's goals.

Whenever possible in feminist work with clients, the practitioner and the client should approach the relationship on an equal footing. This equality means that the feminist practitioners do not view themselves as experts on clients' problems, rather they act as catalysts to help clients empower themselves. Thus there is a reconceptualization of the helping process through a feminist perspective which concerns itself with eliminating the dominant-submissive relationship (Van Den Bergh & Cooper, 1987).

Multicultural Theory

Multicultural theory aims at helping practitioners pursue the understanding and ongoing application of multicultural competence and social diversity. This involves understanding the concept of culture, being aware of strengths in diverse cultures, continuously seeking cultural knowledge, and understanding the oppression faced by many different client groups.

Culturally sensitive social work practice requires more than a generalized knowledge of various cultural groups. Many argue that rather than an achievement, cultural competence means a process of becoming (Castex, 1994; Green, 1995; Sue & Sue, 1990). It involves seeking opportunities to learn about ourselves and others by being open, inquisitive, and accepting. Cultural competence is an ongoing process, a way of accessing and learning about the world of people different from ourselves (Green, 1995).

Narrative Theories of Practice

In recent years there has been a movement in psychotherapy toward a "new direction" (O'Hanlon & Weiner-Davis, 1989) that invites fuller appreciation of human beings and their potential. This new direction focuses more on the strengths and resources that clients bring to a situation rather than their weaknesses and limitations. In this approach, more emphasis is placed on where people want to go than on where they have been. This approach does not ignore the painfulness and seriousness of some situations but it moves away from the conventional psychiatric pathologizing and toward a more optimistic view of people as unique and resourceful creators of their own realities.

"Patients have problems because their conscious programming has too severely limited their capacities. The solution is to help them break through the limitations of their conscious attitudes and to free their unconscious potential for problem solving" (Erickson, Rossi, & Rossi, 1976, p. 18). Following Erickson, the important paradigmatic shift is from deficits to strengths, from problems to solutions, from past to future (Fisch,

TABLE 3.1   **Different Fields That Contribute to Social Work Knowledge**

FIELD OF STUDY	CONTRIBUTIONS TO SOCIAL WORK KNOWLEDGE
Sociology	Understanding of individuals, groups, communities, and organizations in society; social class stratification; social behaviors; cultures; role theory; discrimination including racism, ageism, and sexism.
	The different effects of demographics, social change, and other theories on different types of families and different lifestyles.
Psychology	Understanding different theories of psychology; development of individuals, families, groups, communities, and organizations.
	Gender roles, self-identity, normal and abnormal psychology; learning, motivation, coping and adapting capabilities; interpersonal capabilities and relationships.
Biology	Genetics, health, wellness, and health problems, such as chemical imbalance and dependency; physical growth and development; aging.
Anthropology	Communities and different styles of communication; culture and customs, values, and traditions.
	Living arrangements; styles of housing based on effects of physical environment.
Ethology	Study of animal behavior in terms of territoriality, boundary making, and dominant/aggressive or submissive/passive behaviors.
Economics	Distribution of monies; distribution of goods and services.
	Labor and trade; employment; consumer behaviors; welfare economics; government fiscal policies; and global economy.
Geography	Effects of space; concept of time; weather, climate, styles of housing, presence or lack of resources including vegetation and water supply; effects on lifestyles.

1990), utilizing whatever the client brings in the service of healthy change (de Shazer, 1988). In narrative theories of practice, the worker and clients have a respectful partnership, and the emphasis is on strengths and resources with a hopeful eye toward the future. The theory aims toward the building of solutions with language or "conversation." For example, White (1995) and others have developed a process of questioning that helps clients gain more power over their problems. The questions try to find or attempt to create in the client's language an emotionally resonant name for the problem like "Sneaky Poo" for encopresis (Swenson, 1998). Narrative theories aim at devising creative ways to reduce the practitioner's power in relation to clients. Based on respectful curiosity, the practi-

tioners convey a belief that clients want to change, can change, and have valuable but subjugated knowledge and skills within themselves to bring about change (Swenson, 1998).

The different types of knowledge presented do not cover all the fields from which social work has borrowed, modified, exchanged, or utilized knowledge. For a better understanding of the wide area of social work knowledge, the different disciplines that contribute to social work are presented in Table 3.1.

All these diverse areas of study contribute significantly to how social workers understand and work with people. For instance, theoretical knowledge presented in sociology about individuals, families, groups, communities, and organizations combined with information on social stratification, cultures, and demographics give social work practitioners a theoretical base to begin to understand the complexities of society. Similarly, the study of how geography, in terms of climate, weather, and type of housing, affects lifestyles and the economic status of people helps practitioners better serve clients.

THE CORE KNOWLEDGE BASE OF SOCIAL WORK PRACTICE

Social work knowledge is varied and interdisciplinary. As such, it opens up a number of avenues for helping people grow and develop. Through the years, there have been a number of attempts to select and organize knowledge in a manner that con-

stitutes an adequate knowledge base for social work practice. Kadushin (1959) pointed out that between 1929 and 1959 there were two major reviews and studies of social work education in the United States. Many more efforts were made to systematize social work; one of the most exhaustive was the twelve-volume study by Boehm (1959) for the CSWE Curriculum Study group. Another attempt to broaden the knowledge base of social work was made by Baer and Frederico (1978) in their Undergraduate Social Work Curriculum Development Project. It dealt in great detail with objectives and curriculum content for the bachelor's program.

The categories outlined in this section reveal the core curriculum areas as presented in the social work programs of the CSWE, which serves as the official accrediting body of the social work programs (see Figure 3.1).

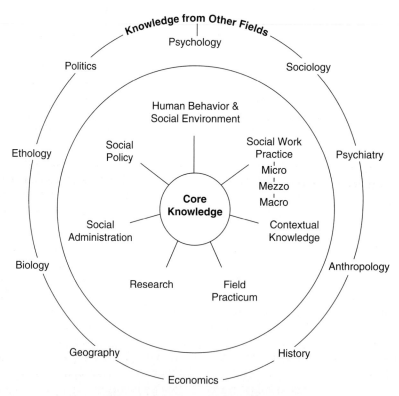

FIGURE 3.1 Core and Related Knowledge Base in Social Work

Human Behavior in the Social Environment

This area covers the development of people from birth to old age, placing particular emphasis on life tasks, human problems, available resources, and the influence of the existing social environment (Pillari, 1997). A broad view, such as an ecosystems perspective, is currently utilized more often than any traditional psychoanalytical framework. Efforts are made to present this knowledge with case examples and a specific emphasis on ethnicity, race, gender, and sexual issues. Problems and issues that are typical of different life stages are examined to help the student become aware of the needs and resources of different people.

In work with different size systems such as groups, families, organizations, and communities and the functioning of people in different systems, knowledge is presented with a broad perspective so that students are prepared to deal with issues at these differential levels (Pillari & Newsome, 1997).

Social Policy

Social policy involves "decisions of various levels of the government, especially the federal government, as expressed in budgetary expenditures, congressional appropriations, and approved programs (Morris, 1977, p. 664). For instance, one social policy determines who is eligible for public assistance. Social workers have a responsibility to use social policies that enhance the social functioning of individuals, families, groups, and communities and to develop a basic understanding of the planning, organizing, and implementation of social services. Knowledge of social policy enables students to participate effectively in efforts to achieve change in social policies and programs, to identify unmet human needs and available human resources, and to implement policies with sensitivity to diverse populations of women, ethnic minorities, and other groups of people who are subject to discrimination and oppression. The values and ethics of social work highlight social justice and make it necessary for practitioners to have

knowledge of inequities in the distribution of opportunities, resources, and services. Poor distribution eventually affects our society and leads to problems for the disadvantaged and underprivileged. These problems need to be understood, analyzed, and addressed by social workers so they can help deal with difficult or biased policies.

Advocacy and social action in social work practice and education are gaining a great deal of momentum. It is becoming apparent that social workers in community settings and agencies are assisting their clients with support and guidelines in facing social problems and in attempting to change debilitating situations and patterns. Social workers also learn how to use the principles of advocacy when they encounter dehumanizing conditions or abusive treatment within service agencies or societal institutions (Skidmore et al., 1997).

Social Work Practice

Various skills need to be developed in order to help individuals, groups, families, organizations, and communities. To make it convenient for students to understand as well as work comfortably with different size systems, practice skills have been introduced at three different levels. Generalists need to learn practice skills so that they can function at different levels of helping: (1) at the clinical or micro-level interventions, dealing with individuals; (2) at the mezzo-level, skills to deal with families and small groups; and (3) at the macro-level, interventions with organizations and communities.

MICRO-LEVEL PRACTICE   In micro practice, generalist practitioners work with populations of various types. To work effectively with different types of people, social workers should develop good communication and interpersonal skills. The generalist practitioner becomes engaged with the individual who is seeking or has been referred for help through an office interview, a home visit, a telephone call, or contacts with other individuals or organizations in the community, or a combination of some or all of the above.

Let us look at Jennifer who had problems with personal boundaries.

> Jennifer allowed anyone to talk *down* to her in her workplace. If people were friendly, she would take a one-down position and present a diffident self. When she met Brad, who was loving and respectful to her, she did not know how to deal with him. She could not believe that anyone would think she was worthy. She dropped Brad after the first two dates because he was too nice. Jennifer had been sexually and physically abused as a child and could not connect to people who respected her boundaries. (Pillari, 1997, p. 62)

In this case, the social worker has to help Jennifer look at issues that place her in a one-down position. This requires good communication skills, combined with empathy and respect.

MEZZO-LEVEL PRACTICE   In mezzo practice, the generalist works with families and small groups. Zastrow and Kirst-Ashman (1990) state that mezzo events are "the interface where the individual and those most immediate and important to him/her meet" (p. 11)

For this level of practice, students are taught to build on their basic interpersonal skills to work with family and group dynamics. However, before applying the dynamics of how to help, social workers must understand how a particular family or group was formed, identify the rules and expectations of the small group, identify the selected leader of the family or small group, and understand the status, distribution of power, and underlying family and group dynamics. In Part III, we will look at how the social worker may collaborate with a family or group in order to help them reach their goals.

Let us look at family dynamics in a family where there is incest. Anita, a twenty-two-year-old woman, talked about her stepfather:

> He was a giant of a man in our community. My stepfather was a well-known businessman and respected minister in a church that had a real big congregation. He was a pillar of our community.

> In church he would preach about moral sins and how sinners should be punished and everybody loved him. But I knew him better. Often I wanted to scream and call him a liar and a hypocrite because he had destroyed my virginity when I was 13 years old. He screwed me so many times that I wondered how he could go to church and act like a man of God. (Pillari, 1997, p. 122)

A social worker needs to help Anita confront her family dynamics, involve her family if necessary, and help them work through their issues. Although Anita did not mention her mother, the dynamics of the parents' relationship would also be an important aspect of family sessions.

The worker should also pursue other mezzo aspects of Anita's situation. Does Anita have friends she can talk to? Do people visit her? How often? Does she have opportunities to get out of the house at all? Is she affiliated with a church or another group? Should Anita be encouraged to join a group for sexually abused clients at a social welfare agency that would act as a support system and help her deal with her trauma in a setting where other people will be dealing with similar problems?

MACRO-LEVEL PRACTICE   Macro practice can be called indirect or strategic practice. Social workers at the macro level function as professional change agents by being organizers, planners, and administrators. They participate in the community to deal with social problems. The problems may be long-term ones, an immediate urgent problem, or a number of short-term problems. Like the micro practitioner who could work in a public or a private setting, the strategist could also work in either a private or a public setting. The activities of the practitioners at this level would include developing and working with community groups, organization and planning, developing and implementing programs (Hepworth, Rooney, & Larsen, 1997).

Macro-level practice involves the processes of social planning and community organizing. The type of work that macro-level practitioners perform depends on their community. A suburban setting requires a different kind of planning than an inner city or a rural area. The practitioner should be knowledgeable and flexible, and understand how to involve people in community power positions to bring about change.

Generalist practice at the macro level involves administration, where the social worker assumes leadership in human service organizations, and has minimal face-to-face contact with clients. According to Sarri (1987), administration involves formulating and operationalizing policy, implementing program designs, funding, allocating resources, directing and supervising personnel, and directing organizational representation and public relations. The overall purpose is to monitor, evaluate, and improve organizational productivity.

Neighbors complained that eighty-four-year-old Matilda had not been seen for a week and was not answering the doorbell or phone calls. Social service workers, with the help of the police, got into her apartment and found her in a disorganized and poorly ventilated bedroom. Matilda had been ill with the flu and had not been able to take care of herself. After initial medical treatment, the county social worker made arrangements for Matilda to receive help at home. This included a meals-on-wheels program that provides regular delivery of hot meals to elderly people. Also available in the community was a visiting friends program where paraprofessionals visit elderly people like Matilda in their homes and help them with shopping, paying bills, making medical appointments, and so on. The county social worker is aware of all services available in the county and helps Matilda to make appropriate use of them.

RESEARCH AND EVALUATION   Research is an important aspect of the knowledge base of the social work profession and a key to the expansion of knowledge. The purpose of basic research is to generate theory. Knowledge is necessary for scientific and scholarly inquiry as well as for knowledge building. Research involves the structuring of inquiry through research designs, conceptualization, measurements, and operationalization for collection of data and data analysis in the social context. Basically, a research methodology is selected based on its ability to answer research questions.

When does a researcher use quantitative or qualitative methodologies? Most researchers use quantitative methodology when they know something about a particular phenomenon. If the researcher can define variables and measure them in meaningful ways, then they can select quantitative methodology such as a structured questionnaire for data gathering or a highly controlled experiment. For instance, a study of parents' child-rearing patterns in a middle-income neighborhood and a lower-income neighborhood can be compared by studying 100 middle- and 100 lower-income families.

Qualitative methodology is chosen when researchers wish to study processes about which very little is known, such as the subjective feelings of a person receiving social support. Qualitative methods can be used to understand what lies behind a phenomenon. For example, a qualitative researcher might attempt to uncover the nature of a person's experiences with a particular illness or any type of addiction (Pillari, 1991). The selection of a research methodology depends on the biases of the researcher.

Of course, there are advantages to both methods of research and they should be viewed as complementary. One advantage of quantitative research is the possibility of measuring the reactions of many people to a limited number of questions. This facilitates the comparison and statistical aggregation of data while producing a generalized set of findings that can be presented elegantly and parsimoniously. In contrast, qualitative research typically produces a wealth of detailed information about a much smaller number of people and cases (Pillari, 1991). Good qualitative research requires an openness to phenomena that is inhibited by researchers who have too much confidence in preexisting formulations.

Evaluation is an important aspect of research. Evaluative research is used to assess the effectiveness and efficiency of agency programs and services. Evaluation is an essential part of micro-, mezzo-, and macro-level practice. The purpose of applied research and evaluation is to apply action, enhance decision making, and also apply knowledge to solve human and societal problems (Patton, 1990). Applied evaluative research is judged by its utility in making human actions and interventions more effective and by its practical usefulness to decision makers, policy makers, and others who have an interest in improving the human condition (Patton, 1990).

FIELD PRACTICUM   A field practicum is an integral part of social work education; it is designed to enhance the achievement of competency in practice and to provide opportunities for the integration of social work knowledge, values, and skills leading to professional practice. The field practicum represents that aspect of undergraduate and graduate social work education that takes place in a human services setting, generally under the instruction and supervision of a social work practitioner. Social work practitioners who provide student educational supervision are guided by values, knowledge, and interventive approaches that are uniquely identified as part of the social work profession.

Spending time in the field helps in the *doing* aspect of generalist practice. The setting can vary from a hospital to a family welfare agency or a nursing home, but should provide students with opportunities to develop practice skills that integrate and focus on the various dimensions of the helping process.

PRACTICE WISDOM   As Mattaini (1995) indicates, practice wisdom refers to two separate but related phenomena: (1) explicit rules are generally handed down by experienced practitioners to others that appear to "work," that is, heuristic rules of thumb that are "good enough" to guide much of practice; and (2) patterns of professional behavior that may or may not be articulated, but have been shaped and refined over years of practice and serve as models for other workers. Experienced social workers have a great deal of knowledge such as "start where the client is," or while working with clients it is "important to meet concrete needs before trying to explore emotional issues" (p. 10). As Mattaini (1995) put it, practice wisdom is a slippery concept, yet there can be little doubt that much of what happens in practice is based on something like it.

There are risks associated with reliance on such rules. First, such rules may be erroneous or inaccurate. Second, those who passed on the rules may believe strongly in the erroneous rules. For instance, social workers in the field of substance abuse often apply codependency theory, which indicates "that a woman married to an alcoholic contributes to her husband's addiction because of her own disturbed personality needs" (Collins, 1993, p. 471). Until recently, this concept was presented as fact and many social workers operated according to this framework, although there was substantial reason to doubt its accuracy (Collins, 1993). Similarly, when objectivity is lost, personal values may also obscure accurate perceptions of the client's issues and needs.

Another problem is that accepted rules sometimes grow from what works for the practitioner rather than what works for the client. There are many instances in which clients are labeled as "unmotivated," "resistant," and so forth, which leaves them without help while social workers focus on less troublesome clients. But as Gitterman (1983) indicates there are reasons for resistance, and it is possible to work effectively with clients who initially seem resistant.

Another type of practice wisdom comprises patterns of professional behavior that are shaped by practice experience, which may be difficult for the beginning social worker to capture. Effective practitioners sometimes find it hard to explain exactly what they do or why, but by observing their timing as well as the inflection of their voices during a clinical session, others can learn important professional behavior. The current practice of audio- or videotaping sample sessions, whether real or simulated, is making a valuable contribution to the learning and observational skills of beginning generalists.

In many ways, social work practice is considered an "art" because it is often shaped through the social worker's knowledge and practice over years of experience. Some researchers have attempted to extract principles from unarticulated practice (Schon, 1983) known as *knowledge engineering*. Knowledge engineering uses computerized systems that interview experts in a structured way in an attempt to extract the rules on which the experts base their professional decisions. Often experts do not recognize the factors that shape their behavior and there is some risk that the explanation presented by experts may be plausible but inaccurate (Mattaini, 1995).

Finally, a word of caution—there can be distortion in using practice wisdom. Therefore it is important for the practitioner to constantly monitor whether approaches are rooted in the field's body of knowledge (or any other) and contribute to meeting a client's goals. If not, other options should be examined. A general rule of thumb is that only knowledge that has hardened by support from multiple sources is practice wisdom. Empirical testing or common rules suggested by multiple experienced practitioners should be used as opposed to knowledge that lacks support.

PERSONAL EXPERIENCE As students move through successive stages of personal development toward becoming professional social workers, they are expected to engage in a process of self-evaluation that develops self-awareness and facilitates self-acceptance in the professional role. It is crucial for social work students to develop their own practice wisdom, so they can learn not to begin anew with every client. Also, the basic interpersonal and problem-solving skills that students have learned as part of their own life process affect and inform their practice.

Personal life experiences can inform or impede practice in different ways. For example, personal values learned at home should ideally be congruent with the professional values of social work. However, there are situations in which dilemmas are created for workers. Abortion is one such example. If a client asks for help to obtain an abortion but your family and spiritual values view abortion as unacceptable, how do you deal with the client? Think about it. Social work advocates

client self-determination as an important value. The appropriate professional behavior would be to send the client to another professional who is perhaps more liberal in outlook so that the offering of help is not clouded by subjectivity. All beginning professionals, even those who have been in the field for years, should take time to think about their life experiences, be aware that their values could affect their work and prepare themselves to deal with the probable conflicts that may arise from them (Mattaini, 1995).

CONTEXTUAL KNOWLEDGE

Social work knowledge has developed in different ways but always within the context of society, that is, diverse cultures and environments and the interdependence of people and environments. While dealing with knowledge in social work research, Fanshel and Shinn (1978) have sought to interest practitioners in developing knowledge of changing situations and the effectiveness of practice skills. In a similar manner, Kahn (1965) and Morris (1977) among others have worked to relate substantive policy issues to the practitioner so as to raise the consciousness of social workers to the content and processes of practice. Thus, contextual knowledge in social work has not been neglected. However, there is a need for constant change and growth.

Knowledge in social work is influenced by the social context in which it exists. Societal values about individuals have influenced the development of knowledge in terms of the needs of individuals, groups, organizations, and communities. Social work knowledge describes what we know about people and their social environments relative to the situation in which the knowledge develops (Johnson, 1995). Such knowledge explains the functioning of persons and their ecosystems. Thus knowledge is used to gain understanding of persons in situations and of larger social systems in order to enhance the individual's social functioning. Knowledge includes human development, diversity, and minority issues within the ecosystems framework. To respond to any need, knowledge about engagement, assessment, relationships, the social work process, and intervention is necessary.

But as Popple (1983) indicates, the social work profession is always in a state of flux because social work is embedded in an institutional context and must interact within this context to reach its goals. For instance, people with AIDS and the large number of crack cocaine addicts have become a major concern in social work. Similarly, the changing American family, the vacillating economy, changing sexual mores, and social and political climate in other parts of the world have all produced profound changes in ecosystems.

As the institutional context changes, the profession of social work takes on new challenges. Social work deals with public and voluntary programs that are concerned with immediate problems and priorities; it also reflects values and beliefs that are constantly shifting. Though the mission of social work is a moving target, it is basically concerned with human needs and human relationships. It is imperative that social workers understand their institutional context, for only then can they understand their own professionalism and the nature the practice (Popple, 1983).

Other areas of knowledge that a social worker needs to be familiar and comfortable with in order to work effectively and empathically include knowledge about human diversity in order to promote social and economic justice, and work with populations-at-risk.

Human Diversity

People who belong to "groups distinguished by race, ethnicity, culture, class, gender, sexual orientation, religion physical and mental ability, age and national origin" (CSWE, 1992, p. 6; 1992b, pp. 7–8) differ in some respect from the majority of others in society and may be subject to the effects of prejudices. As mentioned in Chapter 2, the United States is a nation rampant with prejudice and discrimination against anything that is different. Regardless of whether the nation has had to build its culture on institutional racism, there is no

room or place for this type of discrimination in social work with clients. The best weapon against discrimination is knowledge because often people are discriminated against due to stereotypical ways of thinking. Stereotypes can be described as preconceived and relatively fixed ideas about individual, group, or social status. Such ideas are generally based on superficial characteristics or overgeneralizations of traits that are observed in some members of a group (Barker, 1995). Another definition of a stereotype appears in *Webster's Tenth Collegiate Dictionary* (1996) "a standardized mental picture" that is held about members of a designated group and "that represents an oversimplified opinion, prejudiced attitude, or uncritical judgment" that does not take into account individual differences (p. 1153).

There are various stereotypical ideas that reveal how people are viewed in simplistic ways. A woman of color who had been a U.S. citizen for over twenty-five years complained about the unusually hot weather. A colleague heard her and commented, "but you are from Africa, with a hot climate. Why should you complain?" A healthy, athletic sixty-year-old woman applying for a job as a waitress may easily be overlooked in favor of a pretty young woman of twenty-five and then "logical" reasons are given for not hiring the older woman in order to protect the restaurant against age discrimination. A Puerto Rican adolescent from the inner city has a different social environment than a upper-middle-class Puerto Rican adolescent living in the suburbs of the same city. When these adolescents present problems, they should be viewed based on their class, family, and social history, and not merely be lumped together because they are Puerto Ricans.

It is an awesome responsibility to be an effective and knowledgeable social worker and awareness of human diversity is a critical practice criterion. This is acquired by gaining knowledge and understanding of cultural and situational differences. Reading literature about cultures as well as sensitively asking clients about matters you do not understand are good beginnings. How to talk with clients is discussed in Chapter 8. Critical thinking and effective and sensitive communication is a requirement for generalist practice.

Promotion of Social and Economic Justice

Generalist knowledge also requires information about the promotion of economic and social justice. Barker (1995) describes justice as people living in ideal conditions where all people have the same "basic rights, protection, opportunities, obligations, and social benefits" (p. 354). The CSWE requires social work programs to provide an understanding of "the dynamics and consequences of social and economic injustice, including all forms of human oppression and discrimination " (CSWE, 1992a, p. 6; 1992b, p. 8)

However, it is difficult to attain the ideal social and economic goals for everyone when social inequality is a condition of life. Barker (1995) describes social inequality as "a condition in which some members of society receive fewer opportunities or benefits than other members" (p. 354). For example, there are two public schools in a community. The school that has a majority of white students receives better financial aid for education and classroom equipment compared to a school where a majority of the students are African American. The reasons offered for this may be rational but they do not take away the inequity. It may be impossible to remove all inequalities from the world, but social workers should have a vigorous and active knowledge of the existence of injustice. One should understand the ethics of the profession and vigilantly combat injustice whenever it is possible. Social workers have an ethical responsibility and obligation to use their values and skills to work on behalf of those in need and to promote social and economic justice.

Populations-at-Risk

According to the CSWE, populations-at-risk include "people of color, women, gay and lesbian persons," and others who are at risk "including but not limited to those distinguished by age, ethnicity, culture, class, religion, and physical or mental ability" (CSWE, 1992b, pp. 7–8).

The issue of populations-at-risk is closely intertwined with diversity and social and economic justice. For example, a bright young African American student is accepted into a prestigious university and yet he often hears patronizing comments such as "You got lucky, didn't you?" or "You are lucky to be here" or questions such as "Are you here on an athletic scholarship?" Although the student is from an upper-class background he has still to deal with racism and prejudice. However, the majority of social work clients will not be upper-class people, but poor or lower-middle-class people. Social workers must be prepared to be involved in getting resources and working toward problem solving with people who are diverse and, to a degree, suffering from economic and social injustice.

It is important to have a broad in-depth knowledge base concerning populations-at-risk, to view them empathetically, and to understand in theory the patterns, dynamics, and consequences of discrimination, economic deprivation, and oppression (CSWE, 1992a, 1992b), which in turn should begin to influence your practice skills.

In the next chapter, the skills for helping people coupled with functions of helping and accountability will be presented.

CHAPTER SUMMARY

Social work knowledge is built on a body of information, values, and skills. Historically, social work knowledge did not develop systematically but rather randomly. By its very nature, social work knowledge is interdisciplinary. Knowledge from other fields has traditionally been added to social work knowledge.

Scientific knowledge in any field has the following characteristics: abstractness, intersubjectivity, explicitness, rigorousness, and empirical relevance. Critical thinking and viewing issues from different perspectives is an important aspect of knowledge building.

Borrowed knowledge in social work includes the liberal arts perspective. Professional social knowledge includes both propositional and procedural knowledge. Propositional knowledge is "factual, descriptive and theoretical proposition or information bits" (Siporin, 1975). Procedural knowledge is called the "how to" or the practice wisdom of social workers and is obtained through teachers, coworkers, and supervisors.

In utilizing professional knowledge for social work, five different criteria can be identified in borrowing theories. These include the pathology–wellness balance, practitioner–client control balance, personal–societal impact balance, internal–external change balance, and the rigidity–flexibility balance. After knowledge has been selected and organized, it must be made into a theory that has a fit, understanding, generality, and control.

Different theories have been obtained from different fields and utilized in practice including psychoanalytical theory, ego psychology, social learning theory, role theory, and group theory.

The Council on Social Work Education, which serves as the profession's official accrediting body, has designated the core curriculum areas. These core areas include human behavior in the social environment, social policy, social work practice methods, direct and micro-level practice, mezzo-level practice, macro-level practice, research and evaluation, field practicum and contextual knowledge, human diversity, promotion of social and economic justice, and populations-at-risk.

4

FUNCTIONS, SKILLS, AND ACCOUNTABILITY

In this chapter the focus is on the basic functions, specifically the social functioning of people, for effective social work practice and understanding the beginning professional skills of helping. The concept of accountability and its significant role in managing different responsibilities as a practitioner is also covered.

BASIC FUNCTIONS OF SOCIAL WORK

Understanding the functions of professional social work is the basis of social work practice. The issue of accountability is closely connected. In this era of managed care, short-term therapy, and the use of technology, understanding functions and accountability pave a concrete road for the practitioner. The practitioner needs to understand the functions of social work, the social functioning of people, core social work skills for working at micro, mezzo, and macro levels, as well as professional accountability.

Although our knowledge expands professionally and new ways of helping people constantly appear in the field, the basic functions of social work continue to be the same. What are the basic functions of social work today? According to a major historical curriculum study in social work education by Boehm (1959), social work practice is viewed as having three functions:

1. The restoration of impaired capacity or potential
2. The provision of individual and social resources
3. The prevention of dysfunction

Another variation of the basic functions was put forth by Tracy and DuBois (1987) and DuBois and Miley (1996) as:

Consultancy

Resource management

Education

Within each of these functions there are associated roles that explicate the nature of interaction between clients and social workers at various system levels.

Pincus and Minahan (1973) classify the functions of social work under seven major purposes and identified the goals of professionals:

1. To help individuals enhance and more effectively utilize their own problem-solving and coping capacities
2. To establish initial linkages between people and resource systems
3. To facilitate and modify interactions and build relationships between people and societal systems
4. To facilitate interaction and modify and build relationships between people and the resource systems
5. To contribute to the development and modification of social policy
6. To dispense material resources
7. To serve as agents of social control whenever possible and feasible

An example of social control is the immediate precautions one must take when a client is suicidal to make sure that the relatives and friends of the client are aware, with the aim of preventing suicide. When an adult is involved in an incestous relationship, necessary precautions must be taken to prevent further incest from happening in the family.

All functions of social work highlight how to help and contribute to the well-being of people and society. The functions of social work are based on the assumptions that (1) the person, family, group, organization, or community is important irrespective of age, gender, ethnicity, race, religion, educational background, or socioeconomic status; (2) individuals, families, groups, organizations, and communities have problems that arise out of inner conflicts, conflicts with other people, conflicts due to lack of resources or conflicts due to environmental factors such as change in climate,

and natural disasters; and (3) it is necessary to find solutions in order to alleviate these problems.

SOCIAL PROBLEMS AND SOCIAL FUNCTIONING

In Chapter 1 we looked at some social problems. In this chapter, we will explore how social problems affect social functioning.

What is a social problem and how do people develop such problems? Webster's New Universal Unabridged Dictionary presents a problem as any question or matter involving doubt, uncertainty or difficulty (1996). Barker (1995) defines social problems as "conditions among people leading to social responses that violate some people's *values and norms*, and cause emotional or economic suffering. Examples of social problems include crime, social inequality, poverty, racism, drug abuse, family problems and maldistribution of limited resources" (p. 355). According to Merton (1961), the central criterion for a social problem is that of a "significant discrepancy between social standards and social actuality." This means that there is a gap between an individual's, a group's, an organization's, or a community's expectations and the realities of what needs can be met, as well as how these different size systems can attain their goals, and how different systems should act in order to accomplish their goals in society.

Social problems may be categorized as problems having individual and societal aspects. Individual troubles such as losing a job, misconduct, inadequate parenting, criminal behavior, emotional disturbance, and mental illness are ways that one could be personally affected by social problems. Societal aspects of problems can be seen in social disorganization such as that which displays itself in mass unemployment, a high crime rate, or natural disasters like an earthquake.

A social problem can be understood as a difficulty in social functioning on the part of a person or a group, family, organization, or community. When a person, family, group, organization, or community faces obstacles, they have a social problem that can also be seen in terms of meeting of certain human needs. A social problem can also be expressed as a form of ineffective, inadequate social task and role performance in social relationships and in social living. Tensions, conflicts, and serious social problems can arise out of marital discord, divorce, child abuse, incest, mass unemployment, and widespread drug trafficking and abuse in a community. When people are caught in difficult life situations, they may not be in a position to utilize fully their self-restorative or compensatory powers (Siporin, 1985). This inability diminishes their well-being and the well-being of the people living around them. This is true of individuals, families, groups, organizations, and communities.

In social work it is safe for us to assume that the nature of any problem in the area of social interaction is determined both by the individual, family, group, or community's potential capacity for growth in performance of their social roles and the social resources available to satisfy these needs. Social roles, such as those of parent, group member, organizational leader, or community member, are patterns of expected tasks and behaviors related to a particular status in terms of role concepts and role performance in relationship with others. The generalist practitioner focuses at the same time on the capacity of individuals, members of groups, communities, and organizations for effective interaction and on social resources for effective functioning. In light of this dual focus, the social worker, alone or in conjunction with related professional or nonprofessional community groups, initiates steps for (1) increasing the effectiveness of any size system's interaction with others; (2) mobilizing appropriate social resources by coordinating, changing, and creating them anew; and (3) empowering different size systems to help different clients function effectively.

The emphasis on social functioning and the reduction of social stress helps define the role of social work in collaborative activity with other professions. Thus, social functioning and social stress are enduring concepts in social work. Barlett (1961) explained "social work is always concerned with the same aspect, namely, the lessening of social stress and the improvement of social functioning" (p. 11). Siporin (1975) defines social functioning as "goodness of fit," or reciprocal adaptation between people, individually or collectively, and their environments, that is, family, school, and neighborhood. Social functioning also refers to "the ability of people to perform tasks of daily life and to engage in mutual relationships with other people in ways that are gratifying to themselves and to others and meet the needs of an organized community" (Siporin, 1975, p. 11). On the other hand, social stress denotes "strain or tension that interferes with the ability of people to satisfactorily perform daily tasks or live satisfactorily in community with others" (Carlton, 1984, p. 7). Rivier (1991) defines stress as "any threat—real or perceived which can alter homeostasis" (p. 6). These concepts are all part of generalist practice and cut across social work methods, models and fields of practice (Beck, 1977; Berkman, 1978; Meyer, 1976; Moroney, 1986; Northen, 1982; Saleeby, 1992).

Social functioning includes the transaction between a person and his or her environment. Germain and Gitterman (1995) discuss the person-environment fit—that is, the actual fit between an individual or a collective group's needs, rights, goals, and capacities and the qualities and operations of their physical and social environments within particular cultural and historical contexts. If a person in an executive position has a problem adjusting to a job because he or she does not like being in that position, problems may begin to show up in some area of the organization, depending upon the size of the organization and the number of employees it has, and it would affect the productivity in the company. Problems are also interrelated in family situations; for instance, an alcoholic parent represents a dysfunctional family situation.

Siporin (1985) indicates that self-actualization is achieved through a person's optimal social functioning. Generally, a person's self-actualization takes place in an interdependent relationship, where each person enhances the potential and personality of the other person and where each person is free to grow to be himself or herself. This is also true of families, groups, organizations, and communities.

Social functioning can be negatively affected in many different ways. People may develop problems in their social role performance. Families, groups, organizations, and communities may lack social and economic resources, information and knowledge about a specific situation, or social supports and opportunities. Problems may arise because of interference from others, developmental or acquired physical or mental disabilities, or overwhelming responsibilities in caring for others. Such problems may require professional intervention that focuses on the interaction between the person and elements in his or her social environment. Barker (1991) indicates that social workers help individuals, groups, families, organizations, and communities to learn to deal effectively with the social problems they encounter. This process is viewed as educational, emotionally supportive, and oriented to helping the client use existing social resources. In order to deal with these problems in living and to carry out the functions of social work, a worker needs to develop some basic skills in helping and some specialized skills related to specific problems and populations.

PROFESSIONAL SKILLS

Based on the functions of social work, where dealing with people's issues is an important aspect of helping, practitioners have to develop and use professional skills to perform their work. These skills can be described as the ability to put social work knowledge into effective interventive activities with micro, mezzo, and macro systems.

Cournoyer (1991) defines a social work skill as a set of discrete cognitive and behavioral actions that derive from social work knowledge and from social work values, ethics, and obligations. Social work skills are consistent with the essential facilitative qualities and comfort with a social work purpose within the context of a phase of practice.

Skills are referred to as facilitative conditions, core conditions, or central ingredients in helping relationships (Hepworth, Rooney, & Larsen, 1997). Skill is also explained as technical expertise and the ability to use knowledge effectively and readily in the execution of performance competence (Bartlett, 1970).

When utilizing skills, it is important to keep two factors in mind. In helping the client, the practitioner must make choices based on the profession's knowledge and value base and the specific nature of a client's problem. Skill includes technical expertise assessment, developing a plan of action, and implementing the plan. It also includes the human relations skill needed to engage clients and related others in a position to help in the problem-solving process. The following case presents practice skills in use.

> Ten-year-old Mark would sit in clinical sessions and play with his fingers. He would talk endlessly about his "green" thumb as well as his pets, which ranged from a rat to a spider. Sometimes he would come late for a practice session and seem preoccupied. Mark did little things to annoy me, in spite of our congenial relationship. If we talked about something, he might pretend that he did not hear me or he would ask me to repeat it to him a number of times. His grudging responses were often rude one-word answers. When I expressed annoyance, he would respond in a sarcastic monotone, "I am really sorry" which was meant to provoke me further (Pillari, 1991, p. 50).

The worker saw Mark's passive–aggressive behavior as an expression of his deeply felt anger and as an example of the way he would set himself up to be scapegoated. Accordingly, the practitioner used her skills of listening and appropriate communication to help him deal with his issues including his emotionally starved relationship with his mother (Pillari, 1991).

Skills for working with clients are classified as cognitive and interactive or relationship skills

(Johnson, 1995). For example, cognitive skills can be described as:

1. Those used in developing an understanding of an individual, family or group, organization, or community in their distinctly different social environments
2. Those used in identifying the knowledge appropriate for working with the different clientele

When working with a three-year-old, your way of talking and style of presentation should enable you to reach the three-year-old, cognitively, on the child's level of understanding. Interactive or relationship skills can be explained as skills used in communication with clients that create a sharing atmosphere between worker and clients conducive to carrying out plans of action (Johnson, 1995). This concept will be discussed in greater detail in Chapter 8.

Skills for working with clients rest on a foundation of cognitive and interactive abilities and are refined as a result of practice and experience. Social workers must be aware of the full range of interventive measures encompassed by their profession, not only as skills to be learned but as ways of offering help but empowering people, influencing situations, and bringing about social change while taking into account joint planning and action.

Another important factor is that the development of skills involves not only the application of knowledge and the operationalization of values but also the worker's individual attributes and the development of a personal style of work. Every worker has a unique personality and needs to integrate personal qualities with the cognitive and relationship skills learned in school and on the job. Beginning practitioners who attempt to imitate another practitioner completely are not likely to be totally successful in their work because their own personal qualities and spontaneity will become stifled. The best help occurs when one develops a style of working with different size systems that integrates one's own personality and style with the values, knowledge, and skills of the profession.

What needs to be highlighted in the helping process is matching any size system's coping capabilities and environmental demands. For example, Andrew was placed in foster care after he ran away from his chaotic home a number of times. The foster care family had eight other children and he found the family situation demanding, so he went back to his coping pattern of running away. At this point, the generalist intervened and realized that the environment in which he had been placed was not conducive to his growth. After reevaluating the situation and finding that Andrew's coping capabilities and environmental demands were in disparity, the generalist took him out of this particular foster home.

Core Practice Skills

Although practice skills will be discussed throughout the book, this section introduces the importance of learning basic practice skills. Many efforts have been made to articulate the skills required by practitioners, starting with the beginning practitioner. Several of these conceptualizations will be used to demonstrate contemporary attitudes about core practice skills.

The social work process begins with a *feeling* of concern, which generally arises because there is an unmet need. After *thinking* through the situation the worker assesses the problem in order to help the client take some *action*. Feeling, thinking and action are important aspects of the helping process as seen in Figure 4.1.

Remember that generalist social work provides an integrated and multilevel approach for meeting the functions of social work. Generalist practitioners are aware of the interplay of personal and collective issues that encourages them to work with a variety of clients, which may include communities, societies, neighborhoods, organizations, formal groups, families, and individuals, in an effort to bring about change that maximizes optimal human functioning. Thus, generalists work with different client systems at various levels in order to connect clients to available resources, intervene with organizations to enhance the responsiveness of resource

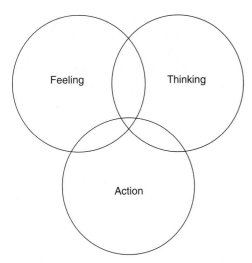

Figure 4.1 **Combination of Core Practice Skills**

systems, advocate just social policies to ensure the equitable distribution of resources, and be able to understand the different facts surrounding a situation through research (Miley, O'Melia, & Dubois, 1997). Our role as practitioners includes working with client systems, interdisciplinary teamwork, organizational development, community practice, and social reform. Varied skills will enhance workers' ability to work with a number of diverse clients.

DuBois and Miley (1996) classify the generalist social work practitioner skills as follows: relationship skills, communication skills, ethnic competence, policy analysis, research skills, computer literacy, and time management.

RELATIONSHIP SKILLS   Relationship skills involve professional relationships created between clients and social workers. A social worker's ability to develop working relationships with clients hinges on interpersonal effectiveness and self-awareness. Practitioners must be skillful in communicating empathy, genuineness, trustworthiness, respect, and support.

COMMUNICATION SKILLS   Communication skills include interviewing, observing, and oral and writing skills. Important exchanges of information

take place in all types of communication when social workers listen with understanding and respond with purpose. Vivid oral communication bolsters the practitioner's ability to work with all clients. Good writing skills lead to effective record keeping and report and grant writing.

CULTURAL COMPETENCE   Cultural competence is an aspect of understanding and working with people of different age groups, socioeconomic classes, sexual orientations, and racial, ethnic, and religious groups, as well as from different geographic regions, all of which affect lifestyles (Lum, 1996). Cultural competence exists on a continuum: Mere understanding of culture is not sufficient, but learning how to address and communicate is the beginning of a working relationship with diverse people.

We are all aware that there is a great deal of stereotyping in North America. Cyrus (1997) indicates that people from Africa and South and Central America are lumped together as having the same cultures. The U.S. Census groups as "Hispanic" people from different places and different backgrounds based on the fact that they all speak Spanish. Similarly the term *Asian* or formerly *Oriental,* covered under its label peoples of nineteen distinct groups who represent different cultures with different social backgrounds. The same is true of Native Americans (or are they American Indians?) who see themselves as members of distinct nations. So how should a social worker employ cross-cultural skills in communication with clients? Probably the first and best rule is to call people what they wish to be called. As Green and Leigh (1985) indicate, social workers should possess ethnographic interviewing skills— skills that elicit a person's view of the problems and situational contexts from a cultural perspective. Listening and demonstrating sensitivity for cultural implications in all your work is an important aspect of a professional.

POLICY ANALYSIS   There are a number of policies that govern the personal practice of generalists as well as that of agencies at the local, state, regional, and national levels. Workers should be aware of their policies when providing public testimony, advocating for legislative positions, improving clients' situations, and participating in policy-making processes. Social workers should also take on advocacy roles in developing policy with reference to oppressed people, the poor, elderly, and gays and lesbians.

RESEARCH SKILLS   Social workers should be proficient as consumers and practitioners. They should use research skills to conduct literature reviews, formulate research designs, analyze policies, and evaluate their practice. Research should be used to collect and apply statistical analysis, analyze data, and present findings. Other important factors include following ethical standards, which means using informed consent and the right to privacy in conducting research (DuBois & Miley, 1997).

In the 1970s, the ideas of Baer and Frederico generated a tremendous amount of discussion among social work educators. Baer and Frederico (1978) identified ten different competencies that social workers, particularly beginning professionals, should develop as part of their skills:

1. Identify and assess situations in which the relationships between people or between people and situations need to be worked through by enhancement, protection, and termination
2. Based on problem assessment, develop a plan for improving the well-being of people by exploring obtainable and available options
3. Enhance the problem-solving, coping, and adaptation skills and potentials of people
4. Link people with systems that offer them resources, services, and opportunities
5. Intervene effectively on behalf of the vulnerable and discriminated
6. Assist in the effective operation of different size systems that provide people with services, opportunities, and resources
7. Actively participate with others in creating new, modified resources or opportunity systems that are just and responsive to consumers

8. Constantly evaluate the extent to which objectives of intervention plans are achieved
9. Continually evaluate one's professional growth; be aware of drawbacks and strengths, and develop those qualities that are effective for social work practice
10. Add to the improvement of services by contributing to the knowledge base of the profession

Through the years, the National Association of Social Workers (NASW; 1996) has identified and refined the skills varying from listening to mediating that are necessary for the generalist.

- Listening to others, eliciting information, creating and maintaining helping relationships, and observing and interpreting verbal and nonverbal behavior
- Engaging clients in resolving their own problems
- Discussing sensitive emotional topics in a nonthreatening manner, and determining the need to end therapeutic relationships and how to do so
- Interpreting professional literature and research findings
- Mediating and negotiating between parties that are in conflict
- Performing interorganizational liaison services and interpreting or communicating social needs to funding resources originating with the public or with legislators

Besides conceptualizing important skills, the NASW has also identified the following abilities as necessary to work effectively with clients:

- Speak and write clearly; teach others and respond supportively to emotion-laden or crisis situations
- Serve as a role model in professional relationships
- Organize workloads to meet responsibilities
- Interpret complex psychosocial phenomena
- Identify and obtain resources

- Assess one's performance, feelings, and function under stress
- Participate in and lead activities with different size systems
- Deal with contentious personalities

In terms of knowledge, the practitioner should develop the ability to relate social and psychological theories to practice situations and to identify the information necessary to solve problems. The practioner also needs to develop the ability to evaluate research studies of agency services, and one's own practice.

The manner by which a generalist acquires skills depends on the individual's past, personality, learning experiences, the social work educational facilities that are available in the area, and the manner in which the individual has been trained. For some, the skills will come more naturally; for others, it will take effort and time.

A Vital Skill—Verbal Following

One of the generalist practitioner's most important skills is the ability to do *verbal following*. This major activity is critical in communication with clients (Finn & Rose, 1982; Katz, 1979; Schinke, Blythe, Gilchrist, & Smith, 1980; Shulman, 1984; 1991). Verbal following in practice involves staying in psychological contact with clients and understanding their verbal and nonverbal messages. Figure 4.2 shows verbal following skills.

Two important variables are embodied in verbal following:

1. *Stimulus–response congruence* involves the extent to which a practitioner's responses provide feedback to clients on how their communication is interpreted. Inaccuracies in communication can be clarified through feedback. For example, twenty-one-year-old Lita informs her social worker between sobs, in a barely audible voice, that she was deceived by her boyfriend just like she had been deceived by her father. The worker responds to the same by offering feedback, "So you are telling

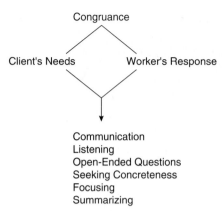

Figure 4.2 **Verbal Following Skills**

me that you were deceived both by your boyfriend and your father."

2. *Content relevance* involves the extent to which the content of the practitioner's responses is perceived by clients as being relevant to their concerns. For instance, a twenty-four-year-old woman who needed money to start her life in a new city was constantly rebuked by the psychoanalytically trained, not-so-sensitive social worker who refused to help the client and insisted that her demand for money was her way of showing anger against bureaucracy. The client discontinued treatment prematurely as she rightly felt that her messages were not being received accurately or empathetically by the worker.

Often, beginning professionals think that verbal following is simply looking and showing that you are listening and you care. However, good client-worker communication includes verbal following. As Hepworth, et al. (1997) state, the key verbal following skills include *furthering* or listening to responses carefully and *paraphrasing* responses or restating the client's messages concisely. Knowing when to pose close-ended and open-ended questions is a necessary part of practice work as well. *Close-ended questions* usually require a "yes" or "no" response or a specific answer to a question, such as "When did you last see your doctor?" *Open-ended inquiries,* such as

"Please tell me more about your family," are unstructured and give clients opportunities to expound on the details of their problems. In some instances, however, they could clutter a client's mind.

Another important factor in verbal following is *seeking concreteness*. While following a client's presentation of the problem, the social worker will find it necessary to seek precise information, for often clients, as well as beginning practitioners, tend to talk in generalities. This involves asking questions such as "What did you actually do?" or "How many times did that happen?" In order to convey ideas clearly, the client has to communicate precisely and the worker has to respond concretely and with specificity.

Focusing is another important skill involved in verbal following. Focusing means encouraging the client to select the topic of concern and then exploring it in depth, always maintaining a focus on the topic. After the discussion of the topic ends, another aspect as verbal following is to *summarize* what has happened with the client and convey to the client the worker's interest and competence.

The verbal following skill is a sample of the different skills that should be part of the generalist's repertoire of skills.

Time Phases

In working with clients there are two types of time phases. The first phase deals with time from the interview through the complete helping process. In the second, time is classified into individual, social, and historical times.

The whole helping process has a beginning, a middle, and an end. In the beginning time phase the generalist gets to know the client, the middle time phase, contains the bulk of the assessment and intervention work with the client, and the ending time phase is known as termination.

In the helping process, every interview involves a series of sequential steps with certain objectives to be followed (Kadushin, 1990). An interview has a beginning or introductory session, which involves getting acquainted, establishing a

relationship, and making a beginning statement of a problem. The middle or working section is concerned with obtaining more detailed information about a problem and working toward finding solutions. The ending or closing phase is concerned with maintaining a mutually acceptable relationship, recapitulating an understanding of an event, and bridging procedures for the next interview. Thus every interview has definite time phases with time distributed from the beginning to the middle and ending phases.

Besides time phases in the helping process, the manner in which time is viewed and experienced is affected by an individual's sociocultural development. *Individual time* refers to the continuity and meaning of individual life experiences over a lifetime (Germain & Gitterman, 1995). Individual time is reflected in the life stories we construct and tell to ourselves and to others. Life stories are a part of all societies, cultures, and people. Laird (1989) indicates that "one's identity then, is built upon the sense one can make of one's own life story" (pp. 430–431). Life stories provide connections among life events, continuity, and a sense of coherence in individual and family life (Spence, 1982). When a worker listens actively, a life story gains increased intelligibility and consistency. The person who tells the story reinterprets and reconstructs the narrative, which will ultimately contain new concepts of self and of relationships with others (Stern, 1985).

Historical time refers to the impact of historical and social change on the developmental pathways of a birth cohort. That is, all people born in a particular time period are exposed to the same sequences of social and historical changes over their life course. People growing up in one decade are different in many ways from a group of people born in another decade (Elder, 1984; Riley, 1985). People in different age groups may experience the same forces but they may experience the effects differently. Although individual and cultural differences are more forceful influences on development than cohort effects, the cohort concept adds an essential social and historical dimension to individual phenomena.

Social time refers to the timing of individual and family transitions and life events as influenced by changing biological, economic, demographic, and cultural factors. Neugarten (1979) indicates, that age cross-overs refer to the changing timetables of many life transitions which have become independent of age. For example, there is no fixed, age-connected time for learning, selecting sexual partners, marrying or remarrying, first-time parenting, changing one's career, retiring, or moving to new statuses and roles. Giele (1980) refers to gender cross-overs that transcend traditional gender roles once considered unchangeable. Such cross-overs are reflected in the exchange of traditional roles in some families, such as solo parenting by fathers and the entry of women into male-dominated occupations and men into previously female-dominated occupations. Individual developmental, behavioral, and narrative processes also merge over social time into collective processes through which families, groups, and communities are transformed (Hareven, 1982).

The individual, historical, and social time phases represents an integrated segment of the person–environment configuration. Understanding these time phases helps practitioners show sensitivity to different ethnic groups and client differences and helps them to be consciously skillful in dealing with differences.

CREATIVE BLENDING OF KNOWLEDGE, VALUES, FUNCTIONS, AND SKILLS

Working with people as a generalist practitioner is a privilege that demands success. To begin this successful journey requires integrating the elements of values, knowledge, and skills into a unified coherent system of thought and action, which can be applied to a wide range of people and problems. Thus, we refer to both the "art of social work" and the "science of social work." The art is acquired through hunches and intuition or personal attributes (Johnson, 1995). Compton and Galaway (1994) have described the art as emphasiz-

ing feeling with an empathetic quality and a high degree of subjectivity and self-consciousness. In essence, social work reflects the individual style of each practitioner as well the shared knowledge and values of the profession.

The science aspect requires knowledge to think and understand a process. The science and art of social work are not in conflict with each other, but are complementary. Let us look at a case in order to understand the blending of values, knowledge, and skills.

Fourteen-year-old Jason, an accomplished guitar player, is placed in a residential setting by the family court because he has misbehaved and threatened his classmates with a knife several times in the playground whenever he was angry with them. One day in anger he actually flashed a knife in the classroom, thus prompting his placement in the residential facility. His family background reveals that his father had murdered his aunt in anger and Jason had witnessed the incident. Jason's father is now in prison. Jason loved his aunt but did not interfere; he could not help her because he was too afraid of his out-of-control father.

Looking at Jason from a *knowledge* perspective, in an on-the-spot assessment, we can see an adolescent who is acting out. He also comes from a disturbed family situation in which he has witnessed a crime. Understanding the developmental phase as well as the crisis aspect of adolescence aids in understanding Jason's unique coping strategies.

In terms of *values*, the worker has to respect the feelings and intelligence of the client and accept him as a person with worth and dignity, in order to help him feel comfortable and willing to participate in the treatment process. As the decision to send him to a residential setting was imposed on Jason, every effort should be made to help him understand the reasons for the decision and how he can benefit from it.

In terms of *skills*, the worker can utilize the family situation to help Jason see the connection between his behavior and his feelings of frustration and anger with his father and allow Jason to vent. On the positive side, the practitioner could highlight some of the positive things Jason could do at the residential setting, such as teaching the other residents how to play the guitar and participating in activities with other boys. Thus even in a fairly restricted situation, there is room for Jason to express his feelings verbally without fear of retaliation and to develop and strengthen his potential for sociable behavior.

Jason's social worker should use practice skills to involve his mother and siblings in planning for Jason's residential care and a treatment program that addresses both the young man's personal issues and the closely interconnected family issues. Other factors would include referring the family members for appropriate services.

This brief example shows how knowledge, values, and skills are brought together and used to help a client. In this case, it also shows how a professional social worker functions as a part of a larger system that includes a residential treatment agency and a court system with authority and power to order that a child be removed from his family and community under specific circumstances.

PROFESSIONAL ACCOUNTABILITY

Accountability in social work has always been a concern, particularly because the discipline is considered to be an art and a science. For instance, when twenty-year-old April cries about the abuse she underwent as a child, a practitioner needs to help her deal with her feelings and at the same time help her accept her past and learn to manage the realities of her present life. Dealing with the case and selecting different skills to reach the client is an art. In terms of science, there is the need to be accountable to the agency and the client in terms of the progress the client has made and as well as time, money, and effort invested in the client.

In examining accountability, this section will look at the following topics: principles of accountability, worker–client accountability, service contract, worker, client, and agency setup, funding agencies, and the bureaucracy and con-

flict between the bureaucracy and the social work professional.

What is accountability? Accountability refers to contractual obligations and legal liability that people face as part of their agency or institution, as well as personal responsibility for the delivery of effective services at a professional level of competence and at a reasonable cost (Siporin, 1985). Barker (1995) explains accountability in two ways:

> (1) The state of being answerable to the community and to consumers about a product or service, or to supervisory groups such as a board of directors.

> (2) An obligation of a profession to reveal clearly what its functions and methods are and to provide assurances to clients that its practitioners meet specific standards of competence. (p. 3)

Accountability is important to the public who have made contributions to social work and other helping professions in terms of taxes and donations and have a right to know how their money has been spent. In earlier days, charitable societies emphasized that gifts should not be wasted and recipients should be worthy. As social work expanded and moved toward professional status, the idea of efficiency and effectiveness was endorsed through the concept of accountability. Today more than ever before, communities and agencies are continuing to coordinate and plan efforts in order to avoid duplication as well as for purposes of accountability.

As Connaway and Gentry (1988) indicate, when we work in agencies that are associated with other funding bodies, we provide data for planning and coordination. As agency funds come from the community, professionals must learn to live within the restrictions imposed by the community regarding expenditures. It is also important that the agency is accountable for its practices and services to community groups. The agency's physical location, condition, and size affect its relationship with the neighborhood. Any efforts that the agency makes toward change are also affected by the surrounding neighborhood.

Accountability has created some problems for social workers. As Siporin (1983) eloquently put it, social workers made a promise that was implicit in the 1962 amendment to the Social Security Act that they would reduce the public assistance rolls in return for vastly expanded federal funding of social work education and of social service programs in public assistance. The increase in the public assistance rolls benefitted the poor people, but it also led to bitter scapegoating of social work as a profession by both federal and state governmental authorities because the caseloads did not go down. Social workers today are more realistic and recognize that poverty, crime, disability, and family dysfunction are firmly entrenched in our social, economic, and political system and will require major commitment by the entire society to be reduced or eliminated.

Principles of Accountability

As Siporin (1983) indicates there are certain principles with reference to accountability. Accountability in social work is basically a process. A generalist with professional competence follows ethical standards and offers efficient services to people. In this case, the process objectives become the outcome objectives. It can be further delineated that the process of achieving change and adjustment is more decisive as the criteria of achievement than the ultimate product of change or adjustment.

Accountability is complex. Practitioners are responsible to clients for upholding their part of the service contract and for providing services that have been agreed upon. At the same time, practitioners are responsible to the profession for upholding social work values and the NASW *Code of Ethics* in delivering services in accordance with their agency's functions and policies. Agencies are in turn responsible to the taxpayers who do not have any universally accepted goals for service.

As shown in Figure 4.3, accountability is multifaceted and is closely related to evaluation. In many ways accountability is responsibility. Accountability also has two components: efficiency and effectiveness. Efficiency refers to the cost of the

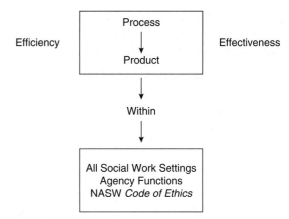

Figure 4.3   Accountability

service based on the nature of human services, such as the amount of time spent in work. However, this component is not sufficient in itself because social costs must be considered. Effectiveness refers to whether the service leads to the goals for which it was intended. Due to the complexity of the human situation and the differing goals of individuals who are concerned with agency programs, it is often difficult to measure effectiveness. However, if measurable goals have been included in the plan of action it becomes possible to determine if those goals have been reached in a particular service situation.

The key factors in accountability are the identification of goals and the evaluation of the service given. Evaluation is important not only as a part of the social work process, but also as a necessity for agency functioning (Johnson, 1995).

Evaluation can be described as a collection of data about the outcomes of a program of action that are related to goals and objectives that have been set in advance of the implementation of that program. Miley et al., (1998) explain evaluation as a method of assessing the outcomes and measuring the effectiveness of social work strategies. In evaluation, practitioners and clients monitor progress and assess what clients can achieve and evaluate what programs can accomplish. Generally, an agency or organization is accountable for its programs, and practitioners are accountable to clients and to their agency. For an agency to be accountable, it should develop an ongoing means of evaluating both the efficiency and effectiveness of programs. As part of the agency and community, social workers should contribute data for their agency to use in its accountability efforts and should also be aware of the evaluative mechanisms that may be useful for developing accountability responses. In a sense, it is the social worker who knows the impact of programs on different size systems, is aware of the data available for use, and who is also responsible for providing primary data (Johnson, 1995). For instance, if an agency takes upon itself to provide recreational activities for older people in an underprivileged area, they have to take into account the cost, the number of older adults who will use the services, and how the seniors will benefit. A careful accounting of the number of senior citizens, reactions to recreational activities, and whether the utilization of services by seniors has increased or reduced would be an indicator of how effectively the services are being used.

Social workers need to become skilled at evaluating to what degree they are being effective providers of services. Today there are a wide variety of evaluation techniques that are available to assess effectiveness of current services and also to identify unmet needs and service gaps. As Zastrow (1995) indicated, one of the most common approaches is management by objectives (MBO). The aim of this technique is to specify the objectives of a program, to state in measurable terms how and when these aims or goals will be met, and to periodically measure the extent to which the goals have been met.

Management by objectives is an effective way of being accountable (Zastrow, 1995). Consequently, large number of agencies require that social workers who have clients do the following: (1) identify and specify the goals of the different size client systems in the initial interviews; (2) write down in detail what the worker and the clients will do to achieve the goals including deadlines; and (3) periodically assess the extent to which the goals been achieved.

Worker–Client Accountability

Change in the clients through the helping process is dependent on efforts put forth by both social workers and clients, and is present as an objective in their working relationship. Accountability between clients and workers is based on mutual agreements regarding problem definition, goals, planning, and action. Mutual agreement makes it easier for the social worker to assess the outcomes with clients at the ending phase.

However, most agencies require that workers complete statistical forms to provide the agency with information valuable for agency use, regulatory bodies and funding agencies. In a sense, these forms encumber the worker with a quantifying responsibility to such bodies. According to Germain and Gitterman (1996), accountability also includes professional responsibility for quality services to clients. Such accountability is not complete until there is an evaluation of outcomes during the ending phase. Accountability in such circumstances is based on mutual agreements and continues with ongoing joint consideration of progress in achieving agreed-upon objectives, including assessment of how the generalist practitioner and clients are carrying out assigned roles and associated tasks. Creating a climate that will encourage clients to be candid in their assessment of the service is one measure of practitioner skill.

Service Contract

Another aspect of accountability that needs to be worked through is the service contract. A contract makes the worker accountable for his or her performance to the recipient of the service. This concept is particularly desirable when there is no concrete final product (Loewenberg, 1983).

In many ways the service contract operationalizes the worker's accountability to the client. The service contract may be said to exist when both worker and client explicitly understand and agree upon the task to be accomplished and how each will help accomplish the same. This contract may or may not be in written form, or it may be established verbally by the worker in terms of what the worker and client will do in order to help accomplish the goals. Normally the service contract is a working agreement. For example, a community may attribute its problems to pressures due to lack of work as well as job discrimination toward members who belong to a new immigrant group. As the task becomes well-defined between worker and the community, the worker helps the community move toward reaching its goal, to aggressively recruit the new immigrants into the appropriate job markets.

The extent to which the service contract is specified in detail is less important than the worker's intent to be completely open. That is, the worker should not have a secret agenda or goals that differ from the client's. A specific contract has many advantages. Both workers and clients can hold each other accountable for the work that needs to be done in order to accomplish a goal.

A service contract includes the following:

1. The purpose of intervention, which includes identification of problems, tasks, and definition of goals
2. The person or situation that needs to be changed
3. Appropriate intervention strategies and how they can be used to bring about change
4. The roles and rules pertaining to both the worker and the clients
5. The administrative procedures that need to be followed in terms of fees, place of meeting, and so forth
6. The amount of time allotted for the contract

When a contract is used in social work it has the advantage of reducing the relative powerlessness of clients in the helping relationship. At every step of the process, clients should be viewed as partners in determining what will be done and how it will be done. Thus clients are not asked to trust social workers blindly, but to have some objectives clearly spelled out.

Accountability deals with outcomes. Many human services organizations are confronted with an increasing emphasis on accountability, which tends to produce confusion about what is efficiency and effectiveness in human service organizations as compared to other organizations (Scott & Meyer, 1994). For instance, in hospitals financial accountability demands rapid discharge of patients, which raises a question of whose interests are being served (Germain & Gitterman, 1996).

Timely assessment and discharge planning are central tasks that all social workers need to be aware of in order to be effective in different arenas of help. It should be remembered, however, that there is a danger too many statistical forms confronting generalists could become an end in themselves. However, the trend today is that social work and other helping professions are required to be more directly accountable to the users and consumers of such services and to the public, the licensing and supportive communities, the academic and helping professional communities, and the employing agency.

Accountability should also include effective outreach efforts, personnel training, and program policy and development that incorporates an appreciation for the concerns and life experiences of all clients. Generalists and agencies should be accountable for knowing and using the results of research and theoretical literature on a particular subject, and keeping a record of what works and what does not work in their own experience. Working with clients is as complex as human behavior. Some clients and their situations improve in spite of incompetent intervention, or with no outside help at all. On the other hand, some clients fail to improve or get worse in spite of the most dedicated and skillful handling. All that we can be held accountable for in any given situation is doing "our best."

What is "our best"? Besides placing an emphasis on ethics and skills, there is an intellectual component. This means being knowledgeable about the latest research and theoretical literature on the problem that confronts us in a client situation. On the other hand, if our best efforts are consistently ineffective or seem to achieve no better outcomes than a control group getting no help, it does raise questions about continuing a particular program. To perpetuate a practice or a program that we know does not work is perpetrating a fraud.

Cost–benefit analysis is an important aspect of accountability that bears further discussion. Agencies and third-party payers are placing increasing emphasis on short-term treatment to cut costs because some research shows that planned short-term treatment is as or more effective than open-end long-term contacts. Managed care has led to a greater degree of accountability in client care, but has also brought with it a number of problems. Figure 4.4 presents the structure of managed care.

What is managed care? *Managed care* is an elastic term that describes a variety of health care financing methods and delivery systems. The term *managed care* usually refers to a system of delivering services and a system of case management (Broskowski, 1991; Corcoran & Vandiver, 1996;

Hoge, Davidson, Griffith, Sledge, & Howentine, 1994; Mechanic, Schlesinger, & McAlpine, 1995; Sederer & Bennett, 1996). Briefly, managed care can be described as an attempt to combine financial administration of a health care organization with responsible patient care. Managed care involves selective contracting and networks of providers, an increase in fiscal management of care, a shift from provider to payer, and a basic concept of what constitutes treatment and outcome (Edinburg & Cottler, 1995).

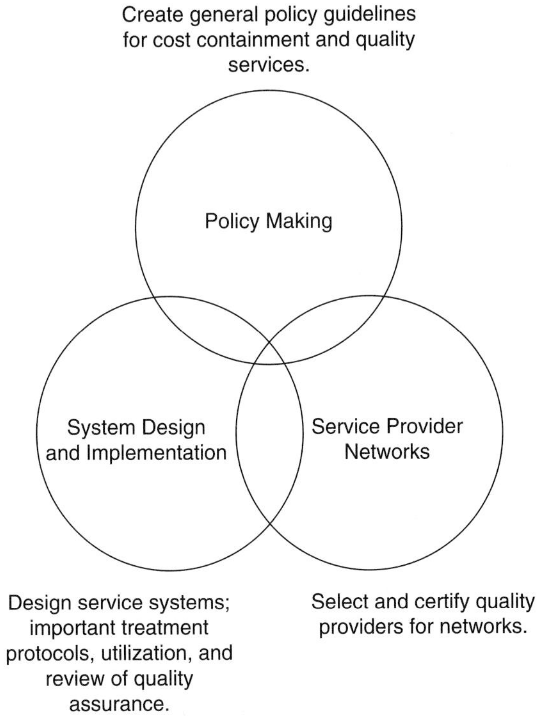

In terms of social accounting, we have a responsibility not only to clients but to the community and society as a whole. This suggests attention to who is and who is not being served and whether social problems are really being addressed. For example, does a program of adolescent pregnancy prevention actually reduce the incidence of adolescent pregnancy? Does a school drop-out program really keep kids in school?

Finally, a practical aspect of accountability stems from the fact that most social workers are not just professionals, they are also employees. As employees, they are required to meet certain organizational expectations such as maintaining an acceptable interview count, keeping statistical records, and utilizing certain models of practice. In other words, along with being accountable to ourselves, our clients, our profession, and our community, we are first and foremost accountable to our employers. The latter aspect of accountability assumes great practical importance because of the agency's power to hire, fire, promote, and so forth.

Workers, Clients, and Agency Setup

If workers wish to help their clients cope with the problems of access to services in the most beneficial manner, it is extremely important that generalists understand the policies and procedures of their agency in order to find ways to overcome or circumvent obstacles. The necessity of handling paperwork efficiently cannot be overemphasized. How workers handle paperwork also reveals how effectively they use their time with reference to deadlines, particularly in terms of their advocacy

Create general policy guidelines for cost containment and quality services.

Policy Making

System Design and Implementation

Service Provider Networks

Design service systems; important treatment protocols, utilization, and review of quality assurance.

Select and certify quality providers for networks.

Figure 4.4 **Structure of Managed Care**

and brokering for clients. There are policies of the agency that workers may have to interpret for the benefit of clients. Social workers have to understand the parameters of the policies of their agency and, at times, the authority available for interpretation. Often, workers who do not understand how organizations function may interpret the policies of their agency in a narrow and traditional way. In such situations, clients get hurt because they do not receive the full benefit of the services that should be available to them. At times, agencies may exclude a particular category of clients or fail to make full use of available resources. In order to bring about change, the responsibility of social workers is to view problems concisely and document them in detail. If there is any suggestion that a policy needs to be changed, or an exception to policy is needed, workers may have to document this information, as well.

Every agency has an organizational structure through which it carries out its functions. In nongovernmental (private) agencies, ultimate responsibility resides in a voluntary board of directors elected or appointed under the agency's corporate by-laws. The major responsibilities of agency boards include setting overall policy, approving budgets, hiring and firing the executive director, and sometimes fund-raising. The actual management of the agency is the responsibility of a paid executive as in any organization. The organizational structure and the levels of hierarchy will depend on the size, the complexity, and the particular characteristics of the agency. There may be an associate director who is responsible for day-to-day operations, while the executive director is involved more in community relations and long-range planning.

There may be department heads responsible for separate major programs of the agency or district office directors responsible for geographically separate units. There may be supervisors who oversee the work of a given number of generalists. Finally, there are line workers who are responsible for service. In smaller agencies the differentiation of roles would not be as great, with administrators frequently taking on responsibility for some staff supervision and even direct work with clients.

In governmental (public) agencies, the director of the agency is likely to report to an elected official such as a mayor or even the governor rather than the board of directors. Thus the social agency becomes part of the political system. In "host agencies" such as hospitals, schools, courts, community settings and more recently, the industrial and commercial corporations that hire social workers, the social work functions are viewed as secondary to the primary functions of the agency, that is, health care, education, law enforcement or making money, and staff social workers report to members of other professions or disciplines. A competent social worker possesses skill not only in work with clients, but in establishing effective working relationships with a wide range of people, including fellow social workers, members of other professions, support staff, board members, volunteers, and others who participate in the social welfare enterprise.

Funding Agencies

Funding agencies for social workers have changed through the years. More often than before, federal and private funding agencies are asking for documentation of effectiveness in terms of outcome measurement of programs that social workers conduct. Many programs and practices that have been ineffective have been phased out or modified. Regardless of how the amount of paper work involved interferes with their work with clients, social workers are obligated to show the funding source that the provider agency has offered the highest quality services. Program outcome studies have taught us about the usefulness of work with clients. Program outcomes have shown, for example, that orphanages are not the best places to serve homeless children, that long-term hospitalization is not the best way to help emotionally disturbed children, that individuals with mental disabilities can be helped best in their own homes along with supportive services rather than by confinement in an institution (Zastrow, 1995).

When the amount of money that will be available for a fiscal year becomes known, an organization must allocate funds and other resources to competing services and departments. If the organization secures all the funds it requested and its original formal proposal was realistic in terms of client demands and organizational aspirations, then the task of allocating funds is relatively simple and the proposed budget becomes the actual budget. However, when there are decreasing funds, the allocation of available resources can be a major struggle with potentially serious effects on many parts of the organization.

The effectiveness of programs will affect the allocation of funds. As services are being provided and funds expended, all transactions must be recorded as a basis for internal and external reports. It is important to record both service and financial information in a planned way for functional accounting and budgeting, cost analysis, evaluating costs of different ways of providing services, and reporting to resource providers, regulators, and constituents. Every social agency has to come to grips with the issue of accountability and carefully and specifically define its services so that the information can be aggregated in the same framework through accounting, personnel, and services (Fellin, 1995).

Historically, the concept of accounting for government and voluntary nonprofit agencies developed around concerns about how these organizations spent the funds allocated to them. In a democratic society, responsibility requires that elected officials answer to their constituents (Johnson & Schwartz, 1997). The concept of stewardship of funds is central to accounting principles in both government and voluntary sectors. Effectiveness and outcome of programs, job performance of personnel, and financial accountability continue to require the close attention of managers of profit and nonprofit agencies.

Improved skills in financial management include not only traditional skills in planning and controlling expenditures but also management indicators, financial ratios, and graphics. The impact of computers in this area is immense; fiscal management in social welfare has increased by means of automated spread sheets to support analysis and reporting through increasingly sophisticated accounting and statistical software. Also, today a larger number of social work students are receiving more information on financial management in schools of social work (Fellin, 1995).

The Bureaucracy, and the Conflict between the Bureaucracy and the Professional

A bureaucratic organization can be described as a formal organization with an administrative design that is expected to operate efficiently and has been considered to be superior to any other form of secondary group structure that has been devised. Of course, this is a traditional perspective that has been discredited to some extent by current organizational research and theory. Current thinking, especially in relation to professional and scientific endeavors, places greater emphasis on egalitarian relationships, democratic processes, and informality where tasks call for imagination and creativity rather than adherence to an established way of doing things. In current organizational theory, a well-functioning organization, like a healthy family, is flexible and adaptable to new challenges emanating from within or without. This does not mean that we can do away with the characteristics traditionally associated with bureaucracy, that is, formal hierarchical structure and standardized procedures. Someone has to be in charge, especially in large complex organizations, and there have to be clear lines of authority. Having a set of rules is also essential in the interest of fairness, stability, and efficiency.

What is an appropriate structure for a particular organization with a particular staff and a particular mission at a particular point depends on the organization, and there is no one best model. A general principle that holds in social work is that the higher the level of professionalism of the staff, the less the need for a rule book approach to practice. In public welfare, for example, where most of the line workers and even supervisors do not have professional credentials, there are volumes and volumes of policies and regulations. In professional family and mental health agencies, there is much more room for professional judgment in addressing client needs.

Bureaucracy is woven into the fabric of modern life and is probably here to stay. However, bureaucracies are not all alike. Some are stuck in the mud and spin their wheels. Others are more flexible and task focused, and are quite successful in achieving their goals.

In the corporate world, as in government at both the federal and local levels, bureaucracy is absolutely essential. The alternative would be anarchy. In a traditional bureaucracy, there is a clearly defined hierarchy, there are contractual relationships that are clearly defined, and employees are given positions based on their technical qualifications. The employees are remunerated with fixed salaries and a system of promotion prevails. The practitioner is subject to strict and systematic discipline and control (Compton & Galaway, 1994).

A bureaucracy that is set up to control work and procedures in order to perform work has some limitations. Historically, these limitations are seen in red tape, officiousness, timidity, exaggeration of routine, and limited adaptability. Often, the agencies emphasize technique and method rather than people and services (Compton & Galaway, 1989). This rigidity creates conflicts between the bureaucracy and the professional.

As Compton and Gallaway (1994) indicate, while working in bureaucratic settings, personnel usually experience conflict with the organization to some degree. Often what the social work professional sees as the ideal interventive action in order to help a client may be inappropriate because it is not within the parameters of the agency. Practitioners often have to compromise in order to meet the needs of the agency and the client who has entered the system seeking professional help.

One of the crucial problems of working within bureaucratic structures is the lack of recognition of the distinction between profit and nonprofit agencies. Money becomes an important criteria in profit organizations. When there is less money, hasty and ill-planned efforts are sometimes instituted to deal with issues. Financial problems affect the manner in which work is carried out with clients and how the services are evaluated. The manner in which a nonprofit organization operates is very different in that the connection between the product and the revenue is indirect.

At the present time, however the distinction between profit and nonprofit organizations has, to a large extent, fallen by the wayside. Agencies looking for ways to cope with increased deficits are looking to client fees as a source of increasing revenues. Preference is given to clients who can afford to pay for service or who are covered by insurance. The treatment process itself is influenced by insurance company preferences for short-term treatment. Often, controversial advocacy in the community is avoided for fear of offending large contributors or other funding sources.

Legal Sanctions

Social workers, like other professionals, operate within a legal framework through formal regulation. The regulation of social work includes registration and statutory certification and licensing. All of these are done through the credential process. As Biggerstaff (1995) indicates, a credential is evidence that a practitioner has met minimum standards to provide services to the public. Registration laws and statutory certification are forms of regulation. These are voluntary statutes that are applied only to social workers who wish to apply for a particular title. The laws that govern registration and certification require that social workers meet minimum requirements of education and experience and provide a state agency with their name and an address. Registration offers two types of protection: title and practice. This protection prohibits practitioners from using titles such as registered clinical social worker unless the person is credentialed to provide that service. Practice protection both regulates the use of the title and limits certain areas of professional practice (e.g., private practice) and the use of the title is given only to those people who have met predetermined minimum requirements (National Clearinghouse on Licensure Enforcement and Regulation and Council of State Governments, 1986).

Another form of regulation occurs through a voluntary certification program such as the Academy of Certified Social Workers (ACSW), which is a form of credentialing established by the NASW. The voluntary certification regulates specialty areas of practice.

Licensing laws establish the minimum standards for entry into the profession and exclude unqualified candidates from practicing in the profession. Licensure is based on the power of the state to enforce standards to practice. Minimum requirements are spelled out by different states, which include education, training, experience, and supervision for entry-level practitioners. In 1973, the NASW adopted a model licensing law that defined social work practice as professional activities directed at enhancing, protecting, and restoring people's capacity for social functioning whether impaired by physical, social, or emotional factors (NASW, 1973). Legal regulation in the form of licensure is present in thirty-seven jurisdictions for all social workers who provide clinical services or those who are in private practice.

Licensing laws in different states define the parameters of the work that can be done. There are sanctions for professional misconduct, and laws and rules that operate to protect clients' legal rights and control professional discretion. There are also many legislative actions and administrative procedures that govern the limitations of an agency's services.

Social workers should have adequate and specialized knowledge in such areas as the marital contract, rights, and obligations of eligibility for public benefits, rules governing confidentiality, the utilization of case records, and videotapes in legal proceedings and testifying in court as an expert witness.

Finally, there are also elements of self-interest in professional regulation. Depending on a particular system, licensure or certification determines and limits who may use a certain professional ti-

tle and who is allowed to provide certain types of services. From this point of view, the intent of licensure and certification is to make the profession more highly valued in the labor market by increasing the status of its professionals. There is no evidence to suggest that the salaries of social workers have been increased, but regulation and vendorship laws have contributed to increased earnings in the private sector (Gibelman & Schervish, 1993).

Part II of the book will focus on the skills required to work with different types of clients. These include understanding the therapeutic environment that is created, worker and client roles, communication and interviewing, and relationship skills required to be a professional generalist.

CHAPTER SUMMARY

The functions of social work are based on the assumption that people are important irrespective of their age, gender, ethnicity, race, religion, educational background, or socioeconomic status. Individuals can have problems arising out of inner conflicts, conflicts with other people, or conflict due to lack of resources. It is necessary to find solutions in order to alleviate these problems. In social work the practitioner's concern is with the interaction between people and social environments.

Social workers need skills in order to bring about changes in people's behavior. Skill has been explained as technical expertise and the ability to use knowledge effectively and readily in the execution of performance competence (Bartlett, 1970). The core practice skills include communication, interviewing, engagement, assessment, and intervention skills. The competencies that workers need to make use of their skills are problem assessment, enhancing problem solving, intervening effectively, evaluating with the intervention plans in mind, and improving services offered to clients. The helping process is an orderly, rational enterprise and is often a humane, merging experience between helper and client.

Based on skills, workers play different kinds of roles including direct roles and system linkage roles. In some agencies, these roles are performed by the same person including outreach worker, broker, advocate, evaluator, mobilizer, teacher, consultant, community planner, data manager, and administrator. In order for a practitioner to be successful, it is necessary to integrate knowledge, values, and skills in working with clients.

Accountability is an important aspect of social work. Accountability refers to contractual obligations and legal liability that professionals face as part of their agency and institution and personal responsibility for the delivery of effective services at a professional level of competence and at a reasonable cost. Changes in the client are dependent on the efforts put forth by the worker and client in their working relationship. Another aspect of accountability is the service contract, which makes the worker accountable for his or her performance to the recipient of service. The service contract highlights the purpose of intervention, the roles and rules between worker and client, the administrative procedures in terms of fees, and the amount of time that is allocated for this contract. Cost analysis and social accounting are also important aspects for social work practitioners, who not only have to be accountable to their clients but also to the community.

Social workers who wish to help clients need to understand the policies and procedures of their agency in order to find ways to overcome or circumvent potential obstacles. Every agency has an organizational structure through which it carries out its functions. In nongovernmental agencies, the ultimate responsibility resides with a voluntary board of directors elected or appointed under the agency's corporate by-laws. In governmental agencies, the director of the agency is likely to report to an elected official such as a county executive, mayor, or even a governor rather than the board of directors.

Funding in agencies has changed as federal and private agencies are asking for documentation of effectiveness. All this happens under a bureaucratic setup that can be described as a formal organization with a hierarchical structure and standardized procedures. Finally, like other professionals, social workers operate within a legal framework that protects clients' legal rights and promotes professional discretion.

THE CONTEXT OF HELPING

CHAPTER

5

INFLUENCE OF ENVIRONMENTS ON GENERALIST PRACTICE

This chapter discusses the person–environment fit and the influence of different elements of environments on practice. Often, it is assumed that learning skills means knowledge of how to work with clients. But work with different clients involves more than skills. It requires understanding the environments of people and deciding what skills are appropriate for a particular client group. For instance, while working with a poor family that consists of six members living in a two-bedroom apartment, it would be inappropriate for the social worker to suggest that children have separate bedrooms. Though ideal, this would be impossible in such a setting. Creative spatial alternatives within the apartment should be worked out with the family.

The study of environments is important because environments may protect or endanger people. We need to be aware of the power of environments if we wish to view issues holistically and offer effective help. It would be considered poor practice if we took little account of the impact of environments on the agency and the profession and those whom we serve (Germain & Gitterman, 1995). Even an agency itself provides an environment that helps or hinders effective practice.

This chapter deals specifically with the following topics:

The influence of environments on practice

Physical environments—natural and built, physical surroundings and behavior, form and context

The social environment

Arrangement of physical space and social outcomes

Interpersonal relationships, temporal environments, social networks

Internal and external environments

Agency environments and other factors that contribute to an effective helping environment

PHYSICAL ENVIRONMENT: NATURAL AND BUILT

The term PHYSICAL ENVIRONMENT implies that there are many environments. For the purposes of analysis, we could extract social, physical, personal, and psychological environments from the total environment. However, these are not separate environments but rather a continuum, all of which need to be considered when analyzing situations. It can also be said that all environments—physical, social, and psychological—interact with each other and people cannot exist optimally except in relation to the total environment. For example, the physical setting, be it a hospital ward, a community, or an organization, is not merely or simply its physical space with its design and the inanimate objects that occupy it. It also includes persons in this setting, their behaviors, and the social context that defines what the space is used for, who uses it, and what should and should not happen within it.

It is necessary to know the different environments within which clients have been transacting and experiencing. Understanding the differential environments of clients enables practitioners to become more knowledgeable and effective as generalists.

The idea of environment is complex in and of itself, and often it is difficult to distinguish what constitutes the inner and the outer environment for a person. There are a number of early contributors to the conceptual development of the implications of environment on social work practice, including Pollak (1952, 1956), Lutz (1956) Hearn (1958), Coyle (1958) Stein and Cloward (1959), Stein (1960), Polsky (1962), and the anthropologist Kluckholn (1958). As our understanding of people becomes more holistic, our knowledge of environments and their influence on people is being codified, and new theories about people–environment transactions are being developed in social work, environmental psychology, planning and architecture, social psychiatry, biology, and ecology.

Historically, transactions can be explained as what goes on over time between two or more entities where each entity reciprocally influences the other (Dewey & Bentley, 1949). Germain (1983) described transactions as processes by which people continually shape their environment and are shaped by it, over time. In other words, people are active participants in influencing their environment and they are also influenced by it. These elements of the environment are important to understanding work with clients.

A physical environment consists of natural and built environments (see Figure 5.1). The distinction between the two is superficial, but for the purposes of analysis it helps to clarify the dynamic nature of different environments in transaction with different people and with each other. Natural environments include the natural surroundings or physical landscape of a place, be it mountainous or tropical, and its effects on people. Other aspects of the natural environment include the climate and weather and their influence on how people dress and feel. The seasons of the year also influence people's behavior

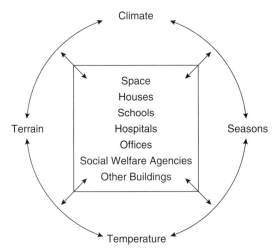

Figure 5.1   Natural and Built Environments

and attitude toward life. For some, winter is a good season because they feel energized to pursue their goals aggressively; similarly, others are highly motivated and energized in summer. Natural factors such as a drought or a hurricane can affect a community and its resources.

Christie, a depressed forty-year-old woman, stated in the clinical session that she hated the spring. She detested seeing flowers bud and bloom and the sprouting of new green grass. She loathed the spring season because of a failed pregnancy that left her childless for a period of ten years. Spring weather made Christie feel resentful toward the season and was responsible for her developing seasonal depression ever since her miscarriage.

The natural environment can also have positive effects on people. Searles (1960, 1996) believes that human beings should not only respect the natural world but should also remain in touch with its restorative and healing powers. According to Germain (1991), Searles specifies four positive effects of relatedness which he termed the nonhuman environment:

1. The appeasement of various painful and anxiety-laden states of feeling—being related to the nonhuman environment assuages our

existential loneliness in the world. This also alleviates fear of death, gives a feeling and sense of peace, and counteracts feelings of insignificance.
2. Relating to the natural world helps us gain a deeper sense of personal identity based on abilities and limitations and stimulates creative abilities.
3. Connectedness to the natural world enhances and sharpens the experiencing of our own existence in this world as real and deepens our sense of reality.
4. By being related to the world of nature, we come to value ourselves and others.

These effects help explain the sense of serenity and wonder that is felt by those who are fortunate enough to experience mountains, the seashores, or the countryside. They also account for the powerful influence of wilderness therapy on people of all ages in different states of physical and mental health (Germain, 1991).

Sixty-five-year-old Nellie lost her husband in a train accident a month ago. She has mothered five children who are all married and live in other states. Nellie is totally lost. You have introduced her to a Widows Group, and she is also in individual sessions with you. Nellie is in good health and constantly talks about how lonely it is in the house. Based on earlier discussions with her, you are aware that she loves cats and plants. You recognize that she is still in mourning. Would the suggestion that she grow plants inside the house or buy the cat that she always wanted for a pet be appropriate at this point? Why do you think this suggestion would be helpful to her?

Tucked away as part of the natural environment are areas that we call urban, suburban, and rural. U.S. urban areas have continued to act as population magnets during the 1980s, according to the 1990 census. By 1990, 75.2 percent of the U.S. population lived in metropolitan urban areas, up from 73.7 percent in 1980. On the other hand, the number of people living in rural areas fell from 26.3 percent to 24.8 percent from 1980 to 1990. In 1990, about 74.5 percent of the nation's housing units were located in urban areas (U.S. Bureau of the Census, 1992).

Between urban and rural communities are the suburban communities. Often suburban families have deserted large cities to move to smaller quiet communities that surround large cities. Suburban families are usually upwardly mobile families. The highway systems, lower property taxes, and the availability of more green space for their dollar has encouraged families to move away from large cities. This has also been called the "flight" of the upper and middle classes from problems in a crowded large city.

Edwards and Minotti (1989) define a rural county as "one in which the largest community has a population of less than 50,000 and in which more than 50% of the inhabitants reside in communities of less than 2,500" (p. 324). Deavers (1992) describe rural communities as small towns with open country and small-scale, low-density settlement. Rural communities tend to be peripheral to the larger society and are not fully integrated into centers of information, innovation, technology, and finance. Lack of such integration means that these rural communities will fall increasingly behind in an age of national and global development. Of course, there is an increasing trend among many rural communities to be connected to new information via computers, the Internet, television, and other technology. Also computer companies, such as the Gateway Computers in South Dakota, are located in more rural areas.

All of these different environments—urban, rural, and suburban—bring their own set of strengths and problems. Generalists need to be aware of the potential issues and problems that can arise in these different settings.

Besides the natural environments that influence our minds and our feelings about ourselves, built environments also exert influence. A built environment includes the houses, office buildings, and other structures of the area in which a person resides. A built environment could be a residential neighborhood with neat, well-kept houses and clean streets, or it could be a city block with high-rise apartment buildings and busy streets. People often take their physical surroundings for granted and tend to accept, and at times, cherish their familiarity. People who have not experienced or lived in inner cities might assume that these neighborhoods are disorganized but this is not necessarily so for their occupants. In reality, they possess rich structures of mutual aid systems and social networks (Kemp, Whittaker, & Tracy, 1997; Lawton, 1980; Stack, 1974; Valentine, 1978; Williams, 1996).

Other adaptive behaviors that people develop center around religion, music and humor that offset harsh environmental exposures (Draper, 1979). Almost all people have a sense of place, and their geographic origins are part of their sense of identity. Some people feel a kinship to the world of nature and others have strong attachments to places like their own homes. They may have some treasured room or objects that create a sense of comfort and relatedness. If these objects are removed, this person might feel a sense of loss of identity and view the loss as a personal assault. Thus, natural and physical environments provide opportunities and obstacles to the development of competence, relatedness and autonomy in people (Germain & Gitterman, 1995).

To understand people who come from places different from one's self, it is necessary to understand their background and history. It is also important that social workers recognize their clients' physical and social backgrounds so that the help they provide is holistic and ecologically oriented.

You are interviewing a client from a physically impoverished home background. You are amazed at her manner of dressing in winter. She is still wearing her summer clothes in layers to keep herself warm. You have never seen anything like this. You are confused. It's extremely cold outside. You ask her firmly why she is not dressed in winter clothes. The client appears to sink in front of your eyes. She avoids eye contact and does not respond. What have you done that has made the client feel inferior or view you as confrontational? If you as the generalist had been more aware and observant of the client's background, would you have asked such a question that perhaps put the client on the defensive?

Physical Space and Surroundings

The effects of physical space and surroundings can be observed in everyday situations. For example, in modern hospitals, the waiting rooms are large and totally impersonal, and they minimize interactions between patients. In contrast, the old-fashioned doctor's office, though incredibly crowded, is often unassuming and personal. The crowded waiting rooms of free clinics often reveal that patients are usually friendlier and closer to one another than they are with the doctors. The physical-built environments in which patients receive treatment reveal information about the goals and values of society in that particular arena, and also their effects on the identity, orientation, and ego organization of the people who operate within those environments. For example, hospital buildings reveal how society views the activities that go on within them. Until recently, the grim facades of our state hospitals for the mentally ill showed how the architects, designers, and providers felt about mental illness. Few and fenced windows, drab colors, and little interior decoration revealed the hopeless atmosphere of such a hospital.

Kathrina, a social worker in a mental hospital, is aware that the care of the mentally ill is short-term due to changes in hospital policies. Kathrina had been working with a group of depressed, mentally ill men. To her frustration, they were discharged from the hospital within three months and, in her opinion, without adequate psychological help and without sufficient protection. Most of these men are poor, and were abandoned by their relatives after admission to the hospital. A large number of such poor, unclaimed, mentally ill patients wind up with new problems when they become homeless. In such cases, their physical environment is dramatically modified from the enclosed physical space of the mental hospital to the open space of the streets where they must try to find temporary shelter on sidewalks and park benches.

Form and Context

The form of a building and the context in which it is built influence people and environments. The ultimate objective of a design is to create a form. Every design begins with an effort to join two entities—the form and its context. This simply means that when we speak of design, the real object of discussion is not the form alone but the ensemble that comprises the form and its context.

For example, let's look at a city and its habits. In this case, the human background dictates the need for new buildings which, in turn, are placed on the available sites and provide a context for the city's growth. By contrast, an old, crowded, drug-ridden city neighborhood is "cleaned up" under new rules and regulations and an investment of money transforms the outlook of the place.

We can also speak of culture itself as an ensemble in which the various fashions and artifacts that develop in that environment are intimately fitted. An apartment building in a poor area of a city in many ways reflects the outlook of its impoverished inhabitants. The apartment building has nonfunctioning elevators. Climbing up the dreary steps, one encounters large cockroaches and rodents. The landing midway between each story is clearly no-man's-land. Garbage is piled up in the corners, and an unbearable stink envelopes the building. However, the people who inhabit the building walk the staircase familiarly and comfortably, revealing their acceptance of the surroundings and the environment. Crime and drugs also exist in this environment. Though illegal, these activities bring families money that they desperately need.

To understand the psychological environment of the people who live and work in a particular area, it is necessary to study how their environment came into being, as well as the processes by which a person perceives, recognizes, and creates an environment for himself or herself. To understand and conceptualize human environments, it is important to include the relationship between the physical world and the world people "construct" from it, in terms of human behavior and experience (Proshansky, Ittelson, & Rivlin, 1970; Germain & Gitterman, 1995).

Sandy lives in the crowded inner city. You pay a home visit. You have never observed poverty. In Sandy's apartment, the floor and walls are damp because water is leaking from the pipes. The children, six of them, are sitting on a couch waiting for you. Sandy is holding a cane and has instructed the children to remain on the couch until you leave. The place has a smell that combines food, dampness, soiled clothes, and human sweat. You are responding personally to the squalor around you with shortness of breath, uneasiness, and discomfort. You are aware that you need to deal with the client but the strong unpleasant odor is overwhelming you. You are confronted with three issues: (1) your own personal discomfort; (2) the physical environment and its effects on Sandy and her family; and (3) your role as a practitioner. At this point it is important to process your feelings so that you can deal effectively with this client.

In order to change human behavior, environments are at times modified. For instance, an office building's setup prevented communication between coworkers. Redesigning the building to provide more open space allowed people to see each other and created a different environment, more conducive to congeniality, a sense of togetherness, and more productivity. There is a close relationship between building structures and the stability and consistency of human responses to that physical setting. Chavis and Wandersman (1990) indicate that the extent to which residents in a community feel a sense of community is a key mediating factor between individual and community well-being. A sense of community is related to the degree to which members believe they can have influence on their immediate environment.

Six-year-old Jacques was constantly in trouble in school. His classroom was painted a dull grey and was extraordinarily plain except for desks and chairs set in rows. The children were kept in their chairs throughout the school day and Jacques, an "isolated active" who was unable to keep still, was often in trouble in the class. After trying to work with the school system for several months with no improvement in his behavior, Jacques's parents decided to enroll him in another school. At this school, the classroom was attractive, the children were encouraged to decorate the walls with their own paintings and drawings, and the seating arrangement of the classroom changed to suit different activities. If the teacher was reading a story to the class, the chairs were placed in a circle; if the chil-

dren had to interact with others, the chairs were placed around small tables where the children could talk comfortably to each other. Over time, it became clear that Jacques "fit" into the classroom. There were no complaints about him to his parents and he, in turn, learned to enjoy school. In time, his positive behavior in the new school setting became enduring and consistent. In terms of the environment, one had been found that appeared conducive to his growth.

There is growing evidence that child and family well-being is fundamentally tied to the well-being of neighborhoods in which there is social cohesion (Elliot et al., 1996). This points to the importance of a focus on the development of community resources and supports as a component of direct practice. Awareness of the tremendous impact of environment on behavior and efforts to change behaviors should be an integral part of a practitioner's repertoire.

THE SOCIAL ENVIRONMENT

The social environment is intertwined with the physical environment. Culture is an important aspect of the life of an individual, a family, a group, a community, or an organization. Culture involves people's perceptions of relationships among individuals and the natural world. Barker (1995) describes culture as "the customs, habits, skills, technology, arts, values, ideology, science, and religious and political behavior of a group of people in a specific time period" (p. 87). Rounds, Weil, and Bishop (1994) present culture as diversity that can be understood in terms of race and ethnicity that contribute to the uniqueness of the individual, family, and community; other factors include socioeconomic status, education, family history, and ethnic group identification. Cultural norms and values influence both social and physical settings. Culture influences the manner in which land is utilized and how buildings are located and designed. In turn, social and physical environments also influence culture. In the twentieth century, the beginning of the information era of television, computers, the Internet, air travel, and technology have affected modern culture in profound ways.

Social environments created by and for people include natural groups such as families and friends, formal groups such as health care, education, and recreation organizations, workplaces, religious groups, and political and economic structures at local, state, and national levels. Differential environmental influences—physical, social, and psychological—affect people in different ways and it would be unnatural to separate people from their physical and social environments (see Figure 5.2).

The term *social network* (Kemp, Whittaker, & Tracy, 1997) refers to the structure and number of a person's social relationships, whereas the term *social support* refers to exchanges within a network such as emotional encouragement, concrete aid, and advice and information that are viewed as being beneficial. As Heller and Swindle (1983) note, social support is a multidimensional construct, consisting of social network resources, types of support, perceptions of support, and skills in accessing and maintaining support.

Both physical and social environments intermingle. Complex transactions take place simultaneously between physical and social settings and people who are part of them. The manner by which people interact may vary as well, depending on their backgrounds. At first we build our physical settings, and these shape the social transactions between people. As time passes, the physical settings are also influenced and shaped by the social patterns, needs, and goals of people. Thus, when we work with clients, we must keep in mind the reciprocal relations between the physical and social environments in addition to the profound influence of culture if we are to provide effective helping. For instance, a physically challenged person may have problems of access not only in terms of moving around a room, but also in terms of social problems because of the attitudes of some people in the room. As one physically challenged professor commented, "I like going only to that particular restaurant, because there is no hassle about access or people's attitudes. I always found them to be helpful."

Feda grew up in a warm climate and a culture in which doors to homes were kept open, people socialized easily and comfortably, and they were congenial and helpful to each other. After a move to a large crowded city, Feda was threatened with a knife and robbed of her money. This was followed by another incident in which her daughter was followed to their apartment by a man who held a knife to her back. This greatly affected Feda and her family. They learned not to trust strangers and to keep their doors locked. They carried this fear with them when they moved to other cities. Being suspicious of people became second nature to the family. Thus, due to environmental factors, a new family cultural pattern developed in a reciprocal response to the environments that this family experienced. How did the environments to which this family was exposed affect their behaviors? How would you work with them if they became your clients?

The next section looks at different types of environments that can affect behaviors. Notice that all of them were created for the well-being of a group of people or the general public.

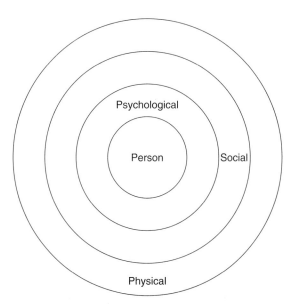

Figure 5.2   Person and Environment

Hospital Settings

Looking at the effects of a hospital setting on human behavior, exemplified in the earlier case study of social work consultant Kathrina, aids in understanding the influence of physical and social environments on people. Does the physical environment of a mental hospital influence the behavior of patients and the staff who occupy and use it? Indeed, there is a relationship between people's behaviors and the physical environments in which they are placed.

The physical design of a psychiatric ward limits the range of behavior that is available to patients. For instance, a patient cannot sleep in a hospital solarium because neither a bed nor a couch is available. If a patient decided to sleep on the floor every night and this was not acceptable to the hospital staff, he or she would be confronted with the constraints of the hospital which require patients to sleep on beds. Another factor that affects the freedom of choice of these individuals is the presence of other patients. If one seat is occupied by a patient, the other patient has to go elsewhere to sit down or read a book or take a nap or eat lunch.

Any physical setting, be it a hospital, a psychiatric ward, a house, an apartment, a classroom in a school, a neighborhood, or a city is part of a larger, more encompassing physical setting. It is influenced by this setting, which it influences in turn. Physical structures and the broader settings that encompass them are expressions of correspondingly inclusive and interlocking social systems. When a physical setting is an open system that undergoes change but maintains stability, the organization is dynamic and the behavior of people within it is interdependent.

The Prison Setting

A totally different type of an environment, prisons are technically known as *rehabilitation-based correctional facilities*. Thomas (1994) emphasizes that the current prison system mirrors the predominant philosophy of modern criminology and conforms to recent court rulings forbidding government entanglements with religion, unlike in the past when religion was used to help prisoners modify their behaviors. The current system lacks any methodical attempt to deter inmates from committing future offenses. Instead, the present prison regime tries to rehabilitate offenders under the assumption that crime is caused by social forces. The use of the term *social forces* is a conscious effort to undermine references to religion and other constructive outlets which could formerly have been counted on to soften hearts and stiffen the discipline of these inmates. With this no longer present, there is no genuine hope of a properly defined rehabilitation.

The lifestyle and regime of present-day prisoners is a troublesome problem. The use of imprisonment as a means of punishment has far exceeded the willingness of the American people to adequately fund new prisons. The present overcrowded physical environment of the prison system mocks the original goal of at least semi-solitary confinement and results in living conditions that are hazardous and all too often fatal for inmates. Today there are nearly a million prisoners in the United States (Gest, 1992). Due to political failures to allocate sufficient funding to prison construction and maintenance, they are packed into prisons with shrinking living space, and increasingly hardened criminals for roommates. Another serious problem that has arisen in this overcrowded prison system involves race. Inmates who refuse to accept racial segregation risk violence or death (Carroll, 1974). White prisoners generally join white supremacist and neo-Nazi groups largely for purposes of self-protection (Taylor, 1992). Similarly, African Americans and other ethnic groups form their own groups. The violent racial fragmentation of the prison system, coupled with too many offenders crowded together in close quarters, has created a situation which is so chaotic that prison administrators are today reluctant to claim that rehabilitation is the penal goal.

Another standard occurrence is homosexual rape, with few inmates leaving a maximum security facility without being sexually assaulted in some manner (Gest, 1992). To escape threats from other prisoners, weaker inmates often "marry" a bigger inmate and exchange sexual privileges for protection (Engel & Rothman, 1984).

Adding to the chaos of this institutional failure is the tragedy of enforced idleness. Federal law essentially prohibits inmates from working. Incarcerated criminals are left to spend their time writing appeals of their convictions, bullying their fellow inmates, or planning their next offenses (Thomas, 1994). Thus, space and time used irreverently and inefficiently has created an atmosphere of hostility and demoralized behavior in the prison system.

Neighborhoods

Neighborhoods are social organizations that depend on local friendship ties and social cohesion. The level of resident participation in formal and informal voluntary association results in a system of informal social controls. Wilson (1996) asserts that in neighborhoods where there is a high degree of social organization, adults are empowered to improve the quality of their environment and neighborhood life. In such situations, members of the neighborhood interact well in terms of obligations, expectations, and relationships and are in a better position to supervise and control the activities and behaviors of children. In the absence of such characteristics neighborhoods can be less conducive for the healthy development of its members.

Neighborhoods plagued by high levels of joblessness more often experience low levels of social organization (Wilson, 1996). In fact, these two factors go hand in hand. In a nonnurturing environment, joblessness can trigger other problems such as crime, gang violence, and drug trafficking. As studies have revealed the decline in legitimate employment opportunities among inner-city residents has led to increased incentive to sell drugs (Wilson, 1996). Generally, the distribution of drugs in a neighborhood attracts individuals who are involved in violence and lawlessness. Violent behavior in the drug marketplace has a powerful effect on the social organization of a neighborhood. Neighborhoods that are plagued by high

levels of joblessness, insufficient economic opportunities, and too much residential mobility are unable to control the volatile drug market and the violent crimes related to it. Therefore, the behavior and norms in the drug market are more likely to influence the actions of neighborhood residents, even those who are not involved in drug-related activities. Drug users and drug dealers cause the use and spread of guns in a neighborhood to escalate, which in turn raises the likelihood that others, particularly youngsters, will come to view weapons as being essential or a prestige symbol for self-protection, settling disputes, and gaining respect from peers and others.

Joblessness and drug use in different pockets of the neighborhood environment create a culture of poverty in the rest of the neighborhood. These pockets of poverty are prevalent in the inner city, where people typically comprise the "underclass." As Kaus (1992) observed, the underclass is represented by out-of-wedlock births, single-parent families, school truancy, crime, and welfare dependency. Other researchers define the underclass as those with a set of deviant behaviors such as drug addiction or mental illness (Corcoran, 1985). Regardless of label—underclass or poor, the results are always desperately painful for a neighborhood's residents. Poor neighborhoods reflect unemployment, teen idleness, crime, births to teenagers, low birth weight babies, and infant deaths (Bailey, 1993).

ARRANGEMENT OF PHYSICAL SPACE AND SOCIAL OUTCOMES

Social work professionals need to understand the use and presence of space as an active factor in assessing intervening with, and evaluating clients. In a built environment, we regard space as being defined by physical barriers that have been erected in order to restrict motion and the reception of visual and auditory stimuli. The spatial behaviors of people, like those of animals, are many and can be defined by the term *territoriality*. Spatial behaviors regulate social intimacy and distancing and also serve to define our relationships in terms of status, role, authority, and hierarchies in families and groups.

Territorial behavior is used to possess and occupy portions of space that people regard as their own, for example, the attitude of gangs toward their "turf." Stea (1970) and Blanckenhorn (1991) indicate that territorial possession is as fundamental as sexual possession. We create territoriality or space that we see as our own by a fence, a compound, nameplates, or other markings that distinguish our property from that of others.

A person also tends to create some personal space around himself or herself. This space signifies an individual at the center of a culturally determined radius. This personal space or distance (Hall, 1966; Lloyd, 1975), which can be understood as an imaginary shell in which a person is encased, varies from culture to culture. The importance of a spatial framework that conditions the relations of distance and the position of human beings one to another is likely to create a feeling of security or insecurity depending on its form and dimension (see Figure 5.3).

According to psychologists, the need for personal space appears in the child around the age of

seven. The absence of territory suitable for the establishment of personal space could be caused by limited space and overcrowding, which could lead to regression. In a 1958 symposium, Searles (1960) reported the most suggestive facts about the significance of space. It was found that in a large, overcrowded, and rather neglected ward of Saint Elizabeth's Hospital in Washington, D.C., space had assumed genuine value because of its scarcity. A dominant patient had full control of the hall, while those below him in hierarchical order had access only to limited space. No other patient could intrude on the territory of a person more powerful than himself. At the bottom of the totem pole was the patient who could not use anything except the bench he slept on. This person could not even go to spit in the drain located in the middle of the hall, and he had no right to use the toilet. These limitations existed not because of the patient's psychosis, but as a result of his social status in the hospital–patient setting.

Searles (1996) in his study of schizophrenia observed the disturbances of space perception in mental patients. He found that some schizophrenics come to the point not only of losing spatial awareness in terms of limits on their own bodies (a well-known phenomenon) but also of connecting and confusing space perception with the limits of the room.

How should social workers utilize space in working with people? Is touching or sitting close to a person comfortable or offensive to that person? How should we arrange space for effective communication? The following section looks at utilizing space for effective interpersonal relationships.

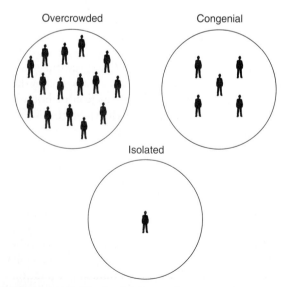

Figure 5.3 Social Space Creates or Disrupts Interpersonal Relationships

Interpersonal Relations

An important aspect of the arrangement of space has to do with the "silent language" of the positioning and distancing of one person from another. Verbal language also borrows from the silent language in expressing both superior and inferior social position and distance. For example, a hostess at a formal dinner party arranges where the guests should sit: left or right, far or near to the head of the table. In fact, all the rituals of propriety correspond to the art of situating oneself and others in relation to oneself. Utilization of space is an art in itself.

When people need to discuss common needs, what is the most effective way to arrange the space? If there were twenty people in a room, how would you arrange the space? Would you arrange chairs in a row and stand on a podium to talk to them or would you place them in a circle so members could see each other? Which arrangement might lead to a better discussion? Social work professionals must consciously plan spatial attitudes and behaviors based on professional ethics and the needs of different clientele.

A couple walks into your office for a marital session. Carrie and Carlton are in their early twenties. You observe that Carlton is extraordinarily good-looking. Carrie, on the other hand, looks unkempt. While inviting them into your office, you make eye contact with Carlton more frequently than you do with Carrie. Sitting down, you invite them to do the same while still making eye contact with Carlton. Carlton pulls a chair closer to you, Carrie sits away from you. When you begin to talk to Carrie, do you find that she sounds hostile? Why? How could you have used body language and eye contact in an interpersonal manner in order to make both the clients feel at ease?

Different cultures have different ways of using space. For instance, Americans often find that Latinos come too close to speak. On the other hand, Latinos tend to think that if they keep a distance, others will consider them to be cold. When a Latino couple visit England, they are surprised to find that there is a degree of aloofness or lack of emotional warmth that appears to border on coldness among the people living near them. In a Middle-Eastern culture, it would be easy for two men to hug each other and hold each other's hands and walk together as friends, whereas this gesture probably would be misunderstood in the American culture as reflecting a different lifestyle.

Although many cultural differences exist, an important factor in understanding interpersonal distance relates to the biological needs of people. As ethologists have found, among all animals there is a *flight*, or *critical distance*, and a *personal distance*. The critical distance can be identified as the amount of space required before an animal reacts by flight to the approach of an assumed enemy. In a similar manner, a practitioner needs to know how much physical distance he or she needs to allow for effective communication with the client.

When Cecelia was working with a group of emotionally disturbed teenagers, she was astonished by the different ways the boys reacted to her. When they were being constructive and friendly, they allowed her to enter their space and even invade their personal space by patting their shoulders or their heads. But when they got angry, most of the boys would warn her away by saying, "You make me too mad. Don't come near me or I will hurt you." In doing so, they implied that Cecelia had reached the critical distance and closeness was a discomfort when they were upset; thus, they distanced themselves and Cecelia respected it. This behavior was also exhibited in their relationships with their families. Not only would the boys distance themselves physically, they also would not communicate verbally, which caused these teenagers more problems.

A client needs to experience comfortable interpersonal spacing and territoriality to achieve the desired level of privacy or social interaction. This is called *healthy boundary making*. Barker (1995) describes boundaries as regions separating two psychological or social systems. Analogous to the membranes of living cells, a function of boundaries in family systems thinking is to differentiate systems and their subsystems and to permit the development of identity. Family systems thinking relates to implicit rules that are created in families in terms of how family members or subsystems are expected to relate to each other and to nonfamily members. Healthy family functioning largely entails clear boundaries or healthy boundaries; less healthy functioning is seen where boundary subsystems are either inappropriately rigid or not consistently clear. But when the boundary regulation is ineffective or negatively affected, it can create problems.

Temporal Behaviors

The relational aspects in behaviors, both temporal and spatial, constitute personality characteristics. One must have time for solitude, time for interacting with people, and time to cope with stress and adapt to new circumstances. Time is a cultural attitude. When a client comes late for an appointment and is new to the therapeutic culture, he or she has to be made aware of social time. This concept of time has great implications for differences in people's behavior, in terms of conceptualizing punctuality, the sequencing and pacing of events, and the rhythms of family life (Germain, 1991; Germain & Gitterman, 1995). Such differences have to be evaluated carefully in working with clients. For instance, in the English language we say that the clock "runs" but in Spanish the clock "walks."

Amy rushes through grief caused by the loss of her spouse by denying it, and Rose stays with it for a long time. What is the appropriate mourning time in different cultures? A label of *merry widow* is a stereotype that implies that a woman did not mourn the loss of her husband for a sufficient or required period of time. At the other extreme is Margie, a widow of three years, who said in a clinical session, "I wish I could lie down and die. But I am required to get up and go to work and I do so reluctantly." Dressed in black for three years, she had no social life and she reviewed her life in terms of how much more time was left before she joined her husband. For her, time froze when her husband died.

Coping has to be instituted in order to increase the level of social interaction in the case of loneliness or widespread isolation. But timing is also important in offering help to individuals, families, groups, communities, and organizations. Improper timing can lead to ineffective helping.

Social Networks

Helping clients network with others is important for their own development? What do we mean by social networks? Barker (1995) describes networks as individuals or groups who are linked by some common bond, shared social status, similar or shared function, or geographic or cultural connection. "Social networks form and discontinue on an ad hoc basis depending on specific need and interest. Included as some of the many types of social networks are the support system, the natural helping network, self-help groups, and groups of formal organizations that address a common problem" (p. 355).

Although there is an awareness of social networking, workers often do not emphasize this sufficiently while working with clients. It is an important aspect of human relatedness and should be utilized appropriately. People are brought up in socialized relationships, and they tend to expand them in widening circles over their lifespan until old age when such relationships contract. Through involvement with others, people develop a sense of self and individuality (Germain, 1983; Germain & Gitterman, 1996; Lewis and Suarez, 1995). Bowlby (1973) and Dubos (1978) which indicate that humanity evolved the structure of small nomadic bands to eliminate the unwanted distance that violated deep needs for relatedness. When people do not feel related to others, they are often in danger of mental disturbances or death. Will (1959) and Searles (1996) indicate that even pain and loneliness can be endured if the sense of relatedness to the human world is maintained.

There are two types of loneliness: emotional isolation and social isolation. Emotional isolation happens when there is a loss of an intimate attachment, such as spouse, a child, a parent, or a lover. Social isolation is the result of a lack of a network of involvement with peers. All adults need both reciprocal attachments and the social integration of engagement with a network of others. For example, widow-to-widow programs allow women with similar issues of grief, pain, and loss of an intimate emotional relationship to meet in a social peer group to grieve and work through their issues. This program helps widows move into their new status and also face coping tasks with the guidance and support of peers who have experienced similar situations (Silverman, 1976). The support that people receive does not replace the lost attachment but it is a constructive way to cope, adapt, and look forward to new beginnings (Sabatelli & Sheehan, 1993).

For the practitioner, it is important to be aware of the social networks of clients, of mutual-aid systems, and self-help groups for two reasons: primary prevention of problems and restorative intervention (Denzin, 1992; Lewis, 1988; Sabatelli & Sheehan, 1993;). The presence of social support systems mediates the effects of stress as a causal factor in physical illness. For example, twenty-eight-year old Rita had a mastectomy. Sharing her feelings and experiences in a self-help group encouraged her to accept her condition and view more realistically the possibilities of leading a normal healthy life.

Also important are self-help and mutual-aid systems that serve oppressed populations ranging from Native Americans, African Americans, and Latinos, to homeless families and people of low income (Lewis & Ford, 1990). When these networks work, the environment is improved for everyone in a kind of recycling process. Lewis and Suarez (1995) note that self-help groups and natural helping networks are fundamental to the U.S. social welfare system. But as Americans emphasize individual growth and attainment, such networks may also be seen as threatening.

When mutual aid networks organize and mobilize for social action against the police or programs of governments or corporations there may be repercussions. Network members may be detained by the police, questioned by authorities, or put under surveillance, such as those who attempted to unionize factory workers at the turn of the twentieth century (Jansson, 1993). However, an interesting phenomenon has occurred since the 1970s. As funds available to address contemporary social problems have dwindled, there is a growing national movement to abrogate the social responsibility of governments in providing for citizens in need and to promote natural helping networks. Therefore, it is not surprising that natural helping networks constantly change to func-

tion better as buffers against environmental challenges faced by members (Gutman, 1982; Lewis & Suarez, 1995; Warren, 1981).

THE EFFECTS OF INTERNAL AND EXTERNAL ENVIRONMENTS ON CLIENTS

Physical and social environments have an influence on people and create psychological environments for them. The influences of these environments have a complexity of meaning based on cultural orientation and a person's sense of self. Individuals contribute symbolic meaning to different environments and to activities they engage in. These meanings are derived from the personality processes of cognition, emotion, and action. Other factors that come into play in terms of the meaning of the environment to a person include a person's cultural and family background, life experiences, and the influences of social, cultural, and geographical factors. Factors such as gender, age, and ethnic group are also important. For example, a home, which is really a physical building, can be comfortable or uncomfortable for a person because it has a symbolic meaning involving a sense of security or insecurity, social contacts, feedback, and the consequences of one's actions. This symbolic meaning can produce feelings of warmth and a sense of being nurtured or pain, stress, and conflict. Through internalization, environments and culture become a part of a person's self-concept (Germain, 1991). The properties of environments are closely connected to a person's outlook and sense of place.

Sometimes people have to be uprooted from their surroundings because they have faced trauma in their home life. This applies to children who have been sexually or physically abused, women who have been physically abused, the elderly who have been abused and, in some instances, men who have been abused. For now, let us focus on children who have unusual problems.

Some children with special needs have to be placed in different environments. Some may have to be removed from their homes because they are in danger of being impaired physically and psychologically. When children are removed from their own homes for protection, they need to be placed in environments that can help create in them a sense of rootedness. But this does not always seem possible. Although foster homes are temporarily available for care and safety of children, permanency in foster homes is difficult to achieve. Moving children from one foster home to another and forcing them to adapt to different environments with different value systems and cultures has not been conducive to their healthy growth.

Twelve-year-old Derrick was removed from his home due to neglect charges. At three years of age Derrick was found tied to his crib. He was undernourished, tiny, and clothed only with a diaper that reeked of urine and excrement. He had been fed sporadically by his mother who was both mildly retarded and mentally ill. She made her livelihood through prostitution and was away from the apartment for days at a time. Fortunately, neighbors reported the situation to the police who, in turn, referred the child to social services. Social services placed Derrick in a foster home. After living with them for six months, Derrick was returned to the agency because the foster family found him incorrigible. For one reason or another, over the next nine years Derrick was moved to six different foster homes with different types of child-rearing practices, rules, and regulations. This transplanting added to Derrick's feelings of insecurity and mistrust coupled with low self-esteem and hostility. At this point, he is in a residential treatment setting. The practitioner who works with him needs to be aware of his exposure to different family environments, some nurturing and others nonnurturing. The worker also needs to keep in mind the inconsistent transitional environments in which he has been placed, as well as the effects of the rules and regulations of different homes on Derrick.

There are nonnurturing environments of physical abuse prevalent in some women's lives. A chilling 31 percent of all women killed in the United States are murdered by their husbands, ex-husbands, or boyfriends (Ross & Goss, 1989) and the percentage continues to increase. Even when these women leave their abusive partners they may still not be safe because they are followed and harassed by their abusers (Gottlieb, 1995). Thus, although temporary, an alternative environment has been created for these abused women. How would you, as a generalist, keep the environments in mind not just for you to offer services but to empower the abused female client to think, grow, and change? Perhaps the temporary shelter in which the women live in can arrange classes for occupational training that may empower them and move them toward emotional and financial freedom.

Abuse of the elderly, a closely kept secret in many homes, is slowly becoming more well known. The elderly are sometimes abused by adult caregivers who, in many cases, are their own adult children (Tatara, 1995). About two-thirds of elder abuse victims are physically abused or neglected. The average age of these victims is about eighty years (Tatara, 1993). The role of the medical profession is crucial in recognizing such abuse. There are different types of services available to the elderly including protective services set up by the American Public Welfare Association and National Association of State Units on Aging (1988). Also, long-term care ombudsman offices and state health departments provide health services. There are prevention services where professional and educational programs are available at the community level and, finally, there are support services such as advocacy and victim support groups, foster care, respite care, group homes, and transportation and socialization services. In each one of these settings a different environment and culture prevails, and the generalist who works with the elderly should be flexible with knowledge, values, and skills to help the elderly cope with their own issues and to empower them to work with different, new, or modified environments.

UNDERSTANDING THE ENVIRONMENT OF AN AGENCY

Generalists are aware that agencies incorporate physical, social, and psychological factors as part of their environment. Agencies are complex organizations created by human beings to solve certain complex problems and achieve particular goals in various areas of life.

Social welfare organizations or social welfare agencies are formal organizations legitimized by the state to deliver personal and social services and other benefits and goods to citizens; participate in deviance control on behalf of the state (Austin & Hasenfield, 1985; Kamerman, 1985) and promote the public interest or common good (Bellah, Madsen, Sullivan, Swidler, & Tipton, 1985). Social welfare organizations are intrinsically embedded in the social, physical, and cultural environments of an area (Pillari & Newsome, 1997). The organization and agency becomes the immediate environment for worker–clientele interaction. The agency also becomes important in creating an environment in which the worker functions as well as interacts with the client. A social worker is not only part of the agency system, but is also accountable to the agency. There is form and content in the agency and the agency provides resources to both the workers and different clients.

The environments of different agencies vary. Some are exclusively social work agencies whose main goal is to offer social services of various types. For instance, in the family services agency the chief aim of all clients is to get help with various physical, social, and emotional problems in the family and related areas. The types of financial resources and the professionals that an agency employs set the tone and establish the climate. Some agencies are very reputable, and others are mediocre. Some agencies receive funding from federal, state, and local governments and remain bound by government regulations. Others ar exclusively voluntary with a governing board of citizens who raise money in the community for agency support. Some voluntary agencies now receive governmental funds in the form of purchase of service and grants.

Social workers are also employed by public agencies such as social services or child protective services, which are funded by state and federal agencies. In such settings the worker is regulated by laws, governmental policies, and various regulations. For example, welfare clients receive monthly checks from such agencies along with what has been described as "poor services for poor people." In some agencies, the bare floors and walls and the hard chairs fixed together in rows create a harsh atmosphere which, at times, is staffed with untrained workers and clerical help who treat clients badly.

There are some social workers who are employed in what are called "host" or "secondary settings." The primary function of such agencies is not social services. Rather, social services are used to enhance the primary function of the agency, such as social workers working in hospital and school settings as part of an interdisciplinary team.

Twelve-year-old Brittany is not concentrating on her studies and is listless in class. The teacher finds that Brittany does not dress properly or attend school regularly. She refers Brittany to the school social worker who focuses on Brittany's poor school performance and her family relationships. She works closely with the principal, the teacher, and the parents to help Brittany work through her family issues, while keeping her school performance in terms of attendance, classroom participation, and proper attire as priorities. If serious issues should come up, Brittany would be referred outside for more help and follow-up work by a practitioner. As generalists, social workers should be comfortable with the different people who are part of the client's life in order to be an effective helper.

All agencies in which social workers function can be classified according to several dimensions. These include size, means of support and governance, nature of the primary service offered, and range of employees. The surrounding community provides financial support and sanctions for the agency, as well as expectations for the nature and outcome of services. The resources that an agency has depend on the nature of the agency structure and the services it offers. As changes take place in the community, there will also be changes in the agency system. Social workers who understand this relationship of agency, community, and the environment should be better able to understand, function within, and use the agency system in the service of clients (Johnson, 1995).

The worker needs to be aware that in all agencies there is distribution of power and control that depends on the organizational properties of centralization, formalization, and stratification (Anderson & Carter, 1990; Daft, 1992; Schein, 1992).

Centralization is the distribution of power in a setting. It is manifested by authority in the formal system and influenced by the informal system. An environment of caring depends to a large extent on who is in power and how authority is used in the setting. Too much rigidity at the top could affect flexibility and adaptability in work practices.

Formalization is the creation of rules in order to maintain impartiality, efficiency, and fairness. Agency rules are of two types. Formal rules support the achievement of agency's goals and may be rigid or may have latent functions to benefit the organization rather than worker or client needs. There are also customs, traditions, and norms that develop in the agency setting. The social worker has to understand the impact of formal policies and informal customs on the quality of services that are offered to clients.

Finally, there is *stratification,* which is distribution of rewards within an agency as manifested by the type of status a person maintains in the organization. High status in an organization is rewarded by position and higher income. People who have more prestigious jobs are likely to enjoy more space and other amenities. In such environments, social workers can gain prestige through professional competence, attractive personal and interpersonal qualities, and exchange relationships with other staff members. At times, stratification of position and power can account for competition between disciplines and departments, as well as allocation of funds.

Due to the presence of distinctive features in organizations, social workers find themselves functioning with two conflicting types of expectations: professional and bureaucratic. These expec-

tations set the tone for the agency as well. Some bureaucratic expectations call for loyalty to and acceptance of authority and require working within the rules of the agency. Bureaucratic expectations emphasize specialization and efficiency. Professional goals tend to be different and involve commitment to professional values and services to clients. At times these different types of expectations create tensions in an agency, and the worker has to understand the organization's rules, regulations, and type of authority in working with clients (Johnson, 1995).

Generally, the professional perspective regards authority as residing in professional competence, but the bureaucratic perspective views authority as residing in the office that is held. When fifteen-year-old Brett gets into trouble, the generalist works toward serving the best interests of the client, whereas the bureaucrat is seeking to serve the best interests of the organization. The bureaucrat has rules about how long Brett can stay in sessions based upon agency workload, waiting lists, and the financial situation of an agency system.

Professional social workers seek their identity from their professional organization, whereas bureaucrats, though sometimes also social workers, identify with their particular stratum within the bureaucratic hierarchy. Again, orientation to power is different. "The professional norm is to influence clients and peers by modes which are oriented toward the pole of free exchange while the bureaucratic norm is oriented toward the pole of coercion" that is supported by the invoking of sanctions (Morgan, 1962, p. 115).

Factors That Contribute to an Effective, Constructive Environment

In order to work with clients, it is necessary that the worker knows what their problems are and understand the physical and social situations and environments they have encountered in their lives. It is the worker's responsibility to create a supportive atmosphere for the client. All clients need to be respected and made comfortable. They should be able to relate problems with confidence as well as understand their rights so that they will not be violated. A constructive environment for clients includes not only the physical setting in which they meet with the generalist, but also the generalist practitioner's ability to create a communicative environment. Thus, to a great extent the constructive atmosphere or environment, besides being a physical setting, is created by professionals through their attitudes and behavior. This includes being caring, warm, and willing to listen and deal with the clients' issues.

Creating a constructive atmosphere also means reaching out and finding the clients' strengths. It means reaching out to the potential in the clients and refusing to accept even the clients' own descriptions of impossibilities. It means bringing about change in different size systems with their input and direct involvement. The social worker and the client have within themselves the potential strength to implement and move toward changes that need to be made in a client's situation. Creating a constructive atmosphere also means that the generalist discusses the meaning of intervention and helps the client understand his or her significant and active role in change. A constructive atmosphere is conducive to the different transactions that need to take place in order to bring about change and make the client aware of the work that has to be done. A constructive atmosphere also means creating a setting where people feel they can talk about difficult and controversial matters and still be accepted as clients and helped accordingly.

Forty-year-old Anita, a single parent, did not wish to leave her home and attend the mothers' meetings that were held in an agency where her ten-year-old son, Daryl, had been placed. She was a loner without any friends. From the time the practitioner met her, it was clear that Anita was overwhelmed by her situation and afraid of contact with people. She literally hid behind the door for several minutes before she opened it for the visiting practitioner. However, through persuasion she was helped to attend the mothers' meetings. Initially she felt that she could not contribute or learn from the meetings, but with the

worker's unconditional support she started to participate, timidly at first. Later she brought in new ideas and became a productive, contributing member of the group. Analyze why the client became a productive member of the group. What was the worker's role in this change?

An apartment building with an absentee owner had a number of missing utilities. The members of the apartment complex belong to two different ethnic groups and are constantly fighting each other, a situation made worse by the lack of heat, broken electrical outlets, and poor water supply. A generalist who had gone to visit a client family was flabbergasted that instead of fighting the landlord the tenants were fighting each other over turf issues in the building. The practitioner, who was seriously interested in helping his clients as well as other young families, decided to work to mobilize them to get the basic necessities taken care of as part of all tenants' rights. In spite of the chaos and hostility, the worker made a special effort to get to know the natural leaders of the building complex. After he got to know them fairly well individually, he called a leaders' meeting and supported them in efforts to get the necessary changes they needed from the landlord. The two ethnic groups slowly began to work together toward a common good and to demand their basic rights. Their cooperation to get building improvements led to better relationships and a more congenial physical and social environment. Discuss different ways by which togetherness can be created between two groups?

Help or empowerment takes place in different surroundings at different times. These surroundings include the physical, social, and psychological environments. Large public welfare settings, particularly those where welfare checks are distributed, are not generally conducive to any form of congenial work. The coldness of a place, with chairs placed in rows and welfare workers behind glass windows with microphones is not conducive to any form of therapeutic work.

The arrangement of furniture has an effect on clients. The furnishings in an office and the seating arrangements affect communication. Agencies in which help is offered in small, sparsely furnished, open cubicles where passers-by in the corridors are visible may make clients feel uneasy. Furnishings and the arrangement of furniture also have an effect on how the clients feel they are treated. When a middle-class client walks into a private practice office of a well-known social work professional group, the whole atmosphere talks to the clients. The thick carpets, the curtains, and well-cushioned couches in the waiting room that is generously stacked with current magazines and tasteful flower-arrangements put clients at ease. There may be soothing music, and the receptionist is helpful and kind. This sets the tone for the therapeutic environment.

The professional's office is also conducive to communication. There may be a couch and a few chairs in the room. The absence of a desk makes it more congenial for sessions. Often there are wall hangings and other decorative pieces that show the personal touch of that particular professional. Communication takes place more effectively in this setting where everything is geared toward the privacy and comfort of the clients.

For group meetings the rooms are tastefully decorated. Comfortable chairs are arranged to create a congenial distance between different group members. The doors are closed when the session begins. Everything about this physical setting is conducive to effective help.

There are some agencies where the practitioner may use a desk and chair that separate the client from the worker. Placing a desk between a worker and a client can create a block in communication as this arrangement emphasizes a difference in power and status. However, in some situations, a desk may provide clients with the structure they need to calm them down and create a feeling of security. One of the easiest ways of spacing furniture for comfortable communication is to place chairs at right angles around the corner of a desk (Scheflen & Ashcraft, 1976).

Through trial and error, social workers should work out a personal space with clients that is comfortable. What kind of space distancing would you like to have in your office? This should be carefully evaluated by all practitioners, since interacting with some clients in the office is a common phenomenon. Usually, a professionally objective level

should be maintained in the office setting. A number of clients may find it easier to discuss more intimate concerns in the impersonal atmosphere of an office where confidentiality is respected and where there are no interruptions.

Another environment that social workers enter are the homes of different clients. Home visits are helpful in understanding clients. People exist in a social world—they live in homes and go to their workplaces, churches, recreational settings, and neighborhood stores. An observant interview in the home may help the worker better understand the circumstances of the family or person than office visits alone. When we visit our friends in their homes we understand their circumstances and life situations better than when we meet them only in the workplace. Social workers do not always have to make home visits, but in order to understand a client better, there is no real substitute for seeing people in their own homes. Usually the nature of the problem and the needs of the client's condition necessitate a home visit. If you have a choice, discretion is important. For instance, it would make more sense to visit the home of an elderly client who has chronic health problems than a well-adjusted client who is looking for a job.

In the case of foster care, it is critical that the worker visit the home of the prospective foster parent to carefully evaluate the physical cleanliness, and socioeconomic and cultural data as well as the psychological attitudes of the foster parents and their other children toward foster children.

Beginning social workers sometimes make unplanned and hasty home visits at the start of a follow-up investigation, thus confusing effort with effectiveness. Instead of creating rapport and a professional relationship with clients, such visits may actually make the client wary and suspicious of the worker. You need a flexible outlook on how different types of space and environment should be used in helping people. A well-timed constructive home visit can strengthen the help offered.

The therapeutic environment is created through proper timing, understanding the needs and problems of clientele, and creating a spatial atmosphere that is conducive to growth and empowerment. All practitioners must work in different environments and play different roles, but the worker needs to be most aware of his or her role and that of the client. Chapter 6 discusses the role of the generalist practitioner.

CHAPTER SUMMARY

This chapter presented the person–environment fit and the influence of different environments on helping people. The agency also was discussed as providing an environment that can either help or hinder effective practice with clientele.

The total environment is classified into social, physical, personal, and psychological environments. The physical environment consists of natural and built environments. Natural environments include the physical landscape of a place. Built environments include houses, office buildings, and the area in which a person(s) resides. All these factors influence people and those who help them.

In the social environment there is an intertwining of physical and social environments with culture. Culture determines people's perceptions of relationships among individuals and the natural world. Cultural norms and values influence both social and physical settings. Social environments include natural groups like family and friends, as well as formal organizations such as health care, education, and recreation facilities, work places, religious organizations, and political and economic community structures at local, state, and national levels. Complex transactions take place simultaneously between social and physical settings.

The physical design of a hospital ward limits the type of behavior that is permitted by patients. Any physical setting be it a hospital, a psychiatric ward, a house, an apartment, a school classroom, a neighborhood, or a city is influenced by a larger and more encompassing physical environment which it also influences in turn.

The arrangement of physical space and social outcomes should help workers understand and use space as an active factor in assessing, making an intervention, and evaluating a client's behavior. The term *territoriality* refers to behavior to possess and occupy portions of space that they regard as their own. A person develops a need to create some personal space around himself or herself within a culturally determined radius.

Another aspect of the arrangement of space has to do with interpersonal relations and the "silent language" of positioning and distancing of one human from another. As ethologists have found, there is a flight or critical, distance and a personal distance. A practitioner needs to know how much distance to give diverse clients.

Clients also exhibit temporal or time-limited behaviors. Time is a cultural attitude. The concept of time has great implications for differences in people's behavior, with regard to conceptualizing punctuality, the sequencing and pacing of events, and the rhythms of family life. Such differences have to be carefully evaluated in working with different clientele.

Although there is an awareness of the social network we do *not* emphasize this while working with clients. It is an important aspect of relatedness and should be utilized appropriately. There are two types of loneliness: emotional isolation and social isolation. Emotional isolation happens when there is a loss of an intimate relationship; social isolation is the result of a lack of network or involvement with peers. It is necessary for the practitioner to be aware of the social networks for clients including mutual-aid systems and self-help groups.

Internal and external environments affect clients differently. Individuals contribute symbolic meanings from their own processes of cognition, emotion, and action. Other factors include cultural and family influences, as well as social and geographical factors.

Agencies are complex organizations, created for the purpose of solving certain complex problems and achieving particular goals in various areas of life. The environments of agencies vary. Some are exclusively social work agencies and others are host, or secondary, settings. In these settings social services are used to enhance the primary function of agency as when, social workers in hospital and school settings function as part of an interdisciplinary team. Social workers function within several dimensions including size, means of support and governance, nature of primary service offered, and range of employees. In all agencies, there is distribution of power and control based on centralization, formalization, and stratification.

Factors that contribute to a client's welfare include not only the physical setting in which sessions take place but also the practitioner's ability to make clients feel comfortable. Besides the client–worker interaction other factors that contribute to a conducive environment are the type of agency settings, public or private, the furnishings in an office, the arrangement of furniture, matters of access to buildings, and the utilization of home visits. Space and environment can be used constructively in work with people.

6

GENERALIST PRACTITIONER ROLES

Generalist practice is based on knowledge derived from varied sources and practitioners need to play a number of different roles in different size systems as they work with individuals, families, groups, organizations, and communities. First and foremost, in working with diverse types of clients it is important that a practitioner be professionally competent. What do we mean by "competency" in different situations and how do professionals know what is expected of them?

PRACTITIONERS BECOMING SUCCESSFUL AS HELPERS

One of the criteria for successful professional practice is familiarity with a number of problem-solving approaches and strategies. A practitioner who has a broad range of alternatives from which to select is better able to choose an approach on the basis of client need rather than personal limitations or preferences. Of course, when these selected strategies are applied, they are filtered through the practitioner's perceptions, thoughts, and feelings and become a distinctive style.

Generalists should be able to deal with clients in the *affective* domain that is related to feelings and emotions, the *cognitive* domain that relates to thinking and decision making, the *behavioral* domain that relates to action and deeds (Okun, 1987), and finally the *ecological* domain that deals with clients' transactions with the physical and social environments. One of the roles the practitioner takes on is that of teaching clients to function more effectively in all these domains. In addition to an understanding of client needs and problem-solving techniques, workers have to develop an understanding of themselves, and a conscious awareness that separate their own needs and problems from those of their clients.

This chapter examines the following areas: helping as a collaborative enterprise, knowledge of self, common concerns and special problems of beginning professionals, anxiety in the beginning sessions, challenges to the practitioner's competence, the myth of the perfect generalist, stress in counseling, burnout, and issues pertaining to generalist roles. The different roles of the professional in social work practice that are covered include clinician, enabler, teacher, mediator, advocate, broker, empowerer, researcher, analyst, and evaluator, among others.

HELPING AS A COLLABORATIVE ENTERPRISE

The practitioner needs to develop the ability to work in the affective, cognitive, behavioral, and ecological domains of clients. However, helping is a collaborative effort between the generalist and the client system. It is a process in which the practitioner and the clients work through issues and problems together. Clients often achieve their goals through facilitation by the worker; but while a worker can help a client achieve a goal, workers do not control outcomes. Clients also have a great responsibility in the production and quality of outcomes.

Discussing outcomes as a collaborative process, Eckert, Abeles, and Grahman (1988) draw a distinction between perceived gain and raw (real) gain. *Perceived gain* can be explained as something that makes the client feel good about the helper and the helping sessions. *Real gain* occurs when the client has made progress in managing problem situations and developing opportunities. Some clients may feel that they have achieved something because they focus only on the helping sessions; that is, they focus on the warmth, respect, and interest of the worker they experienced during the session and the good feelings that resulted. These feelings are not negative because they do stimulate the client in the right direction; however, they do not produce the important raw gain in managing problems and developing opportunities (Egan, 1998).

Sonya appeared very happy and satisfied when she returned to the clinic for her second session. Her problems as presented in the first session centered on an unwanted pregnancy three months after she got married. As she appeared to be content and happy, the worker asked her if she had reached any major decisions concerning the unborn child. Sonya responded with a smile, "I like coming to see you; you are so nice and make me feel nice." Although this was flattering, the worker realized that Sonya had not made any real (raw) gains essential to serious decisions regarding the pregnancy.

It is important and necessary that clients feel good about what they accomplish in everyday life rather than just feeling good about working with a generalist. Fischer and Corcoran (1994) indicate that the most important measure of success is the client's statement of satisfaction with the outcome of the helping process because behavior or attitude changes have taken place and when the client no longer views the presenting issue as a significant problem.

Thirty-year-old Megan was a member of a women's group that worked on self-assertiveness issues and helped women move away from total dependency on others. During the initial group sessions, Megan was uncomfortable and not at all sure if this was the right group for her. However, after a period of three months, she started to become more assertive, took a job, got her own apartment, and stopped blaming her ex-husband for all her problems. The group helped her to make both an attitudinal and behavioral change, and the outcomes proved that Megan had worked on her self-esteem through the group sessions.

An agency was created to help the elderly with services that would better their living conditions. However, the agency was located in a high-crime area. To the elderly, this area was not accessible because they feared for their safety and therefore would not risk going. The agency was suffering due to lack of clients and loss of revenue, and began to trim its professional staff. A survey of problems in the area and discussions with the elderly helped one of the staff's generalist practitioners present the problems to the agency director and board who, after a great deal of debate, decided to work at providing safety measures for the security of the elderly. It also started a discussion about the need to relocate the agency in another setting.

Any type of outcome of social services depends on many factors including the competence of the worker and the motivation of the clients, the quality of their interactions, and a host of environmental factors over which the worker and clients may not have control.

KNOWLEDGE OF SELF

One of the most important factors in working with people in diverse situations is being able to look at oneself honestly and make changes if necessary to be effective practitioners. Essential questions we need to ask ourselves include: Do I have the right to intervene in the lives of clients in difficult situations? Do I really have my own act together?

These are significant questions. As professionals, we acquire extensive knowledge of theoretical and practical ways of working with people. But to every situation we bring ourselves as persons. Practitioners may have a good education and learn good diagnostic and interviewing skills, yet be ineffective as helpers. It is difficult to discuss being a practitioner without considering the personal qualities that we bring to our work—our beliefs, personal attributes, life experiences, and lifestyles, as well as all of our biases and unresolved problems. We have an ethical and professional responsibility to be aware of the latter, and not let them get in the way of meeting clients' needs.

Corey, Corey, and Callahan (1993) and Cormier and Cormier (1998) have listed a number of personal traits and characteristics that professionals should develop. Read the list carefully and ask yourself how many of the characteristics you have as you work toward becoming an effective generalist. Remember also that the struggle to be effective does not end with the acquisition of a degree.

GOOD WILL   All effective practitioners have a sincere interest in their clients. This does not mean simply caring about a particular client, but rather challenging clients to look at themselves in ways that they may not prefer. It often requires that they look at aspects of themselves they would like to ignore.

Virginia complained that her husband had treated her badly like her previous two husbands and stated that she wanted a divorce. Though she was ill-treated as she said,

what aspects of her personality or her background attracted her to abusive men? Only by demonstrating positive regard for the client was the worker able to help remove Virginia's own mask so that she could face her issues more honestly.

In a community setting, the effective generalist must first recognize the natural leaders, network with them, and win their good will in order to work effectively for the community. Only then will the community be able to reach its goals.

RECOGNITION AND ACCEPTANCE OF ONE'S PERSONAL POWER   As social workers we have to be aware of our own power. Although there is mutuality and reciprocity in helping, in most situations generalists are more in control based on their practice knowledge and the fact that they are giving rather than receiving help, including empowering people. This power should not be used to exploit or dominate others or to feel superior; rather, this power should be used to contact our own strengths and vitality. Thus, when clients need emotional support and guidance the worker should be able to offer it, keeping in mind that the general aim of helping is to assist persons, groups, families, organizations, and communities to move toward their own growth with autonomy and competence.

Minnie walks up to you after she worked through her obesity problem and gushingly tells you that she adores you. She would go to school and get an education if this would make you happy. Of course, this adulation is flattering. However, you should not use the power that the client is giving you, but suggest and reaffirm that Minnie must do what she considers important and right for her.

A PERSONAL STYLE OF WORKING WITH CLIENTS   Developing and refining your own personal style of working with clients based on the knowledge, values, and skills of social work is important. Effective generalists develop ways of working with people that are expressive of their own personalities. You can learn and borrow from others, but your style of working is ultimately your own. It is best to work at perfecting your own style rather than imitating another generalist.

A WILLINGNESS TO BE VULNERABLE AND OPEN
Generalists should be willing to take risks, to be vulnerable, to trust their own intuition even when they are not sure of outcomes, to be emotionally available to others, and to be sensitive to the feelings and struggles of other people. Practitioners should also be able to disclose their own ideas, feelings, and thoughts about their clients when it is appropriate to do so.

Twenty-five-year-old Zoe came alone for the tenth session looking like she had seen a ghost. Even her lips were pale. She walked in like a zombie and blurted that her boyfriend would not come for the couple session. Earlier she had gone to his apartment to pick him up, but found him in bed with another woman. Upon saying this, she burst into uncontrollable sobs and her body literally shook. Zoe walked up to the woman practitioner and put out her arms asking for physical consolation. The practitioner held her hands until her sobbing ceased. She was moved by the ultimate deception that Zoe had just faced and expressed. In such situations, factors such as gender differences are important and appropriateness in dealing with the client is crucial.

SELF-WORTH, SELF-RESPECT, AND SELF-APPRECIATION
Practitioners should have a sense of self-worth that enables them to relate to others in terms of their strengths rather than their weaknesses.

Stacy was an effective generalist; however, her weakness was her quick temper. An awareness of her short temper allowed her to see this problem as her personal issue and avoid losing her temper with clients. Stacy consistently worked on her temper. She was a warm, caring, and genuine person, and used these positive aspects of her personality to help clients with their problems.

A WILLINGNESS TO RISK MAKING MISTAKES AND
ADMIT THEM   Practitioners, like others, learn by mistakes and by trial and error. In becoming effective practitioners we have to risk failing. When this happens, and it sometimes will, it is best to learn from mistakes and move on.

Muriel, a beginning professional, asked her new client to stop crying and gave her a tissue. Muriel promised her client that everything would be all right, saying that all situations are reversible without even knowing the reason for the tears. When the client related in between her sobs that her father had died in a plane crash, the worker felt horrible and spent the rest of the session apologizing for not being sensitive. After the client left, Muriel continued to self-recriminate by telling her coworkers and later her supervisor about her own foolishness. It is best to remember that we make mistakes and set them right if possible, but dwelling excessively on the mistakes as Muriel did is not particularly healthy.

A GROWTH ORIENTATION   Growth is a continuous process. Because we have acquired a degree or worked with different clients for a certain number of years does not mean that we have become experts. Professionalism requires a constant search for better motivation and an ongoing desire to work at self-awareness and consciousness of personal strengths, fears, and vulnerabilities that may later foster self-understanding in clients as well. Often practitioners encourage clients to become more autonomous; in a similar manner, workers should live by their own standards of professionalism and empowerment and not be overcome by the expectations of others.

COMPETENCE   The way generalists feel about themselves can significantly influence the way they behave. If we as generalists do not feel confident about our ability to help a group of clients, we may inadvertently structure the helping process to meet our own self-image problems or confirm our negative self-pictures. It is difficult to be an effective helper if you have a fragile ego.

A SENSE OF HUMOR   Last but not least, workers should be able to laugh at themselves and with clients. Humor at the appropriate time in work with clients can ease tension. Humor is one way for practitioners to maintain a sense of perspective in their work.

Martin had seen six clients in one day and each one of them seemed to have a serious issue and were mad at him. At the end of the day, Martin was exhausted from the heavy sessions he had experienced. As he was leaving his office, he looked out of the window and saw that the weather did not offer much to improve his mood either. However, when he met his supervisor, he told her, "I've had a long day . . . nothing went right." Then he added humorously, "But look outside, the sun will begin to shine, I will hear the birds sing, and I am going to have a beautiful day . . . or what is left of it."

A practitioner needs time for self-reflection as well. As a beginning professional, what do you consider your strengths? Why do you consider them to be assets? What are the weaknesses that might stand in the way of you becoming an effective social worker? What qualities do you see in other professionals that impress you? What qualities turn you off?

Meier (1989) suggests that practitioners need to learn to ask themselves the following questions and answer them honestly:

How did you decide to become a social work generalist?

Why do you wish to be a practitioner?

What types of feelings make you comfortable?

What types of feelings cause you discomfort?

Do you set your expectations for your clients?

If clients have intense feelings for you, positive or negative, how will you deal with those clients?

If you begin to have intense feelings for clients, how will you handle these feelings?

To what extent can you be flexible and caring?

All beginning practitioners need to grapple with these issues, so that they will not get in the way of their ability to work with and deliver services for clients.

Besides personal characteristics, it is necessary for workers to have a good understanding of their own lifestyle, philosophy of life, moral code, value system, individual needs, and how these affect their own day-to-day functioning and social relationships. Self-knowledge does not happen in a day. It is an ongoing introspective process in which the worker learns to understand how he or she operates as a person. This process requires understanding how one meets personal needs, deals with restrictions and freedom, and also accepts change in oneself and the environment. The helping person must observe his or her own behavior, spend time on introspection, and seek out others' constructive observations about himself or herself. The worker also takes the risk of self-dissatisfaction because of unresolved issues or negative past experiences or anger or pain about one's role and place in society. This journey of understanding oneself is a major tool for working skillfully and competently with clients and helping them reach their maximum potential.

One exercise that may be used with new students involves personal reflection. Students should take time to think about their feelings and life situations. This exercise is done in a quiet, dimly lit room without any music or noise and with no one else present. After half an hour of reflection, the student writes about his or her weaknesses and strengths. This exercise is carried out every week for a semester. At the end of the semester, students identify their weaknesses and strengths and how they have followed these qualities through the semester. The students are assisted in highlighting their strengths and using them constructively and consciously downplaying their weaknesses in work with clients, particularly if they interfere with effective practice.

Grace, a beginning professional, is impatient and short-tempered. However, when sitting with a client who is slow in communicating Grace learns through trail and error to tone down her style of communication and move at the client's pace. It is not easy to do, but awareness of her professional role and a willingness to work on it helps Grace deal with her impatience.

Other Issues for the Professional

We need to be aware of our own feelings about different issues and problems. If a worker becomes uncomfortable with a specific client or with a particular subject area, it is important to recognize the discomfort and proceed to offer help conscientiously or refer the client to another worker. For instance, a worker who has strong religious views and cannot deal objectively with the issue of abortion with a client may not be able to offer meaningful help. When making referrals of clients to other practitioners because the worker cannot be objective and is uncomfortable, it is best that the worker informs the client of his or her convictions by using "I" messages: "I do not know how to deal with abortion, because my religious upbringing gets in the way, and I don't know enough about it to discuss it with you."

Because of their own insecurities, some practitioners utilize avoidance strategies with clients by dealing with them randomly instead of focusing on the client's issues. As Okun (1976) and Doyle (1998) pointed out, there are people in the helping professions who overfocus completely on clients and avoid their own feelings and problems. In such cases the worker is not helpful to clients and has to make a special effort to work through those issues by constant self-assessment.

Susi tuned out her client Terri whenever Terri talked about her marital problems. Susi had her share of marital problems at home and had not dealt with them adequately. As she followed her own pattern of avoidance she became aware that she was no longer a facilitator. She realized that if she wanted to help Terri, she would have to take a risk and discuss Terri's marital issues with her but separate them from her own problems.

Honesty in relationships with different clients is an important aspect of role performance. Does the worker have a need to always be perfect and right? Does the worker's fear of being disliked influence him or her to be agreeable to clients because confrontation may make the clients dislike the worker? If workers suffer from a strong need to be liked all the time, they will use reassuring, supportive responses excessively, thereby diminishing the client's ability to grow toward responsibility and independence.

At the other extreme are workers who themselves constantly face difficult situations and are always looking for problematic and negative situations. Does this influence the worker negatively? Can the worker learn to identify and use positive feelings and thoughts to help clients focus on their competencies. The worker should have the ability to balance the negatives and the positives while dealing with clients.

A group of people in a rural community had successfully worked together with a practitioner to bring medical services into the community. A few weeks later the practitioner and the community people met to discuss some issues only to have a community member take over and point out all the negatives they still faced, overlooking the new medical services they had just obtained. As dissatisfaction and anger began to rise, the practitioner intervened and commented on how hard they worked to get the medical services in place. She reminded the community that they should rejoice over their success as a group and feel empowered in their own togetherness as an asset for dealing with other issues. The practitioner's comments calmed the group and they began to relax and talk about their achievements and hopes for their community.

At times, a worker may have negative feelings about a difficult client. Because practitioners are people, they may have problems with a particular client, which in turn might interfere with the work with the client. This can be remedied by checking out the negative feelings about a client. For example, every time a client complains about her mother, the practitioner gets angry. As these feelings persist, the practitioner handles the situation by confronting the client using "I" statements such as, "I find myself feeling angry whenever you talk in a derogatory manner about your mother. When you say 'she is dependent on me like a baby' but at the same time she has given you as you say, 'all her money and assets' for good home care. I realize she is old, but she still babysits for you and does all your grocery shopping, besides getting your children ready to go to school. I am having problems dealing with it. I do not wish to impose my values on you but could we talk more about this?" In another situation, a worker might say, "I am having a hard time listening to you talk about wanting to repair the TV when Nat has needed a warm new winter jacket for the past few months. I realize that, for me, a child's health is more important than TV. I do not wish to impose my values on you, but can we talk about this some more?"

It is best for social workers to remember that there are situations in which it will be difficult to be genuine and show unconditional caring and a nonjudgmental attitude. All workers cannot work well with all types of clients. In some situations you may not be able to feel positive regard for a client. At this point you have certain options: (1) locate another practitioner in your agency or through referral; (2) seek consultation with a colleague or supervisor in order to work better with the client; and (3) limit the relationship to the accomplishment of specific, immediate, and concrete goals. The latter would include processing papers and providing factual information to the client.

Another means by which the worker can understand and improve is by maintaining a log for recording feelings and thoughts after working with a client. Recording these feelings and thoughts about work with the clients systematically can help a generalist begin an organized study of self.

The practitioner embodies the qualities of both responsibility and authority. The worker takes responsibility for creating a constructive atmosphere that helps clients; providing alternative points of view with reference to the clients' issues and problems, based on the worker's experiences and knowledge; and providing a structure for the clients, which includes a focus on skillful use of the problem-solving process. The worker is responsible for providing information about resources and, if need be, offering assistance in obtaining those resources. Both the worker and the client are responsible for the outcome of the work.

Irrespective of what the worker says or does, the client views the generalist as a person with a certain degree of professional authority. This authority is confirmed based on the training and field experiences that social work professionals undertake. How should workers utilize their professional authority without encroaching on the client's rights? An example would be by not imposing middle-class standards on the client whose lifestyle and ways of child rearing, though different from a middle-class perspective, are still caring and loving.

Beginning practitioners need to ask themselves the following questions:

> How can I know when I'm working for the welfare of the clients, or when I am working for my own benefit?
>
> How do I view myself?
>
> Do I appreciate myself or do I depend upon others to validate my worth and value?
>
> How can I deal with my sense of insecurity and inadequacy if I am not making progress with a client? (Corey et al., 1993)

Self-questioning is the beginning professionalism.

Social workers need to recognize and accept the responsibility for those areas of a situation for which they are responsible. However, they should not assume the responsibilities of the clients.

Carel had problems with self-assertion in her marriage. Whenever Carel and her husband had a disagreement she would tell him that they should discuss the issue with their social worker, Emily. She viewed the social worker as her ally and felt strengthened with Emily by her side. However, when Emily realized that she was just Carel's crutch, and Carel was not becoming self-assertive, Emily established a rule with the couple that they must work out their minor issues at home and not look to her as part of their everyday decision-making process. Because Carel was nervous, the process was started in small steps with small tasks and assignments that the couple had to sort out and carry out by themselves. Emily was supportive of the clients, and saw herself as being responsible in helping the couple work out their issues, but would not allow Carel to become overly dependent upon her.

COMMON CONCERNS AND SPECIAL PROBLEMS OF THE BEGINNING PRACTITIONER

All beginning practitioners have fears, resistance, self-doubts, concerns, and questions. You soon find out that when you face clients you have to draw on yourself. This can be a frightening experience. In fact, not only beginners but also experienced practitioners find themselves struggling from time to time with doubts and anxieties about their own performance.

What are some of the concerns of the beginning generalist? Reflect on and write down your concerns about being a professional. Ask yourself what assumptions underlie your concerns and if these assumptions are valid.

Here are some of the typical concerns presented by a group of practitioners including Hutchins and Vaught (1997), Doyle (1998), Cormier and Cormier (1998), and Corey et al. (1993):

I am afraid of making mistakes.

I have real doubts about my ability to help diverse clients.

I am afraid to deal with feelings of anger.

I am too much of a perfectionist and I do not wish to fail in any client situation.

I am concerned that the client will find out that I am a beginner and wonder if I am competent.

I am threatened by demanding clients.

What are your concerns and how do you deal with them? Have you set such high expectations for yourself that you cannot reach them? Try asking yourself these questions:

Why should I be all-knowing? Can anyone be all-knowing?

Is making mistakes really fatal? Have you ever made any mistakes in life?

Do I really have to provide answers for all my clients' problems? Has anyone ever done this?

Don't people grow and change through mistakes?

Anxiety

All beginning practitioners suffer to some degree from anxiety. Raising questions about yourself is part of a process of self-inquiry. It is also impor-tant to discuss worries, fears, and questions and to learn to deal with such feelings. Anxiety is common, particularly when there is a degree of uncertainty concerning your work with the clients. Some of the anxiety is due to the fact that the beginning professional may expect instant positive results for clients and this may not happen. Overly concerned workers begin their work by trying to solve every problem that clients present. The fact is that there is no immediate solution to problems and clients also do not usually make immediate gains. Workers need to understand that they may not see the impact of their work until after the termination of the professional relationship.

Beginning practitioners face different kinds of clients with different types of problems for the first time. Practitioners may view certain clients as difficult, particularly if the worker has a need to "win" and therefore views the client as difficult and negative. In a one-on-one session, silent clients who do not participate in a session may create feelings of discomfort in the practitioner. The beginning practitioner who is uncomfortable may overcome anxiety by breaking the silence with unnecessary chatter. The practitioner may assume that silence means that the sessions are not fruitful though, in actuality, silences occur for a variety of reasons. The generalist should not view silence as nonproductive, because it may not be. In some instances, the client is silent waiting for the practitioner to give directions, because the client may be used to the practitioner asking too many questions or making suggestions. At times, the client may be experiencing internally some feelings that have been aroused during the session. In other instances, the client may feel stuck and not know how to move on. Lastly, both the client and the practitioner may be resisting a deeper level of communication.

Amelia and Juergen, a married couple, were referred to a practitioner because, though they had been on civil terms with each other, their relationship had lost its joy and spontaneity. Amelia insisted that their problems stemmed from constant in-law visits and feuds with each other about the interfering ways of Juergen's mother. Juergen remained quiet.

In the second session, after the initial presentation of the issue, both Amelia and Juergen fell into silence. The worker waited for a few minutes and asked if they wished to share more information. Amelia shrugged her shoulders, and Juergen did not respond. The worker in turn shrugged his shoulders and started to browse through a book he pulled off his bookshelf. Amelia looked at her husband, and he looked back at her. After a few seconds, both of them broke out into spontaneous laughter, and the worker, shutting his book, joined them in their pleasant outburst. Silence led the couple to look at the comical side of their own feuding, and the worker used this laughter as the beginning of an alliance to work on their hesitation to discuss the problem.

A practitioner has to ask himself or herself, "How do I feel about silences, particularly long ones? Would I be able to communicate to another person through silences as well as through words? What should I do when a client is very quiet and what does this do to me?" (Corey et al., 1988) Another kind of client with whom it is difficult to deal is the overdemanding client. This client is especially troublesome to beginning practitioners who feel that they have to meet all clients' needs. A common problem among practitioners is the concern that they should be more giving. Because some clients will take and expect more and more, less skilled professionals may not be sufficiently assertive to set limits and may allow themselves to be controlled by clients.

Mary Ellen had been very dependent on Velma, her social worker. Mary Ellen was also needy and persisted in demanding that she be able to call Velma at home whenever she had an issue. This made Velma uncomfortable and she wondered what had happened in the sessions to make Mary Ellen feel this way.

A practitioner working with overly demanding clients needs to question if he or she has a desire to be needed. If a practitioner has to be available to a client at all times, there needs to be an assessment of what benefits have been obtained. A practitioner who likes needy clients should ask why this particular group of people is interesting and work through his or her own issues.

The most challenging type of clients are the unmotivated clients. They come because they are mandated and expected to do so, or to please a family member. They do not invest themselves productively and have very little motivation to change. These clients may be good at playing games and practitioners should be wary.

Forty-year-old Donna came for sessions because she wanted to please her husband who thought that his "dumb" wife needed help. She played the role well. Donna came with her three teenage children and discussed her issues with them and her husband. But she ended up by repeating the problems again and again in every session without listening to anything that was being communicated to her. The worker was getting tired because Donna would not respond to questions about tasks that had been discussed in an earlier session. At times, Donna just sat, smiled, chewed gum, and asked her children to talk to the practitioner. Though she seemed to have a number of issues with her husband, she constantly smiled and tuned the worker out. How would you handle this client? If Donna does not respond to the sessions, why are you seeing her? What, if anything, have her teenage children accomplished in the sessions?

Most of the issues discussed so far could happen to a worker when working with any type of client—a single person, a family, a group, an organization, or a community. However, working with any type of group can be particularly frightening to a beginning practitioner, because of the need to deal with a number of people at the same time. In these different size client systems, a number of individuals share the same therapeutic endeavor. The practitioner is in a position of prominence, but is only one part of the helping process. In working with groups, there are two issues with which the social worker has to deal: (1) a group presents a problem that is unique to itself, and (2) that group members also come together to meet personal needs. If the worker's ego and leadership skills are weak and the group desires excessive attention and recognition, the worker may experience frustration. When the generalist starts to compete with a client, the situation can become nontherapeutic, destructive, and unproductive (Reid, 1997).

Melissa, a social work intern, was leading a group with her supervisor. The supervisor was well respected and liked by the group members who were also aware that Melissa was undergoing her internship in this setting. One day the supervisor did not attend the meeting and Melissa had to lead the group. She found herself becoming overwhelmed when Audrey took over. When Audrey spoke everyone listened to her, though she was not the group leader. This was humiliating to Melissa because she was aware that Audrey was "only" a cleaning woman. Melissa was also embarrassed because some of the interpretations and advice given to the group members by Audrey were very "sensible" and were accepted by the group members without any conflict. In short, Melissa was threatened by Audrey and wanted to hide behind her supervisor, so that she would not feel less important in the group.

Similar problems can arise when working with families.

Forty-year-old Prince was a new social worker who was working with his first client family. The family consisted of a forty-year-old father, Dancy, a Navy man, and his wife, also forty, and three children. Although he was fairly uncomfortable with the family's situation, Prince was eager to please. However, instead of observing the interactions in the family or making the family members comfortable, Prince got caught up in his need to be in charge of the session. When Dancy ventured to present some of the family issues, authoritatively, Prince felt threatened that Dancy knew so much. Because he felt threatened, Prince complained to his supervisor that all the family members were easy to handle but that he did not like Dancy. Although he gave professional explanations beneath his professional veneer he was a beginning practitioner threatened by the fact that Dancy seemed to have his act together. This led to a negative, competitive, and destructive atmosphere in the sessions that would prevent any fruitful alliances between the family members and the practitioner.

Eda, who had just graduated, obtained her first job as a community worker in a small rural town. The suicide of a high school student shocked the close-knit town. It is Eda's role to help people grieve and console people, but she is overwhelmed by the suicide and the demands made on her by the community. Instead of processing the incident and the pain of the community people she fo-

cuses on a prominent member of the community who is loud and angry. Without looking at his pain she takes him on as a competitor to gain the support of the community and fails miserably.

Some of the initial anxiety of a beginning professional occurs because the practitioner is getting to know a person, family, a group, a community, or an organization. If you find yourself in such a situation, you might ask yourself some of the following questions suggested by Corey (1990), Homan (1999), and Reid (1998):

Do I have enough knowledge to work with a family or a group, a community or an organization?

What does this particular system expect of me?

How can I start my work with these participants? Is there a "proper" way?

Should I ask all the questions and be an active leader, or should I let the clients talk first? Should I carry an agenda with me and stick with it, or should I let the group members talk themselves?

What happens if I don't have a plan?

If I lose control of the group, what do I do? Would they respect me if this happened?

Are there any particular techniques I could use while working with groups?

Does intuition matter or is it meaningless?

What if I fail and make blunders?

If I am not effective will the clients participate actively in working on their issues?

Such feelings are normal for beginning generalists and it is best that they are explored while in supervision. Usually, a moderate degree of anxiety can be beneficial because it can lead to honest self-appraisal. But too much anxiety can be counterproductive and might force a person to freeze into inactivity or attempt to dominate the helping process (Corey, 1990).

Beginning Sessions—Initial Anxiety

When working with family members or any other type of group, the beginning professional may fear looking incompetent or foolish. Quite often, the practitioner feels under close scrutiny and obliged to do the correct thing at all times, which is impossible. Practitioners may also feel that it is their fault if some of the group members do not wish to return for the sessions. A worker may be uncomfortable when there is silence in a group and wonder if he or she should continue to talk to fill the void. Also, the practitioner may not feel sufficiently competent and imagines that he or she has "fooled the clients, one more time."

Anxiety level also has to do with a worker's self-esteem. Kottler (1986) notes that many group workers (and sometimes, family, community, and organizational workers) feel vulnerable to annihilation through assaults on their self-esteem. All workers are usually invested in the outcomes of the helping process but the beginning outcomes in most situations reflect only a preliminary success, if any. A worker who is looking for positive outcomes right from the start of the first session may be disappointed. Helping is a process that goes up and down rather than moving in a straight line continuously upward. It is important that workers recognize the nature of the helping process.

When a family member does not improve or when a group, community, or family member is having difficulty, the beginning practitioner may take it personally. When clients become loud or aggressive, the novice generalist may be upset but also worried about how other colleagues will view the situation. Also, when family, group, community, or organizational members begin to reveal their painful feelings about their situation, the beginning generalist may fear that the clients could get out of control and chaos could result (Reid, 1998). The worker may anticipate all kinds of problems, including aggressive conflicts between members in a group, organization, or community, that may be difficult to manage. At times, the generalist may fear that clients will collaborate, establish shared defenses, and scapegoat the worker.

Caroline started a new group for women who needed to be trained in assertiveness. Hilda, a member of the group, made Caroline uncomfortable. Hilda was aggressive and domineering and many times attempted to control the group as well as Caroline. A power struggle ensued. Caroline held her ground and one day, feeling insecure, humiliated Hilda in front of the rest of the group. By the following week, the group dynamics had changed completely. All the group members joined Hilda and fought Caroline. A tense and humble Caroline left the session gratefully when it ended but her worst fears were realized. At the next session Caroline was prepared to take on the group members. When Hilda spoke, Caroline responded to her using a number of technical terms that Hilda did not understand. Caroline was attempting to put an end to the power struggle by appearing to be more knowledgeable. However, she did not succeed in creating a congenial atmosphere. Caroline dealt with her own anxiety instead of the clients' needs by using technical language in order to appear intellectually superior, a situation that cannot accomplish much in the way of help (Reid, 1991).

THE HURT HEALER

At times, a number of irrational dynamics come into play in sessions when clients start to share their problems with the worker. When clients uncover the root of their problems and all types of issues appear, the worker helps them to deal with the problems. Offering help is definitely not one-dimensional. The process is one of give and take, regardless of the levels of functioning.

When a worker and a group, a family, a community, or an organization work together to form an alliance, each person brings to the situation his or her total life experience. Each person carries psychological baggage, which includes values, prejudices, weaknesses, pain, secrets, and blind spots, as well as strengths. Each person in the therapeutic relationship also has a history of relating to others.

Like clients, practitioners have weaknesses and a need for recognition, prestige, and security. Practitioners also have a need to be liked. At times, a practitioner gets into a helping situation because of a desire to be needed and wanted. Sometimes professionals are lured by the need to be in a position of authority, by the dependence of others, and by the image of benevolence. Individuals who have suffered in their own personal lives may feel that by helping others, they are helping themselves.

When Jenny was physically abused by her father, she did not turn to anyone for help because her mother was very passive and allowed the abuse to happen. Now, as an adult and a beginning social worker, Jenny has opted to work with physically abused persons. Jenny helps group members move toward better functioning through constructive confrontation with those who have abused them. In group sessions, whenever an abused person is able to confront the abuser and work out some of the issues, Jenny feels extraordinarily elated. She views it as personal victory because of her life experiences. These situations also provide symbolic gratification of Jenny's needs.

Over a period of time, workers begin to develop a balance between giving care to others and, in indirect ways, receiving care (Maeder, 1989). The need to self-care and care for others often becomes part of the worker's professional attitude. Years ago, Towle (1954) asked to what degree have social workers been misunderstood as children and if, in their persistent need to be understood, they move toward understanding others. However, it is still not known to what degree those social workers who have been hurt as children are more sensitive to the suffering of others. This does not mean that social workers who have unfulfilled needs should not be in the profession. In every profession there are people who are trying to understand and "find" themselves.

Workers have the potential to grow as they become aware of clients' deeper needs. But this growth is futile if workers use clients in ways that are not helpful to clients' own growth (Reid, 1998). For instance, practitioners who work with couples with serious marital conflicts and extramarital relationships become aware of the intense pain that these conflicts cause not only the couple but also their children. In many ways this recog-

nition helps workers in their own growth as a person and as a professional. But growth can be curbed when a person who is working with a couple sets one against the other (which is poor practice) or becomes personally involved in a sexual relationship with one of the partners to fulfill the practitioner's own personal desires. This is true of community work as well.

When Jeff, a natural leader, helps Lisa to get to the community meeting and gives hints about how to handle the community members who are fighting crime in the area, Lisa appreciates and enjoys Jeff's support and constructive counseling. Jeff does not wear a ring on his finger and Lisa is attracted to him. She has an affair with him. However, she soon finds out that Jeff is married. Lisa has put herself in a no-win situation and lost sight of her goals as a community generalist.

Jaffe (1986) presented another point of view which specifies that all professionals should see themselves as people who simply cannot give and remain detached from their feelings. Rather, they should look inward at their own personal roles and needs. There are professional myths which suggest that practitioners, who can also narrowly be called healers, should detach themselves from their own responses to pain. It would be more helpful for workers to be aware of the impact of pain on their own lives as they work with people. Those who work with people's intimate personal issues and problems must deal with painful life experiences and human anguish.

Clients do not ask for help because they are happy. Clients work with a generalist because they wish to set things right. Similarly, professionals may choose the helping professions to work with people's problems and issues. Working with clients who present pain or unresolved issues in many forms requires that practitioners need to pay attention to our own experience of pain and utilize it for personal growth. As they do this, major personal changes will take place that help practitioners approach their work differently (Corey et al., 1993; Cournoyer, 1996; Esten & Willmont, 1993).

CHALLENGES TO THE GENERALIST PRACTITIONER'S COMPETENCE

Challenges to a worker's competence is common in individual, group, family, community, or organizational work. These challenges may be indirect or direct, but workers must be aware that challenges can happen. The following section focuses on challenges practitioners encounter with different types of clients.

Challenges to the generalist's competence usually fall into two categories: (1) challenges about personal qualifications, and (2) challenges to professional credentials. Challenges to personal qualifications vary. When an obviously successful middle-aged businessman and father, looks at the young female generalist working with his family, comments on the generalist's youthful appearance, and questions if she knows how to help them, this challenge can put the generalist on the defensive even before the helping process begins. Even if the father feels strongly about his inability to relate to his teenage son and envies the worker's ability to do so, the worker still feels that her competence is being challenged. Beginning practitioners tend to get caught in the problems of families, groups, communities, or organizations more often than do experienced generalists. Instead of responding defensively, the beginning practitioner should learn early in the career that questions about youthfulness may be relevant and that answering them honestly without defensiveness, and then moving on, is the best defense and a constructive move toward professional practice.

Usually there are high expectations of a generalist. Most clients come with the assumption that good practitioners "have it together" (Anderson & Stewart, 1983). Practitioners, particularly beginners, may believe that they will have all the answers to questions and can resolve all problems quickly. When generalists have such expectations, they are more likely to become defensive when faced with the natural challenges of a client group. One of the reasons that clients may challenge a practitioner is to avoid focusing on their own behaviors.

A couple came for a session in a hospital setting because the wife had attempted suicide, after which couple and family help was recommended. The husband came to the hospital for his first session unwillingly. He was a middle-aged physician, authoritarian and moralistic. As he was successful as a doctor, he did not see the need to consult a professional. One of the first things he asked the worker, who happened to be a woman, was to identify her qualifications, her work experience as a generalist, and the rest of her credentials. When he found out that she was a social worker, the physician stated that he did not need to see her because the family did not have any money problems. When she explained that she was part of a multidisciplinary team that worked with families of individuals who have attempted suicide, he reluctantly agreed to attend sessions.

However, after the second session, he seemed unwilling to participate. By this time he was aware that the worker was a single woman. A couple of days later he attempted to cancel his appointment by informing the worker in a cold and hostile manner that he and his wife had sexual problems. He added that the worker could not help because she was a single woman and could not possibly know anything real about marital sex. This manipulation of the worker got him off the hook and placed the worker in a no-win situation. If she said that she did not know about sex, he could assert that she could not help him, but as a single woman if she said she did know about sex, he would disqualify her on the grounds of being immoral (Anderson & Stewart, 1983).

An inexperienced or insecure generalist can become defensive and lose control of a case when a client is hostile. The challenge is to not overrespond to a client's hostility and resistance, which may be due to pain and uncertainty in the face of a crisis. A client's avoidance of issues can turn the focus on the practitioner in order to let the individual or family off the hook.

Practitioners may be challenged if they become emotionally or irrationally involved by taking sides with different family, group, organization, or community members because of their own personal or professional issues. In such cases, family or group members may feel that the worker is out of line and resist any form of help. In work with clients, however, resistance should be viewed as a valuable cue in terms of timing, accuracy, and appropriateness of intervention.

Marianne, a new generalist, felt sorry for the young adolescent client, Rosy. At sixteen, Rosy seemed as lost and unhappy as the practitioner had been at her age. Moreover, Rosy's parents appeared to be very hard on her in terms of rules and regulations. Marianne identified with Rosy and became very supportive of her. This angered the parents when they saw Marianne becoming too involved with and too supportive of their daughter. They feared the involvement would lead to more problems in the family situation.

Another personal challenge that practitioners face involves questions of ethnicity, class, race, and marital status, any or all of which may be important to the clients. Questions such as, "What do you know about our ethnic group? You are not a member of it and therefore cannot experience what is happening in our situation" or "How do you know when you do not have children?" can put a generalist on the defensive. A challenge to professional and personal credentials could also put the generalist on the defensive. It is best to be aware that some clients are not ready to receive help and it is essential to go through the intricacies of developing trust so that clients feel comfortable in confiding to the generalist.

THE MYTH OF THE PERFECT GENERALIST

All practitioners have lived in families of their own and have had problems of one sort or another. All practitioners have had issues at one time or another with their spouse, parents, or children, some of which may be unresolved and which may predispose them to see helping situations in a distorted way. So, instead of feeling a need to be perfect, it is best to work toward one's own self-awareness and not dwell on inadequacies, or attempt to hide one's own family problems. The task

for beginning generalists is to know and accept their own vulnerabilities. This is the only way we can highlight our assets and minimize our weaknesses (Anderson & Stewart, 1983; Poulin & Walter, 1993). No single practitioner has all the answers to a question. This should be accepted by all generalists without question.

STRESS IN THE HELPING PROCESS

"Stress is not a direct reflection of objective events; it stems in part from the frame of mind of the person experiencing the events. The sense of threat that triggers the stress experience is partly attributable to personal vulnerabilities which vary from one person to another" (Carver, 1996, p. xi).

Lazarus and Folkman (1984) distinguish two levels of stress evaluation or appraisal: primary and secondary appraisals (see Figure 6.1). Primary appraisal assesses the personal meaning of an event and asserts whether the stressor has a positive, negative, or neutral meaning for the person. Positive emotions are connected with challenges that a person likes; negative stressors are distinguished by feelings of anxiety if the stressor is a threat, and feelings of anger and grief if the stressor involves personal damage or loss. Generally, negative stressors involve threats to the physical and psychological self. Neutral stress, as the name implies, happens to another unrelated person or is an unrelated event that affects humankind like a hurricane or a tornado destroying other people's

Primary Stress Appraisal	Personal meaning of an event—positive/negative
Neutral Stress	Unrelated event/person—for example, a hurricane destroying other people's properties
Secondary Stress Appraisal	Exploration of coping capabilities. "What can I do?"

Figure 6.1 **Different Types of Stress Appraisal**

properties. Crime against the elderly could also fall in this category.

Secondary appraisals are affective changes that take place in an individual when the person responds to a stressor with questions such as "What can I do about it?" These processes refer to the thoughts or ideas that a person experiences in exploring the capacity to reduce the threat, damage, or loss caused by an event. These are called coping capacities and be explained as any effort used to manage external or internal demands that are viewed as negative or challenging. External demands refer to the event itself and internal demands refer to emotional reactions to an event (Maes, Leventhal, & Ridder, 1996). Unless they are in a crisis most clients seek help when they make their secondary appraisal.

Social work practice with different clients is a hazardous journey, and often beginners are not really aware of the whole reality. Usually, because novices say they like people and like working with people, they assume they will like the profession. Being a professional requires more than this. Although the worker usually feels a sense of self-satisfaction while working with clients, often we are not told that our profession demands a commitment to self-exploration. This search is full of difficulties. While working with clients, we use our own life experiences and personal reactions as a way to understand clients and work with them. But we find out that as we become partners in someone else's life journey, we are sometimes affected by the client's issues. A client may also open up our own deepest issues. Often, unfinished business comes to the forefront, and old wounds, if not worked through, are opened again.

Lydia's teenage son committed suicide while she was a homemaker. Lydia felt that she had failed as a mother and her pain was intense. Her husband, in pain too, silently blamed her. Lydia wanted to help people. Thus, she found herself in the social work profession. She pushed away her own pain and devoted her life to helping young people. But when one of the young boys she was working with committed suicide, it hit her violently. When his parents came to see her for help, her old wounds opened up and she was deeply distressed.

In work with clients, conflicts that seemed to have disappeared, may reappear. Many beginning and, at times, experienced generalists are not prepared for this (Corey et al., 1998; Koeske and Kelly, 1995).

Deutsch (1984) and Farber (1983) identified some of the factors that cause social workers a great deal of stress and may lead to a premature termination of the work. These include suicide statements, anger towards the generalist, severely depressed clients, apathy or lack of motivation, aggression and hostility, chaos and disorder in an individual, family, group, organization, or a community. Stress also arises when generalists set unrealistic goals for themselves. Such as:

I should always work at a peak level of enthusiasm and competence.

I should be able to cope with any client emergency.

I should be able to help all clients.

Stress occurs when a particular client does not make progress and the worker views it as his or her fault. Stress also occurs when practitioners view their job as their whole life and begin to believe that they have the power to control their clients' life process. In sum, if workers assume complete responsibility for the success or failure of the helping process, they burden themselves needlessly and create insurmountable stress.

Burnout among Practitioners

Even as a beginning professional you need to understand burnout, so that you know when and how to use preventive measures. Burnout is a state of mental, physical, and emotional exhaustion due to prolonged emotional pressures. Practitioners who are burned out reveal physical depletion and feelings of hopelessness and helplessness (Arches, 1991). According to Shulman (1991), the term *burnout* is used to describe a syndrome exhibited by workers dealing with intense stress over a period of time, during which they do not do receive any support. The severe and apparently insolvable nature of clients' problems may affect the worker's motivation and attitudes. Thus, workers may become as depressed and overwhelmed as their clients. These emotions may impact the worker's practice skills and working relationships, and eventually the outcomes of practice.

People coping with burnout also have negative attitudes toward themselves, their work, and their life. This is especially true for social workers who are often involved in emotionally taxing work. They are typically insensitive to other people's problems.

Lloyd (1995) called practitioners who were emotionally exhausted by their work and retreated into detachment "case hardened" (p. 1277). Hardening up is one aspect of burnout. For example, social workers in HIV settings can become emotionally exhausted and develop feelings of depersonalization and decreased personal accomplishment.

Farber and Heifetz (1982) identified some of the causes of burnout in professionals. They found that 54.7 percent of the practitioners interviewed saw burnout as a result of the nonreciprocated attentiveness, giving, and responsibility demanded by the helping process. Another cause was overwork (22 percent). A large number of practitioners (73.7 percent) also indicated that lack of success was the single most stressful aspect in their work (also reported by Shulman, 1999). When people constantly give and do not receive positive feedback, they can burn out. Extreme responsibility to clients can also lead to burnout, as can fragmentation of one's efforts.

Practitioners who do too much, spread themselves too thin, and have too little time for themselves do not do justice to any of the activities that they are performing and can quickly burn out. Some of the questions that practitioners need to ask themselves are:

1. Can some of my work be eliminated or delegated to someone else?
2. Am I setting myself up for failure by holding expectations that are too high?
3. Are my goals clear and am I really working toward them?
4. Do I know how to say No?

It is best that beginning practitioners become their own monitors and pay attention to themselves and their limits. The novice practitioner should remember the adage, "All work and no play makes Jack [Jackie] a dull boy [girl]" and take precautions to prevent the same. Time and workload management are important factors that all practitioners need to utilize in their work situations.

Practitioner satisfaction can be described as the degree to which workers hold positive attitudes and feelings about their work, working conditions, and their employing agency. Practitioners can check out their job satisfaction using the Job Description Inventory (JDI) which explores work, pay, opportunities for promotion, supervision, and relationships with coworkers (Newsome & Pillari, 1991; Smith, Kendall, & Hulin, 1969). Effective worker performance is part of work satisfaction. Patti (1983) suggests that performance has four components: productivity, efficiency, quality of service provided, and service effectiveness.

Worker attitudes and behaviors are also related in that increased job satisfaction can lead to better work performance (Friesen, 1987). The support systems that a worker has are useful in preventing burnout and, as Shulman (1991) indicates, a worker's openness to receive help from supervisors is more positively associated with skill, relationship and outcome measures. Finally, a sense of humor on the part of the worker was associated positively with skill, trust, and helpfulness. These are all factors that beginning professionals should keep in perspective while working with different clients.

Supervision of Practitioners

There are a number of situations that are difficult for a worker to handle, without help, particularly in the beginning stages of a career as a practitioner. One of the best ways of receiving feedback is through a supervisor who is also a trained social work professional. Supervision in the field helps the trainee and the beginning practitioner to become aware of themselves and their strengths and weaknesses. Practitioners are expected to know the areas where they have personal difficulties. Being a practitioner means knowing yourself, not just techniques and theories.

Constructive supervision implies instruction, consultation, and direction to beginning practitioners in how to best work with different clients. Utilizing a competent supervisor to explore issues and feelings about clients is a good place to start. Supervision cannot be concerned merely with the supervisee's issues, but a beginning worker must get a perspective of the other side of the worker–client relationship.

Twenty-five year old Beverly, who came from a small town and had never been exposed to urban life, became dizzy when she was told that she had to work with inner-city children. When the supervisor asked what had upset her, Beverly responded that she did not know. The supervisor asked her whether the idea of going or meeting the inner-city children was a new experience for her. At this point Beverly started to sweat, saying that she was afraid that the children might not like her or work with her. She worried that they would find out that she was a small-town woman and maybe not respect her. The supervisor mentioned that many supervisees have felt uncomfortable in different settings. She herself had been uncomfortable about these children, but after working with them for ten years she said that she would not change her job for anything. Thus began Beverly's search to understand her fear of the unfamiliar and of loss of control.

Most social work practitioners are supervised by more experienced practitioners after graduation. This is an important factor in the social work profession. Some social work practitioners receive supervision for a longer time than others. Though there are attempts to move away from supervision as a general rule to autonomous practice, individual growth-oriented supervision still serves a useful purpose.

When Della had problems with an elderly client who reminded her of her father who had mistreated her as a child, she started to react to him as if he were her father. In discussions with her supervisor she was able to bring this issue to light. Eventually she was able to establish a positive working relationship with the client.

The social work supervisor combines educational and assessment functions with administrative authority and responsibility. Supervisors utilize agency-preferred strategies in guiding their supervisees. The supervisor's role is primarily that of a middle manager responsible for implementing agency policy and conducting a part of the agency's program. This includes responsibility for office staff budgets, program development, and community relations in addition to case consultation and practitioner training. Learning the supervisor's role on-the-job is an important one, and the practitioners who have spent time understanding themselves and being well informed about the agency in which they work do become better supervisors. Although supervisors have developed a number of effective ways to educate, train, and acclimate workers, they still find it difficult to assess accurately the skill and performance of their own supervisees (Loewenberg, 1983; Senge, 1994). Workers are evaluated on the basis of their supervisor's expectations and attitudes, so that many workers pay attention to their supervisor's suggestions and learn to view their supervisor as the model for desirable practice.

Exposure to Multicultural Situations

Workers need to be exposed to multicultural situations. Culture indicates a broader scope than ethnicity. It includes demographic variables such as gender, age, place of residence, and social, educational, and economic status variables, and the formal and informal affiliations to one group or special population. Broadly, culture also includes institutions, language, values, religious ideals, and patterns of social relationships (Pedersen, 1986). Culture shapes the basic characteristics of human beings, including beliefs, emotions, and sense of self.

Overgeneralization can result in cultural re-ification, harmful stereotyping, and the loss of individuality that are extremely important for effective treatment of clients (Matsumoto, 1997). In fact, intracultural differences may exceed intercultural differences in some cases (Lum, 1992; Sue, 1981). As Martinez (1988) notes, "There are some ways in which any particular Chicano is like *all* other Chicanos and there are some ways in which a particular Chicano is like *some* other Chicanos, and there are ways in which a particular Chicano is like *no* other Chicano" (p. 184).

Ethnic-sensitive practice focuses on present-day influences on the daily life of ethnic minority groups with an understanding of historical and cultural perspectives. This type of practice goes beyond the concerns of the individual and addresses the consequences of racism, poverty, and discrimination on a group of people. Minorities are people from racial, ethnic, linguistic, and religious groups who have been discriminated against by a majority. The term also applies to women, gays and lesbians, the elderly, individuals with physical disabilities, and individuals with behavior problems (Lum, 1992).

To become an effective worker with different groups of people, it is important that practitioners understand their own values and assumptions about people. The social worker must develop a capacity to share the client's worldview without criticizing or judging this view. He or she must develop an understanding of the sociopolitical forces that influence attitudes toward oppressed populations. Garvin (1997) notes that oppression is the destructive effects on people when social institutions damage their identities, denigrate their lifestyles, and deny them access to opportunities.

Exposure to multicultural clients requires that practitioners develop multicultural interviewing skills. *Multicultural* is a generic term that deals with cross-cultural matters; that is, the interaction and intermingling of two or more cultures. *Intercultural* interaction occurs within the same culture and *transcultural* interaction occurs when different cultures have factors common to all of them, such as different European or Asian cultures that have some commonalities.

Multiculturalism highlights the complexity of culture and avoids any implied comparisons. It has been suggested that people share a common denominator in the general society though many belong to groups that are identified by beliefs, values, thought patterns, feelings, and behavior—all of which are aspects of different cultural environments in the larger pluralistic culture. Padilla and De Synder (1985) define pluralistic counseling (or practice) as "a therapeutic intervention that recognizes and understands a client's culturally based beliefs, values, and behaviors" (p. 160). It takes into account the client's ethnic historical background, personal life experiences, family history, and sociocultural factors. Also pluralistic practice aims at helping clients clarify their personal and cultural standards.

Multicultural practice also requires an understanding of different racial and ethnic groups, and a sensitivity to how clients react to different, often conflicting, cultural influences. An additional factor involves how practitioners feel about their own membership in a particular racial or ethnic group. The degree of acceptance or rejection of one's cultural heritage adds another dimension to working with different clients.

Sixteen-year-old Mumtaz is the child of immigrant parents from a Middle Eastern city. They are conservative practicing Muslims. However, Mumtaz has grown up in North America. Like her peers, she goes out on dates, much against her mother's will and without her father's knowledge. One day, the father finds out about his daughter's dating and abuses her physically. After intervention by the police the family is sent to the family services agency. Dorothy, a new social worker, interviews them. Dorothy is an Anglo-Saxon. When Mumtaz's father explains in anger that his daughter should not go out with boys even if she was living in America, but only marry a man whom he chooses, Dorothy is puzzled. At one point, when the father becomes hysterically angry when his daughter defies him, Dorothy loses her cool and feels a strong urge to giggle.

Why do you think Dorothy is reacting in this particular manner? What are the issues in the case? How would you handle this case?

The issues in this case are multicultural issues. Dorothy is reacting in a manner that reveals she has not been exposed to different cultures. Her attitude is ethnocentric and also stereotypical. The case becomes more complex as the clients have to overcome the prejudices and ignorance that they face with the worker. Dorothy must learn by asking questions in an empathetic manner—or lose the case. If you are the practitioner who is ignorant of another culture, it would be more professional to be sensitive and to ask questions to better help understand the culture of the family before attempting to intervene.

Holly is the social worker for a group of people with physical disabilities. This is her first job and she feels uncomfortable. One of the young men, Andreo, speaks Spanish and does not seem to fit in with the group. He has a strong accent and is not easily accepted by the different group members. Holly begins to feel sorry for him and makes special efforts to assist him when he gets up from his chair without his crutches. She also walks him to the door. While the group discusses family issues and occupational issues that they need to deal with, Holly looks out for Andreo in an overprotective manner. Instead of being empathetic, the rest of the group is irritated and angry. They pick on Andreo and tease him about his behaviors and pronunciation. Holly is puzzled and wonders why the group members are so hard on Andreo. After all, Andreo is not so different from everyone else in his physical abilities.

Why is Andreo being treated differently by the group members? What are the problems of the group leader, Holly? How would you handle the case? What would you do differently, if anything?

Holly feels sorry for Andreo. She is overprotective and biased toward him. Her relationship with him is no longer a therapeutic alliance. This in turn affects the other group members who are envious and resentful of the special attention that Andreo is receiving from the practitioner. They take out their resentment on Andreo for being the favorite by teasing and ridiculing. Letting others help Andreo if necessary and treating him like the rest of the group would create better relationships among the group members and help them all move toward the therapeutic goals that they have set for themselves.

Forty-year-old Antonio, who was raised in a traditional Italian Catholic family, is a practitioner in a family services agency. Antonio was assigned a case with a hurried, brief note left by his supervisor which merely said "different couple." Antonio walked into the session room where the clients, Jim and Keith, were waiting. Antonio introduced himself to Keith and Jim who were holding hands. Antonio showed his discomfort by turning away. Because they were used to this type of reaction, the men in a

matter-of-fact manner told Antonio that they were married and had some issues about raising their child whom they had adopted. Antonio did not know how to handle this case, at least not in the first session.

If you were the worker how would you handle the case?

First and foremost, it is important to be sensitive to diverse people and respect their lifestyles. Jim and Keith seemed savvy enough to understand Antonio's initial discomfort. Antonio could ease into the situation by admitting his initial surprise, letting the couple know that he is interested in working with them, and getting on with the business of helping this couple and their child. However, if Antonio had unresolved discomfort about the couple's lifestyle, then he should say so, apologetically, and refer the case to another unbiased practitioner.

Bill Park is a small housing complex within a large university community. A large number of African Americans, Latinos, Native Americans, and a few Anglo-Saxons live in this housing. Most of these students are relatively low income or from poor families. The apartments were poorly maintained, with worn out and permanently stained carpets. Some had leaky roofs that had not been repaired for years. Some apartments lacked an adequate water supply and others had broken toilets that had not been replaced. The garbage removal service for the complex was often sporadic, and a pungent stink haunted the apartments. Calls to the landlord for any type of help in building maintenance fell on deaf ears. Finally, the students formed a group for housing betterment. They joined with the Citizens for a Better Community group to get their needs heard and improve the housing in Bill Park. The citizens group, headed by a generalist social worker, was invested in a safer and cleaner community. This group lobbied the city council with letters and public discussions of their issues and problems. Finally, they succeeded in achieving enactment of a property maintenance code for the Bill Park community.

Would you have worked differently as a generalist? State your positive or negative response and provide reasons to justify your thinking.

WORKER ROLES

The efforts of generalists to help people is serious work. The particular characteristics that the social worker brings to the professional setting and the influence he or she exerts in managing processes lead to social adjustment and social change. The ability to approach professional responsibilities with flexibility, creativity, skill, knowledge, and ingenuity can bring about change and growth. Social work professionals are inculcated with knowledge, values, skills, and purpose that cannot be separated from personal and professional attitudes and values. The social worker is no less significant than what he or she does.

There are three major variables that are part of the worker's self: the observing self, the sentient characteristics, and the role characteristics (Goldstein, 1984; Shulman, 1999). The observing self includes how an individual perceives and defines his or her own reality. All the significant relationships a person has, combined with personal experiences, education, and sociocultural factors, result in a professional who has unique attitudes, habits, values, perceptions, and behaviors.

The sentient characteristics have to do with peoples' feelings about themselves and their social reality. Earlier in this chapter, we discussed how important it is for the worker to try to achieve some objectivity about personal perceptions, feelings, and behaviors, especially in professional contexts.

Role characteristics pertain to the worker's position and status in the change system and the attitudes and behaviors that are a result of position and status in that system. Role performance is also influenced by self-perception and the expectations of others in the system, and the requirements of the system itself.

These characteristics can also be seen as entities by themselves. For example, because a social worker is acutely aware (observation) of the undercurrent of feelings (sentience) that are prevalent in a family, he or she will feel more certain about his or her responsive actions (role), and also because these actions are defined by his or her interpretation of the family (observing self).

As a generalist, how do you view your role? What is the meaning of a role? Role can be defined as those recurrent behaviors, normative obligations, and responsibilities that delineate status and position and determine the behaviors that are directed toward clientele. Role can also be de-

scribed as a product of interaction between persons. A role has three components: role conception, expectations, and performance (see Figure 6.2). Role conception is a person's idea of how he or she is expected to perform in a particular social situation. Role expectations are how others actually expect a person to perform, and role performance is the real behavior of a person in a given position (Cameron, 1990; Thomas & Feldman, 1967). When there is a certain degree of congruence between these three components, there is continuity and smoothness in social interaction. *Webster's Tenth Collegiate Dictionary* (1996) defines a role as "a socially expected behavior pattern usually determined by an individual's status in a particular society" (p. 1014). Barker (1995) defines a role as "a culturally determined pattern of *behavior* that is prescribed for an individual who occupies a *special status*" (p. 328).

A role, whether social or professional, is composed of psychological processes that are one's perceptions and feelings about one's status and the status of others in the relationship, as well as the influence of society and its institutional controls on people. The latter arise from the internalized norms of behavior that derive from learning about the expectations of the social environment. Think of your own roles in society as a partner, parent, or child and as a student, a social work internee, or a wage earner. Is there some degree of congruence in the roles you play? Because individuals have multiple roles, people have to prioritize their

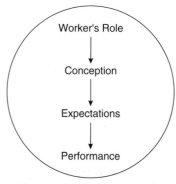

Figure 6.2   **Components of a Worker's Role**

roles and the functions they perform within each role. If an important role—say that of a parent or wage earner—is affected, it invariably affects other roles as well.

The discussion that follows focuses on the social worker's role performance and the influence of actions and responsibilities the practitioner brings to the change experience, in order to complete the meaning of the generalist professional image. These are based on a schema presented by Lister (1987) and represent the different roles that workers play with different clients to help them reach their goals.

The social worker is an agent of change who works on target systems and moves toward bringing about change. The change agent carries a great deal of responsibility in different situations and in work with different size systems.

A change agent is specifically employed in a voluntary or profit-making agency, organization, or community for the purpose of bringing about planned change. A change agent can also be described as any person or group, either professional or nonprofessional, inside or outside the system attempting to bring about change in the system. The change agent who is a paid professional is influenced by the system that employs him or her (Pincus & Minahan, 1973). Barker (1995) describes a change agent as a social worker or a group of helpers whose purpose is to facilitate improvement. An action system can be described as the people and resources in the community with whom the social worker deals to achieve the desired changes. A target system is an individual, group, community, or organization that needs to be changed or influenced to achieve the social worker's goals (Barker, 1995).

Roles that the worker uses to reach the client may be classified into direct provision of services, indirect influences on a system, and system linkages. Work with clients can be done on a face-to-face basis or by referral to consumer groups that provide services. These social roles can be described as constellations of worker activities designed to link client systems to the resources that they require.

Although the various roles discussed might appear separate and distinct, the role definitions are somewhat artificial intellectual constructs. In the real world, roles such as clinician, case manager, family worker or therapist, broker, advocate, enabler, empowerer, mediator, advocate, supervisor, analyst or evaluator, and initiator blend into each other. In actual practice, the social worker engages in a complex of activities custom-tailored to the client's needs and situation. The practitioner needs to be versatile and flexible. A worker often has to choose one or more roles in order to reach all the goals that need to be achieved in a specific client situation. The generalist's many roles are shown in Figure 6.3.

The Clinical Role

The clinical role of the practitioner is to assist clients to modify attitudes, feelings, and coping behaviors that interfere with their functioning. Goldstein (1983) discusses the individualizing practice role that workers play. In typical clinical situations there are people who are confused or hurt, people who get other people into trouble, or people who are trying to grow and live relatively constructive and productive lives.

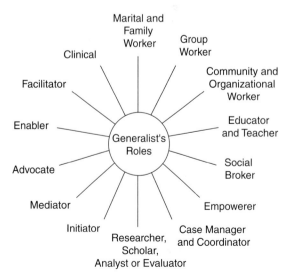

Figure 6.3   **Generalist's Roles**

The clinical role rests on four assumptions. The first assumption states that individual growth, development, and behavior are the result of the complex interaction of the individual's endowment with all of the person's internal and external environments. The second assumption acknowledges complex, potential stressors that interfere with growth, development, and behavior and that are still unknown at the beginning of the helping process. The third assumption recognizes that we do not expect all persons to react in the same way to stressors. The fourth assumption requires that we reexamine the arenas of social functioning and the effects of stress that include the individual, intimate networks, support networks, work, school, the neighborhood, and the larger community (Connaway & Gentry, 1988).

The impact of problems on the individual, group, family, community, or organization is observed in terms of relationships and interactions. The practitioner focuses on what a problem means to the clientele and all the members of the system, how problems change the system, and how severe and serious the problem is.

One of the factors we need to be aware of is the meaning of the problem to a specific clientele. Categories of meaning include group discontent, community and group contexts, family issues, and personal issues such as inability to meet general and significant expectations and changes.

Idge is a worker in a rural hospital where she works with clients suffering from AIDS. Matilda is a twenty-year-old AIDS patient who is unhappy at the hospital. She is angry with herself for being promiscuous and bringing this disease on herself. Matilda behaves in a nasty manner toward Idge. Whatever Idge attempts to do to help is ignored or rejected by Matilda, because she is overwhelmed and angry at the prospect of dying. At times, in the sessions she is totally honest and discusses how she feels about her life and the fact that her family abandoned her after she got AIDS. She insistently talks about her own wasted life and her anger at being unable to be a "regular" person. Idge uses these sessions to help Matilda work through her issues and accept her life situation.

In an individual clinical situation, help is offered to the client on a one-to-one basis, keeping in mind the larger environment. This is also called counseling, where the worker helps a single client to cope and adapt to his or her person–environment situation, keeping in mind the influence of others.

The Marital and Family Therapist/Worker/Practitioner

In the marital and family work, the practitioner works with a family or couple in joint and group sessions. A family typically focuses on one person in sessions, but the family therapist works with the whole family in order to help them communicate and interact in ways that help them understand and work better with each other. Sometimes, a couple is seen separately without their children in order to deal with intimate issues such as sexuality. At other times, couples may come simply for couple sessions, in which the worker plays the role of a marital or conjoint therapist/practitioner. The goal is to help individuals deal with each other in their relationship, communicate their feelings to each other, and work toward a better relationship.

Felicia and Jeremy have been married for fifteen years and they have four children. Jeremy was a very successful businessman and Felicia stayed home and took care of the children. Eventually, all the children were in school and Felicia decided to attend school and improve her own prospects of getting a job. Jeremy was threatened by her new ambitions and regularly sabotaged her attending school. He always came up with an excuse such as having extra work to do in the office. The day before Felicia's final exam, he invited a number of his buddies home. Felicia had to entertain them by cooking and acting the pleasant hostess. This made her very angry and led to a fight between the couple.

Before long Felicia was talking of divorce. Jeremy did not want a divorce and saw all her efforts as an indication that she wanted to leave him. However, Jeremy was surprised when Felicia set up an appointment for them to see a couples' therapist/practitioner. In the clinical sessions, Jeremy mentioned that he was afraid that Felicia's education was her way to become independent of him.

With the help of the worker, both were able to communicate more effectively. Felicia said that she was afraid of being left behind by her husband and that she wanted to be an effective partner, not just the mother of his children. She had started to feel useless when the youngest child did not need her mother to dress her and send her to school. Jeremy, in turn, was surprised because he had felt threatened that she might become "fashionable" after she became educated and have no interest in him. Through weekly sessions, a large number of their fears and doubts were put to rest through communication with each other. Also, based on task assignments, both were able to set time aside for each other and renew their love. The most important role that the worker played for this couple was to help monitor them in terms of family communication and interactions not only with each other but with their children. This type of help is crucial in work with families.

The Group Worker

The group worker's role includes a number of varied services to different clientele. It often involves conducting group activities with support groups, self-help groups, and knowledge and skills development groups.

The purpose of the work is to keep the group focused and goal-oriented and also to assist in member-to-member interactions. The group worker has to explain his or her role to the group members. Group guidelines and pertinent issues such as activities, attendance, risk taking, confidentiality, self-disclosure, and confrontation should be discussed. The group worker facilitates and enhances the positive interactions that happen in the group.

For example, the group worker can end a session by saying that the group has covered a great deal in the session. The group worker might say, "We have talked about confidentiality and the support you group members have received from your spouses; we have also discussed how to find time for ourselves in terms of attempting to make others happy, and also feel confident that we are all doing our job in our workplace. Is there any specific issue you would like to discuss next week?"

In another group session a hospital group worker might suggest: "Well, I would like to discuss with you the anger that some of you feel toward the hospital, particularly about the insensitivity of the staff and the limited visiting hours. We have some time left, about twenty minutes. Is there anything else you are interested in saying about this matter before we move on to another topic?"

Usually, while working with groups in the beginning sessions, the group worker concentrates on becoming aware of the clues about unfinished business. For instance, group members may talk about their feelings and the thoughts that they had while they were returning home from their first group session. They may even talk about their own frustration about what was and what was not accomplished.

Community Worker and Organizer

Helping clients in communities requires that the worker has to work in multilevel systems which include different neighborhoods and different aspects of the community. A generalist working in a community emphasizes self-help and cooperation toward achievement of goals. Some of the key roles that a community worker can play include enabler, coordinator, and supporter of problem-solving skills (Gambrill, 1997). Members of the community are viewed as participants in a shared problem-solving process (Fawcett et al., 1996).

Community problems may vary from preserving neighborhoods, to increasing safety to decreasing crime through neighborhood block organizations (Chavis and Wandersman, 1990; Prestby et al., 1990). As an organizer, the generalist has to empower citizens and help them increase the influence they have over decisions that affect their lives. This is done through knowledge of problems and alternative solutions. The worker should have skill in presenting issues and leading the community in using related strategies in order to access elected officials through meetings. Examples of community work include: teaching community board members to speak effectively at board meetings (Briscoe, Hoffman, & Fawcett, 1975); enhancing advocacy skills of people with physical disabilities (Balcazar, Mathews, Francisco, & Fawcett, 1994); involving community members to identify community needs (Schriner & Fawcett, 1988); and enhancing leadership skills (Seekins & Fawcett, 1987). The most important factor to be remembered is that the people in the community need to gain increased social support and a sense of control, which in turn enhances personal confidence and coping capacities.

Jeffrey is the new social worker assigned to a small town that has a number of needs. In order to familiarize himself with the community and its people, Jeffrey walks the neighborhood streets, goes to their favorite beer shop, and gets to know the names of natural community leaders. His casual but interested attitude creates a sense of good will toward him from the community residents. Jeffrey uses this good will to talk to different types of people including the natural leaders in order to find out and prioritize the pressing needs of the community.

As an organizer and administrator of a social agency, the generalist takes on a number of responsibilities. As an administrator the generalist has management tasks that include budgeting, coordinating activities, resolving conflicts, encouraging compliance with expected standards, coordinating agency needs and goals, and meeting external requirements from regulatory or funding sources (Hasenfeld, 1987). Maintenance roles are key for administrators. As Resnick (1982) indicates, these include the role of a harmonizer who solves disagreements and reduces tension, a consensus tester who checks whether a group of people are nearing a decision, an encourager who is friendly and warm, and a compromiser who changes a position when it is called for. Agency administrators have different styles of providing direction to their employees and this would vary depending upon the generalist's authority styles. Some are authoritarian, others use coercive power, and still others are democratic in their approach to their employees.

Andrew is the new generalist director of a social welfare agency. The agency has had a large number of turnovers in administration. Therefore, Andrew steps into his new role firmly but with an open mind and a democratic approach to the employees. Andrew encourages the employees to reach out to him if they need to discuss anything of concern. This type of a new beginning led to a positive relationship between employees and Andrew, and thus created for Andrew an effective leadership style.

Educator and Teacher

The purpose of practice is to help client systems function more effectively, learn new information, and acquire new skills. Thus the generalist as an educator should be knowledgeable. The clients who use social worker assistance for educational purposes meet their workers in a number of different practice settings: neighborhood centers, in- and outpatient health and mental health facilities, employment assistance programs, women's centers, private offices, community planning groups, family agencies, and many other types of organizations.

Bowen (1978) believes that the practitioner is a teacher who educates clients to understand their roles and the behaviors that create problems for them. The practitioner is also an educator as he or she disseminates information to diverse clientele. This could be information about drugs, alcohol, family planning, or other matters such as better communication or planning and building networks.

The worker also plays the role of a model and simulator. In modeling, the worker utilizes personal behavior to influence the behavior of clients. One of the important ways of modeling is to demonstrate desirable behaviors. For example, in a family interview, the worker might speak to the children calmly and respectfully. In other situations, the worker may use simulation or role play to help clients learn or develop more effective behavioral responses in different situations.

Educating clients includes offering information and teaching new skills and behaviors. For instance, the worker may provide essential information to clients in educational sessions on parenting skills, stress management, and various aspects of mental health and health care. In larger settings such as hospitals, negotiation, networking, and mobilization are effective methods for transmitting information and instructions.

Discussion allows clients to participate and get feedback in terms of reinforcement and recognition of problems and issues and ways to deal with them. For the worker dealing with a group, a community, or members of an organization, it is best to facilitate the active participation of all members. Learning through discussion and active participation is common in groups, communities, and organizations where the members have specific needs and issues.

The Social Broker

A broker is an intermediary who connects people with resources. The resources are used by the broker to assist people to accomplish their life tasks or to alleviate current distress (Curriculum Policy, 1992). The broker links different size systems such as groups, families, organizations, and communities. According to Barker (1995), a broker helps clients put various segments of the community in touch with one another to enhance their mutual interests.

The National Association of Social Workers (NASW) identifies different goals that people would like to reach. Interventions can be used to link people with systems that provide resources, services, and opportunities and help them reach their goals (NASW, 1992). It is necessary for practitioners to have a knowledge of community services so that they will be able to make referrals. In order to carry out this role, the worker has to negotiate and bargain on behalf of clients. Normally, negotiations become important in the face of inequalities between different parties.

It is also necessary for practitioners to have a good understanding of the policies of resource systems and to create networks with key contact persons through working relationships with them.

Sometimes clients have to be helped to overcome their fears and misconceptions of the services that are offered in one setting (Hepworth, Rooney, & Larsen, 1997). Social brokering can be done in different ways: for example, when a worker arranges for clients to learn parenting skills.

Charles and Cindy, a couple in their early twenties, were living together and had several children. Cindy had delivered three children since the age of seventeen but she did not know how to be a mother. Charles became unemployed and Cindy had to get a job. Neither was good at managing the children. The children had not had a bath for over one month. They were frequently left on their own and not well fed. At last they came to the notice of the county department of social services, and the children were taken away. Cindy cried, saying that she loved her children but was overwhelmed by the amount of work she had to do. She complained that she did not receive any help from her boyfriend who, due to lack of work, was drinking heavily. After a couple of interviews it became clear to the worker that Cindy had concerns and fears that the children might be taken away from her permanently. The worker referred Cindy to a parenting class, where there was a long waiting list. Understanding the urgency, the generalist got in touch with the parenting class supervisor and advocated for appropriate connections for Cindy and Charles. Thus Cindy and Charles joined the parenting class where both improved their parenting skills. The children were returned home but the worker visited them periodically to see if Cindy and Charles continued to meet their parental responsibilities.

Through social brokering, clients can be helped in many different ways. For instance, clients who are unemployed may be referred for job placement, and this linkage can help them obtain a job. A practitioner working with a group of unemployed people might invite a speaker to talk about different ways of getting help with a job search. In order to be effective, the practitioner has to be knowledgeable about the variety of services and resources that are available in the community. Workers should possess knowledge of organizations for planning and implementing appropriate matches of needs and resources. Referral or linkage is a process that often requires a high level of clinical skill. Clients may need help to overcome resistance to the referral and be prepared to make appropriate use of the new service.

Specialized broker role strategies are necessary for disaster situations affecting large groups of people. These require being alert to the social networks of the community and attempting to maintain its support systems. In such situations, the usual method of distributing resources to an individual or a family, an organization, or a community of people, may be disrupted. For example, in distributing mobile homes in Eastern Kentucky after a fire, it was found that separating families who were accustomed to close proximity resulted in destruction of kinship systems, an important source of mutual help and also violation of important cultural values and traditions. Of course, results of other disaster relief efforts would have to be examined as a basis for future planning and preparing for responses to disasters.

The broker role is time-consuming if done properly. Many times it is interconnected with other roles, but it is always important in helping different clientele.

Case Manager and Coordinator

Due to acute problems or chronic limitations, some clients cannot take on the responsibility of following through on their referrals to other resource systems. These clients include the homeless, the elderly, the chronically mentally ill, people with developmental disabilities, and dependent and neglected children. Due to the dramatic increase in the numbers of such clients, many articles now discuss the need for case management.

The role of the case manager entails work between the clients and their environments. This role has evolved to a central one in direct practice in response to vulnerable client groups who otherwise would not receive essential resources and services because they lack the physical mobility, knowledge of resources, and mental abilities to get help for themselves. McCreath (1984) and Ely (1985) have found that these clients have vital needs that may

go unmet because the agencies are not providing the services or because the clients do not make their needs known. In such situations, the consequences are more suffering and increased vulnerability to deterioration in functioning.

Social workers are qualified to be case managers because they have a knowledge of community services and skills in communication and advocacy, along with skills in assessment and counseling. Broskowski (1991), Christianson and Gray (1994), and Hepworth et al. (1997), list many objectives in working with clients including: (1) helping people to obtain resources; (2) facilitating interactions between individuals and others in their environments; and (3) making organizations responsive to people.

Also, the role the case manager plays varies from setting to setting, and role definitions may vary within specific settings. In order to work effectively in linking clients to settings, a case manager should maintain close contact with other service providers. The case manager must negotiate for, coordinate, and ensure that essential linkages are in place and that services are delivered in a timely fashion. In order to perform these functions, the case manager must have extensive knowledge of community resources, the rights of clients' and the policies and procedures of various agencies, as well as skills in mediation and advocacy (Wernet, 1999). Besides being case managers and service providers, generalists also perform dual functions in direct work with clients. Assessing clients' needs and helping them to participate in the planning and decision-making process to the extent of their abilities is an essential aspect of case management.

A frail elderly woman was left alone in her home after her husband died. She had been married to him for over fifty years and was used to being taken care of by him. When he died, her whole world fell apart. Instead of getting help, she stayed home until the groceries ran out. The bills were paid sporadically. She found it more and more difficult to leave her house because she suffered from severe arthritis. One day while smoking in bed, she set the bed on fire. This finally brought the woman to the attention of social services. The worker who was assigned to her realized that besides counseling her, he needed to be her case manager because she did not know how to get help or, for that matter, even take care of herself. It was as if she was out of practice, and the worker slowly had to enable her to receive the services that were available to her.

The case manager from one agency has to take on the chief responsibility of arranging and coordinating the delivery of essential goods and services that are provided by other settings and also working directly with the client. He or she works directly with the client to ensure that plans for service delivery are in place. Case management also involves monitoring the progress of a client through professional teamwork using the services of several professional agencies, health care facilities, and human service programs. Barker (1995) indicates that case management can occur within a single large organization or within a community program that coordinates services among agencies. Case management is seen as an important way of limiting problems arising from fragmentation of services, staff turnover, and inadequate coordination of providers. It is important to note that in this role the practitioner functions as the interface between the clients and their surroundings or environment.

Mediator

The role of the mediator is to resolve disagreements and conflicts that happen between a client system and other people or organizations. The purpose of mediation is to assist systems that are in conflict to reach agreement about the issues that form the basis of their conflict. Mediation can also be explained as a process that "provides a neutral forum in which the disputants are encouraged to find a mutually satisfactory resolution to their problems" (Chandler, 1985, p. 346). Mediation is also the art of intervening in a negotiating process that involves at least two systems with the purpose of assisting them in settling differences.

Negotiating is the art of conferring, discussing, and bargaining about differences for the purpose of reaching a settlement. In social work mediation, the negotiators are usually the systems directly involved in the conflict or dispute. In the mediator role, the worker is not one of the contending parties but a neutral and nonpartisan third party whose role is to assist the system in conflict to reach an agreement (Moore, 1986). Thus a mediator is a person who interposes himself or herself between contending parties, usually at their invitation, and assists them in resolving conflicts. As Barker (1995) indicates, intervention in disputes between parties helps them reconcile differences, find compromises, and reach mutually satisfactory agreements. Social workers use their unique skills and values orientation in many forms of mediation such as between landlords and tenant organizations, neighborhood residents and halfway house personnel, and so forth. Mediation also may include assisting couples to work out their own child custody and property settlement agreements which are then instituted by the court. Settling matters outside of the courtroom helps them avoid the adversarial process (Irving, 1981; Blades, 1985).

The mediator is neutral and nonpartisan although he or she is interested in outcomes and agreements. However, the mediator is not responsible for agreements reached and intervenes only to allow negotiating exchanges between contending parties. The goal of mediation is conflict resolution to help preserve the social fabric of families, communities, and nations. In mediation people examine the facts, problems, feelings, and attitudes in order to make decisions about their choices. The goal of mediation is not to bring about personality change or behavior change but rather to modify an interaction and the choices made by participants who are part of the action.

Rhonda and Robert were caught in a custody battle. Originally Rhonda received custody of the children. However, when Robert found out that his wife had sued for divorce only because she had fallen in love with the man next door, he became extraordinarily upset. Wanting revenge, he reopened the case and started a battle for the custody of the children. The children who loved both parents were torn in their loyalties and started to misbehave in school, fail in class, and become disruptive. Rhonda realized that the children were reacting to the custody battle, so they went to their minister for mediation. The minister, also a generalist, was neutral because he liked both the parties. He was also aware that Robert's job as a salesman made him less available as a father and a husband. By being caring and concerned, but neutral, he helped the couple resolve their issues. The children continued to live with their mother, but the father was given liberal weekend and visitation rights.

Mediation takes place when breakdowns happen between clients and service providers to help the clients renew services that they have been denied temporarily due to problems. The goal of this type of mediation is to help get rid of obstacles to service delivery. In mediation, both the client and the helping system attempt to find a mutually satisfactory solution to their problems. If a child is causing trouble in school and has been suspended a number of times, the practitioner who works with this child could serve as a mediator between the child, the family system, and the school system in order to help resolve the problem.

The mediator helps clients and other parties find common ground on which they can negotiate a resolution to a problem. Playing the role of the mediator requires using techniques to bring about the convergence of perceived values of both parties to the conflict. It also includes helping each party to recognize the legitimacy of the other's interests and to assist parties by identifying common interests in a successful outcome. This is also done to avoid situations where winning and losing are paramount. The mediator attempts to localize the conflict to specific issues so that the whole relationship is not jeopardized. The mediator works at facilitating communication between parties by discussion, sharing information, and persuasion procedures (Compton & Galaway, 1994).

Mediators listen carefully and draw out facts and feelings from both parties to discover the cause of a breakdown. After obtaining as many facts as possible from both parties, the mediator

plans appropriate remedial action to remove barriers, clarify possible misunderstandings, and also work through negative feelings that have impeded service delivery.

Today, mediation skills have reached a high level of sophistication. Social work mediators work with attorneys to resolve disputes regarding property settlements and conflicts between divorcing parties as well as personnel disputes and labor-management conflicts.

Advocate

The role of the advocate has been assumed by social workers since the inception of the profession. Advocacy, which is a concept originally utilized in the legal profession, has the same implications in social work. The advocate in social work, as in law, argues, bargains, or manipulates the environment on behalf of the client. Thus, in many ways, advocacy is different from mediation where the worker attempts to maintain neutrality. The obligation to assume the role of an advocate has been reaffirmed many times, including the NASW *Code of Ethics* as revised and adapted in 1993.

As Rees (1991) indicates, "in matters of social injustice, the realm of public affairs should become a political domain where people can be enabled to represent their own interests" (p. 145). Advocacy can also be described as a process of working on behalf of clients to: (1) obtain services or resources for clients that would not otherwise be provided; (2) modify current operating policies, procedures, or practices that adversely affect clients; and (3) promote new legislation or policies that will result in the provision of needed resources or services (Hepworth et al., 1997). Advocacy provides "the opportunity for empowerment, for active, responsible participation in the social or public realm (Lewis, 1991, p. 28). As the definition suggests, the term *advocacy* is very popular now. It has come to mean anything one can do to assist or speak for another and may be extended to mean social reform as well as the protection of existing rights.

Many times in human history, we have been outraged at injustices and violation of human dignity, and we have acted alone or in concert to reverse the negative effects of social structures and norms that discriminate against people and devalue them. This includes efforts on behalf of disadvantaged populations such as the mentally ill, women and children, and older adults (Khinduka & Coughin, 1975; Kutchins & Kutchins, 1978).

Porter Lee (1930) observed that there are two basic tasks or functions that social workers perform: participating in "causes" aimed at changes in law or public policy, and "function" work in structured programs to help people and the community. The purpose of social advocacy is to ensure that new and existing rights and entitlements are protected and secured by requiring that social institutions fulfill their responsibilities to the community. When we use case advocacy, it is to secure and protect entitlements of a particular client or client system. Class advocacy is used to secure and protect entitlements for a group of client systems that share a common status and problem.

Case advocacy is initiated based on a worker's assessment of need and the client's entitlement or rights to be secured or protected. Clients at all system levels are entitled to life necessities, protection of health and safety, and opportunities for growth and development. Entitlement for people are established in several ways. Some rights are established in law or common consensus, some in an organization's policies, and at times in new interpretations of law or an organization's policies.

The generalist has to assess how vulnerable clients are in terms of their characteristics and their immediate entitlement problem. Practitioners have to act quickly and also take responsibility for responding to emergencies and chronic difficulties wherever high vulnerability exists; for example, among abandoned, neglected, and abused persons, as well as the very young, the old, and the infirm, and people with serious illness or mental health impairments. Some minority groups are more at risk because of lack of services, employment, and other entitlements. These include racial and ethnic groups, people with physical disabilities, and gays and lesbians.

Four-year-old Yolanda was found in her apartment with blood on her body and physical marks of abuse. The case was reported to the social services department by a neighbor who would not identify herself. However, Yolanda's stepfather would not allow the child to be taken away from him, saying that he was in charge of Yolanda until her mother returned and the mother would be away for two days. Acting as the child's advocate, the worker made temporary provisions to keep the child out of the house until her mother returned. The worker had already begun to investigate in order to be the child's advocate until the child's welfare was ensured to the extent possible.

Advocacy entails risks for both advocates and clients. The risks range from failure to achieve successful outcomes to increased resistance and negative reaction in the adversary system. The worker may face threats to employment or in finding future jobs. However, worker risks are reduced if this person's agency vigorously pursues client rights as well. Risks are also reduced when agency positions exist specifically for advocates. Barozzi, Park, and Watson (1982) emphasize the need to legitimatize advocacy activities and to integrate them into the structure of agency services.

The role of advocate can be played without the direct involvement of clients, although this has drawbacks. A worker could be tempted to represent a client without having a clear contract with the client to do so. Social workers who do advocacy work should have a contract with a client group whenever possible before they engage in case advocacy.

Enabler

Social workers have the responsibility to help clients become capable of coping with situational or transitional stress. Barker (1995) identifies the specific skills used in achieving the objective as conveying hope, reducing resistance and ambivalence, recognizing and managing feelings, identifying and supporting personal strengths and social assets, breaking down problems into parts that can be solved more readily, and maintaining a continued focus on goals and the means of achieving them. Zastrow (1992) indicates that an enabler helps individuals articulate their needs, clarify and identify their problems, explore resolution strategies to select and apply an appropriate strategy, and to develop their capacities to deal with their own problems more effectively.

In the role of enabler, the worker helps clients bring about change in their life and behavior. By utilizing the enabler's role, the worker helps clients not only to change in terms of relating to others or the environment, but also to empower them to move toward their goals.

As an enabler, the worker helps and encourages clients to verbalize thoughts and feelings, examine the patterns of relationships, and above all, to make decisions and take actions to achieve their goals and objectives. While enabling, the worker is in contact with the clients—an individual, a group, a family, an organization, or a community—rather than with other external systems.

For example, the generalist can enable a parent and teenager to understand their relationship patterns and problems and find a better way of relating to each other. This is done by identifying and selecting alternative ways of behaving that would be beneficial to both clients.

In an impoverished community the generalist can enable the community members to examine their different problems, prioritize them, make decisions about a problem, and take appropriate action.

Facilitator

The role of the facilitator is to expedite the change effort by bringing together people and opening lines of communication. It includes helping people channel their energies, activities, and resources, and providing them with access to expertise (Barker, 1995).

The term *facilitator* means one who eases or expedites the way for others. When there are prob-

lems between individuals and their environment or when there are problems between members of a group, family, or community, the role of the facilitator is very important.

The task of the facilitator is to enable others to function. After pinpointing different factors that impede service delivery, generalists as facilitators have the responsibility to plan and implement ways of enhancing service delivery. Hepworth et al. (1997) indicate that this involves providing relevant input to agency administrators, recommending staff meetings to address problems, working collaboratively with other staff members to pressure resistant administrators, encouraging and participating in essential in-service training sessions, and other similar activities.

Facilitation also takes place when social workers support helpful behaviors of their clientele. The facilitator can provide information about the helping process. In groups, families, communities, and organizations, they can summarize what they have said or decided; they can deconstruct problems by breaking them into parts and prioritizing which part should be worked on first and deciding the order for working on the rest of the problem (Johnson, 1995).

Heather was a single mother of three children and lived in Wala, a low-income area. There were bus services available to go to work in the nearby city, but not much in the way of transportation to the city for grocery shopping, medical services, and recreational activities. People from Wala had either to walk a couple of miles to get groceries or take their own cars. Heather did not have a car. When she was ill and ran out of food, she did not attend work and could not get to the grocery store. Before she knew it, she lost her job. Eventually, Heather went to the city social services agency for help. The social worker found to his dismay that there were a number of single mothers in Wala who were immobile due to lack of transportation. Heather mentioned that she had asked for free transportation service from the agency for the Wala community a year ago, but did not receive a response. The social worker acted as a facilitator for Heather and the rest of the Wala families. With Heather as the chief spokesperson, the social worker approached his agency and suggested that the Wala community should have bus service at least two times a week to take residents grocery shopping. The agency was already aware of this need and the social worker facilitated bringing about this service, which eased some of the problems that Heather and her community were facing.

Initiator

The initiator, as Kettner, Daley, and Nichols (1985) define it, is the person or persons who call attention to an issue. The issue could be a desire, a problem, or concern in the community, family, group, or organization that could be improved, remedied, or prevented. In some ways, the initiator gets the ball rolling, which involves looking at future problems or enhancing existing services in order to bring about a certain degree of change.

For example, a particular policy in social work agency that prevents workers from seeing clients after 5:00 P.M. is causing problems to prospective clients. This could be pointed out to the agency by a generalist. In a military setting, a generalist initiator begins to discuss gay rights in the military and the problems it causes due to lack of acknowledgment by those in authority.

After pointing out an issue a worker has to take on other roles and other types of issues to work through the problem. Pointing out a problem is only a beginning.

Empowerer

Empowerment can be described as the "process of increasing personal, interpersonal, or political power so that individuals, families and communities can take action to improve their situations" (Gutierrez, 1994, p. 202). Rappaport (1987) described empowerment affectively as that which "suggests both individual determination over one's life as well as democratic participation in the life of one's community, often through mediating structures such as schools, neighborhoods, churches, and other voluntary organizations. Empowerment conveys both a psychological sense of personal control or influence and a concern with actual social influence, political power, and legal rights. It is a multilevel construct applicable to individual citizens as well as organizations and neighborhoods. It suggests the study of people in context" (p. 12).

Inequality and powerlessness cause a number of problems to large groups of people in the United States. Racism, sexism, and ageism all cause problems. When people feel powerless, it can be said that their voice is either too soft or too rancorous and in turn, their frustration leads them to diffidence or excessive demands.

To experience real change, clients should be active participants in the process. The end result of empowerment is achieving power. Empowerment also refers to a state of mind such as feeling worthy and competent or perceiving power and control (Swift & Lewis, 1987). Empowerment implies that diverse clientele can exercise psychological control over personal affairs and, in turn, control over their own environments. Empowerment also hinges on having access to resources: psychological, social, and physical. This implies that people know their choices and have opportunities to select their course among many options.

Hea Wan was an Asian immigrant who had moved to New York from Kansas. Hea Wan had a scholarship for tuition but was not aware of other resources available in the university system. A generalist who was a member of the counseling center referred Hea Wan to different resources available to her, including the International Student Association, medical and counseling services, and a networking league for newcomers. With knowledge of these services Hea Wan felt empowered and moved on to create her own networks.

In helping clients become empowered, workers have to share information and knowledge that are necessary for performing actions. They must develop proficiency in interpersonal skills, which is a necessity of effective practice. Eventually, however, empowerment can become a political process. If the social work empowerer is successful, then the population that is served will demand the types of services that are important for their wellbeing. Helping people to become economically self-sufficient is probably the most significant form of empowerment. In this situation, politicians and other groups of professionals play a role in offering the kind of help that the people need (Lowenberg, 1983).

Researcher, Scholar, Analyst/Evaluator

DuBois and Miley (1996) indicate that "as researchers and scholars, social workers add to social work's base of theory and evaluate practice (with diverse clientele) and program outcomes. These activities link social work practice and theory through knowledge–development strategies" (p. 274).

For social workers, research means building theories, designing different practice strategies, and measuring practice outcomes. The task of the analyst/evaluator involves analyzing or evaluating effectiveness (Yessian & Broskowsky, 1983). An analyst can determine the effectiveness of a program or an entire agency or the help offered to individual clients. Generalists have a broad knowledge base of how different size systems function and can be effective in evaluating agency programs and their own interventions.

Understanding and analyzing can lead to professional scholarship that contributes to the profession's knowledge base. Social workers should integrate research and practice as consumers of research and active researchers. All these different scholarship activities are part of the obligation to contribute to the knowledge base of social work by conducting their own research and sharing their findings with colleagues through publication in professional journals and books.

Fran, a generalist, worked with the homeless population in a crowded city. Based on the different services offered and her evaluation of the effectiveness of these services, she wrote an article. Fran utilized her evaluative skills and contributed to the knowledge base of social work through a written article that was published in a professional social work journal.

As you complete your reading of this chapter, take a few minutes and reflect on the different roles you have read about. Ask yourself, which would be fairly comfortable roles for you to play and which would be uncomfortable. Why?

With practice would you be able to play a variety of roles or would you still prefer to concentrate on just one or two? Is this because you feel more competent playing a particular role, or do you wish to avoid another role? Why? What are your own discomforts? How would you learn to ease into the different roles? Think about your responses and connect them to your understanding and awareness of yourself.

CHAPTER SUMMARY

The beginning practitioner has to develop competency in working with people and be able to deal with clients in the affective, cognitive, behavioral, and ecological domains. The worker should have self-knowledge. This includes good will, recognition and acceptance of one's personal power, a personal style, a willingness to be vulnerable and open, self-worth, self-respect, self-appreciation, and a willingness to risk making mistakes and to admit to having made them, as well as a growth orientation and a sense of humor.

In supervision, the emphasis is on the workers exploring their own feelings with reference to their work and their clientele. In order to work with different clients, the worker should understand his or her own values and assumptions about people.

Generalists play different roles. These are not truly separate and distinct, but overlap in many instances. These roles include the clinical role, marital and family therapist, the group worker, educator, teacher, the role of model and simulator, social work broker, case manager, mediator, advocate, enabler, facilitator, empowerer, researcher, scholar, and analyst/evaluator. Finally, the role of the supervisor is an important one, as well. Supervisors also play the role of middle managers and participate in implementing agency policy and conducting a part of the agency's program along with case consultation and clinical training.

7

THE CLIENT

All the work we do as practitioners involves people and their issues. We work directly with diverse clients or we work toward a cause like better housing or rights of oppressed people for a group or community of people. The essential factor is that we must learn to take the pulse of our clients and help them accordingly. In order to understand our role as generalists, we need to be aware of the different roles that clients take on as individuals, groups, families, organizations, or communities. Our awareness of different client roles can prepare us to be sensitive, empathetic, and caring. At the same time, this awareness should prepare us to become involved in the tasks of helping, strengthening, and empowering our clients to reach the constructive goals that they set for themselves.

The term *client* refers to a person or persons who receives professional services from a generalist practitioner. The term *client* may also refer to a multiperson system (Johnson, 1997), such as a family, a small group, an organization, or a community, all of which are constantly influenced by environmental factors. Germain and Gitterman

(1996) further describe the client as an involved system that participates through shared focus and direction and supports a difference-sensitive, empowering, and ethical approach.

This chapter addresses the following topics: the client, the rights of clients, confidentiality, privileged communication and privacy, the right to informed consent, the client as an individual, the family, the group, the community and the organization. Also discussed are important client factors such as motivation, experiences, behaviors and emotions, the complexity of clients' feelings, client resistance to painful feelings, sociocultural factors, and mastery and competence.

Our work as generalist practitioners involves serving a diverse group of clients who need our help. We may help an individual child or adult cope with the loss of a loved one, or we may help an oppressed group of clients organize to obtain better housing, medical care, or child care. Our roles will be different in each situation; however, the essence of our role is the same. We learn to feel the pulse of our clients and work with them accordingly.

Clients assume various roles when we work with them. Just as our roles change in each setting or situation, the roles of clients also change. For example, a client experiencing a painful loss may assume a dependent role with a practitioner, whereas a group of clients who already know their goals may want to assume roles as our working partners. Regardless, all clients expect our understanding and our commitment to their well-being and self-determination.

Clients may come to us on a voluntary or involuntary basis. There are clients who seek help voluntarily for problems connected to normal phases in development—adolescence, parenthood, retirement, and other life transitions. This group includes clients who receive professional services for family problems such as divorce, marital conflicts, and parent–child and other relationship problems. Clients may also receive service when they become involved in crises beyond their control such as natural disasters, illness, death, and accidents. Voluntary clients seek professional services because they wish to work on their own issues.

Involuntary clients are referred by courts, by school systems, or by other organizations concerned about behavioral or social situations that may be a threat to the physical and emotional health and safety of the clients or others in the community. It is not unusual for involuntary clients to express vehemently their displeasure and frustration at having to attend the practice sessions. Sometimes this expression is direct while at other times it is evident in a generally passive, uncooperative attitude. After they have expressed their anger, clients may be ready to participate in working on their issues if they feel that the worker is understanding and accepting. With involuntary clients, there is an obligation for social workers to "provide information about the nature and extent of services, and of the extent of the clientele's rights to refuse service" (NASW, 1995).

There are other clients who are not easily classified as voluntary or involuntary. These clients include people whose spouses threaten divorce unless they agree to counseling, or whose employers threaten termination unless they do something about their problem, such as alcohol abuse or other drug-related issues. Often, these clients begin their sessions with displeasure but many eventually appreciate the clinical sessions and change their own behaviors.

Another type of client is the larger systems, such as communities and organizations. Issues for these groups can involve advocacy or social action with populations-at-risk, as well as organizational change.

Clients who ask for professional help generally have mixed feelings. All of us would like our problems to go away, but do we really want to change our attitudes and our behaviors? Will we receive the kind of professional services we are looking forward to or will it be different? How comfortable or painful would it be to receive help? How well will the generalist understand our problems? Will the practitioner be helpful or will sessions create additional problems? What kind of professional services does a particular agency offer? All these are valid questions that clients ask themselves or practitioners.

Being a client often entails discussing psychological, social, financial, and other life issues and losses. At times, problems are compounded because some clients feel that the worker is in a superior position and they are in a subordinate role. This is the reality in many agency situations.

Just as generalist social workers need to develop knowledge about themselves and their personalities, they also need to understand different client systems and the issues they bring to the professional relationship. This requires understanding the client's lifestyle as an individual, a family, a group, a community, or an organization, as well as their values and moral codes, and how much information these systems are willing to share with the generalist. Understanding the client's background, family, and cultural factors is essential in providing services. The generalist understands clients through their social history, including psychological and social factors such as education and work experiences, as well as concerns, needs, and problems. The practitioner must identify collaboratively with the clients in relation to the strengths and limitations in their situation.

A client's diversity arises from the expectations of the cultural group as well as relationships within the dominant society. Communication patterns and coping capacities are important factors in understanding individual attitudes and behaviors. Diversity in different size systems includes ethnic and racial factors plus age, gender, physical factors, religious affiliation, and sexual preferences.

Most client groups come with a degree of expectation. It is important to start with the presenting problems of clients. The worker's exploration needs to be selective, always focusing on the problem-solving objective. When clients see the relevance of a particular line of inquiry, they are more likely to share information than if questions seem irrelevant. Clients' willingness to share information is in itself a dynamic variable that depends on many factors including the development of the worker–client relationship (which is discussed in Chapter 9). A client who is reticent at one point, may be quite open at another. Also, the worker's active listening and following the client's lead may be more productive than asking a lot of questions.

Ophelia grew up with traditional family values. At fifteen, she found herself in New York City with her mother after her father deserted them. Before long, Ophelia was drinking on the sly and going out with boys. Much to her shock, after her first sexual experience Ophelia discovered she was pregnant. Belonging to a strict Catholic family did not help. Ophelia was too afraid to confide in her mother and she was also petrified about having an abortion. So she became extremely depressed and eventually attempted suicide. Ophelia's mother found her in time and rushed her to the hospital. The mother was horrified when she found that Ophelia was almost five months pregnant. They were referred for prenatal medical care and for counseling. The mother cried, heartbreakingly, "She has forgotten our ways already!" In this simple statement, the mother revealed the history, culture, and religion of her people, which are extremely important factors in working with different types of people. Active listening by the practitioner gave her a great deal of information about the client.

THE RIGHTS OF CLIENTS

Chapter 2 discussed values, confidentiality, privileged communication, and privacy of clients. This section briefly addresses an important aspect of the helping process—the rights of clients.

All clients have rights. Often clients feel helpless and will accept unquestioningly whatever the practitioner says or does. Because an atmosphere of unconditional acceptance is created in the helping process, clients may have an exaggerated confidence in the generalist. Therefore, it is important for the practitioner not only to protect clients rights but also to make them aware of these rights. In addition, clients are our partners in the professional process and therefore need to be made aware of their responsibilities and helped to develop a healthy sense of self and personal power. Informed consent as well as ethical and legal issues are important in the helping process. All clients should receive sufficient and adequate information to make informed choices about entering and continuing the client–practitioner relationship and receiving professional services. When we make clients aware of their own responsibilities, we also help them to develop a healthy sense of self and personal power.

On the other hand, involuntary clients attend sessions with generalists because it is mandatory, and they may refuse to participate in the helping process. Such clients can sometimes be persuaded to participate in sessions, but if they are adamant the generalist has no alternative but to respect their wishes.

THE RIGHT TO INFORMED CONSENT

Clients will benefit by knowing about ways they can make informed choices. Although all professionals seemingly agree on the ethical principle that it is crucial to provide clients with information about the client–practitioner relationship, in practice there is very little consensus about how much or what can be revealed (Goodyear & Sennett, 1984; Monkman, 1991). Frequently, agencies utilize standardized consent forms that use language that can be difficult for clients to understand. Rose (1995) goes further and specifies that clients should be informed about the major procedures of an intervention plan and their approval for implementing the plan should be solicited even when they do not suggest the interventions to be used.

Clients should not be overwhelmed with too much information nor should they be given too little information. Clients give consent more easily when matters are explained to them clearly and carefully (Badding, 1989). Informed consent should be seen as ongoing, particularly in the beginning stages of the helping process. As information becomes more easily available and as plans are tried out by generalist and client, those plans that are found to be inadequate can be revised or even eliminated and new plans can be substituted.

Professionals have a responsibility to their clients to make reasonable disclosure of all significant facts, including the nature of the procedure and the probable consequences and difficulties present in the helping process. Bray, Shepherd, and Hays (1985) also specify two types of liability that practitioners face while working with clients: negligence and malpractice. Practitioners who wish to deviate from the standard professional practice, must inform their clients ahead of time; failure to inform clients is considered negligent practice and a breach of contract. If you guarantee clients certain cures and do not accomplish them, there is a likelihood that you will be sued.

According to Bray et al., (1985), there are three elements in informed consent: capacity, comprehension of information, and voluntariness. Capacity is the client's ability to make rational decisions. If the client is a child, then a parent or guardian is responsible for giving consent. Comprehension of information means that the practitioner must give clients information in a clear manner and observe to determine if the information is understood. Voluntariness means allowing the clients to assert free choice in making decisions.

Corey, Corey, and Callahan (1988) indicate that at the outset of the helping process clients need some answers to their questions, including:

What are the goals of the helping process for specific client systems?

What are the different types of services that the generalist will provide for the client?

What are the generalist's expectations of the clientele?

Should these expectations be clearly specified to the clientele?

What does the generalist think are the risks and benefits expected from the helping process?

Who is the provider of services?

What is the estimated duration of professional services?

Is all information confidential, or is there a limitation to confidentiality?

When should the generalist make mandatory reporting of problems, if at all?

Handelsman, Kemper, Kesson-Craig, McLain, and Johnsrud (1986) and Doel & Lawson (1986) point out that there has been a great deal of writing in the helping professions on the subject of informed consent for treatment. However, the meaning of consent in written agreements has dealt primarily with the financial arrangements of professional services rather than specific goals for client groups, which of course leaves the clients at a disadvantage.

There are other factors that the client needs to be aware of, such as the professional background and education of the practitioner. Costs involved should be discussed at the beginning of the helping process. The estimated length of time required should be discussed. If the practitioner discusses the progress of the clients with a supervisor, it is best to inform the clients that the practitioner will be consulting about their situation with other professionals. This type of information should be mentioned right in the beginning of the process, so that professional services are seen as a process with clear parameters.

Clients also have rights of access to their files consistent with the consumer rights movement that has impacted the health, counseling, rehabilitation, and education fields. Clients, particularly individuals, families, and groups, also have a right to know if they have been given a diagnostic classification. Most clients do not know that they are being labeled or that the labels and other confidential material will be given to insurance companies for third-party reimbursement, so it is best to get their consent. It is important to have maximum openness with clients about all procedures so that they can be active and informed consumers.

Another important issue is the tape recording or videotaping of sessions. There are more and more agencies that require the recording of interviews for training and supervisory purposes. Clients need to be informed of this procedure before they start their initial session. They need to know why the recordings are made and who will have access to them. Clients' written consent to the recording of sessions should be obtained. Also, if the clients wish to hear or see a recorded session of themselves, they should be allowed to do so.

Clients need to be informed about the alternatives available to them if they choose not to use a particular practitioner or specific setting for professional services. Some of the alternatives are individual self-help programs designed for personal-effectiveness training, peer self-help groups, crisis-intervention systems, psychological and psychiatric helping systems, and other institutional helping.

Twenty-two-year-old Patricia, from a middle-class immigrant family, is in clinical sessions in a family agency. She has limited financial resources to pay for her own sessions. Because Patricia is severely depressed, the generalist informs her that she will require at least one and a half to two years of professional help before she can feel really healthy. Patricia is surprised, because she does not have the money for two years of weekly sessions and because two years seems too long. Patricia looks hesitant. The generalist impatiently tells her that if she is not interested in investing that amount of time, she should find another practitioner. How would you handle this situation?

A caring and ethical generalist first makes a careful evaluation of the client and then discusses fees, including alternatives that would be helpful to the client. The generalist has an ethical and professional obligation to give clients a rationale for clinical sessions lasting two years. If clients are not satisfied, the practitioner should help them explore alternative approaches to receiving help, rather than abruptly informing them that the generalist will not continue sessions.

Involuntary clients are mandated to see a social worker often through the court system based on an evaluation by mental health professionals. Treatments may be imposed on clients who have run afoul of the law or to keep them out of conflict to protect other individuals. The generalist plays a role in safeguarding the rights of such clients. They, too, should be made aware of the right to informed consent and given all the information necessary to make reasonable and intelligent decisions regarding their right to accept or refuse treatment, and the treatment options available. They should be clearly informed of the potential benefits and risks of different types of treatment. Despite limited freedom they still have a few choices.

Persons-in-Situation

When dealing with clients in practice, practitioners should pay attention to the interplay between intrapersonal, interpersonal, and environmental systems (Germain & Gitterman, 1996). There is always relatedness and interconnectedness between people and their environment, be it home, school, workplace, or neighborhood. For instance, when forty-year-old Ronald has a problem with his boss, he takes it home with him by being irritable and angry with his wife and teenage children. His youngest son who has faced the brunt of his father's anger feels that his father dislikes him.

Each client brings to the helping situation a unique set of qualities that play a part in the outcomes of the interaction. Much of practitioners' work with clients is based on constructs which suggest that the past life experiences of clients have an impact on the way they experience, react to, and cope with problems. However, when making an assessment of clients, social workers, like other helping professionals, tend to focus on identifying weaknesses and pathology. In many ways, this practice has led to excessive labeling and an overfocus on intrapersonal factors rather than psychosocial or socioenvironmental factors in the understanding of human problems.

Today, this is changing. Generalist practitioners balance their work by looking at clients' potentials and resources, by viewing them as "persons in situation" (see Figure 7.1). This simply means that practioners consider their clients' personal strengths and capacities while offering services. Highlighting clients' strengths makes them feel that they are still worthy (Graber & Nice, 1991; Wolin & Wolin, 1993). Clients who have been constantly mistreated may not even know that they have strengths. They may have learned to view situations negatively because of their family or situational history. For example, the nonoffending parent of a sexually abused child, who was sexually abused as a child, may not know how to protect the child. In this situation we see the intergenerational impact of sexual abuse.

THE CLIENT AS A UNIT OF ATTENTION

Many complexities permeate the way agencies and communities view clients. Clients can be classified in the following categories: (1) clients who seek help for themselves, appropriately; (2) those who seek help for another person(s); (3) those who do not seek help but are in some way blocking or threatening the social functioning of another person(s); (4) those who seek or use help as a means to reach their own goals or ends as required by the system; and (5) those who seek help inappropriately (Johnson, 1995). Figure 7.2 depicts clients and the unit of attention they bring to the helping process.

Irrespective of the different classifications of clients, we need to remember that different size systems ask for and receive different types of professional services. Regardless of the type of help or the size of the system, it is important to emphasize that we always deal with *people*. The generalist needs to have some basic skills in working with different types of people in diverse settings.

When clients start to speak, the worker listens to the clients' account of their concerns and their life history. The worker observes and experiences the clients' style of verbal and nonverbal communication. While observing, the worker notes the

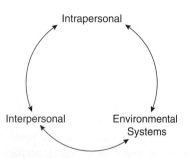

Figure 7.1 **Persons-in-Situation**

Figure 7.2 **Unit of Attention**

clients' ability to tell their story and the affect with which it is presented. The generalist pays attention to the clients' orientation to time, place, and persons and also to their perceptions of different life events as clues about the clients' sense of reality. Distortions of reality could be due to prolonged stress and trauma (Baradell & Klien, 1993). Usually clients can identify their own issues and concerns. Clients may discuss interpersonal situations such as problems with a spouse or a child or symptoms such as anxiety, depression, and sleeplessness.

To better understand clients, Reid (1997) suggests the following questions about clients and their presenting problem:

What is the problem?

How long have the clients had the problem and how have they tried to deal with it in the past?

Why are they coming for help now?

How do they feel about their problem and what are the resources that they may use in order to deal with it.

What is the clients' degree of motivation?

Fifty-year-old Harris is a deeply depressed man who has been in and out of clinical sessions for the past seven years. One spring morning seven years ago, he surprised his wife by coming home unexpectedly and finding her in bed with her lover. He beat her up and she left him permanently for her lover. Harris never recovered. Every spring he goes into depression and is unable to work. He takes his vacation sometime during this period and spends the time in outpatient care which includes psychotherapy. Although his ability to cope and adapt has increased in terms of his office functioning, his personal life has been almost nonexistent. He seeks professional help only during this period and "recovers" enough to function as spring turns to summer. In this case, the client's issues center around the unresolved problems with his wife. How would you as a beginning generalist get to the essence of the problem?

Harris is depressed; depression is anger turned inward. He did not work through his anger when his wife left him, resulting in his inability to express his pain and hurt. These factors will need to be dealt with before anything can be resolved about his seasonal depression cycles.

THE FAMILY AND THE GROUP— THE MULTICLIENT SYSTEM

The Family

The family can be described as a multiclient system. The worker must understand not only the members of one subsystem, such as the husband–wife unit, but also other subsystems in the family. In turn, the family as a whole is a subsystem of the larger structure of society. At the same time, it must also be a structure complete in itself.

For example, when we look at a family that consists of grandmother, father, mother, and two children, we see all these people together as forming a family system (Goldenberg & Goldenberg, 2000). Within this family system there are myriad smaller combinations of people who function from time to time as separate subsystems within the larger structure, at the same time maintaining a life of their own. For example, a special dinner party may involve the three adults of the unit, while a one-on-one basketball game involves only father and son.

Family structures include not only the relationships within the system but also the rules and regulations that control and maintain the family. Added to the family structure are family communications through which process rules and regulations are implemented. In working with families, generalists understand problems and dysfunctions emanating from family communication patterns as the source of the intrapsychic problems of any one individual. Individual symptoms are seen as reflections of stress arising within a larger family system or other social system. Such stress may be caused by the family's inability to negotiate a developmental passage or to weather a nondevelopmental crisis (Okun & Rappaport, 1980; Worden, 1999).

Seventeen-year-old Anu, a daughter of an upper-class Asian immigrant family, went to a prep school. Her classmates talked about their boyfriends and the intense competition involved in going out with the best-looking boy. Anu's parents were conservative and believed in arranged marriages and did not allow their daughter to date. With her good looks, Anu attracted a number of good-looking boys. Though reluctant, Anu started to date without her parents' permission due to peer pressure. This caused a great deal of conflict in Anu's family because her parents were unable to negotiate a developmental passage with their daughter.

The family as a system influences the functioning of its different members. It is the primary system responsible for satisfying the needs of the individual. Problems may arise within the family system when the needs of individual members cannot be met or when problems in individual functioning cannot be solved. In order to bring about change in a troubled family system, it is important to understand the family as a whole. Positive changes in the family as a whole will affect all individuals in the family (Atwood, 1999). A family social history is necessary for understanding the family as a system. The generalist assesses the family's motivation, capacities, and opportunities for change in order to suggest realistic goals and objectives. For instance, in the case of Anu, if the parents compromise, accommodate, and begin to accept the behavior of American teenage dating as part of a rite of passage, then their problems with their teenage daughter could be resolved without too many conflicts.

Some of the accepted or traditional ways of working with the family include identifying necessary information from the family such as names, language spoken in the family, occupation, religion, race, and ethnic group and cultural background. Viewing the family as a system demands understanding the functioning of the family. The practitioner looks at the family with regard to cohesiveness, which includes maintenance of positive feelings, dependable family boundaries, and relatedness to different family members. The concept of cohesiveness also involves the quality of connectedness and separateness among family members, the specification of family rules and norms, and the emotional climate of the family (Brown & Christensen, 1998). Present living conditions, socioeconomic status, and the family's

relationship to the community and the neighborhood are also essential factors. The family's communication patterns and decision-making patterns are important as well. Role performance in terms of parenting and child-care practices, parents' encouragement of support systems, and growth among family members reveals to the worker the family's customary coping mechanisms. Significant events in the life of the family and the normative developmental stages of family life challenge the family's adaptive strengths (Carlson, Sperry, & Lewis, 1997).

Membership in a particular family system may or may not be limited to members of the nuclear family. At times, extended family members such as a grandmother or unrelated individuals such as boyfriends or girlfriends may be significant participants in family interaction. In other cases, a parent or a child may be out of the home or deceased but remain a part of the family's psychological field. Even pets may be an important part of the family constellation. The picture becomes even more complex when we factor in, as we must, relationships stemming from divorces and remarriages.

In order to understand a family fully, it is helpful to utilize a family genogram. A family genogram is a format for drawing a family tree that presents information about family members and their relationships for at least three generations (McGoldrick & Gerson, 1985). A genogram charts births, deaths, marriages, and divorces over several generations to understand the family's cultural background or mix of cultural backgrounds. All these factors contribute to our better understanding of the family.

A generalist needs to find answers to a number of questions: Why has the family come for help? What are the individual needs of the different family members? What are the strengths as well as the weaknesses in the family system? What are the needs of the parental and marital subsystem and how well is it fulfilling its responsibilities? What are the problems that affect this subsystem? What are the family's expectations in receiving services? What is the family's capacity to cope, adapt, and change? Does the family now have or can it access resources to support change?

The ability to adapt to change is a crucial aspect of family functioning. Most changes in families are inevitable and are due to natural developmental changes such as the birth of a child, a child going to school, a child leaving home as an adult (the empty nest stage), and the death of a spouse. While changes are inevitable, the manner in which different families adjust or adapt to them varies a great deal (Munichin and Nichols, 1993).

Andrea was an only child. Much against Andrea's wishes, her mother married a twice-divorced man who had a number of children. All the children lived with their natural mother and he visited them occasionally. Andrea, who was twelve, dreaded him. There was no apparent reason for her behavior because he appeared to be friendly and caring toward her. However, when her mother worked night shifts as a nurse, Andrea was forced into a sexual relationship with her stepfather. Though angry and repulsed by her stepfather, Andrea would not tell her mother about the abuse for fear of hurting her and of breaking up her marriage. Eventually when guilt and anger got the better of Andrea, she complained to her school counselor who reported the situation to the county child protection authorities. The stepfather was immediately removed from the house. A thorough examination of the family history revealed that the stepfather's family had a history of intergenerational incest and that the stepfather was a childhood incest victim, only to become the villain in his stepdaughter's life.

Further examination also revealed that the family's communication patterns were constricted. Anything that caused pain was not discussed. If there were problems in the family, either in terms of marital or parental problems, they were swept under the rug. The history and culture of the family revealed factors that had been a problem for a long time. The parents were advised to go to marital counseling or couple therapy. The father was mandatorily placed in a group for perpetrators of incest. The group discussions helped him to understand his role as a member of a family where this had happened before and who unwittingly had created the same situation in his present family. Also, Andrea was in counseling individually and jointly with her mother. Hopefully, when the time is right the stepfather will join sessions in a three-directional effort to help them work through a number of other family problems.

Groups

Group work is often discussed with regard to direct practice with client groups. But the concepts and issues addressed in client groups are also pertinent to work with organizational and community groups (Schopler & Galinsky, 1995). Most practitioners are involved in some sort of group work. Generalists may facilitate treatment groups, support groups, educational groups, social goals groups, work groups, or recreational groups. Social workers may serve as leaders or members of multidisciplinary teams, task forces, and committees. They may consult with community action groups, self-help groups, or advocacy groups.

Group work can be described as essential and ubiquitous. It takes many forms so that theories, skills, and values important to group practice are applied to all arenas of social work, from services to individuals and families to the planning, development, and management of human services. Group work is characterized by its breadth—it spans numerous purposes and populations, as well as practice settings, practitioner roles, and practice approaches (Schopler & Galinsky, 1995). As in family work, work with groups entails viewing both the group as a whole and its individual members as clients.

As Garvin (1997) indicates, groups provide the means to achieve social goals in a community context as well as a method to encourage individual growth and change in educational or rehabilitative contexts. The following section explores helping groups.

According to Schwartz (1961) and Gitterman and Shulman (1985/1986), groups are an enterprise in mutual aid and an alliance of individuals who need each other in varying degrees to work at some of their common problems. The central factor in a helping group is that members need each other. The practitioner's role includes organizing the group, screening clients for appropriateness, and facilitating the mutual aid process. This creates not one but many helping relationships for each person who receives and gives help. This *mutual process* fosters a common bond, over and above specific tasks for which the group was formed. Some groups come together and develop as mutual aid systems without outside help. In other situations, a professional skilled in guiding group interaction may be needed to create conditions for mutual aid. Along with the general self-awareness required of all social workers, group leaders need to be especially conscious of their own feelings and behavior tendencies in group situations. Social workers leading a group must know if they are talkative or quiet, anxious or secure, cooperative or competitive.

There are many advantages to mutual aid including the sharing of experience among group members who come from different backgrounds. Group members have different life experiences and bring different information, views, and values to share, which enriches the group as a whole (Zastrow, 1997). For instance, in a group of working, single mothers, members may have different and unique problems. They will also have experiences that are similar. They can learn from each other about child care, jobs, available housing, and money management.

An effective group climate is created when members feel free to communicate. As members communicate, information becomes synthesized. Although members might present differing points of view, the group as a whole will arrive at its own conclusions. Confrontation or conflict between group members is inevitable in any group (or family) in which there is honest sharing of opinions and feelings. Such conflicts may be a threat to the group's survival, but if the issues are dealt with openly and if there is a reservoir of good feeling, the group and its members may resolve their conflicts and, in the process, achieve a higher level of functioning and more positive group feelings (Jacobs, Masson, & Harvill, 1998).

Sometimes being part of a group also means developing the ability to discuss embarrassing topics such as sex, anger, authority, and dependency. Often, a group culture is created to help clients challenge some of their own taboos. The belief that there is strength in numbers is true. As group members continue their work, their level of comfort with the taboo topic decreases. First one member takes a risk, then another. Stronger members encourage the more reluctant and frightened members to participate in positive work. Eventually all the members benefit, and the level of anxiety is considerably reduced.

Another important benefit that can be achieved in groups is the relief and support experienced when members discover that feelings or experiences which they consider shameful are shared by other members. For instance, when one member of a group of sexually abused children is embarrassed about a family background of sexual abuse, it quickly becomes clear that the other children are in the same boat. Thus, the guilt, anger, and shame that has been experienced in a isolated situation by the individual becomes a matter for sharing and caring. For group members, hearing about the similar experiences of others in the group contributes to their self-understanding. When the group culture supports the open expression of feelings, the capacity of members to empathize with each other is increased. As group members share common concerns, they are often able to understand and care about their own and each other's concerns. Over time, group members expand their abilities to understand feelings expressed in words, facial expressions, and physical postures and thereby open themselves to richer, more genuine postures in social interactions.

Here is an entry from the journal of a member of a self-help group:

> I sometimes think as a recovering addict that I'm different from so-called "normal people" in that I'm too emotional. After being in the group, I realized that "I'm ok, you're ok," and even though my past experiences or my socio-economic level may be different, we came together where feelings were involved. The group was a real healing time for me. (Reid, 1991, p. 278)

When a member enters a group with a number of unresolved issues, the group members usually attempt to help the member, based upon their own life experiences in relation to the needs of the troubled group member. For instance, when a self-esteem group met for the fifth time, one of its members mentioned and then talked intensely about her totally negative relationship with her mother who constantly put her down because she always kept a messy apartment. While some members helped her to deal with her mother in a different way, others who were also mothers and who had been viewed negatively by their daughters started to explain a mother's perspective. Thus the problem took on a new perspective and the group member was able to deal with her issues constructively.

Organizations and Client Roles

Organizations such as social service agencies, health care organizations, educational facilities, industrial settings, and correctional facilities can be viewed in terms of their dependency on environment, enforced openness, and mapping of the environment (Martin & O'Connor, 1989). Although many social organizations are formal, they depend on their environments for support (Pillari & Newsome, 1998). Social welfare organizations do not have tight control over their settings and therefore function in enforced openness, an environment which provides the agency its legitimacy. The quality of its relationship to the outside affects the organization's well-being; therefore, social welfare agencies interact closely with environmental needs and resources.

Organizations that are in tune with their goals create a distinct culture. An organization's culture can be described as "the set of values, guiding beliefs, understandings, and ways of thinking that is shared by members of an organization and is taught to new members as correct" (Daft, 1992, p. 217). Social services organizations are made up of people who utilize their skills and resources to perform tasks and produce services that are deemed useful by systems of authority. Employees of the organization are responsible for implementing the organization's goals (Ilgen & Klein, 1988).

Organizational generalist roles include work with formal employee groups, interdisciplinary task forces, task-oriented groups, community service clubs, and self-help groups. Functions, structures, roles, patterns of decision making, and styles of interaction are factors that influence the process of change in organizations. In working with organizations, it is important to understand the dynamics of formal groups. Skills are also required in organizational planning, decision making, and conflict negotiation (Dubois & Miley, 1996). The positive factors that organizational generalist practitioners promote are conflict resolution, learning to work with others, developing win-win outcomes, and team building.

Social services organizations in particular have a number of problems of which generalists need to be aware, and despite which they must be able to facilitate solutions. Today's global society, expanding population, and shrinking resources usually means producing quality services with a limited staff while avoiding undue stress. Often goals must be changed to fit available resources. Other important organizational demands include accountability for the number of clients seen by a professional, measurement of client outcomes, and the influence of agency policies including written and unwritten rules.

Accountability is an essential aspect of the work of welfare agencies (see Chapter 4). Barker (1995) describes accountability as the state of being answerable to the community, to consumers of a product or service, or to supervisory groups such as a board of directors. Secondly, it is an obligation of a profession to reveal clearly what its functions and methods are and to provide assurances to clients that its practitioners meet specific standards of competence.

It is difficult to measure the effectiveness of our interventions with clients. For instance, when working with battered women in a shelter and teaching them parent management techniques over an eight-week period, how would one measure success at the end of the intervention? Can their success be measured? Should the women take a test in parenting techniques to demonstrate that they have acquired them? Should a follow-up test be done at some later time? If so, how much time should elapse before a follow-up? Should the parents and children be tested?

Success in changing human behavior is relative and difficult to measure. Evaluating a whole agency or program is more difficult. Holland and Petchers (1987) indicate that "service content must . . . be made clear, with uniform definitions describing program activities. For consequences to be attributed to an activity, it is necessary to state exactly what a client has received from a given treatment or service and to determine whether that content has remained consistent over the course of intervention" (p. 213).

All social welfare organizations have policies, rules, regulations, and procedures that employees must learn and follow. These guide the behaviors of workers and clients. For instance, an agency policy may be that social workers must sign out whenever they leave the agency, an effective form of accountability for supervisors, administrators, and clients. Other important factors that come into play include agency policy and individual professional judgment. A generalist practitioner has to think in terms of autonomy and accountability at the same time. These options depend on your discretion as a professional.

Besides agency policies there are rules and regulations that need to be followed. Written rules are found in personnel handbooks and the by-laws of an agency. Unwritten rules are passed by word of mouth from more experienced long-term employees to new employees. Sometimes there are unspoken agreements about what can and cannot be said or done.

Jackson was told that he had to be at the staff meeting at 9:00 A.M. Jackson was there on time. No one else was in sight, So he sat down and waited. It was about 9:15 before people started to trickle in, leisurely carrying their coffee mugs and chitchatting with each other. Wisely, Jackson refrained from making any comments but observed their unwritten rules and ways of communication. His bservations of group members' communication style helped Jackson learn to fit in as a member of the organization.

Generally, all social work agencies follow the ethics of professional practice. In order to offer effective help, all problems should be handled within the context of the agency and its culture. Most social agencies use the NASW *Code of Ethics* (1996) as the standard for ethical behaviors.

Communities

The term *community* means different things to different people in different contexts. "Communities have multiple meanings, including sociopolitical connotations. Some communities have official boundaries, such as political subdivisions, school districts, and church parishes. And some communities are based on shared interests and values" (Pillari & Newsome, 1997, p. 175). For example, social workers can call themselves a professional community, and a university is called a community of scholars. Informal and small communities may convey a mood of warmth and togetherness, or restrictions and exclusiveness. It has been said that the world can be viewed as a global community or a global village, because technology has made communication among countries and cultures much easier.

Burghardt (1982) and Homan (1999) emphasize that social work practitioners must acknowledge the basic philosophical underpinnings needed for community change efforts. Burghardt believes that people in communities are basically decent and given genuine alternatives will respond to them with trust and authenticity. In community social work practice, we work with people, not for them. People should accept ownership of their problems and work to help themselves (Freire, 1972, Lewis, Lewis, & D'Andrea, 1998). The manner in which we plan to help should be established together with the community members. "We should base our strategies on some sound objective that corresponds to the actual conditions and perceptions of people's lives" (Burghardt, 1982, p. 12). In other words, what the community asks for and desires is where we start.

Community members are partners with social work generalists in working on their problems. Work with communities and neighborhoods involves collaboration for social change. In the past, social workers attempted to reform people who were oppressed, disenfranchised, or powerless. Today, it is obvious that positive social action requires a new approach; that is, working in partnership with those who are oppressed and disfranchised.

The participation of citizens is necessary for constructive decisions to be made about issues that touch their lives. This is true not only because it is democratic, but also because it is synergistic to community members' and practitioners' efforts to promote social justice and social change. When community members work together toward change in one area of their community, other aspects of the community are affected positively, such as cleaning up parks leading to a reduction in crime. Because of the transactional nature of change, changes at one level of the community tend to affect all other levels of the community system. The process of working together stimulates creative change.

Generally, members of a community do not need outsiders to talk to them about their concerns. They are aware of their problems but what they can do about them is another question. Often, the answer revolves around resources, time, energy, and leadership. If a community is in poverty and caught up with bread-and-butter issues on a daily basis they may let other problems slip, although the concerns never really disappear. In other circumstances, they may become accustomed to a problem out of helplessness. However, if there is adequate community leadership and a sufficient number of concerned people in the community they can rally together to change situations. What we need to understand as generalists is that a community of people is a very powerful group and when their energies are focused they can perform a number of constructive actions for themselves (Lewis et al., 1998).

Sometimes the generalist can help mobilize the community members for constructive action, provided there is a good working alliance between practitioner and community leaders.

A neighborhood near the Crestview Country Club in Wichita, Kansas, is an exclusive community with large tree-lined roads and a golf course. One resident stated "you think you are so safe because we are kind of tucked back in here. We feel a little more secure..." (*Wichita Eagle*, August 7, 1998, p. 11a). She felt this way until her home was broken into by burglars who took all that they could, including her jewelry and her fireproof safe with some treasured photos. This was followed by a number of burglaries in the same area over a number of days.

The community members contacted the Sedgwick County Sheriff and, with his help, quickly mobilized to develop a neighborhood "block watch." With the help of the sheriff (a social worker), the natural leaders in the community got word to neighbors to turn on their outside lights at night as well as their alarms and to keep an eye out for anything suspicious. Soon they got the local police and neighbors involved in patrolling their area (*Wichita Eagle*, Friday, August, 7, 1998, p. 11a).

In this example, the community members together had the strength to bring about positive change.

Generally community members attempt to resolve varying community problems in three ways (Fisher, 1984). First, they may take their problems to the power structure in their own community, which is done in a consensual, gradual way that focuses on service delivery. For example, tax money can be used for health and recreational programs in a crowded community.

Second, community members may focus directly on conflicts and challenges present in a community. For example, a tenant organization may be formed to spruce up buildings through negotiations with the owners of the property. Third, community members may combine their own peer system with the legal and political structures to obtain a specific objective; for instance, to improve property values and maintain neighborhoods.

As a generalist you could work with community members in all or any of the three different levels. The important factor is that by using basic skills, one can enable and empower community members resolve community problems together.

CLIENTS' MOTIVATION

Whether they are members of families, communities, organizations or are representing themselves as individuals, clients bring with them their own unique personalities. To bring about change, clients need to be motivated. What is motivation? As Johnson (1995) describes it, motivation is influenced by what a person wants and how much a person wants it. Unless a client wants to work on a problem, it is difficult to offer him or her any help. Factors that influence motivation are the push of discomfort, the hope that things could be better, and the natural tendency in people to grow and to overcome anxiety.

Clients' motivation and attitudes are important factors that contribute to the outcome of their therapeutic work. Some clients are not ready to use the worker's help and therefore find fault with the worker's positive efforts. Others may be positively motivated and have positive views about coping with their problems.

Forty-year-old Manuel, an independent businessman, reluctantly accompanied his wife, Sally, to visit the generalist practitioner in a family agency setting. Throughout the session, he was very quiet and answered questions in monosyllables. After two such sessions, the worker confronted him about his attitude. He looked at her and complained that every hour he was away from his work he lost money and he also did not see the need for him to be in clinical sessions. He viewed the problem as his wife's, although Sally's original reason for being in the sessions was because he rarely communicated with her at home and was always preoccupied with making money.

At this point, Sally interrupted and attacked Manuel, saying that he did not have any time for her. Later she mentioned that she would like to leave him and get her own life together. She wished to go back to school and

get her degree so that she could also spend her time more usefully. Manuel started to perspire and stopped talking altogether. The session ended in discomfort.

When the next meeting was being set up, Manuel commented that he wished to attend the sessions. He said that he did not want a divorce and would like to set matters right between him and his wife. Manuel's motivation was based on fear. He explained that he loved his wife and did not wish to lose her under any condition. Two sessions later, the situation changed. Manuel and wife were ready participants willing to discuss their issues, compromise, and accommodate each other. The practitioner encouraged both of them to discuss their life goals and dreams. As each of them talked about their goals, there was a great deal of compatibility, though Sally's higher education aspirations continued to scare Manuel. With great discomfort he mentioned that he had taken his wife for granted and wanted to do everything to make a better life for them. He realized the more he and his wife communicated, the more powerful their partnership as a couple become. As Manuel continued to attend sessions, he accepted Sally's educational aspirations, he and Sally developed a more positive attitude and a greater willingness to work on family issues.

Thirteen-year-old Esther came reluctantly for sessions with her mother. She did not wish to participate and thought poorly of what she called "any type of shrink." Esther commented that she did not have any problems. However, as her mother described the tension she was causing in the family by her reluctance to accept her mother's new husband, Esther got irritated and complained that she did not care about what her mother said. She was tired of them, both her mother and her new stepfather. At this point the mother, who was feeling vulnerable about her new marriage, started to cry. She said that she felt caught between her husband and her child. Apparently, Esther did not realize the amount of pain she was causing her mother. She looked surprised and confused, pushed her chair close to her mother and also started to cry, saying that she had never seen her mother cry. She mumbled, "I'm sorry." Then she looked at the mother and added, "I will come for the sessions with you and . . . him. I know . . . I know I am having problems too." This acknowledgment of the family situation was an important beginning. More than her own situation, the seriousness of the family situation and her mother's pain became the initial motivation that prodded her to attend the sessions.

Fifty-year-old Chuck was court-ordered to be in a group session for perpetrators, because he had sexually abused his granddaughter. He looked at the generalist who was conducting the session and commented with sadness that the abuse had happened only because his wife had not had sex with him for over five years. After this specific comment he sat back, complacently. Somehow, for him this seemed to be a sufficient reason for the abuse. He was not motivated to look at his behavior, but blamed his wife for his behavior.

In one of the sessions, the members of the group accused him of avoiding responsibility for his sexual abuse of his young grandchild. After a few defensive statements, Chuck became silent. In the next session, for the first time in weeks, Chuck gave the impression that he wished to work at the problem of thinking of himself as a molester and not as a man who had been sexually "wronged" by his wife. The fact that other members in the group had experienced similar feelings but were moving towards positive changes in their own lives helped him to become motivated, feel hope, and begin work on his problem.

A community of homeless people lives in a city park. The city government is attempting to "clean up" the park. A generalist who works in a nearby shelter addresses the homeless people in the park, telling them about the temporary shelter and the available resources. The homeless people are not interested and talk about temporarily "disappearing" from the park but returning after a few weeks. The generalist explains to them that the area will be patrolled to prevent homeless people from returning to the park. They are still not motivated to discuss the shelter.

The generalist observes that the most talkative person is the natural leader of the group and attempts to impress on him the necessity to leave the park and go to the shelter rather than wander away with winter just around the corner. After a discussion with the generalist about the temporary shelter, the natural leader is motivated to talk to the rest of the homeless people. Based on their discussions with the natural leader most of them prepare to go to the temporary shelter.

These four cases reveal how motivation can come from different sources and how motivation should be reinforced to help people work at problems. This occurs when clients reveal their genuine concerns about themselves and significant others.

Another factor that affects clients' motivation is the availability of opportunity in the clients' immediate environment. Opportunity can be described as the energy, time, knowledge, and capacity that clients discover in working on their problem. Opportunity also refers to the availability of resources and services that are needed for problem solving and for change (Johnson, 1995). What are their support systems? How conducive will a resource be in helping clients rework, adjust, accommodate, cope, and adapt to their life situation?

Whenever clients present themselves to a practitioner, they almost always experience some degree of *stress*. Wingate (1972) and Reid and Popple (1992) view stress as any influence that disturbs the natural equilibrium of the body including physical injury, exposure, deprivation, and all kinds of diseases and emotional problems. Distress and strain are commonly used in conjunction with the word *stress* and they share the same sources. Stress develops when a group of conditions prove to be demanding and challenging and the person responds with different types of behaviors (Beehr & McGrath, 1996). Costa, Somerfield, and McCrae (1996) indicate that the hallmark of stress is emotional arousal. Barker (1995) describes stress as any influence that interferes with the normal functioning of an organism and produces some internal strain or tension. He indicates that human psychological stress refers to environmental demands or internal conflicts that produce anxiety (p. 367). The *Webster's New Universal Unabridged Dictionary* (1996) describes stress as physical, mental, or emotional strain or tension. Strain is the exertion that is necessary in order to meet the demand, injury, or change that results from such exertion. *Fatigue* is another word that is commonly used in the same context as stress and is defined as weariness after exhaustion or a long strain. Implicit in these definitions is a model of stress as a constraining force that acts on a person who is attempting to cope with internal or external adversity (Cox, 1979).

Stress is a natural part of being a client. People do not seek professional help unless they are excessively stressed by some situation in their lives. Becoming a client may actually increase stress temporarily. Stress is so much a part of being a client that the experienced worker should assume its presence, and through active listening and verbal following assess the stress level of the client. This will enable the worker to make constructive and helpful responses to the client. Clients need to know they can trust the worker and to what degree the worker can be helpful to them. Usually, clients meet with a social worker only after having made considerable effort to cope with a situation, solve a problem, or meet a need. The worker can expect to hear about these failed attempts. By listening carefully the worker can identify coping strengths in the client and work with them accordingly.

WORK WITH DIFFERENT TYPES OF PROBLEMS

Work with diverse clientele is a *process*. We speak of content and process as intertwined aspects of a problem. Process means what actually goes on between worker and clients: engaging the client, developing a relationship, active listening, responding to verbal and nonverbal cues, evaluating, planning, and working toward goals, and termination. Through contacts with clients, the worker becomes aware of resources that could be made available to them. A great deal of attention is paid to the needs of clients and to their situations, which always include the fit between different environments and different personalities. Concern and understanding by the worker allows clients to share their life experiences.

The capacity, or strengths, of clients fall into two categories: (1) types of coping and adapting mechanisms that the clients use, and (2) their problem-solving strategies. Depending on their habitual patterns of problem solving, clients under stress may restabilize easily, slowly, or only with outside support.

When Mindy was faced with problems on the job, she did not deal with them at the workplace but brought them

home and took them out on her spouse and children. She displaced her angry feelings for her boss to her family and became impatient with her husband and children. This had painful repercussions for her fourteen-year-old daughter, Kelly, who felt unheard and overlooked. Kelly became angry with her mother and withdrew from family activities. Crisis occurred when her parents found out that Kelly had become pregnant, which exacerbated all the other problems that had not been resolved. The family became disorganized and reached a state of disequilibrium. Although there had been chronic disorder in the family due to the mother's problems, Kelly's normal, developmental transition from childhood to adolescence became a crisis and she needed outside help.

At this point they went to a generalist social worker. The clients were experiencing high levels of stress and needed appropriate responses to their concerns. The worker tried to find out about their coping and adapting capacities and their problem-solving strategies. How would the adults and Kelly deal with the pregnancy? What were the options open to them and what type of problem-solving strategies would they use. Based on their own efforts at problem solving, the worker offered useful suggestions to address the various needs of the immediate situation as well as other ways in which the family could be helped.

THE COMPLEXITY OF CLIENT FEELINGS

Experiences

When we deal with clients, we are also dealing with their experiences, behaviors, and emotions. The following section deals with varying ways in which clients present themselves and the different emotions they express or do not express as they engage with practitioners. Examples of case situations are presented to illustrate the complexity of emotions at play. Individuals, families, groups, communities, and organizations are an integral part of society that all display emotions. As generalists, we need to be aware that problem situations carry feelings, thoughts, and sensations, as well as actions that we need to understand in order to be effective. For instance, when a client indicates that he had a bad day, he may also be saying that he had some bad experiences that affected his actions as well as his emotions. This is a simple example but reveals that "a bad day" involves multiple issues—events, emotions, and behaviors that all affect people, their daily routine, and their life that day.

In terms of experiences, as Egan (1998), Okun (1997), and Long (1996) indicate, some clients spend a great deal of their time talking about what happens to them. For example, a client says "My boyfriend treats me badly"; when asked to elaborate, she adds, "I also get headaches when I am ill-treated." Similar statements from clients include: "When my husband goes out of town, he never calls me. He does not care about my feelings"; "My boss yells at me"; "My coworkers do not talk to me"; and "Nothing effective can be done in this agency." These are clients who see themselves as *victims* and talk about their experiences in terms of how they are affected. While constantly talking about what people do to them, such clients are discussing their experiences but not dealing with their own responsibilities for working at issues. If clients present feelings of being a victim, the practitioner may find the clients will feel victimized by the intervention of the practitioner, thus repeating a long-standing pattern. When the timing is right, the generalist has to confront the attitude of the clients as well as highlight their strengths.

Behaviors

Change happens in people not only by thinking through the issues identified in treatment, but also by practicing new behaviors. The ability to utilize new understanding to develop more appropriate, effective, and more satisfying behavior patterns counts more than insight. Insight is developing an awareness and recognition of one's problem, and the awareness of aberrant behaviors (Amador et al., 1994, Cuesta & Peralta, 1994). Insight can be helpful and used behaviorally.

Negative behavior leads to further negative experiences.

A client, Dick, says, "My wife and children are unhappy. My wife fights with me all the time since I lost my job again."

WORKER: Have you been looking for another job?

DICK: I have stopped looking for a job because there are none in this town.

WORKER: So who provides for your family?

DICK: My wife does. But when she yells and screams at me, I get tired of her and go out and drink with the boys. Later after a few days I go looking for a job. . . . Jobs are hard to come by, you know. . . . My wife continues to yell at me constantly and I work through my frustration by drinking, which gets her more mad . . . but I can't help drinking, anymore.

Dick's behavior is the result of his experiences. However, in sessions, he and his wife could work together at developing positive behaviors that might aid in their constructive growth.

Affect

Affect refers to emotion and feelings that lead, accompany, underlie, or give color to clients' experiences and behaviors (Egan, 1998; Okun, 1997). People have different ways of expressing their emotions. Some verbalize them and others do not. Clients who are depressed may tell you that they feel depressed but may not be able to identify what makes them depressed. Others may not talk about depression but are stoic in covering up their feelings until circumstances force them to burst out verbally and express very intense depressed emotions. This sometimes takes the form of a suicide attempt and suicide gestures.

In session, Ray says: I screamed and yelled at my mother for nothing and I feel ashamed of myself now.

WORKER: What made you do so?

RAY: She makes me mad. When she sees my Dad's girlfriend, she always starts to cry and I am tired. He left us a long time ago. I am ashamed that I get mad at her, but I always do when she cries about my dad and his girlfriend. I don't like it either but I don't make a big deal about it like my mother does.

Ray is *implying* that he has control over his emotions unlike his mother who cannot help but cry when she sees her ex-husband with his girlfriend. But, in reality, what was Ray really experiencing? Perhaps his mother's tears were a reminder of his own anger and pain.

In the helping process it is essential to help clients get beyond their disabling feelings and emotions. Clients can be helped to control their emotions. Of course, this cannot be done immediately or directly. Controlling emotions happens indirectly when clients actively refrain from dwelling on disabling thoughts. On the other hand, there are clients who need to learn how to express their emotions in conversation as a way of enriching their interactions with others. Practitioners need to have knowledge and skills to help clients deal with their emotions and also manage the affective aspects of their lives. (Luborsky, McLellan, Woody, O'Brien, & Auerbach, 1985). Emotions should be focused and balanced in the context of experiences and behaviors (Egan, 1998; Westra, 1996), in tune with the self, environment, and culture of a family and place. This is in line with the two general goals of the helping process: (1) to help clients accept responsibility for their actions, and (2) to help them exercise some control over their feelings and thoughts.

Some clients avoid their own emotions. Unless the worker helps the client to focus inward, these feelings will not come up in sessions. Some clients will talk endlessly about their emotions without any change resulting. This often happens when the practitioner does not address the importance of goals as well the importance of feelings. However, if a practitioner acknowledges a client's current affect and assists the client to explore it further, an emotional unfolding should follow.

Sadness, Anger, and Shame

According to Teyber (1992) and Donigian and Hulse-Killacky (1999) a triad of interrelated feelings repeat throughout the client's life and can be easily identified especially when clients are presenting problems. Clients who present problems may experience the first affective constellation of sadness, anger, and shame. The predominant feel-

ings are those of anger. The client's anger is often a reactive feeling to an original set of primary feelings of sadness, hurt, and vulnerability.

Dawn, who while growing up was physically abused by her father, later married a man who abused her. At present, Dawn is upset and hurt that her husband has left her for a younger woman. She covers her hurt and sadness with anger. Feeling angry is easier for Dawn than the sadness and hurt she has denied.

When a practitioner responds to the client's anger in the following manner, it may lead to uncovering other emotions as well: "After you have expressed how angry you are with your husband, tell me how you are feeling now." This is the "open window" (Teyber, 1992) to the original feelings of hurt or sadness. With such questioning and correct timing, clients will reveal their feelings of hurt and sadness and vulnerability. As clients begin to experience the original feelings of sadness or hurt within the safety of the practitioner's session, they may then come into contact with the internal aspect of the conflict—anxiety and guilt. Often, it is easier and safer for clients to be angry than to show the vulnerability and sadness that, if it can be tolerated, could begin to move them toward resolution of their issues. If such feelings cannot be tolerated, clients will continue to be angry. But if the worker persists in the helping process and gently prods them to unfold, a third aversive set of feelings may be aroused: shame, anxiety, and guilt. If as a generalist you inquire why your client Dawn is resisting, Dawn might respond: "If I let the pain in, or let it be there, then it's admitting that he [her husband] really hurt me." If you are successful as a practitioner in helping Dawn experience some of the original pain, then a deeper set of stronger feelings such as jealousy, rage, shame, and humiliation may be expressed. Dawn may say that if she starts to show her hurt and sadness, other people will "go away" or "there will be nobody for me and I will feel alone and empty."

For many clients there are frequent anger outbursts which are defenses against unexpressed sadness that, in turn, can be associated with shame, guilt, and anxiety. However, significant and enduring changes can result when clients express, experience, and then contain each feeling in this triad of feelings.

As Teyber (1992) and Corey, Corey, Callahan, and Russell (1992) suggest, clients resolve their internal conflicts when they: (1) let themselves fully experience and express each feeling; (2) express or share the feeling with a practitioner so that they know they are no longer hiding it; and (3) contain, hold, or tolerate the feeling rather than push it away. When clients begin to integrate feelings in this manner, they have begun to master their conflicts. After this process, clients begin to take on new, more adaptive responses that they could not incorporate previously.

Once the practitioner was able to elicit Dawn's pain and hurt, she started to make a significant change. Dawn had put herself in the victim's role because the direct expression of her anger and her own needs was unacceptable to others in her family. After she had reexperienced her pain and expressed her feelings, Dawn began to claim her feelings as her own as well as develop her personal power. In subsequent sessions Dawn showed and shared the good news about moving away from the destructive relationship she had with her former husband. She indicated that she was giving herself time to heal and grow.

Dawn's guilt caused her to be ambivalent toward her abusive partner. But as the worker helped Dawn examine all her feelings, she helped Dawn to relinquish her earlier victim role.

The practitioner's responsibility is to respond effectively to the feelings that clients are experiencing and to provide a safe, nurturing, and realistic environment within which they can experience difficult feelings safely, so as to reduce their negative effects by greater understanding and supportive containment.

Clients' Resistance to Painful Feelings

When clients are resistant and unable to deal with their issues, the worker can skirt the issues and deal with clients superficially or talk to clients in ways that would be useful. Some clients feel resistant while dealing with feelings that threaten them. Instead of pushing clients to present those feelings, the worker can help clients clarify their defense against them. The generalist worker should understand why the resistance was once necessary. Practioners can ask questions such as: "We don't have to talk about your feelings, but what do you think would happen if we did? If you started to cry in front of me, what might go on between us that would not feel good to you?" (Teyber, 1992, p. 34).

Sometimes clients will tell you that they just do not want to experience painful feelings. It is important to remember that when painful feelings are expressed in sessions, some of the chronic depression and other symptoms may begin to lift. This expression may be too threatening to clients if it means breaking family taboos and rules.

Yolanda told her therapist, "Now that I have told you my fears and I have really cried, I am afraid to go back to visit my parents, because when we go back home, even now after two years of living away from home, we cannot express feelings and we can never cry in front of anyone."

Interpersonal themes from the family of origin are inextricably woven into the client's situation. Clarifying them is necessary and important in freeing clients to experience and share the feelings that have been conflicted and covered up for a long period of time.

The practitioners should work to provide clients with a nurturing environment. When clients express central feelings of pain they usually expect the practitioner to respond to them in the same problematic ways they have been exposed to in the past. But when the practitioner provides a nurturing environment, then the client's feelings can be expressed. Before a child can develop the capacity to manage feelings on his or her own, someone has to provide the nurturing environment. This does not happen in families where the child's sadness cannot be heard or supported. Such is often the case in families where the child arouses the parents' own sadness or guilt or makes the parents feel inadequate. When such parents do not respond, the child is left feeling emotionally alone, confused, alienated, or ashamed of his or her own feelings. The child will then devise ways to deny or avoid these painful feelings. When clients present such feelings, the practitioner should help the client accept and tolerate these feelings (Pillari, 1991). The practitioner should not become overwhelmed or threatened, and should not move away from the client lest the client feel worse for revealing his or her feelings. The practitioner should have a commitment to the client.

Clients do improve when the worker provides an effective nurturing environment that helps them deal with their painful feelings. A corrective emotional experience occurs when the client's pain is not denied, minimized, or otherwise shied away from. Clients are sometimes afraid that the practitioner, like their family and parents in particular, may be overwhelmed, hurt, or burdened, or will have to go away and somehow be impaired by the intensity or unacceptability of their feelings (Teyber, 1992; Worthington, 1989). The clinician must therefore provide a corrective emotional experience by accepting the client's feelings, connecting emotionally to the client, and not being injured, burdened, or overwhelmed by the client's feelings. In such an atmosphere, clients find a supportive context for expressing their feelings and the generalist responds with kindness and understanding to their emotions, thus helping clients feel more powerful about themselves and begin to change.

Inertia

Some individuals, families, and groups, as well as communities, request professional service at the same time they appear inert. Inertia means that a body stays at rest unless something happens to make it move. When clients do not act on their own behalf or seem reluctant to act, then they are suffering from inertia. Egan (1998) and Greenberg and Safran (1989) note that different feelings accompany inertia including passivity, learned

helplessness, self put-downs, vicious circles, and disorganization.

> A group of teenage pregnant girls all in their second or third pregnancies were listening to a talk on family planning and contraceptives. However, when the group leader tried to convince them to use contraceptives because of the advantages to them, the girls responded with apathy. One of them said, "My boyfriend doesn't like to use the condom and I forget to use the pill." She shrugged off the whole discussion in a few seconds. The rest of the group members looked disinterested, giggled, and did not seem to be affected by their status and the problems they would face if proper precautions were not taken.

Passivity

Maslow (1968) and others believe that people use only a small fraction of human potential in taking on the challenges and problems in living. Schiff (1975) discussed four types of passivity:

1. Doing nothing and not responding to problems and options. For example, Brandon says, "Edna tells me that I should do something about my problems, but I have so many and I am getting used to them."
2. Overadapting by accepting in an uncritical manner goals and solutions that are suggested by other people. Thirty-year-old Brandon is depressed and relates that although his wife is unfaithful to him, he has accepted this as a way of life. Problems at the office require all his energy, where he is constantly told that his energies should be focused on work and that his family is secondary.
3. Engaging in random and agitated behaviors or acting aimlessly. Brandon mentions that once he became particularly upset when he found a condom blatantly sitting on the bed after he returned from the office. He got mad, threw things around the room, and broke a window, but then returned to his passive behavior as if nothing had happened.
4. Becoming incapacitated or violent, shutting up or blowing up. After a period of time, Bran-

don became incapacitated and impotent in his relationship with his wife. Although her extramarital affairs became more overt, he remained uninvolved and acted uninformed.

Learned Helplessness

Seligman (1975) and Rothschild (1999) have described "learned helplessness" and the manner in which it is related to depression. Clients learn from a young age that they do not have control over certain life situations and come to accept helplessness as a way of life. Some become depressed and deny their problems. When people feel sad, inadequate, or vulnerable, others are sympathetic and may expect less from them. As a consequence, these people learn that being depressed has a secondary gain—being taken care of by well-meaning others. Others who are less severely impaired may feel minimally helpless and depressed and go to a worker for help. Simons and Aigner (1985) have used the term "learned resourcefulness" to describe clients' learning to challenge their own helplessness.

Corky became physically handicapped due to a crippling car accident. She was a capable computer programmer but spent her life talking about her helplessness. She found her friends and the members of her family catered to her. Her practitioner made Corky aware of her control over other aspects of her life and of her power and ability to pursue her life goals with the many resources available to her. The practitioner particularly highlighted Corky's computer skills. As she redeveloped work skills, Corky found her feelings of helplessness disappear.

Another form of helplessness is self put-downs. Ellis and Dryden (1987) and Grieger and Boyd (1980) have noted that people often get into the habit of talking negatively to themselves and thus keep themselves passive, saying things such as: "I am stupid and cannot do it"; "I cannot cope with life problems, there is so much to do"; or "Nothing works for me; not even this."

Self put-downs are among the most negative things that practitioners experience in working with clients. Typically clients who practice self put-downs come into sessions because someone else wants them to get help. They spend hour after hour in sessions being part of a self-defeating conversation that keeps them from moving ahead.

Vicious Circles

Pyszcznski and Greenberg (1987) have studied another theory about self-defeating behaviors. At times, people are enthusiastic and energetic and have high ambitions. But if their actions fail to get them what they want, they can lose their sense of self-worth and go around in vicious circles of guilt and depression. Still another variation is staying disorganized. Ferguson (1987) and Gunderson (1999) put it succinctly when they say that many times we saddle ourselves with little problems and irritations that distract us from what we are doing in our jobs or our personal lives. In this way we set up our lives to ensure a level of disorganization that allows us to continue to think of ourselves as inadequate. Driscoll (1984) observes that inertia is a form of control. In some cases, when we tell our clients that they should be in control of their lives, the reality is that they already are, albeit in a disorganized manner. As practitioners we need to make them aware that staying disorganized is a way of control. "Action is the antithesis of inertia." According to Ferguson (1987) practitioners need to build in actions as part of the helping process from the first day that clients ask for professional help.

Frustration Tolerance in Clients

Clients have varying levels of frustration tolerance. Tolerance is an altered physiological state that is brought about by continuous use of a specific form of behavior, such as abuse or use of drugs, that leaves the person with a less reactive behavior to that type of treatment (Vaillant, 1999). Levels of tolerance for frustration and, more importantly, coping with frustration should be assessed for all clients. It is important to remember that clients may tolerate a great deal of frustration and hurt at home but will not do the same in a formalized group.

John was sexually abused by his father and later by his male lover. Eventually, he joined an assertiveness group where men who had been battered were learning to become self-assertive. Group discussions brought out different reactions from the members. John appeared to have a high level of tolerance because he experienced constant verbal put-downs at home. When other group members questioned him on his lack of anger or assertiveness at home, he stood up and told the group members that he had had enough and wanted to leave the group. He lamented that he would never learn how to be assertive and did not want to be a member of the group. Although his frustration tolerance appeared high, he was unable to tolerate the frustrations of the group and was simply withdrawing. Eventually, with consistent group support and self-questioning, John learned to become assertive and less tolerant of the verbal abuse he received at home and established a dependable level of tolerance in the group.

COPING CAPABILITIES AND ADAPTIVE MECHANISMS IN CLIENTS

Coping mechanisms are a person's way of organizing and responding to his or her experiences. For example, how does a person respond to short-term discomfort? Can he or she postpone gratification? Does the person have a sense of basic trust? Does the person think positively? (Reid, 1998).

Coping is a stabilizing factor that can help persons maintain psychosocial adaptation during stressful periods (see Figure 7.3). It encompasses cognitive and behavioral efforts to reduce or eliminate stressful conditions and associated emotional distress (Lazarus & Folkman, 1984; Moos & Schaefer, 1993). Coping refers to the different efforts that people make to maintain positive feelings in the face of internal and external stressors. Some stressors precipitate an internal struggle or a trial and focus energy toward a goal (Mechanic, 1974; Murphy, 1974; White, 1974). Thus, techni-

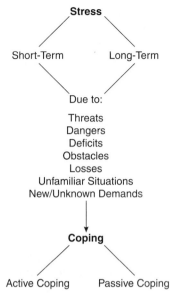

Figure 7.3   **Stress and Coping**

cally, coping is a set of responses an individual presents with reference to threats, dangers, defeats, obstacles, losses, unfamiliar situations, and new and unknown demands from other people and situations in the environment.

Clients can cope when they have the capacity to identify and understand their problems and to use both emotional support and concrete community resources to solve the problems. Coping is adaptive human behavior. Adaptive coping enables people to bring reason to bear on their problems and to deal with unhealthy interpersonal experiences to achieve some meaning and comfort in their lives. It is when people are unable to cope well that they turn to a practitioner for help (Perlman, 1975).

Coping styles vary among clients. For instance, some people deal with their life problems actively, whereas others do so passively. An active, fairly well-adjusted person may be willing to deal with his or her problems directly; a passive person may avoid them. An active person may be energetic and enthusiastic, but may have difficulty with impulse control. A more passive person may be reflective, but have difficulty in making decisions and taking action. Weiner (1986) and Kohn (1996) indicate that the best coping mechanisms are those that implement responsible action.

Clients visit a practitioner when they are unable to cope without help. Their problems vary; some are acute and time-limited, while others may be long-standing and intractable. Some stem from disturbed or negative thinking, some from stressful human relationships, and still others from lack of access to resources in the environment. Most often, clients' problems and their causes are multiple and complex.

Sociocultural Factors

We live in a multicultural society. Clients come for help with expectations that reflect their cultural origins. Lum (1986) and Ivey and Ivey (1999) indicate that when a worker interviews a member of a minority group, the worker has to make an assumption that this person is competent, adequate, different but not automatically deficient, retarded, or maladjusted because he or she cannot speak standard English or behaves differently. Although it appears as though the obvious is being stated, social workers are aware that this could become a factor in working with clients.

Sookja was a Vietnamese refugee who found her way to the social services agency due a large number of hardships, including the fact that she did not speak standard English. The social worker, eager to perform well at her new job, was not thrilled with Sookja. When she spoke, Sookja did not immediately understand her. This was in part because the worker spoke too fast. The worker raised her voice, as if she could not hear Sookja. But the issue was not a hearing problem, rather a language difficulty. This, in turn, intimidated Sookja, who stopped attempting to talk and merely started to shake or nod her head in response to the worker. The new worker muttered under her breath that the client was taking too much time and became impatient. The interview process left Sookja devalued and misunderstood and the new worker feeling like a failure.

As a new worker how could you handle this situation? Observing, asking questions, listening attentively are beginning skills in understanding differences.

Minority clients function within the social environment and an ethnic context that includes unique cultural internalized values, beliefs, and attitudes. Under stress, such clients may draw on ethnic coping mechanisms. It is helpful when workers are able to reach an understanding of the client's ethnic context and to discover these factors. Making an assessment of such clients necessitates learning the client's beliefs, affective expressions, and culturally unique patterns of social interaction.

If a worker has not experienced close relationships with people of different ethnic groups, the worker must first learn sensitivity. Workers who have been successful with clients of different ethnic groups are open-minded, open-hearted, concerned, and willing to be flexible in their approach. Nonverbal communication of acceptance and concern by the worker is "sensed" by clients despite the worker's other cultural limitations.

Forty-year-old Marianna is an African American single parent. Her son had been placed in a residential setting due to behavioral problems and Marianna had been labeled as "unfit" because she had neglected her child. Marianna had been in and out of practice sessions for self-evaluation with the hope that she would be allowed to take her son home. She was constantly told she had not made sufficient improvement and did not have her act together. Ruby, the new worker, had already read Marianna's file when she saw her for the first interview. Marianna walked in angry and irritable and asked the worker if she was going to "get into my head" as her other workers had done. Ruby sensed the client's hostility and, therefore, decided to talk about more concrete things that would help Marianna see her as a caring worker. Ruby talked about the knitting that Marianna had in her hands. "You must like to knit. I do too." was the first icebreaker. They talked about Marianna's apartment, where Marianna mentioned she had knitted a sweater for her son. The interview session was focused on concrete positive information aimed at building the self-esteem of the client. For the first time Marianna communicated like she was talking to another human being, rather than a "stuffy" worker who was there to "make judgments on her as a parent." Marianna's comment at the end of the interview, "You are not like the rest, I like talking to you" signaled the beginning of constructive clinical sessions.

Being sensitive to different cultures and utilizing new and innovative ways of working with clients in response to their cultural orientation is an important factor in understanding and working with diverse clients. For instance, Native Americans traditionally prefer noninterference, and a worker would not be successful if they assumed the active role that might be acceptable with white middle-class families (Lewis & Ho, 1975; Okun, Fried, & Okun, 1999).

Mastery and Competence

Mastery and competence refer to a person's capacity and ability to interact successfully with the environment (Porter & Stone, 1996). In order to attain a goal, a person needs to rely on a combination of mechanisms, including cognition, skills, intentional actions, and an ability to deal with feelings. When studying how children cope, Murphy (1974) concluded that the term "I do" is almost always a precondition to the word "I am." What this means simply is that doing, feeling, and experiencing are important to the client's meaningful functioning.

A member of a group, Mary Jeanne, wrote about her feelings for her group: "Today's group meeting was wonderful. In a sense, it helped me tremendously. I risked talking to people as an adult. I realize that in relationships I must take a risk and also be vulnerable... More important to me now than before is to explore my ability to take risks and continue to take them, in and outside of the group."

Clients' motivation and ability to change depends in large part upon their desire. The more clients wish to change, the more able they will be to attend sessions, and talk about themselves, and to consider interpretations that challenge previously held notions.

ASSISTING CLIENTS IN SELF-EXPLORATION

Self-exploration can be described as the elaboration of self-awareness that occurs as clients speak about themselves. Self-exploration provides clients with a sense of discovery and creative thinking that facilitates adaptive change.

Helping clients self-explore requires the worker to provide a dependable, safe place in which to do it. New generalists may ask too many questions in the initial sessions, perhaps because they feel too strong a need to help clients and are uncomfortable with silence. To help in client self-exploration the worker should avoid giving advice. However, giving information that the client requires is different from giving advice (Cormier & Cormier, 1998). Providing useful information may help the client to work through the decision-making process. To help in the client's self-exploration, the worker should avoid premature problem solving because it deprives the client of the satisfaction of exploring (Egan, 1998). Clients ultimately bear the responsibility for change and, therefore, offering quick solutions may be pushing clients into decisions that they are not ready to make. With regard to problem solving, workers should find out how the clients define their problems and how they have tried to solve them in the past.

A worker should also avoid asking questions repeatedly. Too many questions interrupt the natural unfolding of a client's thoughts and feelings. The worker should listen carefully to what the client says. How clients view the world is illuminated by the their choice of words. Language provides clues to where the client is coming from (Bandler & Grinder; 1975; Sedney et al., 1990). For example, if a mother refers several times to her son's refusal to "obey" her, it may suggest that she is an overly authoritarian parent. Listening is healing because it helps clients tell their stories in their own fashion. Clients' messages represent stories about themselves and narratives about their histories and current experiences from which clients construct their identities and infuse their lives with meaning and purpose (White & Epston, 1990).

The worker should also pay attention to nonverbal cues and messages such as smiles, the tone of voice, and body language. One way of helping a client to explore is to point out discrepancies between nonverbal and verbal communication; for example, "You say it didn't bother you, but you seem close to tears as you talk about it." Practitioners can help clients become aware of their nonverbal clues, provided they have established a level of trust with the client. Clients can usually learn from an exploration of their nonverbal expressions. For example, one client found out that she smiled to hide her embarrassment about her feelings. This led her to explore how she often hid her painful feelings behind a "happy face."

The worker has to keep the focus on the clients. Many clients have problems talking about themselves. Sometimes, the worker may use self-disclosure to help clients get in touch with their own feelings ("I remember how [scared, angry, depressed] I was when . . ."). Self-involving and self-disclosing may encourage clients to reciprocate sensibly. Self-disclosure on the part of the worker can be effective, but should be done sparingly to avoid taking the focus off the client. All self-disclosure should be appropriate and done only in the best interests of clients and their growth.

Clients will often allude to feelings and thoughts that are vague and intangible. In such cases, it is a good idea to try to help clients express these feelings and thoughts more clearly. When discussing a client's tasks and goals, the worker should help the client to be specific and realistic. A vague statement of goals does not generally lead to concrete actions.

Finally, the worker or client can summarize material for each other. A worker can summarize what happened in an interview session to reinforce certain significant points. When clients summarize, it is a way to check their ideas and their biases about the helping process as well as their current feelings.

EMPOWERMENT OF CLIENTS

It is important to understand that people can achieve empowerment through life experiences. Empowerment processes are multifaceted and multidimensional (Rappaport, 1987). Empower-

ment depends on people's ability to obtain organizational and community resources (Gutierrez, 1990). As DuBois and Miley (1996) note, there are many ways to reach empowerment. The combinations and permutations involve persons, situations, and sociocultural and economic factors. Based on the specific combination, resources and solutions are numerous. However, each circumstance and set of clients or combination of influencing factors is unique and the process that leads to empowerment is highly individualized and non-replicable. Practitioners and clients have to generate solutions that are uniquely fitted to the dynamics of a situation. There are some common ingredients for developing empowerment including focusing on clients' strengths in different situations, working collaboratively with clients, and linking personal and environmental strengths wherever possible to empower clients.

Winter was a single mother who worked hard to make ends meet but she had money problems. Her strengths included being a great cook. For office parties, she would often be requested to make her "special chocolate cookies," which were popular among her peers and friends. Winter's practitioner was aware of the popularity of her cookies, so she suggested that Winter might use her talent and ability to market her cookies by selling them at the office and advertising them in the office bulletin. Winter was pleased with the idea and agreed to try it out. She walked out of the practitioner's office with her head held high.

The next chapter will focus on communication and interviewing skills for working with various clients.

CHAPTER SUMMARY

The term *client* refers to a person or persons who receive professional services from a practitioner, including individuals, families, groups, organizations, or communities. Clients may be voluntary or involuntary.

Professionals have a responsibility to their clients to disclose all significant facts, including the nature of the procedure as well as the consequences and difficulties present in the helping process. Confidentiality, privileged communication, and privacy are part of the client's rights.

The family can be described as a system and the worker must understand not only the members of one subsystem such as husband–wife, but also the other subsystems of the family. The worker needs to be aware of the family structures, the relationship between systems, and the rules and regulations for control and maintenance of the family. In working with groups, the worker's role includes organizing the group, screening clients for appropriateness, and facilitating mutual aid. People in organizations and in communities can also have issues and problems. The client's motivation and attitudes are important factors that contribute to the outcome of helping process.

Clients present a complex of feelings such as sadness, anger, shame, and guilt. Clients may also suffer from inertia, passivity, learned helplessness, and negative vicious circles. The worker needs to be aware of clients' coping and adaptive mechanisms and the manner in which they organize and respond to their life experiences. Practitioners also need to be aware of the different sociocultural, ethnic, and racial factors that influence clients.

8

COMMUNICATION AND INTERVIEWING

In generalist practice work, the manner in which we communicate can build or break or block a helping process. Irrespective of the client system—individual, family, group, community, or organization—we need to utilize effective communication skills. Skills of communication include those where the practitioner observes interactive communication patterns and participates in helping clients build relationships and reach specific goals that they have created.

As generalists, we have to use our communication skills to work with individuals, all of whom have individual personalities with their own strengths and weaknesses. Even when working with larger systems such as organizations and communities, we need to keep in mind that we are still working with individuals who, in effect, are possible targets of change or facilitators in the change process. Thus we can work effectively with different systems by varying the manner in which we apply our skills to a single individual.

COMMUNICATION

This chapter focuses on communication and interviewing skills that are necessary for all generalists. Generalist practitioners use communication skills that involve perceiving nonverbal messages (affective and behavioral content), hearing verbal messages (cognitive and affective content), and responding to both kinds of messages. It is necessary to be conscious of personal communication patterns as these are critical to being an effective communicator and interviewer. Often we take our communication style and behavior for granted and have no awareness of how we are perceived by others. One interesting way to develop this awareness is to watch ourselves conducting interviews, either actual or role-played, on videotape.

Communication theory concepts, which include encoding, transmitting, decoding, and noise, provide a framework within which we can begin to understand communication in social work situations. *Encoding* refers to the process of putting a message in symbol form so that it is ready to be transmitted. *Transmitting* is the process of sending the encoded message; *decoding* is the process of interpreting the stimuli that are received. *Noise* refers to extraneous material that interferes with and distorts the message that is being sent from the transmitter to the receiver (Compton & Galaway, 1999). *Feedback* provides a way of overcoming the problems created by noise and by inadequate coding or faulty reception and transmission (Brown, 1973).

The worker is talking to thirteen-year-old Tom.

> **WORKER:**   You said that you got into a fight with your father and he abused you. How did he hurt you physically?
>
> **TOM:**   No, he did not beat me. He used abusive language as he always does.
>
> **WORKER:**   So your problem is that, as you mentioned earlier, you do not have a good relationship with your father because he is verbally abusive to you. Is that right?
>
> **TOM:**   Yes, it's horrible but it's true. He abuses me badly.

Communication can be described as a two-way process (Long, 1996). Listening is one part of the process and talking is the other. Listening, as we all know, is more difficult. For instance, you cannot listen to a two-hour lecture without your mind wandering off to some other thoughts.

Listening is a prerequisite for all communication, as well as interviewing strategies and responses. When a worker does not listen, the client is likely to be discouraged from self-exploring, and the wrong problem may be discussed or an inappropriate strategy of helping may be used. The client may not pursue receiving help due to the attitude of the generalist.

Listening involves three processes: receiving a message, processing a message, and sending a message (see Figure 8.1). All clients send out verbal and nonverbal messages that are stimuli to be received and processed by the generalist. Processing, like reception of information, goes on in the worker's mind and is not visible to the outside world, except possibly from the worker's nonverbal cues. Processing is important because a worker's cognition, self-talk, and mental (covert) preparation and visualization set the stage for overt responding (Ivey, Gluckstern, & Ivey, 1993). Errors creep in and messages are not processed accurately when the worker's biases and blind spots prevent acknowledging parts of a message or interpreting a message without distortion (Nichols, 1995). At times, generalists may hear what they wish to hear, rather than the actual message that is sent.

> **WORKER, CHEERFULLY:**   Good morning, Allison, how are you this morning?
>
> **ALLISON:**   A little depressed, not so good.
>
> **WORKER:**   I love the color combination in your dress. You look wonderful. How is your son doing?

Note how the worker completely overlooked the client's concerns.

The third process of listening involves the verbal and nonverbal messages sent by a generalist. At times a worker may receive a message correctly but may have difficulty in sending out appropriate responses. It is important to listen and plan messages carefully before responding (Ivey, 1994).

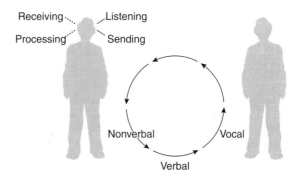

Communication Process

Figure 8.1   **Communication Processing**

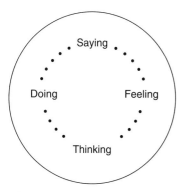

Figure 8.2 **Total Communication**

Lack of synchrony when two people are communicating indicates that there is an absence of listening behavior on the part of both people involved (Connor-Greene, 1993).

Before proceeding to verbal and nonverbal communication, it is essential to understand the term *total communication*. Total communication means that one completely understands what another person is saying, doing, thinking, and feeling, something which in reality is almost impossible (see Figure 8.2). How can practitioners communicate to clients about what is constructive and useful? This purpose requires approximate clarity and understanding. As Bloom (1978) noted, "Communication to clients ought to be simple, clear, accurate, and direct. Social workers should choose words that are precise and cannot be misunderstood, words that are not evasive and vague" (p. 585). The various levels at which practitioners communicate with clients involve verbal and nonverbal communication, including body language and social and emotional ways of understanding and relating to people.

STARTING COMMUNICATION

In communicating with different types of clients, our language should be attentive and communicative to the clients. Egan (1994) classified worker–client communication using the acronym SOLER.

S means that the generalist must adopt a body posture *squarely* facing the client. Adopting such a posture indicates involvement. When a generalist is physically distracted, the body orientation conveys the message of noninvolvement to the client.

O means the worker should also adopt an *open* posture. An open posture is seen as a nondefensive position. An open posture also communicates an openness and availability to the client. In the initial stages the generalist should not sit with arms crossed over the chest all the time or constantly frown and look at one's watch. These are signs of less involvement and unavailability to others.

L stands for *leaning* forward in order to be involved with a client. Leaning forward implies a natural inclination toward involvement. A slight bend and move toward another person says nonverbally, "I am with you, I'm interested in you and in what you have to say." Sometimes it is better to just lean forward and begin with body flexibility and responsiveness that enhance your communication with clients.

E stands for good *eye* contact. Sheafor, Horejsi, and Horejsi (1997) highlight eye contact as a very powerful means of communication. Eyes reveal much about our emotional state; as such they are called the "windows of the soul." When a person does not maintain eye contact, he or she is considered insincere or uninterested in the topic of discussion. Maintaining direct eye contact says to a client, "I am with you, I want to hear what you have to say." Again this does not mean that you have to stare at the client all the time; it simply means that the principle is not violated when a person looks away occasionally.

In North American cultures, steady eye contact generally is not unnatural for two people in deep communication. Direct eye contact can convey different meaning to different people. When two people are in deep conversation, they demonstrate a considerable amount of direct eye contact. However, staring at a person or glaring is seen as rudeness or anger. It is important that we have an awareness of cultural differences. For example, in some ethnic groups such as Native Americans when a person does not make eye contact with an older person, it is seen as a sign of respect.

R stands for another important factor: being *relaxed* while dealing with a client. This relaxation involves two things: (1) not fidgeting nervously or engaging in distracting facial expressions, and (2) being comfortable with your own body so that it becomes a vehicle of contact and expression.

A crucial factor in the helping process is how a worker responds to a client. The SOLER framework should be seen as guidelines and not the only way to deal with clients. It is important to remember that communication patterns have to be adapted to special circumstances, as one practitioner notes:

> I remember a client in [X] agency, a fifteen-year-old boy who was very tense and guarded in the office. However, he became quite verbal when we were going some place in the car and I wasn't really paying attention to him. After that, I found other opportunities to take him outside my office and pretend not to be paying attention (Pillari, 1991).

NONVERBAL COMMUNICATION

Nonverbal communication involves an awareness of the cues and messages that a worker and a client are constantly sending back and forth in a relationship. There are some behaviors that cause clients a great deal of nervousness and anxiety. It is important to reflect on them to discover your biases and weaknesses. What cues are you sending to a client? What are your reactions and how would you communicate appropriate messages? For instance, when a client makes you angry, how do you respond?

Another nonverbal expression that is important when working with clients is the smile. Smiles are associated with being pleasant. Tight lips reveal tension and stress, and quivering of the lower lip implies anxiety and sadness. Facial expressions

convey basic emotions and are the most essential stimuli in interaction because they are the primary communicator of emotional information.

It is also necessary to develop an awareness of body postures and movements that do not have specific social meaning but are learned and culture-specific. For instance, nodding the head while listening is culturally learned. Body movements are not produced randomly, and they seem to be linked to human speech.

A high degree of human communication is nonverbal. Nonverbal communication is the foundation on which human relationships are built. Some anthropologists believe that more than two-thirds of any communication is transmitted on a nonverbal level (Hall, 1969; Mischel, 1973). We send 50 percent of our communication by facial expressions. Facial expressions such as smiles, frowns, nods, and also lip quivering and blushing send messages to the observer. A client may read approval or disapproval from the manner in which the practitioner looks at the client.

Pausing while speaking and maintaining silences in a conversation are part of linguistics or any meaningful units of speech. Paralinguistic cues pertain to how a message is delivered even though, occasionally, these vocal cues represent what is verbally expressed as well. Vocal cues are important because they convey data about clients' social, physical, and emotional states. Remember too that voice levels vary from culture to culture. Sue and Sue (1990) indicate that Americans generally have louder voice levels than people of other cultures.

Pauses and silences are part of effective communication. There are two different types of pauses: filled and unfilled pauses. *Filled pauses* involve some form of phonation such as "uh," as well as stutters or slips of tongue (Knapp & Hall, 1992). Clients make more slips of the tongue when they are anxious or uncomfortable.

Unfilled pauses are periods of silence. Usually, unfilled pauses occur when a person needs time to interpret a message and make a decision about how to respond. An unfilled pause may be started by the practitioner or by the client. When practitioners initiate silences, there should always be a particular purpose in mind, which could be simply to give the client more time to think. The worker might also use silences in attempting to lower the level of activity in the session or for refusing to answer a question that the client repeatedly asks. However, when a worker is at a loss for words or does not know what to say, the silence is probably less effective. If the silence becomes helpful to the process in such cases, it can be said that the worker is fortunate rather than competent (Hackney & Cormier, 1994).

Dress and appearance are important forms of nonverbal communication as well. They tell a great deal about how we see ourselves, and how we wish to be seen by our clients and colleagues. For example, casual clothes may be perfectly acceptable in a particular agency setting but may seem unprofessional in another setting. The setting may also have an official or unofficial dress code as part of the organizational culture. Deviation from these norms will generally bring special attention to the practitioner, which may not be desirable.

Knowledge of nonverbal communication helps practitioners be alert to the needs of clients and at the same time be aware of their own nonverbal communications. As practitioners, we have to ensure that our nonverbal behavior is consistent with verbal behavior. We also have to pick up on clients' cues to help identify the affective (underlying) feelings that are present.

A word of caution. Nonverbal behavior provides us with clues about underlying feelings but does not provide conclusive proof. Some people or ethnic groups show their emotions more than others, or show them differently. Some of us, maybe all of us, sometimes mask our true feelings. We may smile when we are angry or pretend to have feelings we do not really have. While nonverbal communication is usually more honest than words, because it is involuntary, this is not always the case. Nonverbal communication can be misinterpreted. Did you frown because you are angry, or because you have a headache? Did he put his arm around her as a platonic gesture or as a sexual advance? Nonverbal communication requires much interpretation.

Generalists who are effective in helping clients are always mindful of the cues and messages that they send through their body language as they interact with clients. For instance, if your muscles start to tense up while a client is talking, ask yourself why this is happening. What is causing your anxiety? What cues are you sending out to the client and what are your reactions? You can use body language to communicate appropriate messages, and you can use body language to censor messages that are inappropriate.

A thirty-seven-year-old client looked at her preteen daughter and asked, "When did I have sex with your father?" The practitioner believed that this was a totally inappropriate way of speaking and she immediately withdrew from the conversation by stiffening her body and sending out cues that informed the client that her behavior was inappropriate. An awareness of the ability to utilize the body instinctively as a means of communication makes it easier for a worker to communicate more effectively than would otherwise be possible.

What do the following behaviors and nonverbal communication mean to you? Read the cases provided and compare your responses with others in the class:

Rosa, a young client you have been seeing in clinical sessions, walks into your office for her third session, sits erect in the chair, and clasps her arms across her chest before saying a word.

Gilbert, a teenager in a group session, refuses to talk and avoids eye contact with you.

In a family session, Lourdes crosses her legs and moves her foot in a slight kicking motion at the same time she drums her fingers.

In an individual session, Miranda sits forward in her chair, tilting her head, and nodding at intervals.

In the middle of a session, a generalist takes a phone call and carries on a conversation while the client, who has been discussing her divorce, waits.

A client walks into Sara Beth's office. Sara Beth is busy writing. She nods her head slightly, acknowledging the client, but continues to write for another five minutes without saying a word.

Verbal communication

When we talk to people we send out two types of messages: cognitive and affective. *Cognitive* content consists of the actual facts and words of the message whereas *affective* content (which can be both verbal and nonverbal) consists of feelings, attitudes, and behaviors. Processing verbal messages requires being able to understand both cognitive and affective content and also being able to discriminate between the two. Cognitive content is easier to understand because it is stated. Affective content is generally more difficult to understand as its meaning is often less apparent. The manner in which you respond to a client will depend on your ability to hear and understand what is being said and to uncover the underlying message. When you hear only the cognitive message and not the affective message, it makes a difference in that your listening may be ineffective and lead to an inappropriate response to your client. The manner in which you respond will also affect the direction of the client's next statement (Okun, 1987).

Tone of voice generally reveals how a person feels. For instance, a loud, forceful tone of voice generally suggests that the person is aggressive, controlling, or strong. A scarcely audible voice usually indicates that the person is scared and suggests withdrawal, fear, and weakness. A flat or monotonous voice suggests lack of interest or lack of emotion.

Cognitive Messages

Cognitive messages are easier to recognize than affective messages. When people receive cognitive messages they are involved in talking in a simple or complex manner about things, people or events. When generalists focus merely on clients' cognitive messages, then they may never get down to the clients' underlying feelings.

A number of cognitive topics are given in the three cases that follow. Can you pick them out?

Forty-year-old Carmela complains, "My husband does not have a job. I have to pay bills and do not know what to do. My job cannot take care of all the bills. I would like to take an extra evening job of telephone soliciting or become an evening waitress." But Carmela is nervous about doing this because she has three young children.

Jeraldo and Hermania recently moved to a new apartment. Unfortunately for them, Jeraldo just lost his job and they have not paid the rent for the apartment. Hermania explains to the worker in social services, "My son is sick and I have no money to go to the doctor. I am new to the area and do not have friends here. The landlord cut off the heat because we did not pay the rent. I need to pay the bills and I don't know where to go first, but I also need to get all my furniture that just arrived today to be carried and arranged in the apartment."

Jason, a generalist, is completely taken aback at the anger of the community group he is facing. The natural leaders in the community talk to Jason with their hands waving angrily in the air. They complain that the previous practitioner had promised to help the community in different ways but suddenly resigned his job without telling the community people and left the area. They complain that they do not have sufficient medical and recreational facilities in their community. Young children play in the streets and they have to travel to an adjoining city to get medical services. They had attempted to work on their issues, but with the sudden departure of their last generalist social worker, they feel let down.

Affective Messages

Affective messages are communicated both verbally and nonverbally, though this section deals with verbal communication. Affective communication involves feelings and emotions that are expressed directly or indirectly. Affective messages are far more difficult to communicate than cognitive messages and they are more difficult to perceive and hear (Okun, 1987; Uhlemann, Lee, & Martin, 1994). When clients discuss their problems, it seems that they are more aware of their thoughts than their feelings. When the worker starts to talk to them about their feelings, clarifying and identifying those feelings may come as a surprise to them. Eventually clients learn to explore, experience, and also "own" their feelings.

As Okun (1987) and Uhlemann and Koehn (1989) indicate, feelings can be classified into four major categories: anger, sadness, fear, and happiness. A feeling from one category can mask another kind of feeling. For instance, anger and hostility can cover for fear and insecurity. Identifying feelings in a client is difficult when first starting a career; it is also related to how comfortable and proficient we are in recognizing and identifying our own feelings. It is important that we identify the clients' feelings rather than project our own on them. To discuss feelings and to be empathetic to a client takes a great degree of practice.

Look at the following case and specify whether the case highlights cognitive or affective communication or both. Explain your reasons.

> **CLIENT:** Well, I am really tired of doing what I am doing. I have been to one of the best colleges and have a great education, but it seems wasted. What would it take to help me move on to something that is more in line with my qualifications?
>
> **WORKER:** (1) You are eager to make more money.
> (2) Do you wish to move up quickly?
> (3) I guess it is frustrating to feel that you are not working up to your potential.

Among the three responses which one would describe the client's feelings and thoughts most aptly? Why? Give your reasons.

The following exercise deals mainly with affective communication, so when you read the cases ask yourself what the underlying feelings are in the given situations.

Zoe, married for fourteen years with four children, does not have time for anything except housework. All her talents as an artist are submerged. She is tired and tells her preoccupied husband, "Put down your paper and talk to me. The children are all outside playing. You never talk to me anymore."

How is Zoe feeling? Frustrated, alone, angry, neglected? Why do you think so?

Drew, age seventeen, gets a bad grade in English. He tells his classmates, "Ms. Brown is a lousy teacher. She does not explain anything."

Why is Drew blaming the teacher? Is he angry, disappointed, or feeling sorry for himself?

Another exercise involves picking out a number of emotions like anger and fear, and related emotions like hostility, guilt, and jealousy. In small groups, discuss one emotion. Each group member should describe one incident when they have expressed this emotion. Sharing such experiences and discussing them in small groups makes the emotion more alive to you and, at the same time, makes you more sensitive to clients' presentations of their emotion.

Verbal communication is filled with cognitive and affective factors. It is best for the beginning generalist to be aware of and learn how to deal with affective communication, something that practice usually makes easier.

SIGNIFICANT COMMUNICATION

Significant or active communication takes place through active listening. Active listening does not come easily to people, but it is a skill that can be encouraged and developed. In order to be an active listener, the generalist has to pay attention to clients' underlying feelings as well as words. The worker has to use effective body language, communicate attentiveness, and use gestures in order to demonstrate openness and concern. To listen to a client effectively the worker has to use the techniques of clarification, paraphrasing, reflection, and summarizing. Active listening also involves four skills: (1) observing and understanding the client's nonverbal messages including posture, facial expressions, movement, and tone of voice; (2) listening to and understanding the client's verbal messages; (3) listening to the whole person in the context of the social setting of his life; and (4) doing what is called tough-minded listening (Egan, 1994).

Listening and Understanding Verbal Messages

Besides nonverbal messages, generalists also have to listen to clients' verbal descriptions of their experiences, behaviors, and affect. The practitioner has to make an effort to help clients focus and clarify their presentation of their problem in terms of specific experiences, specific behaviors, and specific emotions and feelings. The worker's first job is to listen carefully to what clients say. What are the core messages and *themes* coming through? What is the client's point of view? What is important to the client?

A client, Charlotte, says, "I am worried that my mother will die, even though the doctor has not said so." Charlotte is twenty-eight years old, from a middle-class Catholic background, and a regular churchgoer. She has a bachelor's degree in business administration and is an executive in a large company. As the generalist, you should immediately be alert to the fact that Charlotte is anxious and should make no effort to tell her not to worry about what the doctor has not said. But you should ask her what her worries are and why she *feels* that her mother will die. The theme of the client's discussion is her mother and at the core are the client's feelings of anxiety with reference to her mother's life.

Listening and Understanding Clients and Their Environments

Another important factor to remember in listening to clients is that clients are the sum of their verbal and nonverbal messages and the contexts in which they live and function. As you listen to a client's story, you also have to remember the particular background of the client. In this case of Charlotte, she is from a Catholic background, is very loyal to her church, and has a bachelor's degree. This is the first time in her life that she has faced such a difficult dilemma. She is intelligent and understands the doctor's efforts to prolong her mother's life, but she is aware of the inevitable. What support systems might help Charlotte through a crisis, which will happen sooner or later with her mother. The client is a fairly independent woman; she sees the reality in spite of what the doctor has said or not said. She holds an executive position in an office, which also reveals her responsible behavior. She is from a middle-class background and came up to this level through hard work. There is pain in the revelation that her mother may not live, but Charlotte has to deal with the reality that this might happen.

Her social background, life experiences, behaviors, and support systems all become important in understanding Charlotte. If a generalist focuses only on the inner psychology of the client, insufficient help is given because the client has not been treated from the viewpoint of a person-in-environment configuration or ecosystems perspective.

Another kind of important listening is tough-minded listening. As presented by Egan (1994), tough-minded listening means detecting gaps, distortions, and dissonance that are part of clients' reality resulting from experiences that they have undergone. In this situation the clients' visions, feelings, ideas, and thoughts about themselves and the outside world have to be understood. Sometimes clients' perceptions of their outside world are confused and distorted. Their self-esteem is low and they view the world as hostile even though such a view may not seem realistic. For example, if a client feels that she is ugly when she is fabulously beautiful, the generalist has to take time to listen and understand why she feels that way. But then the client should be helped to understand that her experience of herself as ugly does not agree with reality. The client should be helped to see reality, even while the generalist continues to be empathetic with the client.

Eleven-year-old Holly does very well in school, earning straight A's. She is pretty and does well in sports. One day when she receives a B grade for an unplanned quiz, Holly falls apart, crying hysterically. Holly is brought to you, the school social worker. She responds to your questioning by saying, "I am not good-looking and I am also stupid. I will never be as good as my sister, just as my mother has always told me." Holly's reaction to an unexpected quiz was one of overanxiety. It appears that there is unfair comparison which has probably created low self-esteem for Holly, and perhaps sibling rivalry as well. Would involving the family members in sessions be appropriate?

DISHARMONY AND DIFFICULT COMMUNICATIONS

Although communication is meaningful when there is active listening, obstacles and distractions do occur.

Different kinds of ineffective listening often overlap. For example, in inadequate listening practitioners get involved in their own thoughts and do not pay attention to what clients are saying. Sometimes when you do not listen, clients will exclaim that you have not heard them. Others may look at you desperately as if to say that you have not heard them. At times, you may be preoccupied with your own problems. At other times, you may be tired or feeling sick and not able to give the client the amount of attention and time necessary. Sometimes workers are distracted because of the clients' appearance, or by social and cultural differences between them and the clients that make listening and understanding difficult.

Evaluative listening happens when a person listens attentively but also listens judgmentally (Nichols, 1995); that is, judging the merits of the others in terms of whether what they are saying is wrong or right, good or bad, acceptable or unacceptable, and relevant or irrelevant. Let's look at an example of evaluative listening.

> GEORGIA: Though I have been separated from my alcoholic husband for two months now, there are so many unresolved issues, particularly with reference to the children. I also wonder whether I am doing the right thing.
>
> VIRGINIA (HER FRIEND): Forget about it. Move on with your life. You don't need to think about him. For God's sake, it's over.

Although this may sound like useful advice, the point is that Virginia heard Georgia and responded in an evaluative way. From a professional perspective, clients must first be understood and then challenged, instead of being challenged without being understood about why they are saying what they say. Often, evaluative listening, which can be translated as advice giving, will turn clients off. There has to be an investment in understanding clients' perspectives, by asking clients to expand on what they are saying. There are times when evaluative listening and expressing your opinion are appropriate and necessary. However, this should be a carefully thought-out decision that is based on the client's needs, rather than the practitioner's bias.

All of us use filters to listen to people. Often we are biased to listen in specific ways based on our own socialization. As Hall (1966) puts it, "One of the functions of culture is to provide a highly selective screen between man and the outside world. In its many forms, culture therefore designates what we pay attention to and what we ignore. The screening provides structure for the world" (p. 85). Filtered listening also happens due to prejudice. Like everyone else practitioners are influenced by their own backgrounds. At times, practitioners are also pigeonholed because of gender, race, sexual orientation, nationality, social status, religious persuasion, and lifestyle. Self-awareness and self-knowledge are extremely important in understanding and working with clients, so that practitioners do not allow their biases and prejudices to interfere with the helping process. When clients ask questions that appear to be personal, prejudiced, or biased, the practitioner should view this as an opportunity to respond in a straightforward manner, and nondefensively move the topic of discussion to the clients' concerns.

Some generalists are so interested in fact-finding and getting the facts straight that they do not pay any attention to the client. Of course, fact-finding is important but it is irrelevant unless it takes place within the context of themes and key messages. When a client presents information about his spouse in a negative way, his way of presenting is worth exploring because the negative attitude may be the result of years of unhappiness in a troubled marriage where he was constantly overlooked. This could be an explanation for the manner in which he presents himself while discussing his wife. However, if this practitioner is seeing only facts, the context in which the client experienced them will be overlooked.

When workers are caught up with what they wish to say and how to express it, they do not pay enough attention to what the client is saying. Another problem for practitioners occurs when they learn to "interrupt others." Interrupting clients distracts them from their issues. Though it is necessary to have dialogue with clients, there are instances when clients have to say what they wish to without interruption. To carry on a dialogue is necessary, but to cut off a client in mid-thought is highly disruptive. A worker could interrupt a client benignly by saying, "You've made several points and I would like to make sure that I understand them." If interrupting promotes necessary dialogue and assists problem–management process, it can be considered to be useful (Cormier & Cormier, 1998).

Some Defensive Communication Patterns

One of the most difficult factors to deal with in communication with clients is defensiveness. In interpersonal relationships, defensiveness occurs when people feel they have to protect themselves from real or imagined danger. People tend to feel threatened and become defensive when faced with embarrassment, loss of privacy, and failure to receive an expected social provision. Sometimes it is necessary, particularly in a client situation, to understand if a defensive behavior has served a functional purpose in the past. If the client's pattern is long-term rather than situational, it could be associated with some fundamental rejection by a parent or a breakup in a family, and so forth. Defensive behaviors also develop due to fear and pain. At the point that clients reveal or change their response to a positive or nondefensive behavior, the worker may wish to reinforce the positive changes nonverbally as well as verbally.

People normally use three modes of communication: visual, auditory, and touch. A person may say "I see what you mean" (visual), "I hear what you are saying" (auditory), or "the idea is within my reach" (touch). Every person has a dominant mode of communicating and the worker should try to mirror or match the phrases to suit the client's mode, for example, "I see your point of view" (visual), "I hear your point of view" (auditory), or "we are not going to hurt you in this agency" (touch).

Practitioners can align themselves with resistant clients by using the technique of "joining the resistance": "At last, I am relieved to know that you are angry with your father. You have a right to be angry and I would be too." But practitioners must be careful about labeling the client or the problem as part of a general category, which suggests that people with similar problems are all the same. For instance, a statement such as "men are insensitive" or "women are emotional" are stereotypes and show prejudice. Clients will almost always experience a sense of loss of individuality when such broad comments are made. A client who views the practitioner as prejudiced would probably be defensive and attempt a number of maneuvers to block a worker's engagement efforts.

At times it is important to pursue an assertive way of communicating with the client, particularly when it involves children or individuals who are in a position of dependency with the client. The generalist can pursue the matter by saying, "I realize you do not wish to talk to me about your child being injured, but it is necessary. Let us stay with the topic until we have discussed it." The worker has a responsibility to help clients focus on their problems even though they may be difficult for clients to discuss.

There are clients who persist in making verbal attacks. Shaefor et al. (1997) suggest the technique of "fogging" to deal with such clients. The worker or the person who is under attack can mentally and emotionally behave like a "fog," and the verbal attacks that a person makes have no effect or impact. Without responding defensively or angrily the person who is being attacked can calmly mention that the angry person has a point and might be right in his or her assessment. Calm reasoning may aid the worker in helping the client abandon his or her efforts to cause discomfort. It may also strengthen the treatment relationship by showing that the worker is interested in helping and will not retaliate.

INTERVIEWING AND COMMUNICATION

Effective communication is an essential aspect of interviewing, which is the generalist social worker's major tool. The ability to elicit necessary information, to sort out facts and feelings through verbal and nonverbal communication, and to focus on the needs, desires, problems, and issues presented by clients is an important aspect of the generalist social worker's repertoire. The interview may be described as a conversation with a definite purpose. Because its purpose is definite, its content is directed toward the achievement of that purpose (Kadushin, 1995).

Compton and Galaway (1994) view the social work interview as a major tool to collect data on which intervention decisions are made. Interviewing skills must be developed and refined throughout a person's social work career by communication skills in conjunction with interviewing strategies.

Kahn and Cannell (1957) offered the classic and often cited definition of an interview as a specialized pattern of verbal interaction that is focused on some specific purpose and on some specific content with the consequent elimination of extraneous material. The interview is a pattern of interaction in which the role relationship of interviewer and respondent is highly specialized and its specific characteristics depend on the purpose and character of the interview.

Interviewing is part of the practice of many different professions: medicine, law, journalism, management, and research, to name a few. Some of the techniques and skills are the same but the social work interview is different in that it is concerned with how to achieve social work purposes in social work settings.

As Kadushin (1995) notes, the purposes of the interview can be described as informational; that is, in order to make a social study, to make an assessment of a client system, and to bring about constructive changes in that system. The process of information gathering, assessment of a client system, and bringing about constructive changes is a continuum.

Interviewing can be conducted with a single person, a family, group, a community, or an organization. A worker may conduct the interview alone or with a copractitioner. Because the purpose of an interview is definite, one person has to take the responsibility of directing the interaction so that the interview moves toward its goal. In social work practice, the specific goal is to help clients work through their problems. This is a nonreciprocal relationship because the goal is to meet the needs of the clients, rather than the worker.

In an interview, clients as well as generalists should be task-focused. Both need to think about what happened in the last interview session and what they want to discuss in the present session. Both clients and generalists should feel responsible for the process and the outcomes. At the same time, both workers and clients must be themselves—human beings with their own thoughts, feelings, and behavior patterns. An efficient practitioner is expected to be spontaneous and intuitive, as well as knowledgeable and deliberate.

When a potential client approaches a practitioner in private practice, the worker has a right to accept or refuse the request, just as doctors or lawyers do. If a potential client approaches an agency, the agency has an obligation, as part of the social welfare system, to at least conduct an initial interview, however brief, assess the needs of the client, and steer the client toward appropriate resources. If the presenting problem or initial assessment appears to be an emergency, professional social workers have an ethical obligation not only to give the client information, but also to ensure that linkages are made.

When an interview happens, the generalist has to give it his or her exclusive attention. One of the common practices in the helping process is to set a limit for this structured conversation, which varies from fifty or sixty minutes to, in some unusual situations, an hour and a half for the first of a joint family interview session, or a group, community, or organizational meeting. The interview is always limited in time because the worker has other professional and personal obligations. In an office, usually phone calls and all other interruptions are put on hold until an interview is completed.

Interviews are usually, but not always, planned ahead in terms of time and place. They take place in a generalist's private office, in an office in an agency setting, or at a meeting hall for community help, and, less frequently, in the client's home. Depending on special circumstances, however, interviews can take place almost anywhere: at hospital bedsides or waiting rooms, in restaurants, in the street, in cars or buses, and so forth. The setting does make a difference, but it is less important than clarity about the purpose of the interview.

Information Gathering and the Social Study Interview

The purpose of information gathering is to obtain focused information about an individual, a family, a group, a community, or an organization in order to understand their social functioning. Gathering information about the client helps the generalist develop knowledge and understand clients in their situations. The information gathered is selective and necessary to understand clients, but is also relevant to the kind of help the agency can provide. Gathering information about a client is cumulative. Every time a same client is interviewed, some new and previously unshared information is obtained. For instance, in her third interview, Rita indicates, "I did not tell you this earlier; I am an adopted child. My real mother is my aunt."

Usually, early interviews are focused on information gathering and then the worker moves on to making an assessment. At times, however, a social study interview is the only specific charge, such as when a probation officer is asked to do a social study of an offender to help guide the court in dealing with the offender (Kadushin, 1985). In a social study interview, the worker gathers information about the client's sociocultural and economic background while keeping in mind the client's presenting problem.

Assessment and the Decision-Making Interview

Kadushin (1990) indicates that the purpose of an appraisal interview is to obtain selective information in order to make a needed assessment of a client. The assessment is a process in which the generalist applies theoretical generalization to the data obtained and organizes and interprets the data in order to make valid inferences. Making an assessment of a client can lead to an evaluative product and a decision on how to work with such a client or what a particular agency will do.

This type of decision-making interview facilitates appraisal and determination of eligibility of services. For example, a child welfare worker interviews a child to see if the child needs to be placed in foster care. The protective worker visits a family to observe if a petition of neglect should be filed against the child's caretakers. With regard to family members, the worker assesses the family situation and the motivation of the family to work on their issues. With groups, the worker assesses whether the members have primarily the same issue, such as alcoholism, abusive parents, or self-esteem issues, including their motivation to be group members and follow the norms of the group. Communities are evaluated in terms of realistic objectives, and the motivation and the goals for change in organizations are reviewed and worked through. In assessment, workers look for definite, limited kinds of information. The decisions that are based on such information will move toward offering constructive help to clients.

The Constructive Helping Interview

The purpose of this interview is to bring about changes in the client and also in the social situation. Therapeutic interviews use remedial measures to bring about changes in feelings, attitudes, and behavior. In this interview, the worker utilizes a deliberate, controlled influence on the psychological functioning of the client, with the client's permission, for the purpose of effecting changes and empowering the client (Sommers-Flanagan & Sommers-Flanagan, 1995; Taylor & Schneider, 1992). For example, when a couple has marital conflicts the generalist helps them with the purpose of bettering the marriage. If a child has problems adjusting to the structure in the classroom setting, the school social worker helps the client deal with this issue. At times, this is done for the client through advocacy and brokering. The worker in such a situation would interview people in strategic positions in an attempt to influence them on behalf of the clients. The aim of such interviews is to balance forces in the social environment on behalf of the clients.

The chief goals of any and all interviews are to help clients deal effectively with their own problems in living. The different types of interviews are part of an overall process aimed at helping clients. There are sequential steps that are followed to achieve the goals. These include gathering facts for making a social study based on an understanding of clients, through assessment, and then achieving the goals that clients have set for themselves, which may involve constructive interventions that have a therapeutic intent. Also interviews in the helping process can be used with one single client, a dyad, a family, a group, a community, or an organization. Interviews may be conducted in different ways depending on the philosophy of the worker or the agency and the specific modality of helping that an agency or a particular worker wishes to use (Kadushin, 1990; O'Connor & Schaefer, 1994).

There are four special characteristics in an interview.

1. The interview has a context and a setting.
2. The interview is purposeful and directed.
3. The interview is limited and contractual.
4. The interview involves specialized role relationships.

Clients have certain expectations of the generalist based on clients' past experience, and also an image of how the interviewer should behave (Morrison, 1995). Clients may expect a generalist to be warm and understanding as well as patient, or unfeeling and officious. Clients prefer workers genuinely interested in their well-being who can help them work toward coping and adapting to their own unique life situations. Usually, the chief concern of the client is to see if the interviewer has the capacity, ability, and willingness to help.

The Participants—The Generalist and the Clients

The generalist may use a wide array of skills to interview and work with different size systems such as individuals (micro), families and small groups (mezzo), and organizations and communities (macro). However, there is a high degree of overlap among people from different systems since all systems are interrelated and interact constantly with each other.

THE INDIVIDUAL AS THE CLIENT   When an interview takes place, the participants in the session react and respond in terms of their understanding of the current realities as well as their family's biopsychosocial history and life experiences. The parties involved bring many affiliations with them including gender, age, race, occupation, class, religion, and ethnicity. When the young male bricklayer from a lower-income Mormon family tells his worker something about himself, the worker should attempt to understand the client's behavior, feelings, and attitudes in terms of family, religious, and cultural background as well as the young man's own uniqueness. The forty-five-year-old single, Caucasian, Protestant female nurse who lives with her elderly mother provides us with a different but specific picture of who she is.

Both these clients by their race, status, age, and sex tell us who they are. Besides these affiliations a client is also a member of several primary groups including a family, a peer group, a job, a congregation, a friendship group, an organization and a community. These are important factors that the generalist should keep in mind in working with individuals and their environments.

THE FAMILY AS A CLIENT   In the preliminary family session, the generalist observes the interactions between the different family members and focuses on the spousal and parent–child relationships through communication. Practitioners must also keep in mind the child-rearing practices in the home, the differences in history and family background of different members, and the influence of different environmental factors such as job situation, influence of peers, and so forth. However, the focus of the family session always remains on how individuals in the system communicate and function with each other.

A single mother with three teenage daughters has recently married. Her husband was single and does not have a clue about how to handle the hostility he is facing from the daughters. His response to the children's attacks on his inability to be a parent is silence or sudden burst of anger yelling, "I am your father now and you should listen to me." This is usually followed by their reply: "You are not our father and you cannot tell us what to do." The mother removes herself from the discussion having determined that they should work out their issues for themselves.

THE GROUP AS A CLIENT   With small groups, the generalist works toward improving the well-being of all members. The generalist may lead small face-to-face groups that have specific goals. In such groups, individual members communicate with the leader and other members with the purpose of relieving tension and stress and enhancing their problem-solving skills.

A group of teenage mothers and a generalist are brought together in an agency to discuss their issues. Individuals are asked to share their problems with other members of the group and discuss ways to resolve them. They may exchange information and views about resources and techniques for resolving problems, as well as share emotional experiences in a controlled setting that enables the members to look to each other for support through understanding their similarities and differences of background and upbringing.

THE ORGANIZATION AND COMMUNITY AS A CLIENT   The generalist facilitates social change through work with large organizations, neighborhoods, and larger communities. In these situations, the generalist works with groups of individuals to achieve change through neighborhood organizing, community planning, locality development, public education, and social action.

A group of elderly people are not receiving enough services in their own community. There is a scarcity of housing, meal delivery, protection, and support workers. As a generalist, you alone are not able to help these people, so you get in touch with people in other county agencies so that they can develop a new program to help these clients. For this purpose you approach the agency leaders to explore the opportunities available for funneling funds and resources to meet the critical needs of these elderly. With knowledge of the elderly, the community, and the agencies' outlook, you are able to communicate with people and effectively secure services for them. As a generalist you are able to work to convince different people to bring about changes in policies and distribution of resources to the needy elderly with whom you work.

CULTURAL AND GENDER FACTORS   Other factors that come into play and affect the interviewing process are the diversity of people who need professional services. Individuals from different racial and ethnic groups often present different types of communication styles. An African American adolescent from an inner-city neighborhood has a different socioeconomic background and would need a different communication style than an African American adolescent from a upper-middle-class family from the suburbs. The values and orientations of different groups of people will affect members' personal lives and styles of presenting themselves.

Another cultural factor that comes into play in interviews is eye-to-eye contact. The Euro-American pattern of direct eye contact is considered intrusive and rude in some cultures. Many Native Americans, Latinos, and people from other cultures prefer less eye contact. Haase and Tepper (1972) and Dupree, Spencer, and Bell (1997) indicate that some African Americans tend to use eye contact patterns that are directly opposite to standard Euro-American usage. They may gaze at you more while talking and avoid direct eye contact while listening.

Clients who are discussing intensely private issues may feel more comfortable if the practitioner avoids a direct gaze or eye contact. Eye contact is essential, but it must be modified to meet individual cultural needs.

Other nonverbal behaviors are culturally determined. For example, Russians shake their heads up and down to indicate "no" in direct contrast to typical North American style. Body language varies from culture to culture. In the North American culture, people are generally comfortable when they keep others at arm's length irrespective of race or ethnic group. This is a contrast to those of recent Arab descent who may be more comfortable with six to twelve inches of distance separating conversation partners.

Many Asian American groups also have a different style of communicating. They may tend to view the helping professionals as authorities who can solve their problems by providing advice. Some Asian cultural patterns prescribe deference to authority and therefore some Asian clients may speak little unless they are spoken to by the practitioner, who in turn may perceive the clients as being passive and ingratiating. Thus long gaps of silence may occur as the clients wait for the practitioner to structure the interview, take charge, and provide the solution (Tsui & Schultz, 1985). Such gaps in communication could engender anxiety in both parties as well as affect the development of rapport and hinder the helping process.

It is essential that the generalist is not only ethnically and racially sensitive but also sensitive to gender differences. There are a number of gender stereotypes. Gottlieb (1987) notes that "sex inequality is based on the belief that a woman's role is a family role" (p. 562). Gender stereotypes specify that women tend to be warm, dependent, emotional, and supportive, while men tend to be aggressive, strong, unemotional, and independent. Both are negative stereotypes because they place all women and men at a disadvantage when they need professional help. Men do cry and woman can be strong. It is also important to remember that women more often than men experience difficulties in overcoming traditional stereotypes (Gottlieb, 1987). Therefore, when interviewing women, practitioners need to be sensitive to the potential for low self-esteem and nonassertiveness. Practitioners should master constructive communication skills to address the needs of women.

Learning how cultural differences and gender play themselves out in the diverse cultures of the United States is an important and ongoing learning process for an interviewer (Evans, Haern, Uhlemann, & Ivey, 1993).

Finally, attitudes, behavior, and beliefs that are associated with the roles people play greatly influence communication and are pivotal to the interviewing process. Significant family roles such as wife, husband, mother, father, daughter, son, aunt, uncle, and grandparent will affect how clients participate in the interview as well as how they will deal with issues. Other significant roles that clients carry are occupational (employee, employer, etc.) and social.

Problems can at times form a continuum; that is, one problem can lead to another.

Fogerty, a factory worker in the automobile industry, lost his job due to the unstable economy. Fogerty's wife and three teenage children were supportive of him and the family stuck together in spite of economic hardships. But as time passed, there was no sign of any positive change. With the financial situation deteriorating, the couple developed a number of problems, which led to a lack of respect toward Fogerty by the rest of the family. Another problem arose when Fogerty turned to alcohol for companionship. His drinking affected the couple's sex life. Fogerty's overburdened wife constantly threatened to divorce her husband. Problems in one role led to problems in others and eventually the family ended with a practitioner when the threat of the marriage dissolving scared Fogerty. With appropriate efforts at building constructive communication between the husband and wife and other family members, the practitioner was able to help the family. Fogerty joined Alcoholics Anonymous, stopped drinking, and found himself a temporary construction job.

THE INTERVIEWER   Like the client, the worker also brings to the interview a configuration of determinants. The worker has a group affiliation in terms of race, religion, ethnicity, and educational training and qualification. How a practitioner has learned to play the professional role and what he or she has undergone in training will affect how he or she conducts interviews.

The professional affiliation and socialization of the practitioner help to explain why certain types of behaviors are encouraged in an interview.

Professional behavior is modified to suit the needs of the agency where the practitioner works. An agency may have a particular theoretical orientation that influences how the workers are expected to help clients. The different conceptual frameworks include the Freudian psychoanalytical model, the learning theory model, behavior modification, short-term therapy, the ecosystems perspective, and the strengths perspective. These perspectives not only explain problems in human behavior, but also affect the helping process in different ways, including how interviews are conducted. Some settings emphasize the deficiencies in an individual's personality, while others emphasize the social environment as the main factor in causing people's problems. The clients will be offered help based on the philosophy of the agency.

The National Association of Social Workers (NASW) *Code of Ethics* is enforced with sanctions and can be applied against individuals or organizations who violate the code, which emphasizes the rights of all individuals, irrespective of race, ethnicity, class, or lifestyle. One aim of professional and in-service training is to help reduce unprofessional attitudes that interfere with a practitioner's ability to accept and respond appropriately to clients from different social classes and cultural backgrounds.

One area in which professional norms and rules of social etiquette seem to conflict is in how to respond to verbose clients. As one worker commented:

> When my client started to talk and talk and be irrelevant, I did not know whether I should be polite and listen or whether I should be rude and interrupt. But through the years I have learned that letting a client go on and on irrelevantly when he or she is unfocused is a waste of his or her time and mine. I gradually learned how to break in without being rude and help the client focus on the relevant details by saying that she was talking about different things, and I did not understand how they fit together and that we should begin to focus and remain with topics that were crucial.

According to Cross (1974), the interviewer needs to keep two things in mind. One is diplomacy and the other is boorishness. *Diplomacy* requires that the worker be warm, empathetic, and sensitive to clients and their needs. At the same time, in order to get the job done the worker has to be somewhat *boorish,* too. This simply means that the worker should be able to ask questions that sometimes may be embarrassing and uncomfortable for the clients. The clients' discomfort can be eased considerably if the worker's manner is matter-of-fact and professional, and if the client can be helped to understand why the subject is being introduced. For instance, the practitioner might say to a client who keeps focusing on his children's actions, "Children's behavior often reflects tensions in the home. Perhaps you can tell me more about your marriage."

In social work interviews, the communication is to some extent reciprocal, but ordinarily the practitioner has more and greater varieties of power and influence that can be used to empower clients. In all interview sessions, the worker has to observe and employ the affective and cognitive materials and be a good communicator. The power of the worker comes from the fact that he or she generally has more professional knowledge and skills and is objective in dealing with clients' problems. The practitioner's influence also comes from the ability to influence others who carry power in a client's life such as judges, doctors, teachers, and welfare workers. Also, it is important to remember clients may feel stigmatized or humiliated—less powerful—because of their inability to solve their problem by themselves.

Once work begins between practitioner and client, the worker has what is called *referent power,* which derives from professional training and skills, to influence the client. However, there are clients who will not allow themselves to be influenced. One classic example is the involuntary client who may react to the worker with indifference. At times, clients may wish to reverse roles and attempt to take over and ask the interviewer questions that may not be relevant to the interview, or they may refuse to discuss a topic that needs to be focused on. The best way to respond to this situation is to not allow a power struggle to take place. "I can't make you talk about it if you don't want to. Perhaps you're happy with the way things are."

Forty-year-old Darcy had been ordered by the family courts to undergo therapy because he had sexually abused his stepdaughter. Although Darcy was aware of his responsibilities, he tried to get into a power struggle with an attractive young female social worker. Darcy told her, "I don't think you know what it is be denied sex in your own home. I do not need help. My wife does. She is responsible for my behavior toward her daughter. She was always tired or unresponsive to sex, and I had to find a way out and that was why I got involved with the daughter."

As the worker nonverbally shows her disapproval while Darcy is talking, he starts to bang the desk in front of him to make his point. Then he says that he is a religious man and God has forgiven him; therefore he does not understand why he should be required to attend sessions. When the worker attempts to enter the discussion, he pooh-poohs her by saying that she does not understand everything that happened in his family.

There is an attitude of self-righteousness about Darcy that intimidates the worker. Although she is aware that he needs help, she does not know how to help him. She is caught in the cross fire of his anger. She feels manipulated and does not respond to him appropriately. A worker who is experienced and is comfortable dealing with sexual abuse cases would stay with the facts and help to focus Darcy on what he needs to do in order to modify his attitudes and behavior so that he could begin to work at his problems and the family situation. The worker might say something like "The facts are that you have committed a crime, hurt your family, and refused to accept responsibility for any of this. I think it would be too risky to allow you back into the house, just as you have been told by the authorities."

In an interview session, the practitioner can influence clients by selective responses to what they say or do. When clients attempt to discuss their role, the worker can help "condition" them by responding in ways that encourage them to talk more about their role and what they have to do in order to modify their behavior. Using verbal conditioning, the worker conditions clients through deliberate, controlled use of words and vocalization. The worker rewards clients by his or her approval of what they have done or hope to do and also uses words to discourage the clients from talking about matters that are not important by saying, "Let's discuss that later; it is really not important now."

The competent and experienced interviewer is likely to use his or her power and influence selectively, and will usually be less controlling, less active, and less inclined to offer advice and suggestions than inexperienced workers. New workers tend to talk more and are apt to take more responsibility for the interview, perhaps because the new worker is often more governed by anxiety and insecurity than the experienced worker. This does not mean that experienced workers are passive; it just means that they are comfortable with clients and can afford to be discriminating and modulate their activity.

The task of the interviewer is to induce the client into the session and keep the interview going. The whole purpose of interviewing is to help clients achieve their goals. This happens when the worker encourages the development of some aspects of the client's role behavior and discourages others as inappropriate. The worker not only has to challenge the client to focus on the goals in the interview, but also to do a lot of mental work. This involves receiving and processing complex data and making complex decisions about how to respond and evaluate.

Forty-year-old Herbert and his wife, Ida, were in sessions for couple and family problems. Herbert's background history revealed that he had served seven years in prison for drug abuse before he married Ida, his old high school sweetheart. Ida had two daughters by her previous marriage, aged ten and eleven. The whole family attended a family session. In this session there were four females including the worker, Hillary. While discussing family rules, Herbert, who due to his own past experiences in the prison system had developed a very strict adherence to rules, mentioned that the girls were not well disciplined.

His wife presented an incident and explained that he wanted them to behave like robots. Herbert, feeling angry about the discussion of his rules, turned around and called out, "You girls [the worker, Ida, and his stepdaughters] don't understand" and started to take control. The inexperienced worker was intimidated and lost control of the session. Later, the worker discussed issues raised in the session with her supervisor, including the new worker's feelings toward men and self-assertion. In the next session, the worker started to become self-assertive and also focused on the husband–wife issues, attempting to keep herself objective and untangled from the situation.

Kadushin (1990) and Schubert (1991) note that the worker is only one participant in an interview; the other is the client. The role of the worker is crucial but this role only partially determines whether an interview session will progress successfully or fail.

The responsibilities of the worker in terms of data collection can be seen in three different areas. First and foremost, the worker is responsible for creating a productive climate in which clients can constructively and comfortably share relevant thoughts, feelings, perceptions, and factual information at their own pace. Creating a conducive environment also means asking questions that help motivate and encourage clients to respond. Usually short, straightforward statements set the stage and also encourage client participation.

A second responsibility of the worker is to help clients focus on the interview. At times, clients may move away from the topic of importance because they are uncomfortable and want to discuss a more comfortable but not really relevant topic. The worker's responsibility is to help the client return to and focus on what is important.

A third responsibility of the worker is to sort out clients' responses. For instance, what is the client saying verbally? How does the client look? How does the client behave? How does the client perceive the interview situation (Benjamin, 1987; Kadushin, 1990)?

Like driving a car or playing tennis, interviewing skills are based on certain concepts that must be learned. Proficiency is developed with experience, through practice, and by trial and error. There is a repertoire of techniques that should be developed by workers as they become more experienced and efficient in their styles of interviewing.

THE INTERVIEW PROCESS

In social work a great deal of work between the practitioner and the clients happens through the interview process. Clients are seen for varying periods of time, ranging from one meeting to as long as nine to twelve weeks or more. If the client is willing to pay out of pocket, the sessions can go on for an even longer period. In terms of community and organizational issues, the number of interviews depends on the urgency of the problem. Every interview is part of the process of helping, with the purpose of reaching the goals that have been set between the clients and the worker. Every interview is a process itself, with a beginning, a middle, and an end. Thus each interview is a consciously implemented, dynamic movement through successive stages to accomplish the purposes of the interview, even if it is in small steps.

In the beginning part of the interview process, niceties are exchanged and the tone is set based on issues related to the goals that are presented by the clients. The middle part is the essence or "meat" of the session, when the problem and solutions are discussed. Lastly, the ending is used to highlight certain aspects of the interview and certain decisions that have been made, as well as to set the agenda for the next session. For example, "You agreed to set aside time to talk to each other without arguing, every night. Next time, I'd like to ask you about your first marriage." The next appointment is set or reaffirmed and the client and the worker say their farewells.

The section that follows examines the different phases of the interview process from the standpoint of one family in their first interview. The phases may also be applied to different size systems.

The Initial Phase

The initial phase of an interview includes the greeting, the beginning of the interview, the introduction to new surroundings, and also the invitation to speak. The worker introduces himself or herself, takes the family to the office room where the sessions will be held, acknowledges everyone's presence, and tries to adapt to the family's speech and style so that the family members feel comfortable. The practitioner wants to create an atmosphere in which the clients can begin to entrust the therapist with the leadership of the interview (Herson & Hassett, 1998; Stierlin, Rucker-Embden, Wetzel, & Wirsching, 1980).

A family of four is coming to their first session. The mother comes early with her daughter and a younger child, an eight-year-old boy named Archie, the identified client. The father, who had to leave his workplace early in order to attend the session, arrives late. In the initial, or beginning, phase of the interview, the worker greets them and makes a mental note that the father is late, but does not comment. How do they begin? The worker observes where they seat themselves; who sits next to whom, and who sits away from others. As introductory comments are made, the climate between the worker and the family warms up a little. The worker is watching the family's relational dynamics. Archie is fidgeting with his shirt, and his mother asks him to keep still. Archie's sister joins her mother and asks him to stop fidgeting. Archie looks at the practitioner in an uncomfortable manner.

The practitioner is also trying to understand why the family has come for help. What are the different problems being presented? Is there a specific problem to be discussed? How did the family difficulties begin and are they being solved? What outside help has the family sought so far? What were the different attempts made to solve the problems and did they fail? Why? What course is the interview taking at this point?

In the family case, the practitioner attempts to understand the motivation for the family coming in for family sessions. Did they come through the advice of a friend, a family doctor, or an agency? The presenting problem is Archie's acting-out behavior in school. However, the worker observes that there is no eye contact between the father and the mother. The mother talks about all the efforts she has made to help Archie, emphasizing the word *she*. However, she adds this has not helped Archie from acting out in school.

The Middle Phase

It is important in the middle phase of the interview for the practitioner to identify issues and establish parameters for the helping process. These include how the family is organized. What different transactions are observed during the interview? Are the family members well individuated or is there poor individuation? Are the family members enmeshed with each other and how do the husband and wife communicate? Which transactional mode of functioning seems to be operating in this family? Are family members close to each other or do they push each other away and stay distant? What are the rules for different family members? Is anyone being scapegoated in terms of excessive demands, and are there conflicts in the family? From a multigenerational perspective, what are the parents' family backgrounds? What are the relational legacies that they have inherited and what, if any, are their family myths (Pillari, 1991)?

The worker also has to ascertain the state of mutuality. How are the family members communicating? Is there a state of malign stalemate with all participants deadlocked or are they ready to establish a dialogue? How quickly is the practitioner drawn into the family dynamics and rendered powerless? Are family members caught up in a power struggle where no one can win? If so, how far? To what extent is the family really stagnated? How is the worker performing? Is the worker conscious of the powers that are operating in the particular family system? What is the focus of the helping process? What do family members hope to achieve and how? What are the dynamics of the husband–wife relationship? What are the relationships between the parents and each child and the family as a whole? Moving the family to look at the important issues becomes the essence of the session.

In the family case, the worker observes that Archie's acting out is perhaps a symptom of other issues in the family. The mother and daughter look at each other and smile while discussing Archie's problem and the father squirms in his seat. The mother comments that the whole family has problems. They do not communicate with each other; the father sighs. The worker moves quickly to focus on the husband and wife as they appear to have problems. Dealing with them would perhaps also lead to an understanding of Archie's problem.

The Ending Phase

What are the strengths and weaknesses of the family? What type of motivation or resistance to change does the family reveal? What are the different resources of the family? What are the family's expectations of the practitioner? What are the long- and short-term goals for the family? What does the practitioner believe is the problem that the family is facing? Does the family need to be referred to any other agency? Does the family show resistance?

At the end of each interview the practitioner should consider whether he or she has succeeded in eliciting some important family information and how to pursue it in the next session. Also, the practitioner should have a hypothesis of the family's relational dynamics so that he or she can assess their motivational situation. In this phase, the practitioner also motivates the family to come for additional sessions and helps them to arrive at a family therapeutic contract that begins to set the direction for further professional help (Herson & Hassett, 1998; Stierlin et al., 1980).

In the family case, the beginning therapeutic contract was to work with issues between husband and wife. In the course of the interview the behaviors of the mother, the father, and the daughter made it obvious that there was a family secret. However, focusing on the husband and wife should help the whole family. Thus a basic goal of helping the husband and wife becomes the aim of sessions, though this can be modified or changed in the course of the helping process.

Skills and Techniques of Interviewing

There are basic interviewing and communication skills that can be learned and practiced. The skills discussed in this book are classified as listening responses and action skills (see Figure 8.3). Listening responses include clarification, paraphrasing, reflecting, and summarizing, which were briefly mentioned earlier in this text. Action skills include probes, confrontation, interpretation, and information giving (Cormier & Cormier, 1998).

Listening Responses

Clarification is asking a question when you do not understand what a client is saying. When a client gives an ambiguous message, the practitioner asks for clarification, saying for example, *"Do you mean*

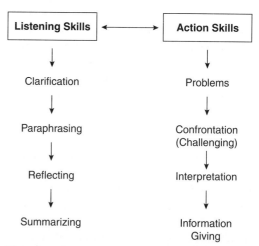

Figure 8.3 Listening Skills and Action Skills

that . . ." or *"Are you saying that . . ."* The purpose is to encourage client elaboration and to check the accuracy of what the client has said. Clarification also means restructuring the client's perceptual field. Clarification distinguishes between subjective and objective reality and also presents various options and alternatives for consideration.

Feda, a Lebanese woman married to an American, was very upset when her mother-in-law, whom she disliked intensely, gave her a green sweater for Christmas. Feda hated the color green because she thought it was unlucky. She was in tears about what might befall her due to her mother-in-law's intentional "bad luck" gift. However, after some specific questioning, it became clear that the mother-in-law, whom Feda saw rather infrequently, was unaware that her daughter-in-law did not like the color green. This threw new light on the problem and also helped Feda to understand that her mother-in-law was making special efforts to accept her in the family. If Feda were your client, how would you clarify the situation for her? Think of at least two relevant questions you would ask. Why are they relevant?

Clarification efforts aim at increasing specificity. Usually, the interviewer requests clarification to check understanding of what a client is saying and to provide clarification when there is a feeling that the client is not clear in his or her thinking and feeling (Kadushin, 1990). Quite often, when a relationship has an undertone of hostility rather than friendship, the motives ascribed to the disliked person may be inaccurate, as in the case of Feda who misunderstood her mother-in-law's positive attitude toward her. Clarifying dispels any confusion that both the interviewer and the client may face in trying to understand a complicated issue. The clarification process also specifically increases the mutuality in the interaction. In turn, this motivates the client to participate actively as it is difficult not to respond to a practitioner who is trying to understand and be helpful.

Okun (1987) indicates that often a situation may appear to be simple, but it is easy to be sidetracked while working with clients, particularly when dealing with certain types of content.

CLIENT: I'm having family problems. My fiancée and I have mutual friends that we grew up with, and I also have an aunt whom I love very much, as do my parents. But my fiancée's mother does not like this particular aunt and has not spoken to her in nine years. My fiancée has been forbidden to invite this aunt home. My fiancée will not invite her to the wedding, as this would upset her parents.

WORKER: That's tough. This probably makes you feel guilty about your relations with your aunt.

CLIENT: Yes, but the problem is the wedding. My mother is insisting that this aunt should come to the wedding, but my fiancée says that this is impossible.

WORKER: So you are really in a bind and you don't know how to get around it.

CLIENT: I think we should elope. You know about big family weddings; I don't know how we can make everyone happy.

WORKER: Let's talk about the different ways with which you can deal with the wedding invitations.

Did the worker deal with the real issue in this case? No. She avoided it. The practitioner should have maintained the focus on the aunt and the problems surrounding it.

CLIENT: I'm really having family problems. My fiancée and I have mutual friends that we grew up with, and I also have an aunt whom I love very much, as do my parents. But my fiancée's mother does not like this aunt and has not spoken to her in nine years. My fiancée has been forbidden to invite this aunt home, and she will not invite her to the wedding, as this would upset her parents.

WORKER: You are really upset that your fiancée's parents have so much control over her.

CLIENT: Looks like it to me.

WORKER: It's uncomfortable for you to be caught in the middle of two families and for your fiancée to not take a stand with you.

CLIENT: You are right! I think she should be loyal to me, first. We are ones who will be married, and I am going to be her husband!

WORKER: Sounds like you are wondering how things will be between you two after you are married, particularly in terms of how she will react to her parents' pressures.

CLIENT: You are right. That's really it.

The worker in this second case study was able to clarify the real issue that was bothering the client rather than being sidetracked by another issue or changing the topic of conversation.

It is important for the practitioner to identify the core problem and its ownership; if this is not done, a large amount of problem-solving activity is futile. *Problem ownership* involves identifying the problem a client is facing. A person, a family, a group, an organization, or a community has to "own" a problem before they can invest energy into it (Holland & Petchers, 1987; Meenaghan, Washington, & Ryan, 1987; Okun, 1987; Sarri, 1987).

PARAPHRASING   Beginning professionals sometimes confuse the restatements of content or cognitive aspects of a client's statements with the repetition of the client's message. When parroting occurs, the interview becomes stale, circular, and repetitive rather than progressive, which can make clients uncomfortable. Empathy is not parroting. The mechanical helper corrupts basic empathy by simply restating what the client has said, sometimes adding statements like "Well, I just said that to you."

To paraphrase, practitioners have to ask themselves questions such as "What is this client's point of view?" and "What are the core messages in what the client is saying?" Thus the practitioner is engaged in a process that is more than mere repetition. In interviewing, the worker should pay careful attention to the essence of a client's statement rather than to the words that the client uses. After hearing the client, the worker has to rephrase the client's statements in his or her own words.

Paraphrasing has several purposes. Cormier and Cormier (1998) list the following:

1. Paraphrasing shows that you have understood what the client has said. If your understanding

of their issue is clear, then clients can expand or clarify their own thinking.

2. Paraphrasing can encourage a client to elaborate or expand on an idea or a thought.

3. Using paraphrasing helps clients focus on a particular situation, event, idea, or behavior.

4. Paraphrasing can help clients to get back on track and not wander off.

5. Paraphrasing helps clients to move toward decision making.

According to Ivey, Ivey, and Simek-Morgan (1993), paraphrasing is often helpful to clients when they have to make a decision. The repetition of key phrases and ideas helps clarify the essence of the problem. When clients are caught in the affect aspect of presenting a problem, paraphrasing helps them to understand what has been said.

Paraphrasing is done through attending and recalling the message, and first restating it to yourself covertly. Next, select an appropriate beginning that can match the client's choice of sensory words. Translate the key content or constructs into your words and then verbalize them in order to paraphrase. Lastly, assess the effectiveness of your paraphrase to be sure that it sounds like a statement rather than a question. If the paraphrasing is accurate, then the client will verbally or nonverbally confirm its accuracy and usefulness (Cormier & Cormier, 1998; Ivey, Ivey, & Simek-Morgan, 1993).

CLIENT: I suppose all my problems are caused by what is going on at home.

WORKER (PARAPHRASING): You think your problems are caused by your difficulties at home.

To paraphrase, it is necessary to accurately reflect the content of what the client has said to you. If the worker had said the client had a problem in his or her marriage, the worker might be assuming too much from what the client said.

In order to accurately reflect the content of a client's statement, a worker should paraphrase the main idea contained in the statement. In other words, the essence of the client's communication should be reflected in the worker's response. By reflecting content, the worker reassures the client that he or she does understand what has been said. Reflection of content can take place in the form of a simple or complex sentence or a sentence fragment, but should be similar in grammatical structure to the client's statement. For instance, suppose a client says, "Yeah. It's my fifteen-year-old niece, you know; we are having trouble with her. She stays out all night." The worker might respond: "Your niece not coming home at night is a major problem." The worker who came out with, "I guess you do have a number of problems with your niece" would be incorrect and assuming too much from the client's statement.

REFLECTING CONTENT AND FEELINGS A practitioner can reflect content either by paraphrasing a single statement or summarizing a number of statements. In addition to clarifying the accuracy of a client's statements, the worker should also be able to relate messages revealed in these statements about significant situations and events in the client's life and the client's feelings about those events. That portion of the message that gives or expresses information or describes a situation or event is called *content* or, as discussed earlier, the cognitive aspect of the message.

When speaking about cognitive content, we tend to think of events, objects, people, and ideas. There is a second portion of the message that reveals how the client feels about the content; this emotional tone is the affective aspect of the message (Hackney & Cormier, 1994). For instance, a practitioner discussing community issues with residents of an inner city hears their verbal statement of their problems, but can sense the underlying feelings of hopelessness and defeat. Affective content can be transmitted verbally and nonverbally. When it is verbal, it is reflected as happiness, anger, sadness, and fear.

Reflection of content and reflection of feelings are not mutually exclusive. Using the technique of reflection of feelings, the practitioner attempts to rephrase the affective aspect of the client's message. The purpose of reflection is to use response effectively and accurately so that clients feel they have been understood. Reflection also encourages clients to express their feelings, both positive and negative. Most of a client's concerns involve feelings and emotional factors that need to be resolved (Ivey, Ivey, & Simek-Downing, 1987). Clients become aware of lingering and, at times, conflicting feelings. Often it is through ambivalence that clients express their feelings about problematic issues.

Another purpose of reflection is to help control and manage feelings. Dealing with feelings of fear, dependency, and anger is an important way of working toward a client's growth. Clients also need to be taught to express their negative feelings about the type of help they are receiving. When a client gets angry, there is a tendency to become defensive; by using reflection in such instances, the worker can lessen the possibility of an emotional conflict that can arise when two people are trying to make themselves heard, but neither one is listening (Kahn, 1991; Long & Prophit, 1981).

Finally, reflection helps clients distinguish among their different feelings. Sometimes clients are anxious and at other times they are nervous or sad.

A worker reflects feelings to a client by listening to the feeling or affect words in a client's messages. Okun (1992) indicates that positive, negative, and ambivalent feelings are expressed by one or more affect words. These fall into seven major categories: anger, fear, uncertainty, sadness, happiness, strength, and weakness. Another way of observing the client's feelings is through the nonverbal behavior that accompanies delivery of the verbal message. After the feelings reflected by the client's words and nonverbal behaviors have been identified, the worker should attempt to reflect the feelings verbally back to the client using different words. When a client says he is irritated, you might then use words like *annoyed* or *bothered* to convey the emotion.

The next step would be to reflect to the client what he or she has said by using the term that the client used; for example, saying "It looks like you are irritated now."

The final stage in reflecting feelings is to assess the effectiveness of your reflection. How does the client respond? Does she say, "That's exactly what I meant," or does she say, "Well, sort of"? If a client denies your reflection of his or her feelings then your interpretation was inaccurate or the client is too defensive and is in denial, in which case you need to understand that the timing for reflecting feelings was inappropriate.

One of the important factors in working with clients is knowing when to respond to feelings. The worker has to attend to the affective component of what the client presents to determine the appropriate time. Discussing feelings in the beginning session(s) or too frequently may overpower the client. Overuse of feelings may make the client uncomfortable or lead to a client's denial of feelings. However, depending on the problems and how clients experience them, clients may present feelings right from the first session. If the feelings are intense, they may get in the way of constructive discussion. When a client is preoccupied with certain feelings, the worker will have to identify them, normally through posture, voice, and other mannerisms. The worker should utilize a wide range of words to label emotions. When reflecting feelings, the worker also should give a clear and concise summary of what the client appears to be feeling. Again, reflecting the client's feelings often makes him or her more aware and willing to explore feelings, and helps to develop a strong relationship between worker and the client.

The client, a middle-aged woman, says in a loud, high-pitched voice, with clenched fists, "You can't imagine what it was like when I found out that my husband was cheating on me. I saw red! What should I do, get even? Leave him? I'm not sure."

1. Were any overt words used that expressed the client's feelings?
   None, except for the affect phrase, "saw red."
2. What were the feelings expressed by this woman?
   Anger, pain, outrage, hostility.

3. What are the choice affect words used to describe the client's feelings at a similar level of intensity?
   Angry, vindictive, totally outraged.
4. What is an appropriate statement that matches the sensory words used by the client?
   From the client's use of image words like *saw red* the worker can use visual phrases like "it appears," "it looks like."
5. What is the context of the client's feelings that you can paraphrase?
   Finding out that the husband was cheating on her.
6. How will you know if your reflection is accurate and helpful?
   Watch and listen to the client's response—whether she confirms or denies being angry and vindictive.

Some examples of reflection that the worker could use are:

1. "It looks like you are extremely angry about your husband's going out on you."
2. "It appears that you are full of rage at your husband's actions."
3. "It seems like you are both furious and vindictive now that you've discovered your husband has been cheating on you."

At times, a worker can reflect feelings that distract the client and also impede the progress of the interview. For example:

CLIENT: I have a date with my neighbor. You should see him. He's something. He's so good-looking.

WORKER: You are very excited about this.

Here the worker is responding to the feelings aspect rather than the cognitive aspect of what the client has said. But if the worker responded by saying, "Well, that's only a date, don't get your hopes up," the response could be viewed as a piece of advice and not a reflection of feelings.

If a worker accurately reflects the client's feelings, he or she is indicating perceptions of the client's world. If that does not happen, the progress of the interview will be affected.

SUMMARIZING Summarizing is a pulling together of the content and affective components of several messages. Summarizing also draws together the main affective and content elements of what has been discussed in the interview session (Shaefor et al., 1997).

Summarizing involves themes. A client may present a number of messages that suggest consistencies and patterns called themes. When a client expresses similar messages continually, the client is presenting a specific theme. For example, Christian repeatedly mentions his unhappy marriage even though he is in clinical sessions to work through some childhood issues. So the worker summarizes the theme by saying, "I am aware that in the last three sessions you have consistently spoken about your unhappy marriage. Perhaps this is an issue you wish to focus on."

According to Cormier and Cormier (1998), there are five purposes in summarizing:

1. To pull together different and varied elements of a client's message. Summarization becomes a good feedback mechanism for extracting meaning from vague and ambiguous messages.
2. To find a common theme or pattern after the client has spoken for some time.
3. To focus on the interview when the client is rambling and "storytelling." Focusing gives direction to the interview.
4. To slow down the pace when an interview is moving too quickly. Summarizing offers psychological breathing space during the session.
5. To review the progress a client has made during the sessions.

To help clients organize concerns, and the interviewer should present a concise, accurate, and timely summary of what has been said. Reflection of content should not be overused in a parrotlike effect that could inhibit the client's communication.

> **CLIENT:** I lost my temper and hit my daughter during an argument about her sleeping around. Then my husband got upset and I started to worry about his blood pressure, which is very high. The next day, I had trouble concentrating and made a couple of big errors on the job. I realized that I could not solve anything by losing my temper.
>
> **WORKER:** So the stress caused by your daughter's sexual activities, your response, and your husband's blood pressure is affecting your performance at your workplace and you are searching for a solution.

The response is accurate and brief; it reflects what the client said. As the client has mentioned, the problems at work are her focus of concern and the other two issues, though extremely important, are contributing factors as presented by the client.

When you summarize, you have to pay careful attention to the client's verbal and nonverbal messages. It is helpful to restate these messages to yourself and process what the client has told you over time. Identify the different patterns and themes, because without them it is possible to get caught in the content and not pay attention to the process. While summarizing, address the client by name and make a summary statement, utilizing a sensory word that the client has used. Assess how well your summarizing is being received by paying close attention to see if the client confirms or denies, and also whether your summarization adds or detracts from the focus of the session (Ivey, Gluckstern, & Ivey, 1993).

Over the course of three sessions, Felix, a middle-aged client, relates to the practitioner that he has had affairs with a number of women. He says that his affairs are ruining his marriage. His wife is a good woman, but he cannot help his own behavior. The affairs make him feel better, momentarily, and he is able to take his job stress better. Most of the time, he chooses women from the office who are in lower positions than he. He adds that in the long run it will hurt him, but it is hard for him to keep away from women. Having an affair makes him feel good.

As a helpful and nonjudgmental practitioner you ask yourself the following questions: What has Felix been trying to tell me today and in the earlier sessions? What is the key content and the key affect? What theme is he presenting? In spite of the problems it causes him, he likes having affairs. Does Felix use a particular sensory word a lot? If he says, "I am feeling" or "I am sensing," use those same words to restate his situation to him.

Summarize what Felix has told you and note how he responds. Here are some possibilities: "I sense that you like affairs and it's worth the trouble in spite of the problems they cause you in the marriage," or "Felix, I feel that your affairs have created great difficulties in your marriage, but I sense your reluctance to give them up." Another way to summarize this situation would be to say, "Felix, I sense that despite all the problems, having affairs feels satisfying to you but is painful to your wife."

If Felix agrees that having affairs is the issue then you have summarized the theme correctly. If he denies it, then you have to ask Felix to clarify how the summarization was inaccurate, realizing that the summary may be inaccurate or that Felix may not be ready to acknowledge his problems at this time.

A practitioner's demonstration of listening skills and attending skills usually models socially appropriate behavior for clients (Gazda et al., 1995). Listening is hearing, observing, encouraging, and remembering. "Active listening combines the talking and listening skills in such a way that the client feels understood and encouraged toward further self expression" (Cournoyer, 1991, p. 77). Often clients have not learned the art of listening in their own relationships and social contacts. However, they may incorporate new interpersonal skills when they experience them firsthand by contact with a significant person who could be a practitioner.

Action Responses

While the listening process can be considered the foundation of the entire therapeutic helping process, there are also action responses that reflect the practitioner's attitude. Listening responses to clients show that the practitioner is following what the client has to say. These are messages that primarily reflect the client's point of view and perspective. However, when working with clients, practitioners also have to present responses that influence the client directly or indirectly. These responses are labeled as action responses because

they are active rather than passive and reflect a more practitioner-directed than client-centered mode of communicating.

Ivey (1994) indicates that listening responses influence the client indirectly whereas action responses have a more direct influence. According to Egan (1990) and Germain and Gitterman (1996) action responses are aimed at helping clients see the need for change. Performing action lends a sense of competency, and action also leads to a more objective frame of reference.

PROBING   Effective inquiry as discussed by Evans, Hearn, Uhlemann, and Ivey (1993) is similar to probing. The worker has to master an effective style of inquiry that facilitates communication. Effective questioning or inquiry requires knowledge of open inquiry, closed inquiry, and minimal encouragement.

The term *probing* should not be misunderstood. There is no abrasiveness or harshness in professional probing, but an invitation for a person to follow or pursue a particular area of interest. Questions like "Can you tell me more about that?" or "I'd like to hear a little more about this particular person or situation" are useful. Probing is used when it becomes essential to prompt and encourage clients to explore situations when they fail to do so spontaneously. Probes and prompts are verbal tactics that help clients talk about themselves and define their problems concretely in specific terms, including feelings, behavior, and experiences (Egan, 1994).

Probes, questions, or inquiries are the building blocks of an interview process. How effective they are depends on the type of question and how it is asked. Questions can help in the development of desirable or undesirable patterns of interpersonal exchange, depending on the skills of the worker (Long, Paradise, & Long, 1981). Many times, beginning workers may ask so many questions that the session is more like an interrogation than an attempt to understand the client. Sometimes experienced workers may similarly overuse questioning (Long et al., 1981). A generalist should not ask questions unless they serve a particular purpose. The two types of questions that the worker can ask of a client in a session are classified as open-ended and closed questions.

In interviews, the most effective questioning is done in an *open-ended* fashion. Such questioning normally begins with words such as *what, how, when, where,* or *who.* Research studies have shown that "what" questions usually tend to elicit facts and information; "how" questions are usually associated with sequence and process or emotions; and "why" questions produce reasoning and intellectualization (Ivey, Ivey, & Simek-Downing, 1987). "Why" questions can also often provoke defensive feelings and are not generally recommended. Questions that deal with "when" and "where" elicit information about time and place and are associated with getting information about people. Also, open-ended questions have a number of purposes in different helping situations (Hackney & Cormier, 1988; Ivey, 1988; Long et al., 1981). "Could" and "can" questions also provide the client with the greatest flexibility for response.

Beginning an interview session with "What would you like to discuss in today's session?" encourages clients to express more information about a subject that is bothering them. Gathering information about the particular behaviors, thoughts, and feelings of clients so that the practitioner can better understand the conditions that contribute to the client's problem would involve a question such as: "What are you doing [thinking or feeling] in this situation?"

Creating client commitment to communication by asking the clients to talk and guiding the client to move in a focused interaction is important in interviewing. It is also crucial in community sessions where there are opportunities to be sidetracked by negative issues. For instance, members of a community meet with a generalist practitioner to discuss their problem of lack of water supply. In the middle of the discussion one of the community members begin to talk about the lethargic attitude of the community officials, which produces a long debate about community officials and distracts from finding solutions to the water supply problem.

Open-ended questions are good questions to start with because they allow applicants a great degree of latitude in beginning to communicate. Even asking questions like, "Tell me more about yourself [or the agency or community]" is a comfortable way to begin an interview with a client. Open-ended questions give the clients greater opportunity to discuss topics that are relevant to them, which leads to productive information gathering and at the same time helps clients explore and clarify their concerns. Open-ended questions generally put clients at ease and facilitate the elaboration of a point, which elicits specific examples of general situations.

In contrast, practitioners use *closed questions* when they require a definite answer. Closed questions tend to be more focused. They generally begin with words such as *are, do, is, can,* and *did,* and are answered with a short "no" or "yes." Questions are the major tool in gathering information as well in making an assessment of a client's situation. Closed questions are particularly effective in obtaining or verifying factual information about a client; for instance, "Did you receive a check this week?" While the response to an open question is nonspecific, to a closed question the response is almost always brief and definite. Closed questions are useful with clients who do not know how to express themselves, or when a person has difficulty talking. Asking a number of direct closed questions lets clients respond more easily with fewer words.

A word of caution. In interviewing, closed questions should be asked sparingly. This is because too many closed questions discourage discussion and also give the client permission to avoid sensitive and important topics. When making closed inquiries, ask questions on a specific topic. Closed questions should be used infrequently, and only when specific information that is important to the progress of the interview is needed. Other forms of closed questioning that need to be avoided are multiple questions in one sentence.

Asking leading questions and cross-examinations are forms of closed questioning.

Practitioners need to make sure that their questions are understood by clients, irrespective of whether they are open or closed. Checking whether you understand the client also is a good form of feedback and can be phrased as "I seem to be hearing you say this . . ."

To help clients continue their discussion, it is necessary to use minimal encouragement with phrases or vocalizations such as "and then," "umm hmm," or "right." Repeating a few words from the client's previous statement can provide minimal encouragement, too. When you use this technique, you encourage clients to continue and you also indicate that you are focusing and following.

Hackney and Cormier (1994) and Shainberg (1993) have developed some important guidelines for the effective and efficient use of probes in questioning.

1. The practitioner must develop questions that are centered around the concerns of the client. Effective questioning comes from what the client has said and not from the worker's curiosity or need for closure or disclosure.

2. After asking a question the worker should pause to give the client sufficient time to respond. Clients are usually under stress and the practitioner should not expect an immediate answer. Pressure to answer is threatening to the client and could encourage the client to give a response that pleases the practitioner.

3. Clients should be asked only one question at a time. Stacking questions may confuse clients and, at times, they may respond to the least important question and avoid the rest.

4. The worker must avoid accusatory or antagonistic questioning. Accusatory questions can happen when you ask a question that begins with "why," which typically puts the client on the defensive.

5. A worker has to avoid allowing questions to become a primary response mode during an interview. In some cultures overuse of questions seems offensive and intrusive, which could lead

to problems in the professional relationship and create resentment in the client (Gazda et al., 1995). Questions that are most effective are those that promote new insights and yield new information.

Many generalists ask too many questions. Clients should not be assaulted with a volley of questions that could put them on the defensive or overburden them. Questions should prompt clients to talk more freely and concretely. When asking questions that are information related, the practitioner should make sure that these questions are useful to the client. Questions should lead the client to talk about specific experiences, behaviors, and feelings.

> **JIMMY:**   I have principles I was brought up with. I can't be socially active and study and be an A student. What options do I have? Maybe I should give up all my social activities.
>
> **WORKER:**   Is this what you really want to do?
>
> **JIMMY (PAUSING):**   I guess not. Who would want to give up all their social activities?

At times, probes and prompts can take the form of statements and requests in order to help clients talk and clarify relevant issues. While probing, the worker has to keep the following factors in mind:

1. What is the purpose of my probe?
2. Can I anticipate the client's answer?
3. Given the purpose of my work, how should I word my probe so that it will be most effective?
4. How do I know if my probe is effective (Gazda et al., 1995)?

For example, Claire, who had been accused of neglecting her children, expressed a great deal of anger as she talked to a child protective worker.

> **CLAIRE:**   I just don't know where to start. I have a mother who is very ill, seven children, a boyfriend who disappears on me frequently, and no job. I am so angry.

The practitioner asks herself what the purpose of probing is and whether it is therapeutically useful to Claire. To be able to focus specifically on what issue is most important to Claire at this point, she wonders if she can anticipate Claire's answer?

Because she can't, the practitioner considers how to word her probe in order to make it most effective? Perhaps, "Which one of the problems . . ." or "Do you want to discuss . . .?" Finally, the practitioner wonders if the probe was effective.

Examine the responses of the client, both verbal and nonverbal and the resulting dialogue to see if the purpose was achieved; that is, if the client wishes to focus on a specific concern.

The worker can respond in the following manner, after thinking through the above.

> WORKER: Things must feel overwhelming to you now. Of the four concerns you just mentioned, which is the one that concerns you the most, right now?
>
> CLAIRE: My children. I want to keep them together, but I don't know how to.

This last statement is accompanied by direct eye contact. Claire's body posture is tense, but begins to relax. From Claire's verbal and nonverbal responses, the worker concludes that her question was effective because Claire focused on a particular concern and was not threatened or turned off by the question.

Making probing statements should place some demand on the client either to talk or become more specific. Probing statements are also indirect requests of clients to elaborate their experiences, behaviors, and feelings. For example:

> WORKER: I realize that you often get angry when your sister visits you and stays with you for more than a day. But I'm not sure why this makes you so angry.
>
> CLIENT: First of all, she comes uninvited and, because she took care of me as a child, she thinks she has a right to throw out my schedule for the day and put in hers.

Interjections may help clients focus their attention on the discussion:

> CLIENT: After cleaning up after my husband and children and fixing dinner, I am almost totally exhausted.
>
> WORKER: Exhausted?
>
> CLIENT: Yes, tired and angry because my children and husband do not do anything to help with the housework.

Some interjections can be nonverbal:

> CLIENT: There are lot of things about my husband I don't like [pause].
>
> WORKER: Uh-huh.
>
> CLIENT: For instance, he spends too much time working and too much time by himself. He hardly spends any time with me.

There are a few hints to keep in mind while probing. The first is to determine whether the probe is legitimate and therapeutically useful. Second, because probing depends on a specific purpose, decide what type of question will be most helpful to ask. Open-ended questions tend to foster client exploration, while closed or focused questions should be reserved for times when you need specific information or to narrow the topic of discussion. Finally, constantly assess the effectiveness of your questioning and determine whether its purpose has been achieved (Welch, 1998).

Probing and prompting are really the salt and pepper of interviewing, and should be used judiciously as condiments rather than as the main course (Egan, 1998). However, if there is reason to suspect such serious problems as child abuse, alcoholism, risk of suicide, or AIDS, precise factual information is essential. In such situations, human lives may be at stake. Consequently, probing may be the best course of action.

CONFRONTATION In everyday use, confrontation is often seen as hostile and punitive. However, in social work interviewing confrontation is a high-level skill the worker uses to draw the attention of the client to discrepant aspects of the client's verbal and nonverbal behaviors. Egan (1998) uses the word *challenge* rather than confrontation, because he notes that many people see confrontation as unpleasant. Challenge is an invitation to examine internal and external behaviors that seem to be self-defeating or harmful to others, or both, and to change if necessary. Confrontation includes conflicts, and client's feelings, thoughts, and actions. Patterson and Welgel (1994) indicate that confrontation is a tool to focus the client's attention on some aspect of his or her behavior that, if changed, would lead to more effective functioning.

Confrontation should be tentative and encourage the client to explore the discrepancies in his or her communication. Once a confrontation has been made, the interviewer should use skills that have been presented previously to discuss and resolve discrepancies. Confrontation is based on the worker's effective listening and careful observation of the client's behavior. It is used to help the client explore other and different ways of perceiving self or an issue that lead ultimately to different actions or behaviors.

According to Egan (1998; see also Cormier & Cormier, 1998; Ivey, 1988), there are six major types of mixed messages and accompanying descriptions of practitioner confrontation.

1. Verbal and nonverbal behaviors. A client says that she loves her husband but frowns and wrings her hands while she says this.

> WORKER CONFRONTATION: You say that you love your husband, but you are frowning and wringing your hands.

2. Verbal messages and action steps or behaviors that are discrepant. The client says that she will visit her mother the following week, but does not.

> WORKER CONFRONTATION: You said you would visit your mother but as of now, you have not.

3. Two verbal messages that state inconsistencies. A client says that his wife is sleeping around but he is not worried or bothered about it, and then adds that he believes their relationship should mean more to her.

> WORKER CONFRONTATION: First you mentioned that it was all right for your wife to sleep around, but then you said you are feeling upset because your relationship is not as important to her as it is to you.

4. Sending out two nonverbal messages that are apparently inconsistent with each other. For instance, a client cries and smiles at the same time.

> WORKER CONFRONTATION: You are crying and also smiling at the same time.

5. A situation between two people that is contradictory. Edith wants to move to another part of the country, where she has relatives because her caregiver daughter, Marcia, lost her job; Marcia does not wish to move because of her close friendship ties in the community.

> WORKER CONFRONTATION: Edith, you would like to move. Marcia, you are feeling strong friendship ties and wish to stick around.

6. Verbal messages contradict the context or situation in which confrontation happens. A young married couple has had conflicts and problems for the past three years, yet they wish to have a baby.

> WORKER CONFRONTATION: The two of you have separated three times since I have seen you in sessions. Now you are saying that you wish to have a baby to improve your relationship? The truth is, having a child and being parents increases stress, rather than relieves stress. How can the two of you deal with such a situation together?

To confront a client effectively there should be trust and rapport. Confrontation should not

A second factor that affects interpretation is *focus*. Research studies show that focusing helps give the client control to move effectively toward change (McGrath, Tsui, Humphries, & Yule, 1990). Focusing on controllable causes is more effective in the helping process than focusing on external forces over which the client has no control. Focusing is most useful when clients are overwhelmed with so many problems that they need the worker to help them focus on what is important, and when the important issues have to be discussed concretely.

Paolo exclaimed with his hands up in the air, "I have had the most horrible week! My girlfriend and I had a bad fight and she will not talk to me; my car broke down; my boss is mad because I have not completed my assignment; and I have not returned my mother's call. My brother borrowed my best suit for a night but has not returned it. I know what must have happened!"

Because Paolo presented many issues, the worker simply focuses by summarizing with the following statement: "Let's stop for a moment before we go on. It looks like you encountered a number of bad events this week."

In the given situation, the client is committed to communicate and the worker invites the talk and guides the client along a focused interaction. The purpose is to regulate the pace in the session and give focus.

When a client speaks, the worker should be able to focus on what the client is saying and at the same time be able to follow the information through eye contact, nonverbal behavior, and verbal following. For instance:

WORKER: Could you tell me what caused you to run away from your home?

CLIENT: I am scared to talk about it . . . it makes me nervous.

The best response in this situation is to look directly at the client and encourage him or her to talk. The worker should avoid staring, which can make clients uncomfortable. It is also not appropriate to take notes when clients appear nervous and hesitant, which might mean that they do not know

how much the practitioner can be trusted. In responding to the runaway, the interviewer could say:

> I realize you are uncomfortable and that is natural. I am here to help. I realize you are nervous, but everything that is said in this room is confidential [unless you are aware that something cannot be kept confidential]. I hope you will feel comfortable soon, and talk to me about it.

When there is silence, the worker does not push the client by asking too many questions, but respects the client's need to be silent, which might be the client's way of focusing.

CLIENT: I ran away from home because my parents are always fighting and my father almost beat me when I interfered in one of their fights. My friends' parents are all really nice. I wish I had parents like my friends.

Even if a client's information comes as a surprise, the worker should not avoid a client's gaze. Developing natural eye contact with clients is necessary for the helping process; however, when there are natural breaks in the conversation the interviewer can take brief eye contact breaks, particularly when the worker and client are thinking. When focusing, worker's body posture should be relaxed and attentive and facial expressions should be appropriate based on what is being discussed. The worker's verbal responses should be made in a warm, expressive manner. Also, the worker should follow the client's story and should not change the topic or interrupt the client.

The third factor is the *connotation* of the interpretation; that is, whether the worker reframes the client's behavior and attitudes in a positive or negative fashion. According to Madanes (1981) and Beck and Strong (1982) structuring interpretations to reflect a positive connotation promotes more enduring change.

To make a constructive interpretation, a practitioner's statement should be only slightly different or discrepant from the client's beliefs. It is constructive to recast the client's information into a new or different frame of reference, usually in a positive light rather than a negative one. Interpretations are based on the client's actual messages rather than the worker's biases and values projected onto the client. This requires self-awareness on the part of the worker.

There has been positive research data to show how interpretation can lead to expression of greater self-understanding, self-exploration, and behavior change (Beck & Strong 1982; Elliott, 1985). However, as Pope and Singer (1978) specify, interpretation often reveals information about experiences that a client may resist learning about, because of the anxiety aroused by a particular topic or situation. There are times when clients react to interpretations with anger and defensiveness because they do not wish to hear what is being said about them.

Therefore, when making interpretations the most important factor for a worker is *timing*. The client has to be ready for the interpretation. Although the worker may be able to identify the issues that are causing a client's problems in the first session, it is better to hold off until the client shows some degree of readiness to deal with the problem and the interpretive response. Brammer et al. (1989) indicate that a worker usually does not interpret until clients can almost formulate an interpretation for themselves.

It is important that interpretations are made in the beginning or middle part of a session so that the client has an opportunity to react to them. Making interpretations at the end of the session leaves little time for the client to react and does not provide useful or constructive help.

Milne and Dowd (1983) suggest that interpretations should be made tentatively, using phrases such as "perhaps," "it is possible," or "it appears as though." Also, it is useful for the worker to ask the client if the interpretation has been accurate in terms of the message. Practitioners should examine the effectiveness of interpretation by assessing clients' reactions. Are clients learning something from the interpretation? What are their verbal and behavioral cues?

INFORMATION GIVING   A social worker is expected to have specialized knowledge about human behavior, social problems, and community resources and to share the information with clients as needed. Information giving is essential to shared treatment planning and problem solving. As with other aspects of interviewing, pace and timing are important. Information should be presented when the client is ready for it, with enough time allowed for discussion of how the client wishes to use the information.

There are certain steps that facilitate information giving that practitioners can use as a cognitive learning strategy. With regard to the problem, what information does the client lack? What are the most important aspects of the information and how should they be sequenced and included in the sharing? How does the practitioner make the information easily understandable for the client? What is the possible emotional impact of this information on the client and what steps can the practitioner take in order to ensure that the information given is effective?

According to Selby and Calhoun (1980), to convey information about the psychological and social changes that accompany a problem situation is a highly effective addition to any helping strategy. For example, a client who is suddenly physically disabled may need information about lifestyle adaptation in terms of personal and occupational life, rehabilitation services, and support groups.

When practitioners do not have necessary information, it is preferable to say that they do not know and will find out. It is crucial that workers are honest with clients.

There is a difference between providing information and giving advice. When a worker gives advice, he or she usually recommends or prescribes a particular line of action, whereas in information giving the worker gives relevant information about the issue or problem. The decision concerning how this information will be used remains with the client.

The client, a young married woman with three children is also taking care of her mother who recently became a widow.

> **CLIENT:** I find it very difficult to refuse numerous requests made by my mother, though she is overdemanding. I do care about her, but I also need to take care of my children and other household chores.

> **WORKER:** Why don't you say that you can't take care of one or two requests—anything you feel comfortable with refusing—and then see what happens. (Advice giving)

Or the worker might respond in the following manner:

> **WORKER:** There are two things we need to talk about that affect the way you handle this situation. First, you need to understand what it means to you if you say no. Second, how were requests handled in your family when you were growing up? Often, even as adults, we respond to our parents the way we did as children—the way we were brought up—in such an automatic way that we don't even realize it's happening. (Information giving)

Advice giving involves the worker providing clients with direct suggestions for actions. Social workers are often uncomfortable about giving advice. However, when clients have no experience coping with a particular situation, the worker only damages them by expecting clients to find something that they do not have available.

It is important that advice is given tentatively so that clients do not automatically reject it. A tentative offering of advice can help the client summon more energy and ensures them of your concern and your willingness to join in the change effort (Simon, 1990).

The social worker needs to be aware of what kind of advice he or she is qualified to give and also when and how to give advice. For instance, when a pregnant client complains of pains the worker cannot advise, but only recommend that she see a medical doctor for advice and consultation. A worker cannot give advice about technical, medical, or scientific matters but can and should recommend the client to the appropriate source. In contrast, when a client complains of boredom, a worker can prescribe a different course of action for the client to follow.

Your client, Vonya, has a boyfriend who is constantly sleeping around with other girls. Though aware of the situation, Vonya, does not deal with it until she finds her boyfriend and another girl in her own bed at her apartment. She is still shocked and very upset during the session, as this event happened the previous evening. You have to hold off giving advice at this point, as the client is shocked and therefore the timing is not right. Also, how you approach the topic becomes crucial to whether the client will respond to you.

Simons and Aigner (1985) and Feld and Radin (1982) indicate that information giving in practice should be a tool and not an end in itself. They identify the major guidelines in information giving as when, what, and how information is given. In order to be effective, information giving should be well-timed. As a rule it is best to present the most significant information first so that it will be remembered by the client as the information is sequenced. Information should not be imposed on the client, who is eventually responsible for what and how to use the information. The information presented should be discussed in such a manner that it is "useable" and the client can "hear and apply" it in daily life (Gazda et al., 1995). Clients recall information when it is given in small pieces, rather than when they are overwhelmed with a lot of information at one time (Drake, 1994; Levy, 1976). Also, it is important not to give too much information, because at some point the client may start to ignore it and not take action (Gelso and Fretz, 1992).

Factual presentation of demographic date does not have a real emotional impact on a client. But when information is given about test results that indicate a person has a type of ailment, the client may react with pain, anger, and anxiety. It is best in these situations to discuss the client's reactions to the information that is given. The worker should not complicate matters by using jargon. The worker should even use a pencil and paper to draw a picture or figures if necessary to make information understandable to the client. The worker should ask the client to verify the information by summarizing or repeating it.

To summarize, information giving is a means of providing data to clients according to their need. Information should be given in a direct, concise, and concrete manner. After the information has been given, the worker should check with clients to note whether they have attended to the facts provided. The worker should also evaluate the client's response for any distortions and use other interviewing techniques to correct them. Information giving is utilized to orient clients to the interviewing process, to provide them with instructions and directions, feedback, and alternative perspectives, as well as to direct clients to other resources.

INTERVIEWER STYLES AND PROBLEMS

An interviewer's style is a blend of the worker's personality and skills. Some interviewers are "folksy," others more formal; some speak slowly, others more rapidly; some are outgoing, others more introverted. There is no one best interviewing style or technique. However, there are certain kinds of problems that are fairly common in therapeutic interviewing.

Interviewees can evoke a number of feelings in interviewers and some of these feelings may cause problems during a session. There are interviewers who have preconceived notions about different types of people based on prejudice and perceive clients accordingly which denies their preferences and individuality. Sometimes, practitioner dislike is based on a client's unwillingness to cooperate. Some clients make it difficult for the practitioner to work with them because of their attitudes and reluctance to work at their issues. At

times, the worker's personal issues may lead to misuse of the therapeutic role and to undermining or undercutting of the client to boost the worker's own self-esteem. In any of these situations the degree of awareness that a worker has is important. How does the worker view his or her role with the client?

There are workers who suffer from self-doubts about their ability to help, and such people do not have sufficient self-assurance to work with the information that is provided by the client. Some workers have problems with gratification. Workers may sometimes use power and control in order to impress clients with their wide knowledge and experience with the subject matter of the interview. The positive power that interviewers have in their position should not lead to misuse of this power in the interview session.

Also, there are generalists who are sensitive about the pain they might cause in asking about a client's failures and personal tragedies. Just as inexperienced medical doctors and nurses may be hesitant about giving an injection, novice social workers are sometimes too timid to probe into sensitive areas so they offer reassurance or change the topic.

Some workers themselves are in pain and are anxious to avoid sensitive areas (Day, 1995). If workers themselves have problems such as marital interaction and conflicts, parent–child problems, earning a living, financial problems, and dealing with issues of illness and death they may avoid these subjects because they hit too close to home. At times, problems overlap from home to the workplace and what is discussed in interviews may remind workers of unresolved or partially resolved problems present in their personal life. If workers are uncomfortable with unresolved issues, then they will be uncomfortable and not willing to discuss these issues. At times, workers may act out their own need to avoid a topic, which may indicate disapproval and direct hostility to the client (Kadushin, 1995).

A worker can reveal his disapproval in a number of ways:

1. Disapproval

   CLIENT: I was mad, I blew my top.

   WORKER: Just for that you called her names?

2. Topic changes

   CLIENT: My husband annoys me.

   WORKER: How old is your husband?

3. Ignoring hostile feelings

   CLIENT: I am really mad when I see tardiness.

   WORKER: We can all be tardy sometimes.

Another problem that workers face is a natural fear of hostility. When clients present inconsistent information, the worker may be too afraid to ask questions that could lead to a hostile reaction. A worker may also be afraid to challenge an inconsistent client because the worker imagines that he or she is being disrespectful. Trained to respect clients, new practitioners sometimes do not know whether they should confirm that an interviewee is not telling the truth. The worker needs to feel confident enough to call for honesty and responsibility without being punitive.

Worker burnout, which happens more often with experienced workers or workers who have been involved in the same problem situation for a long period of time, can also be a problem. Constant interaction with clients around certain problems may leave workers depleted, especially if they feel that they have not been very effective. Constant interaction and frustration leads to boredom and sometimes such workers may distance themselves from clients in order to self-protect. Obviously, such feelings are counterproductive to any constructive interview situation.

Other factors to consider include control and interview structure. Control should not be misunderstood as being inherently coercive. Skillful control of an interview situation implies stimulation and guidance without bias and pressure. In the final analysis the ultimate purpose of the interview

is helping the client, and the worker has a professional obligation to direct the interview toward the specific aim of meeting the client's needs. At the same time, different workers will choose to exercise different degrees of control, depending on personal interviewing style. Two examples follow.

WORKER: Tell me about yourself.

CLIENT: Where shall I begin?

WORKER: Wherever you feel like.

There is minimal structure in this situation. To achieve more structure, the worker would help direct the session more actively:

CLIENT: I have a lot of problems and I don't know where to begin.

WORKER: You are here to discuss the problems you have had since you broke your leg. Would you like to begin there?

Subtly, the worker is asking the client to focus and is structuring the interview a little bit more aggressively.

Some workers are active and others more passive in the practice session, which is also related to control and structuring. Greater activity on the part of the worker involves taking more initiative, whereas workers who prefer low control and limited structure take a lower profile and allow the interview to take shape as the client starts and works through the interactions. A worker could also be passive in one session but, depending on the client's needs, become more active in another session (Kadushin, 1995).

A worker's individual interviewing style develops from skills that the worker has learned such as focusing, reflecting feelings and content, and the more sophisticated techniques of interpretation and confrontation. In practice, the worker begins to integrate skills and develop a personal style. Developing style is also related to how the worker masters each skill and learns to respond to clients in a way that is comfortable.

Communicating Feelings and Immediacy

Immediacy or direct communication is the ability to discuss directly and openly what is happening in a relationship and that which is related to the professional relationship. Workers, like clients, have feelings. These feelings need to be communicated appropriately in a situation. Generally, appropriate communication between the worker and the client is focused on immediate concerns and deciding when it is appropriate to focus an interview on immediate concerns. The worker's ability to recognize personal feelings makes it easier to identify others' feelings. Communicating feelings is similar to reflecting feelings except that the emphasis is on the interviewer's feelings rather than the client's.

> CLIENT: I got this great new job that I really enjoyed and I was getting into it in a big way and then bang, there are budget cuts and they let me go.
>
> WORKER: I'm sorry they let you go. That's terrible news!

Another example of a worker expressing feelings can be seen in the following example:

> CLIENT (HAVING FAILED TO BRING HER DAILY JOURNAL TO SESSION A COUPLE OF TIMES): I'm sorry I left my journal at home, again. It's not that important, is it?
>
> WORKER: I'm upset that you forgot your journal again because it is one good way of understanding what you have been feeling for the past few weeks.

In the first example, the worker communicated empathy; in the second, irritation and disapproval. In addition to the words, it is important to be aware of the feelings conveyed by bodily reactions in response to the client's messages. When you communicate your feelings, it is necessary to maintain eye contact, a relaxed posture, and an appropriately moderated tone of voice.

A young woman who has been living with a man has decided to leave after she found out that he was cheating

on her. She told the worker, "I really don't know where to begin today," as she looked out of the window and became silent. "I told my ex-boyfriend that I want to find a place of my own," she said as she glanced out of the window again. "We had a long sensible talk [looking down at the floor]. It was a really good talk," she concluded as she continued to look down at the floor and fidget.

Communicating immediacy of feelings, the worker replied "I get the feeling that you are so upset that you can't talk about it."

The worker has to focus on what is and is not being said. To do so, practitioners focus on how clients express themselves as well as the feelings that have developed between the worker and the client or the nonverbal behavior that accompanies the discussion. Also, it is good to respond to clients in the present tense (Ivey, 1988).

> ANGRY CLIENT: I have been coming to see you for the past few months and yet you are not able to help me get a job. What the hell are you doing? I only came to you because I needed a job.
>
> WORKER: From what you are saying I get the feeling that you don't think I have helped you or that I am doing my job. It seems like I am not doing what you want me to do.

It is always good to respond in the present tense and also to express yourself carefully and sensitively and be ready to follow up openly and nondefensively. When a client gets upset and accuses you of not being helpful, it is important to respond immediately in a nondefensive manner and to highlight some of the emotions that the client is presenting.

Immediacy responses are also necessary when the client engages in aimless, circular discussion or agrees to achieve a particular goal but does nothing to attain it.

> CLIENT (AFTER TWENTY MINUTES OF LISTLESS TALKING):   There is nothing to say, nothing happened last week.
>
> WORKER: As I listen to you, I am wondering why we're not discussing more important things.

When discussing immediate concerns, it is best to promote and direct mutual communication, resolve tensions and discomforts, focus on and resolve incompatibilities, clarify the issues concerning trust, and resolve client inactivity and the client's feelings during the initial and final stages of the interviewing process. It is also essential that the worker send the client "I messages." All too often people send out "you messages" (e.g., "you should have more confidence in yourself," and so forth). Using I messages enables the practitioner to communicate in a noncritical and nonaccusatory fashion. As Sheafor et al. (1997) indicate, I messages are a basic communication technique that is used frequently with clients, professionals, and family members. It can also be taught to clients as a method of helping them deal with common interpersonal problems. For example, instead of blaming or accusing another person by saying, "You are making me angry," you could say, "I am angry because . . . "

Self-Disclosure

There have been several discussions about whether self-disclosure is useful and helpful in the helping sessions. Self-disclosure means sharing with the client personal information about yourself, your life experiences, attitudes, and feelings. Constructive self-disclosure helps you conduct the interview without distraction.

There are some practitioners who feel that self-disclosure should be avoided and that helping is most effective when objectivity is effectively maintained. But this author believes that self-disclosure is useful and helpful when utilized at the appropriate times. Barker (1995) specifies that, within the social work interview, the social worker's revelation of personal information, values, and behaviors to the client constitutes self-disclosure. The profession does not declare that such revelations should or should not be used, and in certain limited cases they may be considered useful. However, there is consensus that self-disclosure should not occur unless it is designed to help a client by achieving the client's goals.

Self-disclosure is related to authenticity and genuineness. It requires that the practitioner be aware of personal feelings and accepts responsibility for these feelings, both positive and negative. If there is a need to share feelings, the worker does so openly and honestly and without defensiveness and apology. Regardless of intent, we do disclose a lot about ourselves in a practice session. Sex, age, race, and class are fairly obvious. Even marital status is clear when the practitioner wears a wedding ring. Diplomas and certificates hanging on the wall reveal additional information about the practitioner. However, personal matters like parenthood, marital problems, frustrations, and disappointments in life are generally not revealed without a worker's choosing to share this information (Kadushin, 1995; Oz, 1995).

> CLIENT: I want to go away to college but I'm worried because my mother just got divorced.
>
> WORKER: You must feel a lot of pressure. I was faced with a problem like yours. That is, my mother got divorced when I went away to college too. I attempted to identify the main and immediate problems and tried to deal with the situation bit by bit, because it is scary to face the whole thing at once.

Self-disclosure on the topic of concern will help clients to sort out their way of handling the problem. When using self-disclosure, a practitioner can share information that relates to personal life experiences, current situations, or possible events in the future. Usually self-disclosures about the present and current situations are more powerful because they help the client to focus and deal with a particular problem concretely.

> CLIENT: I am a little overwhelmed. I am not sure if I can leave my parents and go off to college. I am not sure they can manage without me. I guess I should talk to them, but I'm not sure if this would be useful.

WORKER: Let me share this with you. Many times, I have felt responsible for one or both of my parents. When I felt this way, I often underestimated how well they could cope.

This self-disclosure focuses on the present and helps the client identify an important aspect of the problem.

When self-disclosing, the worker must focus on relevant personal material and respond with appropriate affect. When a worker self-discloses, it encourages the client to share information that is personally meaningful. It also increases the level of trust between the worker and the client. While using self-disclosure, the worker should focus clearly and accurately on problems and available resources and the worker's response should never overshadow, deny, or negate the client's communication.

CLIENT: I am afraid to leave home and go to Cincinnati for my new job because I don't know anyone there and I am not good at making friends.

WORKER: I have found it beneficial to sort things out ahead of time. This really helps me.

The best response is one that reduces the client's anxiety. Such a statement is sincere and nonjudgmental and encourages the client to explore appropriate ways to work through his or her anxiety. Self-disclosures should only be used in moderation after a constructive professional relationship has been established with the client.

Cultural Issues in Interviewing

Some people have stereotypical ways of viewing people belonging to different cultures, races, and ethnic groups. This is a legitimate concern and affects interviewing in the helping process. Maslin and Davis (1975) define stereotyping as ascribing traits to a person on the basis of presumed knowledge about a group to which a person belongs. Sue (1992) indicates that stereotypes are conventions that people use in order to refuse to deal with one another on a person-to-person basis.

The most important and damaging stereotyping takes place in terms of ethnicity and gender. America is becoming more and more diversified as people of many cultures make the United States their home, so there is a need to understand and work with different cultures.

As Hepworth, Rooney, and Larsen (1997) indicate, it is necessary for practitioners to develop an understanding and knowledge of norms related to a client's cultural background that are different from their own. Without that type of a knowledge, practitioners can make errors in assessing both individual and interpersonal systems, because cognitive, emotional, behavioral, and interpersonal patterns that are deemed functional in cultural context may be deemed problematic in another culture. For instance, asking unacculturated Hispanic women to assert themselves to their husbands may subject them to violence, because such behavior is contrary to cultural norms. In the same manner, asking an Asian American woman to stand up to her controlling in-laws would be potentially damaging because her cultural norms demand respect for older persons and that maintenance of strong family ties is crucial for family living (Lum, 1999). Cultures vary widely in their prescribed patterns of child care, child rearing, adolescent roles, marital selection, marital roles, and care for the aged.

Although it is essential to have knowledge about the client's culture in transcultural work, practitioners should guard against stereotyping clients on the basis of that knowledge. For example, there is considerable variation among different Native American nations, which are distinct groups with 250 distinct languages (Edwards, 1983). Filipinos embody diverse cultural groups who speak eight different languages and about seventy-five or more dialects. Cubans, Puerto Ricans, and Mexican Americans also differ widely from each other, although they share a common Hispanic heritage (Queralt, 1984).

In assessing the functioning of ethnic groups it is necessary to consider their degree of socialization into mainstream American culture. Clients from the same group may vary in their degree of acculturation, depending on a number of factors. Even then, mistakes can be made if practitioners fail to attend to a client's uniqueness. For example, generally unacculturated Asian Americans are regarded as emotionally unexpressive and are assumed to prefer structure and direction by a practitioner. However, Sue and Zane (1987) found that "many [Asian Americans] . . . seemed quite willing to talk about their emotions and to work with little structure" (p. 39). Other authors report that varying degrees of acculturation occur in the members of the same family and same generation (Kumabe, Nishida, & Hepworth, 1985).

There are clients who may need an interpreter to bridge the language gap. If an interpreter is not available, the practitioner should speak slowly, deliberately, and respectfully, so that clients have ample time to process the information they receive and respond effectively to it.

It is also crucial to keep in mind that cultural groups define problems differently (Green, 1982). In most Native American cultures, for example, family members actively seek counsel from elder members of the extended family unit in coping with their family problems. The wisdom of the elderly is highly valued (Hull, 1982).

It is important to remember that what people do in a specific situation depends on the behavioral options that have been made available to them. A culture presents acceptable options and condemns others. For instance, in some Eastern societies marital problems will have to be resolved within the family. Going outside the family is considered a shame. How should a practitioner deal with such a couple living in the United States who, due to lack of options and extended family networks, goes to a clinician? Would the worker understand the concept of shame that is involved in the couple's going to a practitioner?

In the majority Anglo-American culture there are differences between men and women. It has been found that white females use more reflective listening responses (Evans, Hearn, Uhlemann, & Ivey, 1993) and also utilize responses like paraphrasing and reflection of feelings. There is also evidence to show that African Americans tend to give more directions and advice than whites do (Ivey & Autheir, 1978). Even in the Anglo and African American cultures, however, we should be careful about overgeneralizing and ignoring individual differences.

It is crucial that a person in the helping profession be open to learning about a client's culture and yet understand that a person would be able to attain only a superficial knowledge if he or she is addressing that culture for the first time.

A worker has to be sensitive to both individual and cultural differences when interviewing a person belonging to a different culture. All cultures use listening skills, but they use them in different ways. The task of the practitioner is to learn how to use listening skills in different settings and to make appropriate adjustments in order to communicate with clients.

Okun (1987) reports that another common form of stereotyping in the helping process involves ageism. For instance, the stereotype that older persons cannot hear well or are not interested in sex can discourage workers to make assumptions that may affect the manner in which older persons are treated. If a worker has stereotypical ageist attitudes, he or she should be aware of them, particularly if they interfere with the interview process. The worker has to either modify his or her attitude or refer the client to another worker.

People with disabilities often require special help, education, training, and services. People with disabilities are protected by the Americans with Disabilities Act (ADA) of 1990, which became effective on January 1, 1992. The ADA requires employers to make reasonable accommodations to facilitate the employment of an otherwise qualified individual with a disability. A number of practitioners work in rehabilitative programs (Hepworth et al., 1997). Practitioners must be knowledgeable about various types of disabilities and relevant resources in the community or region as well as relevant laws, policies, and procedures. While working with clients who have disabilities, communication and interviewing skills should highlight empathy, care, understanding, and knowledge of available resources for a specific disability.

A variety of skills are necessary for effective interviewing. A person will adapt skills to reflect personal interviewing style. In order to be a competent practitioner, you must practice these skills. As a worker gains experience in interviewing, he or she will develop skills that will eventually establish an effective style. Remember to use your skills as required and to continue to integrate and sharpen skills as you move forward in the process of becoming a practitioner.

RECORDING

After an interview has been conducted, the practitioner records the interview for agency record keeping, time accountability, agency finances, and also for learning experience. Kadushin (1995) discusses recording of interviews and some of his thinking is incorporated in this section.

Record keeping helps maintain a client–agency contact that allows another worker to take over if need be without difficulty, or be involved in the case at a later point in time. The case records also meet requirements for the agency's accountability to the community. Another reason for record keeping is to achieve more effective practice, supervision, and administration. Recorded material may be used for in-service training, teaching, and for research purposes.

Case records are an integral part of becoming a professional social worker. According to Miles (1965) and Timms (1972), the record is used to organize a person's thinking about a case and also to plan a future course of action. Studies of case records show that the principal use has been to prepare and plan for direct or indirect service to clients. When workers read case records and also document what they do, the workers organize their thinking in terms of plans for the case.

Recording helps the worker to move toward more effective interviewing. Recording requires a systematic formulation of experience, which also helps to individualize the person, family, a group, a community, or organization along with the experiences of these different size client systems. If a worker has a large caseload, it is easier to recall a specific case if it has been noted in writing. Recording contributes to retrospective analytical reflection about the interview experience. Recording an interview also encourages cognitive and affective integration of the worker's experience with the clients (Kagle, 1991).

Documentation is important for third-party payments, as in Medicare and Medicaid, and also for peer review of worker performance. The court systems frequently use case records as evidence in order to terminate parental rights, facilitate divorce proceedings, and support adoption. A recorded interview may justify why a child should be placed in foster care.

A case record should note the purposes of the interview and whether they were achieved; the type of interventions the worker made and whether they were useful; the client's strengths and weaknesses; and plans for the next interview session. Also, case records should include identifying data that would help a worker recognize particular clients and their situation at a glance. Such information is usually presented in what is called a *face sheet*.

Normally the time lag between the interview and the recording should be brief. The longer the period of time between the interview and the recording, the greater the danger that the information in the interview may be forgotten or distorted.

The content and form of the interview record varies from agency to agency depending on the purposes of the agency and the purpose of recording.

The oldest form of recording is called *narrative recording*. This began by the second half of the twentieth century, when recordings included facts such as who received services, what resources were available and offered, and the impact they had on the client situation. For the first time, practitioners were "making a case," that is, judgments about clients' needs, resources, and responses. The concept of accountability was held in place not only through documentation but through explanation and evaluation, which came to be known as narrative recording (Kagle, 1995).

Schubert (1991) indicates that there are different types of interviews as well as recording that are part of a social work agency. These include:

1. A social history interview that covers a specific topic in a client's life.

2. Process recording includes considerable details about the content of an interview and the sequence in which the discussion took place. This includes the worker's comments as well as the kinds of emotions that a client revealed. The general behavior and appearance of the client and the worker's reaction are also recorded in the interview. The process recording is an important tool as a basis for supervisory or consultative help to the interviewer. The process of detailed recording helps in reflection as well as analysis of the material being presented. There are some agencies that still require process recording of all cases.

3. Periodic summary recording is done at specified times, indicating the dates of the interviews that are covered and a statement of the major findings at that time.

4. There are detailed or brief opening and closing statements that include dates of interviews and also the persons involved.

5. A summary is made when a client is transferred to another worker in the same agency or is transferred to another agency.

6. A summary is prepared for the purpose of psychiatric or other consultation or is prepared for staff discussion.

7. A checklist form is supplemented, if necessary, by a brief narrative. Checklists are less detailed than process recording and concisely list different items. At times the checklist form is supplemented by a brief narrative statement.

The different types of summary recording are effective in providing a description of services given and maintaining adequate continuity of service to the client. Criteria for a good record would include clarity, accuracy, selectivity, utility, easy retrievability, and brevity of information (Kadushin, 1995).

There has been an adaptation of the problem-oriented record that was originally developed by the medical profession, but has been standardized for other professions (Hartman & Wickey, 1978). This record involves: (1) systematic recording of relevant data; (2) identification of the principal problems that have been derived from the data; (3) development of an assessment plan for each identified problem; and (4) implementation of the plan. Although the problem-oriented record offers a streamlined format for organizing the record, as Kagle (1995) indicates, it partializes and oversimplifies assessment, deemphasizes strengths and resources, focuses on biomedical rather than psychological concerns, and disregards the complexity of service delivery.

Due to the vulnerability of agency records, two types of records are recommended. One is the official record that consists of more objective data, which includes a face sheet, health and test records, and summaries of interviews. A second group of unofficial records which the worker maintains for worker and agency use includes worker's notes, subjective impressions, and diagnostic references that relate to interview interaction (Kadushin, 1995).

In contemporary social work practice, audio- and videotaping have been used fairly regularly in recording interviews. Playing back an interview to a client has some therapeutic value. When clients see and hear themselves, it gives them an opportunity to view themselves in ways that they never have before. It may give clients a different perspective on their behavior and could be a subject of further discussion. Audiotaping and videotaping of interviews also help in worker supervision sessions. Workers view tapes of themselves and discuss their performance with a supervisor in order to understand their own strengths and weaknesses and how to nurture those positive qualities that would further enhance productive work with clients. This can help workers become better practitioners.

Computerization and standardized recording are also used in agency settings. As Kagle (1995) indicates, computers are used to log appointments, perform billing, budgeting and accounting, collect and analyze information about clients, services, personnel, and prepare reports and other documents. Many agencies use standardized forms to collect specific information about clients, service, and workers. They are an efficient means of ensuring that particular information is systematically documented. This type of documentation simplifies and routinizes record keeping and permits easy access to information that is necessary for caseload, fiscal, and agency management. One of the chief drawbacks, however, is that standardized forms fail to capture the unique nature of the client situation as well as the special qualities of the service transaction. A number of agencies balance the use of forms with the use of narrative reports (Kagle, 1995).

A Practice Exercise

After reading the chapter and assimilating it, interview a person, a family, or a group of people with a common problem for fifteen minutes.

Before the interview is actually held, consider the manner in which you will conduct the interview.

Make a transcript of the session. Classify your interviewing leads by skills and focus; classify the client's focus as well. Identify the specific stages of the interview as you move through the stages. You may not follow the order sequentially, but you must have covered all the needed stages.

Make comments on how you conducted the interview. Include both strengths and drawbacks. How could you improve it? Make notes on the same.

Develop an interview plan for the next session.

CHAPTER SUMMARY

Practitioners utilize communications skills in working with clients. In practice, it is important to understand affective, behavioral, and cognitive messages.

Verbal communication is both cognitive and affective. Significant or active communication takes place through active listening.

Good communication is an essential aspect of interviewing skills. The interview may be described as a conversation with a definite purpose. The purposes of interviewing are informational, in order to make a social study, to make an assessment of a client system, and to bring about therapeutic changes in the client system. The worker needs to develop self-awareness and be professional in his or her attitude toward all clients, keeping in mind factors such as race, ethnicity, religion, educational training, and qualification.

The interview process consists of the initial, middle, and ending phases. The skills and techniques of interviewing include listening and action responses. Listening responses include clarification, paraphrasing, reflecting content and feelings, and summarizing. Action responses include probing, confrontation, interpretation, and information giving.

Cultural issues should be viewed carefully in interviewing. Stereotypical ways of looking at clients, in terms of race, ethnic group, or gender will be detrimental to the helping process.

Recording is an important part of the interviewing process. It is necessary for keeping records, for time accountability, and for agency finances. There are different types of records such as the social history, process recording, periodic summary, checklist, and also audio and video recording of therapy sessions, but all serve the purposes of practitioner learning, helping clients, and for accountability to the community.

9

THE PROFESSIONAL RELATIONSHIP

Work with clients ranges from dealing with intimate personal issues to general problems in living. However, every aspect of helping carries an emotional aspect. Personal situations such as husband–wife conflict have an obvious intimate and emotional aspect. Even community issues such as housing problems or water supply involve both the heart and the head. In working with our clients, irrespective of whether the problem is short-term or long-term, we develop a professional relationship.

CHARACTERISTICS OF THE PROFESSIONAL RELATIONSHIP

Brammer, Shostram, and Abrego (1989) and Whiston and Sexton (1993) describe the professional relationship as important because it constitutes a principal medium of eliciting and handling the significant feelings, thoughts, and ideas that are involved in the helping process. This includes changing clients' feelings, thinking, and behaviors in conjunction with environmental factors. A pro-

fessional relationship is also used to help a group of clients move toward action.

An empathetic relationship plays a vital part in nurturing and sustaining clients and also provides the vehicle through which the practitioner becomes emotionally significant and influential in clients' lives. The type of professional relationship that is built with clients will vary depending on whether the client is an individual, a family, a group, a community, or an organization, as well as on the type of professional services they require. Nevertheless, the ingredients that determine the professional relationship are the same despite different clientele situations.

This chapter examines the characteristics of the helping relationship, the purpose of the helping relationship, the process of the professional relationship, professional relationship enhancers, and issues affecting therapeutic relationships.

As Coady (1993) and Bachelor (1995) indicate, being able to work with individuals is the first step in learning how to practice generalist social work. All of us should learn to understand interpersonal dynamics and have relationship skills in order to work not only with individuals but also with families, groups, communities, and organizations.

Goldstein (1984) explains that most practitioners and researchers view a professional relationship between the helper and the client as being necessary but not sufficient for client change. However, on the basis of that relationship a foundation is built that exists for no other reason than to yield the intended effects of change in different clients. Some literature refers to relationships as a therapeutic alliance (Barnard & Kuehl, 1995; Kokotovic & Tracey, 1990; Matziali & Alexander, 1991). Coady (1993) suggests that social work's historical emphasis on the helping relationship has been diluted in recent years and highlights the need for renewal. Matziali and Alexander (1991) found that a productive relationship includes an agreement between worker and clients to be aware of the objectives of the helping process, the tasks of the helping process, and an interpersonal bond between clients and workers, however brief this might be.

Pincus and Minahan (1973) indicate that descriptions of the professional relationship have largely focused on one-to-one or one-to-group relationships, but they point out that workers engage in many other types of relationships. In working with clients, workers may be involved with landlords, teachers, employers, and board of directors, a community of people, or the staff of an organization, among others.

When generalists and clients get together, some kind of a professional relationship develops between them. A generalist aims to develop a constructive working relationship with a client, but the degree to which that happens depends on both generalist and client. The generalist has the additional burden and responsibility of being the person who is knowledgeable and skilled in working with different kinds of people. The generalist's attitudes and skills are important determinants of the quality of the relationship that a generalist can enhance. An effective generalist should work toward achieving a balance of interpersonal and professional competence (Cormier & Cormier, 1998).

THE PURPOSE OF THE RELATIONSHIP

The professional relationship is a working alliance—an alliance in which there is safety for clients to better cope with their problems and issues and in which persons are freed to direct their energies and capacities toward making changes. It is important that professional social workers accept this responsibility as part of their skills and know what a helping relationship consists of, what its components are, and how to incorporate them consciously into their dealings with people (Perlman, 1975).

When we feel connected to another person, it is said that we are in a relationship. Most of us are capable of being involved simultaneously in a number of relationships. In professional relationships there are both normative and operational purposes. Normatively, the professional social work relationship is aimed at helping clients deal with their problems in a manner that is helpful to them. How the relationship is developed and utilized is called the operational aspect of the relationship.

A professional social work relationship is deliberately and consciously shaped and distinguished by its particular type of purpose, which is to increase the coping and adapting capacity of different clients. This relationship grows out of mutual consideration of what clients want and need coupled with the practitioner's obligation to participate fully in the problem-solving process. A professional relationship is established when a client and worker get together with a purpose in mind and ends when the worker and client recognize that the purpose has been achieved or that they have gone as far as they can go. This understanding or perception of purpose sets normative behaviors by establishing how people will and can behave toward each other. (Mayer & Timms, 1970; Maluccio, 1979). A classic study by Mayer and Timms (1970) reveals that there is difficulty in establishing a helping relationship with certain clients due to their lack of understanding of the purposes and values of the professional helping process.

When working with clients, it is important for the practitioner to clearly explain to the individual, family, group, community, or organization what their responsibilities are. It is presumptuous to assume that a client is looking for a helping "relationship" upon entering the social work situation. For that reason, the practitioner does not talk about the need for a relationship; rather, one grows out of purposive work and the problems and difficulties presented by the clients. The nature of the relationship depends on the issues that clients are facing and the goals that they have set. The growth and development of the professional relationship ceases when the goals have been achieved or when the clients choose to leave.

In the professional relationship, workers devote themselves to the interests of clients and the needs and aspirations of other people, rather than to personal interests. Workers also form relationships based on objectivity and self-awareness that allow them to step outside of their own personal troubles and emotional needs and become sensitive to the needs of others (Hepworth, Rooney, & Larsen, 1997; Pincus & Minahan, 1973). Practitioners are human, too, and do experience personal satisfaction and frustrations in their professional activities, but the expectation is that they will be able to set these aside and focus on their clients' needs and their professional obligations.

Practitioners receive sanctions from specific client systems, from the community that establishes and also pays for social work services, and from their own profession. The sanctioning sources expect practitioners to use their knowledge and skills to provide impartial, objective services in the best interests of the client. The practitioner is expected to be motivated primarily by ideals of service rather than by personal profit and gain (Pincus & Minahan, 1973).

From research findings, Goleman (1985) determined that the quality of the relationship between the client and the practitioner is the best predictor of the success of the helping process, an even better predictor than the kind of help. Though there is agreement that the helping relationship is important in working with clients, all do not agree about why that is so. Some indicate that the relationship in itself is therapeutic, whereas others stress the work that needs to be done through the relationship. Another view is that both factors operate in varying degrees in different cases.

RAPPORT

Deffenbacher (1985) and Egan (1994) discuss the kinds of characteristics that practitioners have to present in order to foster a relationship. When practitioners work with clients, they establish *rapport* that increases trust and creates an interpersonal climate where clients can openly discuss and work on their problems. Clients view the worker as a caring, positive, hopeful collaborator who helps them understand and make changes in their world. Good listening by the worker in an open, nondefensive, and careful manner helps in tracking the clients' concerns. Direct, honest feedback creates a context in which further exploration and strategies can be implemented.

Rapport is developed through effective communication. Rapport is crucial to offering effective help to clients. Unless practitioners successfully engage clients, they may be guarded about revealing vital information and feelings, and they may not pursue their request for help after the first meeting. When clients are engaged successfully with the practitioner, they have established rapport. Rapport reduces the level of threat and it helps clients gain trust in the practitioner's helpful intent. Thus a condition of rapport exists when clients perceive a practitioner as understanding and genuinely interested in their well-being.

Establishing rapport at the exploration stage of helping starts when there is focused and empathetic communication with all the attendant values and attitudes manifested in the professional services. When developing a relationship with clients, the worker has to be accepting and show respect for the clients' worth and dignity. Achieving rapport requires that the practitioner gain the trust and good will of the clients. This will help clients risk revealing personal and sometimes painful feelings and information to the worker. As such, it is best to remember that the majority of clients have not had any contact with social work agencies and therefore enter the interview situation and the beginning professional relationship with apprehension and uncertainty. A large number of people view seeking help with their problems as evidence of weakness and their inability to manage on their own.

Cultural barriers can prevent the establishment of rapport with different ethnic groups. For instance, many Asian Americans who have strong cultural ties will generally not discuss personal or family problems with outsiders. They believe that revealing problems to others is a reflection of personal inadequacy and therefore a social stigma suggesting disloyalty to their own families (Kumabe, Nishida, & Hepworth, 1985; Tsui & Schultz, 1985). Also Native Americans, African Americans, and Hispanics may experience difficulty establishing rapport because of the distrust established during a history of exploitation and discrimination (Hepworth, Rooney, & Larsen, 1997).

The best way to develop rapport with such clients is to employ a warm-up period. This is particularly important with ethnic and minority groups. A warm-up period is also important in gaining rapport with adolescents, particularly those who are emancipating themselves from adults. The worker has to be sensitive to timing and alert to different cues that the clients send out to the worker. For example, Native Hawaiians and Samoans may begin their narrations by participating in a "talk story" which involves sharing warm, informal, light personal conversation that it is not really a discussion of serious problems. It

would be considered rude and intrusive if the worker did not participate in the warm-up period (Hepworth, 1993). Similarly, Perlman and Pablo (1978) recommend that when practitioners are working with Native Americans, they should be low-keyed and nondirective.

In establishing rapport, the worker should start where the client is to lay the foundation for both beginning help and a sound professional relationship. This means focusing on the immediate concerns and emotional conditions of the client. For instance, when the client appears to be emotionally distressed, the worker should focus on the clients' feelings rather than the client's problematic situation.

For example, Minerva, is obviously distressed in the first session. She sounds broken-hearted as she talks about her mother's accidental death. She sobs deeply and gasps for breath. The worker should not focus on what happened but should deal with the emotional state the client is presenting, offering her a tissue and maintaining a respectful silence. If the worker interposed immediately with factual questions, she would appear insensitive and not tuned in to the client. A worker who is sensitive and focuses on the client's emotions fosters rapport, as the client begins to view the practitioner as concerned, perceptive and understanding.

In building rapport, the worker may have to slow down the pace of communication when talking with clients who have limited educational backgrounds or language limitations. The worker has to be sensitive to nonverbal cues when a client seems confused, because clients and people in general, are often reluctant to admit that they do not understand what is being said. This is particularly true when the culture is different or knowledge of English is limited.

VARIABLES IN THE PROFESSIONAL RELATIONSHIP

Variables in the relationship include the purpose of the relationship, as well as the setting in which the worker and the client system come together. The time limits set by the individuals, families, groups, communities, and organizations and the interests they represent are also variables, as are their capacities, motivations, expectations, and purposes. The goals for the resolution of problems, the qualities, knowledge, and skills of the workers and what they bring of themselves to the relationship are also important (Compton & Galaway, 1994).

The relationship is not an end in itself; it is rather a means to an end. A good relationship is essential and effective in helping clients achieve their goals. The goals cannot be achieved if the relationship is poor or if too much focus is placed on the relationship itself.

Helping at its best is a professional and humane venture and the helping relationship works in different ways. It could be a short-term relationship focused on case management and crisis intervention. An example would be a practitioner working with clients who call a teenage hot line. If a teenager calls just once about a destructive relationship she has with her boyfriend and to get information about agencies that could help her, the relationship begins and ends with this specific phone interview.

In some relationships the focus is on case management. The primary objective of this approach is to keep individuals in their own environments with the support of formal organizations (Moore, 1990). Case management services that are targeted toward a particular client group are managed through a professional relationship that requires the practitioners to have different types of skills. The targeted populations in case management include vulnerable groups such as families with multiple needs, developmentally disabled, frail elderly people, chronically mentally ill people, and other at-risk populations. The case manager needs to have expertise with special population groups and knowledge about available services to the designated groups in order to mobilize appropriate services. In the role of case manager, the worker can create a relationship as a problem solver, advocate, broker, planner, and counselor.

In professional relationships of eight to twelve weeks or more, which is the focus of this chapter, workers can aid clients by helping them tell their stories, particularly when their stories are difficult to tell. Help may also be given by clarifying their problems from their own point of view. Clients can be helped to develop alternative solutions to their problem situations, and workers can aid them by helping them tap into their inner resources and create realistic and meaningful agendas. Lastly, clients may be helped by brainstorming their options. Throughout this process, workers can be both supportive as well as challenge the clients to involve themselves fully in the helping process.

The relationship itself is a forum for social–emotional reeducation that takes place through interactions between practitioners and their clients. Clients learn to care for themselves. They also learn to trust themselves and challenge themselves, skills they may begin to learn through their interactions with the practitioners. As one practitioner noted at the termination of a relationship with a client:

> Because I trusted him, he trusts himself more; because I cared for him, he is now more capable of caring for himself; because I invited him to challenge himself and because I took the risk of challenging him, he now relates better both to himself and to others. Because I respected his inner resources, he is more likely to tap these resources. (Egan, 1990, p. 59)

THE MYTH OF THE PERFECT RELATIONSHIP

There is no one kind of perfect professional relationship. We deal with diverse types of clients who have different needs at various times in their lives, and these needs are best met through different kinds of relationships. A combination of skills and techniques is required to work with different clients. For some clients it is important that the worker is more objective and businesslike. There are some clients who fear intimacy, and still others to whom we need to communicate a great deal of empathy and warmth. Effective workers blend a number of skills and techniques to create the kind of relationship that is best for their clients.

One way of helping clients is to focus on values. Workers need to be proactive when we use beliefs, values, and norms in our interactions with clients. Particularly in social work and other helping professions, values are not only ideals but a set of criteria for making decisions. Working values become important while interacting with clients.

Gerald was a haughty, arrogant client who had an I'm-always-right-and-nobody-knows-better-than-me attitude which turned the worker off. She realized that she could respond to Gerald in one of two ways. She could either challenge him and put him down, or she could respond so that he understood her openness but did not feel belittled.

THE RELATIONSHIP PROCESS

In their practice with clients, workers need to follow the steps in the relationship process and have a set of working values (see Figure 9.1). Okun (1997) identified five steps in the helping process: (1) initiation/entry; (2) clarification of the presenting problem; (3) establishing a structure or a contract in the helping relationship; (4) intensive exploration of problems and; (5) establishing the goals and objectives of the helping relationship (see Figure 9.1). The professional relationship is also a tool for practitioner and clients who are working on solutions based on goals and objectives, implementing a treatment plan and evaluating outcomes, and finally terminating. (These aspects of helping will be presented in Part Three).

Whether a practitioner is working with a single client, a group of clients, a family, or members of an organization or a community, the basics of creating a professional relationship are the same. Working with different size systems involves human interaction and an intricate web of commu-

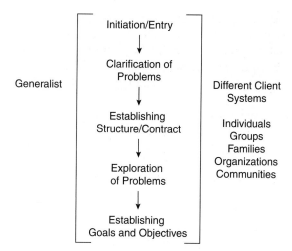

Figure 9.1 The Professional Relationship— A Tool

nication. For instance, when a generalist is working in an urban neighborhood where there are drug addicts, the ability to reach and help them would involve creating a relationship that would move toward helping them: This might entail hospitalization, rehabilitation, or initiating a needle exchange program. Similarly, if you wish to help a community open a recreational facility, you have to create a relationship with community residents and the decision makers.

The Entry Stage

When the worker meets a client, the worker has to do two things simultaneously: begin a relationship and also begin to interview the client. Usually a warm, friendly smile is a good way to start with a client. Workers must help clients understand that they are glad to see them. In a first meeting with a client who is obviously not comfortable, it is best to start the session with small talk about the weather or whether the client had problems with directions or parking. However, although asking and making icebreaking comments is a practical way to open an initial interview, the social chit-chat should be brief in keeping with the professional purpose of the contact. Quite often, beginning practitioners are uncomfortable themselves and attempt to keep a conversation going by asking too many questions. Simple statements such as: "Tell me what I can do to help you" or "Discuss with me what is going on in your life and perhaps that would help me to understand how we could work on your problem," are positive ways to initiate therapeutic discussions. Also, it is best to allow the client to talk, with the worker making responsive listening statements rather than asking questions.

During the entry stage it is important that the worker communicates support and understanding, while also seeking clarification if the situation presented by the client is not clear.

Bernadette constantly cries in the initial session and covers her mouth when speaking. The worker acknowledges her discomfort and responds in a nonthreatening and honest manner.

> WORKER: You seem uncomfortable. I realize you are having trouble relating your family situation to me, but please do take your time. I am here to assist you to deal with your situation as best as I can. I am glad you have come to see me.

In this situation the worker is waiting for the client to communicate and she is patient and understanding. In the situation that follows, the worker responds to the request for an explanation, again in a manner that is nonthreatening to the client.

> CANDY: I am not sure whether I should come to you with this information and I do hate to complain. But my daughter is having a very difficult time with her new teacher, Mrs. Susan, and is very unhappy.
>
> SCHOOL SOCIAL WORKER: I am glad you have come to see me. Please do tell me what you think is troubling your daughter about her teacher.

Here, the worker is reassuring the client that it is all right to deal with the issue and at the same

time, it is also acceptable to ask for further information. She does not feel a need to defend the teacher or the school.

Statements made to clients in a nonthreatening, open, and direct manner are called "door openers." The helping relationship begins when the worker starts communication flowing and does not judge, confront, or manipulate. Using statements such as "Tell me more about . . . ," "I am wondering . . . ," "It seems to me that . . ." can keep communication flowing, when supplemented by nonverbal behaviors such as head nodding, smiling, and being attentive.

A word of caution. Being supportive and helpful should stop short of false reassurances. For instance, when a client says that things are not all right with her marriage, it would be premature and false on part of the worker to say, "I am sure everything will work out fine." Such statements confuse clients, and help them avoid rather than approach the real concerns that they have. There is danger in the worker being too reassuring and denying clients the legitimacy of talking about their concerns. It is best to make the beginning questions open-ended and specific in order to concentrate on responsive listening. False reassurance also show the worker's lack of sensitivity and understanding.

Clarification of a Problem

Generally, clients who are seeing a practitioner for the first time are reluctant to immediately relate their real issues. They do not know who the practitioner is and feel a need to test the situation. Often, they may present superficial concerns until they can trust the worker. It is important for the worker to listen actively and respond to the client accordingly so that issues do not get sidetracked by other, and at times, superficial concerns.

A client comes to family session without her husband, but with her five-year-old daughter and discusses the child's behavior problems at home. Throughout the session, the client does not remove her dark sunglasses, which cover a swollen eye. The worker realizes that it is too early to ask the client any questions about the injury. After spending forty-five minutes of the session focusing on side issues concerning the child, the client finally makes the statement that her real problems are with her husband. She is very angry with him because he physically "pushed" her around, and she wants to talk about her troubled marital relationship.

It is a paradox that clients may go to a practitioner yet not be ready to discuss their issues, either out of lack of trust in the worker or their own insecurities. They may at times present many issues, and the worker must listen in a responsive manner in order to determine which problem the client needs to focus on.

Twenty-five-year-old Marisol was upset when leaving her clinical session.

> **MARISOL:** I will not be able to come for the next session. I just will not be able to make it, even though I know I need to see you. But I will be here the following week.
>
> **WORKER:** What is your reason? Looks like something is upsetting you.
>
> **MARISOL:** Not really. I need to be looking for a new apartment anyway. I need to have a place of my own.
>
> **WORKER:** What is happening to your present living arrangement? Is it not working out?
>
> **MARISOL:** You can say that again. The lady I am sharing the apartment with is very bitchy. She is always ridiculing my accent and laughing at my English. She's really nasty. I need an apartment of my own and I am not sure how I will manage. I don't know if I can manage.
>
> **WORKER:** It looks like you are torn between getting an apartment of your own or putting up with a bad situation in terms of your roommate.
>
> **MARISOL:** You're right. I have never been on my own before and I don't know if I can do it. Everything seems to cost so much.
>
> **WORKER:** Let's see if I can help you plan how much it will cost.

By taking time to listen to what the client was relating, the worker was able to identify the client's underlying fear and insecurity, rather than being sidetracked by the client's discussion of her roommate and the feelings she had for her.

It is best for workers to remember that a client's presentation of a situation can cover up more pervasive underlying problems and it may take a few sessions before these problems begin to emerge. A great deal depends on developing rapport and a trusting relationship so that the client will confide in the worker. Often, the client is unaware of the kind of problem he or she needs to discuss. At times, a client may begin with a presenting concern that needs to be dealt with immediately and later will talk about newer, emerging situations.

Abigail is a member of a support group for dieters.

> **ABIGAIL:** I have to discuss my weight problem with you. I realize that you also help with feelings about eating and I need help with mine.

The worker addresses the presenting problem of the group and all the members cooperate and everything begins to work well. However, after three weeks, a new problem begins to emerge for Abigail.

> **ABIGAIL:** I am upset. As I am becoming serious about losing weight, my husband is trying to sabotage me. We are having problems. He is sarcastic and jealous and jokes about my dieting.

Now, the worker is faced with a different and additional problem situation.

Contracting

When a client presents a problem, the worker is more or less aware of whether the problem can be handled in a particular setting. If a worker is not able to provide help, then the client should be referred to another setting to receive appropriate help.

For instance, assume that you are working in an agency that advocates and encourages pregnant teenagers to have their babies. The teens are helped toward taking care of their babies or advised to give them up for adoption, but the agency will not sanction or even discuss abortion as an option. A frantic teenager walks into the agency, and you are the intake or initial worker she meets. She talks about wanting an abortion and seems clear-headed and firm about this decision. Your professional and ethical responsibility in this situation, irrespective of your own feelings about abortion, would be to refer this teenager to another agency immediately so that she could take care of her problem in a way she feels is best for her. Hypothesize that you are the worker who is opposed to abortion. How would you deal with this situation? Would you attempt to persuade her to have the baby, and if she reacts negatively, would you reject her?

When dealing with a situation that you are aware cannot be handled in your agency you need to make a *referral*. Referrals are made for clients in order to see a designated worker or another agency for a specific purpose. In helping relationships early referrals are essential, because they take time to become effective. At times there may be a waiting period in another agency and if the client chooses to come to you during that period, you may have to offer a supportive, helpful relationship.

As Hepworth et al. (1997) indicate, there are guidelines to assist you in making referrals.

1. Make sure that clients are ready for a referral by eliciting their doubts, misconceptions, and apprehensions. If clients are not ready for a referral, the rationale for not referring has to be given. Often the rationale is that if they are not ready for a referral, they may not follow through irrespective of the worker's expressed interest in their well-being.

2. The worker and client have to work together to find resources that best suit the needs of the client. The worker has to be knowledgeable about the different resources available in the community and should have some idea of the quality of service that is offered in various settings. The worker is obligated to share relevant information with the client and also render informed judgments.

3. While exploring possibilities, the client's right to self-determination must be respected including recommendations about which resources are most likely to be beneficial to the client.

4. The worker should avoid making false promises and unrealistic reassurances about another agency. Usually clients are apprehensive about going to a new or different agency, so it is best to allay their fears and remind them of their apprehension in meeting you for the first time. Remind them how you both succeeded in developing a professional relationship.

5. The worker should be helpful about the referral but it is unnecessary to discuss the functions and methods of the agency selected more than briefly. Also, do not speculate about the kind of practitioner the client will work with or the kind of help that the referral practitioner can offer. False promises made to clients sets them up for failure. There is really no way to know what they can expect from another worker in another setting, because styles and techniques of dealing with clients vary among agencies and agency personnel.

Weissman (1976) and Mathews and Fawcett (1981) have defined connection techniques and reported impressive findings regarding successful referrals. These techniques include:

1. Writing down necessary facts about contacting a referral setting including the name and address of the resource, how to obtain an appointment, how to reach the resource, and what to expect when a client arrives at the setting. The initiative for making the appointment and following through is the client's responsibility.

2. The worker must provide the client with alternative contacts in the setting whom the client can call.

3. If the client has a complex problem and requests help in presenting it, the worker should assist the clients in writing a brief statement addressed to the resource, detailing the problems and the services desired by the client.

4. If the client wishes, the worker may call the referral agency from the office, so that the client may make the appointment with the contact person.

5. In the event that the client is reluctant to go, suggest that the client go with a family member or a close friend at least for the first time.

After taking these steps, the worker's responsibility to facilitate the referral officially ends. But it is best to ask the client to report back, if he or she has been receiving help and working with you for a period of time. Your continued interest may help in making this referral a successful one and enable you to suggest other alternatives if the client does not get the help he or she needs.

CONTRACTS A contract can be described as a consensual, mutual agreement and acceptance of reciprocal obligations and responsibilities with commitments to perform certain tasks and to deliver certain goods within a particular period of time. Contracts can also be described as agreements between two organizations or entities (practitioners and clients) which specify that one will provide certain services in exchange for payments from the other (Coley & Scheinberg, 1990).

A social services contract can be described as an agreement between a worker as a professional practitioner and as an agency employee and clients about their reciprocal role expectations, conditions, and objectives of service. It includes the operating procedures and individual and collaborative efforts that need to be carried out to establish a contract.

Hepworth et al. (1997) state that many researchers agree that a contract should include the following:

1. Goals that can be accomplished (ranked by priority)
2. Roles of different participants based on different size client systems as individuals, families, groups, organizations, and communities
3. Interventions or techniques that can be employed
4. Time frame, frequency, and length of the helping process

5. Ways of monitoring progress
6. Stipulations for renegotiating the contract, whenever necessary
7. Housekeeping factors such as beginning date, provisions for canceling or changing scheduled sessions or meetings, and financial arrangements

Making an explicit contract is one way of clarifying expectations. For instance, when you tell a client you will meet with him five times, then you should work toward five sessions. You can always agree to lengthen or shorten the time. The terms of the contract can spell out length of sessions/meetings, the site of sessions, fees, an estimated number of sessions needed and who may attend sessions, procedures for changing the terms, and identification of worker and client expectations.

There are three different types of contracts although they specify the same goals. *Written* contracts, which are signed by practitioners and clients, are not legally binding. This should be stipulated in the written contract or presented verbally by the practioner. The document is not legally binding, because clients are dealing with fluid personal issues and may choose to drop out of sessions or change the issues being discussed. In addition, by not legally binding clients to the contract, the practitioners are protected from clients who believe they are justified in filing for malpractice if they do not achieve the goals set forth in the contract. Written contracts are most commonly used by public agencies. *Verbal* contracts stipulate an agreement between practitioner and clients to reach some goals but it is not written. Finally, some contracts are partially written and partially verbal in identifying the expectations and goals. Any type of contract can be used with different clients. Research to compare the efficacy of written and verbal contracts with respect to process and outcome measures disclosed that there was no superiority of one method over the other (Klier, Fein, & Genero, 1984).

Obligations and responsibilities assumed by the clients are also spelled out in the contract. For example, the client has the right and opportunity to initiate suggestions for tasks and goals, as well as the means of reaching them. Clients also need to be clear on their options and limitations for choice. For group contracts the agreements may need to be based on a resolution of differences among group, community, or organizational members. Actually, the contract itself represents a resolution of such differences, and a commitment to mutual work on common or similar problems. Such an agreement must be acknowledged openly so that it can help activate pressure for change and compliance. Also, the members need to actively demonstrate their willingness to implement the agreement.

One of the problems in the helping process is that an individual client can sometimes be caught in an endless process with no frame of reference. For instance, a client receiving professional help talks about different topics at every session and does not focus on any particular areas of concern. The worker in turn, does not help the client to focus, so they go in circles. It is best to establish a framework when the client begins to discuss his or her issues that relates to specific goals in their contracts.

As mentioned in Chapter 7, there are two types of clients: those who come voluntarily for help and those who are mandated to receive help and are called involuntary clients.

Nineteen-year-old Gayle was referred to the university counseling center where she met the social worker. Gayle was not doing well in school. She was listless and homesick. This was her first time away from home and she did not seem to have made friends. At the end of the fifty-five minute session, the worker concluded that Gayle was suffering from low self-esteem and feelings of inferiority, inadequacy, and loneliness.

WORKER: Our time is up. How do you feel about what we discussed?

GAYLE: I guess it's okay.

WORKER: Would you like to continue to come?

GAYLE: Yeah. I think so, unless you think otherwise.

WORKER: Really, it's up to you. If you wish to, we could talk some more about what you are doing and how you are feeling.

GAYLE: Okay.

WORKER: For now, let us plan on four more sessions and go from there. As you are aware, it will be one hour per week.

GAYLE: That sounds good to me. Should I make an appointment with you or with your secretary?

WORKER: Talk to my secretary. She has my schedule.

In the session the worker realizes that the client is feeling diffident and unsure of herself. There is more probing to be done and more material to be gathered before the worker and client can come up with options, so setting a certain number of sessions provides the client with a frame of reference within which to function.

Ervin, a fifteen-year-old in a residential treatment setting, did not want to see the female social worker. After the worker made a couple of phone calls to his cottage, the client came to her office reluctantly.

WORKER: Ervin, I understand that you don't want to see me.

ERVIN: I hate you people. You talk and talk and talk and I don't see why I should come here. You are all full of garbage.

WORKER: I guess it makes you angry that you cannot make a choice but have to see me.

ERVIN: Yeah.

WORKER: What are your options if you don't come to see me?

ERVIN: I guess I would have to do some stupid chores in the cottage or . . . I don't want to talk about it.

WORKER: I am wondering what would happen if we decide not to meet again.

ERVIN: Look here, let me tell you this. If I don't come to see you, there will be a lot of trouble for me. I will not be able to visit my mother every other weekend.

WORKER: Do you want me to set up an appointment for you for next week?

ERVIN: Yeah. Set it up. I will come and see you only because I like to go home.

WORKER: Sounds like you wish you were living at home. I realize you are frustrated and we will see what we can do to arrange the sessions.

The immediate problem is that Ervin is tired of social workers or anyone else who he sees in that role. But as a resident in a home for disturbed children, he does not really have a choice. The only reason Ervin wants to attend the clinical sessions is because of his need to visit his mother, but with further exploration the worker may be able to help Ervin in more constructive ways. The practitioner does not become defensive or fight the client's reluctance to see her, which would be counterproductive.

Intensive Exploration of Problems

By listening actively the worker can begin to work with clients on the aspects, implications, and ramifications of their problems. In the exploration process a fuller, more complex picture of the presenting problem, and often other problems, may emerge. The nature and severity of the problems, the people who are involved, and the extent to which the worker can help the client is dependent on some initial problem-solving strategies.

Generally, the practitioner tries to learn as much as possible about the client, the system, the possibilities for change, and the different choices that exist. During this process the practitioner learns more about the thoughts, feelings, and behaviors of the client, both within and outside of the helping relationship. The worker attempts to learn about the client's values, beliefs, attitudes, defenses, coping and adapting strategies, and relationships with others, as well as the client's hopes, ambitions, and aspirations. Also, the worker encourages the client to express whatever thoughts or feelings are being experienced without being judged or instructed. While the client is communicating, the worker is promoting the development of trust, genuineness, and empathy to create a safe climate in which the client feels free to explore personal self-awareness (Okun, 1997).

The following excerpt is from the third practice session with Gayle. It demonstrates intensive exploration of her problem.

WORKER: So you felt for a long time that you were not capable of doing things on your own?

GAYLE: Yes. As you know, I am an only child and my parents have done everything for me.

WORKER: How do you feel about it?

GAYLE: Kind of funny. They were overprotective, I guess, and growing up, even in high school, they used to check my homework. My mom tried having another child but she had a number of miscarriages and finally gave up. Instead she invested all her energies on me.

WORKER: Sounds like your mom invested a lot of energy and time on you.

GAYLE: My parents always told me that they wanted me to go to college as they did not have a college education.

WORKER: Is college important to you, too?

GAYLE: I don't know, really. I haven't even started to think in terms of what is important for me. But all I know is that I don't wish to upset my mom.

WORKER: How about your dad?

GAYLE: Usually he says he wants what my mom wants. He always goes along with anything mom says.

WORKER: It sounds like you are angry.

GAYLE: It's so tiresome to think that my dad has no opinion of his own. At times, I wish he would stick up for me.

In this session, the worker is learning about Gayle's background and her feelings of low self-esteem and inadequacy. It is important that some exploration take place before goals and objectives are established. Intensive exploration is one of the most challenging and important steps of the helping relationship.

The members of a housing community are not clear about their goals, and they continue to quarrel with each other about their priorities. Their priorities appear to vary from safeguarding the entrance to their building, to putting up lights in the parking lot, developing a recreational place for young children, regular in-house baby-sitting services, shopping services for the elderly, and so forth. Opinion is divided about every issue. Finally, the worker asks the members of the housing unit to think through their issues together in terms of needs and wants and prioritize them accordingly. The worker highlights the fact that a decision that is agreeable to all or most members should be the priority. A follow-up meeting is scheduled for another time so that the members can think through and informally discuss their issues before they reach a consensus decision.

Establishing Goals and Objectives

After the problem has been explored, the worker and the client can develop more specific goals and objectives for the long- or short-term relationship. The practitioner should help clients choose their immediate and long-term goals because it is important that clients and the worker agree on these. In the case study involving Gayle, the practitioner and Gayle may develop specific goals for helping Gayle stay in school and working at her self-esteem in terms of the school setting, rather than working on long-term, more diffuse goals such as solving family problems.

One of the goals of the professional relationship is to provide a vehicle to the client for self-understanding, as well as working toward the development of alternative forms of behavior. The practitioner needs to explain to the client why the relationship exists and what are the goals in this relationship.

If the worker and client formulate several goals they should decide which goals have priority. Goal setting is important with clients because it increases their motivational abilities and results in better performance due to the client's active participation. Goal setting (Goldstein, 1973) for clients includes:

1. Obtaining some concrete services or needed resources such as employment, health care, or housing or financial assistance
2. Relieving immediate distress and other barriers and making important life decisions

3. Modifying structures in different size systems such as a family, an organization, or a community by changing community patterns, interactional behaviors, or rules and roles
4. Fulfilling some future aspiration through rational planning
5. Becoming aware of the value of growth and change and seeking social service to realize their fullest potential.

Goals should be explicitly stated and must be specific and arrived at mutually (Kishardt, 1992). When goals are clear and specific, it is easier to evaluate outcomes and minimize exploitation and confusion.

RESISTANCE

No discussion of the professional relationship is complete without discussing resistance. Resistance may appear when the worker and the client have not collaborated on establishing or striving toward goals. According to Anderson and Stewart (1983) resistance to change in general and resistance to being influenced in particular always occurs when individuals, groups, communities, or organizations are required by circumstances to alter established behaviors. For instance, a client is keen on bettering her communication skills with her husband, but the worker is concentrating on focusing on the client's own self-esteem issues and does not pay attention to the client's immediate needs. At times, group members resist because the worker is highlighting one member's needs and not paying attention to other members' needs.

Sometimes resistance happens when the client is threatened by the material that is being discussed.

The practitioner, Toya, discusses the negative effects of abortion as soon as her client mentions that she just had an abortion. The client is uncomfortable and hints that she does not want to listen to this information, but Toya continues to present the negatives of abortion. As a result, the client becomes resistant.

Resistance also happens when the worker is probing and interpreting sensitive issues before a trustful relationship has been developed.

An inexperienced beginning worker addresses a community of homeless people living in a park and continually asks them if they do not have any relatives who will take care of them. He also makes blanket statements such as "Don't you feel bad about the way you live?" The homeless walk away from him in disgust.

Kerri, a new client, sobbed and stated that her husband was having an affair and she wanted to leave him. The practitioner rather insensitively started to question Kerri about her sex life with her husband and proceeded to carry on a discussion about whether sexual inadequacy at home could have brought about the affair.

There are subtle forms of resistance, such as inattentiveness. This occurs when a client does not listen to what the worker is saying. Another way clients show resistance is when they constantly break appointments. Some clients become very ambivalent toward the worker, and still others may reject the worker outright.

A worker becomes sensitive to a client's resistance by attempting to understand the client's unique defensive style. The worker tries to reduce the client's defensiveness by changing the pace, topic, or level of the discussion and also by communicating support and acceptance of the client.

Mrs. Shasta, a forty-year-old, was angry when she walked into the session. She took one look at the worker and exclaimed, "I know how you social workers are. You will get into my head and ask me a million questions and then conclude that something is wrong with me. I've heard this too many times before. I don't like you people."

The new worker immediately took the hint and started the interview by focusing on the physical appearance of the client. Mrs. Shasta, an adult woman, had chewing gum stuck on her lips and wore a dress that was more appropriate for a young child. The worker focused on Mrs. Shasta's positive features and highlighted how good grooming would make her look very attractive. This discussion was so different from the kind of professional relationship and type of interview she had experienced with other practitioners, that Mrs. Shasta broke down her resistance and started to respond positively to the worker.

There are situations where the relationship is so well established that the worker can reflect to the client feelings of resistance and decide with the client how to deal with them.

Jamie had been in sessions for six months. But every time her practitioner attempted to discuss Jamie's conflictual relationship with her mother, Jamie would change the topic. The practitioner pointed out that Jamie's pattern of behavior was avoidance of any constructive discussion of the daughter-mother relationship. Although Jamie became uneasy she agreed to discuss her relationship with her mother in the next session because she also realized that it was important.

A worker can reduce resistance by changing strategies in helping, or as a last resort referring the client to a different source of help. It is not constructive to start a power struggle with a client. Struggling with a client can cause the worker and client anxiety, frustration, and anger. The more you pursue resistance, the stronger and more manipulative the struggle becomes. Resistance is often the client's problem but, out of a need to help or because the worker is deeply involved in the situation, it can at times lead to inappropriate behavior on the part of the worker. In such situations, blaming the client for resisting is not the issue, but understanding and recognizing the value and inevitability of resistance is part of the change process.

A group of older Mexican women, who were new immigrants, were learning different ways to understand the American work ethic and way of life. These women developed friendships with other women based solely on gender lines. These workers, unaware of the cultural differences, tried to bring men of similar interests into the group to make it more heterogenous. The new workers faced a great deal of resistance. One woman in the group commented, "I've never had an *amigo*. Men cannot be trusted too much. They might mistake or misunderstand your motives and some may even try to make a pass at you."

In the following case example, choose the response you think would best facilitate the development of an empathetic relationship and aid in clarifying the presenting problem.

> CLIENT: I don't understand why my husband and I are always fighting. We cannot seem to talk to each other anymore about anything.
>
> WORKER RESPONSES:
> a. Tell me more about it.
> b. All married people like to fight sometimes.
> c. It is scary that you can be so angry with your husband most of the time. Think about what happened that changed your relationship.
> d. What do you and your husband fight about?
> e. Maybe you need a change. How about you guys changing your routine a bit? Like going out to a dinner or a movie or something that is different?

This exercise allows you to experience the power of the worker–client interactions. Think of a situation you have experienced with a client, write down the different ways you could respond to one of the client's questions, and ask yourself the reasons for the different responses.

Involuntary or Reluctant Clients

Reluctant clients present a special challenge, especially to a new worker who lacks self-assurance. In such situations, Rooney (1992) suggests that the worker should use affirmation techniques, including responsive listening and acknowledging the reasonableness of the client's perspective on the situation. When a client is unwilling to communicate, the worker can exacerbate the situation by devaluing the client or by being sarcastic or impatient. Statements such as, "I have seen people like you before," or "We don't have all day . . . you

have to talk about your problem," are a demeaning and extremely unhelpful way of communicating with a client. On the other hand, if the practitioner communicates genuine caring and respect for clients, then the clients may begin to trust and communicate. As in many other situations, open-ended questions can help clients focus on self-examination. More often, however, workers get caught in an "I am here to help you" game with clients which is viewed by clients as threatening because the worker is implying omnipotence. One way to avoid this problem is to help the client structure the interview by highlighting what they wish to focus on in that session, which empowers clients (Okun, 1997).

In a residential treatment center, thirteen-year-old Nilé walked into the social worker's office for her first appointment. She did not lift her head but sat with downcast eyes, staring at the floor. The worker felt that he had momentarily seen her eyes but was not sure. Nilé was obviously pregnant. The worker resisted the desire to ask questions. At first, the worker was also uncomfortable, but he smiled and told Nilé who he was and added that she must have heard there was a new worker in her cottage. Nilé did not reply. The worker looked at her and commented that when she is ready to talk, he would be there to work with her. Nilé came for two sessions and did not say a word, but the proximity of the client and the communication of caring and genuineness by the worker's nonverbal communication and presence turned out to be useful. After two silent sessions, Nilé dropped her fears and slowly started to share thoughts and feelings that bothered her about the unborn baby. What appeared to be a test of endurance between two people ended in a meaningful therapeutic alliance due to the worker's patience and his ability to communicate positive feelings to the client.

When a worker is feeling fragile, as sometimes happens among beginning or overworked practitioners, there is the danger of feeling guilty or hurt when rejected by a reluctant client. One way to avoid feelings of rejection is to study aspects of your approach to the client, as well as the setting and situation, that could contribute to that feeling. Sometimes a worker's manner of communication may be ineffective with a particular client. In that case, the worker must modify the style or arrange for a referral. Modifying one's style might include using humor and being more openly supportive. A frank discussion of the resistance and clarification of the consequences of not working together may be necessary. When nothing works and the client refuses a referral to another worker or agency, leaving the door open for the client to return will sometimes lead to a different attitude at a future point.

Forty-year-old Vinny came reluctantly for the sessions. He was hostile to the worker, telling her in the first session that she reminded him of his first wife who was a manipulative woman. The worker fell for the bait and tried to tell him how she was not like his ex-wife. The harder she tried, the more he stereotyped her and as she attempted to extricate herself from this situation, he called her manipulative. Thus began a power struggle between worker and client that did not lead to any constructive helping. The worker understood the futility of the situation, as she saw herself becoming very defensive, she decided to refer the client to another worker. She realized that the client's "I am the strong man, and you are the weak woman" attitude had aroused feelings that she had been dealing with in her own life.

Angry Clients

It is extremely important for the generalist to openly address clients' anger and complaints. Generalists should be able to handle themselves assertively and competently in the face of anger. Workers who are not able to handle themselves assertively and competently in the face of anger and resistance risk losing the respect of the clients and the ability to offer help.

The worker is called in as a consultant to an organization, where she had been invited once before. As she enters the meeting room to talk to the employees she observes anger and hostility. As she begins to discuss their rights as employees, there is angry protest from the hundred or so organizational staff. One of them yells, "You have been here before, but we still don't have rights in this place. Why don't you talk to those people about our rights? You make your money anyway." There is chaos and angry laughter, and a number of staff members begin to talk at the same time.

The generalist responds empathically to reflect the clients' anger and their underlying feelings, "I sense you are angry at me and that you may be disappointed because things are not changing quickly enough. Please let us discuss this. I will definitely take your concerns to management as I did before and also express to them your disappointment and specify constructive actions that you would like them to take to ensure your rights in this organization."

The following section looks at the different ways by which relationships can be enhanced.

RELATIONSHIP ENHANCERS

In all practice relationships it is important that the worker be a knowledgeable person with curiosity and a desire to learn, in addition to having a warm and caring personality. Cormier and Cormier (1998), Egan (1999), Cournoyer (2000), and Chang and Scott (1999) emphasize several qualities that workers need in order to develop a professional relationship and work effectively with clients. These qualities include intellectual competence, energy, flexibility, support, good will, and self-awareness (see Figure 9.2). Related qualities include empathy, authenticity, expertness, pragmatism, genuineness, and a commitment to client self-responsibility.

Generalist's Qualities

Intellectual Competence

Energy

Flexibility

Support

Good Will

Self-Awareness

Figure 9.2   **Professional Relationship Enhancers**

One important quality that the helper should have is intellectual competence or expertness (Cormier & Cormier, 1998). Although working with clients is seen as a process which deals with emotions, it is necessary for a worker to have an adequate and thorough knowledge base in different fields in order to make informed decisions with the client about treatment and choices. For a generalist this knowledge should include information about different social policies and programs, community resources, normal and deviant human behavior, and family processes, in addition to knowledge and skill in counseling strategies and techniques. Competence is not just a goal to be achieved; it is a lifelong pursuit. To be competent is to continue to learn.

Another way to demonstrate competency is to model the kinds of behaviors that you might challenge clients to emulate. For instance, if you want clients to be open, you should be open. Competency also requires assertiveness. That is, if you are good at what you do, you should not apologize but just do it. Beginning workers should not be afraid to assert themselves. Workers should learn to do things that help clients and not be uncomfortable about being helpful. Most clients are not as fragile as we make them out to be.

LaVigna, Willis, Schaull, Abedi, and Sweitzer (1994) suggest that competence does not lie just in behaviors, but is also found in accomplishments toward which these behaviors are directed. For instance, a group of women meet every week with a group leader in order to become effectively assertive. If after a year of weekly sessions they are still nonassertive, then the worker's competence, other things being equal, comes into question. Trust in the worker can disappear quickly when little or nothing is accomplished in the helping sessions.

Workers should also have a sense of competency, combined with feelings of personal adequacy. When workers have feelings of inadequacy or incompetence, they may be overwhelmed by feelings of failure and fail to accomplish much. Such feelings hamper work with clients.

Unresolved questions of power can cause a worker to be too controlling or lead to impotence, passivity, and dependency. Using power to manipulate clients to meet and satisfy a worker's need to be omnipotent is a negative way of viewing and working with clients. In addition, workers who have not resolved their own intimacy issues may not be helpful to clients because such practitioners experience problems with closeness and affection. Because of their own problems, these practitioners avoid listening to emotionally intimate information and ignore the expressions of clients' positive feelings.

Workers also need to be empathetic. Empathy requires that the worker have the ability to understand people from their own perspective and point of view rather than the worker's. When a worker responds empathetically to a client, he or she "attempts to think with, rather than for or about the client" (Brammer, Shostram, & Abrego, 1989, p. 92). For instance, if a fifteen-year-old girl says, "I am trying to get along with my mother but it is not working out. She's too hard on me . . ." an empathetic response would be "You are attempting to work out a relationship with your mom and if it's not working, that must be very frustrating." On the other hand, "You should try harder" is not an empathetic response.

Short empathetic responses are more effective than long-winded discussions and speeches, which hamper the helping process and prevent workers from getting at the core meaning of what the client is saying. Also, when a client speaks enthusiastically, the worker has to respond accordingly. When a worker responds in a flat, dull voice, it is not fully empathetic. This does not mean that the worker should imitate clients, but he or she should share information in an emotional tone that suits each client's situation.

There has been a great deal of confusion about the terms *empathy* and *sympathy*. The word *sympathy* has more in common with pity, compassion, commiseration, and condolence than empathy (Gladstein, 1983). These qualities of sympathy are not totally useful in offering help. By behaving sympathetically the worker shows compliance with the patient's behavior and problems. This compliance bogs down the practitioner and the client's experience. Sympathy that merely agrees with the client lacks the objectivity of empathy, and the collusion of sympathy will not prove useful.

The professional relationship has an aura of commitment. Commitment means that the worker is willing to work with the client as demonstrated by being on time for appointments, reserving time for exclusive client use, maintaining confidentiality and privacy, and applying skills to communicate a sense of commitment (Cormier & Cormier, 1998).

Clients will feel respected to the extent that they are aware that the worker is trying to understand and help them work through their problems. This is done by asking questions and indicating both verbally and actively that the worker is interested in understanding the client.

According to Gladstein (1983), there are particular strategies and helping interventions that may be technically correct but therapeutically impotent unless they are combined with the right emotions. Being warm to a person reduces the impersonal and sterile nature of working with clients. As Traux and Mitchell (1971) and Hepworth et al. (1997) indicate, most clients respond with warmth to any warmth from the worker. Caring and being warm can disarm and diminish the negative feelings that the clients may have toward the worker.

Warmth and *spontaneity* enable workers to express themselves without contrivances or artificial behaviors. This means being tactful without being deliberate about everything you say and do. However, this does not mean that the worker should express every thought, particularly negative ones. Rogers (1961) suggests that practitioners who constantly express negative thoughts or feelings may find it difficult to convey empathy.

The worker also needs *energy* for an effective relationship. Dealing with emotions can be draining and it can affect the worker emotionally and physically. When a worker is energetic, enthusiastic, and dynamic the client learns and becomes more self-confident.

Workers also need to be *pragmatic*. They have to keep a client's agenda in focus. Because clients

are our customers, they deserve whatever we can give them. Otani (1989) recalled rather painfully his first attempts at being a practitioner. He focused more on theories that he had learned in graduate school than on the client's pain when the client complained that his homosexual lover was beating him up. Instead, Otani talked to him about his "real" problem which was the dynamics of his sexual orientation. Otani's success at pinpointing the dynamics did not last long because the client did not return for help. Focusing on and working out what the client needs is the only appropriate process of helping (Driscoll, 1984).

Another factor that workers need to be aware of in the initial stages of working with clients is *concreteness* (Cormier & Cormier, 1998). Often, what clients talk about can be an incomplete representation of their experience. Their words and language do not always represent their experience. Sometimes there are gaps in the presentation of their experiences that include deletions, distortions, and generalizations. Deletions occur when matters are left out or omitted, distortions happen when matters are not as they seem or they are misconstrued, and generalization means that a whole class of things or people is associated with one feeling or the same meaning and conclusions are reached without supporting data.

Because clients often leave gaps, it is important for the practitioner to use linguistic tools to achieve exactness and concreteness. This requires that practitioners not project their own sense of meaning onto the client, because that meaning may be irrelevant or inaccurate. For instance, a client could say, "I am sad." One worker responds to the client by saying, "About what, specifically?"; this allows the client to respond in specific ways about her sadness. Another practitioner responds by saying "Sad? I have been there, too. Oh, yes, I do know what it feels like. How sad are you?" The first worker is more likely to get a response that would be exact and concrete. The second worker, on the other hand, is caught up with personal issues and views the client's reality like his own.

Being concrete means that the worker is able to ensure that common and general experiences and feelings like sadness, anger, anxiety, and pain are all defined idiosyncratically for each client. The worker defines that experience or emotion by requesting specific information from clients and by not making assumptions or searching for equivalent meanings and interpretations. According to Lankton (1980), "to translate a client's words into your own subjective experience, at best, results in valuable time and attention lost from the clinical session. At worst, the meaning you make of a client's experience may be wholly inaccurate" (p. 52).

Flexibility is an important quality of personality for helpers. It is important that practitioners not be tied to any one single ideology or methodology. Flexible workers help clients with techniques that are useful to them, rather than pushing clients into the theoretical modes and strategies that the workers may prefer.

The generalist should be action-oriented. It is best to ask ourselves what we can do that will help clients act on their own behalf in a prudent fashion. At times, workers may assume that the client will need to be in the helping process for a long period of time, and this may not be true. The worker should focus on getting to the point and help the client as quickly as possible. Although some clients may continue to receive professional help, others will not because of money, time, and other commitments. This is particularly true now, in the era of managed care and the focus on short-term help.

Practitioners should do only what they think is necessary for the client and avoid generating resistance. If resistance does occur in the beginning stages of the relationship, they should assess what is being done that the client sees as coercive and then alter it in order to maintain a cooperative relationship in which issues can be dealt with productively.

Fifty-year-old Lana admitted leaving her children with her husband when she left home suddenly fifteen years ago. She explained she was depressed at that time and then became clearly uneasy. The worker, Shannon, who was also in her fifties and married with children, had been watching the client critically, wondering how a mother could leave her children and disappear. Lana "caught"

Shannon's nonverbal judgmental communication; she became insecure and uncomfortable and stopped talking. Because Shannon was self-aware, she realized that what she had done was incorrect and went back to building rapport. Shannon explained that her mind had wandered for a minute, and added that "it must be difficult for you to talk about your family."

The helping relationship is basically a supporting relationship, in which clients should view the practitioner as someone who respects and cares about them. Effective practitioners are *supportive* of all kinds of clients. As part of the professional relationship, they work with the client's anxiety and feelings. Being supportive of a client does not mean encouraging the client to lean on you. The worker as a supportive person should not be misconstrued as someone who "rescues" clients and thus robs them of their self-support.

When a worker has good will toward a client it means that the motives and intentions of the client are viewed as positive and constructive whenever and wherever possible. Another important factor in the creation of the professional relationship is *trustworthiness*. Fong and Cox (1983) relate that trust involves the client's perception that the helping person will not mislead or injure the client in any way. Trusting the worker means that the client accepts the worker's role and reputation for honesty, and views the worker as someone who demonstrates sincerity, openness, and a lack of any ulterior motives (Strong, 1968; Strong & Clairborn, 1982). Fong and Cox (1983) suggest that trust can be described as a series of relationship interchanges. Johnson (1995) indicates that trust is not a fixed phenomenon, but changes constantly depending on the actions of both persons. Particularly in the beginning stages of the helping process, most clients trust workers based on their reflecting professionalism and ethical behavior. Generally, clients place their trust in a worker initially on the basis of role and reputation and, over the course of time, they will continue to trust the worker unless the trust is abused in some way. But LaFromboise, Coleman, and Gerton (1993) and LaFromboise and Dixon (1981) indicate that members of minority groups frequently enter professional relationships suspending trust until workers prove that they are worthy of being trusted.

The important factors that contribute to trustworthiness include the congruence or consistency of the worker's verbal and nonverbal behaviors, including nonverbal acceptance of client disclosures and nonverbal responsiveness and dynamism. For instance, direct eye contact is seen as genuine interest rather than persistent gazing at a person. But if the worker tends to be incongruent in communications with the client, is judgmental, or shows evaluative reactions or passivity, the client's trust in the worker can be eroded quickly. By being genuine, the worker shows appropriate supportive behavior and a willingness to collaborate with a client in dealing with problems. When a worker is genuine, the emotional distance between worker and client is reduced considerably, which fosters an effective relationship.

A group of batterers is court ordered to participate in a group. At first there is a great deal of stiffness and silence. As the generalist deals with their issues directly and empathetically, the trust level begins to build. Group members then begin to participate by effectively communicating about their problems, including their anger and their impulsive abusive behaviors.

In order to be *genuine* and *congruent,* it is necessary to seek two things: (1) an honest knowledge of ourselves and what and who we really are; (2) a clear knowledge of different agency procedures and policies and their meaning to us; and add to that our acceptance of clients and commitment to their welfare, and to the authority aspects of the worker's role and position. A genuine, trustworthy, congruent person is also authentic. Authentic people do not hold back interactions that build the professional relationship but share feelings and thoughts when necessary, even if this is uncomfortable.

In creating a professional relationship with a client, we try to understand the individual. Similarly, clients also wish to know where we come from. When clients request personal information about a worker, they are interested in more than the facts. "Do you have children?" could mean that if you do, perhaps you can understand them better. At times, clients will test you by asking for a favor such as borrowing a book or having you call them at home. Again, it is not your immediate response that is important, but how you handle the request and also how reliable you are in following through. If a client looks at a book you are reading and asks to borrow it, you could respond by saying that you will lend it to the client after you are finished with it, or that you cannot lend it as it belongs to another person, or you do not lend books as a policy. A good rule of thumb is not to promise more than you can deliver and also to be sure to deliver what you have promised (Cormier & Cormier, 1998).

At times clients will put themselves down in order to see if they can trust you. The test of trust in the beginning stages of the relationship is determined by whether the worker can be accepting of the different aspects of clients that the clients themselves view as negative, dirty, or bad. Sometimes clients will say things to shock workers and to check out their level of acceptance. In all such situations the worker has to respond neutrally to client self-put-downs rather than condone or evaluate the clients' statements. Clients also test the worker by trying to change appointments, cancel at the last minute, or request a different location where they can be seen. The worker has to set limits in order to help the clients understand that the worker is dependable and consistent, which in turn can make the clients feel secure.

There are workers who have a tendency to view professionalism and objectivity as if these qualities mean "coldness" and "cautiousness." Presenting oneself in a cold and cautious manner is truly unprofessional and unrelated to one's need to be self-protective.

Another important enhancer of the professional relationship is *self-responsibility* with reference to the client. Workers do not make decisions for clients, but rather help them find their own solutions to their problems. What practitioners and clients do together determines the success or failure of the helping process. However, if clients are not urged to explore and assume responsibility, they may not do the things needed to manage their lives better, or they may do things that aggravate their problems (Egan, 1999). At times, workers may assume responsibility for the clients, which may cause the clients to work less. When workers and clients engage in the helping process together, they should share responsibility and work as a team to accomplish their goals (Patterson & Welfel, 1994).

Fisher and Corcoran (1994) have pointed out a number of hypotheses with reference to client self-responsibility:

1. Clients can change if they so choose
2. Clients have more resources for managing problems in living and developing opportunities than they or most workers assume
3. The psychological fragility of clients is overrated both by clients and workers
4. Maladaptive and antisocial attitudes and behaviors of clients can change significantly no matter what the degree of severity or chronicity
5. Effective challenging can provoke in the client a self-annoyance or a desire for a better way of living that can lead to a decision to change

Today we are also aware that highlighting and helping clients work on their potential competence and strength as well as respecting their opinions about their action options successfully brings about change. However, it also needs to be remembered that change involves a great deal of effort and sometimes pain.

Schwarz (1994) indicates that understanding clients in terms of assumed self-responsibility enables workers to tailor their responses. For instance, Brenda was anxious and confused in her behavior at the outset of the helping process and the worker literally had to hold her hand. But as Brenda started to feel better, she was also able to see herself as responsible for her own behavior and allowed the worker to challenge her more frequently about taking better care of herself.

Developing self-responsibility in clients means empowering clients and avoiding the danger of increasing a client's sense of powerlessness (Saleeby, 1992). The client and the worker have to accept helping as a two-way process, and the worker has to focus on the client's enlightened self-interest. Although it is difficult to change things that are beyond one's control, the practitioner who articulates what the client can control becomes an important strategist for developing the client's own power. Walter and Peller (1992) describe this process as an "enhancing agency." They ask questions that reflect the assumption that the clients are capable and are already solving their problem. In addition, clients have a responsibility for solving the problem and they have the freedom to do what they wish to do. Clients are the experts on what they want in their lives and what they will do.

In addition to the qualities and characteristics that enhance the worker–client relationship, there are other issues that the worker has to be aware of while developing a relationship with clients. These are discussed in the following section.

ISSUES AFFECTING THE THERAPEUTIC RELATIONSHIP

Although relationships with individuals, families, groups, communities, and organizations differ, each therapeutic relationship is defined somewhat by the type of clients we encounter in the helping process. However, certain issues affect professional relationships, including dependency of clients.

Client dependency can be seen as an ethical issue particularly when the client is vulnerable and looking for direction. In American society we believe dependence is not a positive factor and overemphasize independence. In reality, we are all interdependent people; we need each other. If this need is underemphasized, clients may view their dependency on a worker as a sign of weakness.

A word of caution. It is true that social workers sometimes encourage client dependency inappropriately, but it is also true that some social workers fail to respond to their clients' realistic needs for emotional support or practical assistance. Workers need to have an awareness of the healthy dependency that happens to all people in times of need. Persons in pain or trouble need to have their hand held until their usual coping capabilities are back and intact. Healthy dependency needs to be acknowledged, accepted, and dealt with accordingly.

Nevertheless, there is a real concern when workers deliberately encourage dependency behavior on the part of clients. Beginning practitioners sometimes keep clients in the helping process because they believe they would look bad if they "lose" a client. Some workers will not challenge clients who show up for sessions regularly and pay their bills, though they may be going nowhere in the helping process. In such situations, we may say that it is the worker who is dependent on the client, both financially and emotionally. This situation is more apt to happen in private practice than in agency setting, particularly if accountability is at a minimum. Some practitioners will allow clients to be dependent because it makes the practitioners feel important. When clients are not encouraged to grow, they may come to view their workers as all-knowing and all-powerful and thus continue to be immature and dependent. Some workers feed off this dependency in order to gain a sense of significance.

In many ways the mystification of the social work professional relationship tends to intensify clients' dependence and reduces their ability to be assertive in the helping process (Gelso & Carter, 1994). Mystification is the ability to purposefully bewilder and also play on a person's credibility in order to involve him or her in confused obscurity (Laing & Esterson, 1970). Gelso and Carter (1985) also describes how practitioners keep clients dependent and mystified in order to maintain their power.

Although the purpose of the professional relationship is to help clients reach their highest potential, Patton (1991) claims that powerlessness among clients is common. Powerlessness is a learned state of generalized helplessness in which clients believe that clients are unable to have an impact on their immediate environment, which could be a family or work situation. Clients also learn to believe that they need some external source to intercede on their behalf. Thus dependency among these clients becomes a self-fulfilling prophecy whereby their expectation of helplessness is reinforced in the helping situation and their expectations of powerlessness feed on their experience of being powerless.

Elena and her husband had been receiving professional services for two years. Elena was the original client but as her marital and family problems opened up, her husband and children joined in the helping process, which included family sessions and marital sessions. Elena would sometimes come by herself and discuss her issues with the worker. One day while in a marital session, her husband asked, "What is it you wanted to talk about in front of Ms. Meredith?" Elena giggled and informed the worker, "I truly love you and cannot discuss family matters without involving you in all of it." Instead of helping the client understand that her dependency was unhealthy, the worker felt flattered by how much Elena needed her. In many ways, the worker had encouraged the client to be dependent and helpless even in her relationship with her husband.

There are also practitioners who feel powerless and therefore cannot prevent their clients from feeling powerless. The issue of encouraging dependence in clients is often not clear-cut in the helping process.

In the following two cases, how would you deal with the situation in terms of fostering dependence or independence in the client?

Thirty-year-old Carmen is single and was involved with a married man for a number of years before she went back to college to get her master's degree. While in college she sought professional help and broke off with the married man, who had made promises to her that he did not keep. Carmen continued to see the practitioner to work on her self-esteem. However, as her graduation drew closer, she talked ambivalently about being on her own, getting a job, and giving up the security of student life, where she had rules and regulations to follow. Due to her earlier life experiences, Carmen did not trust her own decisions because she thought her earlier choices had been disastrous. Her style was to plead for advice about applying for a job, finding a date, graduating from college, and so forth. When the worker did not give her advice, Carmen got angry and accused the worker of not being directive enough: "Why should I come here if you cannot tell me what to do? If I knew how to make decent decisions by myself, I wouldn't be coming here in the first place."

How would you work with Carmen if she were your client? How would you respond to her continuous prodding and asking you for answers? What do you think of her statement that you are not doing your job if you are not giving her advice? What would you do to challenge her to move forward positively? How would you empower her?

Guillermo is a beginning social work practitioner who encourages his clients to call him at home any time and as often as they like. He believes that he is being helpful. Because most of his clients come from abused backgrounds, he feels that he needs to take care of them. He often lets sessions run overtime, lends money to clients, and devotes more hours to his job than he is expected to. He overtaxes himself by taking on an unrealistically large caseload because he feels "sorry" for the clients. Guillermo says that he lives for his clients and that social work is his life in that it gives him a sense of being a valuable person. He believes that the more he can do for people, the better life will be to him.

Point out the different ways that Guillermo keeps his clients dependent upon him. What is he getting out of this for himself? How would his life be without clients who need him? Are there any qualities in yourself that can be identified with Guillermo? Does your need to have clients more than they need you make you feel like a worthy person? If Guillermo was your friend, what would you tell him about giving too much?

Manipulation as Unethical Behavior

Unfortunately, practitioners can deceive or negatively manipulate clients under the guise of being helpful or concerned. There are ways of fooling clients. For instance, practitioners have kept the helping process mysterious and maintained a rigid "professional stance" that excluded the client as a partner in the relationship (Corey, Corey, & Callahan, 1988). One of the ways this problem could be prevented is through definition of the professional relationship in the contract between the worker and the client. This contract should emphasize the partnership between worker and client, demystify the therapeutic process, and minimize the chance that the client would be led astray.

One of the best ways to avoid manipulation is the worker's self-presentation as open, trustworthy, and vulnerable. As Jourard (1968) indicates, "If I want him to be maximally open, but I keep myself fully closed off, peeking at him through chinks in my own armor, trying to manipulate him from a distance, in due time he will discover that I am not in that same mode; and he will then put his armor back on and peer at me through chinks in it, and he will try to manipulate me" (p. 64). Manipulation can work in other subtle ways that can be unethical.

David works with a group of preteen school dropouts. He wants them to attend sessions so that they will return to school and be responsible. He attempts to win them over by taking them to restaurants and to movies whenever he observes discontent in the group. When there is a disruption in the group, he will manipulate them by offering to take them to a movie if they participate constructively in the group activity.

Dr. Andreo had a good relationship with his client, Mindy, a middle-aged woman suffering from depression and loneliness after her husband's death. Within six months Mindy recovered by accepting her husband's death and was ready to move on. Dr. Andreo, however, did not terminate and allowed her to come for sessions although it amounted to an hour of social talk. In fact, he encouraged Mindy to come, constantly stressing the need for her to remain in the helping process. Mindy's son was a football player and got free tickets to go to football games. Dr. Andreo liked football and Mindy supplied him with a large number of tickets that he wanted for his family and friends.

Was it unethical for Dr. Andreo to continue to see Mindy in clinical sessions when the nature of their sessions became basically social? Was receiving tickets from the client to see football games ethical? How would you handle the case? When does the helping process become exploitation?

Amanda is twenty-two years of age and on her own. She had eloped with an older man of a different religion of whom her parents did not approve. Subsequently, he squandered all of Amanda's money and then disappeared from her life. Amanda was too ashamed to go back home and went to work as a waitress. She was depressed and was referred to a social worker, Melanie, through her boss, who also had been in sessions with Melanie. Amanda had a number of issues to work through and the worker was helpful, but the issue of contacting her parents was never discussed. To make matters worse, Amanda ran out of money. By this time, Amanda had become more vulnerable and dependent on her relationship with the practitioner. Melanie, who was in need of a good babysitter, suggested that Amanda babysit her three children in a barter for therapeutic help. However, Amanda disliked babysitting Melanie's children and found Melanie's husband to be as critical of her as her father had been. Amanda found herself comparing her home situation to Melanie's home situation. This upset Amanda and she informed Melanie that she did not wish to continue and that perhaps she did not need any more help. This upset Melanie who assured the client that she had a great deal of "unfinished business" that she needed to address.

Was it appropriate for Melanie to barter Amanda's services? Who was really benefitting in this situation?

Is it appropriate for a worker to keep a client in the helping process when the client wishes to leave? What are the negatives in this case in terms of manipulation and misuse of the professional relationship?

Rational and Irrational Elements in Relationships

While a relationship is being formed with a client, it is necessary to remember the cognitive elements that are present in a relationship. Both the worker and the client bring to the relationship all of their human traits; that is, appearance, personality, knowledge, values, and so forth. The therapeutic relationship has the capacity to generate a great deal of emotional intensity. To some degree, workers have to be emotionally involved with clients in order to be helpful. But feelings, attitudes, and inherent patterns of behavior can be irrational as well. If a worker is cool and distant that may turn the client away. But if the worker is too involved,

this might cloud the worker's judgment and the emotional intensity might be threatening to both worker and clients.

There are two terms commonly used in discussing therapeutic relationships: *transference* and *countertransference*.

Transference is a process in which the client transfers to the worker past feelings and attitudes that they have experienced toward significant people in their lives. These feelings are triggered by the present situation but are brought to it relatively unchanged from earlier experiences. In transference clients' unfinished business with others distorts the way in which they see the worker. A high level of emotional intensity affects these clients, and they lose their objectivity and begin to relate to the practitioner as if he or she was the person with whom the clients had issues. These feelings are irrational in that they are usually unconscious and the manner in which they appear is inappropriate to the present situation.

Feelings experienced in transference can be either positive or negative. These feelings are connected to the client's past, but they become directed toward the practitioner (Kahn, 1991). Transference is a reenactment of an earlier important relationship—a replay of how the client wishes it were (Kahn, 1991). Mallinckrodt, Gantt, and Coble (1995) suggest that transference can be analyzed from the point of view of attachment theory. Transference is a misperception of the helper and of the therapeutic relationship resulting from the client's use of long-established working models of self and others to resolve ambiguities in the new caregiving attachment and to look forward to the motives and behaviors of the new attachment figure.

When Julie started receiving professional help, she seemed to take an immediate liking to her practitioner. She talked comfortably and divulged a lot of information that was irrelevant to the session. Sometimes she acted childish and silly. She talked as if she were close to the worker, although in reality this was not the case. At one point Julie called the worker, "Mom" and backed off, laughingly commenting that the worker reminded her of her mother. Fortunately, in this case a positive transference had taken place between the worker and the client. At times, transferred feelings are negative as when the client does not seem to like the worker and projects negative feelings toward the worker. This is called negative transference. In either case, the worker needs to talk to the client in order to clarify these feelings and work toward helping the client move in a positive direction in terms of receiving help.

Positive transference can be used for the growth of the client, and positive transference that facilitates treatment need not be discussed unless the transference is directly related to the issues being worked (e.g., the relationship with her mother in Julie's case).

Transference, especially negative transference is sometimes used as a cop-out. A client's reaction may be realistic based on his or her past, but the worker has to address the client's attitude by highlighting the differences and the need for the client to vent about his or her situation. The worker must also use the reaction to help the client rather than merely view the client as a difficult person.

Harris, a social worker, had a sweetheart when he was in junior high school who reminded him of his mother. Many years later, a bad marriage and a messy divorce coupled with the death of his mother left Harris feeling sad and lonely. He immersed himself in his work as a practitioner. Eventually a female client who had qualities of his mother and his childhood sweetheart was referred to him. Haris fell for the client and became involved in a sexual relationship with her. Of course, this was totally unethical. It was also extraordinarily detrimental to the client as she had started sessions to work on self-esteem issues.

Countertransference involves the feelings and attitudes that the worker has about a client. These feelings and attitudes may be realistic or characteristic responses to transference or they could be responses to material that troubles the practitioner (Kahn, 1991). Countertransference can be viewed as the point at which the practitioner loses objectivity and develops a strong emotional reaction to the client. As Watkins (1985) relates, countertransference also can play either a positive or a negative—constructive or destructive—role in professional relationships. Negative countertransference occurs when a worker's own needs or unresolved personal conflicts become entangled in the therapeutic relationship and obstruct or destroy the sense of objectivity. In that sense, countertransference can become an ethical issue.

Countertransference arises from a practitioner's own woundedness. It occurs when practitioners are blinded by an important area of exploration, when they focus on an issue that is more their own and pertains less to a client, when they use clients for vicarious or real gratification, when they put out cues that "lead" the client, when they make interventions that are not in the best interests of clients, and when practitioners adopt the role the client wants them to play in his or her own life script. In short, countertransference precludes a meaningful therapeutic working alliance with clients.

According to Corey, Corey, and Callahan (1988), countertransference can be seen in the following ways: being overprotective of some clients and revealing an oversolicitous attitude, seeing clients as fragile and infantile and protecting them from experiencing pain and anxiety that thwarts their own struggle, and not challenging clients to grapple with their own personal problems and conflicts; thus clients do not learn how to face and cope with their issues.

Watkins (1985) indicates that a worker may treat a client in benign ways which may stem from the worker's fears of the client's anger. The worker creates a benign and bland atmosphere with the result that exchanges between worker and client are superficial. In such a situation, the worker loses the therapeutic alliance and the worker–client interchange ends in a friendly conversation or a general rap session.

At the opposite end of the countertransference spectrum, the worker begins to reject clients based on his or her own perception of them as being needy and dependent. In such a situation, the worker keeps himself or herself distant and aloof and moves away from clients.

Similarly to how some clients feel, workers may start to experience the need to receive constant reinforcement and approval from clients. These workers have an excessive need to please clients and receive reassurance concerning their effectiveness. Ellis (1973) indicated that practitioners need to let go of their irrational need to please clients so that they have the ability to challenge and confront their clients' own irrational and, at times, self-defeating thinking. Practitioners are able to do so only when they risk their clients' disapproval.

At times the worker sees himself or herself in a client and become lost in the client's world and loses objectivity.

When fifteen-year-old Blake came for the clinical sessions with her parents, the worker observed that Blake's mother, Nadine, was overly controlling and authoritative. The worker immediately started to take sides with Blake against Nadine. It seemed to the worker that she, like her client Blake, had been "picked on" as a child. She identified with Blake and felt sure Blake experienced the same kind of discomfort that the worker had faced with her mother. By being supportive of Blake, the worker thought that she was trying to make Blake feel better. However, in the process she was alienating Nadine from Blake, as well as from therapeutic help. In reality there was no evidence that Blake felt the way the worker assumed she did. Nor had the worker faced the fact that she and Blake were two different people with two very different childhood situations. The worker's response to Blake and her mother was an irrational one rooted in the worker's own painful childhood.

Another manifestation of transference and countertransference is the development of sexual or romantic feelings between clients and workers. In such situations workers exploit clients, particularly because their clients are vulnerable. At times when a client behaves seductively, the worker may do the same, particularly when the worker is unaware of his or her own dynamics and motivations. If this is not handled in an appropriate manner, it can cause both the worker and the client a number of problems. It is best that feelings of attraction be recognized and acknowledged without becoming the focus of the therapeutic relationship. If a worker has not resolved his or her sexual feelings and needs and if they seem to interfere in the helping process, it is best that the client be transferred to another worker. The affected workers should go through a self-evaluation or consult another practitioner when they encounter difficulties due to feelings toward certain clients. Sexual encounters between workers and clients raise serious clinical and ethical questions and often end in practitioners losing their licence to practice.

In order to handle transference and countertransference, practitioners need to be aware of the dynamics that lead to them. Clues to transference and countertransference include a sudden eruption of feelings and strong emotions either by the worker or the client. Generally such emotions seem inappropriate in timing, intensity, and the context in which they happen (Perlman, 1971). The worker who does not see this transference or countertransference may respond inappropriately to the client. It is important that practitioners are constantly aware of the various levels of impact that they have on clients and the impact clients have on them (Brammer, Shostrom, & Abrego, 1989).

Racial and cultural barriers can also affect therapeutic relationships. Although practitioners may work toward a congruent working relationships across racial, cultural, and social class barriers, problems do arise. A person might spend a lot of time mastering knowledge about the history and culture of another race and plan to use this information in a therapeutic situation, but when he or she encounters a person of another race, feelings and thoughts may arise that are quite contrary to the plan. Such individuals may condemn themselves for inappropriate thoughts and feelings and may even deny them to others, yet these feelings persist because they are the result of irrational responses most likely learned as part of growing up. Every individual who grows up in our racist culture absorbs some of the irrational attitudes toward race (Compton & Gallaway, 1999). Workers should recognize such irrational elements as being part of the helping relationship because this realization helps the practitioner understand and accept clients' expressions and also helps practitioners exercise appropriate self-discipline in relation to their own behavior.

When working with families, and groups, organizations, or communities, generalists must develop an understanding and a discipline about their own status and needs. They must come to terms with facts and feelings about a group or a family, an organization or community, and their innate responses to open conflict among group members in a family, group, organization, or community situation.

In any group, there is conflict. Conflict is inevitable and a normal part of all groups and is also an important and necessary part of the therapeutic process. Conflict has the potential to enhance the understanding and strength of relationships among group members (Northen, 1982). But conflict can also overwhelm a group and drain its life energy, create resentment and hostility, and cause psychological damage to its members. Few workers are comfortable with conflict and a worker may become excessively warm and friendly in an effort to smooth differences. Some workers may become apathetic and do nothing, which in turn can lead to group conflict, greater divisiveness, scapegoating, and acting out.

Rather than avoiding conflict the objective of the worker should be to help group members grow and profit from conflict. One way is to hold the system steady by ensuring stability and continuity within the group (Henry, 1992). Even though a conflict can cause group members to experience hurt, pain, anger, and hostility, the worker can provide a stable environment in which members can talk about their feelings and work through their conflicts. The best track for a worker to take in such a situation is to address the conflict openly and to avoid defining situations in ways that suggest participants are winners or losers (Cowger, 1994).

Here are some questions that you should think about and deal with as part of your own professional growth (Corey, Corey, & Callahan, 1988). These questions pertain to self-awareness and therefore there are no right or wrong answers.

Do you react in overprotective ways toward certain people? Why?

Can you allow other people to face their pain, or do you have a tendency to want to take their pain away quickly?

Would you prefer not to deal with certain people, and do you have a tendency to move away from them?

If you reject certain people, can you spend time trying to understand why you do so?

Do you want the approval of your clients? Can you risk a confrontation with a client or are you afraid of taking that risk?

Can you confront some types of clients but not others? Why?

What are some of the qualities that clients have which would most likely elicit over-identification on your part?

What would you do if you were sexually attracted to a client?

How would you know if this sexual attraction is countertransference or not?

When do you think advice should be given to clients?

Do you give advice easily to clients? What does this do to you?

Would your own need for a social relationship with a client interfere with therapeutic activities and defeat the purpose of the helping process? Why do you feel the need for this social relationship? How should you deal with it?

Sexism in Professional Relationships

What is sexism? There are two ways to define or conceptualize sexism. One is based on discrimination with reference to the individual's gender.

Kieffer (1984) defines sexism as the range of attitudes, practices, and policies discriminating against women or men on the basis of their gender. Barker (1995) describes sexism as individual attitudes and institutional arrangements that discriminate against people, usually women and girls, because of sex role stereotyping and generalizations. Sexism is also based on cultural beliefs that one sex is superior to the other. For instance, in social work there is an assumption that female social workers will prefer direct service over administrative roles and thus they are openly advised to pursue their clinical education. Another way to conceptualizes sexism is at the societal or institutional level (Simon, 1994), which emphasizes the idea of male privilege and the subordination of women as a class in a caste system. Institutional sexism can be described as a process of exclusionary procedures, rules, and actions that are sexist in their consequences and cause a greater burden to be placed on females than on males (Van Den Bergh & Cooper, 1986).

The U.S. Bureau of the Census (1995) indicates that more than half of the U.S. population is female, yet women are shortchanged in the workplace. Even though their wages have increased, women still earn 30 percent less than men. Nearly 38 percent of female-headed households have incomes that are below the poverty level. Issues that women face such as poverty, homelessness, domestic violence, and inadequate child care are at the core social and economic inequities.

Trisha went to a male practitioner for help. There is a widely held belief that the worker is more aware of the client's needs than the client, and some practitioners like to keep the client in a dependent state. It is generally accepted that this is more prevalent with female clients than male clients. After several months in sessions, Trisha expressed the wish to discontinue receiving professional services as she felt that the relationship was not comfortable and too controlling. The worker spent the whole session explaining to Trisha that she would experience anxiety and depression if she stopped receiving help. Perceiving the worker's reasons as valid, Trisha went back to the worker for a few more weeks. But Trisha became uneasy and felt that the worker was setting her up to feel weak and powerless in the relationship. Finally Trisha stopped her professional services, she received a number of phone calls from the worker but did not return them. Angry and upset, Trisha set up a four-week contract with another worker. She needed to validate her perceptions about her own growth and the controlling relationship with the former worker. She felt that she was ready to break away from any dependency that the first practitioner had tried to create in her and had the right to "fire" the worker just as she had "hired" him. When she left the clinical sessions after four weeks with the second worker, Trisha believed that she had done the right thing. She called the second worker for a few months to reaffirm that she was doing well and that she was right in walking out on her first practitioner/helper.

Some practitioners are so preoccupied with being overly responsible and keeping female clients dependent that they neglected such reality factors as attitudes, personality traits, setting, circumstances, cultural differences, and socioeconomic conditions of clients (Boyd-Franklin, 1993).

Kathleen, went to see a male psychiatrist for help. She was attractive and well dressed and mentioned during the course of the session that she was a lesbian. The psychiatrist refused to accept her lifestyle, mentioning that she probably had not had a "really good time" with a man, which was why she was stuck with a woman. A lot of energy was spent in attempting to prove to the client that she should be a heterosexual. The psychiatrist focused on her anxiety and depression and stated that her current lifestyle was self-destructive. At this point, Kathleen dropped out of the sessions. Kathleen's relationship with her lover did not last. In the pain of this breakup and feeling like she had nowhere else to turn, Kathleen went back to the psychiatrist, whose first response to Kathleen when she mentioned that she had broken with her lover was, "Thank God, that's over. Now we can get down to the real problems." This made Kathleen angry and she did not return.

In order to be truly helpful to clients, practitioners have to establish a mature relationship with clients rather than treat them as if they were dependent, immature people. Instead of encouraging clients to be helpless, dependent, and childlike in clinical sessions as some of them might have been in other relationships, workers have to help clients move toward growth and self-actualization. In some cases, helping clients move toward independence requires accepting their dependence and allowing them to move toward independence at their own pace.

Through exploration, clients can proceed at their own pace to bring up issues and decide whether they can cope in their own way. Clients should also be encouraged to regain a sense of power over a small area of their lives through a more or less egalitarian relationship with a supportive professional.

To work with clients without being perceived as being sexist, practitioners must be aware of their individual and collective sensitivity to the role of sexism in society, and utilize practice models that respond both to individual, group, and community clients and to environmental issues that represent areas of change. Practitioners should make special efforts to overcome personal and professional sexism and test methods and models that are congruent with professional values and the cultural and socioeconomic environment of clients. Recognizing the dynamics of power involved in relationships and increasing sensitivity in the development of value-congruent models is important for social work practice (Boyd-Franklin, 1993). To move away from oppression of others would help practitioners achieve their full potential in their personal and collective efforts to be more sensitive and caring.

To explore some of your own feelings about sexism, think about the following questions. Again, there are no right or wrong answers.

What feelings and thoughts come to mind when you think of women and men? Why?

What is it that you dislike about women and men? What are your own experiences that contribute to those dislikes?

What are your expectations of women and men? Why?

What is it that you actually give to and get from women and men?

What do you expect will happen in the helping process with women and men in general?

What do you fear about women and men?

What are your feelings for women and men?

A different and totally negative form of abuse of clients occurs through sexual contact. The National Association of Social Workers' (NASW, 1993) *Code of Ethics* indicates that the social worker should under no circumstances engage in any sexual activities with clients. However, as in other helping professions this tenet has been abused in social work. Gil (1994) indicates that sexual abuse by practitioners is best understood along a continuum of three levels—psychological, covert, and overt abuse. In psychological abuse, the client is put in a position of becoming the emotional caretaker of the practitioner's needs. In such a situation, practitioners work at fulfilling their own personal need for intimacy through the client and thus reverse roles and start to self-disclose without any useful purpose being served for the client. In covert abuse, the boundaries between the worker and the client are diffused and the confused client is faced with sexual connotations by the practitioner that further invade into the client's intimacy boundaries. This type of abuse includes sexual hugs, professional voyeurism, sexual gazes, over-attention to the client's clothes and seductiveness through clothes, and gestures. At the end of the continuum are overt forms of misconduct that include sexual remarks, passionate kissing, fondling and sexual intercourse. Such behavior by professionals when reported by clients normally results in practitioners being suspended or losing their license to practice. To prevent abuse of clients, all helping professions have specific statements that condemn sexual intimacies between workers and clients. As in the NASW code, workers can be sued for malpractice; there are also definite procedures for processing ethical complaints by the NASW.

It is essential to remember that feminism adds a perspective to the strengths of women as survivors of patriarchy, inequalities, and oppression (Simon, 1994). Simon reports on the works of two feminist social work scholars from Great Britain, who view women as active, resilient, and enduring actors on their own behalf, rather than as sorry objects of other people's actions or words. Women discover their identity and self-worth in their ability to survive. Survival means more than perseverance or living a life of quiet desperation, it means self-assertion, however unobtrusively this may be expressed. Survival means taking on what has to be confronted, preferably on a woman's time, as well as on her own grounds and around her issues (Simon, 1994).

Racism in Professional Relationships

Pinderhughes (1989) examines the themes of race, ethnicity, and power from a cross-cultural perspective. Starting from the key role of culture in service delivery, Pinderhughes develops a strong case for cultural sensitivity and cross-cultural awareness; that is, understanding difference, ethnicity, race, and power. Often clients from non-dominant groups have experienced oppression, discrimination, and overt and covert racism. Therefore they may feel more vulnerable in interpersonal interactions that involve self-disclosure with a person they perceive as holding unequal power. During the initial meetings, clients from diverse backgrounds are likely to behave in ways that minimize their vulnerability and that maximize their self-protection (Sue & Sue, 1990). Often, Euro-American practitioners are seen as part of the establishment (Sue & Sue, 1990, p. 80).

Stevenson and Renard (1993) observe that the dynamics of hostile race relations still exist in U.S. society. It is important that practitioners question whether these relations are played out in any manner in the sessions with clients. Sensitivity to oppression issues allows practitioners to build credibility, which is critical to cross-cultural relationships especially in practice settings. A practitioner who refuses to recognize oppression only fuels a minority client's legacy of mistrust (Stevenson & Renard, 1993). DeJong and Miller (1995) recommend that practitioners understand and ad-

dress the impact of mistrust during the entire helping process from engagement to termination.

Practitioners have to keep in mind a number of factors, including professional social work values and skills. In terms of racism, specific factors are important in determining the outcome of intervention efforts. These include the historical place of racism in society, professional ideals, individual practitioner–client relationships and family, group, organization, and community practice relationships.

While working with clients from different groups, it is important that social workers consider cultural and lifestyle differences. Developing the ability to work sensitively despite racial and ethnic differences is an important aspect of a social worker's training.

Schulman (1991) lists the following as the major racism issues in social work:

Ensuring access to services

Sensitivity to cultural differences in any treatment or intervention by a social worker

Learning to speak in their language, when a large majority of clients belong to a different ethnic group or culture

Developing an awareness of the place of religion, beliefs, history, or tradition that may affect different clients, as well as of the special social or health needs that are prevalent within a given minority group

Using specialized treatment modalities such as empowerment strategies that may be more effective with minority clients

Understanding the client's unique values

Developing an awareness of newly emerging special problems of the clients in a particular minority group, like delinquency and alienation among some Asian American groups (Lum, 1996)

Providing special staffing or organizational structures that may be needed for more effective treatment of a particular minority client

Meeting special needs for particular kinds of services such as delinquency prevention, alcoholism, drug services, special health needs, special educational problems, and advocacy

Developing an awareness of special ways of coping that a minority group uses such as the availability of church or family as a support system among African American and Hispanic clients, with particular emphasis on child welfare and aging, also the role of the godparent in the Hispanic culture and the bodega (small grocery store) which are social and help centers among Puerto Ricans

Learning about special attitudes that are prevalent among some minority groups such as the male role in Hispanic society or the stigma that is associated with receiving certain types of assistance such as welfare or mental health services among many ethnic groups is necessary

People of different ethnic groups use emotions differently based on the language they speak. For example, Hispanics usually vary their emotional expression when they switch from Spanish to English. Schlesinger and Devore (1995) indicate that Hispanics generally offer more carefully weighted, rational, and intellectualized messages in English and more emotional messages in Spanish. Hispanics may come across as relatively guarded and businesslike in English, and yet when speaking Spanish, they frequently become much more open, expansive, informal, jovial, friendly, jocose, explosive, negative, or positive. It is as if two personalities reside in the same person at once. It is best to be aware of the language differences that could cause a barrier when ethnic groups who are more comfortable in their own languages have to express their thoughts and feelings in English.

Another negative instance of racism occurs when a worker is uncomfortable with a client and behaves accordingly. The following case study is based on a case study by Cooper (1973).

A twenty-two-year-old African American male who was recently released from a mental hospital attends an out-

ing that is arranged by the staff at his day treatment center. He is not sociable but engages sporadically in conversations with different group members and participates half-heartedly in group activities. While on the bus, a white social worker, a bright young woman conscious of the injustices done to African Americans, sits next to him and he begins to talk. He talks about performing violent acts. As they pass an affluent neighborhood, he looks at the homes and comments that he would blow up the houses because the people who own them have it "so good." The worker did not comment as she felt that neither she nor any other white worker had a right to discuss this with him. White guilt about racism prevented her from saying anything. But an African American worker might have been able to intervene constructively. Yet the white worker was aware that this client was angry and had overwhelming impulses. He was not just talking and he needed strength to control his impulses as he took his first faltering steps toward fitting into the community. However, overwhelming and misplaced guilt about the dominant group's past history overshadowed the worker, and the client was denied the help that he needed (Cooper, 1973).

In working with a group, the worker needs to keep racism in mind. A noneffective group dynamic may occur if latent but unconscious prejudices are aroused that could cause anxiety, fear, anger, and flight and appear individually or collectively among group members. Being sensitive to ethnic differences is important. However, to believe that people of a particular racial or ethnic group are best qualified to help each other can be taken to an extreme, due to stereotypical values and one's own inadequacies.

Knowledge of the norms and behaviors of different groups is necessary to work with them effectively. Without this type of knowledge a person can make serious errors in creating a relationship, which may be doomed from the start if the client views it as condescending, patronizing, or simply "foreign" to his or her way of thinking and feeling. Interpersonal relationships that are deemed functional in one culture may be viewed differently in another culture. For instance, based on therapeutic work with depressed, first-generation, lower-class Italian American women, McKee (1985) indicated that workers had to weigh the consequences of encouraging the women to be increasingly assertive in their marriages or become independent in their relationships with extended family members. The authors analyzed that participation in such middle-class mores of behavior would be at variance with the women's norms, and treatment would be viewed and experienced as being disruptive rather than helpful. These observations are also true for groups such as Mexican American, Puerto Rican, and Cuban women (Hepworth et al., 1996).

The social work profession cannot afford to sustain practices that would diminish the humanity of any group of people. Social workers should stop thinking that only African Americans can treat African Americans, that only Anglo-Saxons, can treat Anglo-Saxons, or only people of the same culture can understand and work with each other successfully enough to provide constructive help.

It is extraordinarily important for social work to teach that different is not "better," nor is it "worse," but that it is just *different*. Pinderhughes (1989) emphasizes the need for the social worker to highlight cultural strengths that enable people of different racial and ethnic groups to cope with social conditions. This entails empowering clients so that they have a higher level of self-differentiation and strong sense of self, as well as changing the social context of the problem situation.

After reading this chapter, students should discuss the differences in cultures. Discuss special different cultural events such as rites of passage into adulthood, marriage ceremonies, and the meaning and roles of different family members. After a couple such discussions with examples from different cultures, student should ask themselves in the privacy of their minds what they think of a culture or a group of people. Then they can constructively discuss multicultural issues to help to dispel some of their own preconceptions or biased thoughts. Finally, they should maintain a journal in which they can note differences and how they affect them, their sensitivity to such differences and the level of comfort they experience in creating relationships with clients from groups different than theirs.

Chapter summary

The professional relationship constitutes an important medium for eliciting and handling feelings, ideas, and actions that are aimed at helping clients. Rapport with clients is developed through effective communication and empathetic communication is necessary to build a professional relationship.

The relationship process consists of five steps: the initiation or entry stage, clarification, establishing a structure or a contract, intensive exploration of problems, and the establishment of goals and objectives. No examination of the professional relationship is complete without discussing resistance. A worker has to be sensitive and gain an understanding of clients' unique defensive styles.

There are a number of relationship enhancers. These include intellectual competence, expertness, assertiveness, empathy, commitment, spontaneity, energy, pragmatism, concreteness, flexibility, trustworthiness, being genuine and congruent, and encouraging client self-responsibility.

Issues that affect the therapeutic relationship are client dependency, using manipulation as unethical behavior in working with clients, and the role of rational and irrational elements in relationships which includes transference and countertransference. Transference is a process whereby the client transfers to the worker past feelings and attitudes that they have experienced toward significant people in their lives. These feelings can be positive or negative. Countertransference happens when a worker loses his or her objectivity and transfers feelings from the past to the client. These feelings could be positive or negative and are called positive or negative countertransference.

Sexism in the professional relationship includes the range of attitudes, practices, and policies that discriminate against women on the basis of their gender. Treating people differentially due to their gender role is unethical. Racism in professional relationships is a similar concern. It is important for social workers to be aware that being different is not worse or better, just different.

PART three

three

THE PROCESS OF HELPING

10

THE ENGAGEMENT PROCESS

The environments in which clients live, the roles of the generalist and the clients and styles of communication are covered in Part Three by examining the six stages of the helping process: engagement, assessment, planning, intervention, evaluation, and termination. These basic stages of helping are utilized with all different types of clients, cutting through every modality of practice

with different size systems. The only model that does not fit is the crisis intervention model where a person needs immediate directive help.

THE HELPING SITUATION

In the helping situation the generalist plays many roles as a provider of services. Generalists are both

apartment. The situation was devastating. When the policewoman and Mrs. Gonzales entered the apartment, they had to adjust their eyes to the darkness. Four children, who ranged in age from five to two months, were huddled in a corner of the unheated apartment. They looked weak and malnourished. At the sight of the police, they began to cry incessantly. Mrs. Gonzales learned from the neighbors that the mother was unemployed and prostituted herself to make money. At times, she left her children with a babysitter; at other times, they were on their own. Mrs. Gonzales decided to take the children to the city emergency shelter. She left a note for the children's mother explaining what she had done and asking the mother to contact her as soon as she returned to the apartment. Within two hours the mother was at the agency demanding her children. Angry, upset, and concerned, she complained that when she needed help in the past, she did not get any.

Imagine you are the worker in this case. What specific questions would you raise with the client? How would you engage this client in the helping process? How would you go about exploring the problem situation?

The First Face-to-Face Contact

To develop a good working relationship with clients, the practitioner has to lay a foundation. Most beginning workers feel uncomfortable meeting clients for the first time; presumably, clients feel the same. In the first session, the practitioner and the client size each other up and form their initial impressions. Workers ask themselves several questions:

1. Who is the client?
2. What is the client's background?
3. Are there any special problems or needs?
4. How should I deal with this client?

As Sheafor, Horejsi, and Horejsi (2000) and Conrad and Schneider (1992) indicate, there are several guidelines practitioners can follow in creating positive interactions with clients. First and foremost, the worker should be prepared to respond in an understanding manner to the client's fears, ambivalence, confusion, and even anger in the first meeting.

The physical setting in which the session takes place should be comfortable in terms of temperature and furniture arrangement. Chairs facing each other without a desk should be used for a person-to-person session. Also, the worker should use good communication skills, including both verbal and body language, in attending to the client. The worker should dress in a way that conveys professionalism.

Russell, a thirteen-year-old in a residential treatment center meets the new worker and comments angrily, "I hate you guys. You are nothing but trouble!" Is Russell insulting this particular worker or would he do it to any worker? How would you react?

Amanda, a new client, enters your office. You are busy talking on the phone, so you acknowledge her with a nod and continue your conversation. She stands awkwardly in the center of the room because you have not invited her to take a chair. You are on the phone for another five minutes and ignore Amanda. After your phone conversation, you invite her to sit down. Amanda, is hesitant and a little hostile. Why is Amanda uncomfortable?

If a client has requested the session, the worker can begin with some small talk, such as a comment about the weather or a question about whether it was easy for the client to find the agency. After a few moments, the worker can move on by asking the client about the concerns that brought him or her to the agency or indicating why the client was asked to come in. In either case, the worker has to explain his or her role, qualifications, the agency he or she represents, and what he or she hopes can be done together to work with the client's problems.

Another important factor in engagement is confidentiality. The worker has to reassure clients that anything they divulge will be held in confidence. This reassurance often puts clients at ease so that they can present information without fear of their confidences being violated. However, in some situations the worker plays a different role. For instance, in a court-mandated case, a practitioner may have to tell a client that the information he or she is giving cannot be held in complete confidence. In such cases, the practitioner might say to the client: "Before you start to talk to me, I need to let you know that I am preparing a report for the court based on our sessions. Whatever you tell me will be included in my report to the judge. I hope you understand this clearly. Nevertheless, my primary objective is to help you work on your problems."

If you have limited time, the client should be made aware of this during the first session, so that matters of highest priority will receive the necessary attention. The worker should also give a great deal of attention to what the client describes as his or her concerns. Often clients are not sure of workers and will attempt to test their competency and trustworthiness before they begin to relate their real problems or the whole story. The social worker has to start where the client is, with whatever the client considers essential. Professionals should not jump to conclusions about a client's problem. Rather, they check out their assumptions and perceptions to avoid jumping to premature conclusions. If the client says something that a practitioner thinks is impossible, a professional does not react with disbelief or surprise. Neither does a professional jump in and give advice.

A professional will respect the client's feelings, and not push the client to make statements. If the client needs to remain silent and pause before speaking, the practitioner sends a verbal or non-verbal message that says, "I will give you the necessary time to develop and arrange your thoughts and decide what you wish to say."

The practitioner should avoid using technical or complex language when dealing with clients. Professionals communicate at the client's level and capacity for understanding. To make clients feel at ease, they ask open-ended questions unless they need specific answers. Professionals also take precautions not to ask questions that clients may be unwilling to answer.

Seventeen-year-old Lisa was obviously pregnant. The practitioner wanted to know if this was her first pregnancy, so he forced the question on Lisa in the first session. Lisa was not comfortable and did not want the worker to label her or make it difficult for her. She also was not sure of this new worker, so she quickly said that this was her first pregnancy, although in reality it was her fourth. The worker's question was too hasty and prevented a positive engagement from happening.

Clients sometimes ask a service-related question in the first session about which the practitioner does not know the answer. The practitioner should not feel embarrassed because no one can knows all the answers. The worker should explain and offer to find the answer, but not make promises to get information quickly if this may not be possible.

There are two points of view about note taking during the initial session. Sometimes it may be necessary to take notes on pertinent client information, which might also demonstrate the worker's concern and desire to remember some important facts. However, for some workers and clients note taking can be distracting. If it bothers clients, practitioners should explain why it is necessary to take notes, such as filling out an agency form. As a formality, the practitioner should let the client follow the information as he or she writes it down. Because it is the practitioners who make clients feel at ease in the clinical session, at times they may have to stop taking notes.

The practitioner should plan the next session before ending the first session, taking the name, address, and telephone number of the client. This may not be necessary for an organizational worker who can reach clients through the agency, but in that case the worker should give the clients his or her name and specific telephone number at the agency.

Helping Clients Tell Their Stories

When we communicate with clients, we attempt to help them engage in self-disclosure or tell their stories. Clients explain the situations or concerns that are causing them problems, situations they have not managed well, and opportunities that they have not used.

Twenty-nine-year-old Vicki has been abandoned by her boyfriend of seven years and ends up in public housing in the inner city. In the first sessio\n the engagement of the client takes place in the following manner.

VICKI: I really don't know where to start. I have too much on my mind.

WORKER: You say that there are too many things bothering you. What kinds of things?

VICKI: Well, I moved into this public housing building recently. The people don't take care of the building. It's dangerous to live there. I've got four daughters and I'm worried about their safety. You hear gunshots and fights at all times in the night. I worry about myself, too, but mostly I am worried about my girls.

WORKER: It's bad that you have to worry and be afraid for your own safety and more importantly the safety of your children.

VICKI: The elevator is broken all the time, and using the staircase worries me the most—it scares me.

WORKER: The staircase?

VICKI: It's dirty and dark and there are no lights. That's not the scary part. It looks to me like no one really cares about anything. Strangers walk in all the time; women have been raped. Nothing has been done about it. This building is definitely not at the top of anyone's list. I can tell you that. I don't know whether to stay or leave, but I really don't know where to go.

WORKER: So you don't feel safe in the building. Worse still, it looks like no one seems to care. Plus, the circumstances that you are in at the moment make you unsure, and you cannot move even if you wanted to.

The worker here is engaging the client using skills of active listening, empathy, and probing, all of which are used to build a relationship with the client and help her tell her story in her own fashion. When the engagement begins positively, as seen in Vicki's case, the client and practitioner will work successfully together and the client will reveal the main concerns of the problem situation. By discussing the problem situation, the client and the worker will come to understand the situation more fully. At the same time, the worker will develop an understanding of the client and his or her needs.

Problems

Problems can be classified as concrete or psychological. *Concrete problems* deal with lack of resources such as unemployment, financial problems, housing, transportation, child care arrangements, and physical disabilities. *Psychological problems* include role uncertainty, life transitions, and interpersonal and intrapersonal problems. However, in reality problems are likely to be interrelated. Problems may stem from concrete situations or individual inadequacies and become combined at some point.

The problems that clients present fall into categories of choice issues or change issues or a mixture of the two (Cormier & Cormier, 1998; Dixon & Glover, 1984). In *choice issues,* the clients may have the resources to deal with a problem but do not feel ready to do so. In other situations, the clients may have the prerequisite skills and opportunities but feel conflicted and uncertain about an option, a choice, or a decision. For example in Vicki's case, she is uncertain about whether she should move. At times, clients do not have the information they need to make a decision, or they run into emotional blocks.

In *change issues,* there are some deficits or excesses in a person's behavior or situation that need to be remedied. Clients are dissatisfied with themselves or a situation and wish to make changes either in themselves, in the situation or both (Dixon & Glover, 1984; James, 1991). This calls for some kind of restructuring. In Vicki's case, she would like to live in safer surroundings due to her living experience in public housing; the situation is frightening to her as presented by her affect. She does not mention making moves to change her situation, as in remedying matters through action perhaps due to financial reasons. Thus her situation involves both change and choice issues.

In engagement, practitioners face different types of clients and also different types of issues. The following case studies illustrate some of these issues.

Wendy comes for help, because she has a number of problems with her two adolescent sons who have been placed in a residential treatment agency. She has problems taking both the sons home at the same time because she sees them as quarrelsome and uncontrollable. When Wendy meets her sons' social worker in the residential setting for an initial session, she says that she wishes to discuss a number of issues. She talks about her mother whom she describes as being dependent on her. She moves to another topic and talks about her boyfriends and how every one of them let her down. She talks about her father who died suddenly. Then she explains that she lives twenty miles away from her family and feels guilty about it. But Wendy likes her freedom. Her newest boyfriend is married and hopes to get a divorce soon, and she hopes he will not be like the others. Wendy talks about her job and her supervisor whom she does not like. She would like to change her job. At a later point she talks about her sister whom she loves very dearly, but Wendy feels abandoned by her because the sister left town three months ago and has not been in touch with her. At the end she adds that she has a degree in psychology and is aware of her issues.

Wendy's complex story comes pouring out like a gushing river. She jumps from topic to topic and tells her story in her impulsive style. At one point, she stops and smiles, "I didn't know that I had so much to talk about!" In spite of her overflowing problems, Wendy does not seem to be overwhelmed by them. Wendy's problems are a combination of choice and change issues.

Twenty-one-year-old Kathleen needs help to work on her problems with her boyfriend. In another relationship two years ago, she found out that the man was cheating on her and she ended the relationship abruptly. Kathleen wishes to maintain a "healthy" relationship with her new boyfriend Skip. After the introduction and preliminary formalities and some basic information, Kathleen just sits there and does not say anything. She does not even look up. As Kathleen does not talk, the worker uses a number of probes to help her tell her story. Even when the worker is empathetic, Kathleen is withdrawn and she volunteers very little information. Finally, Kathleen begins to cry. Gradually she talks in bits and pieces. She is having trouble with Skip, who is domineering and controlling and threatens to leave her whenever they get into an argument.

Now look at a third example of an involuntary client who has been mandated to seek professional help. Involuntary clients may be abusive and neglectful parents, abusive spouses, prisoners, probationers, or psychiatric inpatients. The coercive power that brings them in touch with a practitioner may be a legal authority such as a judge, probation officer, or a child protective agency (Sheafor, Horejsi, & Horejsi, 1991). The problems that involuntary clients have are attributed problems (Reid, 1997) because others attribute problems to them and the clients may not necessarily acknowledge these problems. Because involuntary clients appear to lack motivation to change, workers must possess skills to enhance their motivation.

Stella is sixteen years old, a runaway, and a prostitute. She has been arrested a number of times for street prostitution. The practitioner already knows a great deal about Stella, because of her court record. Stella is street smart, cynical about herself and others, her occupation, and the world in general. She is also very hostile toward the social worker.

STELLA: If you think I am going to talk to you, you are out of your mind! What I do outside of this hole is my business.

WORKER: If you don't want to, you need not talk about what you do outside. We are meeting here to discuss what've we are doing in this meeting.

STELLA: I am sitting in front of you because I have to. And you are here because it is your lousy job and you get paid for it . . . Probably, because you couldn't get a decent job. You people are no better than people on the street, except you think you are better. Makes me want to throw up!

WORKER: So you believe that nobody could be interested in you?

STELLA: Why should anyone be interested in me. Even I am not interested in me!

In this case, the worker attempts to help Stella to focus on the story of them—worker and client—living here and now. Although hostile, Stella, shares a lot of information about her distrust of the "system," which includes the worker, and emphasizes her contempt for people who try to help her.

These three examples show how different clients approach engagement in the helping process differently. Some will tell long and detailed stories; others will be brief. Some will reveal their stories with great emotion, while others will tell theirs coldly and angrily. Some will talk about their problems and issues directly from the start; others will tell a secondary story before they feel they can trust enough to disclose what is really troubling them. Some clients will talk about their inner world and make statements such as "I don't like myself," or "I can't trust myself," or at a different level, "I hear voices." Some present inner and outer concerns. A client presenting his or her story is the starting point for possible constructive change. Often, just telling the story will begin to help the client view it more objectively.

While clients are talking, generalists need to concentrate on identifying the core theme in their story, observing and making note of the core experiences, behaviors, and feelings of the clients. When a client finishes, the practitioner gets back to the salient features and helps the client explore further. As Egan (1994) indicates, certain expressions can be used to review the core parts of the story and show empathy. The worker might say, "There is a great deal of pain and confusion in what you have just said. Let us see if I have understood some of the main points you have made," or "You have said a great deal, so let me see if we can piece it all together." When you show empathy, the client is aware that you have been listening intently, but getting the client to tell the story is only a first step and the beginning of the helping process.

Clarity

Clarity in understanding the client is not sought for its own sake, but to move the whole process of engagement forward. In working with clients, we need to think of clarity in terms of specific experiences, behaviors, and feelings. Long (1996) indicates that if practitioners can find a way to expand the statement of a problem to the specific behaviors, experiences, and emotions that constitute it, then major obstacle to the solution of the problem will be overcome. That is, the initial ambiguity with which most people analyze interpersonal and situational problems tends to contribute to their feeling of helplessness in coping. Knowing which specific behaviors will solve the problem provides a definite goal for action and having that goal can contribute to a great sense of relief.

Exploring Expectations

After some degree of clarity has been reached, practitioners have to explore the problems to the satisfaction of both their clients and themselves. What are the client's expectations? A great deal depends on the type of problem, the client's cultural, religious, and ethnic background, socioeconomic status, level of sophistication, and degree of experience, if any, with previous workers. At times, clients' expectations differ markedly from what workers realistically may be able to provide. If workers are unable to deal effectively with the unrealistic expectations of clients, they may feel disappointed and disinclined to return after the first session (Hepworth et al., 1998).

Sixteen-year-old Dillon was referred to the practitioner by the school social worker for acting-out behavior in the classroom. In the initial session, Dillon shared his fears that his father was having an affair and would leave his mother. However, his parents told the worker over the phone that they expected Dillon to get straight A's in school so that he could go to medical school. The parents expected the worker to help Dillon with his "personal problems" so that he would become a high achiever in school. The parents talked as if Dillon's problems existed in a vacuum and would disappear in a similar manner; the worker's role was to help Dillon with his grades. The parents overlooked the fact that Dillon was a C student. The parents saw Dillon's problems as his own and did not view the family as part of the problem situation.

The practitioner quickly informed Dillon's parents that their expectations were unrealistic and that they might also be called in to be part of the helping process. The practitioner used this opportunity to clarify the nature of the helping process and helped them work through their feelings of disappointment. Meanwhile, in the first session the worker aimed at exploring Dillon's expectations to help her vary her approaches and intervention strategies according to Dillon's needs and expectations.

At times, clients come into the helping process with absurd notions of what is possible, or likely to happen. As noted by Kottler (1995), such unrealistic expectations from clients include the following:

> "I will tell you my problems, you will tell me yours, and then I have to figure out what I should do by what you have done."

> "I will tell you my dreams and then you will tell what they mean to me."

> "You are like a lie detector. Whenever I am not telling the truth, or exaggerate a little bit, or tell you a sob story, you will interrupt me and tell me I am full of crap."

> "You have a tissue box in your office. You will give me a tissue, hold my hand, and tell me everything will be all right. That's what a social worker should do."

> "I will tell you my problems. You will tell me what to do so that I can change situations that keep me from getting what I want and then everything will become all right."

Images of a friend, a person with a magic wand, a teacher, or a coach could all be models in a client's mind for what role the worker assumes in engagement. Many of the misconceptions about expectations will be cleared up in the initial engagement session. The worker must explain his or her role, the helping process, and how and why it works. Such explanations help modify the client's thinking to reflect a more accurate portrayal of the helping process. The worker and the client should also discuss who will do what and what is most likely to happen as a result of these expectations.

The Overall Quality of Client Disclosure

Listening attentively to a client is both an empathetic and a reality-checking activity. Egan (1999) suggests a number of questions to help a worker check a client's reality. These can be triggered by what the client says and how the client acts. The questions that follow should remain in the back of your mind and, of course, should not interfere with your listening ability.

> How appropriate is the client in his or her self-disclosure?

> What is the quality and quantity of information that is being given to you relative to the problem situation?

> How easily does the client talk about himself or herself? Is this talk rewarding or punishing to the client?

> Is the client getting some gratification in telling his or her story?

> How open is the client in the disclosure?

> To what degree is the client getting something out of what he or she says?

> To what extent is the client relating his or her story to other parts of the helping process, such as setting goals?

> What signs, if any, are there that the client is trying to con or manipulate you?

> Is there anything that the client is leaving out?

> To what extent is the client expressing or discussing thoughts, emotions, and feelings?

> To what degree does the client talk about experiences rather than his or her own behavior?

If what the client says triggers in your mind one or more of these questions, it is a good idea to intervene to help him or her tell the story better. For example, if a client does not reveal any emotion while discussing a painful topic, you could ask, "I have a vivid idea of what happened, but I'm not sure how you felt about all this." This tack is based on the assumption that when a client spells out a problem situation, it is expressed in terms of experiences, behaviors, and emotions. However, in some situations strong emotions may not play a role, in which case there is nothing unusual when the client does not express emotion.

A word of caution. Self-disclosure is not a "cure" in itself. In some cases, as Corey and Corey (1998) indicate, self-disclosure in the beginning engagement session can release "healing" resources in the client. For example, self-disclosure may remove a burden of guilt that the client may have been carrying for a long time and move him or her toward a better frame of mind and eventual behavior change (Egan, 1999).

Negotiating contracts and goals

When a worker and a client believe that they have adequately explored the problems, the next step is to plan the process of strengthening the client. If the client cannot be helped in one agency, referral to another agency that would be in a position to help should be done as soon as possible. However, if the client's problems match the functions of the agency and the client wishes to proceed further, it is appropriate to negotiate a contract.

As noted in Chapter 9, contracting happens when the worker and client reach an agreement about the nature of the problems and the systems involved. Hepworth et al. (1997), Pincus & Minahan (1973), and Johnson (1995) describe contracting as a natural culmination of the first major phase and the introduction of the change-oriented or goal-attainment phase that is the heart of the helping process. Contracts specify goals to be attained and the means of accomplishing them.

There are preliminary contracts that include a client certification for service and there are sec-

ondary contracts that deal with time-limited tasks for the client to accomplish with regard to specific behavior changes. In some cases contracts are written down; in others, contracts are verbal.

To develop contracts, the practitioner and the client have to take an active role and assume the primary responsibility in negotiating the tasks of a service contract. The worker must also clarify and obtain agreement about what is required, keeping in mind that the contract terms should be formulated to get maximum participation from the client (Bassin, 1993; Goulding, 1990; Shulman, 1992).

Goals

There are research findings that attest to the value of contracts. Rhodes (1977) commented that "ambiguities about the contract and its unsystematic application as a principle of practice may account for a consistently high percentage of unplanned client withdrawal" (p. 125). There is more evidence offered by Wood (1978) who reviewed a number of studies in direct practice and reported that a substantial number reporting negative outcomes by practitioners did not utilize explicit contracts. In order to reach the specified objectives of a contract the worker needs to work with clients to identify goals. Goals can be described as the end results that will be attained if the problem-solving efforts are successful (Bandura & Cervone, 1983; Grinnell, Kyle, & Bostwick, 1981; Rooney, 1992).

The importance of goals has been highlighted in social work literature. Egan (1994) reached the conclusion that being overly general in specifying goals leads to unrealistic aspirations and to repeated shifts in direction. Wood reached a similar decision and cautioned that unrealistically high goals subject clients to disappointment, frustration, and a reduction of confidence in their own abilities.

The Purpose of Goals

A practitioner who engages in understanding the client's wants, needs, and problems is working with the primary goal of prioritizing. As Bandura and Cervone (1983) reveal, goals have valuable functions in the helping process. They ensure that practitioners and clients are in agreement about what objectives need to be reached. They also provide direction, continuity, and focus to the helping process. Well-planned goals facilitate the utilization of appropriate strategies and interventions. Goals help practitioners and clients monitor progress. Goals help in evaluating the effectiveness of specific interventions and serve as outcome criteria.

There are two types of client goals: discrete and ongoing (see Figure 10.3). *Discrete goals* consist of one-time actions or changes that ameliorate problems or choice issues; for example, finding a job for an unemployed client or finding medical care. *Ongoing goals* involve actions that are continuous and help ensure progress on incremental change issues. Examples of ongoing goals are working on one's self-esteem and self-confidence, learning to express feelings, learning to control anger, and learning to be self-assertive. Changes in goals for individuals include changes in feelings; for instance, getting rid of self-defeating depressive feelings and making behavior changes like reducing the number of cigarettes a person smokes per day or reducing alcohol consumption. Thoughts, feelings, and behaviors are interrelated and the purpose of achieving goals is to bring about change in behavior. For example, when a person changes his or her thinking from irrational, unproductive, self-destructive, negative thinking to more positive thinking about self and others, behavior ultimately changes. The client learns to accept self and aspects of situations that cannot be changed when feelings that are worrisome and negative are changed to more positive ones. Similarly, when behavior changes from destructive, inappropriate, impulsive behavior to more positive constructive behavior, the person feels good about himself or herself and becomes more socially appropriate in his or her behavior towards others. Generally, goals relate to what clients will do in order to overcome, reduce, or eliminate concerns or problems.

Guidelines for Achieving Goals

As Hutchins and Cole (1992) indicate, practitioners work with clients in order to establish realistic and achievable goals.

1. The worker and clients have to present achievable goals. Goals should define what the client will be doing in positive rather than negative terms. When a client curses easily and then starts to denigrate herself for being impulsive, she could be helped to develop a positive mental image. For example, "I will count to ten before I say something." This supports self-control with an alternative to self-denigration.

2. The worker and the client must narrow the goals from general to specific. In the initial stage of engagement, the clients may present vague goals. With worker's help, they should be narrowed to achievable goals. For instance, a client is disorganized in his or her work. What steps should the client take to become more organized? Specific positive goals would provide useful ideas about what the client will do to overcome problems and issues. As another example, a group of people in a community need a large number of facilities. Through discussion with the community members the specific needs can be narrowed down and prioritized.

3. The client and the worker specify the conditions under which new behavior will take place,

Figure 10.3 **Goals**

including when this behavior will occur, where it will occur, and with whom or under what circumstances such behavior will occur. For example, a client who is very timid might present the goal in the following manner. When the client meets new people, he will think positive thoughts, feel relaxed, and engage, in conversations (act) that are appropriate in the time available (circumstances).

4. When goals are achieved the client and the worker examine both the positive and negative consequences and the possibilities of unintended consequences that may result. The worker has to help the client to think in terms of what could happen on achieving some specific goals. It is important to be aware that nothing happens without consequences or trade-offs of various kinds. If you are working on one thing, you may need to give up other things or modify them in some ways. When consequences are disregarded, this may lead to other problems. A change in one part of a system changes the whole system.

For example, Hudson had a responsible position, a good salary, and good relationships in the community, but he resigned his job to go to graduate school to get his master's degree in business administration in order to achieve his goal of attaining a higher administrative position in his office. The consequences were that his family was very unhappy because they had to move to a university town. After Hudson resigned his job, they lived off the savings but after a year had no money. This led to a great deal of bickering, and eventually Hudson and his wife separated. Hudson was so emotionally upset that he dropped out of school and salvaged what he could of his family life.

All too frequently, people make plans without anticipating the consequences. The worker has to help the client examine the realities of what might happen should the desired goal be achieved. Both the positive and negative aspects of a situation should be discussed before the client starts to work on issues.

5. The client and worker should break the goals down into smaller manageable parts. For example, a general goal is to interact effectively with others; the subgoals are to learn nonverbal aspects of interaction, to tell others about selected personal interest without appearing self-centered, and to interact positively in an conversation.

In the process of reaching goals, practitioners should select goals mutually with clients; that is, elicit goals from clients and suggest other potential goals, then mutually select those that are appropriate. The client and worker should define goals explicitly and specify the degree of desired change. Finally, the worker must assist clients in making the choice to commit themselves to goals and to prioritize goals.

Exercises

1. After a presentation of a case that highlights the manner in which a worker and client engage, students should discuss the case, looking specifically at

Problem and situation

Client motivation

Exploration of expectations

Negotiating a contract

2. Two students role-play the first session in which the worker attempts to engage an extremely ambivalent client in the helping process. After the role play, the class should discuss the role-play and the engagement process, emphasizing pros and cons and offering suggestions.

3. How would you engage a 10-year-old bed wetter in the helping process? She appears to be afraid of you. What are the skills you would use to reach the child? Role-play and discuss the factors you need to remember when working with children.

ENGAGEMENT IN FAMILIES

A family begins the helping process even before the first session. Usually the initial contact is made through a phone call. The worker will want to indicate that he or she would like to see the entire family rather than a single family member.

The initial session is the only time when the worker and clients are strangers to each other. This gives the worker an opportunity to observe how the family system relates to those outside the family. The manner in which the family members seat themselves reveals how they feel about each other; it shows how allied some family members are with each other and how removed they are from others. It also reveals to some degree the power distribution in the family.

One of the factors the worker must keep in mind is that the initial contact with the family also reveals the nonverbal affect of those present. Some workers may respond to the affect communication by making statements about facial expressions of sadness, anger, or frustration. These comments should be based on the practitioner's comfort and clinical judgment as well as awareness of consequences. Some families may feel affirmation and empathy, whereas others may become defensive because they feel invaded. Defensiveness could mean that a family rule was broken by identifying affect, especially if a specific individual is identified. Such a response often results in amplified cautiousness (Barnard & Corrales, 1979; Franklin & Jordon, 1999).

Joining

After the introductions have been made, the worker "joins" the family and they start the process of induction into the helping process. According to Minuchin et al. (1978), "the therapist has to join the field of stabilized family interactions in order to observe them. He must gain experiential knowledge of the controlling power that the system exerts. Only then can he challenge the family interactions with any knowledge of the range of thresholds that the system can tolerate" (p. 94).

This method of joining is characteristic of family work in general. As a rule, if a stable alliance is not achieved between the family and the practitioner, any interventions aimed at changing the structure of the family will remain unsuccessful, and contact between the two parties will break off after the first interview.

Conceptually, this can be explained in a number of different ways. Looking at families from a systemic perspective, it can be said that the family system is capable of change only when it is receptive to information that challenges or changes existing structures. In this situation, the socially established authority of the worker creates a precondition for the worker and family to come together (Carlson, Sperry, & Lewis, 1997; Rucker-Embden, Wetzel, Stierlin, & Wirsching, 1980). As Minuchin and Fishman (1981) note, joining is more an attitude than a technique and it is the umbrella under which all therapeutic transactions occur. When a worker joins a family, he or she is letting the family know that the worker understands them and is working with and for them. Under the worker's guidance the family can securely explore alternatives, try the unusual, and change. Joining the family can be described as the glue that keeps the therapeutic system together.

McDaniel, Hepworth, and Doherty (1993) indicate that this process is analogous to the medical setting in that just before surgery the doctor administers an anesthetic. In family work, joining is like administering an anesthetic prior to the attempt to restructure, which is the counterpart of surgery.

The initial session is the appropriate time to indicate what will be done in the helping process to bring about change and to decide what the participants wish to do. They will also be responsible for doing work to bring about change. The family also learns that there is no magic and that they will have to work together. Once the introductions have been completed, the family can move into the helping situation.

The initial interview is described by Satir and Baldwin (1983) as the *sensing interview*. In family work the assumption is often made that the mother is the person who is most familiar with the family dynamics, followed by the person who is the identified patient or the person with the problem. As these two people are critical in the family sessions they are not asked to comment until the rest of the family has spoken first. The reasoning behind this is that if these two family members speak first, they may skew the system by affecting what the other family members say. Usually, it is important to talk to the youngest child if this child is not the identified patient, because the youngest is usually looked upon favorably by most family members. One of the general questions to ask is, "What is it like for you in your family?" From the youngest child the worker moves up, skipping the "identified patient." The worker may then speak to the father and later the mother. Beyond this, the worker will try to explore what each member values in the family, along with what is perceived as being worthy of change.

Family members frequently monitor the behaviors or communication styles of other members. It is fairly common in the first session for one member to "clarify" what another member is saying. For example, a mother may interrupt a child's statement in the helping session by saying "that's not the way it is!" The worker can respond by saying "I appreciate your interest, but I would like to hear what Matthew is saying; your turn will come." This comment acknowledges family members and at the same time draws boundaries around each individual family member as a subsystem within the larger system. This serves as a joining mechanism and it also communicates to the family that the practitioner is capable of introducing structure into the already chaotic family system. If members from the father's extended family are also present, then they are asked to speak first, followed by the mother's extended family.

After the interviewing process has been completed, the next step is to arrive at therapeutic goals and finalize the contract. As the worker listens to different family members presenting their concerns about the family and its functioning and how they would like to change, goals can be iden-

tified for the therapeutic contract period. Identifying goals in the family helps facilitate the success of the helping process in family work.

Goals

In many ways the most significant task for the family practitioner is goal setting. Unfortunately, this process is often not carried out. Too many practitioners, especially beginning practitioners, start to "intervene" before formulating, in conjunction with the family, a clear set of goals for the helping process. As a consequence, the helping process often gets bogged down, meanders aimlessly, or is prematurely terminated.

The goals have to be defined as being behaviorally specific. It is wise to suggest that the family agree on the number of sessions needed to achieve the goals. This is done to ensure success and also to suggest the idea that if one change can be achieved in one system, others may result from it. At the end of the contract period, the worker and the family evaluate the progress and decide whether it is time to terminate or negotiate a new contract.

After the number of sessions has been agreed upon, the worker and all the family participants should commit to the process. This will prevent dawdling by clients who may believe an endless amount of time is available. Some practitioners believe that the initial contract should not exceed ten sessions, with an average of six to eight sessions after goal setting. The initial session ends on the same note that it began, that is, acknowledgment of the practitioner's concern and commitment to the family group.

There are several therapeutic tasks that are part of the initial engagement process with families. They include:

1. Establishing a bond between the worker and the family members, particularly the chief family members
2. Providing preliminary information about family work and how it operates

3. Assessing client problems and expectations
4. Instilling a sense of hope in the clients
5. Obtaining a commitment to be patient and work hard, in sessions and between sessions

With these small beginnings rests the future of the helping process.

Exercises

1. Students should be asked to volunteer to play different roles in a family situation with one person playing the generalist. The rest of the class pays attention to the processes of moving through the family carefully with sensitivity and careful observation.

How does the worker join the family members?

Whom does the worker join first and why?

What were the different observations made of the family members by the worker? Why?

2. Thirty-five-year old Lorna is a busy, working single parent with three children. Her youngest child, age twelve, is acting out in school. The family has been referred to you for help. How would you begin to engage reluctant Lorna and her children, particularly the acting-out child in the beginning helping process?

ENGAGEMENT IN GROUPS

Engaging group members is somewhat different from engaging individual clients. Therefore, this section is devoted to some of the peculiar issues involved in being a group member and how the worker should function in order to help move the group members toward engagement with each other and the practitioner.

No matter how well-prepared group members are, the first session generates both excitement and anxiety. Group members may be excited about the possibility of meeting people with similar problems. At the same time, they are anxious about the possible differences and, consequently, may be afraid of taking risks. Once the session begins, group members look to the worker for direction. The worker's sensitivity to beginnings in group sessions is a vital factor in reducing anxiety and enhancing each individual's commitment to the group.

In the beginning of the group session the worker's responsibility is to help individuals find a place to take hold and emotionally join the group as active participants. The more easily and quickly the group members get into action in the group, the more readily each member can direct life energy toward dealing with the situation, rather than protecting himself or herself against its impact (Reid, 1991).

According to Shulman (1999) and Reid (1997) the structure of the first meeting with the group should meet the following specific objectives:

1. The group members should introduce themselves to each other.
2. The worker should make a brief, simple opening statement clarifying the purpose of the group and the agency's role in sponsoring the group. In turn, the group members should raise issues and concerns they feel are urgent.
3. The worker must obtain from group members a sense of the match between their ideas of their own needs and the agency's view of the type of help it can provide.
4. The worker must clarify his or her method of attempting to help group members work.
5. The worker has to deal directly with any specific obstacles that may hinder this particular group's efforts to function effectively.
6. The worker should encourage group members' interaction instead of interaction only between the group leader and each group member.
7. The worker should help develop a supportive culture in which group members can feel safe.
8. The worker should help group members develop a tentative agenda for their own and the group's future work.

9. The worker should clarify the mutual expectations of the agency and the group members.
10. The worker should gain some consensus on the part of group members about the specific next steps; for example, determining what themes or issues they want to begin with in the next session.
11. The worker should encourage honest feedback about the session's effectiveness from group members.

A large number of these objectives can be dealt with quickly, whereas others are interdependent and can be addressed sequentially. Objectives that deal with encouraging honest feedback will require a number of sessions.

Creating Togetherness by Highlighting Similarities

When group members become aware that they have similarities in their life experiences and share difficulties, concerns, and feelings, commonality and togetherness can be nurtured. Members should be encouraged to talk briefly about themselves and to relate what they hope to get from the group. Just learning that other members have similar problems can in itself be very supportive to the group.

Genny talked about her first group experience in the following manner:

> I was full of anxiety and fears about what would and would not be discussed in the group. I was self-conscious. But as everyone started to talk to each other and to the group leader, some of my fears started to disappear. I began to feel comfortable when we talked about our expectations in the group, the rules, regulations, and confidentiality issues that I was really worried about before I came into the group. Once I started to share my feelings, it was comforting to note that Melanie and Max did the same. I gained a lot from other people sharing their feelings and I knew I was going to make it in the group as a productive member.

The generalist should direct questions to the group as a whole and not concentrate on any one member. In this way, group members who are more comfortable begin to speak and there is no pressure on others to communicate unless they wish to talk. The worker begins by asking openended and indirect questions. As Cournoyer and Byers (1999), Cournoyer (1996), and Brown (1991) indicate, it is an axiom that once a group member has said something, however simple or general it is, the person will find it easier to speak a second or third time.

Based on Cournoyer (1996) and Brown (1991), a worker should keep in mind the following practical techniques in the beginning stages of a group:

1. Encourage group members to share their thoughts, feelings, and expectations about being a member of a group.
2. Do not be rushed at the group's beginning, but set the tone purposively and move at a comfortable pace, although some members may appear ready to move on.
3. During the initial session, encourage the group members to share something about themselves.
4. Focus the group members' attention on their feelings if there is doubt about a particular point.

Beginning a Group Session

Preston-Shoot (1989) and Wickman (1993) observe that a group should have unambiguous leadership, clearly defined rules, open communication channels, effective reality testing, and a congenial atmosphere with a relaxed leader. This can be accomplished only through a structured approach to group leadership.

There are some factors that the group leader needs to be aware of when opening the first group session. It should not be started with a lecture about the rules, meeting times, or frequency of meetings because, by doing so, the worker is establishing a leader-dominated group (Jacobs, Harvill, & Masson, 1988). In the first group session, members are usually anxious and self-conscious and may not pay attention to the presentation. Another important factor is that group members may ask questions that are irrelevant and unrelated to what is being said (Benjamin, 1987). In a dependent situation the worker must plan how to reply and react. The worker's role in this session is to convince group members that they have been heard, although all of them may not receive definitive answers to all their questions.

Reid (1997) observes that group structure and leader activity should not encourage group dependency. In such a situation, the group members will also look to the group leader to provide topics, resolve conflicts, offer advice, and also be the one person who can confront objectionable behavior. They come to expect the group leader to do the work *for* the group.

Contracting in Groups

In groups, contracting means clarifying the purpose of the group, the leader's and group members' roles, and soliciting client feedback in response to these matters (Reid, 1996; Schwartz, 1976). When a practitioner explains the agency's purpose, the group members should also be determining the common ground for their own purpose in comparison with the agency's, the group members' needs, and their sense of urgency. Making a contract between a worker and the group members makes the worker's role explicit, presents the need for mutuality among group members, and establishes the mutual expectations and obligations of the group leader and the group members. The purpose of the group, the group members' roles, and the role of the worker may have to be reiterated in the second session as well, so that members who were anxious in the first session will get another chance to hear and respond. The practitioner has to present himself or herself as a facilitator assisting group members to reach their goals. A practitioner in a group helps keep the discussion on topics of concern to the group and stops the group at several points to process what is going on. Another role for the worker is that of a teacher who shares information and responds to problems that group members face in their situations.

Clarifying Group Members' Roles

New group members are sometimes overwhelmed with questions and concerns, and it is best that the leader address them as soon as they appear. For example, are group members expected to self-disclose? If so, how much should they disclose? Is it all right for the group members to disagree with the group leader? Group members usually want to know ahead of time what is going to happen in the group. They also may wonder if they can say what they really feel.

Reid (1991) offers a number of practical considerations for working with groups. The leader should not overwhelm group members with information. The group leader should be very clear about his or her role, as well as the group members' roles and the purpose of the group. Often, group members do not listen to everything that is discussed in the group, so the generalist should be prepared to repeat information that has already been discussed. Finally, the worker should be attuned to the group members' discomfort and anxiety.

The engagement session is the initial stage of the group and a time for orientation and exploration. It should include determining the structure of the group, getting acquainted, and also exploring each other's expectations. Members are trying to find an identity in the group and determine the degree to which each one will become an active group member. However, Norman (1981) cautions that group members should move away from group pressure that may force people to relinquish their uniqueness.

Some of the questions that group members ask themselves initially include the following:

Will I be an accepted as a member of the group or will I be an outsider?

To what extent can I take risks?

Is it safe to take risks?

Can I really trust these people, who are strangers to me?

Will I fit in as a member and belong to the group?

Whom do I like and whom do I not like in this group?

Will the group members accept me or reject me?

Can I present myself as a person and at the same time be accepted as a part of the group?

Group Goals

Group goals should be realistic and attainable. Often in the first session group members are vague about their goals. They may come up with statements like "I want to feel better and be happier." Egan (1999) indicates that such statements could be *declarations of intent,* rather than goals.

Goals should be expressed as specific outcome statements (e.g., "By Friday, I will have applied to ten more jobs"). These goals are related to end results, and everyone who is involved can clearly note the changes that will be accomplished (Nelsen, 1981).

Group members have to create goals that are attainable and not too ambitious. The latter can lead to frustration and depression when a person does not reach them. Before setting a goal, it is important that the group members understand their individual capacity, the resources available to reach the goal, and the situational factors that may prevent them from reaching the goal.

Group goals should also be measurable and verifiable. After each group member formulates a goal, it should be discussed so that the group's negative and positive consequences are taken into consideration. There are many goals in a group. For example, if a goal is to ask a person for a date, the consequences are that this might work very well or the group member who asked for the date may be rejected. In this process, the richness and freedom of being a group member should not be lost because of the danger of a disappointment to group members who are consumed by their goals.

Goals can also be identified when the worker motivates, inspires, and challenges people to get the most from their group. At this point, the members must identify their goals in terms of what they want from the group. There are general group goals that vary from group to group depending on the purpose of the group, and there are also group-process goals that apply to almost all groups. In group process, Egan (1999), Cooley (1994), and Pillari (1996) discuss the several processes that happen. They include self-exploration, experimentation, staying in the here and now, making oneself known to other group members, challenging other group members and oneself, taking risks, giving and receiving information, listening to others, responding honestly and concretely to others, dealing with feelings that may arise in the group, deciding what to work on, acting on new insights, applying new behavior in and out of the group, and making this a way of life.

While establishing the group-process goals, the worker has a challenging task of bringing into the open the hidden agendas of clients. For instance, one group member may have a great need to be the center of attention; another may plan to sabotage intimacy in the group because he or she is personally uncomfortable about getting close to people. Group leaders have to do whatever they can to bring these hidden agendas into the open. If such personal but unproductive goals are not brought out and dealt with, they may seriously undermine the effectiveness of the group (Corey, 1990).

Group goals focus on group dynamics and include the following:

To provide mutual support

To share information and problem solving

To increase self-esteem and assertiveness

To help reduce behavior that prevents intimacy

To learn and be able to trust oneself and others

To recognize that other group members struggle too

To increase one's ability to care for others

To learn to be more honest and open with selected others

To deal with group members directly in the here and now

To support as well as challenge others

To become sensitive to the feelings and needs of others

To be able to confront others in a caring and concerned manner

To be able to provide others with useful feedback

Corey and Corey (1998) have identified some of the general goals for different types of groups:

- Goals for an incest group are to help group members talk about the incidence of incest; to discover and vent common feelings of anger, hurt, shame, and guilt; to attempt or be able to work on unfinished business with the perpetrator; and to undertake ongoing work on personal self-esteem.
- Goals for a group of elderly people are to review life experiences; to be able to express feelings about their losses and to improve their self-image; to work at coping with life stresses more effectively; to provide a supportive network; and to learn or build more appropriate social skills.
- Goals for groups of children who act out are to accept their own feelings; to learn constructive ways of expressing and dealing with their feelings; to develop skills in making friends; and to channel impulses into acceptable behavior.

Trust: The Foundation of the Group

When a group of people with different backgrounds and similar problems are brought together in a group, there is a strong likelihood of chaos and challenges. There may seem to be no place for trust, but trust happens. What initiates it and how does it develop? To a large extent, trust in a group is built on the attitude and activities of the generalist. When workers have carefully thought through the purpose, goals, and structure

of groups and present these in a straightforward and honest manner, they can inspire trust in group members. When group members are provided with guidelines, responsibilities, and expectations, the members learn that they have to take the group seriously.

Anderson (1984) and Wartel (1991) indicate that members' initial trust in the group comes when they understand that the group has a structure as they fumble for clues on how to act and behave in the group. Structure is presented to them in the form of their roles and the role of the worker. Additionally, they grope for norms, assertion of status and power, a sign of approval, respect, and domination, or anything that would shed light on how the group is structured and how they should function. The group members expect the group leader to provide them with answers and also validate them as group members; in turn, they carefully scrutinize the group worker's reactions with regard to expectations and rewards (Reid, 1991).

Corey and Corey (1998) indicate that the worker should teach group members through example. When the members experience the worker as a caring person, they may adapt behaviors and attitudes that are similar:

The group members begin to trust in the group process and to have faith in the ability of the group members to make changes in their own lives

The group members begin to listen nondefensively and perhaps respectfully

They learn to accept group members without imposing their own values on them

Group members begin to participate in appropriate self-disclosure

Unless the generalist begins to reveal himself or herself, the members may have unrealistic attitudes about the worker and what they can do in the group. When a generalist is attacked in a group, how should he or she handle it? A generalist who is honest and remains strong in dealing with such situations reveals a great deal about himself or herself. When the group members observe the worker, they learn what to expect and become free to take risks themselves as well (Corey, Corey, & Callahan, 1993).

Maintaining trust in the group is not solely the worker's responsibility; it is also a responsibility of the group members and a part of the group process. How much group members invest in the group depends on their ability and willingness to share. Some members are unwilling to take risks and will resist the notion of sharing anything but superficial material. Other group members may expect the group leader to bring about change magically without any work of their own.

The first session is an important and crucial session and a significant factor in the development of the group. At the end, the worker should summarize what has happened in the group and make plans for future meetings. Some members may not return because they have had a positive experience and feel that they have learned a great deal and do not need any more sessions. Others may not return because they are ambiguous and not really sure how well they may be helped in the group. If the group members express their opinions at the end of the first session, then the worker should address their concerns and deal with them openly and honestly. While closing the first session, the worker should leave ample time for summarizing; Reid (1991) suggests ten to fifteen minutes. When the session is summarized, the worker should follow up and ask the group members what they did or did not like in the sessions, raise questions, and identify unfinished business. At the end of the session, the worker can assign tasks and homework and encourage members to share their expectations and desires about future meetings.

Exercises

1. In this group session, about eight to ten students play group members in an initial group session and one student plays the group leader. The group leader gives a brief orientation and explains the group's purpose, the role of the leader, and also the responsibilities of the group members. The group leader also explains the ground rules, group-process procedures, and any other information that a practitioner needs to keep in mind. The group members then begin by expressing their expectations, fears, experiences with previous groups, and so forth. After about half an hour, the rest of the class can describe what they observed. Later, the group members give the leader feedback in terms of how they felt as members of the group and what constructive suggestions they have to offer. The leader talks about his or her experience as the group leader, which can be done either before or after feedback from the rest of the class.

2. The class divides into small groups in which students can brainstorm in order to create trust. Group members can explore as many ideas as possible that might facilitate the beginning of trust in the group. The group members can also discuss what can lead to trust in groups and what it takes as a group member to develop a sense of trust in the group. They should also discuss the major barriers to the development of trust.

ENGAGEMENT IN COMMUNITIES AND LARGE ORGANIZATIONS

In most communities the initial challenge is to develop identity and a connection and to establish priorities among the needs (Brueggemann, 1996; Gambrill, 1977).

Identity of Client Systems

The generalist has to identify the type of client system with which she or he is working. There are different types of communities, such as large metropolitan areas, ethnic neighborhoods, small towns, and rural communities, and large institutions. A generalist needs to have some idea about the cultural setting, the economics of the system, and political atmosphere. In terms of organizations, the practitioner also needs to know the membership of the organization, general organizational activities, type of leadership, and linkages available in the community.

Establishing Communication with Members in the System

Brill (1995) specifies that the engagement process begins when generalists involve themselves in the situation with a community or a large organization to establish communication with significant people; begin to identify and define the parameters within which the worker and the clients will work; and create an initial working structure as the needs are being identified. The next step is to determine what needs will be addressed based on community consensus. Generally, there is identification of the problems by the community or organization members who are directly affected by it. For example, a large organization became concerned because it was dedicated to improving the supply of low-income housing, but realized that over 8,000 people in the community were living in cars, shacks, or other substandard housing. The generalist who worked in the organization assembled a community meeting to rally support for the agency and raise money to help the homeless. One of the ground rules was that in this project the low-income individuals and families pay about 1 percent of the cost of the building, maintain their payments on the no-interest loans, and take living skills classes.

Community members have to describe the problems clearly. That is, people need to understand with clarity what needs to be done. Lastly, the problem needs to researched carefully (Kirst-Ashman & Hull, 1997). For instance, how prevalent is the problem in the community? How many people are affected by it? What are the needs of the community? Should time be spent in educating the community members about this problem?

Creating an Initial Working Situation

As the problems are being identified, the generalist is simultaneously using different individual, group, and community skills to engage the com-

munity members in dealing with their issues. Constructive participation by the generalist creates an assurance among the community members that they can begin to trust the generalist by his/her participation in the community issues with concern and care.

BASIC SKILLS OF ENGAGEMENT FOR ALL CLIENT SYSTEMS

Generalists need a large number of skills to work with different kinds of clients. There are special skills that a worker utilizes in the engagement process. These include structuring, focusing, working with differences, timing, withholding evaluation and judgment, and worker activity in the engagement phase (Corey & Corey, 1998; Cormier & Cormier, 1998; Lowenberg, 1983). When the client is unaware of role expectations, the generalist should use the skill of structuring with regard to the client's problems. When the client fears depersonalization and is anxious about what might happen, the generalist has to use the skill of focusing. When there are differences between generalists and clients that interfere with communication, the generalists should use their skills to bridge the gap.

The concept of time has different meanings for generalists and clients, so generalists should use timing skills in planning. When clients fear that they will be judged by generalists, then generalists should suspend judgment or evaluation. When clients wonder if generalists are interested, then the workers should become active. When clients wonder whether generalists are competent and ready to help, generalists should set the tone. When clients are anxious about dealing with problems by themselves, then the generalists should end that anxiety as best they can.

Generalists also need to be aware that they cannot utilize skills without responsibility. When generalists work with an individual, a family, a group, a community, or an organization, do they have full responsibility for the direction and outcome of the process? No, it is a joint responsibility of clients and generalists. Why? Because generalists should *never* forget that they are privileged to deal with other people's lives.

Corey (1990) indicates that one way of conceptualizing the issue of generalist responsibility is to think in terms of a continuum. There are some workers who assume a great deal of responsibility for the direction and outcomes in their work. They are highly directive and they keep clients moving in ways they think are productive. A disadvantage of this method of responsible leadership is that it robs clients of the responsibility that is rightfully theirs and can produce dependence upon the generalist. At the other end of the continuum is the worker who proclaims, "I am responsible for myself and you are responsible for yourself. If you wish to leave with anything of value, it is up you. I cannot do anything for you; that is, make you feel something or take away any of your defenses, unless you allow me to do so."

Hopefully, every generalist will find a balance between empowerment of clients and acceptance of their rightful share of responsibility, without jeopardizing clients' responsibility. This is central and necessary in understanding the generalist's approach to other's responsibilities as well as personal responsibilities.

Structuring

Structuring is used to help people function more effectively as clients both in terms of their role behaviors and their outcome experiences. Structuring is done directly or indirectly, positively or negatively. In direct structuring, clients are given messages that tell them what is expected and what is possible. Structuring occurs when the generalist says, "Tell me in what ways you can improve your behavior." In indirect structuring, the worker uses nonverbal communication, such as smiles and shaking the head, to encourage appropriate and discourage inappropriate client behaviors. In positive structuring, the client will be told what to do and what not to do and also what to expect; in negative structuring, the worker will point out clients' mistakes or unacceptable behaviors. In pos-

itive structuring, the worker might tell the client, "I think your mother would be more cooperative if you spoke more kindly"; negative structuring might be a statement such as, "You lost control and started yelling at your mother, again?"

Becoming a client also means learning new role behaviors. There are workers who will point out patterns of behaviors and there are others who will remain passive and silent, leaving it to the clients to select those behaviors that they think are meaningful for them. However, the generalist must find an appropriate balance. Too much passivity on the part of the worker is not helpful; clients participate better in the helping process when they know what is expected of them. As noted previously, too much directiveness takes responsibility away from the client. Even when working with impoverished communities, generalists prioritize the type of work that needs to be done based upon the needs and desires of the people.

Shulman (1999) uses the phrase *demand for work* as a specific structuring skill. Besides expecting clients to participate verbally, the generalist expects clients to work on agreed upon tasks between sessions. Until this kind of agreement is reached, the engagement phase is less than complete. Sometimes clients talk to the worker as if he or she were a friend or an acquaintance, but the worker has to draw the line and create a professional atmosphere. For example, Mrs. Hall looks at the worker and mentions that she likes the way the office is decorated. She goes on to describe her house in an elaborate manner as if she were talking to a friend. The worker gently reminds her that she is there to discuss her marital difficulties by presenting a task assignment that was given to her a week ago, which specified that the client state at least three incidents where she and her husband argued seriously during the previous week. Statements such as "I am glad you like my office but we are here to discuss the marital conflict between you and your husband and also your task assignment. How did this assignment work out for you?" would be appropriate. Whenever the client becomes distracted from the main problem situation, the worker should gently remind the client of the purpose of their meeting.

Another factor to be clarified is that clients, particularly those who have never been to a worker, may expect the worker to solve their problems much in the way a physician does. But that is not the generalist's role. The generalist's role is to help clients find and implement their own solutions wherever possible, even if they have to spend several sessions getting used to each other and the process before they begin to do something about the problem.

To provide structuring is important particularly in the initial stages of the helping process. It is also important when group members are unsure about what is expected of them. Structure may be useful, but too much structuring can inhibit communication. In such situations, structuring may make people feel and act dependent.

Structure in any form of the helping process should be such that it allows members to identify their feelings and express fears, expectations, and personal goals. For instance, in a group members are encouraged to participate in dyads, in go-arounds, and structured questioning while getting acquainted and learning each other's situations. The worker helps members become aware of their feelings and encourages them to express their feelings openly. The purpose of the intervention is to promote a high degree of interaction within the group and not to allow a few members to dominate while other simply observe. Corey (1990) indicates that the type of structuring he uses is designed to let members assume increased responsibility for getting the most out of the group by learning basic norms that let them take the initiative, rather than waiting for the worker's direction. Similarly a community's anxiety can paralyze a large number of people into inaction, but structuring with the community can help prioritize their needs into achievable goals.

Yalom (1983, 1985) mentions a number of research studies where structure is valued in the initial stages of building group or family relationships. When there is ambiguity with reference to the goals and procedures, the group members' behavior changes to anxiety, frustration, and disengagement. Yalom indicates that the basic task of a group leader is to give general direction to the members while avoiding the pitfall of fostering dependency on the leader. Yalom stresses structuring the group in a way that promotes each member's autonomous functioning.

Dies (1983) and Itzhaky and York (1991) indicate that when therapeutic goals are clear, when appropriate member behaviors are identified, and when the therapeutic process is structured in order to provide a framework for change, group members can engage in therapeutic work more quickly. Mondros and Wilson (1994) indicate that early leader direction in a group tends to facilitate the development of cohesion and the willingness of members to take risks by revealing themselves to others and giving others feedback. Mondros and Berman-Rossi (1991) developed a model that shows the value of some types of group and community structures. Structuring in these models increases the group's cohesion, and members gradually begin to feel safer and share themselves in meaningful ways in giving feedback and providing support and challenge to others. The models created by these authors specify that initial ambiguity and anxiety is reduced by increased structure, which is accomplished by giving specific instructions, encouraging members to take increased risks, and increasing group cohesion and personal responsibility.

Focusing

Focusing is an important aspect of the helping process and is especially important in the engagement phase. When clients come into an agency for help, they often feel depersonalized or believe their "case" is being turned into a number. Right from the beginning, the worker should help the client focus on the problem without being unduly rigid about tangential issues. Even the small talk made in the corridor or waiting room is an attempt to introduce the client to the helping system and to help the client begin to focus on the important issues that are being discussed. With communities and large groups the generalist joins the conversation with the goal of helping individuals or groups to express, understand, and redefine their daily experiences in social rather than personal terms. The use of dialogue is to facilitate empowerment in terms of their specific focus (Kemp, 1995; Rupp, 1991).

As Hepworth et al. (1997) indicate, generalists are responsible for giving direction to the helping process and avoiding aimless verbal wandering that consumes valuable time. Effective helping relationships are characterized by sharp focus and continuity. Clients come to practitioners because they are in need of expert guidance in concentrating their efforts on their problems. Quite often, clients tend to be scattered in their thinking and dissipate their energies by shifting their focus from one topic to another. Practitioners perform a valuable role by helping them focus on problems in greater depth and maintaining focus until they have accomplished the desired changes.

Working with Racial, Ethnic, Gender, and Class Differences

There may be a number of differences between the generalist and clients, such as race, gender, age, ethnicity, socioeconomics, and so on. Differences can create problems. However, the worker who is aware of human differences in values and lifestyles and who has learned the skills of communication will be able to work with a wide range of clients. An awareness of different cultures is also important. Lum (1996) describes the dimensions of culture in terms of how the content and specifics of cultures vary. Because of the differences among cultures, there is a natural tendency towards ethnocentrism, which assumes that everyone views the world in the same way, and leads to cross-cultural misunderstanding.

In working with clients from different cultures, the first session is critical. Research indicates that up to 50 percent of all clients of color do not return for a second session (Lum, 1992; Sue, 1992;

Sue & Sue, 1990). This underscores the fact that clients do not feel safe, or that their needs are not being met. Sue and Zane (1987) argue that culturally different clients must leave the first session with a sense that their problems are understood and that they will receive concrete benefits. For this reason, while setting goals during engagement, the generalist should establish a positive beginning relationship that aims at gaining an understanding of clients' problems and what they expect from the helping relationship. This should include communicating clearly about what the practitioner can offer; providing clients with the experience of being heard and understood; and whenever possible and appropriate offering them hope that the helping process can offer immediate help. Being sincere, warm, and respectful is a good beginning for a practitioner with diverse clients. Mutual introductions are also important.

As a practitioner if you do not understand a culture, do not become anxious. Ask questions respectfully or do some extra homework by reading about the culture. As would be done for any client, you should give a brief description of the helping process and the specifics—how often meetings will be held, when, where, and so on. Be sure to explain that confidentiality is an important part of the helping process as most ethnic groups are nervous about divulging information that is personal. Let the clients describe in their own words what they see as their concerns, and ask questions for clarification, if needed. Summarize what you understand and help them proceed further in telling their story. Periodically check with clients to note if they would like other family members or significant others to be part of the helping process. Throughout the engagement process try to evaluate what help the clients expect with the problem. Based on the information that clients present, let them know what can be accomplished in terms of immediate and long-term goals. If the clients experience any problems in understanding the helping process, take time to explain it. Lastly, the first session should end with a formal good-bye, along with concrete plans on what can transpire in the next session.

The entire process is attuned to the needs, concerns, and problems of each unique client and is based on their individual circumstances and personality. Stereotyping of clients based on a cultural group should be avoided at all costs because practitioners lose clients quickly when they begin to look at different clients in the same stereotypical manner. While working with a community of people belonging to a different culture, open-mindedness and sensitivity toward the client will produce effective acceptance of the worker, without resistance.

For example, to view a group of Asian Americans as a single group will create problems for the generalist. Asian Americans may identify themselves as Chinese, Japanese, Indians, Koreans, and so on. However, the name was developed for the bureaucratic purposes of the U.S. Census Bureau and should not be used to imply sameness. In actuality, as Atkinson, Morten, and Sue (1993) indicate, the term *Asian American* refers to "some twenty-nine distinct subgroups that differ in language, religion, and values" (p. 195).

There are other diverse groups besides ethnic groups that need to be engaged cautiously and sensitively. For instance, there are a large number of alcohol and drug counselors who believe that people who have not used drugs themselves cannot become effective helpers for drug users. People who are married may feel that unmarried workers may not be able to help them as much as married workers. Adolescents sometimes feel that older persons do not understand their problems. While there are significant benefits to be gained from contact with others, "who have been there before," there are often advantages to be derived from a more objective and professional approach to problem solving.

Another group of clients who need deeper understanding are those with developmental and psychiatric disabilities. In recent years, life with a disability is viewed as being different rather than deficient (Gerber, Ginsberg, & Reiff, 1992). People are more mobile even if they are confined to wheelchairs. However, there is still a degree of prejudice, stereotyping, and discrimination that persons with disabilities face. The generalist should be sensitive to this, meaning that practitioners may bring their expertise to clients, but it is the clients as consumers who either accept or reject all or part of the help that is being offered (Hahn, 1991). This also means that the natural place for persons with disabilities, even if there is a difference of opinion among professionals, is in control of their lives, living independently from custodial environments, with the same rights and opportunities as persons who have no disabilities (Mackelprang & Salsgiver, 1999). While engaging a person with disabilities, it is crucial that the generalist be aware of the need for them to develop healthy self-identities. This process has many similarities to the process of positive identity development for gays and lesbians (Chan, 1989; Troiden, 1993). Like the gays and lesbians, persons with disabilities may experience a coming out process as they integrate their disability with their self-image.

To understand some of the problems that people with different sexual orientations face, the practitioner must develop awareness of and sensitivity to the client's experiences (Onken & Mackelprang, 1997). These experiences include *preawareness conformity,* which is characterized by an unquestioning acceptance of societal stereotypes and oppression. The person is unaware of alternate views of disability or sexual orientation and blames himself or herself for personal deficits. *Contact* occurs when a person is oblivious to the personal implications of the societal oppression but may feel different by the virtue of having a disability or being different. With *denial* or *avoidance,* the person rejects the implications of ableism or heterosexualism and oppression. A few individuals may acknowledge the implications while others deny being personally affected and still others would "pass" or "overlook" people who are similar to them. Others will distance themselves from similar people and reject membership in a marginalized population.

Comparison is a state in which a person begins to develop an awareness of the reasons for feelings of difference. The person develops a heightened sense of not belonging to the larger society and begins to recognize the disempowerment of being different. This leads to *confusion* and *dissonance,* followed by a personal sense of isolation and lack of group identity. At this point, there is a dawning sense of belonging to a different group but there is a hesitance and a refusal to claim membership. However, constant feelings of isolation can lead to tolerance, which helps the person to acknowledge membership in a similar community. *Connection* takes place when the person seeks out the community by choice; that is, a community of persons with disabilities, or a community of people with a gay sexual orientation. In some cases, *immersion* and *resistance* happen when some individuals take an extremist perspective and reject everything that represents the larger society and have exclusive contact only with people who are similar to them. Some people find permanent happiness in this state. Acceptance and pride are related to immersion and resistance, but in this case, the reactions are not extreme. People may challenge the larger society in terms of practices and beliefs and develop a sense of pride in themselves. *Introspection* and *synthesis* occur when a person is able to balance current personal and community circumstances with past identities, memberships, and relationships. There is a renewed appreciation for diversity and multiculturalism. At this point, a person continues to acknowledge the societal implications of being different, but may feel less anger and stridence.

The primary function of the helping process is to enable diverse individuals to cope and function in life within their social environments as well as the larger society. It is important that engagement begin with a focus on people's strengths and potentials. Assistance is offered to help people understand the larger societal culture and how to use their strengths to overcome oppression and reject devaluation (Mackelprang & Salsgiver, 1999).

However, we should remember that there will be always be differences between the backgrounds of clients and workers. Being sensitive and learning to understand other people's cultures can help tremendously in engaging clients. There are two

types of understanding. In *passive understanding,* as described by Lum (1992), persons read extensively about a group of people and see movies about them. Although they have an extensive understanding of the culture, they do not have any direct interaction with individuals of that culture. What is required in social work is *active understanding,* which is based on actual experiential activity with clients. Active understanding implies understanding matters as they happen while interacting with people. This includes attitudes of respect and acceptance of behavioral and cultural differences in addition to intellectual understanding (Loewenberg, 1983).

There are situations in which there are gaps in socioeconomic, gender, and age differences. Nevertheless, practitioners and clients may have had similar experiences such as divorce or dealing with teen children that can be used, if appropriate, to help clients realize that the practitioner can understand their situations. This occurs as part of self-disclosure discussed earlier. Most of all, it is important that the practitioner is open-minded and able to work with different clients, keeping in mind that there is a contract to work on mutually agreed-upon goals.

Timing

As Loewenberg (1983) and Germain and Gitterman (1996) mention, there are two types of timing. One is *clock timing,* which is based on the time and place for the interview. All agencies and institutions run on clock time, and this is also true of helping sessions. Clients are given a specific time for the appointment, and each client is expected to come on time. Some clients do not pay attention to time and may come late or not show up at all. Depending on clients' culture and background, the practitioner has to highlight to them that coming at the right time is important, otherwise they will not have sufficient time with their worker. It is better to reason with clients, and work out an agreement that is meaningful than to hastily label the client as resistant.

Cultural attitudes toward time are often reflected in the language. As mentioned earlier, in the English language, the clock "runs" but in Spanish the clock "walks." When necessary, differences in concept of time should be part of the initial discussion, in a positive manner, so clients are ready to work within the time constraints of the agency.

Another kind of timing that the generalist should keep in mind can make the difference between being an effective or ineffective practitioner. Introducing topics that are painful for the client at a premature and inappropriate time can cause the loss of a client or represent the beginning of an unproductive helping process.

Jumping to early conclusions about a client may lead to errors in judgment and action. Though there are generalists who based on experience can evaluate more easily and quickly, there are many others who need to take time to get more information. When the timing is not right, the client and generalist will not be able to engage in productive helping sessions constructively, because the client who is sensitive to his or her problems is alert to the generalist's hastiness.

Evaluation and Withholding Judgment

As Biestek (1957) and more recently, Hopps, Pinderhughes, and Shankar (1995) indicate, the nonjudgmental attitude that is expected of social workers does not mean rejection of the values of society or condoning antisocial or immoral behavior. It does mean that social workers have a professional obligation to differentiate between clients and their behavior, and to provide service based on client need, regardless of who clients are or what they have done. One of the most difficult areas that social workers have been placed in is work with abusive parents. The goal in such situations is to help these people stop the physical or sexual abuse and become better parents. In order to do this, a positive relationship has to be established in which the clients felt accepted as human beings; otherwise, the contact will be pointless.

The worker who reveals an overly critical attitude and has expectations that are unrealistic may be more harmful than helpful to the client. When generalists are critical of clients, the clients get the message that their behavior or performance is not good enough, which in turn makes them feel more diffident and even less sure of themselves. For instance, Thelma, a generalist had a forty-year-old client, Emma, who dressed like a child and looked ridiculous to Thelma and her colleagues. If Thelma had ridiculed Emma or questioned Emma about her style of dress in the first session, Thelma would have surely lost a client. The practitioner's expectations must be based on what is appropriate and realistic for the client rather than what the worker thinks is appropriate. As Loewenberg put it, there is a great difference between expecting the "best" from clients as the worker defines "best," or expecting the best from clients based on what they are capable of. Being helpful requires setting goals with clients that are realistic and keeping in mind what clients are capable of doing.

Activity in the Engagement Phase

Very little attention is given to the skills of engagement in terms of worker activity. Studies show that when the worker is active, there is greater client satisfaction (Maluccio, 1979). Parloff and colleagues (1978) found no evidence that high practitioner activity was related to positive outcomes, although they did find that worker activity led to easier communication, a reduction in client tension, and a decrease in one-sided terminations. Further, as Brower and Nuruis (1993) and Germain (1985) indicate, the manner by which people perceive their place in the world frames their view of what is possible within: consequently, community engagement and interventions should be responsive to their aggregate experiences.

The type of practitioner activity can vary depending on the clients and their needs. A practitioner going to the door, shaking hands with the client, and welcoming him or her into the office sets a tone of acceptance, but also reveals that the practitioner is ready for the client and ready to help. As we proceed into the stages of helping, it will become clear that there is a great deal of practitioner activity, but it is in the engagement phase where clients, with the practitioner's help, have to indicate the type of help they require.

A word of caution: There are workers who may become overactive in the engagement phase and take over, which is counterproductive because it allows clients to be overly passive. An overactive worker can overwhelm a client and create feelings of stress.

When Mrs. K, a single parent, brought her five-year-old overactive son for help, the worker made plans for the boy to join a group and also arranged for him to be medicated without discussing the plan with Mrs. K. Mrs. K and child dropped out of the sessions because she felt so uninvolved. The mother is so significant a person in the life of a child, that the worker should have involved Mrs. K at every stage and helped her become involved in the decision-making process to determine what help was given to the child.

FIRST-SESSION (ENGAGEMENT) AGENDA REVIEW

A number of practitioners have developed a structure for conducting the first interview including appropriate modifications based on the client system, whether an individual, a couple, a group or a family, an organization, or a community. Practitioners who have contributed to the first-session agenda are Kadushin and Kadushin (1997) and Reid (1985).

The following list summarizes the steps that many practitioners consider important in a first session. They involve the worker collecting information and establishing a therapeutic relationship that is productive and caring.

- *Opening:* The practitioner begins the first session dynamically, sensitizing the client to the anticipation of change.

- *Route:* The generalist finds out what type of help the client wishes and why the decision was made to seek help.
- *Reason:* The generalist determines the purpose for which the person is seeking help.
- *Expectations:* What are the client system's expectations for help and treatment? Whom has the client system seen before and how was that experience?
- *Definition:* The generalist needs to correct misconceptions and unrealistic expectations. How does the process of helping work and who has the responsibility for each part?
- *Confidentiality:* Discussion of confidentiality is important in establishing trust.
- *Search for Content:* Areas that are appropriate for the helping process include presenting problems, self-destructive behaviors, unresolved conflicts, and interpersonal tensions.
- *Important People:* The practitioner explores the most important people in the client system's world; that is, if there are people who have a vested interest in the outcomes.
- *Functional Level:* The client system is assessed across a broad spectrum of behaviors: resilience, intelligence, confidence, flexibility, perceptual and cognitive capacities, life skills, and values.
- *Structure:* The generalist determines a structure for a client system that should enable the client system to make significant progress.
- *Commitment:* The generalist secures a commitment from the client to change and to work toward goals.
- *Goals:* The generalist works toward realistic goals for offering help that are then reduced to subgoals for between sessions.
- *Summary:* The generalist reviews or lets the client system evaluate what his, her, or their experience has been after the first session.
- *Homework:* The generalist translates the issues that have been highlighted into a summary for a self-determining homework assignment so that action may continue between sessions.

- *Closing:* When ending the first session, the generalist works to solidify relationships and set up future appointments as the final step in the engagement phase.

Although these steps seem detailed, they offer structure in the engagement process. However, the generalist should not alienate clients in the process. An important goal that the generalist needs to keep in mind is to create an alliance with a degree of trust and intimacy. Major therapeutic tasks in the first session are:

1. Establish a beginning working relationship with the client system
2. Provide the client with information about the helping process and how it works
3. Find out the issues and expectations of the client system
4. If appropriate, create a sense of hope in the client system
5. Obtain a commitment from the client system to be patient and work hard in the sessions

This is the beginning of the helping process and on this foundation rests the remainder of the process.

A DIFFERENT CLIENTELE

The Involuntary Client

All the steps of engagement that should be carried out easily with "regular clients" may not happen with involuntary clients because involuntary clients are required or mandated to receive professional help. Mandated clients include abusive and neglectful parents, abusive spouses, prisoners, psychiatric patients and so on. They are placed with the generalist through the legal authority of a judge, a child protection agency, or the influence of a powerful family member or an employer. The worker often has some degree of legal authority with involuntary clients. When workers function in a vol-

untary agency they can make suggestions to clients, but generalists in court-related relationships have the authority to impose a certain amount of action (Rooney, 1991; Shaefor et al., 2000). Successful work with involuntary clients demands a high level of motivation, self-awareness, and also self-discipline. Often, close supervision and peer support are important for developing these abilities.

Although the generalist has a certain degree of authority based on knowledge, role, values, and skills in working with involuntary clients, many generalists are uncomfortable with such authority and reluctant to use it. Hardman (1960) a probation officer and Egan (1998) suggest that generalists make their authoritative role clear to clients and consistently function within its limits for appropriate use of authority. They should not use vile threats or behavior that might be interpreted as unclear, as this clouds the whole process of helping and also does not clarify the generalist's limits.

Rooney (1988) suggests that authority be used in a warm and supportive manner, which demonstrates an understanding of the client's problems. Generalists have to present themselves as carrying *reasonable* authority. Also, clients need to be aware that there is no hidden agenda, which may have to be verbalized periodically. Generalists have to make the protective service role and function clear to the clients and workers should not retreat from the responsibility of making clients aware of expectations. They should demonstrate caring to the client using professional competence to help them, while avoiding a cold and impersonal approach. For example, if a child has to be separated from its parents because of unforeseen reasons, the worker should make the family aware that he or she understands that trauma. Never give the parents the impression that they are the "enemy" and the worker is "protecting" the children from them. Avoid being insensitive to parental feelings that could elicit responses of anger, hostility, and resistance in clients and make it difficult for the generalist to establish a positive working relationship.

Ivanoff, Blythe, and Tripodi (1994) and Shaefor et al. (2000) suggest that practitioners be clear about what requirements are nonnegotiable and what choices and options are open. They should anticipate clients' feelings about their loss of freedom. Give clients facts about the manner in which they are involved in the agency and correct any misinformation. Generalists should explain their role and responsibility with the agency and what is expected of the client. If the rules of confidentiality cannot be followed, the client should be informed and offered explanations. If the client does not cooperate with the generalist, the consequences need to be discussed. The generalist must respect the client's wishes to choose the consequences rather than professional services.

When clients present angry, hostile, defensive reactions and feelings, practitioners cannot take it personally. A client's negative feelings and behavior must be dealt with directly. The practitioner should ascertain the client's experience with the system and any preconceived ideas they have about social workers. Be aware of the sociocultural background of clients. As Rooney (1988) suggests, practitioners can sometimes begin to engage clients through "let's make a deal"! For instance, criminal charges could be reduced by talking to the prosecuting attorney in exchange for cooperation in the helping process.

It is important to be aware that there is no such thing as an unmotivated client. All clients are motivated to an extent. This simply means that their wants, needs, and preferences are different from what practitioners want for clients. To reach involuntary clients, the generalist has to find out their needs and wants and establish intervention goals that are consistent with the clients' goals, at least to some degree. Once there is an agreement about goals, then the client can be engaged in problem solving more easily; for example, "You wish to get out of this setting. Also, we both want you to get off probation so that you don't have to talk to me weekly. What can we do together so that you can reach your goal?" The generalist should also highlight the client's strengths and be positive in recognizing any small gains the client makes in the helping process.

Dangerous Clients

At times workers have to work with potentially dangerous clients and there are certain precautions that need to be taken with such clients. Workers should never enter a situation that is known to be dangerous without first consulting and informing others of their plans. A client's history of violent outbursts should be recorded carefully, so that a new worker can take necessary precautions. When you make a home visit to such a client, your office should be informed and you should check by phone at a prearranged time (Bolton & Bolton, 1987). In an office interview you should position your furniture and yourself so that you do not feel trapped and it would be easy for you to escape. Often, aggressiveness and anger stem from a feeling of being controlled and trapped by others. The best way to work with clients who feel this way is to offer them options, even small options (e.g., "Think about what we talked about and decide what course of action you would like to take.").

The worker should also be alert to bodily signs of imminent attack, including flaring nostrils, dilated pupils, loud outbursts, and so on. In all potentially dangerous situations, the practitioner should dress professionally and maintain a sense of self-confidence that gives the impression that he or she can handle the job. Finally, workers in dangerous settings should be trained in some self-defense techniques and seek guidance from experienced peers and the police. It is important to understand your own limitations and strengths but never under- or overestimate either.

Besides involuntary clients, there are drug abusers, and others who can be destructively manipulative. It's important that workers be aware of such clients and prepared to learn and understand how to work with them.

Exercises

1. Role-play an individual client situation with one person being the worker and the other the client. After the role play, let the worker analyze the emotions, thoughts, and behavior of the client. The person who role-plays the client can give feedback to indicate whether these observations were accurate.

2. Role-play a group situation with a group leader. Afterwards, let the members discuss how they felt playing the role of group member. The group leader should make his or her observations and comment on difficulties and comfort in playing this role.

3. Role-play a family situation with four or five students. Let a student who plays the family practitioner analyze the family situation, then the class can provide feedback on their impressions of the family scene. Students who role-play should also present their thinking and feelings about the roles they played.

4. Role-play a situation in which a worker is working with an abusive mother after her three children have been taken away from her for both neglect and abuse. She is extremely hostile and unwilling to talk to the worker. Because this is a mandatory situation, how should the worker handle the client and develop a working relationship with her?

CHAPTER SUMMARY

In the engagement phase the worker has to identify the problem situation by specifying the concrete aspects of the situation in which the problem occurs. This includes identifying the person, where and when the events occur, and the immediacy of these problems.

In the engagement phase, intake is the process which begins with a request for help by the client or on behalf of the client and culminates in a decision by the agency and the client with regard to the type of service that is needed and will be provided to the client. Problem exploration is an important aspect of engagement because comprehensive information must be gathered before all the dimensions of a problem and their interactions are understood.

The worker provides the clarity to understand the client and move the whole process of helping and toward exploring expectations. Based on the overall quality of a client's disclosure, the worker and client begin to negotiate contracts and goals. Goals are classified into discrete or one-time action goals and ongoing goals.

Engagement in families happens when the family comes for the first session. After the introductions have been made, the worker "joins" the family. The most significant task is setting behaviorally specific goals. A number of sessions are agreed upon in order to achieve these goals.

Engaging group members is somewhat different from engaging individuals. There are specific objectives that need to be followed in structuring the first meeting. The group should have unambiguous leadership, defined rules, open communication channels, effective reality testing, and a congenial atmosphere. Contracting in groups means clarifying the purpose of the group and the leader's and group members' roles, and soliciting client feedback in response to these matters.

In communities, identifying the client system and establishing communication with community members regarding their concerns is important. This is followed by creating an initial engaging phase using individual and group skills.

The basic skills of engagement include structuring, focusing, working on differences, timing, evaluation and withholding judgment, and worker activity in the engagement stage. The first-session agenda includes appropriate modifications based on the client system which include individuals, couples, groups or families, communities, and organizations, as well as involuntary and dangerous clients.

11

ASSESSMENT

The second phase of helping is called assessment. After a worker has engaged a client system and even as the preliminaries are undertaken a worker begins to assess the person–problem configuration and the potential for change.

WHAT IS ASSESSMENT?

Assessment is a process involving procedures and tools that are used to collect and interpret data from which a plan for helping is developed. Johnson (1995) views assessment as an integrative approach that combines a variety of information into a meaningful pattern that reflects relevant aspects of a situation or a client system. Assessment does not depend upon one single measure, nor does it deal with one dimension at the expense of another. In order to make an assessment profile meaningful and useful, it is important to provide a perspective of the client system that is as broad and integrative as possible. For example, an assessment of a political candidate's suitability for elective of-

fice may include a measure of past performance, a review of related experiences and accomplishments, recommendations from knowledgeable observers, and a self-statement of goals and objectives. This would provide all pertinent sources of information from which an integrated picture could be built of the candidate's characteristics, qualities, and aptitudes. Although a political candidate is not a client coming for help with a problem, we access politicians as much on their political philosophy and party affiliation as on the assessment criteria mentioned. A thorough assessment based on the problem or concern of a client system is similarly necessary.

The purpose of assessment is to help clients expand their ability to identify and analyze the relevant factors that are present in a particular situation, and how they influence each other. As noted, assessment leads to a plan of action in which the practitioner and client together make decisions about which aspects of a situation to deal with, the goals for making changes, and the means of achieving the goals.

Problem assessment is not an end in itself but a process, and its purpose is not to classify, categorize, or assign diagnostic labels to a person or a situation (Pincus & Minahan, 1973). Gutheil (1992) points out the importance of understanding the physical environment and its influence on behavior in the family, the agency, and the interview. Tracy and Whitaker (1990) propose developing a "social networking map" to use as a means of assessing a client's sources of social support. The social network map provides a tool for clients to identify both the number of significant people in their lives including household, friends, and neighbors and also the nature of the interactions that provide concrete support, emotional support, information, and advice. Identifying these actual and potential resources is important in helping clients develop strategies for effective stress management.

When generalists and clients make a decision, they are choosing between two or more alternative goals, tasks, or courses of action. The purpose of problem assessment is to help identify the alternatives, select one alternative, and forego others. A pitfall in this process occurs when generalists need to hold on to and continue to act on their initial assumptions in the face of new information or new developments. It is important for the generalist to keep in mind competing theories, hypotheses, and assumptions. Problem assessment is an initial guide for the planned change process. It is not static but continuous.

Cormier and Cormier (1998) and Hepworth, Rooney, and Larsen (1997) have identified many important dimensions in assessment.

1. To make an assessment, it is essential to obtain information about a client's presenting problem as well as other related problems. These include the nature of the client's concerns and difficulties, with special attention to developmental needs and stressors associated with life transitions that require major adaptation. For instance, marriage or a first baby are life transitions likely to produce stress due to the significant change in role and function required of family members. Be-

coming the head of a new organization would be a similar example.

2. The generalist has to identify and evaluate the importance of various factors contributing to or associated with the problem.

3. The generalist has to determine the counseling outcomes required by the client's goals and expectations.

4. The coping capacities of clients and significant others, including strengths, skills, personality factors, limitations, and deficiencies should be considered.

5. The generalist should understand the relevant systems that are involved in clients' problems and the nature of reciprocal transactions that take place between clients and these systems. These systems include the family and the workplace, as well as other relevant systems in a person's life.

6. The generalist should gather firsthand baseline data that can be compared to subsequent data in order to assess and evaluate a client's progress and the effects of treatment strategies.

7. The generalist should locate available resources in a client's social network, in the agency, and in the community to remedy or ameliorate problems.

8. The generalist should clarify, educate, and motivate the client by sharing his or her view of the problem and possible solutions to increase the client's receptivity and readiness for treatment. At times, behavior changes may take place as the result of an assessment interview rather than as the result of a particular action or change strategy.

9. The generalist should use information that is obtained from the client and elsewhere to plan effective treatment interventions and strategies. This information should help answer the question: What type of help, by whom, is most effective for this client system with that specific problem or concern, and under which set of circumstances?

The manner in which an assessment is conducted is largely determined by the setting and the generalist's role in that setting. In some settings, social work is the primary professional function, whereas in other settings such as hospitals, courts, and schools, it is secondary. Depending on the nature of the problem, the setting, and the specified role of the generalist in the setting, the social worker may have sole or primary responsibility for assessment and planning. At other times, the generalist's role is important but secondary, with the primary professional and legal responsibility for pulling information together and deciding what should be done resting with another professional, such as a physician, a teacher, or a judge.

NATURE, CONTENT, AND PROCESS OF ASSESSMENT

Generalists need to be aware that the process of assessment takes place in the context of a helping relationship. Generalists and clients are involved together in processing and assessing the person and situation to the fullest possible extent. This means inquiring about and explaining to the client why certain questions are asked and why a particular subject is important. It also means listening closely and respectfully to the clients who may have important information and insights that the worker has not considered. This type of sharing and assessing a client's situation has numerous benefits. It can further the helping relationship and the client's commitment to the helping process. The worker will probably find it easier to convey his or her understanding of the problem to the client, which can help the client develop a more realistic and objective perspective of the problem. At the same time, the client's participation and knowledge that someone else understands and is ready to help is likely to diminish feelings of anxiety and helplessness.

The assessment process is both cognitive and interactive. The cognitive aspect refers to the mental work of sorting out objective and subjective information, applying theoretical and empirical in-

sights, and making decisions. The interactive work involves engaging clients, establishing open lines of communication, negotiating differences, and obtaining commitments to bring about positive change. The steps of assessment include identifying the client system, assessing the client–environment configuration, gathering information about client needs and problems, and identifying client strengths (see Figure 11.1).

Assessment should be viewed as both a systematic and dynamic process. The purposes of study or fact-finding are achieved in an orderly, thorough manner utilizing checklists and outlines. However, as Shulman (1999) indicates, the assessment process is an open affair with boundaries that are not sharply defined. It is possible to add on to assessment in different stages of helping if new information comes in. As well, it is essential to understand that assessment and treatment do not operate in a linear sequence but in a spiral. In actual practice, it is difficult to say which comes first because treatment itself yields the most telling assessment, that of the person's ability and willingness to engage in working at his or her problems. Because of their shifting, emergent natures, assessments or diagnoses are sometimes called "preliminary," "working," or "terminal." The words *diagnosis* and *assessment* have been used interchangeably for at least two decades, but today the term *assessment* is used more often.

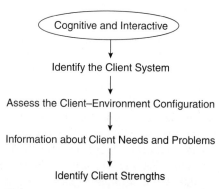

Figure 11.1 **Steps in Assessment**

An analysis in assessment includes various factors such as the problem, the personality of the clients (or characteristics of the client system), and the significant situation. What is the nature and present status of all the significant characteristics? The nature includes the definition of the problem (e.g., child abuse, divorce, or marital conflict), how long the problem has existed and its severity, the degree to which it has affected the clients, the number of people it has affected, and where it began. It is important to know how long the problem has been prevalent—its duration and developmental history. What are the reasons that this problem is present? What needs are met in terms of results and rewards of behavior? For instance, in considering child abuse, the reward for the parent could be taking out frustration on the child; the child, in turn, is too afraid to complain but soon begins to have terrible nightmares. How do the people who have the problem view it? What does it mean for its participants? How is the problem viewed by the people who suffer from it? Is it seen as a crisis or a defeat, and how has it affected clients' self-concept and self-esteem? Do the persons view themselves as failures or accept the problem as something that has been prevalent in their lives for a long period of time?

One of the most important things that the generalist has to remember is that assessment is a cooperative process between the worker and the client system. The purpose, the content, and the questions need to be clarified and explained so that clients understand and become a part of the process. A generalist's interpretations or conclusions should be checked out with the clients. Not only does this provide a reality check for the generalist's thinking, but this cooperative process emphasizes to clients that they are respected and viewed as intelligent people with the competence and willpower needed to resolve their problems.

Also, to be an effective helper, the generalist must emphasize the existing resources within individuals, families, communities, and organizations, as well as within situations, through which positive changes can be made. This does not mean that pathology or other differences are overlooked. However, the helping process does place emphasis on the assets and resources of people.

Statement of the Problem

The first order of business is to obtain a clear statement of the problem being presented to the generalist. Every problem statement comprises five interrelated factors: (1) a statement of the problem and problem identification; (2) understanding the functioning of the clients, including the intrapersonal aspects; (3) understanding the dynamics of the social and cultural conditions; (4) motivation of clients to work on their problems; and (5) the reasons and basis for this beginning assessment. Defining a problem represents a specific perception and determination of the nature of a difficulty and also implies how it should be treated. It is also important to realize that a problem definition may reflect a value stance, a goal, and a policy (Kahn, 1973; Weiner-Davis, deShazer, & Gingerich, 1987). For example, racial incidents in different parts of the country have been attributed variously to anger against police brutality, to a breakdown in law and order, to racial discrimination, to unemployment among minority ethnic groups, and so on. Each of these interpretations points to a different plan of action.

The statement of the problem also identifies and describes a pattern of behavior, unmet need, or other troublesome difficulty and what this means to others in the network of relationships. For example, how does the wife feel about her husband's excessive drinking? The generalist needs to describe the actual behaviors that are either too excessive or too deficient to allow the adequate functioning of a person or family, and whether the presenting problem or complaint is the chief difficulty or is symptomatic of other more serious problems.

As indicated by Siporin (1975), and later by Shulman (1999), and Cormier & Cormier (1998), the following principles apply to the statement of the problem:

1. Whenever possible, the problem should be defined in terms of specific social situations as related to certain specific events or behaviors. In addition, a problematic situation has to be described as being precipitating, acute, or habitual, if symptomatic, and also as primary or secondary. For instance, problematic situations become obvious when a person loses a job and is without a salary for two years and then develops a headache which causes a lot of pain and therefore affects performance in getting a job. A low-income community with children who have a great deal of free time on their hands needs a place for recreation particularly during the summer months when schools are closed. When none is provided for many years, the end result is likely vandalism and crime in that community.

2. From the generalist's perspective, the problem definition should focus on an area that is of immediate concern and interest to clients and one in which some constructive action can be taken.

3. When discussing problems and concerns, the generalist should indicate not only the tasks and needs that have not been identified but also the difficulties that are workable and resolvable without identifying or specifying a particular solution. Depending on the agency, the generalist will usually prepare a prioritized written problem assessment statement.

Written Problem Assessment Statement

A written problem assessment statement provides a clear idea of what the problem is and how it affects the client system. A written statement has many advantages. It forces generalists to think clearly and to make explicit what they know and do not know about the particular client system and the problems that are the focus of attention. It also helps the generalist to bring into play theoretical and value assumptions about a particular situation. Written assessment statements are also used for supervision, consultation, administrative monitoring, and research purposes.

To be useful, the statement of the problem has to be specific and clearly written. Universal statements that talk generally about clients do not necessarily apply to a specific client system. Specific descriptions of behavior and events should accompany and document the use of evaluative or assessment words. For example, a boy might be labeled "aggressive" if he is argumentative, if he gets into fist fights, or if he attacks other younger children. However, the implications of each of these examples of aggressive behavior is quite different and thus, obviously, more information would be necessary to move toward constructive help.

Assessment is not permanent but is gradually reshaped as new information is obtained. Though the initial assessment serves as a blueprint, it is modified as ideas are tested out and new data and information are gathered. The generalist continues to reassess the nature of the problem, the need for supportive data, and the effectiveness of the approaches chosen to cope with it.

Stating specific factors forces the practitioner to make explicit what he or she knows and does not know about the relationship of the person and situation. It also helps to identify the assumptions the practitioner is making, which act as a tool in negotiating and establishing contracts that measures progress. It even facilitates communication about different situations.

Assessment as an Ongoing Process

The written assessment is like a snapshot taken at the end of the assessment stage. However, what must be emphasized is the ongoing nature of the assessment process. That process begins with the initial contact and ends with the last meeting with the client, a time period lasting from a single session to a few weeks, or even a few months or years. In many ways, assessment is a fluid and dynamic process that involves receiving, analyzing, and synthesizing new information as it emerges throughout the entire course of the case (Hepworth et al., 1997). During the first few interviews, clients normally present an abundance of information that has to be processed and understood. After a sufficient amount of data has been received, the generalist analyzes it and, in collaboration with the client, integrates the data into a tentative formulation of the problem and a plan of action.

Often, the assessment has to be modified during the problem-solving phase because of new developments in the client's concerns or because the client provides information that casts the case in a new light. Sometimes a client may withhold important information because of discomfort with the worker or fear of being judged negatively.

A woman who came for help mentioned that she had a number of problems with her husband including emotional and verbal abuse. She felt that she deserved these problems because they had constant money problems due to her fiscal mismanagement. Learning assertive communication styles and money management skills did not seem to help her.

One day after almost five sessions, she revealed that she had been sexually and verbally abused by her stepfather. She felt that she was not a worthy human being and did not have the right to make decisions for herself. She had withheld information about herself because she was afraid of being condemned or criticized by the worker, based on her relationships with people in authority. In this case, the preliminary assessment was not accurate and had to be drastically revised to help this woman.

Assessment per se does not stop at the end of the problem-solving stage. Practitioners continue to assess clients into the termination phase of service. Even during termination, the worker continues to make an assessment of residual difficulties that clients may face and the reactions that some clients may have to termination.

METHODS OF CONCEPTUALIZING CLIENT PROBLEMS

Clients present their story as they experience it. When clients present issues, the practitioner has the task of deciding what additional information to obtain, how to put it together in some meaningful way that can lead to ideas for problem solving. This mental activity, called *conceptualization*, describes the manner in which a practitioner thinks about a client system's problem.

Cormier and Cormier (1998) suggest four ways of conceptualizing problems. First, they suggest a framework that the practitioner may use to develop hunches or hypotheses about the client's presenting problem. Second, they recognize that the problems and concerns are multifaceted and affect how people think, feel, and behave. Third, an understanding of the social and physical environment in which the problem or concern occurs is important. Finally, information about the problem or concern must be provided so that the practitioner can select and plan relevantly together with the client.

A combination of case conceptualization models has been described by Kanfer and Saslow (1969), Lazarus (1976, 1989), and Morran, Kurpius, Brack, and Rozecki (1994). *Case conceptualization* in any helping profession, including social work, is based on the following formula: There are clients who present normal, difficult, or deviant behaviors as manifested in the degree of stress, maladaptive behaviors, habits, and defenses versus supports, strengths, and adaptive habits and defenses. Other important factors that need to be considered in understanding clients include major environmental contingencies, cognitive themes, affective themes, behavioral patterns, and interpersonal relationships.

Sixteen-year-old Cliff is a troubled teenager. He fights with other young people, steals from others, swears at teachers, and has received low grades in five of his six classes. Cliff feels anxious in unstructured situations. He is always compared to his older brother who is considered to be smart, well behaved, and well liked in school and elsewhere. Cliff also carries the tensions of his parents' relationship with him into every situation. He compares himself unfavorably with his older brother and assumes no responsibility at home.

Available supports for Cliff include the fact that the school social worker is willing to work with him and his family. Cliff is also a member of the swim team and performs well in competitions, so the coach wants to help him remain on the team. Cliff is in good health, has normal sleep patterns, and has received high scores on intelligence tests. He appears to be fairly well adjusted in competitive situations. By conceptualizing the normal and deviant behaviors, stresses and maladaptive defenses and behavioral habits, Cliff's social worker can begin to understand the supports, strengths, and adaptive habits and defenses of this particular client.

In any given case, the practitioner obtains a great deal of information which must be synthesized and integrated to be of value in the helping process. If this is not done constructively, it is of little use to the client. The task of the worker is to obtain information, put it together in some meaningful way, and use it to generate clinical hunches or hypotheses about client problems that could lead to tentative ideas for problem solving.

In Cliff's case there are environmental contingencies that include consequences and history. There are also cognitive themes—both misconceptions and irrationalities—that are evidenced by clients. In Cliff's case he sees his older brother as a "superman" to whom he can never match up; therefore, he feels he will never be liked by his parents or teachers. There are affective themes that comprise barriers or emotional conflicts. In Cliff's case, there are felt and expressed emotions that form counterproductive barriers. All behavior patterns consist of overt, observable behaviors, including verbal and nonverbal behaviors that are revealed outside of counseling. These behavior patterns often are connected to problems such as low self-esteem, overeating, poor study habits, and also periodic drug and alcohol use. In Cliff's case, poor study habits and stealing reveal his low self-esteem. All these factors would help a worker draw conclusions in terms of how to plan and work out a treatment plan.

Other factors that a worker has to look at are overall appearance, physiological complaints, and general health and well-being. At times problems may arise due to physical factors. Most social problems occur in a social context and are also functionally related to internal and external antecedents and consequences. All these different areas should be incorporated into an assessment.

Andy is not good-looking and wears heavy glasses. He is intensely disliked by children of his age group who joke about him all the time. His ambitious parents pressure him to be a straight-A student and nothing less is acceptable. Instead of socializing with others Andy isolates himself in the library. His excellent performance in school makes his classmates dislike him more. Under all the different pressures, Andy attempts suicide, bringing him to the attention of the school authorities. The school social worker who interviews his now repentant parents understands their high expectations.

Keep in mind that there are different ways to assess problems, particularly when there are so many factors involved in working with clients. In order to assess a client system, be it a person, family or group, a community, or an organization, the worker needs to have extensive knowledge about that system as well as the multifarious systems that include economic, religious, social, and interpersonal factors. The generalist needs to consider biophysical, emotional, cultural, and behavioral factors, motivational subsystems, and the relationship of those transactions to problem situations (Hepworth et al., 1997).

Another important factor of the assessment and planning process is the worker's conceptualization of what is happening between the worker and client system. From an ecosystems perspective, workers assess problems from the point of view of the person–environment configuration. That is, most of the problems are the result of behavior patterns, environmental factors, and affective and cognitive themes present in persons, families, groups, communities, and organizations. However, a successful assessment depends on specific guidelines and training in the field in order to receive accurate and valid information for treatment planning (Dudley, 1987).

History Taking in Assessment

To begin an assessment and to understand a client's situation, various kinds of information must be solicited. To make an accurate assessment, it is better that the generalist solicit this information rather than wait for the client to give it. Usually called *history taking*, this interview is the first phase of assessment. While taking a client's history, the generalist should observe and ask questions in the following areas:

1. Identifying data including information about sex, age, ethnic group, gender, occupation, marital status, and location of community.

2. Information about general appearance, including height and weight, as well as a brief description of family members, group members, organization or community members. This should include dress, grooming, and the overall physical look of the clients, and in the case of an organization, the place of that specific organization in the community. Because some communities have more resources than others, the community itself should be part of the assessment as well.

3. The history of the given system and how it is related to the present problem. This includes when the problem started; what other factors were prevalent at that time that might precipitate the problem; where, when, and how often the problem occurred; and what were the feelings, thoughts, and behaviors associated with this problem. The extent of the problem is also gauged by assessing to what degree it interferes with the clients' functioning.

In history taking, the generalist asks numerous questions. What solutions have been tried with this client system and what were the results? Why has the client system sought help at this time? Is this a referred client and what are the purposes of the referral, or did the client volunteer to get help? What is the client's past history in terms of service and what kind of help has this client obtained? What was the period of help for this client system and what was the presenting complaint? What was the outcome of the helping process and the reason for termination? What previous help has the client received with regard to physical, emotional, and psychological factors?

What is the education and job history of this client? What problems did the client encounter in relationships with teachers and peers? What different kinds of jobs this client held? Has the client ever been terminated from a job, and why? Also, what was this client's relationship with coworkers?

What is the client's medical and health history? Has the client had any health problems? What is the social and developmental history of this client? What are the client's current life situations, social and leisure time activities? What predominant values, priorities, and beliefs does the client express? What significant incidents happened in the client system's developmental phases? What is the family, marital, and sexual history for an individual client?

The generalist also has to identify data concerning family relations when working with individuals, families, and small groups. Data on parents and family patterns, methods of rewards and punishments in the family, relationships with each parent, relationships with spouse, children, and in-laws are all important. Also, if relevant, which sibling is most like the client? Was there was favoritism in the family? Were there any serious illnesses in the family? In terms of the client, what is the family history, the relationship between the client and the immediate family including wife and children, and any problems that have or should be addressed in the helping process? There should also be a brief assessment of the client's communication patterns, including verbal behaviors and nonverbal behaviors such as the use of eye contact, gestures, voice pitch, fluency, and vocal errors (Cormier & Cormier, 1998).

Some questions should be asked in the first session, and still others have to be brought out at later points in the helping process. For example, questions regarding health and medical history, social and developmental history, and the history of marital and sexual relationships could be asked in later interviews. The first session with community members should allow them to tell the community story in their own fashion, point out the problems and concerns, and discuss them further. In the second meeting there will a fine-tuning of needs and concerns, and items to be worked on will be prioritized accordingly.

CATEGORIES IN ASSESSMENT

Cormier and Cormier (1998) suggest that practitioners address the following categories in conducting assessment interviews.

The Purpose of Assessment

The worker should explain the purpose of an assessment and why it is important for both the client and the generalist. The generalist must let the client know that he or she may be asking difficult questions. The worker should explain that the purpose behind this questioning is to help the client and the worker identify the area they should be working on.

While presenting these ideas, the worker should look at the client for some confirmation or indication that the client understands and is willing to go along with the plan. If not, the worker must continue to provide further explanation. The process should be geared to the client's level of understanding. For example, when the worker asks questions after a standard description of the assessment process, Aileen does not understand and becomes suspicious and withdraws. Observing the client's withdrawal and discomfort, the worker starts to explain the purpose of assessment in simple terms so that Aileen is ready to present her problems without feeling inhibited.

The Different Types of Problems

The generalist and the client identify the range of problems that are part of the client's life. While discussing these, the generalist and the client identify the most crucial problems as well as other related problems. Pictured as a sphere, the crucial problems are a part of the inner circle, followed by problems of intermediary importance which form the middle circle, with the least important problems on the outer circle (see Figure 11.2). This approach has been recommended by Lazarus (1989)

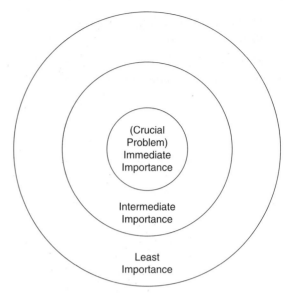

Figure 11.2 Problem Assessment

to help clients disclose problem areas. Topics in the inner circle are very personal and problems in the outer circle are more public. To make it easier for the client, the worker can suggest that letters of the alphabet represent each circle: A could be crucial problems such as lack of food or the threat of suicide; B could represent items such as sexual issues; and C might represent job history. In this way, the client can be asked to talk about the circles and highlight why one particular circle is more important than another.

Some clients will not own a particular problem or see it as stemming from them, but will blame others for the problem and minimize their contribution to it. For example, an employee is having problems with his coworkers and siblings because he curses at people. He does not take responsibility for this behavior and points this finger at others saying that they irritate him a great deal, which makes him lose his temper. One way of working through this pattern would be to ask if the client or someone close in the family wants the problem solved and also to check on the communication patterns in the family.

Prioritizing and Selecting the Most Important Problems

At this point the generalist and the client prioritize and select the problems that best represent the client's purpose for seeking help. When a client presents problems, they appear in more than one area because a client usually has many unresolved issues. For example, a client reports that she has problems with her teenage daughter, but after a while it is clear that the daughter is not the only problem. The husband is an alcoholic and the family has financial problems. After the problems have been discussed, a decision has to be made in terms of which problem will be acted on. Though the selection of the problem is the client's responsibility, the worker can help the client make a choice. If the client selects a problem area that appears to clash with the worker's or agency's values with the result that the worker is not able to work with this client, then a referral needs to be made to another worker or agency where help can be offered without reservations and with objectivity. For example, Jessie was receiving free services in a Catholic agency when she brought up the fact that she was pregnant, single, and a student, and wanted an abortion desperately. Because of the worker's religious values and the philosophy of the agency, Jessie was referred to another agency.

When prioritizing problems, the worker should start with the presenting problem because this will make most sense to the client. Fensterheim (1983) and Field and Steinhardt (1992) observe that just having the opportunity to tell one's story to an empathetic listener will often bring on emotional relief, improve the client's level of functioning, and also make other related problems more accessible. The worker can then move on to the other problems that the client has identified and ask the client which one he or she would like to deal with.

Asking clients to establish in order of priority what they think is least important to what they believe is most important helps them to move in the appropriate direction with the worker's support. Bringing about constructive change in the most important issue area can also be generalized to other areas. For instance, twenty-year-old Carey had a number of problems, one of which was her inability to date men. Her self-esteem was low and she hid herself behind her obesity. Helping Carey consciously work at reducing her weight helped her see herself as attractive. Carey developed confidence in herself, her self-esteem improved, and she moved on to dating men and finding herself a suitable job, which was another issue area for her.

When clients achieve success in solving one problem, they are likely to move with greater ease toward facing other problems. Consequently it is best to ask clients with a serious problem to work with it in the form of smaller tasks or problems. After these have been broken down the worker can ask the client, "Which problem do you believe you can manage most easily and with the greatest success?" The client should choose this problem and work on it. Success with one problem inspires the client to work on others more willingly.

At times, one problem can start a chain reaction of other problems unless the first problem is resolved. For instance, a man loses his job and experiences financial difficulties. His wife and children are unhappy. Later, the wife starts to nag the husband and his children become disrespectful. He gets drunk at night because he cannot bear to hear the family complaints and bullying. Which problem should he work at first? If the client gets a job, will there be a chain reaction with other situations falling into place? The generalist has to help the client make a decision.

Problems and Behavior—Understanding Both Cause and Effect

Once a problem has been identified, the worker should note the extent to which the problem is precipitated by the client's attitudes and thinking, as well as the ways in which the problem affects the client's functioning and behavior. For example, if a person is experiencing marital conflict and is seeking help in this area, then the worker's efforts in this process are to help the client work at this relationship. In so doing it is necessary to identify the feelings that this client is experiencing. Then the worker must look at the client's actions as well as the thoughts and beliefs (cognition) that occur as the result of the problem situation at home. Under what conditions and in which context do these problems arise? Another area is observable behavior. Do the problems arise because the client has a feeling of worthlessness that accompanies feelings of anger and mistrust of the spouse? Or is the client sending out a message that says, "You are okay, but I'm not okay"?

The generalist is called in by Keith, who says his employees seem to resign their positions faster than he can hire them. Based on a brief intake, it is clear that the company pays its employees well and has good benefits. Armed with this information, the generalist meets the employees of the organization by standing at the front door with Keith. During the next half hour, the generalist observes that the employees do not make eye contact with Keith and avoid or leave his presence in a hurry. This trend of avoiding him started a few months ago when he had fired four employees for not performing well. More information on Keith reveals that his wife had an affair with one of his employees, whom Keith caught red-handed. The employee and some of his coworkers were fired and Keith separated from his wife. His mistrust of his wife and that particular employee permeated the company culture and there was tension and an underlying sense of suspicion and uneasiness. New employees sensed the tension and left after a few weeks, believing that Keith also mistrusted them.

Without information about the origins of the problem, it is meaningless to plan intervention strategies. The end result of such specificity is that the problem is defined or stated in ways that are understood by (Brown & Ballou, 1992).

Antecedents

After the specificity of a problem is understood, it is important for the worker to identify the an-

tecedents. More often than not, the problem situation is the result of a number of factors which led up to it or happened before the problem began, which made the problem more likely to occur. Some of these same factors may still be operating to perpetuate and possibly exacerbate the difficulty. Some antecedents may have happened immediately before the problem occurred and other events may have taken place a long time ago.

There are at least six possible types of antecedents. When a person is experiencing an *affective* antecedent the worker can ask, "What do you usually feel before this happens?" Understanding the *somatic* antecedent, the worker will ask, "What goes on inside of you just before this happens?" With *behavioral* antecedents, the worker asks, "If I were to take a picture, what actions and dialogue would I pick up before this happens?" To explore *cognitive* antecedents the worker will ask the client "What happens in your mind, in pictures, before this happens?" *Contextual* antecedents involve questions such as "Has this ever happened at any other time in your life, and, if so, describe it"; while *relational* antecedents involve questions such as "Are you with certain people during and after the problem? What happens to the problem then; does it get better or worse?"

According to McClam and Woodside (1994), behavior is situationally located. Antecedents may elicit emotional and physiological reactions such as anger, fear, pain, and agitation. For instance, Rachael constantly chose abusive boyfriends. With the worker, Rachael explored what events or antecedents led up to this. How did this pattern start? During the assessment it became clear that this pattern started in her family, with a father who was abusive to his wife and daughters. This understanding provided a clearer idea of how Rachel could work constructively on this issue.

Consequences of Behavior

All behavior has consequences. When you complete an assignment on time, there is a positive consequence; when you do not complete an assignment on time, there is a negative consequence. Normally, the consequences of a behavior are events that follow the behavior and exert some degree of influence on the behavior. These events can be functionally related to that behavior. For example, if a woman needs help because she binges on food, the purpose of the helping process is to help her stop overeating. There are negative consequences when she overeats, and she needs supportive help in order to overcome her negative eating habits. If she stops overeating, she has taken care of the problem, which leads to positive consequences known as rewards or reinforcers.

To identify consequences after a problem occurs, the worker can ask questions that are affective, somatic, behavioral, cognitive, contextual, and relationally oriented (Cormier & Cormier, 1998). Affective questions include "How do you feel?" and "What do you feel after the problem happens?" Somatic questions deal with some of the body sensations that seem to occur after the problems and how that affects the problem. These would include illness, diet, or exercising. Behavioral questions would ask the client to identify particular behavior patterns that occur after the problem and whether these patterns help to keep the problem going or stop the problem. Cognitively, are there any thoughts that pass through the client's mind after the problem occurs and how does this affect the problem? Contextually, what happens after the problem? Does the problem continue or does it go away? Relationally, can the client identify the people who are present after this problem occurs, and do these people make the problem better or worse?

In a group meeting for alcoholics, Floyd was intensely disliked because he considered himself to be a little better than the other members. When the group leader was unobservant and passive, fights generally erupted with group members swearing and walking out unceremoniously as Floyd constantly tried to prove that he was better in managing his problems and his life. The generalist realized that unless she was actively involved with the group, Floyd would take over and create a high degree of disruption by initiating negative discussions and arguments.

Identifying Secondary Gains

Although highlighting clients' strengths is an important aspect of the helping process, there is a reality that generalists need to understand: For some clients there are secondary gains to maintaining a problem.

A sixty-year-old client, Nadine, spent all her time in bed and described herself as being a "sickly person." Her family accepted Nadine's situation and everyone, including her children and husband, constantly catered to her. In essence, Nadine "ruled" the house from her bed. Because her illness made her so powerful, Nadine continued to be sick throughout her life. She came for help six months after her husband had died of a heart attack, because the secondary gains of her illness had receded and the "vested interest" of remaining sick was no longer paying off. With the help of counseling, Nadine found a job.

Vested interests help to maintain the status quo of a problem as long as there are payoffs that result. For example, a client who has been overeating may have problems losing weight because her weight prevents her from making efforts to have a sexual relationship, helps her escape from social situations in which she does not wish to participate, and helps her maintain an uneventful but safe lifestyle that she is reluctant to give up (Fishman & Lubetkin, 1983; Gelso & Carter, 1994).

Exploring Earlier Solutions

One of the important aspects of the assessment interview is to find out what the client has done previously to resolve the problem and what the results have been. Getting this kind of information is crucial. It helps the generalist to avoid making ineffective recommendations for problem resolution, which might either create new problems or make the existing problem worse. For example, at an apartment complex in a run-down part of town, residents are attempting to get rid of the drug dealers and stop the drug trafficking prevalent in the area. The generalist who initiated the process initially met with apathy on the part of community members. After a long dialogue with them, he realized the history of the apartment complex and how previous efforts had been thwarted and understood the difficult task the community members had ahead of them.

According to Fisch, Weakland, and Segal (1982), and Fischer and Corcoran (1994), most people suffer from difficulties, and none of us handles them perfectly, or even adequately, all the time. However, a difficulty becomes a problem under two circumstances: when the difficulty is mishandled or when the difficulty is intensified. In this way, the original difficulty is escalated and a vicious circle develops that makes the problem worse, sometimes to the point that the situation may no longer have any apparent similarity to the original difficulty. Thus, asking clients questions about previous solutions they have attempted is helpful. If solutions have not thus far been successful, the client needs to find alternatives to resolve the problem.

Dollie had a disagreement with her mother-in-law, which greatly upset her. The next time she saw her mother-in-law, Dollie became a little sarcastic in her comments to her; this angered the mother-in-law, who retorted angrily. The behavior continued escalating to the point that Dollie dreaded visiting her mother-in-law. This in turn affected her relationship with her husband who was close to his mother.

Developing an Awareness and Working with Clients' Coping Skills, Strengths, and Resources

When clients come for help, particularly when they come voluntarily, they are often overwhelmed with intense emotions and can relate only to their concerns and pain. Often they are shortsighted and find it difficult to believe that they have any external or internal resources that might help them deal with their problem more effectively.

Forty-year-old Eva felt that there were no choices for her when her husband blatantly took a lover. Instead of being angry with him, she saw herself as ugly and blamed herself for his behavior. She accepted her husband's constant complaints that she was "not a good wife." Eventually, when he became more abusive, Eva decided to seek help.

One of the things that practitioners have to keep in mind in cases such as Eva's is to focus not only on the problems and the pain, but also on the person's positive assets and resources. Practitioners must ask questions that help clients identify their strengths and the internal resources available to them, which may help them look at the problem differently. When practitioners look at clients' strengths and weaknesses, they are able to see the problem as a whole. Such information may help the worker to gather data on the potential problems that may crop up during intervention. Last but not least, information that reveals both positives and negatives can be used to help the client, particularly the positive "success" stories that can be applied to current problem situations. For instance, highlighting Eva's strengths as a loving wife who always had a hot meal for her husband when he came home for dinner is a positive way to make Eva aware of her skills as a caring, loving person, which her husband has attempted to downplay.

Acquiring information about the client's strengths and resources is useful in planning intervention strategies. Highlighting strengths and empowering clients help in increasing their social competence. The purpose of empowerment is to foster self-sufficiency and to develop the ability to change the situation and perhaps prevent a recurrence (Gutierrez, 1989). Information should be obtained about clients' behavioral assets including problem-solving and cognitive coping skills, and how clients use them and discriminate between rational and irrational behavior and thinking. Also important are clients' self-management skills, including self-control. Clients' strengths can be heightened so that they can assume responsibility for self-direction, withstand frustration, and assume responsibility for themselves by either self-reinforcing or preventing self-punishing consequences.

The Client's Perception of the Problem— An Exploration

Though practitioners may have worked with a number of clients and believe that they can understand certain problem situations easily, their ability to be competent social workers depends largely on how well they listen to clients. Each person and each problem is to some extent unique. It is extremely important to find out how clients perceive their problems, because their perception is critical to the worker's accurate understanding of the problem. The exploratory process not only provides essential information about clients and their problems, but also provides valuable insights as to how they view their situation. To ignore how the client views the problem and to seek a solution based on strategies without the client's participation would be useless because the issue is the client's, not the practitioner's. Also, this could lead to resistance on the part of the client (Fisch et al., 1982).

Clients should be asked to describe their problems as briefly as possible so that they are able to focus on the essentials. Lazarus (1989) recommends that the problems be described in one word such as *anger, guilt,* or *disgust,* and then further explained in a sentence; for example, "I am angry because I mistreated my child" or "I am guilty because I was unfaithful to my husband." This becomes a first step that the worker uses to help clients identify, describe, and explore problems. The client becomes more focused at this point. Remember, however, more complex interpersonal problems, as well as family, group, organizational, and community concerns and issues will take more time.

Intensity of the Problem—Frequency, Duration, and Severity

How has the problem affected the client's daily functioning and his or her lifestyle? When a client says, "I am upset," does this mean just a little upset or very upset? Is the client upset all the time or just at different times? According to Cormier and Cormier (1998), the client faces three kinds of intensity that need to be assessed: (1) how intense the problem is; (2) how long the client has experienced the problem; and (3) how often does the client have to face it?

The generalist begins by finding out the client's subjective degree of discomfort and stress, which is useful information in assessing how the problem has affected the client. For instance, the generalist could ask a question such as, "On a scale of 1 to 10, where would you say your guilt feelings are?" Consider the frequency and duration of the problem behaviors before planning on an intervention strategy. Questions about how often problems happen, how many times, and how much goes on every day would be good indicators of how the client feels.

Thalia indicates that she starts to binge on food after she finishes her morning chores, and she spends the rest of the day overeating at least five times. But recently, due to problems in her marriage and her husband's constant bickering, Thalia has started to eat even before she gets out of bed in the morning. She keeps cookies near the bed. This overeating is causing serious marital conflicts, but Thalia's reaction is to fight back with food, and recently the frequency and duration of binging has increased considerably. Though obvious to the practitioner, it took a lot of overt discussion before Thalia was able to understand her situation. She was unaware that she was using food to get back at her husband and hurt herself as well.

It is important not to overlook the fact that clients have the ability to learn and grow from their experiences. Most often when faced with a negative situation, people recognize that a life lesson is learned. A person's ability and attitude play an important role in working out issues (Pillari, 1997). When people learn not to be caught in self-blame and defeatism, they take the first step to a different and better level of functioning. Similarly, when clients are helped to tell their stories, the worker who listens carefully finds most of these stories provide new and different learning. There is a lesson in the client's story and the worker's job is to help all clients tap those same strengths in their own lives.

Elsa, a thirty-one-year-old woman, was in love with a married older man who promised her the whole world. In reality he gave her a house, a car, and a child. His promise to divorce his wife never happened. After fifteen years, Elsa awakened from her fantasy and recognized that he would never marry her. Realizing that she would always be second best, she decided to give the man up although she knew it would be very difficult. In the helping process she cried, "I have learned my lesson. I do know I have inner resources. All I want to do now is to get a job and become economically independent. I'm even willing to go back to school to get a degree if that would make my life easier." Finally she was able to mobilize the inner strength to take control of her own life. Elsa's feelings of anger and pain were intense as she worked to abandon a relationship that had lasted for so long. Although her ex continued to profess his love and again promised to divorce his wife and marry her, Elsa moved away from the neighborhood and started a new job with the hope that she could make a new life for herself and her daughter.

Another factor under history taking is to conceptualize a client situation, which includes the people and the different interpersonal relationships involved in the problem situation. There are people who are directly involved in a client's problem situation and there are others who are part of the problem system but their involvement is indirect. The worker has to identify the roles that these different people play. For example, in an alcoholic family with a large number of children and in which there is a great deal of abuse, the family system is very complex. In order to work with the family, detailed information is needed about the roles family members play, how each person affects and is affected by others, and how patterns and problem situations are enacted. All these factors help in conceptualizing and making an assessment of a problem.

ASSESSMENT SKILLS

The worker needs to have certain skills in making an assessment.

Collecting Data through Problem Exploration

How much information does a generalist require in order to work with clients? The initial assessment is made usually within the first few sessions and the worker should collect only as much information as is required in order to make an assessment. Getting irrelevant and unnecessary data can interfere with problem assessment and analysis and undermine the clients' confidence in the worker and the process. Also the amount of time that is taken to collect this additional data and assemble nonrelevant information could be used and spent in the more useful aspects of intervention (Hartman, 1994; Loewenberg, 1983).

If the clients are voluntary, the worker needs to know why they made the choice to ask for help at this particular time in their lives. Have clients reached the point where they feel unable to continue without help? Or, if a problem has existed for a long time, why did the clients choose to come to you at this point? Is this a new and sudden problem which has overwhelmed the clients? Has the problem occurred previously and what were the clients' attempts to change it? Clients' responses to these questions provide some idea of their coping and social skills and knowledge of social situations. Practitioners need to become aware of clients' problems, the situations that led to their inability or difficulty to solve their problems and their need to see a practitioner, as well as to ascertain how much sustained effort will be required on the clients' part to work at their problem.

The manner in which the information is obtained is as important as the information itself because it sets the tone for the intervention process. Besides responding to questions, clients should be allowed to talk about a subject in their own way. Also, if the generalist does the collection of information disinterestedly, haphazardly, or condescendingly, clients may not cooperate or share information willingly. Clients should be informed in the beginning that the information they provide will be used for effective social intervention.

Often social workers are asked for help with a request for a specific service; for example, "Can you help me find a nursing home for my grandmother?" An assessment of the situation, including problems, people, and environments is just as important when the presenting request is for specific services as it is when the client requests counseling. A thoughtful and thorough assessment is even more critical in situations involving vulnerable people who are facing major changes in their lives. The generalist and clients must work together to decide what information is needed to understand the problem better and to evolve a plan of action.

Dealing with Feelings and Facts

An important aspect of the worker's role is dealing with feelings and facts. Affect refers to the feelings and emotions a person experiences that lead, accompany, underlie, and add color to a client's experiences and behaviors (Egan, 1999). Some clients are good at expressing their feelings and others are not; at times, expression of feelings depends on the situation. Clients respond to emotions in different ways. Practitioners need to work with clients by focusing not only on the client's emotions but also on experiences and behaviors. Generalists have to pay attention to cues and hints, whether verbal or nonverbal, that might reveal the person's feelings.

The generalist must focus on themes, key messages, and context. For example, there are some clients who will present a "pessimistic self-explanatory style" in talking about themselves (Peterson, Patrick, & Rissmeyer, 1990). They have a need to attribute causes to negative events and make statements such as, "this problem will never go away" and "my headache affects everything I do." In such cases, the generalist has to assume that there is a connection between a person's poor health complaints and attitudes, and it is important to explore the theme that the client is presenting (Egan, 1999).

Some clients present disparities between their thoughts and feelings. In such situations, the generalist has to carefully observe how clients respond and present the facts. Practitioners use observational skills to read body language when dealing with clients, to see if there is congruence between what clients say and how they express their feelings. Empathetic and observational skills are needed to help clients discuss their problems. For example, a client may have a serious problem but present it with a smile, which depicts a high level of disparity and incongruence in behavior.

Dealing with Information That Is Contradictory

As Simon (1994), Parsons (1991), Breton (1993), and Lee (1994) indicate, sometimes practitioners gather information from collateral sources that is contradictory to what a client is saying.

Without question, it is essential that the worker consult the client before making any contact with collateral resources. If the client objects to getting in touch with a particular person, this should be respected as well as the right of the client to withhold information. The worker can still play an active role by suggesting information sources that have been overlooked by the client. The worker will also want to explore the reasons for the objection.

Inability or Unwillingness to Request Help

In information gathering, there are situations in which a person who needs help is unable or unwilling to request it. This could be a disturbed teenager who needs to be calmed down before he or she divulges the information that you need. It could be a mentally ill person who needs to be medicated before communicating. At times, the client is not willing to share information because he or she has been forced into the helping process by the court system and feels angry and hostile. When a client is unwilling to communicate, it could be because the client senses that the worker has not yet accepted him or her as a person or has not yet recognized the real problem that the client is ready to work on. In such cases, it is best to allow the client to start where he or she wishes, even though it may appear to be irrelevant to the problem.

Gathering Relevant Information

The framework for this book is the ecosystems perspective—the notion that our understanding of most human problems arises from recognizing the maladaptive or difficult transactions of persons and environment. It is essential that the social worker collect data that will help clarify not only the problem or concern but how the clients interact with the social systems and how these systems impinge directly or indirectly on the problem situation. In the case of Clinton who has had problems in the classroom, the worker will need information about his personality, his behavior in and out of the classroom, and how he gets along with his family and friends outside of the classroom. Information gathering reveals that he is the oldest son of a low-income, single-parent, new immigrant family and lives in a drug-infested neighborhood with his mother and three younger brothers. Physically, Clinton is blind in one eye. His father, who had recently separated from his mother, is an alcoholic and Clinton has a poor relationship with him. All the necessary the information about Clinton must be assembled in order to make necessary choices and to set priorities.

In addition to information about the person–situation configuration, the worker also has to gather information about who the client is and what kind of help he or she is seeking from the agency. Also, how has the person coped with conflicts and problems in the past? Such information provides clues about the strengths and coping capabilities of a client and his or her social networks. Strategies of helping are developed based on this knowledge.

Analyzing and Interpreting Data

As Johnson (1995) notes, all the information about the client has to be discovered, explored, identified, and ordered in a given sequence. In this second phase, the worker analyzes and interprets the data. Analysis means breaking up the information that is presented into parts in order to discover the nature, purpose, and function of the whole. Analysis of data is important because problems are highly complex and rarely simple or isolated. Interpretation is explaining the meaning of something. Before making an assessment, the worker has to understand how various aspects of problems are related to each other. Analysis and interpretation occur side by side.

To elucidate the process of analyzing and interpreting, the information that has been gathered about Clinton is placed in sequence in the following section.

ORDERING The worker sorts the information into more or less relevant data. For instance, the fact that Clinton has a British accent is not as important as the fact that he is blind in one eye.

DISCOVERING The worker has to make connections between various data items. There is a significant relationship between Clinton's problems in school and the fact that he comes from a newly immigrated, low-income family. His mother's need for acceptance, his physical disability, tension in school due to lack of acceptance, the drug-infested neighborhood in which he lives, and the added disadvantage of having an absentee alcoholic father with whom he had a poor relationship are all factors that may or may not be important. At this point in the analysis, the focus is on discovering relationships and not trying to establish causal factors.

EXPLORING Information needs to be explored in terms of the person's cultural setting. Where did Clinton live earlier, what are the child-rearing practices in his family, and what is the history of education in his family?

IDENTIFYING Factors that have contributed to the prevention of resolution or alleviation of the problem situation should be identified. Without identifying them, it would be difficult to organize information that will permit an effective intervention strategy.

Though we are viewing problems and persons from a ecosystems perspective, and systems are interrelated for the purpose of study and understanding, in the next section we look at each of the given systems—the person, the family, the group, the community, or an organization—separately in order to understand how to make an assessment of these different systems. It is important to bear in mind that there are intricate interrelationships among all these systems.

PERSONALITY ASSESSMENT

When attempting to help a person or persons, it is crucial to work at understanding the context of the life or the life situation of a client system. When making a personality assessment, the worker tries to understand the client's capacities and social functioning patterns as well as the role or roles involved in the difficulty. Personality is now understood as a set of internal, psycho-physical systems, a repertoire of behaviors, and a set of competencies that are related to life cycle developmental capacities. It includes a complex array of factors like temperament, values, traits, a configuration of coping patterns and lifestyle, and a set of social, personal, and self-identities. The personality system with its structural capacities and behavioral functioning patterns defines what is expected of a person in a specific situation and what one expects of oneself.

When working with individuals it is often easier to highlight their weaknesses than their strengths. The assessment should focus on both and identify the functional patterns of coping as well as what the client will not do or cannot do. The principle behind this thinking is that a successful intervention plan must be built on a client's strengths.

How do we recognize strengths in clients when they are dealing with problems? The worker might ask questions such as, "Despite your prob-

lems, which parts of your life are going well? What is it that you like about yourself? What do other people like about you? In spite of what you are facing in your life now, what do you continue to do well? What about yourself would you not change, even now?"

Shaefor, Horejsi, and Horejsi (1997) offer the following list of client strengths with regard to attitude and behavior. This list can be applied to individuals, families, groups, communities, and organizations.

> The client recognizes that a problem exists.
>
> The client looks for and accepts information and guidance from others.
>
> The client shows affection, compassion, and concern for others.
>
> The client seeks employment, holds a job, and is a responsible employee.
>
> The client attempts to meet his or her family and financial obligations.
>
> The client exercises self-control.
>
> The client makes plans and thoughtful decisions.
>
> The client is trustworthy and honest in dealing with others.
>
> The client has feelings of sorrow and guilt for having hurt others.
>
> The client seeks to understand others and their situations.
>
> The client is willing to forgive others.
>
> The client expresses his or her point of view.
>
> The client stands up for his or her own rights and the rights of others.
>
> The client attempts to protect others from harm.
>
> The client has special aptitudes, for example, mechanical or interpersonal.

Coping Strategies

The worker also needs to be aware of the client's coping strategies. Investigators have utilized two approaches to classify coping. The first approach highlights the *focus* of the coping mechanism—a person's orientation and activity in response to a stressor. In this approach an individual can acknowledge the problem and make active efforts to resolve it, or try to avoid the problem and focus on managing the emotions associated with it. An alternative approach emphasizes the *method* of coping people employ; that is, whether the response entails primarily cognitive or behavioral efforts (Moos & Schaefer, 1993).

Holahan, Moos, and Schaefer (1996) combined these two approaches into an integrated conceptualization of coping. They separated coping strategies into approach and avoidance domains. They then divided the categories to reflect cognitive and behavioral coping, further classifying the two domains as: cognitive approach, behavioral approach, cognitive avoidance, and behavioral avoidance (see Table 11.1).

Active coping strategies involve negotiation and optimistic comparisons that have been linked to reductions in concurrent distress and to fewer future role problems (Menaghan, 1982). Generally, people who rely on approach coping tend to adapt better to stressors and experience fewer psychological symptoms. The strategies that people use in approach coping include problem-solving and problem-seeking information that can moderate the potential adverse influence of both negative life change and enduring role stressors on psychological functioning (Billings & Moos, 1981). A larger proportion of problem-focused coping in relation to total coping efforts is associated with reduced depression (Mitchell, Cronkite, & Moos, 1983).

In contrast, avoidance coping occurs when people use denial and withdrawal, which is associated with psychological distress (Holmes & Stevenson, 1990; Suls and Fletcher, 1985). Purely emotionally focused coping usually entails avoidant-oriented fantasy and self-blame, which often is associated with more depression (Endler & Parker, 1990). Menaghan (1982) notes that efforts to manage unpleasant feelings by resignation or withdrawal may increase distress, which can amplify future problems. Adults who rely on ineffective escapism—avoidant, helpless, reckless coping behaviors—experience more current and future emotional distress (Rohde, Lewinsohn, Tilson, & Seeley, 1990). The use of avoidance cop-

Table 11.1   Four Basic Categories of Coping Strategies with Eight Associated Coping Subtypes

BASIC COPING CATEGORIES	COPING SUBTYPES
Cognitive Approach	Logical Analysis ("Did you think of various ways to deal with the problem?")
	Positive Reappraisal ("Did you think about how you were much better off than other individuals with similar problems?")
Behavioral Approach	Seeking Guidance and Support ("Did you talk with a friend about the issue?")
	Taking Problem-Solving Action ("Did you make a plan of action and carry it out?")
Cognitive Avoidance	Cognitive Avoidance ("Did you try to forget the whole matter?")
	Resigned Acceptance ("Did you lose hope that matters would ever change?")
Behavioral Avoidance	Seeking Alternative Rewards ("Did you get involved in different activities?")
	Emotional Discharge ("Did you yell or scream to let off steam?")

Note: Sample coping items are shown in parentheses.

SOURCE: From *Coping Responses Inventory: Adult Form Manual*, by R. H. Moos, 1993, Odessa, FL: Psychological Assessment Resources.

ing, such as wishful thinking and self-blame, in dealing with life events predicts subsequent psychological problems, particularly among the elderly (Smith, Patterson, & Grant, 1990).

The purpose of a coping strategy is to solve a problem or to reduce the discomfort caused by stresses. Carver, Coleman, and Glass (1976) believe that all people, irrespective of culture, have built-in emotion-focused coping capabilities that are used in their initial reaction to intense emotional pain. The following section outlines some of the common coping strategies in American culture.

Crying is a common and accepted means of alleviating tension and also responding to loss. When people cry, they are often dealing with "grief work." For example, when Shelly found out that she did not get a promotion, she gave way to tears and grieved, because she had done her utmost and expected some reward for her hard work.

Talking it out is another coping strategy that individuals use when they have undergone traumatic experiences. For instance, Sonia had seen her sister murdered by her husband. Sonia was traumatized and constantly talked about this incident. Talking about it was a way to alleviate tension and a natural form of desensitization so that she could eventually accept and tolerate the painful thoughts and feelings associated with the experience.

Some clients will joke about and view painful experiences with a *sense of humor* that releases tension and places them in a broader context. For instance, when the promotion Johnny expected was given to a less-experienced newcomer, Johnny was amazed. But he dealt with his pain by laughing with coworkers.

In times of stress it is natural for children and adults to *seek support*. Receiving attention and affection from people they care about often help individuals regain their emotional equilibrium.

Dreaming is a common reaction to highly traumatic experiences. Dreams and nightmares are often repetitive and so function like the process of desensitization. Talking it out in a recurring dream forces a person to grapple with feelings and to mentally integrate negative experiences.

People with constructive coping strategies will use them with positive motivation, capacity, and opportunity. Such individuals are usually able to identify their own social and emotional needs and also to learn socially acceptable means of meeting those needs. They will also model behavior on people who behave in an effective and appropriate manner. They are able to recognize that one has choices and can exert influence on one's own behavior, feelings, and life events. However, there are many clients who do not possess adequate coping skills. When working with such clients, the generalist has to use an appropriate intervention plan that helps the client learn specific coping skills. Maladaptive behaviors can be unlearned and replaced with adaptive behaviors by learning new coping skills (Shaefor et al., 1997).

Role Performance Problems in Clients

Each human role has three interrelated parts: *role concept,* that is, how people believe they should act in a specific situation; *role expectations,* which indicate how people believe others should act when they occupy a specific status position; and *role performance,* which indicates how people really act (Goldstein, 1973). All roles have psychological components including perceptions and feelings, as well as social components that include behaviors and expectations of others (Miley, O'Melia, & Dubois, 1995).

The concept of a social role derives from the notion that there are predetermined behaviors and norms prescribed by society for certain role relationships. For instance, being a parent requires caring, nurturing, and providing food, clothing, shelter, guidance, supervision, and love. The traditional role expectation for a husband and father is to provide for and take care of his family. The role of a teacher is to impart knowledge; in turn, the student's role is to learn what the teacher judges to be important.

Role performance is what actually happens when a person performs a role. At times, role performance may not coincide with the standard role expectations. Often clients come into the helping process because they have difficulty in performing role-related behaviors. For example, Andy played the role of a husband and was a good economic provider, but he was verbally abusive to his children and occasionally hit his wife. Andy's role performance did not really live up to the traditional ideal role expectation.

A number of terms have been used to describe problems in role performance. *Inter-role conflict* refers to an incompatibility or clash between two or more roles. For instance, a woman has to play the role of a caring and nurturing parent and a wife at home, but in her workplace has to be a hard-nosed and competitive business executive and often travel out of town. There are clients who cannot perform their roles due to *role incapacity*. This means that the person cannot perform a role due to physical or mental illness, alcoholism, drug use, or other physiological reasons. There are others who suffer from *role rejection*. This occurs when a person refuses to perform a specific role, as when a student refuses to study participate in classroom discussions and frequently cuts classes.

Role conception can be described as an individual's beliefs about a role and how he or she expects to behave in that particular role. An individual's role concept may not coincide with the role expectations of society.

At times there may be confusion about roles, which is called *role ambiguity*. This happens when there are few clear expectations associated with a role. Consequently, a client may be confused and not know how to evaluate his or her own performance. *Self-role incongruence* is the discomfort that a client feels in a specific role. For instance, Martin was appointed acting director of his department while the department head was on leave. Martin was unhappy and functioned poorly in the assignment because he was more comfortable as a follower than as a leader. There was little congruence between the requirements of the role and Martin's personality.

Role overload refers to a person's inability to adequately perform all the roles that he or she occupies. The reality is that there are many people who are unable to conform to all the expectations of their different social roles.

The worker has to make decisions concerning the appropriate intervention based on all the role performance problems that individuals have. The practitioner must also keep in mind the discrepancies between actual performance of a role and role expectations (Johnson & Johnson, 1994; Shaefor et al., 1991).

An assessment should also consider a client's stage in the life cycle and also the developmental tasks and roles that are common to that stage. Working with a family consisting of a father, a mother, two children, and a grandmother, the practitioner should pay attention to the developmental stage of each member of the family, acknowledging that certain roles and tasks exist and certain crises are resolved during each stage in the life cycle. The developmental stage of one family member may impact on the developmental tasks and crises faced by another member. For example, an elderly grandmother may need increased attention and care from her adult children, at the same time they are struggling with the problems of their own adolescent children.

The Self-Concept of Clients

Convictions, beliefs, and ideas about ourselves are among the crucial determinants of human behavior. Rounds, Weil, and Bishop (1994) conclude that when beliefs about ourselves are consonant with reality they lead to well-adjusted behavior, but unrealistic beliefs lead to maladjusted behaviors. Rounds et al. (1994) purport that self-perception determines how people present themselves. That is, the postures people assume invite praise, interest, or criticism from others. It is helpful to have high self-esteem and be realistically aware of one's positive attributes, accomplishments, and potentialities as well as limitations and deficiencies. People with positive self-esteem can laugh and joke at themselves. Others are tormented by feelings of worthlessness, inadequacy, and helplessness.

Low self-esteem can make people underachievers in life; they may pass up opportunities for growth due to fear of failing, avoid social relationships, permit themselves to be taken for granted and exploited by others, and gravitate in social relationships to people with low status. People with low self-esteem need to be helped to enhance their self-esteem. It is vital to assess this dimension of clients' functioning. Asking clients what they think about themselves is an important step in making an assessment. The generalist can say to a client, "Tell me what you think about yourself." If the client has a problem responding, then the generalist has to ask the client to respond to him or her spontaneously: "When you think of the kind of person you are, what comes to your mind?" This could be the beginning of helping a person think and talk about his or her self-esteem.

Siporin (1975), Miley et al. (1995), and Gilliland and James (1997) offer the following list of appropriate guidelines for personality assessment.

1. In order to understand clients well, it is important to understand them in relation to others. How do they see and value themselves as people and as role performers in their relationships with significant others in life? This simply means that clients have to look at themselves and focus on how they feel about who they are, and how they are functioning in their various roles and relationships.

2. It is important that the assessment process not become a "grading" of clients, irrespective of their life circumstances. Personality classifications that attempt to place a single label on a client should be avoided whenever possible, because there are as many sides to personality as there are clients. Practitioners have to pay attention to self-put-downs, self-stereotyping, and social typing and stigmatizing processes. It is detrimental to think of a client as a socially inept person or a criminal. Generalizing personality qualities tends to have more negative than positive effects on the person and the generalist should avoid such comments.

3. Clients should be helped to understand that they cannot be controlled by their past, unless they allow themselves to be. A person is not doomed for life because of an incestuous relationship or parental rejection. Different aspects of a client's personality can be put together in either helpful or unhelpful ways. Clients have to be helped to put matters together and view them in helpful ways so that they can take control of their own lives.

4. Miley et al. (1995) stress that while assessing clients practitioners should not lose sight of the building block of change: that is, the strength of client systems. Strength of client systems is closely related to competence in clients. Competence usually refers to the abilities and potentials of human systems to negotiate favorably with their environments based upon the assumption that all human beings strive toward competence (White, 1960).

Cultural Factors

It is imperative that the generalist have some knowledge of the cultural norms of clients. Without such knowledge, the worker can make mistakes in assessment that lead to ineffective and inappropriate interventions. Speight, Myers, Cox, and Highlen (1991) found this problem in their therapeutic work with low-income Italian American women who were depressed. Teaching these women assertiveness was not considered an appropriate intervention because assertiveness would mean participating in middle-class norms not found in their own reference group; their assertiveness would be seen as disruptive rather than helpful in the family. This is generally true of women from other cultures, such as Puerto Rican and Middle Eastern cultures where traditional men exhibit autocratic behaviors and women are viewed as dependent. In some Eastern cultures, as well in some Native American cultures, married men and women will communicate and have more intimate friendships with members of the same sex. The degree of communication between parents and children also seems to vary from culture to culture.

Remember, however, that understanding a culture does not mean the practitioner who has worked with one client from a culture, can lump all people from that culture into one category and make generalized statements about them. To do so would obscure rather than clarify the meaning of individual behaviors. For example, Asian Americans represent many different cultures. Although they may have certain similar characteristics, they still differ significantly from each other as individuals. Similarly, in subcultural groupings such as Anglo-Saxons in the United States, there will be differences among families and individuals. All clients should be viewed as unique and should be helped accordingly.

Another important factor about minority groups is the degree of socialization that has taken place with respect to the mainstream culture. Clients from different ethnic groups as well as from different families may vary greatly in their degree of acculturation. Crohn (1995) and Fairchild, Yee, Wyatt, and Weizman (1995) identified six factors with reference to the degree of bicultural socialization and interactions in which different ethnic groups participate to maintain their role in the mainstream.

1. The degree of commonality between two cultures with reference to norms, values, beliefs, and perceptions.
2. The degree of interaction in terms of cultural translators, mediators, and models.
3. The kind of feedback, negative or positive, that is provided by each culture regarding its attempts to provide normative behaviors.
4. The problem-solving style of different ethnic persons and how they mesh with the majority culture.
5. The individual's level of bilingualism.
6. The degree of difference in skin color, facial features, and other characteristics from the majority culture.

A crucial factor to be considered with clients whose first language is not English is their degree of bilingualism. Some clients will speak English better than others. But if a client does not understand English well, the worker has to speak slowly and provide time for the client to process material before he or she responds. There are some workers who assume that a client is stupid because he or she does not speak English. This insensitivity has a lot to do with ethnocentrism. In fact, minority clients may be quite intelligent and have a solid educational foundation; just because clients do not understand English workers should not assume that clients are not of normal intelligence. Of course, there are disadvantages for the client who has not learned the language, but for some it takes more time to learn English than for others.

Another important factor has to do with problem-solving skills. It is important to remember that members of different cultures define problems differently (Green, 1995). Behavior that is viewed as normal in one culture may not be viewed so in another culture. For instance, a close Hispanic family with a high degree of involvement might be viewed as "enmeshed" or dysfunctional in the majority culture. Clearly, helping should be undertaken within the norms of a client's specific culture. If necessary, the worker should consult experts or people from similar cultures before making an assessment of a client.

Problem-solving methods vary from culture to culture. Among traditional Native Americans groups, family members actively seek counsel from the elderly members of the extended family. The wisdom of these elderly relatives is highly valued and the elderly are much respected (Hull, 1982). Also, Native Americans often pass on their wisdom in the form of story telling which does not insult the intelligence or integrity of the listener because, if one does not like the information, the hearer can always ignore it (Hull, 1982). In a similar manner Asian Americans look to the extended family for direction in problem solving.

To work effectively with different ethnic clients, the practitioner has to achieve credibility by being perceived as competent, caring, and trustworthy. How can this be done? Sue and Zane (1987) suggest that three essential guidelines are necessary. First, the generalist must conceptualize the problem in a way that is consistent with the client's belief system. Imposing anything different is considered ineffective help. Second, if there are expectations in terms of change, change should be made in a way that is compatible with the cultural system. Third, the treatment goals should be consistent with the client's perception of the desired objectives rather than the worker's imposed treatment agenda. Unless the worker is sensitive and asks questions to understand the culture, there is a real danger of making an inaccurate assessment of clients and their problems.

Twenty-nine-year-old Meena, from a traditional Eastern culture, was hospitalized for depression. Her history revealed that she had entered an arranged marriage when she was sixteen years of age and her husband had died before the marriage was consummated. She had remained a widow. When her brother invited her to visit his family in this country, she was eager to get away from her traditional family environment. Meena's depression began because she wanted to remarry but felt guilty because of her traditional upbringing. When Meena was hospitalized, her social worker realized that Meena was a virgin. Without checking the history of the family or her cultural background, the worker concluded that Meena was either asexual, frigid, or abnormal.

Workers need to find out what indigenous cultural resources are available to clients and how they can be tapped. Particularly when an agency is located in an area where the majority of clients come from a different culture and language, it is imperative that the generalist make special efforts to understand that particular culture and use indigenous nonprofessionals to serve as client advocates, if necessary. The agency also should provide direct outreach services to impoverished clients from different ethnic groups (Atkinson, Morten, & Sue, 1994). For instance, indigenous nonprofessionals in a housing project have organized tenant groups among the impoverished minority groups to obtain essential repairs of physical facilities such as air-conditioning and heating systems and have also used legal means to get landlords to comply with the housing laws.

Cross, Bazron, Dennis, and Isaacs (1989) believe that generalists and professionals from other helping professions should familiarize themselves with a client's culture so that behavior and motivation is understood with the client's cultural context. Interpreting the behavior of a person who is culturally different without considering cultural context or our own ethnocentricity can be dangerous. For example, many years ago, during the time of heavy immigration from Southeast Asia, children's protective services agencies received a rash of abuse reports on Vietnamese whose children went to school with red marks all over their bodies. A special attempt to understand the cultural implications revealed that the children had been given an ancient remedy for colds called "cupping," which involves placing heated glass cups on the skin, leaving harmless red marks for a day. This resulted in a group of angry Vietnamese parents who were hyperattentive to the needs of their children being deeply insulted by accusations of bad parenting and the practitioners feeling foolish about their cultural ignorance (Diller, 1999).

As the United States becomes more multicultural, it would be unreasonable to expect any generalist to be conversant with all of the diverse cultures and subcultures. However, it is possible to learn to identify the kind of information that is required to understand what is going on in the helping situation and to have available cultural experts with whom one can consult whenever necessary.

What is the attitude of clients from ethnic groups toward receiving help? Among the Japanese it is considered shameful to receive mental health services (Mokuau, 1985). Sue and Zane (1987) note that Koreans view mental illness as a source of shame in the family. They attribute the causes of mental illness to supernatural forces. Displeasing the ancestral spirits creates psychological distress and interpersonal disharmony in families.

There is a certain degree of mistrust by members of some minority groups who are skeptical about placing their trust in a majority culture. The degree of trust is based on the history of the minority group in this country, and whether they feel exploited and victimized by overt or covert racism. The behavior of ethnic clients in transcultural relationships must be assessed accordingly and workers should be culturally sensitive to clients. Social class status and religion are also important cultural variables to which the worker should pay special attention (Lum, 1999).

As Lum (1999) indicates, in many ethnic cultures prolonged eye contact is considered rude staring or even as casting an evil eye on a person. Avoidance of eye contact by people of some ethnic groups expresses respect, humility, or shyness. The worker should follow the client's lead in interpreting these nuances of manner. Nonverbal cues such as smiling, eye avoidance, silence, and other mannerisms may be culture-bound. The worker should not view them as signs of depression, avoidance, detachment, and inappropriate affect; rather, the practitioner should seek clarification from clients or explore the cultural dimension with an ethnic colleague or consultant, if need be, before making an assessment.

Situational Analysis and Environmental Analysis

Along with the social functioning of the person, the generalist has to keep in mind the situations to which clients are exposed. While making an assessment, the worker has to focus on the transactions that take place between the person and the environment and the problem-solving efforts that may be used to assist people to cope and adapt to their environments.

In a situational assessment there is a review of different social systems and social situations in which the client has role status, identity, and a set of responsibilities. This includes the family, friendship groups, workplace, school, community and the self-help and formal welfare organizations that are part of the client's situation. The worker has to identify situational foci and evaluate the functional and dysfunctional factors that are present in the situation that contribute to a client's problems or concerns and that affect their behaviors. When making a situational assessment the worker has to keep the following factors in mind (Cowger, 1994; Siporin, 1975):

1. The generalist should give priority to clarifying the nature of the client's understanding of a situation. Priority should be given to participants and their own perspectives in relation to their actual strengths and limitations.

2. In order to highlight strengths, a generalist should be able to redefine a situation based on an assessment that deliberately emphasizes a more positive alternative perception of it. The first step in the process is to develop alternative assumptions and beliefs through a process of cognitive reexplanation of a situation.

In order to help clients, the practitioner may have to redefine situations whenever appropriate. When a client describes a situation as a "disaster," the worker will want to help the client view it as "challenging." In this manner, life circumstances are understood as having elements of choice and control and are also seen as subject to one's efforts.

In making an assessment, it is important to pay attention to the environment in which the problem situation is occurring. For instance, in some situations there are obvious threats to health and safety such as overcrowding, poor housing, and unsanitary living conditions, or serious neglect and abuse. Environmental assessments are based on the different and varied lifestyles of clients, their personalities, state of health, life stages, interests, goals, and aspirations. All clients need a certain level of environmental resources. The practitioner has to always keep in mind the clients' unique needs and availability of resources and opportunities within their environment.

Support Systems

Hepworth et al. (1997) compiled a list of basic environmental needs, though of course these vary among individual clients. Clients who have adequate support systems—family, relatives, friends, and neighbors—and social networks can cope and adapt better to problem situations.

The generalist also has to find out about access to specialized health services such as physicians, dentists, physical therapists, hospitals, and nursing homes. What types of facilities are available to single mothers in terms of day-care services? What types of recreational facilities are available to the client? Does the client have opportunities to socialize, utilize resources, and also exercise rights as a citizen? How is the client's housing situation in terms of sanitation, safety, and privacy and also protection from weather hazards and noise? Is there adequate police and fire protection? How are working conditions at the place of employment. Is it safe and healthy? Does the client have adequate financial resources to buy essentials? Is there a sufficient food supply in the family? Are the arrangements and utilization of rooms sufficient for the family? What are the client's opportunities for education and self-growth? Are legal resources, religious organizations, and employment opportunities accessible?

Does the client help the generalist understand the kind of environment and supports and resources that are available? What are the obstacles in the environment that do not help the client reach personal goals? What ways are there to remedy these situations, if any?

Rooney was a divorced man who was still in love with his ex-wife. He became depressed when he attempted to contact her and found that she was with another man. This affected the way he felt about himself and subsequently the manner in which he maintained his apartment. He had dishes and clothes unwashed and piled all over his one-room apartment. He stopped socializing and did not have any friends. He also kept away from his family and neglected his health. His social worker realized that Rooney had to first work through his grief over the loss of a relationship and his expectations after divorce. Then he could work on tidying his home and feeling positive about himself. The generalist also helped him get back in touch with his family and friends who served as positive social supports and assets in rebuilding a meaningful life.

Exercises

1. In response to a case study provided to the class, make an assessment of a client using the history-taking questions discussed on page 292 and keeping in mind the person–situation configuration. After each student has written an assessment of the case study, discuss the case as a class. Critique your own assessment of the case in terms of strengths and weaknesses. How could you have presented it differently?

2. One student can play the professional generalist and another, a client, an angry teenager. After the role play, the class can complete the following:

> Distinguish between facts and feelings.
>
> Deal with contradictory information as presented by the client and discuss how to work with it, without losing the client.
>
> Identify the role-performance related problems.
>
> Discuss how the students would analyze and interpret data in this role play.

3. Have one student role-play an involuntary client with a student generalist and another student role-play a very manipulative client with another student generalist. As the class views the cases, discuss how data were collected and the problem explored. Constructively speaking, what were the strengths and/or drawbacks of the role play? How could it have been done differently?

FAMILY ASSESSMENT

Family assessment occurs when a client referred for treatment is living at home or when a family needs to work through unfinished business with their family members. Sometimes the presenting problem is one that affects the entire family system, such as the classic example of the husband or wife having an affair in the workplace. Family therapy is also used when worker and clients agree that it would be the appropriate modality.

The family is the primary unit that meets the social, emotional, educational, and health care needs of its members (Hartman, 1981, 1994). Problems in families arise due to dysfunctional rules, poor communication patterns, personality disorders, illness, and so forth.

The family is a matrix of identity, and a person's identity is primarily the result of countless interactions that take place between an individual and his or her significant others. Particularly in the formative years, the development of a person's self-concept is highly connected to the manner in which family members relate to him or to her (Worden, 1999). Different roles and rules also influence different family members. The family system consists of subsystems such as the father–mother relationship and the brother–sister relationship. The family is a system with its own rules and regulations. It is governed by implicit rules, specific roles, a hierarchy or power structure, and different ways of communicating and solving problems.

A family develops coherence, balance, or homeostasis in order to maintain itself. All families have implicit or explicit rules and regulations about how to behave. Family members develop familiar ways of behavior and the ability to restore equilibrium in the family. Families prefer to maintain particular accepted patterns of behavior and, if things go awry, there is an attempt to reestablish the accustomed patterns.

Rules and Family Patterns

There are patterns that affect the whole family and create different types of rules. The concept of rules helps one understand how a communication process takes place and defines relationships. Rules are the result of a continuing interaction between two or more people. They are the dynamic fiber of the construct of boundary. Every time a person interacts with another person, this further defines the relationship, so it can be said that every interaction is a push for a change in rules. Explicit rules govern how the family overtly behaves toward each other. Covert rules, or implicit rules, deal with matters that family members do not talk about, although they are aware of them. For example, there may not be a verbal rule against swearing, but family members know they must not swear.

When rules are obeyed for a long period of time, they become patterns of behavior and part of the invisible family structure (Ford, 1983). Patterns are recurring interaction sequences based on rules that govern relationships. These patterns are also called injunctions, or family laws. Examples of family rules include that young teenagers be home by 10:00 P.M. Another family rule says that everyone should eat dinner together every Wednesday and Sunday night. Family members generally follow injunctions without question. Rules demand loyalty among family members and may be used as a guilt-inducing mechanism.

The generalist has to pay special attention to implicit rules in the family while making an assessment. Both implicit and explicit family rules can be dysfunctional and the generalist needs to be aware of them, however, it is more difficult to check an implicit dysfunctional rule than an explicit one. In some families, implicit family rules that guide the family's actions also limit opportunities for growth. Their damaging impact on the family often goes unrecognized and family members' lives are dictated by rules of which they are unaware. By following dysfunctional rules, the family members reinforce the problematic behaviors they complain about.

Ross, a forty-year-old client, was brought up in a family where feelings, particularly negative ones were not shown. Ross remembered that, as a child of eight, he was bitten severely by a dog and had to take injections for a week. His grandmother, who lived two blocks away, would visit every day and take him to the hospital. Ross wondered why his parents would not take him and, worse still, why they were not upset about the severity of his injury. Not one emotion of fear, anger, or pain was expressed. Everyone in the family behaved as though there were nothing wrong and Ross had a sinking feeling that he was unwanted and unloved. At the same time, he subtly learned the family rule that you do not express emotions to anyone, that it was considered wrong to express any kind of emotion. Twenty-five years later he started to question some of the things that had happened to him while growing up. In conversation with his younger brother, Ross learned that when he was taken to the hospital, his mother would fall apart and cry, and her husband ordered her to a bathroom because he did not wish Ross to see his mother's tears. Ross seemed to be healthier than his younger brother who had no friends, and had never dated, lived in apartment that had only a bed and a chair, worked at a repetitive job, and devoted all his life to the church. Ross's brother used the Bible to supplement his style of life and his lack of involvement with people. Ross, on the other hand, became a teacher, and had several intimate relationships. He lived with one woman for three years until one day, according to him, she walked out without any warning. Later, he married his best friend's wife. Unfortunately, they were made for each other in the sense that they both came from families where there was subtle abuse and no display of emotions. They had serious marital conflicts. To understand and break the implicit family rules that these people had lived through was very difficult, because the worker was intruding without permission in an area that the clients preferred to pretend did not exist.

When family rules are flexible, they allow the family to respond well to environmental stress and outside pressures and, of course, individual and family needs. They help family members become capable, adaptive, and healthy and eventually, in the case of children, independent adults. Some positive family rules include the importance of showing others that you care about them, the ability to share both negative and positive thoughts with other family members, and the notion that there should be room for disagreement among family members.

When rules are dysfunctional, they tend to create barriers to communication, secrets, and unhealthy ways of communicating. "Don't be angry" is a negative way of responding to a family member, as are statements such as: "Do not discuss your father's extramarital affairs"; "Do not discuss family problems, they will go away"; "It is important to win an argument, because losing a argument means losing face." In one case, all the

problems in the family were blamed on one child. He was considered not as smart as the rest of the family members; he was "troublesome" and "no good." He was, in short, the family scapegoat, who could not do anything right. The implicit family rule set standards that were beyond his reach and he would thus continue to be the family's "bad child" and the scapegoat (Pillari, 1991).

As mentioned earlier, all families have both implicit and explicit rules; otherwise there would be anarchy. In order to make a meaningful assessment of a family, the worker has to identify both types of rules. Family rules, especially the implicit ones, are identified by being alert to the patterns of behavior. There will be many opportunities for the worker to observe stylized family behaviors that are an integral part of family functioning. For example, in one family the worker may observe that all family members take their cues from the father before saying anything, whereas in another he is all but ignored.

Rules are powerful. When members violate rules, the family has a way of pushing offenders into conformity unless new rules and new behaviors are introduced. There are also habitual ways of forcing the family to return to an earlier state of equilibrium. Trying to change the rules or behaving in ways that are not acceptable may end in negative feedback from other family members in terms of "oughts," "shoulds," and "don'ts" aimed at moving the family back to a more comfortable way of communicating. Violations of rules lead to anger, depression, and guilt as well as other behaviors that prevent the family from working constructively. There will be attempts to invalidate anything that is different with family members, such as using "put-downs" to compel members to obey.

Seventeen-year-old Reema, from a Asian family, is determined to do something different from the rest of the family. She talks to her mother during an evening chat:

"Mom, I really don't want to be a doctor. I would like to study something different, like music."

Her mother responds, "But you have the grades and have been accepted in a number of colleges for pre-med. What is your problem now?"

"Mom, I only applied because everyone was pressuring me, but I would really like to be a pianist and not do medicine. It's so boring. Everyone in this family, Dad, Grandpa, all my uncles, some of my aunts, and my brothers are all doctors. I don't want to be one."

The mother says angrily, "Is this what we get for everything we gave you? You will disappoint your father. And worse, your grandpa who just had a stroke will take it very badly—it might kill him. You just think you want to do something different, but really you would hate yourself if you did anything different from the rest of the family."

Feeling guilty and with no permission to change family rules or the family lifestyle, Reema lapses into silence that reveals both guilt and resentment.

Reema's mother employed effective mechanisms to put down her daughter's need to be different, using the grandfather to add the additional burden of guilt, an effective way of bringing her back to the family reality.

In order to function effectively, a healthy family must be flexible and ready to make changes or new rules. However rigidity and inability to view the family differently as they grow older can make for dysfunctional behavior in some family members. Goldenberg and Goldenberg (1996) indicate that the redefinition of family rules is important as children and adults pass through different adult phases. Disequilibrium in the family system can create a sense of loss and strangeness until new patterns of transactions are created to restore the family balance.

Assessment is crucial in determining the appropriate treatment. Some treatment modalities are clearer than others. Lewis, Beavers, Gossett, and Philips (1976) have identified five levels of family functioning: optimal, adequate, midrange, borderline, and severely disturbed. These categories represent a continuum from the most flexible, adaptive, and goal-achieving systems at one end to the most inflexible, undifferentiated, and ineffective family system at the other. Lewis (1992) believes that in terms of relative size of population, families who are midrange also comprise the largest group, which is greater than family groups at either end of the continuum.

In making an assessment the worker has to conceptualize massive data that is presented in a family session. The worker is equipped with con-cepts, theories, and a methodology for sifting data to form an assessment map of the family as a whole as well as its various subsystems—including rules, boundaries, power structure, and the communication patterns of the family. Not only do developmental changes and family events need to be taken into consideration but also the flexibility of family rules. External stressors like a job change or loss, relocation of the family, illnesses or accidents can cause problems. It is important to identify important family rules and behavior and also to grasp the concepts of content, that is, information and the manner in which information is processed at different levels of interaction.

Assessing family structure refers to the organization of relationships and patterns of interaction between family members, family norms, family roles, balance of power within the family system, and intergenerational factors. Communication is an important aspect of family structure and in assessment and through out the helping process.

The following section covers some of the dimensions that practitioners need to keep in mind in order to understand a family.

Family Boundaries

What are the boundaries of the family? Boundaries protect the differentiation of a system. For example, a man can be a son to his parents and a brother to his siblings. A person's personal and interpersonal development is based on clear boundaries that are found among subsystems in the family. As Minuchin (1974) notes, "for proper functioning, the boundaries of subsystem must be clear. They must be defined well enough to allow subsystems members to carry out their functions without undue interference and they must allow contact between the members of the subsystem and others. The composition of subsystems organized around family functions is not nearly as significant as the clarity of subsystem boundaries. A parental subsystem that includes a grandmother or a parental child can function quite well so long as lines of responsibility and authority are clearly drawn" (p. 54). Boundaries in families are drawn in terms of a family's relationships with the outside world. This includes families developing diverse transactions with other environments such as the workplace or school. For example, a father who is a real estate agent has phone calls coming home all the time, as prospective clients inquire about buying property. This is understood in the family and it is not considered an invasion of privacy when such calls reach home at any time during the day.

Kantor and Lehr (1975) have identified three classifications of spatial and temporal arrangements in families: open, closed, and random.

There are some families with an open flexible family system where outsiders are invited to enter; members are also allowed to engage emotionally in relationships, and information and materials are exchanged with the outside world. Features of the open family include incoming and outgoing traffic in the family system, numerous guests in the family, visiting with friends, and participating in external activities.

There are also closed family systems which function in such a way that they create discrete family space that is separate and apart from the rest of the larger environment. There are rules and regulations that restrict incoming and outgoing traffic. There are locked doors, tight parental control over input from media, and close scrutiny of strangers and outsiders.

In random families there are no real boundaries and there may be as many boundary patterns as there are members in the family, and a conglomerate of individual styles. Random bounding deemphasizes defending the territorial parameters of the family so that limits on entry and exit are not imposed on any family member.

Family Subsystems and Their Effects on Internal Boundaries

All families develop a network based on gender, generation, and functions in the family. These subsystems are called the spousal, parental, and sibling subsystems. Based on lifestyle and other factors, stable and well-defined alliances and coalitions are formed in the family. This is critical to the well-being and health of the family. An alliance or coalition is made between two or more people, which automatically tends to set them apart from others within the system. An alliance in one part of the system "whose components are interdependent and which reverberates to produce change in other parts of the system. . . . The study of such sequences over a period of time, as the therapeutic process unfolds, will help reveal how the various levels of functioning in the family system are dramatically linked and experientially separated or dissociated" (Wynne, 1961, p. 97).

A family functions best when there is a strong and enduring coalition between husband and wife. But if conflict reverberates throughout a family, children are often co-opted into one warring faction or another as parents struggle for power and control. The three basic family subsystems must be clearly defined and permeable to allow members sufficient differentiation to carry out the functions without undue interference (Minuchin & Fishman, 1981).

When there is deviation from the clarity of subsystem boundaries, then the family situation can go in two different directions: (1) enmeshment and (2) disengagement. Enmeshment refers to the tendency of people to emphasize togetherness, belonging, and conformity at the expense of separateness, that is, individual development and a sense of personal autonomy. In such situations, personal and subsystem differentiation become diffuse. Conversely, disengagement refers to the tendency to tighten the boundaries between subsystems and even between individuals so that meaningful interaction and functional cooperation become increasingly difficult. In such a situation, separateness and autonomy are emphasized at the relative expense of belonging and togetherness.

Power in Families

Another factor that needs to be understood in making an assessment of a family is the power structure. According to Haley (1973) all families develop patterns of power and control in their different relationships. Haley believes that people are constantly attempting and struggling to define or redefine a relationship.

As Haley (1973, 1984) has described, families have power and authority many times this power can be a struggle between husband and wife in terms of what and who they are. Though a family may understand that the father has more power than the mother, or the other way around, this may not always be true as power is not monolithic. More often than not, power is shared and there are multiple power structures. However, it is also important to note which family member is the most influential in determining which decisions are made, as well as how and when these occur.

While working with families it is necessary to understand power and how families and individual members are using it. Is there an alignment between different family members in order to make some decisions and how does this work for all of them? As Sluzki (1978) notes that while observing families in communication it can be said that relationships are "affect-laden processes and they are accepted, modified, locked, tested, qualified, broken, rejected or betrayed in a constantly flowing process" (p. 201).

Based on content and conversation, it is important to understand who makes the decisions, who speaks for whom and who interrupts, and also who decides and who seems to hold the ultimate authority for making decisions, irrespective of where the authority originated.

Decision-Making Power

Another area to assess is the decision-making power of a family. The worker needs to find out how decisions are made in the family. Are decisions made unilaterally by one family member or do all members participate in decision making? Are alternatives made available for different family members or are all options closed? Does one person seem to make the decisions? Decision making requires that family members allow time for negotiation and adjustment of earlier decisions. In assessing family decision-making style, the worker

has to elicit information and view processes. The worker also has to view who the client is—knowing a client's family culture and the environmental culture provides the frame of reference needed to understand their patterns of decision making.

An assessment also needs to be made of the range of feelings expressed by the family. Beavers (1982) indicates that feelings expressed in a family are intimately related to the structure of the family. In families where differentiation of members is rigid and inflexible, the prevailing mood is one of depression, hopelessness, anxiety, hostility, and apathy.

How do these families express affection? Is it expressed verbally or nonverbally? How are caring behaviors perceived? Are individual family members dissatisfied? How do individual family members feel about sending out caring feelings? How flexible are family members and the system as a whole with regard to making adjustments, and how does this work? (Hepworth et al., 1997).

Family Goals

What are the different family goals? To what extent do family-originated goals guide the family? Is there a shared consensus regarding major goals, and what priorities are assigned to these goals? Again, are these goals functional for the whole family, or do they seem to cause problems and conflicts for some family members? To what degree do family members manifest dysfunctional interactional patterns and how are they related to the overt and covert goals of the family?

Forty-year-old Brad runs a family business with his sister. His elderly parents supervise them. When the company makes profits, the parents are pleased with both the children. However, when there are family losses, Brad gets blamed. The sister is married but Brad has to provide for her, her two children, as well as for his elderly parents. The family goal makes Brad the family provider and no one wants or encourages him to get married, which is not part of the family plan. There is a great deal of enmeshment and dysfunctional interactional patterns between different family members with providing money as the established criteria for Brad's self-worth.

Shared Family Myths

Family members have shared myths about each other. Family myths are well-integrated beliefs that are shared by all family members concerning their role and status in the family (Pillari, 1986), although these myths may represent reality distortions. Examples of some myths that might be part of the family belief system are: "Father does not care about the children, but mother does"; "it's a sign of weakness to apologize in the family"; "Johnny is a troublemaker, but Julie is a good kid"; and "Boys do not cry, because crying is a sign of weakness." In dysfunctional families there are rigid myths that are almost impossible to escape. Myths lock in family members and the resulting rigidity is reinforced by another myth which says that open divergence about assigned roles will lead to personal and family disaster.

What are the different family roles played by different members? For example, Albert is a son to his parents, a husband to his wife, a brother to his siblings, a father to his children, and a wage earner. Thus within this nuclear family, Albert plays a number of diverse roles. Besides family roles, what is the role of culture in determining family roles? Each subculture that is part of the United States has a culture that determines the definition of roles and distribution of labor in the family. Also, what are the communication styles of different family members? Do they listen to each other? Do they speak prematurely, overgeneralize, and ask excessive questions? Do they direct, order, threaten, or admonish others? The worker must also make an assessment of problematic communication in the family at both the nonverbal and verbal levels.

Development of Self-Esteem

Development of self-esteem is a necessity in every family. How does this happen? Is self-esteem encouraged or are there problems in the family cre-

ated by put-downs of different family members? Healthy families have a way of validating the worth of different family members including warm expressions of feelings, verbal and nonverbal attentiveness to messages, and attention to activities in which all others are engaged (Hepworth et al., 1997). Roger makes straight A's in his exams; a positive, supportive statement by his parents is "You have done well, we are very proud of you." Conversely, Roger is not praised but merely told, "You better continue to get the same grades or else." The former statement builds self-esteem, the latter takes away from Roger's developing self-esteem.

Different family strengths and weaknesses are important. It is crucial to point out the positives as well as the negatives. It is necessary to pay particular attention to the strengths of the family and to take into consideration the strengths of ethnically diverse cultural groups. It is essential to understand the family life cycle and how different family members have passed through the different phases as well as an awareness of the developmental stages of the family.

Duvall (1977) and Carter and McGoldrick (1988) offer a conceptual framework for the middle-class American family. Carter and McGoldrick identify six stages of development: the unattached young adult, the new couple, the family with young children, the family with adolescents, the family that is launching children, and the family in later life. How do family members deal with these different stages, adjust, and grow up? If there are variations in the family life cycle, how does one work with them? Minuchin and Fishman's (1981) understanding of the family crosses class barriers in terms of how family members grow up in families and includes the hierarchical structure and roles of parental and sibling relationships, couple formation, and presentation of families with young, school-age, adolescent, and grown children.

Practitioners need to identify the processes that are relevant to all family members. How would you utilize the different family dimensions in order to guide your exploration of family behavior, and how would you utilize the dimensions for compressing raw data and determining the couples's use of data? Also, how would you develop a written profile of individual family members and how would you assess the relevant behaviors of the entire family? Dysfunctional ways of responding include labeling and frequent expressions of anger.

While making an assessment, it is important to remember the different cultures that families belong to. Also, to assess the need for basic resources such as the need for food, financial aid, job training, as well as the family's ability to secure such resources. Finally, in terms of family assessment, it is important to look at the different support systems that are available to the family.

The Crawford family consists of six family members—a father, mother, and four children. The family myth says that all members should be harmonious in their behavior toward each other. The children, aged two to ten years, are dressed alike. The three daughters are wearing pink dresses and the youngest, a son, is dressed in a pink suit. Although they have been referred to a social worker due to the ten-year-old's acting-out behavior, it is clear that the family is not willing to face the problem. The family power structure is such that the mother is in charge and she presents the issues as "the school's problem." The father speaks only after nonverbally consulting his wife; when she nods her head affirmatively, he begins to talk.

Ten-year-old Nellie begins after "getting permission" from her mother. She echoes her mother's thinking; it is the "school's problem." After an hour-long interview, the worker makes the assessment that the family has enmeshed boundaries and rigid implicit and explicit rules about the family myth which dictates that the family members have to present "togetherness" at all times when outside the family. The communication patterns are skewed in favor of the mother's thinking. In terms of power, role, and status, it is obvious that the mother has more power than the father reporting what can and cannot be discussed in the family. Both parents minimize the problem at school and the worker is aware of the implicit and explicit family rules which say that everyone should follow the mother's directions. The communication patterns are rigid and the family members speak only with the permission of the mother. The family culture reveals rules, regulations, and restrictions in the presentation of emotions, feelings, and thoughts. The family culture sends out a message of "togetherness" to outsiders.

Exercises

1. Several students role-play a single- and a two-parent family. As a class, discuss implicit and explicit rules and the role and effects of power and authority in the family.

2. Read a case study that displays power as distorted authority. Keeping in mind the developmental stages of the different family members, how would you deal with this family in terms of family boundaries and shared family myths?

3. Analyze and make an assessment of the family situation as presented by Mrs. Ken in the following case study.

During the orientation conference at her daughter's school, Mrs. Ken was concerned that there was no lock on the bathroom door. She asked how one ensured privacy for the five-year-old children. The teacher explained that the children went to the bathroom singly, closed the door, and left the door open when they came out again. She added that it may not be easy for a small child to lock the door from the inside.

Mrs. Ken responded, "I hope your rules are always imposed, because I feel strongly that using the bathroom is a private matter. In my home, we follow this rule firmly, right from the time children are three years of age. We do things privately. My whole family dresses privately, because I know it is a sin to view other people in the nude." She ended her comments by saying, "I want my daughter to be as modest as my husband and me. We never see each other in a state of nudity." The teacher responded curtly that she would make an extra effort to ensure her daughter's privacy.

4. A few students can do a role-play of any specific family situation. Based on the role-play the class should make an assessment of the family keeping in mind the different factors that are necessary to make a valid and useful family assessment with application of knowledge and skills outlined in this section.

ASSESSMENT OF SMALL GROUPS

There are two types of groups: task groups and treatment groups. Treatment groups are designed to target growth, remedy problems, provide education, or enhance socialization. Such a group could consist of members whose problems range from drug and/or alcohol addiction, incest, or domestic violence, to self-esteem and self-assertiveness problems. Task groups are formed to get something done, that is, accomplish some specific goal or task such as raising money for a cause or lobbying a state legislature. Before we assess groups let us look at the norms that different groups create for themselves.

Group Membership

When individuals join groups, their group experiences cause many of them to begin to change. Once within a group, individuals display and express behaviors that may differ from their out-of-the-group behavior. It seems that, in a group, people's individuality or the sum of qualities that characterize and distinguish them from others somehow changes (Napier & Gershenfeld, 1993). According to Bennis and Shepard (1987), the most powerful factor that alters people's behavior in groups is mild to extreme anxiety and uneasiness brought about by an unconscious or conscious feeling of danger, not necessarily real, and a readiness or preparation to meet that danger (Brill, 1972). The basis of their anxiety is internal uncertainty, feelings of self-doubt, and the fear of unknown dangers that the members may pose. Most people feel such uncertainties in new situations that involve strangers.

A second prevalent emotion involves the role shift from individual to group membership. Sudden role shifts create conflicts as the person fluctuates between a wish to belong and the self-protective impulse to withdraw. Individuals are caught between the desire to interact with others and the desire to protect their own individuality; between the desire to contribute to the group's tasks and self-doubt about the ability to contribute (Turquet, 1978). Internal uncertainties and ambivalence spring from sudden role shifts that may cause anxiety and with it, distortions, misperceptions, and miscommunication (Bennis & Shepard, 1987; Rioch, 1979).

Group Norms

Based on the type of group and the composition of their members, all groups develop norms. Napier and Gershenfeld (1993) describe norms as a set of standards that groups develop for themselves. Norms are complex. It is often difficult to determine which norms take precedence, which are time specific and which are general, which apply to all members or only to some, and which must be strictly adhered to or may be totally ignored.

WRITTEN RULES   Some of the norms are codified in by-laws and code books. Formal, written statements are intended to be taken literally as group rules and enforced by organizational sanctions, that is, actions to ensure compliance. At times, formal rules may be ignored just as the old statutes that remain in the books but are no longer enforced.

EXPLICITLY STATED NORMS   Some norms are stated verbally and are easily recognized by members. For instance, "everyone should get here by 9:00 A.M.," which means anyone who comes in late is viewed as tardy and meets with disapproval.

NONEXPLICIT INFORMAL NORMS   Within each group there may be nonexplicit, informal, or silent norms that influence member behavior. For instance, in a group of incest perpetrators the norm is that everyone should assume the role of the perpetrator and explain what they did as a beginning step to acceptance of their wrongdoing and working through their own problems. A new member who had sexually molested his stepdaughter kept saying that the ten-year-old had acted "seductively" toward him. At this point, the group members literally jumped on him, insisting that he rethink and talk about his own adult behavior. Being honest was a nonexplicit informal norm in the group. Thus norms are related to a variety of group member behaviors including communication within the group.

The process by which a group brings pressure on its members to conform to its norms or the process through which a member manipulates the behavior of others is called *social influence*. This is true of church groups, political parties, and professional societies. Generally, if the norms of the voluntary group are compatible with an individual's needs, desires, or goals then that person will conform to the norms of the group.

Assessing Behavior Patterns in Groups

As with other systems assessment is an ongoing process carried out from the time a group is formed through intervention until termination of the group (Toseland & Rivas, 1995). One of the first steps in making an assessment is understanding the issues and concerns of each member and what brought the person to the point of seeking help. Some clients facilitate this process with complaints such as, "I am unhappy in my marriage," whereas others might speak of their problems in vague terms.

Reid (1997) notes that in order to make an assessment, the worker has to get responses to specific questions:

How long has the problem been present?

Is this a chronic problem or something of recent origin?

What brought the person to seek help at this point rather than earlier?

What precipitated the situation?

How does the person feel he or she can deal with the problem?

What are the client's strengths and potential to solve or reduce the problem?

How motivated is the client?

Answering these questions may shed some light on the person's coping abilities and the relative sense of confidence or helplessness in the person regarding his or her own situation, which is the foundation on which a generalist's understanding of a group is based.

Through engaging group members in discussion the generalist begins to work on the assessment process. One relevant area for assessment involves communication and interaction processes. The generalist's responsibility is to monitor the openness of communication including encouraging participation of all group members and establishing and maintaining the group goals and structure so that the group can progress constructively and continuously.

At times, self-monitoring questionnaires are given to the group members at the beginning, middle, and end of the sessions to assess their progress. Another form of assessment involves role playing where the generalist requesting group members to role-play what they have learned in the group and soliciting information and assessment about their participation. This feedback further helps the group members to assess and move toward their goals. For example, a group of emotionally disturbed children who use foul language are asked to role-play a parent and a child. Through the course of the role play the observers who are the group members assess whether a specific member even when being provoked by a parent avoids using foul language that detracts from the family problems.

Reid (1997) further indicates that when assessing a group member, a number of specific factors have to be considered including the individual's adaptation to reality and use of effective boundaries in relationships with other group members and the generalist. Their perception of their own problems and ability to test reality is crucial, as well as their judgement, adaptive mechanisms, and their competency and mastery in dealing with issues in their life issues. The generalist also has to evaluate the group members' motivation to change.

When group members are mandated to attend group sessions their motivation may be limited. In such groups, the members should be encouraged to talk about their feelings of anger, frustration, and lack of control over their own lives before beginning any group work. Finally, assessment in such groups could take longer when the members spend a few sessions in ventilating and coming to understand the need for the group meetings. When the group is ready, the group members should be assessed like any other group.

ASSESSMENT OF COMMUNITIES AND LARGE ORGANIZATIONS

When we work with people in communities or organizations, we practice the same people skills as we do with families, small groups, and individuals. After all, communities and organizations are made up of people; in this case, the focus is on making positive changes that could impact large numbers of people.

The most important factor is to understand the context of the community you are assessing, including the attitude of the community regarding needs assessment. To make a needs assessment you need to know what information to gather, how difficult it will be to gather this information, and how to involve the natural and formal community leaders in this process.

Working with communities is complex because the role of the generalist must be subsumed in a task-focused group. Because communities usually have formal leaders in place, what is the role of the generalist in the community? The generalist helps by organizing, not leading. As Staples (1984) explains, there is a clear distinction between leading and organizing:

> It is the organizer's job to get other people to take the lead. They have to be motivated and recruited, encouraged and convinced that they can really do it. Their knowledge and skills must be developed, their self-confidence bolstered, and their commitment to collective action deepened . . . Whoever acts as organizer shouldn't be a formal officer or the organization's formal voice. S/he shouldn't

make policy decisions or tell people what to do. (p. 8)

Regardless of the milieu of the community—whether a neighborhood, a residential setting, or a hospital ward—the generalist's role is to promote the well-being of the community. In a mental hospital ward where the patients felt disempowered, the community worker may help them develop a newspaper to discuss their problems and communicate with staff.

In any community setting, the generalist has to highlight decision-making skills in order for the group to understand its goals. This includes brainstorming, nominal group techniques, and reaching a consensus on needs assessment.

Brainstorming

Achieving some consensus on the needs of a community or an organization can be done through brainstorming, which involves generating ideas about an issue. Brainstorming is a specific technique for generating ideas, possibilities, or alternate courses of action, using freewheeling discussion in order to produce as many ideas as possible without any evaluation of which is best (Hepworth et al., 1997). The free-flowing nature of the brainstorming process unleashes creativity and cooperation and is used for planning and later assessing the best course of action. It encourages an open sharing of ideas and helps create a nonevaluative climate. Also, one person's ideas are added to by others so that creative and unique combinations are generated.

Nominal Group Approach

The nominal group approach was developed by Delbecq and Van de Ven (1971) for use as a problem identification technique in social program development efforts. In this approach the potential users of the service are involved in identifying needs from the point of view of the community or organization that one is trying to serve. The main orientation is to respond to consumers' needs rather than independently develop programs for them. In order to achieve this goal, the nominal group approach is designed to receive input from *all* community members rather than just the more vocal or aggressive ones as often happens in conventional groups. Nominal group is also a useful process to help community members reach consensus or to at least to give members information on the thoughts of other members. The nominal group technique provides members of a task force or planning group with information about their own priorities.

The practitioner met with an interagency council in a medium-sized county to help them define and assess their priorities. The council leadership believed that the group could influence the United Way and the county commission if they spoke with one voice. The problem was that service providers each emphasized their own area of concern, such as aging, juveniles, developmental disabilities, and so forth. In order to reach a consensus, the generalist met with more than forty representatives of all the service providers in a one-day planning session. Using the nominal group approach, the generalist asked participants to identify two groups that they considered especially in need of services and then at a later stage of the process list two specific kinds of services that should be started or strengthened, which effectively canceled out the individual biases of the participants. By the end of the day the participants had agreed on two specific service areas that they would propose to the funding bodies.

Needs Assessment

As the term implies, *needs assessment* refers to the comprehensive appraisal of problems and needs (Zastrow, 1995). Needs assessments also are used by communities to evaluate the needs of the clients, as when a community family service agency conducts a needs assessment of its clients. Whether of a broad or narrow scale, needs assessment refers to acquiring and making sense of information to use in decision making. An agency or a community may conduct a needs assessment to determine whether its efforts are addressing the crucial needs of the agency or community. At times a needs as-

sessment is conducted in order to determine which area needs the most attention.

There are different types of needs assessment. They include understanding the profile of a community with regard to ethnicity, race, age, and length of residence; assessing the profiles of domains of living which include economic and employment data, family lifestyles and patterns, educational patterns, physical and mental health of the population; understanding home management, including housekeeping; assessing criminal justice issues including crime and juvenile delinquency; evaluating life satisfaction, knowledge, and utilization of services and their availability, as well as barriers to service utilization including physical barriers, such as inadequate transportation, and feelings of social stigma because the services are for the needy. Finally, existing community information, resource assessment dealing with identification of existing and potential resources for allocation, and political resource assessment including potential mobilization of political and community leaders and the population at large are crucial areas for needs assessment since decisions are generally made in the political arena.

A needs assessment can be a long complex process or a relatively simple one and is designed to fully yield information needed to make the decisions. The assessment is an important aspect of the helping process which offers information about costs and benefits to different client systems.

CHAPTER SUMMARY

Assessment is the process of collecting and interpreting data from which a plan for helping is developed. The nature, content, and process of assessment involves both the clients and the generalist. An analysis of assessment includes factors such as the personality of the clients, the characteristics of the client system, and the significant environment.

The first step in assessment is the statement of the problem. Assessment is an ongoing process and clients conceptualize their problems in different ways. One of the most important steps in assessment is history taking where identification factors such as ethnicity, race, health, and developmental history are collected. Categories in assessment include the purpose of assessment, the different types of problems, prioritizing and selecting the most important problems, as well as understanding behaviors in terms of cause and effect, antecedents, and consequences of behavior. Identifying secondary gains, exploring earlier solutions, developing an awareness of and working with client's coping skills, strengths, and resources completes the assessment process. The client's perception of the problem is an important factor for exploration, followed by the intensity of the problem in terms of frequency, duration, and severity. Data is collected through problem exploration where feelings and acts are dealt with as well as contradictory information. Relevant data is collected, analyzed, and interpreted through exploration and identification. Personality assessment, coping strategies, role performance, self-concept, cultural factors, and support systems are important assessment tools. Generalists need to be aware that there are some clients who are unwilling to request help.

In family assessment, the family rules and patterns, family boundaries, power and decision making, family goals, and family myths, as well as the development of self-esteem and the culture of the family are important assessment factors.

Assessment of small groups includes group membership, group norms, and the role of group members in pursuing their goals.

Assessment of communities and large organizations includes brainstorming, nominal group technique, and needs assessment.

12

PLANNING

Planning is the next stage after assessment, although in reality these stages tend to overlap. Planning can be defined as an outcome of the assessment process and as a "deliberate, rational process that involves the choice of actions that are calculated to achieve specific objectives at some future time" (Perlman, 1986, p. 246). The planning process has also been defined as "policy choice and programming in the light of facts, projections, and application of values" (Kahn, 1979). Sheafor, Horejsi, and Horejsi (2000) explain that planning has to identify the following: problems, concerns, or issues that need to be addressed by intervention; the objectives or outcomes of the intervention; actions to be taken by the generalist and the client system; and, finally, the amount of time required from the beginning to the end of the intervention. Planning is most successful when practitioners identify goals, plan how to achieve them, and pursue appropriate ones. As in every phase of the helping process, joint decision making is an important factor.

Siporin (1975) views planning from an ecosystems perspective. Siporin elaborates that a comprehensive action plan is "multitarget, multilevel, and multiphasic in design" (p. 259) and includes the following:

Measurable, concrete broad objectives

Prioritizing the objectives into immediate, medium, and long-term goals

Identifying strategies to use and actions to take to meet the objectives

Setting time frames for implementation

Identifying targets for change

Making an inventory of required resources such as financial programs or staff

Clearly dividing actions among the client system, the worker, and others

Evaluating criteria and procedures

Identifying processes for altering the plan

Establishing a defined point of resolution

Regardless of the style of planning, there is mutual discussion between clients and practitioners in terms of examining goals and how to accomplish them. All styles share the perspective that clients are the experts on what they want and what they are willing to do (Siporin, 1980). Practitioners contribute in terms of emotional support, technical skills, and knowledge of available resources, and how change can be implemented.

Like assessment, the planning process begins with the first interview. The generalist and the client system consider the range of possible solutions and the implications of these solutions. They then select the most viable approaches to change and develop a plan of action. There must be mutual agreement between the client and the generalist concerning the goals that need to be pursued and the methods of achieving them. Finding and working toward goals is a process of timing.

In the planning process stage, the shifts from problem definition to problem solution. Resting on a foundation of accepted social work values, theories of human behavior, and practice principles, the plan for problem solution evolves from the needs of the client system within that client's environment. The plan also identifies potential resources and barriers to implementation.

Raphael was fired from his job because he has a drinking problem. Raphael's wife continued to support her husband and wanted to help him get back on his feet. Probing into their family life in sessions reveals that Raphael's father was killed in a car accident several months ago, which has led to Raphael's binge drinking. Armed with these facts, the generalist and clients work to help Raphael work through his grief over his father's sudden death and to join an Alcoholic Anonymous group.

Having a plan that indicates the process, the objectives, and the time frame is a necessary precondition for developing a contract with a client. A clearly documented plan makes it possible to hold the generalist and the agency accountable for the actual performance of the professional and tangible services that are planned and contracted,

as well as the expectations and hopes for outcomes. A well-developed plan also has room for flexibility and change, as the process of work with the clients develop.

In developing a plan of action, the generalist should consider with the clients the realistic possibilities and choices available to them, that is, goals that can be accomplished. Some clients may know what they want to do and only need help determining how to accomplish their goals.

However, a plan works better when it is chosen from a number of possibilities. Some clients decide what they want and implement the first strategy that comes to mind. Although their bias toward action may be laudable, the strategy may be ineffective, inefficient, imprudent, or a combination of all three (Egan, 1998).

In a community where there are a large number of concerns ranging from poor school facilities to lack of medical and recreational facilities, the natural leader encourages people to discuss building a recreational facility while the community medical needs are overlooked. The new community organizer, a generalist, goes along without questioning the community about the medical facilities, even though AIDS and drug addiction are rampant in the area. Halfway through the planning of the recreational facility, community members abandon the project because medical and health problems of the community have overwhelmed them.

FACTORS THAT AFFECT PLANNING

Five factors are influential in the development of the plan: (1) the community in which the clients are living and where the plan is being carried out; (2) the agency that is sanctioning the plan; (3) the social problem/concern to which the plan is a response; (4) the generalist who is involved in the plan; and (5) the clients who are involved in the plan (see Figure 12.1).

Because clients are part of the community, the plan of action should fit community's culture attitudes about receiving help. The generalist should

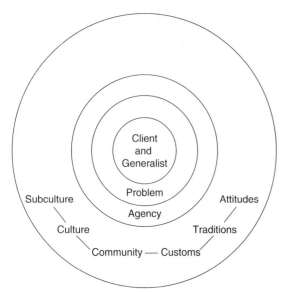

Figure 12.1 **Factors That Affect Planning**

develop a basic understanding of the culture and customs of people of the community. For instance, in a community of Asians, it may be a taboo for a person to seek professional help. The constraints and resources that are found within the helping agency can restrict the plan of action. Social agencies are dependent on the community for their resources and the type of services they offer.

Societal expectations and attitudes affect how generalists deal with social problems. There are three organizing dimensions for describing a field of practice: the social problem, the social task, and the social service system (Shulman, 1999; Studt, 1968). Generalists bring to the helping process a unique primary tool—themselves. Generalists are also influenced by agency needs, rules, and regulations. Generalists function within their agency community and a professional code of ethics, as well as a theoretical level of comfort in working with clients.

CONTRACTS

Developing a contract is important as generalists and the clients work together in the assessment process and make a plan of action that describes what needs to be done and who should do it. Contracting is an active way of involving clients in the planning process, with the generalist and the client working together to design a comprehensive intervention plan. No plan, however, is written in stone. The overall plan could change as work progresses. There are also plans within plans.

Gambrill (1990) has suggested that there are two parts to every contract. The first part includes the client's objectives, a statement of potential consequences, and a time limit. The second part specifies treatment methods, the tasks of the client and others who may be involved, any available support networks and resources, and the role of the worker. Contracts are variously referred to as working agreements, social service plans, and service plans or agreements. No matter what name is used, all contracts specify the product and the process. Contract forms have been developed in the different fields of social work practice including public welfare, social services, community services, adult services, mental health, and community councils (Hoff, 1995).

It should be noted that contracts often are not legally binding on clients; rather they are flexible and open to change. For instance, if clients fail to adhere to the requirements stated in the contract there are usually no legal ramifications. There are exceptions, such as cases mandated by the court system where the generalist works with involuntary clients.

Characteristics of Contracts

Five characteristics of working agreements, as described by Garvin & Seabury (1997), are as follows:

1. Clarification of rules and responsibilities so that each party understands what is expected of them, including each party's individual perspective.
2. Declaration of a mutual process in which both the worker and clients agree on the goals.
3. A contract supports the credibility of the change process.
4. The contract is documented in writing.

5. The written document can be changed or amended and provides for monitoring.

THE COMPONENTS OF A PLAN

To manage the complexity of a contract, a plan has three components: goals and objectives, units of attention, and strategies that include the tasks to be performed (see Figure 12.2). The plan should include objectives, goals, and subgoals or action steps, which could also be called tasks. This requires identifying the work or the service to be done in a situation and the procedures necessary for achieving it. There is a continuous spiral of planning, testing, evaluating, and replanning of the helping process.

A plan is developed in a pragmatic manner. In order to reach an outcome goal, there are a number of subgoals or action steps that the generalist must take in order to help the clients. When we are expected to achieve the overall goal in a short period of time, it can be overwhelming, uncomfortable, and discouraging. The overall goal is therefore broken down into subgoals and action goals.

Subgoals help the clients move toward the solution of problems in a planned manner. When clients work on subgoals, they deal with small pieces of the life puzzle. For instance, if a family business goes bankrupt, how would the members

of that family cope and adapt? Their first counseling session might be spent on helping everyone accept that bankruptcy has occurred. The next step would be to help the family members deal with the necessity of cutting down on expenses, perhaps by letting go of a live-in maid. When this subgoal is reached, the family next works at cutting back on restaurant meals. These are both discrete action goals, but their purpose is to help the family adapt to a new lifestyle.

How the generalist uses the process in helping is as important as the process objectives, which should aim toward providing a learning and growing experience for clients. The process should help the clients help themselves. When the process objectives and the generalist's plan are rigid, problems occur for both the generalist and the clients. There needs to be a certain degree of flexibility in order to help clients deal with their problems, as well as change plans in midstream if alternatives would be more helpful. However, it is clients' needs, desires, and hopes that ultimately give content and form to the helping process.

Principles

Garvin and Seabury (1997) and Hepworth, Rooney, and Larsen (1997) specify that certain principles need to be included in planning intervention. The intervention should be designed in such a manner that the process itself becomes an educational and integrative growth experience for clients. Both goals and subgoals have to be relevant to the issues under consideration by clients.

The primary responsibility for the plan is the clients' with some exceptions, as in the case of those not competent to manage their own affairs and young children. Priority should be given to the client's choice of goals. The generalist has the initial task of identifying and working with the client's strengths in formulating goals.

The specifics of the helping process should be developed in a pragmatic manner based on overall objectives, short-term limited objectives, goals, and subgoals and subtasks to achieve these goals, including concrete services for the clients. The

Figure 12.2 **Components of a Plan**

generalist's responsibility is to help the clients complete their own tasks and also to see that the necessary conditions are provided for their work.

In crisis situations, practitioners may have to take responsibility for helping clients complete tasks and also to see that necessary conditions are provided for their work.

Goals and Objectives

Goals can be defined as long-term and short-term. Long-term goals are reached most easily when they are divided into smaller objectives and tasks. A long-term goal is usually reached after the intermediate goals or objectives have been attained. Broad or abstract goals such as "greater happiness" or "improved mental health" are not very useful unless accompanied by more specific objectives such as "spending more time with friends" or "improved grades in school." In order to evaluate the end result of a broad goal, more specific and short-term objectives are required. A goal should be realistic in that there is a good chance it can be achieved. The amount of time and energy necessary should be taken into consideration.

Goals and objectives work toward the identification of blockages to need fulfillment. They are the desired ends toward which an activity is directed. Objectives refer to the intended outcome of terminal, consummatory behavior and also the end state of altered behavior. A basic goal in social work is to help client systems improve their social functioning. As behavior is purposive, goals, and objectives carry important functions in the helping process as they do in life.

Objectives can be defined with reference to problems, persons, and situations and also as elements of the helping situation. The objective while working out a problem would be to change the situation, to endure it, or to flee from it. Such objectives are usually concrete and are used as a means to reduce stress. With reference to persons, the objective would be to improve competence and self-esteem, and in the process, improve communication and the client's sense of well-being. Ob-

jectives that are formed with reference to a particular situation may be used to help a client deal with a situation, such as to get an apartment or develop a meaningful concept of money management. Objectives are reached through the completion of tasks. It can be said that a task is a piece of doing a job or work or service that is present in a situation.

Purposes of Goals in the Helping Process

When goals are clearly defined, they reflect the area of client concern that needs the most immediate attention (Kisthardt, 1992). Goals aim for results toward which effort is directed and they clarify the client's expectations of the helping process (Compton & Galaway, 1994; Hepworth et al., 1997; Johnson, 1995; McMohan, 1990; Sheafor et al., 2000). Goals also help to show what both the worker and the client can and cannot accomplish through the helping process.

Defining goals structures the manner in which the counseling and other services are provided. If the clients feel responsible for setting their goals, they are more likely to work at their problems than if someone else sets the goals for them. Exceptions include court-mandated clients and the mentally disabled. Without goals, the helping process is directionless and based only on the daily needs of the client or the personal preferences of the generalist. Clarity about goals helps generalists determine whether they have the skills, competencies, and interest to work with a particular client or issue, or if due to lack of training or personal biases, the client should be referred to another worker.

The generalist has also to keep in mind the purpose of goals and their role in human motivation and problem solving. Taussig (1987) found that members of minority groups respond positively to goals. Goals that are clear and concrete instill confidence in minority clients that something will be achieved through the helping process. Goals also help in the fulfillment of successful performance as well as problem resolution because they direct the attention of the practitioner and client toward the resources and components in the environment that are most likely to help in the solution of a problem (Dean, 1989).

Goals reveal the difference between what and how much the client is able to do now, and what and how much the client is likely to do in the future. With goals in mind, the generalist and the client can monitor progress as well as compare progress before and after a counseling intervention. This provides continuous feedback to both the generalist and the client (Siporin, 1985). The feedback, in turn, helps the worker assess the feasibility of the goal and the effectiveness of the intervention.

As Lee (1994) explains that when workers help a client to set goals, there is a clearer focus on case planning and treatment. Workers who are conscious of their goals are more motivated to have clients work on them as well.

There are different types of goals that workers can utilize in the helping process. *Immediate goals* and are utilized to relieve stress. For example, a worker might ask a client to breathe deeply until he or she is comfortable and can speak about a stressful issue without too much difficulty. In the case of a hungry homeless person, providing food to eat would be the immediate goal. An *intermediate goal* is not as urgent as an immediate goal, but it is also important. For example, helping a client learn to dress more appropriately could lead to the client being accepted more readily in the workplace. *Long-term goals* help clients become more effective in their social skills.

Let us look at the immediate, intermediate, and long-term goals of one case. Andrew, who has been without a job for a few months came in for help due to anxiety related to his unemployment. However, it became clear that there were also marital problems, which escalated due to financial pressure. Low self-esteem was another identified problem. The immediate goal in this case was to help Andrew find a job. The intermediary goal was to work at his marital relationship, which would change once money started to reappear regularly and they could take care of basic physical needs. Lastly, the long-term goal for Andrew was to continue to work at developing good self-esteem.

Monitoring Procedures

Monitoring is an immediate and short-range form of feedback that is carried out to reinforce or raise questions about interventions by members of the action system (Garvin & Seabury, 1997). Because monitoring processes are not only focused on the ultimate outcomes of service but also on specific actions and activities along the way, monitoring should be built into planning. Long and elaborate measurement procedures in monitoring are not necessary, although they may become important mechanisms in evaluating the overall outcome of service; however, brief methods of evaluation are necessary.

Monitoring has two dimensions: process and outcome. *Process monitoring* provides feedback about whether a certain action has been completed, if it is still in the process of being carried out, or has yet to be attempted. *Outcome monitoring* involves the effects or results of specific actions. Any action, activity or intervention that is planned by members of an action system can be monitored along these two dimensions. The outcomes of certain actions can be successful and desirable as intended or unsuccessful either intentionally or unintentionally.

In addition, unintended consequences can be either positive or negative. For example, when a student at a university was arrested for destroying university property during a campus demonstration, a social work professor referred him to his lawyer. The student and lawyer developed a friendship, which led to the student working in the lawyer's office, attending law school, and becoming a successful attorney. On the negative side, a generalist once worked with a single-parent family in which the mother loved her children, but was overwhelmed by financial difficulties and childcare responsibilities. One of the things that the generalist did to help the mother cope was to take a walk with the family to the nearby public library, where they could attend story hours and borrow books and records at no cost. This seemed like a very successful intervention until a few weeks later when the mother called in a state of panic saying that she owed the library a lot of money for books that were either lost or overdue. This led the worker to review the case in terms of money management capabilities.

As Garvin and Seabury (1997) indicate, the information that is gathered in monitoring may be gained from the client, from other service providers through direct observation, or any combination of these. Monitoring procedures should be planned in advance. The time frame (weekly, monthly, or less often) has to be clear to all parties and established before intervention begins. There is no specific way in which monitoring takes place. This decision is based on the particulars of a case, the type of intervention planned, and the members who are involved. In some cases, monitoring is required by law such as periodic ninety-day monitoring of children in foster care. Such routines should be treated by social workers as "routine requirements" of practice.

Unit of Attention

A unit of attention is the person, family, group, community, or organization with which the generalist interacts for the purpose of accomplishing some or all of the goals agreed upon with the client. The unit of attention may be part of the client system, as when we work with a mother to effect change in the family structure, or it may be another person or system whose help is needed to accomplish a particular change objective. An example of this would be making the classroom teacher and school principal the unit of attention to involve them in modifying the classroom environment for a child with special needs. These units of attention are systems that are the focus of the change activity. The change process consists of a number of activities that are related to specific objectives and miniplans that are generally worked on at the same time. In planning it is important to pinpoint how a specific unit of attention is related to each plan (Johnson, 1995).

When planning, the generalist must be clear about two important factors: (1) selecting goals

and (2) defining goals. In selecting goals the worker and client have to understand the purpose of the goals and the specific positive changes that the generalist expects of the client. How realistic are these goals, what are the advantages and disadvantages of reaching these goals, and can the client own these goals? After all these factors have been discussed, the generalist and the client must make the decision together (Cormier & Cormier, 1998).

Some of the factors that need to be remembered in defining goals are the overt and covert behaviors that are associated with goals. What determines these conditions or changes? What is the level of goal behavior or event that could occur? What are the subgoals and the intermediate steps that need to be taken to reach the end results? What is the sequence of action steps that need to be taken in order to reach the goals and what are the obstacles that prevent goal attainment? It is also necessary to identify needed resources and review progress. The interview is used as a tool to help clients in the process of selecting and defining goals.

Selecting a Goal through an Interview

When selecting a goal, the worker's role is to help the client take ownership of the decisions that are made. Examples of some of the questions that clients might be asked to facilitate this process include, "How would you think you could benefit from this work with me?" and "What do you wish to accomplish as part of the therapeutic process?" Self-report questionnaires or inventories, such as the Behavioral Self-Rating Checklist (BSRC) developed by Cautela (1977), can be very helpful if used in conjunction with the interviews during which the responses are discussed. This BSRC includes about seventy-three adaptive overt and covert behaviors that the client needs to learn in order to function more effectively (Fischer & Cautela, 1994).

The practitioner helps the client set goals in positive rather than in negative terms. For example, "I will take an exercise class three times a week, and I will talk to a friend or relative on the phone every day" is preferable to, "I will not be depressed." It is important to help clients picture themselves doing something positive rather than negative. If the client is reluctant to respond or responds negatively, the generalist must pursue by saying, "I realize this is what you do not want to do. What is it that you wish to do?" or "What do you want and can you see, hear, and feel yourself doing it?"

Remember that it is important in the helping process to recognize whose goals the practitioner and client are working on. Often clients say that the worker did not hear them or made plans for them that they did not wish to work on. In such cases, there is often a residue of anger that the client associates with the helping process. Practitioners can prevent this from happening by involving clients in every part of the plan, which brings us to the question of *who owns the goal*. If the worker is overly active, clients minimize their own efforts. Also, clients will find fault with others rather than with themselves.

Who owns the goals is a particularly important consideration with involuntary clients who are not there because of their own needs or wishes or goals but because their functioning is defined as unacceptable by other people: the fifteen-year-old adolescent who does not want to go to school, but is told he has to; the twenty-three-old mother whose child, whom she loves dearly, is taken away because she is a prostitute; and the forty-year-old man whose wife threatens to take the children and leave him unless he stops gambling. Issues of goal setting as mentioned in Chapter 10 on engagement are difficult with involuntary clients.

A large number of clients who see a practitioner individually tend to project what they need to change onto other significant people in their lives; for example, "If Willie will study well in school, I will start to think of losing these extra pounds," or "If Marc is kind and attentive to me, then I will go back and get my degree." There are clients who blame others for their problems. In

such situations, the worker must take the position that the person presenting the problems is the identified client and therefore needs to look at himself or herself in order to find solutions. In the case of families, groups, organizations, and communities, the blame often must be shared and the chief interest of the clients should be bringing about change for the better. In these situations those affected need involvement in the selection of the desired outcomes. In situations where there is more than one client, the worker's role should be to protect the rights of those who are in "low power" positions, including elderly and the very young. Also, whoever has responsibility or control over change must be taken into consideration.

Eighty-year-old Jaclynn is receiving help along with her sixty-year-old daughter, who has a family of her own. The daughter would like to place Jaclynn in a nursing home because she says that she does not have enough time to cater to her mother as well as her own family. Jaclynn is mentally alert, lives in her own home, and is economically self-sufficient. She does not wish to live in a nursing home. In the interview session, the daughter dominates, verbally pushing Jaclynn into the nursing home. In this case, the responsibility obviously rests with Jaclynn and the generalist needs to help her present her point of view, as well as prevent the daughter from being too intrusive.

In the interview, the practitioner and clients explore the goals. Are they realistic and feasible? Realistic goals correspond to outcomes that are based on realistic expectations rather than unrealistic, irrational, or perfectionist ideas, standards or self-demands (Cormier & Cormier, 1998). Setting goals very high is a cop-out, and a sure prescription for failure. Clients who set goals that are inconsequential often feel "hollow" and experience no sense of victory or accomplishment (Dixon & Glover, 1984). Challenging goals are more helpful than "easy goals," but they must still be attainable (Gold, 1990).

Clients should be helped to understand their intent and to assess the degree to which a goal is attainable. Clients with unrealistically high expectations will need help in setting more limited but achievable goals. Others who are pessimistic may be encouraged with the generalist's support to reach a little higher.

Advantages and Disadvantages of Goals

The generalist should look at goal making with clients from a cost-benefit point of view: how much should the practitioner give versus what is being gained by the client (Dixon & Glover, 1984). The first step after goals have been discussed is to consider together the possible positive and negative effects of goal attainment. Clients eager to get out of a difficult situation, or to take advantage of a new opportunity, may make a decision that will produce major changes in their lives without considering the costs.

Amy wanted to divorce her husband because she had "outgrown" him. However, she had not really thought about the extra responsibility of single parenthood, the economic insecurity, the anxiety, and the loneliness that lay ahead. After several interviews during which the generalist was able to get Amy to consider the possible consequences as well as alternative courses of action, Amy decided to try couples therapy. When her husband refused, she decided to go ahead with her original plans, but with full awareness of the risks she would be taking.

Goals that are selected by clients with thought and care are more likely to result in positive outcomes. In identifying positives and negatives, the worker should also try to help the client consider both short-term and long-term consequences of the decisions. However, it is important to remember that the decision belongs to the client who ultimately will have to live with results that are not totally predictable.

If there are any major reservations after the strong and weak points of the goals have been discussed, the worker should make the final point that he or she will continue to be part of the helping process until the client can attain the goals. It is essential to add that all important decisions involve uncertainty; that is why they are difficult. That is also why it is essential that the client *own* the decision.

The generalist can summarize the goals that have been discussed with the client in the following manner: "Now that you and I have discussed all the possible advantages and disadvantages and, as you indicated, the positives definitely outweigh the negatives, we need to move toward attaining these goals." Once a decision has been made, clients may be able to proceed on their own. Clients are the primary agents in choosing goals, but while working on the selected goals, circumstances may change and it may become necessary for the worker and the client to reevaluate the goals.

Defining Goals Related to Behaviors

The term *goal* has been used in two different ways throughout this chapter. One definition involves the treatment goals that give focus and direction to a social work intervention plan. The other involves client life goals, which are broader and more encompassing.

In the helping process, clients usually select more than one goal. However, according to Resnick (1995), in order to achieve any goal the worker has to see if the goal is being achieved both functionally and realistically. To do so the worker must begin a sequence of activity by defining the goal. Defining goals is overlooked by a number of practitioners. It involves specifying operationally, in behavioral terms, what the client will do as a result of the helping process. Will the client think, feel, and behave differently and how can this be done?

Shaefor, Horesji, and Horesji (1997) indicate that most clients have multiple problems. Both research and practice wisdom reveal that in order to be effective, the helping process should concentrate on available time and energy and on just one, two, or three problems. If priorities are not clear, then no clear focus has been established. In such a situation the helping effort flounders and ends in frustration for both the client and the worker. From a task-oriented approach to social work practice Epstein (1988) provided guidance with regard to how the worker and client can set priorities among the client's many problems:

1. List problems that the client wants to see changed as presented by the client.

The Chin Mein family who came to the United States as "boat people" from Vietnam are directed to a shelter for help. They do not have any money and are obviously hungry. They speak very little English and are frightened and overwhelmed. Of the four children in the family, three are ill and they are all poorly clothed for winter. The family indicates that they need help in every area in their life.

2. All defined problems should be listed followed by the worker's recommendations if any.

The worker's recommendation is to work on something tangible and feasible that will give them immediate relief and hope.

3. In order to understand the combination of interrelationships and overlap, the many problems of the client have to be identified.

The unmet needs of the family include food, clothing, medical attention, and financial help until they get themselves on their feet with a job, as well as help in learning English and dealing with culture shock.

4. All the problems have to be reviewed and the client has to identify the two or three of highest priority.

The client presents food, medical attention, and clothes as immediate problems.

5. The generalist offers his or her opinion about which problem has the highest priority.

Later, the worker agrees with the client's priorities: food, clothing, and medical attention.

6. The worker and the client discuss each problem and decide its relative importance by considering the following:

Which problems tend to weigh most heavily on the clients?

If not taken care of, which problems would have the most adverse affect on the clients?

If taken care of, which problems would have the most positive effects on the clients?

Which problems are of greatest interest and relevance to clients?

Which of the problems could be changed with a minimum or moderate investment of time, effort, and resources?

Which problems are essentially unchangeable and would demand an extraordinary amount of time, energy, and effort to effect change?

It was obvious in the given case, that the emergency problems presented by the clients had the highest priority. The next step would include engaging the Chin Mein family in an assessment of the total situation, then planning a program of help and self-help. One high priority would probably be to help the father get a job to support the family, which would begin after his skills are discussed. Learning to speak perfect English may not need immediate attention but could become a long-term goal, if the family so chooses.

7. After answering these six questions, the three problems designated as having the highest priority are selected. Three are chosen because both experience and research suggest that it is usually counterproductive to try to address more than three problems at one time. Task-oriented practitioners have termed this principle "the rule of three."

The worker has to remember that the client's problems and concerns will almost always affect or involve significant others in their lives including spouse, children, parents, close friends, and employers. Usually, these people are either a part of the problem or a part of a solution and they should be considered in the intervention planning. By participating in the helping process with the identified client they may either better the change process or, at times, create obstacles and deteriorate the change process.

Bandura, Cioffi, Taylor, and Brouillard (1988) indicate that by focusing on the distant future, it is always easy to put off efforts at change in the present. Bandura (1991) suggests that sequencing goals into smaller goals is more likely to produce results for the following reasons: completion of goals may keep failure experiences at a minimum.

Also, completing smaller goals helps clients maintain their motivation to bring about change. Bandura (1993) also found that when there were progressive subgoals, there was a higher degree of client motivation and the overall outcomes were not difficult to attain. Arranging the ultimate goal into subgoals helped the immediate daily goals.

As Cormier and Cormier (1998) note, after the subgoals are identified, they should be rank ordered in a series of tasks according to complexity and degree of difficulty and immediacy. They suggest using a pyramid to show the series of subgoals, drawing a blank pyramid and writing the different subgoals in terms of priority in each blank space and working at it accordingly. Identified goals are sequenced so that the most important can be handled immediately according to the client's thinking and needs. Identifying and arranging subgoals is important for the client's success at the overall outcome goal.

After these steps have been taken, the worker should identify obstacles that may hinder a client from moving toward a goal. Questions may be raised about the obstacles that may prevent a client from reaching goals. The worker should help the client discuss them and, at the same time, point out the apparent obstacles that the client has overlooked. If there are significant obstacles, the worker should help the client plan counteractions to prevent such obstacles from interfering with the achievement of the goal.

The practitioner asks the overweight client who wishes to lose weight if there are any hindrances in the home that might prevent her from following through on her goals. This question makes her remember that her husband loves cookies and she is tempted to eat them sometimes. Asking her husband to hide the cookies or, better still, asking him to buy and eat them outside the home might be a good prevention method.

STRATEGIES

A strategy is a set of actions designed to achieve a specific goal. Goals are divided into related outcomes or accomplishments and all subgoals also

Figure 12.3   Strategies

have sets of strategies (see Figure 12.3). One of the reasons that clients fail to reach their goals is because they do not explore the different ways by which a goal can be accomplished. When a worker and clients come up with a number of strategies to achieve a goal, it increases the possibility that one of the ways or a combination of several will suit the clients' needs and resources. There are usually many strategies available to clients. Brainstorming (which is also part of assessment) and fantasy can help a client identify different strategies for achieving goals. This has been referred to as "creative problem solving."

Like his father, thirty-year-old Starling has been a construction worker since he was sixteen. His current job is a dead end. He is tired and unmotivated. Starling is not familiar with ways by which people can find new jobs. Recently, Starling has taken to drink for "relief from his boring job." He has gotten into trouble due to his drinking, which has brought him into the helping process. Now Starling and a worker are carefully planning strategies for him to change. What are his resources and what type of home and work environment does he come from? What are his needs as he moves toward accomplishments in his life?

Starling indicates that he would like a desk job. The worker does not limit Starling's options with one or two suggestions, but instead gives him a brief article on career development which includes many different ways of getting a job. Starling reads the article and makes the effort to find a new job. In about two months he has landed a new job and is satisfied. Nevertheless, Starling's drinking, which was his original presenting problem, is still an issue. Starling will not view it as a problem, however, because he holds a job. Using task assignments, the practitioner succeeds in helping Starling work at his problem by encouraging Starling to read material on drinking and asking him to point out ways by which a person could stop drinking. Constant discussions on the subject help Starling to accept reluctantly that he has a problem, and finally join Alcoholics Anonymous.

Planning is the crux of any form of work with clients. Planning sets a tone for the progress in the helping process, and often creates a sense of hope in the clients. Practitioners must recognize that formulating a plan is a step-by-step process for accomplishing goals. Practitioners must also set realistic time frames for each of the steps. This is a necessity. Clients will be likely to do what is expected of them if they know what they are going to do first, and what they are to do second, third, and so on.

Exercises

1. Students can bring in assessments that they have made of a single client, a group, or a family and then plan how they will intervene. The plan should have broad goals as well as small goals, and performance of tasks should be based on how small goals have been set up.

2. A role play may be set up in the classroom for students to enact a family scene such as a single mother with two teenage daughters setting rules about weekend activities and curfew time at night. After the role play, make an assessment and draw up a treatment plan accordingly.

COMMUNITY AND ORGANIZATIONAL PLANNING

Many of the factors that are discussed as part of micro practice are similar to macro practice, though working with communities and organizations involves getting the support of a larger number of people. Goal planning with communities and organizations starts with discussions with community and organization members. After assessing the risks, strengths, weaknesses, and benefits, the generalist works toward pursuing a limited and achievable project. This project may involve the development of a program in a community or a change in agency policy.

Utilizing Ideas

Brainstorming the most important need in a community or organization is an essential aspect of assessment and planning. The ideas that the agency or community members support or have brought to the generalist should be given priority. It is important to remember that just as in working with individuals, families, or groups, the community or agency needs affect the welfare of the people in those settings and their needs should have priority.

Gathering Support

After a need for change has been recognized, planning for change can move forward. One of the most important factors to remember is that generalists in a community or an organization do not have agency or community-based power. Therefore, they need to involve natural leaders and those with relevant influence and power to undertake the planning and decision making and move toward an action plan or intervention.

At times, a community or an organization may not go along with an action plan. If discussions do not help, then the generalist must adhere to the decision of the majority.

There are many issues that need to be settled in an organization where workers are overwhelmed by paperwork. Creating more efficient methods of documentation is crucial for accountability purposes; however, there are some workers who believe that all such work should be done only by the secretarial staff so the generalists can spend more time with clients. Although this is a valid point, evaluation by the workers is necessary in this particular agency situation. The majority agree that confidentiality issues require that they do the paperwork. Some of the staff believe that the agency should set up a different system even though this might sacrifice total confidentiality for the clients. In such a situation the worker should go along with the majority after making efforts to convince the few who oppose it.

We need to remember that productive work with all clients is achieved through effective planning, followed by evaluation of the plan to test its effectiveness.

Chapter summary

Planning can be described as the next stage after assessment, though the stages may overlap. The planning process involves the worker and clients in reviewing the range of possible solutions. There is a shift from problem definition to problem solution as the planning involves the worker, the client, and other significant people in the client's life. A clearly documented plan makes it possible to hold the worker and the agency accountable.

There are five factors that influence planning, including the community where the client lives, the agency sanctioning the plan, the social problems to which a response is required, and *both* the worker and the client. After the worker and client work together in assessment, they reach a contract through a plan of action. The components of a plan consist of goals and objectives, units of attention, and also strategies that include the roles of the worker and client and the tasks that need to be performed.

A plan is developed in a pragmatic manner. In order to reach an outcome goal, there are a number of subgoals or action steps that need to be considered so that the overall goal will not overwhelm the client. There are certain principles that need to

be remembered while working with clients, which vary from being educational and a growth experience for the client to being relevant to the issues under consideration.

Goals and objectives can be classified into long-term and short-term goals. The purpose of goals is to direct our efforts toward results. Before establishing goals, the worker needs to be aware of monitoring procedures including process and outcomes. The unit of attention for planning can be an individual, a group or a family. While planning, the worker must be clear about selecting and defining of goals. After selecting goals, it should be clear that the client owns the goals and the worker should not be overly active in creating them. Also, when selecting goals, the worker and client must look at the advantages and disadvantages of goals and weigh the positive and negative effects of goal attainment. Goals should be defined in specific operational and behavioral terms, so that the client can carry them out. The worker and client must set priorities for working on goals. Obstacles have to be identified so that, if need be, the worker and client can plan counteractions so that the obstacles do not prevent the achievement of goals. Resources should be identified and strategies created. Strategies comprise a set of actions designed to achieve specific goals. It is best to formulate a step-by-step plan, which serves as a guide even if all the steps are not carried out.

While developing a plan for working with a client, the social worker has to keep a number of factors in mind. They should plan with clients to choose interventions that will be cost-effective; they should do everything possible not to arouse excessive anxiety, resistance, or retaliation; and they should try to produce observable, helping consequences. This is a difficult set of criteria but an ideal toward which practitioners should strive.

13

Intervention

Intervention is the fourth phase in the helping process. It is in this phase that the worker begins to implement the plan of action for helping a client; though in some case situations, intervention takes place as the generalist begins the work, for instance, being supportive of a client who has just been fired without any earlier warnings or complaints. In this phase the generalist and clients work together toward implementing goals that have been reached through the assessment and planning process.

THE CONCEPT OF INTERVENTION ROLES AND TECHNIQUES

Siporin (1975, 1985) describes intervention as the application of a repertoire of methods and processes of differential, influential, and planned actions that are taken by a social worker and clients in order to reach their selected goals. Intervention is an active, influential, effort by both client and generalist that is needed to provide a combination of resources and services both physical and mental, as a direct participation in the client's situation. Barker (1995) describes intervention as an interceding in or coming between groups of people, events, and planning activities, or working with individual internal conflicts. In most cases, the worker and the client can be full partners and engage in activities that would lead to more efficient and effective problem resolution.

Intervention in social work practice is the implementation of a plan, that is, the actual doing or action that happens with clients. Today, *empowerment* is a frequently used term in intervention and is prominent in the social work practice literature (Breton, 1994; Cox & Parsons, 1993; Dubois & Miley, 1996; Gutierrez, 1994; Hartman, 1993; Lee, 1994; Mondros & Wilson, 1994; Parsons, 1991; Simon, 1994). The common theme in the literature is that the helping relationship is a partnership in which generalists and clients work toward emphasizing clients' strengths. There is collaborative power in the process of engaging, assessing, and planning with clients—generalists assist them in mobilizing their power to solve problems. Pinder-hughes (1983) defines power as the ability to exert a beneficial influence on factors that affect one's living; powerlessness is the inability to exert such influence. Dubois and Miley (1996) note that empowerment means exercising psychological control over personal situations as well as influencing the course of events in the sociopolitical arena. Parsons (1991) speaks of empowerment as an active process where the clients participate actively in order to influence outcomes. This includes active participation, control, and influencing institutions and events that affect people's lives. However, there are exceptions to this principle, as when clients lack the competence to make their own decisions.

The goals of direct intervention with clients include giving ongoing support to help maintain a client system as it is carrying out its contracted tasks, and helping a system work toward bringing about change in itself (Dubois & Miley, 1996).

Some generalists minimize their own activities so that they do not interfere with the client's attempts to engage in their own problem-solving activities. There are other generalists who agree that clients must have a chance to engage in problem solving but also believe that passivity is not usually helpful. How active should the worker be while working with clients? Usually, that depends on the clients. The worker has to be active with some clients, whereas with others the worker can be less active. There is no research evidence to show that a high level of worker activity results in more successful outcomes, although it can be said that worker activity does seem to ease the flow of communication between clients and worker and reduce unilateral termination of contact (Garvin & Seabury, 1997).

One of the intervention roles that generalists play is educational, which is done through information and advice giving. Another type of intervention used by generalists involves practical help. In some settings generalists utilize a combination of practical help and some form of counseling. Loewenberg (1983) identifies three types of practical help: concrete but nonmaterial services, nonconvertible things, and convertible things. (See Figure 13.1.)

Figure 13.1 General Types of Intervention

Concrete Services

Concrete but nonmaterial services include all the services that are real but intangible, such as finding jobs, job training, medical services, and other forms of concrete help. Nonconvertible things which are also concrete services include receiving goods in kind, such as food, free housing, and furniture even if it is for a temporary period of time. Concrete and nonconvertible items have to be used as given. Convertible things give clients a wider margin of choice to change or exchange what is given to them. The most common form of convertible item is money, which is exchanged for other items. Food stamps and clothing donations are other convertible items.

Giving concrete help is not a routine decision but is based on the needs of clients. There are agencies that specialize in concrete services combined with other psychological services. However, in every situation the worker makes an assessment of the problem presented and the request made by the client. Even if it is practical help, the worker notes whether the client is motivated to receive it. There is no use in forcing help on a client.

Mrs. Watson, a mentally imbalanced, poor homemaker needs help badly. She has chronic health problems including asthma and arthritis, however, she vociferously objects to anyone coming to her home to give her help. Her first social worker, new and enthusiastic, decided to go to Mrs. Watson's home, anyway. This greatly upset Mrs. Watson, who rightfully felt that her wishes had been violated. After this incident she refused to even talk to social workers on the phone. The message here is that help has to be given in a manner that is appreciated by a client when requested, not forced on a client, however much the worker thinks the client needs it.

In another case, an overzealous worker tried to convince a distraught, nervous, and overwhelmed mother to keep her child at home, when realistically the mother needed the child placed temporarily in foster care. Unless appropriate help is given, there can be no contribution to real problem solving. At times, a person may need both concrete and other forms of help. For instance, if it is found that a client, Erik, loses his jobs easily because he is never punctual to work, the worker not only has to work at helping Erik find a job but, more importantly, to find out why he is late to work and how this could be remedied.

Although the notion of concrete help may appear simple, in reality it requires as much thought as the selection of any other intervention activity. Attention must be given to psychological needs as well as service needs. Practitioners need to remember that practical help is only one form of helping, and a dominating worker must not take away the client's responsibility for solving the problem. For example, Lucy became a welfare recipient after her job search took her nowhere. She is a proud but desperate single parent who needs to find a job. With such clients there must be a receptive focus on job placement as well as building the self-esteem of the client who may need some "hand holding" until the client becomes fairly self-sufficient and financially independent. Although concrete help may be provided, the ultimate goal of any form of helping process is to enable clients to become self-sufficient and assume greater control over significant aspects of their life.

INFORMATION, ADVICE, AND DIRECTION GIVING

Clients' needs vary from person to person. Some clients need information before they make a

choice about the kind of service they require. Others may need advice, and still others may need to have decisions made for them. Although practitioners generally view advice giving as compromising the client's self-determination capabilities, it is generally not true. There is research evidence to show that some client systems not only desire advice, but benefit from it (Davis, 1975; Middleman & Wood, 1990). For instance, Asian American clients who come to see helpers are seeking clear directions and advice (Uba, 1994). The whole process of helping is intended to strengthen and empower clients to cope and adapt to their lifestyles.

As Loewenberg (1983) indicates, in information giving the worker offers another person tools for making a decision about any issue the client wishes to deal with. Moreover, information is given without any attempt to influence the outcome of the decision-making process. On the other hand, when a worker is giving advice there is an attempt to influence the decision making, though the actual decision is left to the client. Direction implies that a decision is being made by the generalist or someone else because the client is thought to be incapable of making an appropriate decision. This may happen in crisis situations, for example, with a client who is in shock and not able to make decisions. The generalist may also assume a decision-making role in work with young children and the mentally disabled who are not able to make decisions on their own. There are other situations in which the social worker represents legal authority.

Quite often, giving information, advice, and even directions are intertwined, because clients may need more information before they can make informed decisions. This aspect of intervention is, at times, underestimated by social workers.

Information should be provided in a logical, well-organized, step-by-step fashion. If it is provided haphazardly, clients can become confused. Giving clients time to think about what has been said and inviting them to ask questions to clarify any uncertainty is an effective way of working with clients. It is best not to assume that the client understands everything you have presented. It is important to look for nonverbal signs of understanding, particularly with clients who are under a great deal of stress. For clarification, ask the client to repeat all the key points you have made. When giving complicated information and directions, write them down. Write down names, addresses, and phone numbers that are needed by clients. When clients receive information personally from social workers they tend to be more satisfied with the intervention efforts and the outcome is also more successful than when clients only receive written information (Davis, 1975; Gambrill, 1983; Fisher & Ury, 1983; Locke, Garrison, & Winship, 1998).

How do you feel when someone gives you advice? Do you like it or not? Remember that people do not usually follow advice, even if they originally sought it. Only on rare occasions do people follow advice that is given to them, even when this advice comes from trusted people whom they have known for a long time.

It is best not to give advice unless a client asks for opinions and suggestions. Generalists must remember that they are not experts on everything. We should never give advice about a topic that is outside of our own training and expertise, except to recommend seeking appropriate expert outside help, if necessary. There are exceptional situations in which you would certainly want to offer advice: for example, advising pregnant teenagers to get medical care or a victim of spousal abuse to see a lawyer.

When giving advice it is best to phrase it as "this is what others have done" or "this is what I would have done." Again there are exceptions; for example, advice should be clear and strongly worded in certain situations. ("Mrs. F., I think you are making a big mistake in letting your twelve-year-old son sleep with you, every night"). The issue of legality can also come up as when clients ask if they should get a divorce or quit a job. In such situations, it is best not to give any advice, because this is not the role you play in their lives and also because you would not want to be held accountable for the consequences of the decision.

We should also be aware of manipulative clients who may use you for their own survival. Such clients can very easily turn the tables on you: "I took your advice and it did not work. It's all your fault that I am divorced now." Such clients may become dependent upon you when it suits them but if matters do not go the way they want, they will not take the responsibility for decisions but blame you (Shaefor, Horesji, & Horesji, 2000).

Giving too much advice can turn off a client; at other times, clients become too dependent and expect everything to be decided by the generalist. Information, advice, and direction should never take the place of client activity and responsibility. The goal must always be to strengthen the client's social functioning, coping behaviors, and decision-making capacities. Asking questions that cause clients to think through a problem or decision is more effective than giving advice because clients are more likely to take "ownership" of the decision or conclusion. For example, when Dottie talked determinedly about leaving her husband, the worker's advice came in the form of questions: Did she think couple counseling might be useful in working out her problems? When she remained firm about leaving her husband, the worker asked Dottie to think about the options open to her, keeping in mind the reality of three young children and the necessity of finding a job. These questions, although not giving advice directly, were aimed at helping Dottie address her issues in the given areas.

Taking an authoritative or directive role is generally frowned on as a violation of a client's right to self-determination. However, there are situations in which this can be a useful intervention strategy. For example, when working with members of a multiproblem family who lack skills in child rearing and homemaking, the practitioner can give direction and advice and may actually model appropriate behavior in the home environment.

Loewenberg (1983) indicates that the likelihood of directions or advice being followed is greater when: (1) the worker indicates clearly and specifically the type of behavior expected from clients; (2) the worker elicits a verbal commitment that clients intend to comply with the given directions; (3) the worker provides training in the expected behavior through modeling, role playing, or such similar techniques; (4) the worker provides or arranges for someone to provide support and recognition when clients comply with directions; and (5) the client also knows that positive consequences such as rewards or recognition will result from following the directions that have been given.

There is a common belief that advice and direction are more appropriate for lower-income clients than for middle-class clients. Maluccio (1979) and McClam and Woodside (1994) indicate, however, that such a view is oversimplistic and that advice and directions are activities that are equally important and appropriate for different clients from various socioeconomic levels. This depends on the problem situation, the support networks available, and the desires of the client.

ENCOURAGEMENT, REASSURANCE, AND UNIVERSALIZATION

In order to enhance the problem-solving capabilities of the client, the worker must use the interrelated techniques of encouragement, reassurance, and universalization which are applied in every social work practice setting. Client encouragement usually takes the form of supportive statements such as expressions of praise and approval of attitudes, behavior, and feelings. It is best to recognize successes in the client's life, however small, and acknowledge and encourage them. For instance, a worker could tell a client, "You are so neatly dressed; now you can go to any job interview," "Your homework is very well done, you are capable of handling this kind of responsibility and I am proud of you." Instead of making vague statements such as like "you are great," it is best that the worker relate the remarks to specific behavior patterns or changes.

Reassurance helps clients find confidence in their own actions. However, reassurance must be used cautiously. Hollis and Woods (1981) indicate that reassurance should be used with discrimination and delicacy. When reassurance is overused, the worker may either convey that he or she is uncomfortable or is not able to fully comprehend the reasons for guilt or anxiety, or is deficient in terms of moral standards and is not a person whose judgement matters.

Universalization is a form of reassurance that consists of statements that explain to the client his or her thoughts, feelings, or behaviors. For instance, when a client feels guilty about leaving an elderly parent who is suffering from Alzheimer's disease in a nursing home, the worker supports the client by saying, "There are other people who have similar feelings to those you are talking about. It is very common." Universalization is used to counteract the client's feelings about being different, deviant, and separate from others. Here again, the worker's statements should be specific and realistic to be accepted by the client.

COGNITIVELY FOCUSED INTERVENTIONS

Besides basic information and advice giving, there are other cognitively focused techniques. In this intervention, the worker uses cognitively focused techniques in order to find solutions to a client's problems. The client uses factual information to make appropriate decisions, and also use inductive and deductive thinking processes more effectively.

To help clients the generalist may have to talk to them to obtain relevant factual information about all sorts of factors from child development to community resources. More often than not the clients have the information, but when in stress they cannot see it because they are unable to think clearly about themselves and their situation. In such circumstances the worker's role is to help the client toward developing more effective decision-making and problems-solving skills. When clients are overwhelmed by a mixture of emotions and thoughts, these emotions can prevent effective thinking and planning. In the helping process, the worker helps clients to weigh different facts, re-solve conflicts, deal with their own frustrations, choose an alternative course of action, and cope with various life problems by overcoming their own indecisiveness.

We are well aware that when problems over-whelm clients who have acquired an unproductive and debilitating thought pattern, they should be encouraged to develop a more constructive and ra-tional thinking process through trial and error. Clients may need encouragement in learning to think inductively and creatively. Clients think in-ductively when they generalize from a limited set of observations. In order to foster creative think-ing, a worker has to help clients use a variety of methods, including observation, analysis, conclu-sion, and verification. For example:

What do I observe about this process?

What is the meaning of this information for me, my family, and my friends?

What inferences, suggestions, and conclu-sions can I draw from this process?

How do I try these ideas to see if they are realistic?

There are methods used by practitioners to en-sure openness to new ideas and to gain new per-spectives. Creative problem solving can be encouraged by using brainstorming techniques to generate ideas. The purpose is to ask some open-ended questions that will foster imagination and help create new lines of thought. One way of do-ing this is to ask clients relevant questions such as, "In two years what would you like to be doing? After two or three years how would you look at this problem? In five years where would you like to live?"

Clients should be helped to understand how to resolve problems by using analysis and by view-ing problems from another perspective. This helps them move away from conclusions that are based solely upon deductive thinking. In addition, the practitioner and clients should work together to develop alternative solutions to problems. Clients

can be assisted to integrate this information into meaningful conclusions for themselves.

FEELINGS-ORIENTED INTERVENTIONS

Generalists have to focus on clients' feelings and observe their beliefs, attitudes, and values. Clients have to be helped to develop a better sense of self, a stronger ability to deal with their own emotions, and a sense of improved self-worth, as well as to gain better acceptance and appreciation of others. Encouragement and reassurance are essential in-gredients in working with all types of clients and a crucial part of the whole helping process.

At the beginning of the contract clients should be helped to vent. Ventilation is a process whereby clients are allowed to talk about things that are of concern to them. They examine, discuss, and in-vestigate feelings, thoughts, opinions, and experi-ences. This ventilation aids in making clients psychologically healthier (Okun, 1997). The worker should create an open and accepting ther-apeutic atmosphere in which clients have the free-dom to discuss whatever is bothering them. Later in the contract, the worker may need to downplay ventilation in favor of focused discussion of issues and problems that need to be solved.

Catharsis

Catharsis is an affectively oriented helping strategy that is thought to be a more complex and focused intervention than ventilation. Catharsis is used when clients are not able to express a deeply felt emotion but specify a desire to be freed from this burden. In catharsis, the worker helps clients re-lease pent-up tensions and bring the emotional blockage into the open, thus allowing clients to purge themselves of this restrictive feeling.

Doyle (1992) calls catharsis a cleansing and purging action that results in release of tension and emotional blockage. Catharsis is based on the con-cept that one's emotions can control the way one thinks and acts. Feelings that have not been ex-pressed build up until the resultant pressure or tension causes a person to behave in maladaptive ways (Bohart, 1980). Such pent-up feelings can keep a person from functioning effectively; they also waste a considerable amount of internal energy and often result in avoidance of situations, withdrawal from life, and considerable emotional distance from significant people in the client's life. The unexpressed feelings may be relatively recent, but they are based on traumatic experiences that have occurred a long time in the past. These buried feelings are associated with experiences that have not been expressed but need to be brought out so that built-up tensions can be discharged and the person is restored to more adaptive behavior. The objective of catharsis is to allow clients to vent and experience the release of tension that is blocking their ability to function.

Catharsis encourages the client to relive past grief, fear, shame, anger, and tension (Scheff, 1979). According to Doyle (1992), catharsis takes place in two stages. In the first stage, the client is encouraged to vent by recollecting past experiences. In the second phase, besides helping the release of emotions, the worker focuses on helping the client deal with these emotions.

Twenty-five-year-old Anna got herself into several destructive marital relationships with men. She sought out men who hurt and abused her verbally and, at times, physically. Her third marriage was to such a man, and she had a child with him. The verbal abuse started immediately after the baby was born. Anna confessed that she was always intimidated by men who were like her father: she married them not because she liked them, but because they liked her and she was afraid to say no. She was afraid of confiding in them as she feared that they might control her and that they "always" had more power over her. She distanced herself from the man which, in turn, led to dissatisfaction in the marriage and a great deal of verbal abuse followed by physical abuse. After a number of sessions, Anna remembered herself as a little girl taking a shower with her father. She was in great emotional pain and the worker supported her while she released her emotional blockings. Further work revealed that she had had an incestuous relationship with her father. Her father was an abusive person, and the kind of person to whom she was unconsciously attracted to in her relationships. Understanding the early

childhood sexual and verbal abuse and helping her view her emotional patterns as well as the release of her pent-up anger and hurt about her father, helped Anna regain control of her life. She began to look more constructively at relationships and what *she* wanted out of marriage.

Insight Development and Self-Awareness

Insight is the process of looking inside oneself in order to gain a deeper understanding of oneself. Clients can gain insight in the following three areas: (1) complete knowledge and awareness of themselves, (2) a better understanding of the relationship between themselves and significant people in their lives, and (3) exploration and a better understanding of their own experiences in the world. Insight development and self-awareness employ ventilation as described by Barlow and Durand (1995). The worker provides a warm, open, and facilitative climate for ventilation.

An insight-oriented approach is used with clients who lack self-knowledge and have a subjective view that is incongruent and confused. They may be only vaguely aware or completely unaware of their own lack of self-knowledge. Insight development is also used with clients who function at a fairly high level but need help sorting out the meaning of their own existence, because they may suffer from a painful or traumatic experience.

In this process, the worker helps the client ventilate and uncover answers. With self-understanding, clients eventually move toward developing a deeper productive understanding of themselves. Horowitz (1986) indicates that insight and self-awareness can be fostered by the help of the worker in the following areas:

- Clients are helped to understand their own self-perceptions and how these affect relationships with others
- Clients start to learn how others in their lives feel about them and also how the clients believe they should be treated
- Clients discover the importance of their relationships with significant others
- Clients perceive how their own behaviors affect their personal and social growth

PERFORMANCE AND ACTION-FOCUSED STRATEGIES

These are also called strategies for initiating and sustaining action and there are a number that could be utilized by clients to help them initiate and sustain problem-managing action. Workers need to be aware of and empower clients to use them.

Carkhuff (1985) mentions two types of stages called "check" and "think" steps. Check steps are actually "question steps." In this stage, clients ask themselves questions about the implementation stage, using three types of check steps to do so. Before steps indicate what clients should think about before performing a certain type of behavior. During check steps indicate what the clients should think about while performing the steps, and after indicates what clients should think about upon completion of the step (Auslander & Litwin, 1987). The worker must draw a course of action and set up a list of practical check steps. This technique extends from thinking about the person and the problem to thinking about the field of action.

Louise is a client who has spent a number of years in prison for repeated shoplifting. She also had a problem with alcoholism and wandering behavior. After serving her prison term, Louise was ready to go home; however, she was surprised to find out that her husband had moved to another area and was living with another woman. The children were grown up and on their own and nobody really seemed to appreciate her return. She got in touch with a social worker at an emergency shelter and found out that there were some families willing to take individuals into their homes temporarily.

With the help of the social worker, Louise decides to talk to a couple of families and also a few single individuals about living arrangements. These informal conversations are useful. There is no pressure because no decisions need to be made immediately. This makes Louise feel free but she still wants to put her best foot forward. The worker helps Louise deal with any misgivings by using the following check steps:

- *Before* Louise goes into the interview, these are some of the questions she asks:

  Is it clear in my mind about what I want to say about myself?

  How do I control the feeling that people will reject me even before I get there?

  What can I do if people appear to be putting me down or making me into a "case"?

- *During* the interview, Louise asks herself the following questions:

  To what extent am I being myself rather than some person I think these people would like me to be?

  Am I listening well to these people and trying to understand their point of view?

  How should I handle lack of enthusiasm on their part?

- *After* she returns to the temporary shelter, Louise asks herself:

  If matters do not go smoothly how do I avoid getting depressed?

  Is there any additional information I need to give them?

  Are there any more questions I need to ask of them?

In addition to probing and challenging, Kanfer and Goldstein (1991) formulated six "think rules" that are based on cognitive–behavioral approaches to helping. These rules can be classified as action-oriented and can be part of the helping process.

1. The client has to think in terms of behavior because helping is about performing action.
2. The client has to think in terms of solution because helping is about problem managing
3. The client's thinking has to move toward being positive because action needs should be based on resources and strengths rather than on problems and weaknesses.

4. The client has to think in terms of small steps because action is needed to accomplish small steps and they need to be clear and specific.

5. The worker has to think flexibly as clients adapt their action programs to changing circumstances.

6. The client has to think in terms of the future because helping equips clients to transfer what they have learned from dealing with current problems to future problems.

Action as Intervention

Activity is a way of doing or performing, rather than talking about feelings and ideas. Clients perform different types of activities to work through their life issues, which can vary from developmental tasks, nondevelopmental tasks, and crisis situations. Different types of activities are used to enhance the helping process.

Activity is a powerful means of influencing and bringing about change in systems and persons and the manner in which they function (Johnson, 1995). Clients learn new skills through action, developing social skills and moving toward accomplishments. Action helps people develop competence and better self-esteem. Action can also be used to assess a person's level of competency.

Activity serves many purposes. It enhances physical development, neuromuscular control, and stimulates intellectual growth. Action can also be a means of releasing feelings and emotions, and it teaches patterns of behavior, providing discipline and adding to a person's self-esteem.

While working with clients, it is best to keep in mind some actions that clients need to perform and consciously plan for them. DiClemente, Prochaska, Fairhurst, and Velicer (1991) suggest that the role of the practitioner is to assist an individual, a family, a couple, a group, a community, or an organization to negotiate the process of action and change as efficiently and effectively as possible. Clients who are committed to performing action to bring about change need external confirmation of the plan in order to receive support and gain a

sense of greater self-efficacy. According to Resnick (1980a, 1980b) an action system might involve a planned change process to change a person or an agency policy, or to develop a new program or to institute a project such as setting up training programs in an agency.

Vinter (1967) and Germain and Gitterman (1996) have identified three aspects of activity: (1) the physical surroundings as well as the social objects that are involved in the activity; (2) the behaviors that are necessary to carry out these activities; and (3) what type of behavior can be expected from the client. Before a worker decides to use any particular activity, the worker should consider the different aspects as they relate to a specific activity. Some dimensions that are discussed by Vinter include:

- prescriptiveness as to what the clients can and are expected to do
- the types of rules and other control activity
- the provision the activity leaves for physical activity
- the degree of competency that is required by the people participating in the activity
- the kind of participation and interaction that is required
- the type of rewards that are inherent in the activity.

The activities that are performed should be done for the well-being of the client and not because this is a particular strategy the worker uses for all clients. Moreover, while planning activities, the worker has to keep in mind the client's unique needs and interests, the capacity of the particular client to perform the required activity, and the client's motivation and readiness and ability to perform a particular task. Finally, the ability of the client to support and to accept the activity that is being used must be considered. Activities that are used with clients should be supportive and positive and they should have appropriate limits set.

Amelia, a twelve-year-old girl, was overweight and behaved in childish ways in school. She was referred to a generalist through the school system. The worker found out that Amelia is an only child, abandoned by her father when she was six months of age. She and her mother lived with Amelia's maternal grandmother, who has thoroughly spoiled Amelia. Amelia ate candy for breakfast and would have a temper tantrum if she is told that she could not eat candy. Amelia had become so big and bulky that she refused to bend over to tie her shoelaces; her grandmother and at times her mother tied them for Amelia. In the helping session it was clear that Amelia could get away with anything. At first, her diet requirements were discussed with appropriate referral to a medical doctor. Three weeks after Amelia had lost a few pounds, the worker felt that it was time to work on the task of tying her shoelaces as this was an object of ridicule in the school and, more importantly, a task Amelia needed to learn. After this activity was practiced appropriately once, with her mother assisting and encouraging her daughter, Amelia was given the task assignment of tying her shoelaces. She was asked to tie them every day when she went to school and also to remove the shoes by herself when she was ready for bed. When Amelia returned after a weekend she was fairly proficient in tying her shoelaces, and the worker along with the mother praised Amelia for her accomplishments. Amelia is happy and also eager to take on a new task assignment, as she feels more self-confident.

Action as Mediation

Mediation strategy was developed with small groups but it can be used effectively with individuals as well as families, communities, and organizations. In mediation the generalist does not create a new linkage but improves established connections and relationships that the clients have with resources in their environment. There are two important factors with reference to mediation:

1. The mediators must not appear to be partisan in any conflict that may emerge. Mediators who are successful must be neutral or at least appear to be neutral to all parties involved (Gallant, 1982).
2. Besides being seen as neutral, the mediators must be recognized as legitimate by all parties (Garvin & Seabury, 1997).

Workers who use the mediation while working with involuntary clients have to find common ground between the agency and the client in order to work together with both the parties. This involves helping the clients find individual purposes for the use of social services that are acceptable to both the clients and the worker (Albert, 1994). For example, the involuntary clients who are inmates in a prison system wish to work as a group on their plans for discharge, whereas the prison officials are concerned about the behavior of inmates in the institution. The worker seeks to help the officials and the inmates negotiate a common ground for the content and purposes of the group.

The purpose of mediation is for the worker to be an advocate. The mediator does *not* challenge one system or the other, but rather helps the two systems reach out to each other and pursue a common goal. The generalist functions as a helper so that each of the two systems accomplish the tasks necessary but does not do the work to accomplish the goals.

First, the worker has to "tune in" and be ready to enter the process of transaction in the situation. Then, the worker should help various people involved in the situation reach out to one another and identify what needs to be done. The result is often that contracts are worked through. Discussion of the work that needs to be done follows. Also there are transitions and endings.

Mediation activities can be used to resolve conflicts between people, between agencies, and between minority and majority groups and also neighborhood groups. Practitioners usually maintain a liaison with the main organizations in order to facilitate mutual awareness of changes in policies and procedures which would, in turn, affect the ongoing relationships and availability of resources (Hepworth & Larsen, 1990). Historically, the term *mediation* has been a process through which individuals and their societies reach out to each other through a mutual desire for self-fulfillment. Later it was described as a means of helping people negotiate in difficult environments (Schwartz, 1961). Both Schwartz (1977) and Shulman (1999) have written exclusively about the type of strategy and action that is necessary with clients. Shulman has identified about three blocks (difficulties) in the interaction of individuals with environmental systems.

1. There is a complexity in the system that includes the functioning of institutions and the bureaucracy which has made it more difficult for individuals to understand how to approach these different systems and also how to use the resources that they provide. These complex systems (e.g., the welfare system) are often impersonal and overwhelm the clients.

2. The self-interest of the system is often in conflict with the interest of others or of the larger system to which they belong. When there is a dominant self-interest, it is necessary to make the system aware of the interdependence and thus of the mutual interest that is necessary for the functioning of the larger system. For example, the individual practitioners in an multipurpose agency are making more money than the other systems particularly the one set up to help HIV and AIDS victims. There is a special effort made by administrators to share the money funding among all the different activities performed by the multipurpose agency.

3. There is a communication problem in terms of the inability of systems to work together due to lack of communication or inaccurate communication and thus there are misconceptions about each other. This is true of multipurpose agencies where people work in departments and do little together as a whole. It is the responsibility of the agency administrator to arrange joint meetings with all the different divisions so that there is a sense of give-and-take.

ENVIRONMENTAL MODIFICATION

This is a strategy that brings about change in the environment of clients to enhance their social functioning. Environmental modification recognizes the effect of forces outside the individual and strives to modify these effects through techniques such as providing or locating specific resources or interpreting the client's needs to others through advocacy (Barker, 1995). There are three factors that are considered to be appropriate targets for change: space, time, and relationships.

Environmental modification is a social work strategy dating from the time of Mary Richmond, the pioneer social worker. This term has been used in different ways by different thinkers. Hollis (1979) calls it environmental treatment, and Siporin (1975) describes it as "situational intervention where actions are taken in order to alter cultural, structural and functional patterns." Siporin (1980) also indicates that environment has a profound effect on the behavior, feelings, and self-images of people who use a particular setting. When a major cause for a client's discomfort is described as a reaction to the environment in which the person is living, the generalist has to help modify the pressure or deficiency directly in locating another apartment, changing a school setting, a job, or even medical services. At times, there may be people who create difficulties for the client that can be altered through clinical contact. This is called environmental intervention and is psychological in nature (Woods & Hollis, 1990). Some people may function better due to an external change that produces permanent shifts in the inner balance.

Eight-year-old Jon was having trouble in school. Every day there was a note from the teacher saying he was not doing his homework well or not paying attention and laughing loudly in the classroom. This concerned Jon's mother because she saw her son as reasonable and well-behaved. A visit by the school social worker revealed that Jon's teacher was turned off by him. After a brief conversation the worker found out that the teacher had had a student resembling Jon in an earlier class and attributed a number of his qualities to Jon. The worker tried to work through the situation tactfully, but was unsuccessful. Though objective with other children, the teacher was caught in her own needs and problems which turned into dislike and disapproval of Jon. She was upset and the worker could not work with her meaningfully. The worker decided that Jon had to be moved to another school setting so that he did not have someone constantly pointing a finger at him. The change in the school setting was good for Jon. His new teacher seemed to like him, he got along well with other children, and even put in extra effort to do better in his homework. Thus the creative change in Jon's environment was for the better and conducive to his growth.

When the environment of a person is modified it leads to change, often physical and psychological. The worker may concentrate on the individual system or other systems such as family, school, or office setting that seem most accessible to change and not necessarily the most dysfunctional ones. There is a great degree of preparation involving both the resources and the client, and the assessment of the "fit" between them. This information is required before the current difficulties can be resolved, and the client should be involved in the decision-making process as fully as possible.

OTHER INTERVENTION TECHNIQUES

There are a number of techniques that are used to bring about changes in client's lives.

Behavioral Rehearsal

This is a technique that is drawn from behavioral modification, which teaches clients how to handle a specific interpersonal exchange for which they are unprepared. The client rehearses or practices a specific behavior that would be performed in a future situation. When a person is allowed to rehearse a type of behavior, it reduces the anxiety and also builds the client's self-confidence in handling a situation. Behavior rehearsal is a form of role playing that makes use of coaching and modeling.

Behavior rehearsal is used with clients during the one-on-one interview, however, in a family or a group session the steps are basically the same (Garvin, 1987, 1997). Clients identify their prob-

lem or concern and then describe and demonstrate how they will behave in a given situation. The worker makes further suggestions about how a particular situation could be handled.

Usually role plays are used to demonstrate behavioral changes suggested by the worker and verbally agreed to by clients. Clients enact the behavior if they feel ready and understand the changes being suggested. When clients are satisfied in terms of how they ought to behave and enact it, then the behavior performance is satisfactory. Homework outside the session can also be utilized to further clients' learning of new behavior.

One of the serious drawbacks of behavior rehearsal is that the client may successfully learn what to do in front of the worker but may not be able to carry through in a real-life situation.

In a group meeting, women are learning self-assertiveness skills. Latisha brings up the issue of being passive when she is yelled at unnecessarily by her mother and her boyfriend. The group members and the generalist work on using I statements to be assertive. Latisha role-plays well in the group but returns the next session to relate that she was not assertive with her mother or her boyfriend. The group members suggest practicing before the mirror at home and Latisha agrees.

Self-Contracts and Action

Clients can benefit by making contracts with themselves to initiate and sustain problem-managing action. Contracts specify what clients have to do in order to receive rewards for success and sanctions for failures (Cormier & Cormier, 1998; Benson & Stuart, 1992; McConnaughy, Prochaska, & Velicer, 1983). Self-contracts can help in the most difficult situations of action programs, because they focus on clients' energies. Self-contracting is a commitment to oneself, which is an act of empowerment. There is also a degree of self-control that is involved in the self-contracting. When a worker helps clients draw up a contract, a stipulation should be made stating when the contract will be reviewed.

Emily and Andre have a number of problems in their marriage. They care minimally about housework and each one does his or her own thing. Housework is nobody's business in the family. The dishes are unwashed. Meals are irregular and cooked impulsively. The couple spends hardly any time with each other. In many ways, they are punishing each other, and their chaotic behavior at home is not at all helpful. An initial contract is made with Emily and Andre by the generalist in which each one will assume the housework chores on alternate weeks. Emily is asked to keep the house clean and orderly for a week and Andre is asked to stick to a schedule so that he can be home at a particular time and prepare dinner every day for a week. He has to take care of his commitments at work but also find time to be at home with Emily. The following week they have to alternate their roles. Though these appear to be individual contracts they reduce the chaos in the family. Emily and Andre agree to carry out the contract regardless of what the other does. However, after a period of one month there is less chaos at home and more togetherness between the couple.

Though following self-contracts is useful, workers and clients should not assume that simply fulfilling these contracts guarantees all the problems of the relationship will be solved. What the worker is doing is helping to create some degree of order in the clients' lives, as well as an atmosphere conducive to sorting out problems.

Social Support

When clients ask for help they are relieved, but at the same time they are afraid of the unknown. While the helping process requires them to adhere to agency rules, they also need social supports. When the client works with a generalist who is supportive and caring, problem solving becomes easier. Working through problems is a challenge but with support they can set goals and move to action (Maguire, 1991; Whittaker & Tracy, 1991; Wills, 1985; Germain & Gitterman, 1996).

Clients develop social supports that can be both positive and negative. Social relationships are comforting and helpful but can also be stressful (Fleming, Baum, & Singer, 1985). When there is too little support, the relationship can become alienating. Too much support can be suffocating; at the same time, this could relieve clients of their own burdens of self-responsibility, which is not useful.

People need different kinds of support systems. Some people need very active support systems, while others need a support system that does not overwhelm them. For example, a woman in an abusive relationship needs an active support. On the other hand, a person who is introverted and has problems in the workplace would need a support system that does not make excessive demands. Social support does not mean an admission of guilt, defeat, or abdication; rather such support systems may be a necessity in a highly fragmented society (Wall, Kleckner, Amendt, & Bryant, 1989), and a positive strategy in the helping process.

Feedback

According to Kirschenbaum (1985) and Egan (1990), feedback is an important part of intervention. The purpose of feedback is not to pass judgment on the manner in which clients are performing, but rather to provide guidance, support, and challenge. At times, the worker has to confirm what the clients are doing, affirming that they are on the right track and moving successfully through the steps of an action program toward a goal.

Feedback can be negative or positive. Negative feedback is judgmental, vague, and not at all helpful. Positive feedback helps clients make corrections and move forward.

CLIENT: I am not able to control myself. I realize too much makeup makes me look unprofessional. I did very well in the early part of the week, but by midweek I was not feeling so good about myself and I overdid it again and I could tell, because I saw people staring at me. Yet I feel I should congratulate myself.

WORKER: I feel that you are not motivated enough to give up this bad habit of yours. I think we, together, had originally worked out a good plan for you.

CLIENT: I know it was a good plan. What's wrong with me? Maybe I am lying to myself, perhaps I do not wish to look decent!

Another worker deals with the situation differently and gives the client a different kind of a feedback. In this scenario, the worker is offering some confirming and correcting feedback without adopting a judgmental tone.

CLIENT: I am not able to control myself. I realize too much *makeup* makes me look unprofessional. I did very well in the early part of the week, but by midweek I was not feeling so good about myself and I overdid it again and I could tell, because some people were staring at me. Yet I feel I should congratulate myself.

WORKER: Tell me specifically what happened, in concrete terms.

At this point the client describes specifically what she did and did not do the previous week.

WORKER: Okay. That's pretty clear. Tell me what you think really went wrong?

CLIENT: I guess I just blew it. I have so much makeup on top of my dresser that I picked it up and used it when I was not feeling good about myself.

WORKER: When you followed the plan about not using makeup, I guess you felt good about yourself. It looks like you were motivated and the incentives were there. First, you forgot to put up immediate rewards for keeping your makeup plan. Second, probably you are right in thinking that you can do something about controlling your impulses. You would not have put on too much makeup if you had not lingered near your dresser, and opened up the drawers to look at the extra makeup you have. Perhaps as we discussed before, you just need to get rid of it once and for all. How can you put what you have learned into practice this coming week?

All clients need feedback. Sometimes this will come from the worker, and at other times from friends and family. Feedback is necessary and clients need to ask for it without waiting for others to offer it. It is also useful for clients to give feedback to themselves.

Finally, all helper feedback should incorporate the principles of effective feedback (Egan, 1994) which include:

Feedback should be confirmatory, corrective, and motivating, and to the point.

Feedback should deal with behaviors, rather than elusive personality characteristics.

If the feedback to be given is not positive, it is the worker's role to give it constructively and in a moderate manner.

The client should be invited not only to comment on the feedback but also to expand on it.

When feedback is corrective, clients should be helped to discover alternative ways of behaving.

The manner in which feedback is given is more important and should be experienced as rewarding when it is done in the proper spirit. If feedback is given constructively, the worker can correct the clients and provide them with information they need to get back on course, if they have strayed.

Finally, even if the clients are motivated, adequate and inadequate implementation is discussed and suggestions made about improving performance. Feedback is an integral part of the helping process and should be used at appropriate times.

Role Reversal

This technique is usually used with two clients in a family or group situation where one client wishes to understand the feelings and behavior of a significant person in his or her life. The focus is on interpersonal conflict, with the purpose of helping a person understand how another feels about or perceives a situation.

In family sessions, role reversal is done when there is an impasse and family members are stuck on a particular perception (Shaefor, Horejsi, & Horejsi, 2000). Impasse is the family members' conviction that their present solution is the best available and their insistence on continuing the pattern (Whitaker & Keith, 1981).

The technique of role reversal is described in the following example from Brilhart & Galanes (1995). During a role reversal, the client can take on the role of another person (for instance, Jeffrey) and present the viewpoint of that person (Jeffrey) as if the client were he. Also, in order to use role reversal, the helper asks the client to present the position and attitudes of that person whom he/she would like to role-play. Once the client (Sheila) has identified the person, Sheila has to represent the attitudes and positions as if Sheila were the person. At times, it is helpful for Sheila to switch back and forth between her position and the viewpoint and position of another important person in her life. In such a case, having Sheila switch chairs as she switches viewpoints helps Sheila and others in their process of understanding differences. Sometimes it is possible to have the worker play the role of the other person and then periodically have the client and the other role player switch roles. Also, the person who is being represented in the role play (if present) should be asked to observe to see if the roles are being played accurately.

The worker may initiate the role reversal by saying something like "Would you mind reversing roles in order to see how the other person feels? Let us switch chairs and also try to assume the posture of the role you are taking." For example, a father and son have a conflicting relationship. The father will not make eye contact with his son, which makes the son feel unwanted, and inferior in his father's presence. In the role reversal situation, the son and father change chairs. The son looks at his father and says, "Tom, you are stupid, you will never make it in life." The exchanging of chairs has already made the father uncomfortable and his son's statements surprise the father, who is not aware of how he is perceived by his son. After a few minutes of this type of role reversal, the players are asked to return to their own seats and discuss their own experiences. The worker can preface this by saying that while sitting in a particular chair they are themselves and when sitting in the other person's chair, they become that person.

Role reversal provides insight into communication and relationship patterns among family members and an opportunity to correct their behaviors and communication patterns.

Managing Self-Talk

Self-talk refers to messages that we give ourselves. All of us are influenced by our own interpretation of reality, which may or may not conform to the objective reality. As Holmbeck-Grayson and Lavigne (1992) and Woltersdorf (1992) indicate, many clients need to learn to manage emotional reactions by modifying distorted interpretations of reality.

Self-talk is a cognitive approach of helping that evokes feelings, which in turn give rise to behaviors. For instance, if you think you are treated badly, if you feel angry, or if you think you are in danger, then you may become anxious.

Research has shown that people with emotional disorders systematically distort their experiences and the type and direction of distortion determines the nature of the emotional disorder (Emery, 1981). Utilizing the cognitive theory, Thyer & Wodarski (1998) have identified four types of distortions:

1. *Arbitrary inference* is the process of drawing a conclusion when evidence is lacking or is contrary to the conclusion.
2. *Overgeneralization* is the process of making an unjustified generalization on the basis of a single incident.

3. *Magnification* is the propensity to exaggerate the meaning and significance of a particular event.
4. *Cognitive deficiency* is the disregard of an important aspect of a life situation.

People who have dysfunctional emotional reactions and problem behaviors do so as the result of distorted, unclear thinking as well as faulty beliefs about how they should behave. McMullin (1986) indicates the following sample distortions:

"Driving over a bridge is not safe, it may hurt me, I should never do it."

"I must fit into everyone's values, otherwise I will be totally alone and rejected by everyone."

"If I learn to be assertive then people will see me as arrogant and egotistical." (pp. 55–56)

As Weiner (1990) indicates, changes may be brought about by using a five-step approach to help modify a client's distorted self-talk.

1. Clients should identify their feelings and thinking to the point at which they are talking.
2. Clients should examine their own self-talk and say the words out loud. They should pay attention to extremes of thinking, and look at words such as *never, can't, always, everybody, completely,* and so on (e.g., "I can't make it").
3. Clients should examine the objective reality of their own situation. Once the facts and distortions have been identified, clients should be helped to relax, take deep breaths, and repeat each fact out loud at least three times (e.g., "I have a great job and I have a great future").
4. When clients start to emphasize the facts and avoid using inaccurate words, they begin to feel differently and things do not seem as bad as they did before.
5. The worker must keep the facts of the situation clearly in mind, and consider what he or she can do to help clients.

The following is a dialogue between a generalist and a client who had been in the helping process for six months. They have both been working on helping the client develop better self-esteem. This dialogue occurred on one of the days when the client felt she had overeaten.

SABRINA: I cannot believe I could be so stupid. I ate a whole pint of ice cream this morning and I have blown it. I am never going to lose weight. I will always look fat and ugly. I am a complete failure. I don't deserve to be married to my handsome husband, who would never do anything as crazy as this.

WORKER: Just a minute. That is a lot that you have you said. You are putting yourself down. Remember, you were not going to do that. Let's do something different here. Why don't you tell me what you are feeling and thinking right now.

SABRINA: I was tired and angry after I had an argument with my husband and I wanted to get back at him and did so by eating. Now I know I will never lose all this weight and he is going to leave me, maybe. I hate myself.

WORKER: Sabrina, look at yourself and think about your self-talk. You are putting yourself down. Try to recognize what you are saying to yourself. Also notice your extreme language. Let's look at reality. It's not unusual for people to eat when they are upset.

SABRINA: I know, but how could I be so stupid? I was just beginning to lose some weight.

WORKER: Also, you know your husband is not going to leave you because you blew it and ate ice cream in the morning.

SABRINA: No, he would not leave me, but I am so disappointed with myself.

WORKER: Well, your eating ice cream this morning is not the end of the world.

SABRINA: I realize I am overreacting. But I do not know how to stop these thoughts and actions.

WORKER (HANDING A WRITTEN STATEMENT TO SABRINA): "I would like you to repeat aloud after me, 'The reality of my situation is as such: I flunked once in keeping up my diet these past months. I am feeling unhappy. I will try again and I will not eat ice cream in the mornings. My marriage will not break because of this incident. I will begin to be careful about food again. My life is not over. I am going to be a beautiful person inside and out, to the best of my ability.' "

[SABRINA REPEATS THE SAME.]

WORKER: How do you feel after your self-talk?

SABRINA: I guess it is not as bad as I thought it was. I also feel less upset than ever before.

WORKER: Our emotions arise from what we tell ourselves about our experiences. If you start talking to yourself in a negative way, then your feelings will start to get out of control. Your situation is not as bad as it appears to be. You can use this technique when you do anything "wrong," as you see, because you know your situation is not as bad as it seemed when you were telling yourself all those awful things. But you are going to try not to overdo the eating when you are frustrated. Now let's talk more about it.

The Empty Chair

The empty chair technique is also called the double-chair technique and is a part of family therapy (Minuchin & Fishman, 1981; Corey, 1995; Sherman & Fredman, 1986), but it is used in many situations, without any particular reference to specific modality. This technique deals with issues that need to be clarified in interpersonal and intrapersonal conflicts. Using the empty chair technique, clients view conflicts from a different angle and gain insight into why they are feeling and behaving in a particular manner.

The worker uses this technique when the client has a specific problem and/or conflict that needs to be explored, but the person with whom the client needs to speak is not available, because that person lives far away or is dead or is not willing to participate in the helping process. The worker pulls up a chair and places it in front of the client. The chair symbolically becomes the person or situational incident that troubles the client, the person with whom there is either a conflict or connectedness due to loyalty or guilt. The client is asked to speak to the chair talking about his or her own perceptions and feelings. Later the client is asked to sit in the chair and play the role of the other person. The client can carry on a dialogue by moving back and forth between the empty chair and his or her own chair, asking questions, answering them, and attempting to resolve the issues.

Molly, a fifty-year-old widow, prepares elaborate foods that her husband used to like and all her children have to eat them. Though he has been dead for over ten years, Molly acts and behaves as though her husband was alive. If her children do anything that she disapproves of, she says that their father would not approve of their behavior. Now that the children are grown, the youngest being an adolescent, Molly suddenly feels alone and lost. She is receiving clinical help because the children are leaving her. She is unhappy that her children do not visit her because they do not like all the "rules her husband made" for them.

In the helping process, the empty chair represents the husband and Molly talked to him throughout the session. In her voice there was frustration and anger. When Molly played the role of her husband from the empty chair, said that the children had to be in bed by 10:00 PM, that they should help their mother wash the dishes, and so forth. At last, he (Molly) spoke asking what Molly would do without him and all that he was doing for the family. This was said jovially but when Molly went back and sat on her own chair, her voice was suddenly angry and bitter. She responded with a sarcastic, "of course, dear." Exploration revealed that Molly felt cheated when her husband died suddenly of a heart attack. There had been absolutely no warning and she felt betrayed and alone. Then she admitted the truth: She had not really grieved his death; instead, she made him her "ghostly" companion and made rules and regulations based on what he would have liked about how to handle the children and later on added her own, but called them his rules to keep the children "in line." She was angry that he was gone, but was too guilty to be angry and too loyal to go out with men who attracted her. Thus, she had created a prison for herself and her family. As the children grew they resented Molly's rules, bullying, and nagging. The worker allowed Molly to continue her dialogue with her husband and then invited Molly to express her feelings to him. She started rather timidly, but by the time she was finished, she was a volcano of anger, hurt, and pain. She added desperately that she was so mad at him that she did not want to cry and then added, "There! See, I didn't cry for you . . ." Saying this she started to cry. It was clear that the grieving had not been done, and that Molly had successfully hidden her angry feelings behind the role she played of the "good" widow.

The empty chair technique can be adapted to many different situations. As you become more skilled you can use it more effectively. Another technique called the rolling chair technique will be discussed in the section on family techniques.

Confrontation

The purpose of this technique is to help clients develop self-awareness, with the intention of helping them move forward. Cormier and Cormier (1991) have described confrontation as a "responsible unmasking of the discrepancies, distortions, games, and smoke screens the client uses to hide both from self understanding and from constructive behavioral change" (p. 158). In his more recent writings, Egan (1994) similarly explains confrontation and indicates that clients should be invited to challenge themselves in order to change. Writers who present helping as a social influence note that some form of challenge is central to helping (Dorn, 1984; Ellis, 1984; Strong & Claiborn, 1982). More recently, Egan uses the word *challenge* rather than *confrontation;* he describes a challenge as an invitation to examine external and internal behaviors that appear to be self-defeating, harmful to others or both, and to bring about a change of behavior if this is necessary.

Clients should be challenged to

Talk about problems that they are reluctant to talk about

Overcome evasiveness and talk about specific problems and clarify them

Move away from distortions and develop new perspectives for themselves

Work toward developing new goals, committing themselves to reasonable agendas, and not living in the past

Achieve new goals in the face of obstacles

Have clear, specific plans rather than be disorganized

Implement the plans when they are tempted to give up

In short, clients should be helped to participate in more effective processes of problem management.

A confrontation is usually initiated by a social worker. In order for the confrontation or challenge to be effective, it should be done with concern for the client's feelings and perceptions and a strong measure of encouragement and reassurance. There are important guidelines for challenging or confronting effectively in the helping process. A worker should not challenge when she or he is angry or frustrated; it must be done with the client's attitude and welfare in mind. A worker can only challenge if he or she is going to become deeply involved in the helping process with the client. When a client is challenged by a person whom they do not like, it has no therapeutic value. Challenges should always be accompanied by a couple of positive observations about the client. The worker should be descriptive and apt when detailing the client's self-destructive or negative behavior. *I* statements should be used throughout the confrontation or challenge. For example:

CLIENT: I am an unattractive woman. My boyfriend and I just broke up, and I am afraid I am going to end up as an old maid.

WORKER: You broke with him because he was drinking too much. You asked him to leave your apartment and move his things out. You are going out with a young man right now, although you have mentioned that the purpose is to overcome your heartache. If you were not attractive, you would not have somebody to be with in such a short time. Also, you tell me that all your friends think that you are attractive.

CLIENT: Of course, but I am no raving beauty, I guess others find me attractive. I am bright, interesting, and energetic. At times, I wish I was more attractive. I like to think I could be more attractive.

WORKER: So you have gotten into the habit of putting yourself down. I wonder when and why you started to do that.

CLIENT: I know, it's a bad habit. If I go back to my early childhood and the kindergarten I went to, I would end up telling you a long, unhappy story.

Reframing

The purpose of reframing is to assist the client to view the behavior of significant others from a different perspective and also in a more positive light. Minuchin and Fishman (1981) talk about reframing from the perspective of helping a family:

> They (the family members) have made their own assessment of their problems, their strengths, and their possibilities. They are asking the therapist to help with the reality that they have framed . . . Therapy starts, therefore, with the clash between two framings of reality. The family's framing is relevant for the continuity and maintenance of the organism more or less as it is; the therapeutic framing is related to the goal of moving the family toward a more differentiated and competent dealing with their dysfunctional reality. (p. 74)

The practitioner emphasizes the positive and the appealing aspect of the most disturbing communications. The practitioner lets the family define a situation as they see it and then through manipulation of the family, they begin to see the practitioner's viewpoint and eventually follow it. In another situation, a couple comes for help complaining that the husband has to drink before he can have sex. The wife is upset about this. The husband, in turn, complains that the problem is his wife's lack of interest in sex. The worker reframes by saying the husband wishes to please his wife so much in bed that he drinks before bedtime so that he can be relaxed and be a good and caring lover in bed. Thus a new frame of reference is created for looking at the problem. Reframing is a way of taking the focus off the identified client and helping family members look at the dynamics of the interactions in a different way. For example, when a mother is overprotective, the worker labels her as being caring; or a child who is labeled as a troublemaker is really keeping the number of family rules within reasonable limits.

Task Assignments

Task assignments may take the form of specific requests on the part of the worker during the session (Minuchin & Fishman, 1981). For example, "Hold your wife's hand every time she looks anxious." It could also take the form of homework like, "Each night, after the kids are in bed, I would like you two to sit down, with the TV off, and tell each other about your day."

Learning a new skill or developing a new pattern is essential to the solution of many problems in social functioning. The new skill or behavior should be practiced in the client's natural environment and not just during sessions with the practitioner (Schaefer, 1987).

Task assignment is not appropriate for all clients. As a technique, it works well as an intervention when it emphasizes client training and skill building. Task assignment presumes that the client is willing to accept direction from the worker and also willing to practice new behaviors outside of the sessions with the practitioner.

Envelope Budgeting

The purpose of envelope budgeting is to help clients manage money. There are many clients who are poor money managers and quite a few are poor. A large percentage of these people do not have checking accounts, so their transactions involve cash. Envelope budgeting is taught to clients who need a simple approach to money management. This technique provides some structure and a means of monitoring cash outflow, but has the flexibility needed to handle emergencies (Sheafor et al., 1997).

The client identifies the key categories of expenditure, which usually are food, rent, clothing, transportation, household supplies, and so forth, in order to plan the budgeting system. Then, with the worker as a support system and a consultant, the client begins to determine how many dollars would be needed for each category during a particular spending period, generally of one to two weeks. An envelope is prepared and labeled for each category and all the envelopes are placed in a single box. For example, one envelope may read "rent" another may read "electricity" and so forth. When clients who have budgeted in this manner open any envelope to use money, the amount of money they have for a particular item is instantly clear. When clients obtain additional income, they do the same thing. This technique is useful for clients who do not know how to budget their money and have been in trouble because of this. At times, clients with mental retardation and those whose financial skills are poor may need this type of help. Others may seek similar help after a specific event; that is, they have gone overboard and are overwhelmed by debts and expenditures that far exceed their income. In such cases, credit counseling, debt consolidation, and even bankruptcy should be discussed as options. Because money is a major source of conflict in families, improved money management can and also improve functioning and relationships in other areas.

Resolving Interpersonal Conflict

Often in the helping process there are people who cannot resolve their conflicts with each other and may need the help of a third person. It is important to understand that the dynamics of a conflict are much more complex than the parties are revealing, and also that the conflict is often about issues that no one wants to talk about. People often fight about small issues when they cannot fight about the real issues. Bisno (1988) identifies different types of conflicts including those characterized by a clash of opposing interests or commitments and those created in order to achieve some hidden agenda.

While trying to resolve conflicts, the practitioner should not take sides. The practitioner should be fair and respect the views and feelings of everyone involved. The worker needs to remind clients of the things that they share and already agree on. The purpose is to create a helpful and constructive atmosphere to allow people to resolve their own problems.

As Minuchin and Fishman constantly demonstrate in their work (1981), the practitioner should help clients move toward a demonstration of mutual respect and a willingness to at least listen and understand differences. The practitioner should set rules and regulations to avoiding threats, name calling, moralizing and attacking sensitive spots, or bringing up past hurts and disagreements.

The practitioner needs to ask those in conflict to question their own motives before they start to communicate with each other. The clients have to ask themselves if what they wish to say is reasonable or if they have a hidden agenda, and also ask themselves if what they are saying is relevant or pertinent and whether it is at all constructive. One of the most negative situations in the helping process occurs with couples when one partner wants to be out of the marriage because he or she has fallen in love with another person, but is coming to sessions to appease the other partner temporarily perhaps out of sense of guilt. With such a hidden agenda, the result may be to destroy any type of constructive communication through constant blaming.

Clients involved in a discussion should think in a constructive fashion about identifying and defining problems and issues. Each one of them should be asked to do the same, and each person should state his or her ideas and concerns. Others in the session should respond to what they have heard, and if there is a miscommunication, then the process should be repeated. The purpose is to help the clients communicate with each other and gain each other's empathy.

The practitioner should use techniques of reflection, clarification, paraphrasing, and summarization (see Chapter 8) to help each person express his or her point of view, needs, and concerns. The practitioner should help clients use I statements to express their side of the conflict. This is because often in conflict situations, saying "you" reflects an undercurrent of anger and blame. Throughout the helping process, the practitioner constantly recognizes and reinforces efforts between the parties to control anger, attempt to understand the other party, and to honestly express their own needs and concerns. Once all the relevant issues have been presented and it is clear to the practitioner that the clients are working toward bettering their relationship rather than sabotaging it, the practitioner helps the clients move toward mutual understanding potential solutions and the development of a more harmonious relationship.

Client Advocacy

The purpose of client advocacy is to secure services for clients who are unable to do so on their own (Mickelson, 1995). Advocacy was described earlier in the section on practitioner roles (see Chapter 6), however, client advocacy is highlighted again because it is an important intervention technique that practitioners frequently use when working with clients who cannot fight for themselves or their rights. When the practitioner takes on the role of client advocate, the worker argues, negotiates, and bargains on behalf of clients. This is because clients alone are not able to obtain the services that they require. Before the worker begins to advocate for a client it is essential that the client's approval is obtained.

A practitioner's desire to advocate should arise from genuine concern for the client and not because of some hidden agenda. As with other in-

tervention strategies the worker needs to get the facts concerning various systems involved and develop a plan of action. To be a successful advocate, the practitioner needs a high level of interpersonal skill and respect for the system and its staff. A confrontational approach will likely backfire not only against the practitioner, but the agency and the client as well. If the agency cannot serve the client who has come to you for help, the worker should ask how to appeal and whom to speak to about the matter. Finally, when pursuing appeals the worker should follow the specified appeals procedure and prepare detailed documentation of the clients' needs and how these can be obtained. All information should be documented with names, dates, content of communication, and copies of all correspondence. There are many clients who fail to get the help they need simply because a practitioner did not take the trouble to ask for an exception to policy. An important part of a practitioner's professional responsibility is to look for ways to make his or her agency more responsive to client and community need.

INTERVENTION WITH A CULTURALLY DIVERSE CLIENTELE

Generalists have to keep in mind that they will meet clients from all kinds of backgrounds. This means that all types of intervention must be handled sensitively in order to be effective. Awareness of cultural and ethnic variables is very important. Even more important is sensitivity to individual differences especially in the United States where people may have roots in several different cultures or subcultures and ties to different ethnic groups. Generalists cannot be expected to know everything about every culture and ethnic group but they can be expected to be adaptable enough to relate to a wide variety of people.

Culturally diverse practice requires working with clients from a perspective of cultural awareness (Lum, 1999). Green (1995), an anthropologist who applied ethnographic interviewing principles, developed a help-seeking model that enhances cultural awareness from a

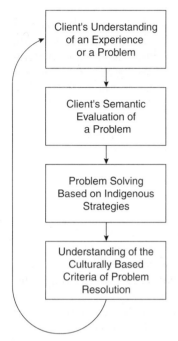

Figure 13.2 **Cultural Awareness**

client's perspective. The Green model consists of four major components (see Figure 13.2).

1. The individual client's understanding of an experience or a problem. Green presents this information as perspective taking; that is, the willingness and ability of the generalist to elicit the client's understanding of his or her needs. The primary function is to gather data about the client's willingness to communicate and to give feedback that the client's position is being heard by the generalist.

2. Clients may have a semantic evaluation of the problem. Language is the medium through which knowledge is gained about an individual or an ethnic group. It is important to understand the meaning of cultural and ethnic words, what Green calls the "cover terms" or specific categories of objects, concepts, ideas, or relationships that are familiar and part of a client's cultural experience. Such cover terms have cultural and psychological reality to the client. For example, for a traditional and conservative East Indian middle-aged woman, marriage is a sacrament, not a legal

contract. Green also emphasizes the importance of a cultural guide whenever available for the generalist to interpret the subtleties and complexities of a particular community as well as cover terms.

3. Problem solving should be based on indigenous strategies, which means seeking appropriate sources of help that are part of a client's culture. Rather than utilizing external social work intervention modalities alone, Green suggests using ethnic community resources, family and extended family support, indigenous advice giving from respected community authority figures, religious resources, and exercise and meditation.

4. An understanding of culturally based criteria of problem resolution. Green suggests that there should be a focus on how people generally solve problems in their own communities and what are the reasonable outcomes of those efforts from their point of view. The generalist should become familiar with the recent history and daily experiences of the client's ethnic community as well as develop an awareness of the variations of differences that may be prevalent in a community and how different clients may respond to specific therapeutic techniques.

Thornton and Garrett (1995) believe that ethnography is a crucial bridge to multicultural practice. It also is important to remember to avoid stereotypic explanations of human behavior. Practitioners avoid stereotypes by using the same helping strategies for all clients who are members of a particular ethnic group. The nonracist practitioner has the ability to feel warmth and genuine concern for people regardless of race, color, and ethnic background.

Grinter (1992) provides a number of guidelines for working with ethnic minorities in terms of interacting and interventions. They are:

> All clients should be seen as individuals first and then as members of a minority group.
>
> The worker should not assume that ethnic status identifies the cultural values and patterns.
>
> Whatever you have read about cultural traits should be viewed as a hypothesis that needs to be tested anew with each new client.

Exercises

1. You are working with a middle-class, single, lesbian client. She has just broken up with her girlfriend, who had been cheating on her. She is in shock and devastated. How would you *advise* her or give her information in her crisis situation?

2. Role-play the following case situation: A woman in her late twenties is constantly losing jobs because she is preoccupied with her relationships with her boyfriends. In fact, the boyfriends seem to leave, in the same way as she quits her jobs.

One student plays the worker, and another, the client. After the role play discuss the cognitive aspects as well as the feelings and behaviors of this client. How can you be helpful to her?

3. In another role play, use feedback as an intervention technique in helping a client view some of his/her strengths and weaknesses.

4. Use any one or more specific intervention techniques in dealing with the given case. Discuss your reasons for your choice of interventions.

A married man aged 24, is talking to a generalist about trouble with his mother-in-law. "The way I see it," he says, "is that she is trying to destroy my relationship with my wife. She does not like me at all. She's very cunning, and it's hard to catch on to what she is doing. Well, I'm tired now. My wife and I fight about her all the time. I have had it: she is attempting to destroy our marriage, and it looks like she may succeed."

THE INTERVENTION PROCESS WITH AN INDIVIDUAL CLIENT

Although we have discussed a number of techniques and ways of intervening with clients with problems in social functioning, there are clients who present other problems. These clients appear to get along with their families and at their workplace and do not believe in making waves; they firmly believe that they should adhere to status quo. Sometimes, these individuals suddenly seek help for problems that they have pushed aside, which leads to a high level of stress.

The practitioner's task in such cases is to identify the clients' conflicts, and draw their attention to the manner in which they have adapted themselves in order to avoid facing their own internal conflicts. The worker has to observe the patterns, themes, and feelings that recur when the client presents the information.

In these cases, the relationship becomes the intervention tool through which the client is helped. This relationship becomes crucial to the client, because within the relationship they enact their own conflicts through the interpersonal process with the worker. Teyber (2000) notes that clients do not just talk about their problems in the abstract. The therapeutic process usually enacts the same conflict that the client is struggling with in other relationships. This is the reason for seeking help. When the helping process fails, it reflects to the client the failure of yet another relationship.

Working with the clients allow conflicts to be resolved as part of the therapeutic process. Beginning practitioners often feel pressure to *do* something for their clients; however, if intervention is premature, they may lose the client because they have not fully understood the interpersonal process. Sometimes the most important thing to do is to *listen*. When practitioners understand the value of corrective interpersonal experiences, they can intervene with selective use of a number of intervention techniques. The worker should first ask "what does this mean?" rather than "what should I do?" When you understand what this means, you will know what to do.

In working on deep emotional problems, the first change occurs in the worker–client relationship. When the worker encourages and gives appropriately timed advice, some clients who function well will feel better and successfully adopt new behavior. This corrective emotional experience becomes a powerful agent for change but one trial learning is not enough to bring about permanent change. In the working-through phase of the helping process, some clients will need more help than others in assimilating and applying new and different ways of responding to their lives, although, in working through issues with these clients, the worker should still be prepared to respond to the conflicts, resistance, and defenses that they present. New symptoms and problems may arise as clients attempt to gain control of their emotions. The worker's task is to identify underlying conflicts and draw clients' attention to the compromise solutions they have adopted to avoid their internal conflicts.

In this case, the worker's role is not to give advice, explain, reassure, self-disclose, or even focus on the behavior or motives of others; rather, the worker should follow the client's lead and listen to patterns, themes, and feelings that occur in the material that the client presents.

Using Process to Resolve Conflicts

When the sources of a client's problems are deeply rooted and out of awareness, it may not be sufficient to train and direct clients to try new and more adaptive responses in their environment. Practitioners often fail to understand how clients are enacting conflict in their interpersonal process and react with impatience, irritation, and even anger. When the helping process fails it may mean that clients were unable to put their problems into words, although they were actually enacting the conflicts in the clinical session. If the worker does not understand what is happening beneath the surface, the helping process is likely to die, either suddenly or slowly over a period of time.

Conflicts Resolved in the Therapeutic Relationship

Practitioners often prematurely emphasize intervention techniques before they understand the interpersonal process that is occurring. It is important to identify and conceptualize what is happening between the practitioner and client in terms of each party's broader dynamics, beyond the pertinent information about the person and the problem. If this is not done, the intervention is likely to fail. In contrast, if the practitioner understands what is occurring in the process of helping, it is usually easier to find effective ways to intervene.

Two critical incidents that are summarized in relating the treatment of an incest victim in the case that follows, which is based on a case study from Teyber (1997). It is not the intervention techniques per se (that is, validating resistance and role play) that have an effect on the client. In this case both the interventions are effective because they follow from the practitioner's *understanding* of the client's dynamics. The practitioner is able to work with these dynamics in the here-and-now immediacy of the client–worker relationship.

Twenty-four-year-old Sadie sought help after a failed suicide attempt precipitated by a series of failed relationships with men, which were increasingly destructive to her self-esteem. While the client was presenting her problems, the practitioner hypothesized that she was an incest victim and anticipated that trust would become a central issue in their relationship. Sadie was sexually abused from a very young age by her maternal uncle who lived in her mother's house. Although this was not part of the presenting problem it came out in the course of the helping process. The helping process got off to a good start, but after several sessions Sadie started to repeat herself in therapy and progress came to a halt. Sadie talked again and again about relational themes with men that were relatively safe. While this type of work was going on, it was clear that Sadie had profound concerns about her safety, betrayal, and vulnerability, which were now being activated with the practitioner.

It was clear that Sadie liked the practitioner and was finding him very helpful. However, when the practitioner pursued the trust issue further and asked specifically whether Sadie felt "safe" with him, her answer, though positive, was distant and unconnected. It was clear that Sadie was removing herself emotionally from the practitioner as they talked more directly about the safety in their relationship.

The practitioner's response was to accept both sides of her feelings. He attempted to tie her concerns directly to the relationship by saying, "I realize you have ambivalent feelings toward me. I am aware that one part of you likes and trusts me and there is another part of you that does not feel at all safe with me. I am also aware that both sides of your feelings make sense and they are important for us to work on." Sadie smiled weakly and nodded her head in order to indicate that this was true.

The practitioner, instead of simply reassuring Sadie that she should learn to trust him, validated the client's distrust in the following manner:

"I want you to know that you have confided in me in asking me to help you. You took a risk in doing that. If I violated your trust, then it would be really bad for you. If I tried to approach you in a sexual manner or even tried to foster a different kind of a relationship between us, it would still hurt you very much. In fact, I think, it would hurt you so much that you would not know or be able to risk trusting another human being again or asking for help."

Sadie started to cry, looked at the practitioner, and nodded in agreement. Observing the response, the practitioner continued elaborating Sadie's concern about the relationship, "If I take advantage of you and our relationship in any way, you will be without hope and I also believe you would be very depressed again and enter into another relationship that will be destructive for you. You might even start to think seriously again that you do not wish to live."

As the worker spoke, clarifying Sadie's concern about the relationship, Sadie's whole demeanor changed. She continued to cry, but agreed with everything the worker was saying. "I understand that it would hurt you a lot if I betrayed your trust, and there is nothing in me that wants you to have that terrible experience again. In fact, I like the part of you that does not trust me. That distrustful part of you is actually your friend and your ally. In therapy we need the part of you that is committed to not letting you get hurt. It is important that we move at your pace in this situation. You have control over the talks we have. You can say No to me and know that I will honor your limits."

Acknowledging Sadie's "resistance" and working through the conflict in terms of their relationship, immediately led to important changes. In a matter of six weeks, Sadie began to recall the abuse she had faced at home by her uncle; before she had only alluded to it. She spoke of being sexually abused by her uncle from the time she was six years of age. She recollected her mother's reactions to Sadie's fears and complaints. Her mother who was a single parent became punitive and scolded her for lying. Her mother denied that any abuse was happening and told Sadie never again to talk about it. Sadie did not seek the support of her biological father who lived nearby, but was unresponsive and distant. Sadie poignantly recalled that she spent too much time sitting in her room with the door closed feeling afraid, ashamed, and deeply alone. The worker responded to this deep sharing by comforting Sadie, validating her experience, and helping her begin to make significant connections between her family problems and her current life.

The sessions became very intense as time passed and Sadie recaptured the experience of her childhood abuse.

The worker used a role-play technique to evoke a different type of response to the trauma Sadie had suffered. The worker said, "I wish there had been a person in that situation to stop his behavior and protect you. But as you know there was no one there for you. But if I had been there I would have walked into the bedroom when he was there with you in the dark, turned on the light and said in a loud commanding voice, "Get away from her, right now. Stop it, immediately. Leave her alone right now. I see what you're doing. It's cruel and it's not fair to her. You are hurting her in the worst possible way and I will not allow it."

After speaking these words loudly and forcefully, the worker stood up and rolled Sadie's coat into a ball. Using the coat as a little doll, he held it close and said in a reassuring voice, "You are safe now. He is gone for good. I will call the police now and they will protect you. You do not have to ever worry about this man hurting you."

By the worker giving this message to Sadie in a symbolic way, the full intensity of her pain and rage was evoked. After these feelings were ventilated, Sadie became composed and said in a quiet voice, "I am going to be all right." The worker took the rolled up jacket and carefully tucked it in the client's arms and said, "That is the little girl that you were. The little girl in you needs you to open up your heart and give her a home. You also need to take care of her and not push her away anymore, like they did to her and you have done. I would like you to hold her and talk to her and listen carefully to what she tells you. I also want you to join me in taking care of this part of you, so that this little girl is no longer hurt and alone in the corner of her room."

Sadie accepted this responsibility. She bought a doll that she used to represent the part of her that needed to be cared for and protected. Although all of Sadie's problems did not go away, she made progress and many of her longstanding symptoms disappeared permanently.

When she started, Sadie was almost incapable of leaving home at age twenty-four. Two weeks after the final session, she got her driver's license and began to drive for the first time in about seven years. She also got a job as a waitress. Later she started going to college on a part-time basis and did well in school.

In what three significant ways did Sadie become stronger? Several factors made this intervention possible. In sharp contrast to what happened in the family, this time Sadie experienced protection, validation, appropriate boundaries, and a very supportive environment. The worker's compassionate and protective response helped

Sadie shift from an identification characterized by her parent's rejection of her and her own resulting shame and self-hatred to an identification with the worker resulting from his compassion for her predicament. This allowed Sadie to take care of herself and for the first time in her life feel like she did matter. Role playing was used to dramatize the source of Sadie's conflicts and provide her with an additional corrective emotional experience. In this manner, far-reaching consequences were set in motion by the worker supporting, confirming, and comforting Sadie when she presented her vulnerability. The immediacy of the worker–client relationship provided a suitable environment for symbolically enacting and dealing with the past abuse. As a result, Sadie received a corrective emotional experience that also helped her become stronger and capable of protecting herself.

The Working-Through Process in Intense Verbal Therapy

The form of corrective emotional experience that was so therapeutic for Sadie can become a powerful agent for change. However, such one-trial learning is not usually sufficient and clients generally need several trials to learn new experiences of change. Initially change begins to occur with the worker in the therapeutic relationship; later, changes occur with others who are important such as caring family members, friends, teachers, and mentors. While the client is working-through with the worker, some clients will easily assimilate and learn to respond in new ways and will readily apply these techniques throughout their lives. There are other clients who will deal with conflicts slowly and uncomfortably and will take more time to learn new ways of responding. Also, there are clients who will repeatedly confront the same conflicts, resistance, and defenses and not benefit from the helping process.

As a worker using interventive skills and techniques, how would you work with the following clients? What is the rationale for your use of a particular skill or technique?

Andrew is a fifty-year-old man who lost his job with a well-known company after working there for over thirty years. He looks healthy and is well dressed. You find out that he is married to a good-looking woman who is in her thirties. This is his second marriage; he divorced his first wife five years ago. He does not have any children by either of his wives. He is presently employed as a real estate agent.

Andrew came to see you because his brother, who is a medical doctor, urged him to do so. Andrew has been complaining of migraine headaches, backaches, and fatigue, although he looks healthy. He tells you that he feels cheated out of his job, which was almost his whole life and he feels no amount of counseling will help get his job back. All he really wants is to get his old job back or some comparable job in a prestigious company. The only reason he is seeking help is because, "My brother has been on my back, asking me to talk out my feelings, about my lost job. I am not sure how much that will help."

After assessing the case, what are your interventive plans for this client? Present your rationale for the same. How would you handle the case beginning with the first intervention step.

Thirteen-year-old Leonard is not doing well in school and was referred to you, the school social worker. Leonard is of average height and is in good health. He comes from an intact, working-class, two-parent family with four siblings. Both of Leonard's parents work outside the home. He was referred to you because the assistant principal indicated that Leonard had been accused of stealing money in small amounts from other children in his classroom. Leonard firmly insists that he has not stolen and adds that he is accused of "everything, everywhere." By way of explanation, he adds that everyone picks on him including a parent, his siblings, his classmates, and his teachers. He goes on to say that nobody likes him at home or at school and nobody trusts him. He is worried that he may fail in his subjects. He wants so much to do well, but perhaps he will never be able to do so. He does not have friends in school or outside. However, talking to the worker, he appears to be comfortable in the office and also volunteers information.

Role-play the given case. One student can be the client and another, the social worker. After the role-play, the class can discuss and present an assessment, a plan of intervention and specific interventive techniques that could be used with this client.

Mrs. A is eighty years old and has recently been admitted to a nursing home. Mrs. A has worked until her seventieth birthday and she has always been active in the community. Her husband died not long ago of a heart attack. One day while cleaning her bathtub, Mrs. A slipped and broke her back. She has been in a great deal of pain ever since. Her married son is not able to take care of her and admitted her to this home. She has lived in the home for one month and is very angry with everybody, particularly her son, who has visited her twice a week since she has been admitted. Mrs. A is feeling restrained in this structured setting. She is in bed and would like to move about more often than she is allowed to do. She criticized her son for placing her in this setting and adds that she will never forgive him for what he did. You work with Mrs. A and quickly find out that she enjoys books and is very adept in discussion about the current state of political affairs in the world.

How would you work with Mrs. A? After making an assessment, plan an intervention. Elaborate on the specific intervention strategies, and offer your explanations for the same.

INTERVENTION AND FAMILY THERAPY TECHNIQUES

This section focuses on using intervention techniques with families and groups.

Enactment

Enactment is a technique in which a worker asks a family to "dance" in his or her presence. The worker constructs an interpersonal scene and asks the family members to deal with it as they would do at home. In enactment, many dysfunctional transactions among family members are likely to be played out (Minuchin & Fishman, 1981). Such transactions occur in the context of the session, in the present, and in relationship to the worker. While the practitioner works through and facilitates the enactment, he or she is in a position to observe how family members verbally and nonverbally signal each other, and is able to monitor the range of tolerable transactions. In this way, the worker can intervene in the process by increasing the intensity and duration of the transactions and

also introducing experimental probes that will give both the worker and the family information about the nature of the problem and the flexibility of the family's transactions in problem solving. It will also give the family members possibilities for alternative ways of coping in a family situation.

There are three different "movements" that highlight enactment. In the first movement, the worker observes the spontaneous transactions of the family and decides which dysfunctional areas to highlight. During the second movement of enactment, the worker reorganizes the family members to dance their dysfunctional steps in front of him or her. In the third movement, the worker makes an information prediction and brings hope to the family (Minuchin & Fishman, 1981).

The Andersen family consisted of two parents and four children. While enacting the situation assigned to them by the family therapist, Mrs. Andersen started to say something to her husband. He responded without looking at her. Anna, the youngest daughter, ran and sat on her father's lap and he lovingly stroked her hair. Mrs. Andersen raised her voice because she was not satisfied with her husband's response. At this point, their oldest son, Derek, the identified client, started to fall off his chair. His mother got angry with him. The father joined her and called him "a troublemaker." The therapist asked the family to highlight the second part of the family's scene after Derek "fell" off the seat. The role playing that started rather self-consciously on the part of the couple suddenly became serious business. The mother looked at the worker in a distressed manner and commented that Derek always behaved badly at home and was always "troublesome." The therapist said that there was hope for the family as they at least knew whom to get angry with, when matters did not go right in the family. Derek was young and surely he would change with help from the rest of the family, particularly his parents, whom he so lovingly distracted in order to avoid having a bad quarrel in front of the therapist.

Family Sculpting

Family sculpting is an extremely important and powerful tool when working with families. This technique facilitates the expression of each family member's experience in a single visual representation (Vondracek & Corneal, 1995). That is, each family member is asked to imagine other members as malleable, and to place them in spatial and postural relation to one another. In the process, each member's body can be shaped in whatever way is desired in terms of expressing feelings, relationships, and also what might be just vague verbal expressions. Then the sculptor also shapes and places the person in relation to the rest of the people. Each individual has a chance to be a sculptor and, in this sense, the picture that is presented, in many cases, is worth more than the proverbial "thousand words."

A family that Satir (1983) was seeing in therapy wanted to learn how to stop fighting. All the family members agreed that they fought a great deal. To make this real, Satir did the following:

> Because I like to make an "alive" as quickly as possible, it seemed natural at this point to ask the older girls to get up and point their fingers at each other in order to see what other family members did when this happened. I find that words are more useful when there is a picture, which I call "sculpturing" or "posturing." I found that when I asked the two girls to point at each other, they were very reluctant to do so. They talked about how they fought, but actually putting themselves in the position of doing it made it more real. They seemed embarrassed." (p. 250)

While the girls were enacting what they did at home, Satir encouraged the rest of the family to get involved as they would at home. At this point, the mother joined them and started pointing her finger at one daughter, the father verbally told them to stop fighting but did not interfere. The oldest son stood near his mother to be the auxiliary father, trying to help the mother with the problems between the two girls.

This is a technique that can be used effectively with families that lack verbal skills, as well as a highly verbal family. By communicating in physical ways, many intellectualizations and other verbal defenses can be eliminated. This kind of sculpting has value because it makes explicit what is going on in the family. Family sculpting can be used diag-

nostically to develop a picture or map of a family and it can be used in an evaluative fashion. After each person portrays how other members are seen in relation to each other, they can also portray how they would like the family to be. Once this ideal has been achieved, periodic evaluation can be used to determine how useful the helping process is in moving the family toward a specific goal.

Another essential element of sculpting is the therapeutic processing that takes place after its completion. This involves a discussion of how each member felt while in the family sculpting process. This also includes arriving at the family members' impressions of how various members presently perceive relationships in the system and how they might bring about change (McGoldrick, Garcia-Preto, Hines, & Lee, 1989; Satir, Banmen, Gerber, & Gomori, 1991).

Marital Sociogram

The marital sociogram employs nonverbal methodologies and depicts each spouse's experience in relation to the other in the relationship. While appropriate for the marital relationship this technique could also be used in a two-member subsystem of a family.

In a marital sociogram, one spouse is placed in a specific location and asked to remain stationary. The other spouse is placed directly opposite the partner and asked to begin moving slowly toward the stationary spouse. This spouse moves closer and closer until he or she has found a comfortable distance. The roles are then reversed. The experience is then processed.

The marital sociogram technique adequately demonstrates the degree of distance each spouse desires in the relationship. The different means of arriving at a mutually agreed on "distance" is also a natural outcome of this technique (Barker, 1998). As with family sculpting, this technique is used as a trigger for discussion of the marital relationship.

Rolling Chairs

Rolling chairs is a useful technique to illustrate emotional distance. In this technique, each of the members in the therapeutic system are asked to take advantage of chairs with casters and to roll over close to a person. When they experience discomfort in closeness, they can move away to another position; the only limitation imposed on the participants is that the members stay in the emotional field, which implies that everyone stay in the room. The technique becomes counterproductive and the possibility of observable interaction is negated when members leave the room. This technique can be valuable in bringing new energy into the therapeutic system and also facilitating therapy with the family.

Home Visits

Visiting a family at their home is a valuable and useful technique when the therapeutic process seems bogged down or when extra family information is needed. When using this technique, the worker views the "home ground" of the family and also determines what the physical affects are on the interactions of the family (Wasik, 1990; Weiss, 1990). The number of insights that one can gain by conducting at least one session in the family home is amazing.

Kim and her family had been in therapy for a period of two months with her oldest child, Andy, as the identified patient. Andy was the one with the most troublesome problems. The worker was aware that Andy was the son of Kim's previous husband, and she had five more children by her present husband. When the worker visited the family, she found it was extremely clean but with scant furniture. In the dining room, Kim had placed a cake cut into small slices; she wanted the worker to have a piece of the cake, and she also allowed the rest of the family to have a piece. However, when Andy attempted to get a piece she yelled at him saying that the cake was for the younger children. He frowned and walked away, perhaps because the worker was there. Later the worker found out that Andy's room was in the attic separated from the rest of the family. He was the only child who had to ask permission to watch TV ostensibly because he was "dull" in school, which of course overlooked the fact that the rest of the children did not do too well in school, either. The family situation, in many ways, revealed symbolically the boundaries that this family established. They also subtly indicated that the boy, Andy, was excessive "baggage."

Home visiting has a number of potential uses. An area of study that is receiving increased attention is home-based services in which social workers actually teach parenting skills and homemaking skills in the home environment. There are also clients who cannot get to the practitioner's office because they are too old, too sick, or too poor for whom home visits offer real help.

Dreams

Dreams can be used in individual, family, couple, and group therapy. They can be used effectively and therapeutically with the entire family. Barker (1996) identifies goals for discussing dreams with couples. When a spouse discusses a dream with the practitioner in front of the spouse, the practitioner uses it to improve the communication between the couple and create a better awareness of what each spouse thinks of himself or herself and the other.

Dreams often are volunteered in the helping process. The family members respond to their dreams with questions such as "What does that mean?" and "Why did that person have such a dream?" If the dreams are presented voluntarily, the worker can encourage family members to use a pad and a pencil to write their own thoughts, feelings, reactions, and associations about their dreams. Dreams are a part of self-disclosure and useful for gaining new insights.

One-Way Mirrors

One-way mirrors can be used effectively in two different ways. In one case, the family and the worker are observed by a supervisor or a team of professionals who watch the clinical session closely. When they feel that there is a need to intervene with a new technique, they will call the worker on a telephone in the room where the helping session is happening. They may ask the practitioner to come out of the clinical session room and give instructions regarding how to work with different family members.

In other cases, family members or subsystems of the family are allowed behind the glass to observe different members of their own family interact when they are not present on the scene. For example, the parents of a child can observe how the worker models effective interpersonal skills with the child from behind the one-way mirror. By removing one or more family members and placing them behind the mirror, can help them see how the remaining subsystems change as a result of their absence. The most valuable diagnostic information provides a basis for future intervention. This technique was written about and elaborated by Minuchin and Fishman (1981), Boscolo, Cecchin, Hoffman, and Penn (1987), and others. (See Liddle, Breunlin and Schwartz, 1988, for more information on how training influenced family therapy.)

Sometimes parents sit behind the one-way mirrors with a copractitioner. Together they reflect on the behavior of their children who are working with the practitioner on the other side of the mirror. Using the one-way mirror forces the parent to observe, reflect, and learn about containment of impulses. This is reassuring to the parents. At the same time they are learning about the here-and-now, as the therapist is seeking to identify the prevailing mood. The generalist seeks to gradually change this mood by either allowing the family to join, by overlooking the characteristic family emotions, or by exaggerating them so they become obvious.

Videotaping

The use of videotape adds another dimension to the treatment process. It enhances the observers' ability to see small movements and repetitive patterns (Nichols & Schwartz, 1995). Videotape equipment can be used the same way the agency employs it in training its practitioners, giving the family therapist an opportunity to observe himself or herself interacting with the family. Family members who witness themselves in the videotaped session see the manner in which they send out double-messages, such as displaying affect nonverbally which undermines the verbal aspect of the message.

Videotape is used to provide feedback to members in situations that would be difficult to capture and explain verbally. It is a valuable technique to help family members understand to what degree they have progressed. Reviewing excerpts from the first session, the middle sessions, and the most recent sessions helps the family understand how they have achieved their goals. This, in many ways, reinforces the family and the work they have done. It also encourages them to continue their efforts beyond the formal treatment contract.

There are two factors that play an important role in the use of video equipment: (1) the possibility of obtaining objective data and using it for immediate integration as an ongoing transaction is making a significant advance in the development of the therapeutic art; and (2) there is a shift in role position in which the worker and the family step back from the usual hierarchical positions to that of being cooperative researchers, which is a common task and marks another significant move in making the helping process a more elastic form of offering help.

Family Photographs

Another technique involves the use of family photographs. In this situation, families either volunteer photographs or produce them at a worker's request (Nichols & Schwartz, 1995). Photos tell stories about people. Often they represent various developmental stages in a person's family. As there are a large number of photographs available today, it is best to limit the number of photos for each family to a few that they consider important and reflective of their perception of the family. Different interpretations by various family members of the same photos can lead to some productive discussion about the family. Family members may be asked to identify the "most" representative of the photos. This process helps provide valuable treatment clues regarding the family's interactional patterns, rules, and roles.

Looking for "absent" members might also be fruitful. Sometimes it is the person who always took the picture. At other times, the absence might be an important part of the family's story.

Looking at photos seems to activate a sense of connectedness and create a bonding element as the individuals share their hurts, joys, and pains. Photos are a valuable tool and assist in the therapeutic process.

Emphasizing the Positive

A family system can be changed by modifying one aspect or element of it. For instance, a family can be asked to select a behavior that is the real concern of the family so that the "real" problems can be effectively changed (Pillari, 1997). Families are sometimes fragmented and alienated. The worker can ask the family to identify one thing that is satisfying to all members. If they suggest that watching news is satisfying, then all the members would be asked to sit down together and watch the news. A session is devoted to identifying one factor that is mildly satisfying to all members. It is wise to ask the members to process this item without the worker's assistance, which results in more freedom of observation. If observation by the worker reveals that the family is feeling a certain degree of togetherness, the same assignment, for instance watching the news together, would be given as repetitive assignment with the hope that more and better communication will evolve between family members, before venturing to other assignments.

Positive outcomes generate more motivating goodwill in the family. As the idea that watching television is the most satisfying time together were employed the next television show assigned was "Growing Pains." The session following the assignment was the most dynamic compared to any previous experience in the family. This was because there was laughter in the family from insights gained by comparing their own behaviors to the *Growing Pains* family.

All these techniques and others should be used as part of a carefully thought-out overall plan for working with families. All of these techniques can also be used selectively while working with different types of families.

Exercises

1. Form into groups of five to eight students and practice *sculpting*. That is, each person sculpts another person depending on what his or her perceptions of that person are. Once this has been verbally processed, they can put together a simulated family from the group and physically implement the sculpting process. Once completed, someone in the group may want to volunteer to sculpt his or her own "re-created" family, which then becomes part of the group. The volunteer assigns group members to various roles, thus portraying family sculpting. Based on this process, the group members who have played family roles can attempt to describe to the sculptor how they felt in their role and how they perceive the family. Special attention should be paid to the type of information that this exercise may bring into the sculpting process.

2. As a practitioner dealing with family situations, how would you work with the given cases?

Twelve-year-old Neal, the referred client, attends the helping session with his parents. They are not able to communicate with him because they complain that Neal sits with his head bent and does not look up. Later, the mother provides a list of things that Neal does or does not do in the house which are causing the family a great deal of pain. He is "so good" at creating a chaotic situation. His older sister, who is the picture of a "perfect child," obediently nods her head and agrees with her parents. By the time the worker is ready to speak, Neal has become very withdrawn and will reply only in monosyllables, further aggravating his parents who see him as a "bad child." When he avoids talking to the worker, the mother looks at her husband and her daughter and then at the worker and comments in a prophetic way, "I told you, he is a very difficult child." Neal responds by lowering his head further.

As a social worker how would you analyze the family? What patterns of interaction seem evident at this point? What would you do next?

Thirty-five-year old Holly is unhappy in her third marriage. She and her husband, Keith, are in therapy. Holly complains that Keith makes too many rules in the family and also tries to control her daughters from her second marriage. He tries to punish them by taking the TV away from them for a week and not allowing them to take showers, but only baths. He inspects the bathtub after they have bathed to see if they really used soap. Holly behaves and talks in a helpless manner, as if she has no control over her children and is also afraid of Keith.

What are the family problems as you understand them at this point? What alternative explanations of difficulties are possible? How would you begin to intervene in this family situation?

Cindy and her husband Charles have been in couples session for six months. One of the problems presented in the marriage is that Charles had an affair a few years ago and had a child by his lover. The child is five years of age and has a lot of problems because his mother is a drug user. As the child's home situation became unbearable, he started to call his father on the phone "just a little too much," Cindy complained. At this point, Cindy, a mother of three children, adamantly talks about wanting a divorce. Charles is not willing to deal with the situation. He constantly turns to religion, saying that he is a born-again Christian and does not believe in divorce. After a couple of such sessions, Cindy is extremely angry and tells him she wants to get out of the relationship. Charles looks at her and says, "God told me that divorce is bad, and I will not divorce you under any conditions, and I love you." Charles is in the Navy and if Cindy leaves him, she will have to leave empty-handed. She says, "the Navy is very protective of its men." Cindy is very angry with him for the affair he had a few years ago and is not willing to forgive him.

As a practitioner how would you handle this case? How would you deal with the divorce issue? What intervention strategies would you use to work with this family?

GROUP INTERVENTION

In group treatment, as in individual and family treatment, the major therapeutic medium is called the interpersonal process of communication. The major activity is talk—verbal interaction. Other activities are used in the area but they are secondary. More important is how clients process their experiences, and how the activities and processing together contribute to problem solving and goal attainment. Activities do assume a greater significance with some groups, such as work with children, because children relate and communicate through play. Also in work with clients who have serious physical, mental, and social handicaps, group activities can meet their basic human need for social and recreational outlets.

While moving toward treatment in a group, a number of factors have to be considered. As a productive group proceeds, there is a healing attitude when members begin to experience the problems and issues of others. In such groups, cohesion is high and the group members develop deep emotional bonds. There is also a shared sense of hope. Overgeneralizing, speaking for another, focusing attention on the worker, rambling and irrelevant information are generally counterproductive in a group and if they happen, often hinder the goals of the group (Brown, 1991).

Silence in a group session can be an anxious experience for beginning generalists. It can imply that nothing is happening or that there is a degree of tension in the room. Silence may indicate that a particular subject has been exhausted and it is time to move on. On the other hand, a group's silence is often productive, however, if the worker resists the temptation to jump in and start talking too soon.

Conflict is an inevitable and necessary aspect of the group process. The worker should confront rather than avoid conflict. The worker should avoid fostering a win-or-lose situation. Further, the worker should clarify and interpret the process as it happens. In contentious situations, the communication process may become entangled. The worker should maintain a relationship with the group as a whole and establish ground rules for dealing with conflict appropriate to the age level and maturity of the group. In certain situations, the rules may have to be as basic as "It is all right to be angry, but there should be no hitting and name calling."

In groups, members take on different roles and ways of behavior. Each member enters a group with an established pattern of behavior.

These are likely to be reflected in fairly well-defined roles within the group context. There could be a placater who talks in an ingratiating way and rarely disagrees with anyone (Satir, 1988). Another kind of group member is referred to as the "assistant group leader." He or she attempts to take on the functions and role of the leader because of strong status needs. The group member who plays the clown can be relied on to offer a practical joke or a quick punch line. The scapegoat provides an outlet onto which other group members can project their own anxiety and pain. The intellectualizer will often sidetrack the group's discussion away from focused problem-solving activity. The silent and withdrawn member may not speak too much at meetings but is still involved in the group. The gatekeeper guards the gates through which the group must pass for the work to deepen. For instance, when the group discussion gets too close to a difficult subject, the gatekeeper intervenes to divert the discussion. There are also social isolates, persons who do not reach out to other members and may have a limited capacity to get along with other members. Finally, there is the rescuer who is quick, sometimes too quick, to come to the assistance of the group members when they are in trouble or confronted (Napier & Gershenfeld, 1993; Shulman, 1999).

Each of these roles may prove beneficial or destructive for the group and for those who perform the roles depending on circumstances. It is the worker's responsibility to assess each individual's role performance in the group, and consider the meaning of the behavior for the individual client as well as the group as a whole.

The success of a group treatment program is evaluated in terms of group members' functioning outside the group in the real world. If group members do not make changes outside of the group, particularly in their work, play, or home life, the intervention cannot be viewed as successful. Improved functioning in the group may be a step forward, but it is not enough.

There are group members who will disown responsibility, act helpless, and be powerless in different situations. Such individuals can be helped and motivated to change through the group process. There are many clients who are in a state of inertia. They do not act on their own behalf unless something significant happens to them.

Angela joined a women's group where she spoke very little. She was intimidated by her husband who always said that she was useless and worthless. However, with positive comments and empowerment from the group members, Angela started to move ahead in developing self-confidence and feeling better about herself. She found herself a job that paid minimum wage and bought herself some makeup and new clothes. She changed from a "doormat" to a more self-confident assertive person. Her husband, who was used to a wimpy timid wife, was uneasy at the way Angela dressed and conducted herself. One day when she walked home dressed well and bringing with her some groceries that she wanted for herself, he was furious and ready to hit her. For the first time, she stood up to him saying that if he hit her, she would divorce him. Angela's presence in the group helped her become more assertive and empowered her as a person.

Moving from inertia to proactive choices takes time and effort and happens in small steps. Having group members take on action assignments is useful and can result in a breakthrough. The purpose of homework in individual and family work is to help members think about and work on their goals and new behaviors, as well as to contemplate what they have learned in the group (Sue, 1992). At each meeting, the group provides members with opportunities to gain success in a particular aspect of life. Homework can come in the form of task assignments that vary from learning to talk in an assertive manner with a person to accomplishing some task that is related to a persons' life, such as preparing a job resume or taking the family on a weekend outing.

While the group process is in the middle phase, the generalist encourages group members to ventilate their feelings, including anger and guilt, that the group members might feel in the group or because of the group. The worker should be clear about the guidelines and goals for the group and its members, and the group should pay special attention to group composition. The worker should particularly avoid bringing together a group of members who are different from each other in terms of their needs and problems. It is important to establish group norms that promote and support individual group members. If a group member cannot be protected in a particular group, the individual should be asked to leave. This group member could be referred to another group or for individual treatment.

Interpersonal relationships in a group can become painful when destructive confrontations and severe scapegoating occur. In order to accomplish intervention, both the group members and group leader must understand their responsibilities and roles, and the rules and guidelines for behavior, so that they can move with the tasks to be accomplished. Individual differences should be tolerated and high-pressure tactics should be banished (Shulman, 1999). To move forward in this process it is important to have effective leaders who are rated as moderate in terms of stimulation and high in terms of caring (Glassman & Gates, 1990).

In the intervention phase, the group generally moves to commitment and sharing. There is a greater degree of exploration, self-disclosures among group members, cohesion, feedback, hope, caring, acceptance, and willingness to risk and trust as well as commitment to change. It is during this phase that productivity increases and members are committed to working on their identified goals.

When working with groups, the leader should select specific activities that meet suitable treatment objectives. Corey and Corey, Callahan, and Russell (1992) indicate that the worker has to pay attention to variables such as the degree of skill an activity requires; the degree of competitiveness an activity stimulates among the players; the degree of leeway that is required when an activity permits group members to respond on impulse; the kinds of rewards and punishments that are available to participants in the activity; and how long the activity delays such feedback.

Basic Group Rules

According to Vinter (1967), Brown (1991), Falsck (1988), and Ephros and Vasil (1988) there are nu-

merous areas that are relevant to each group activity. These are the basic rules in the use of activities in group work utilized in different types of agencies and with different kinds of groups.

1. How prescriptive is an activity and what are the rules and regulations that govern the behavior of such members? Some clients have difficulty with activities that are highly structured. For example, there are people who may have problems with the rigid rule structure of a game such as chess, but no difficulty with an activity like swimming.

2. Who is the person who controls the participants' activity and behavior in a group? For instance, what are the controls exercised by a group leader, a group member, or a referee at any given time?

3. How much skill and competence does a particular activity require, keeping in mind that performance should not be equated with excelling, but rather with participation. For example, in planning activities the worker should consider whether a group of children with poor hand-and-eye coordination will be able to enjoy cutting paper figures and coloring within a set of lines. If only a few group members find success, the worker should redesign the activity so that all members will be likely to experience some degree of success.

4. How much interaction and participation is required of group members? Also what is the quality of participation in a group?

5. What are the rewards present in an activity and how abundant are they? Rewards or gratification can be intrinsic, such as the satisfaction of being able to do something well, or extrinsic, such as an attractive object that is created by the participants. Group members with little or no motivation may be induced to participate in an activity by giving them additional extrinsic rewards immediately and frequently but with purpose.

6. Some of the factors you need to remember while working with a group are:

- Your enthusiasm is an important asset to any group activity

- An activity should be time-limited, and ended when it is going well and the group members are enjoying themselves
- Try an activity before using it in a group
- Be prepared to switch activities in midstream if there is such a need

7. While working with groups, a worker should consider the following elements:

- *Timeliness:* The worker should be aware of the current group processes and introduce an activity naturally without superimposing it.
- *Appropriateness:* A new activity may require new types of behaviors. These behaviors should not be so new that they would overwhelm or surprise the group members. For example, asking a group of older women and men to participate in an activity that requires excessive physical movement when they are accustomed to sedentary activities would be ineffective. Also, activities should be entered into voluntarily. If a member chooses not to participate in an activity, then his decision needs to be respected. There should be safety when group members need to be protected from harm. Activities can easily get out of control and could cause participants physical or emotional harm.

Skill Training

Skill training is a highly structured activity that involves attainment of specific goals. Usually there is a time limit for accomplishing goals, and skills are built on from session to session. Ordinarily, the group leader structures the content of the group activities and facilitates the group's attainment of the agreed-upon goals.

There are certain activities that are part of every client's daily routine. Dickerson (1981) worked with a "club" of adults with mental retardation and used activities as a way of teaching and a way of structuring every member's life. Ac-

tivities were age-appropriate and required four stages to be completed. They included preparation activities that would help the group members to plan, prepare, and serve lunches for their friends, improve their ability to take care of themselves, and interact socially with other people.

Dickerson also made decorations that would provide them with a way to personalize their meeting rooms and enhance their sense of belonging. The worker initiated shopping activities so that clients would learn how to use a variety of stores in the community and practice using money. The worker introduced games the clients could play by themselves or with one or two others. Playing games taught them to accept simple rules and take turns. Dickerson introduced conversations that taught social skills such as initiating a conversation, giving a compliment, and refusing or accepting a date.

As specified by Reid (1997), Corey, Corey, Callahan, and Russell (1992), role playing and assertiveness training (Forsyth, 1990) can help group members develop skills in self-growth and positive group dynamics.

Role Playing

Role playing can be used by group members as a way to extinguish undesirable behaviors and acquire new behaviors. It is also used for problem solving and conflict resolution. Role playing in groups should be open-ended and unstructured. It allows for spontaneity and learning and all the procedures for role playing are flexible (Reid, 1997).

BEHAVIORAL REHEARSAL In this situation a group member can play by himself or herself. Behavioral rehearsal leads to insight into group members' feelings, thought processes, and behaviors. Group members have an opportunity to practice new behavior in the safe atmosphere of the group. By using simulation, group members practice new behaviors and receive input from the other members of the group and the worker (Sprafkin, Gershaw, & Goldstein, 1993). The drawbacks of personal behavior become clear and the worker, with the help of the group members, can help the clients to look at themselves.

ROLE REVERSAL   In role reversal, a group member plays the role of a significant person in that member's own life, perhaps the role of a wife, a spouse, a parent, an employer, or a teacher. This helps group members experience a special situation from another person's point of view. This technique is also used to teach empathy (Etcheverry, Siporin, & Toseland, 1986). Role reversal can be especially helpful when two members of a group are in conflict and are having a difficult time listening to each other and communicating openly.

Etcheverry et al. (1986) indicate that role playing done poorly in a group can be destructive. Problems include encouraging group members to play when they are not ready or are unable to self-disclose or participate; when there is too little or too much direction; when the group leader is planning, implementing, and also closing the role play; and when there is failure to protect and support the protagonist or other player. Another reason for failure would be failure to follow the agreed-upon procedures to achieve indicated objectives.

Assertiveness Training

Assertive behavior includes the direct and honest expression of both positive and negative feelings in interpersonal situations. Lack of assertiveness includes denying one's own rights, not accepting compliments, and being afraid to speak up; maintaining poor eye contact, and using inappropriate facial expressions such as smiling when angry or upset, and assuming nonassertive body postures, such as maintaining too much distance, turning away, and so forth (Forsyth, 1990; Reid, 1997). The elements that are part of assertiveness training are as follows:

- *Education:* First the group worker discusses the differences between aggression and assertion, then asks group members to realistically explore the differences between aggression

and being assertive. Before group members can become assertive, they have to understand that it is all right to be assertive. Also they must come to grips with the problems of being nonassertive.

- *Modeling:* The group leader serves as a model for the group by demonstrating assertive behavior. Members observe the worker's assertive behavior, then they practice what they observed in simulated situations while role playing.
- *Role playing:* Rehearsing behavior acts as an important vehicle for assertiveness training. Group members and group leaders contribute by coaching and playing the roles of significant others in the situation. As the group progresses, the members should rehearse more challenging situations.
- *Home work:* The worker encourages group members to practice the assertive skills they are learning in the group between sessions and report back to the group.
- *Brainstorming:* Brainstorming frees people from self-criticism and the criticisms of others in order to generate creative and imaginative solutions to a specific problem (De Bono, 1992).

In a brainstorming session the participants are given the following instructions:

- They are encouraged to develop a number of solutions. The goal is to obtain a quantity of solutions; quality is determined later.
- Members are allowed to freewheel in their thinking. Even really wild thoughts are accepted without judgment.
- Members are encouraged to combine and elaborate on the solutions that are offered. They are not allowed to criticize or evaluate another person's proposed solutions.

During this session a recorder writes down everything that is verbalized as the ideas come up, using a blackboard or a flip chart. If there is criticism of ideas, either verbal or nonverbal, whether implied by tone or nonverbal gestures, it should be put to an end quickly by the leader, who should also remind group members that all ideas are welcome and the sorting out will take place later.

As mentioned earlier, brainstorming has been used effectively in treatment and in one-on-one counseling. Brainstorming should not be allowed to take place unless there is adequate time. Brainstorming is used in the problem-solving process to get information and evaluate proposed solutions.

Indirect Discussion of Self in Small Groups

By indirectly discussing self, it is easier for group members to discuss and talk about issues that might otherwise be very painful for them. The purpose is to stimulate and structure small-group discussion of the group members' problems and also to protect a person's privacy (De Bono, 1992; Kottler, 1995).

Using this technique, group members are given cards and are asked to make a sign like a postcard mark at the corner of each card and mark letters (A, B, C, and so forth) on the cards. All members then take the card with the postmark sign A and are asked to complete a statement such as "Before a battering episode, I feel . . ." Each group member completes the card saying what he or she feels. Another statement is made: "During the battering, besides the pain, I feel . . . " and members respond on the B card; on the C card, the statement says, "After the battering, I feel . . . " Each card is passed around to different members and they are asked to fill it up and then the cards are gathered and reshuffled and given to different members who do not know which person responded. The members then discuss and analyze the responses, problems, and concerns that are found on the cards.

The next step would be to form small groups with three or four members and study and discuss the cards that have been given out. At first, group members generally identify the frustrations and difficulties that they have experienced as people in

battering situations, be it a spouse, daughter, a son, or any other relative. The members have to identify the different reasons for the behavior that they have experienced. They also should identify immediate solutions before looking at long-term solutions. Later the group members are encouraged to exchange their data with other members so that they can obtain more data on the subject.

This technique works best in large groups, but it can also be used in small groups. The worker helps by writing down the feelings that everyone will be interested in discussing.

Facilitating the Group Process

As Reid (1997) and Napier and Gershenfeld (1993) indicate, rounds and dyads are important methods to facilitate genuine sharing of group members' thoughts and feelings.

ROUNDS   A round is an activity in which every member responds in turn to a particular question (Duffy, 1994; Jacobs, Harvill, & Masson, 1994). Rounds are usually used to gather material, involve group members, get group members focused, deepen a group's intensity, and build comfort, trust, and cohesion within a group.

One of the exercises that could be carried out is called "finish the sentence." The worker might introduce a round by asking each member to complete the sentence such as:

> The person whom I love is . . .
>
> The most beautiful thing that happened to me is . . .
>
> The thing I would like to change about myself is . . .

This exercise is done by limiting each member to a single word or a phrase, which encourages the member to be brief and to the point.

Rounds are a way to encourage group members who do not participate actively to become a part of the group situation. The group worker should spend some time at the end of the session summarizing what happened in the group. This activity can be an eye-opener, as members listen to different perspectives from people who are usually silent. The worker has to remind them that each description is one person's perspective.

DYADS   A dyad is an activity in which two group members are paired in order to discuss an issue or solve a problem. Dyads provide an opportunity for individuals to get to know each other more intimately than they could in the group as a whole. Jacobs, Harvill, and Masson (1994) indicate that dyads are useful in helping to develop comfort within a group, to help group members process information and finish a topic, and to get certain group members together, increasing member interaction, offering a change in the group's format, and also providing time for the group leader to think.

Dyads are used as a way of making things become personal. Instead of having to talk to eight or more members, a group member talks to one other person, which is not as threatening. After working in dyads, group members get more comfortable and are willing to participate in larger group activities. Group dyads can vary from two to twenty minutes, depending on the needs of the group members and how the group responds.

It is important to remember that in cohesive groups the group members feel supported in their attempts to change and are willing to use different new skills, to risk new behavior, and achieve behavioral changes.

Exercises

1. A few students role-play dyads for about five minutes. Later, the students who participated in the dyad can constructively point out some of the feelings and thoughts they experienced with their partner student in the role-play.

Case Situations

2. As a practitioner working with groups, how would you work with the given cases?

Jackie constantly complains in the group that her husband and children take advantage of her. She laments in an aggravated manner, "If they were different, my life would be much more meaningful!" The group members can challenge this by indicating that the family is not going to change on its own. How would you as a group worker intervene in this case? What are the different steps the client has to take in order to bring about change in her life?

Ronnie complained that he was feeling tired and drained in the group. He asserted that everyone in his life was too demanding. In the group, his style of involvement and interaction was that of a helper. He was always very attentive to what others needed and rarely asked anything for himself. At last, in one session he admitted that he was not getting what he wanted from the group and did not wish to return to the group. As a leader of a group, how would you confront him? What type of intervention would you use?

At times, group members make sweeping statements. It is often difficult or impossible to respond to such global statements. Freddie makes a sweeping declaration and comments, "I would like to know what you think of me, and I'd like some feedback from you people." His sudden and spontaneous request for feedback puts the group members in a difficult spot. How would you intervene in this situation as a group member? Why?

INTERVENTION IN COMMUNITIES AND ORGANIZATIONS

All of us are part of a community. What affects the community as a whole affects all of us. A tornado, lack of clean water, and inadequate schools affect all members of the community. In a similar fashion we enjoy the benefits available in a community including economic, educational, political, social, and cultural resources. Problems may arise in communities due to a weak economy, riots against any group of people, a strike organized by workers against a large company during negotiation for a new contract, limited health resources, and lack of social services (Felin, 1995). We are tremendously influenced by the events and situations that affect our communities.

Bringing about change in communities, for whatever immediate or long-term reason, requires the generalist to function in ways that empower community members. This requires the generalist to use some of the same strategies and intervention skills used with individuals, families, and groups. The method of community or organizational change is to bring together a group of people with common interests to structure community change through collective action (Barker, 1995).

Miley, O'Melia, and Dubois (1998) and Lewis, Lewis, and D'Andrea (1998) suggest that the process of working with different size systems applies to communities and organizations as well. When generalists find themselves in a community where some degree of improvement or change has to be made, the most important thing is to first create partnerships with community residents and local government officials as well as natural leaders of the community who have no official titles.

In the next step, the generalist discusses the different challenges facing the community. This is followed by discussing the manner in which interventions can be made and highlighting the purpose and direction of the interventions. When discussing the purpose of intervention, the generalist has to identify the relevant community resources and understand the potentials of community resource capabilities. For instance, in a situation of drug use in the community, are there any organizations with financial backing that could help find solutions to the problem? Where are the indigenous paraprofessional talents present in the community? Based on this knowledge, the generalist and the community members can frame different strategies to bring about change.

Creating alliances between different community members for activating and mobilizing community resources in terms of people, services, and goods is the next step. It is important to use existing advocacy work, bringing about policy changes so that drug abuse is seen as a crucial problem. Whatever successes the community members have made in terms of dealing with this specific problem is recognized, measured, and complimented.

This is further pursued through integrating and stabilizing the gains made in the social and political networks of the community.

Community change occurs by educating the public about urgent social issues and creating social policy that can be used to work on a particular problem. This is called community education. It includes the amount and number of resources available for a specific purpose; for instance, the drug problem.

Often money is scarce for new or different public problems. One of the most important resources that the generalist can provide is to identify the problem and write a grant proposal to secure funds to combat a specific problem. Though this will involve more time, using funds from grants is a good way of ensuring that communities with limited resources and services can be helped.

The mobilizer role is an aspect of empowerment in the community. As Simon (1994) notes, the mobilizer acts "to animate one's client group to advocate for itself collectively and at the same time, to advocate as vigorously as possible for that group's interest" (p. 164).

The generalist as mobilizer should understand the intricacies and the heartbeat of a community. When community issues are being identified, whether it is a drug abuse problem or teen pregnancy, the generalist should dramatize the issue, explain how urgent the need is, build support through advocacy and talks with community members, and maintain the momentum until the changes happen. The generalist has to always remember that the power of a group of people in a community is crucial for all types of community or organizational change.

Some of the ways of bringing about change include the following (see Figure 13.3):

Strategies

Negotiation

Collaboration

Co-optation

Confrontation

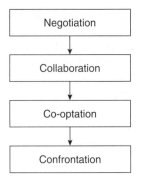

Figure 13.3   **Change Strategies in Communities**

Negotiation, as the term implies, is a positive strategy when a community is willing to work toward a specific agreement and your prospects as a generalist are good for working out a favorable settlement; for instance, when there is a conflict between two groups of people belonging to two ethnic groups in a community. Both the natural leaders of their own ethnic communities are willing to sit down and negotiate after the generalist convinces them that they have a great deal to gain as a larger community rather than as a fractured and compartmentalized group. Both the groups are anxious to put aside their differences and minor disruptions to work together to build a recreational facility for the community. In this case the negotiation is not difficult as the generalist has seen progress in the relationship between the two natural leaders and both have identified that both sides can work together to meet their community interests.

Collaboration is another strategy to bring about change. This happens when two parties are willing to share resources to accomplish an important goal. For instance, in a gang-infested neighborhood, two social welfare agencies who have been in the area for a long period of time decide to pool their funds to take an active part in working with the gang members or ex-gangs. When they come together one agency opts to work with young gang members and their families while the other agency takes an active role in educating the community about gang membership and beginning

signs of gang membership in young children. Collaboration is possible when two agencies or parties work together to accomplish a similar cause. Whatever the reason for collaboration the common goal unifies their respective motives and provides the impetus to work together (Homan, 1999).

Co-optation is described as a strategy for minimizing anticipated opposition by absorbing or including an opponent in the group's membership (Barker, 1995). This strategy is usually geared to opponents. As Homan (1999) relates, co-optation occurs when the beliefs and attitudes others hold about a situation conform to yours. Co-optation takes place when a formerly antagonistic party changes its viewpoint in regard to its opponent. This party, for instance another agency, may be more accepting of its previous opponent and invite the adversary into a relationship of greater congenial contact. It is not uncommon for key leaders of the opposition to offer jobs in the competing organization. Or even an appointment with a special committee that seems to carry some status or special privileges that are arranged for this person (Crowfoot, Chesler, & Boulet, 1983). The purpose is to weaken the opposition or risk losing this new-found acceptance by the former enemy. This reinforces the new moderation by finding merit in a previously scorned point of view. When this happens the former opponent accepts and begins to take a position that furthers the interest of the co-opting party (Homan, 1999).

Confrontation

Confrontation is generally used when you need to force a system to change its position or behavior (Harvey & Brown, 1991). This could happen because the opponent system refuses to meet with you and is unresponsive to your need for change. You wish to crystalize the issue and give the opposition the type of attention that they do not want and in so doing draw attention to your group. For example, you are in conflict with a manager of a social welfare services system which is part of the state government. The state government is, of course, more powerful than your local agency but in this specific instance you may be more powerful than your opponent because your power is focused on a fixed area of operations. In this case, you may be able to use your power to force the local welfare agency to change procedures that have caused you and your agency a great many problems.

In such situations, the vulnerability of your opponent weighed against the strength of your organization is an important factor in winning. Confrontation is never pleasant but sometimes necessary. The bonus you receive is that it increases community pressure and contributes to an atmosphere of controversy that often bothers the opposition.

Social Action

Social action is a coordinated effort to achieve institutional change to meet a need, solve a social problem, correct an injustice, or enhance the quality of life (Barker, 1995). Coordinating with other groups who have similar interests is an important aspect of social action, simply because there is rarely just one group of people who are interested in a specific issue. Coordinated influence brings more strength than one single group asking for a new policy or a policy change. Lobbying is milder form of working toward the same end through persuasion.

Economic injustice is a factor for which social action is appropriate. For example, the Hispanic population represented 26.5 percent of all federal prisoners in 1990. The number of juvenile offenders among the Hispanic population is also increasing. Hispanics do not complete college education comparison in numbers comparable to African Americans or caucasians. However, the rate of increase of the Hispanic population in the United States doubled between the period from 1980 to 1991. Currently, there are debates in the United States that focus on reducing the ability of Hispanics and other immigrant groups to benefit from social, health, and economic services that are routinely available to caucasians (Okun, Fried, Okun, 1999). Coordinated efforts with other

groups and effective help can bring about required changes.

Policy development in the social work profession is an integral part of committing ourselves to social justice and expanded opportunities (Pierce, 1984). Social work professionals on their own and as part of the National Association of Social Workers are in a position to frame public policy and debate the consequences of policy directives. Generalists can offer critical information to direct and shape the development of policy.

Social workers get involved in policy making by examining the social, economic, and political variables evident in the process of formulating policies (Gilbert & Specht, 1986). Many authors propose comprehensive models for policy analysis including Martin (1990), Chambers (1993), and Karger and Stoesz (1994).

Policy development is also an integral part of working with agencies in the community. Consumer participation in agency policy protects the rights of clients, and the relevancy of program services is accountable to targeted populations. Chambers (1993) indicates that consumer participation curbs the career and professional self-interest of staff members and focuses policy making on the needs of clients. Turner (1994) rightly suggests that client consumers should be a part of the advisory committees and boards of directors in order to increase the comprehensive connection between the agency goals and those of social service consumers.

CHAPTER SUMMARY

Intervention is the fourth stage of the helping process. In this stage the worker begins to implement a plan of action to help the client. The intervention roles the worker plays vary from concrete to psychological help. General interventive helping includes: concrete services; information; advice, and direction giving; encouragement; reassurance; and universalization. Helping can be further classified into cognitive, feelings-oriented and performance- and action-oriented strategies. Information and advice giving are part of cognitive interventions. Catharsis and insight development tend to be more feelings-oriented strategies and action as mediation and environmental modification are more behavorially or action-oriented interventions. Other interventions include behavioral rehearsal, self-contracts and action, social support, challenges in helping clients, and feedback. Role reversal, managing self-talk, the empty chair technique, confrontation, reframing, task assignments, envelope budgeting, resolving interpersonal conflicts, client advocacy, and intervention with people belonging to different cultural and ethnic groups are some of the interventive ways of helping that can used with clients.

While working with individual clients the worker can use a number of techniques and skills to improve their social functioning and resolve issues. This process allows conflicts to be resolved in the therapeutic relationship, which is done through verbal therapy.

Family therapy intervention techniques include enactment, family sculpting, marital sociograms, rolling chairs, home visits, dreams, one-way mirrors, videotaping, family photographs, and emphasizing the positives in treatment.

In group treatment, as in individual and family treatment, the major therapeutic medium is what is called the interpersonal process of communication. While moving toward treatment in groups various factors have to be considered such as overgeneralizing, conflicts, and silences. Group members take on different roles and patterns of behavior and the roles may be beneficial or destructive for the group. According to Vinter (1967) there are six different areas that are relevant to group activity, ranging from prescriptive activities to other factors that need to be remembered while working with a group.

Skill training in a group is a highly structured activity that requires a number of goals. There is a time limit to accomplishing goals, and skills are built on from session to session. These include methods of role play such as behavior rehearsal, role reversal, assertiveness training, brainstorming, indirect discussion of self in small groups, and facilitating the group process through rounds and dyads.

Intervention in communities affects community members. The generalist in communities functions in ways that are empowering and helpful to community members. Being a mobilizer is an important role for a generalist working in a community. Some of the ways to bring about change in a community include strategies, negotiation, collaboration, co-optation, and confrontation. Social action is a coordinated effort to achieve institutional change to meet a need, solve a social problem, or correct an injustice. Bringing about policy development is an integral part of working with agencies in the community.

14

EVALUATION

After the client has been through engagement, assessment, planning, and intervention, the worker and the client must evaluate the end results. Evaluation is also done for accountability purposes after the clients have been offered the service just before termination and in some situations after termination.

WHAT IS EVALUATION?

Evaluation is an ongoing process even as the practitioner is making an assessment and intervening. The worker must look at a problem or issue, gather information, generate options, compare options, select the best solution, develop a strategy, implement options, and evaluate results (see Figure 14.1). When the practitioner assesses a client, he or she is at the same time evaluating the situation to determine if the planning for the client will be effective. Thus evaluation is a part of the whole helping process. Evaluation is a means of finding out if the goals are being reached.

As Johnson (1995) indicates, evaluation identifies the *spin-offs* that are unexpected outcomes, both negative and positive, from the helping activity.

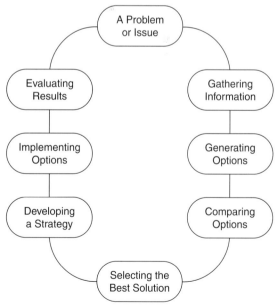

Figure 14.1   **The Evaluation Process**

Evaluation of how practitioners meet professional obligations and activities is also a continuous process in which workers evaluate their work and learn from it.

Evaluation can be described as the act of rendering judgments to determine value, worth, and merit. All genuine evaluations produce findings that are better than speculation (Berk & Rossi, 1990). In evaluation we make sure that both the expectations of the client and the purpose of the helping process are fulfilled. We are also accountable to the agency and the profession for the kind of work we do with our clients. As mentioned in Chapter 4, accountability is a crucial aspect of evaluation. Often money for agencies is provided by government and private funding who require proof to show that their money has been put to good use. The worth of an agency is measured by the accuracy of its accounting in output terms, and this accuracy leads to further and better funding by outside sources.

Without specifying the goals and objectives, it is impossible to measure what has taken place. For this reason evaluation always requires some degree of measurement of achievement in relation to objectives. Bloom, Fischer, and Orme (1995) have identified the following criteria for measurement purposes:

- Measures must be *reliable*. They must be consistent and produce similar results when used under similar conditions.
- The information obtained must be *valid* and measure what it purports to measure.
- It must be *useful*, providing information that can make a difference in making decisions.
- It has to be *direct* and accurately reflect the real problem. The closer it is to the real problem the more useful it will be for future reference.
- It must be *nonreactive*. The measuring process should have minimal influence on the change process being measured.
- It must be *sensitive* to change; that is, the measure you select must show changes as they come about.

- Measurement procedures and scales should be *standardized* so that comparisons can be made.

It is important to remember that not all aspects of the therapeutic outcome are measurable. This is particularly true of the intangible feelings that people experience at different points in their lifetime.

PRACTICE AND PROGRAM EVALUATION

Broadly speaking, social work agencies deal with two different types of evaluation. *Social treatment,* or *practice evaluation,* aims at assessing the effectiveness and efficiency of an intervention with a specific client system. In social treatment evaluation, the worker and the client monitor and assess change. The other type—*program evaluation*—is aimed at assessing the effectiveness and efficiency of a program in serving a large number of clients and in meeting community needs.

Practice evaluation is a method of assessing outcomes as well as measuring the effectiveness of social work intervention techniques and strategies. The client and the practitioner monitor progress and evaluate what the clients have achieved or not achieved. Similarly, program evaluations look at what programs have or have not accomplished. Programs for the elderly, the homeless, and teens are among the many social programs that compete for limited funding. Evaluation provides evidence of programs' fiscal responsibility and goals achievement. Additionally, program evaluations trace the gaps in services and what they suggest may need to be addressed.

Some social work practitioners are concerned primarily with measuring the effectiveness of direct service activities, while others do practice and program evaluations. Both types of evaluations, practice and program, complement each other and create better accountability and effectiveness in agency settings. Practice evaluation is the straightforward method of comparing baseline measures against the latest measures from one interview to the next, or from the beginning of the process to termination. *Baseline* is the measurement of frequency, duration, and intensity of client behavior.

Evaluation may also refer to clients' perceptions of the helping process in terms of what was useful or detrimental. Clients provide feedback about what enhanced or blocked their progress. This helps generalists evaluate their skills and differentiate among techniques and strategies that are more or less useful in achieving desired outcomes. At times, such feedback may be highly informative or confidence building; and at other times, it may be a humbling experience. For example, a worker may believe that a client made significant changes in his or her life due to an extraordinarily useful technique only to find out that the client was "ready" for change because of willingness to reach out and hold on to hope. There are intangible factors that are nevertheless crucial for movement in the helping process, and feedback is necessary to ascertain if a client has reached the goals they set forth.

Another practice evaluation example is studying a client's behavior in the problem situation and noting how the helping process is pertinent to this client, as when a practitioner observes a child in the classroom. Changes that take place in the thoughts, feelings, and actions are used to evaluate the progress—constructive behavior such as better grades and congeniality with classmates—of the client. Similarly, in program evaluation it is important to ask whether the program is achieving its goals. The generalist evaluates this information by considering each client's outcome and compiling the results to determine whether a particular program has met is goals. Often, there is a follow-up with former clients and referral agencies to check for the efficiency and effectiveness of a particular program. Program evaluation is also conducted through a review of case files and clients' progress toward the overall agency goals and mission. Practice and program evaluation combine to provide a more comprehensive view of service delivery.

Purposes of Evaluation

There are at least two purposes for conducting evaluations. The primary purpose is to assess the therapeutic outcomes. For this type of evaluation to occur the worker and the client must determine the type, direction, and amount of change in behavior, both overt and covert, that is shown by the client. According to Schwartz and Baer (1991):

1. The worker and client must determine if the client has changed in global ways
2. Less frequently, the worker measures to see if a client has made specific changes as a result of the treatment
3. Measures may be used to find out if a client has changed enough during treatment to improve everyday functioning

The second purpose of an evaluation is to assess the helping process. After the data have been collected, practitioners monitor strategies to help clients determine whether they are using the strategies accurately and systematically. The evaluation process includes observations of client behavior during termination that are compared to behavior base rate data assuming the same target behavior. This provides workers with an objective measure of success with their other learning interventions. If the data show that there is little or no behavioral change, then the learning strategies would have to be reevaluated and possibly changed.

Social workers are usually called on to justify the efficiency and effectiveness of the type of service they have offered to clients and as well as their own intervention plans. Effectiveness refers to whether the services or intervention plans accomplished their intended goals. Efficiency refers to the amount of time, effort, and resources used.

Working with colleagues to evaluate programs and services offered by an agency helps practitioners select approaches to intervention that lead to improvement in both effectiveness and efficiency. At times, program evaluations may identify unintended consequences of a given program or strategy.

DIFFERENT TYPES OF EVALUATION

Evaluation can be described as the application of scientific methods to measure both the changes and the process of helping that takes place. Evaluation is aimed at measuring the outcomes of specific interventions, the nature of change processes, and the nature of intervention.

In making an evaluation, the worker must think of two different forms of evaluations: formative and summative. Formative evaluation addresses the key question of whether an intervention plan or program activity plan is being implemented as set forth. Summative evaluation refers to the study of program or intervention outcomes.

Formative Evaluation

The terms *summative* and *formative* are used to describe two different types of evaluation. A formative evaluation is conducted throughout the intervention process, starting when the client is beginning to be seen and continuing until the relationship is terminated. Formative evaluations are viewed from two levels: the conceptual and the operational. The *conceptual level* refers to the written plan for accomplishing the objectives.

A social worker practiced with immigrant families who had health and educational issues and family problems. The social worker's role was to conceptualize their needs globally and move toward satisfying their needs as much as possible. After surveying their needs the worker concluded that she would deal with these needs as best she could, first by taking care of health issues such as lice, ringworm, and other diseases. Her initial survey of the immigrant culture showed that these afflictions were not because the people were poor or dirty but due to the fact that their camp often lacked water, bathrooms, and the facilities for proper hygiene.

The *operational* level refers to the intervention activities themselves, that is, what we actually do and the type of worker and client engagement that happens in order to accomplish the goals. At the operational level of the case just mentioned, the generalist working with the immigrant families started the children's summer camp by washing their heads to rid them of lice and sending supplies home with the children so that the camps where they lived could be fogged (Wilshere, 1996).

In formative evaluation, the worker must look at two major aspects of helping: client behavior and the helping process. As Hutchins and Vaught (1997) indicate, there are three questions that need to be addressed with regard to the client's behavior:

1. What type of problem is the client presenting?
2. What are the client's goals?
3. At this point in the process, how is the client functioning in working out the problem?

Evaluating the client's behavior and the helping process occurs simultaneously. Helping is a collaborative process based on the type of problem presented, the person presenting the problem, and the theories, strategies, and techniques used to help the client. If help does not move the client to change in positive ways, the manner in which help is offered needs to be reconsidered.

> WORKER: When we talked two weeks ago, you were going to set aside time to talk to your thirteen-year-old daughter. I believe you said that you would spend about twenty minutes doing so, every day.
>
> CLIENT: I got a new job where I work in shifts, and I am finding out that when I am home I am very tired and impatient with everyone. So it seems to me that right now there is no right time for us to talk to each other.

In this case, the helping strategy might be good, but it did not fit the client's new work patterns. New and different techniques will have to be found to work with this client.

In another example, when a client was not willing to accept or participate in action to bring about changes in his life, the worker evaluated the action strategy and determined it was ineffective. She made shifts in the working plan with the client, and intervened by moving appropriately to a discussion of feelings. When the worker began to explore the client's feelings, she found out that the client was not ready to take action because he was apprehensive of the consequences.

This case study relates the beginning of work by a generalist with the Raskal gangs in the highlands of Papua New Guinea.

The generalist, John, makes a home visit to Dick, a former Raskal gang member who will help him meet other gang members. He finds Dick and the rest of his family already sitting around the fire, drinking coffee, and eating sweet potatoes. John joins them and is given a large plate of sweet potatoes and a big cup of coffee. After a discussion of various topics, the conversation turns to a review of plans that John had worked out with the community people in the last few days on how to farm potatoes in Dick's village and sell them on the northern coast of Papua New Guinea. Finally John steers the conversation to the plans of the day which are to meet two gang leaders and prepare a conference with gangs of other tribes in a particular valley.

John has already conducted such conferences at more or less regular intervals in different communities and is excited. Through trial and error he understands that he needs to evaluate his broad plan to help gang members move away from criminal behaviors. As a generalist involved in community work, he spends time in analyzing and understanding the economic, political, and social structures and developments in the highlands. Within this community framework, he engages gang members in discussions about the reasons for criminal activities. There is an eager discussion of problems, lack of financial resources, and the need for constructive change through active participation. A broad understanding of gang activities provides a base from which to develop economic projects that use the relational and social resources of the Raskals to generate income for gang members and their families. This plan works well because it is based on an evaluation of earlier interventions by Dick and people in similar communities and is firmly based on the desire of the gang members to change (Schwab, 1996).

In many ways a formative evaluation helps the worker to make adjustments in theoretical orientation as well as in complementary techniques. This leads to a corrective adjustment in the helping process.

Evaluation as a Corrective Process

Evaluation is also a corrective process because it points out procedures that have to be changed to help clients move toward realistic and concrete goals. In the process, clients are helped to evaluate what happened in the hope that this will open up alternatives which might be helpful.

WORKER: Last week we made a plan that you spend 20 minutes of leisure time with your wife at least four times in the evening. How did this go?

CLIENT: Not too well. I work on a shift system in my new job so I was not home at night and, therefore, could not carry out the assignment.

WORKER: I guess we need to look at other options perhaps. Why don't you tell me what type of task assignment would be helpful to you to develop a positive relationship.

A community generalist found herself working with several Haitian and Jamaican families who actively practiced voodoo. Because her interventions were being overlooked she reevaluated her value system and concluded that Americans have stereotyped voodoo as black magic. Her initial attempts to move them away from voodoo resulted in hostility, because voodoo was interpreted differently by the Haitian and Jamaican families. To them, it was ancient herbal medicine practiced in a place where there are few medical doctors or medical facilities. It became crucial for the generalist to put aside her own beliefs and values and open herself to a different culture and way of thinking. With this new open-minded perspective, the generalist began to work constructively with the families. Evaluation helped the generalist to communicate and work well within the culture of the families based on their belief system.

In these cases, evaluation was used as a corrective process when the initial procedure did not work. As a result, these workers will be more careful to plan activities that will be useful, helpful, and effective. Activities custom-tailored to the needs of clients have a high probability of being helpful.

The helping process involves questions that eventually lead to a change cycle such as the following: Why is the client system asking for help? What does the client wish to do? How are goals to be achieved? In this way, the work toward solution of a problem becomes a joint effort in bringing about action and empowering client systems. The responsibility for evaluation is shared. The generalist also can work more easily when evaluation becomes a mutual effort.

Another way of evaluating is to ask clients whether they observe any progress. For instance, the generalist can ask the client how things are going since they began to work together, citing the client's plan for work, relationships, and so forth. Making specific inquiries about the client's progress in terms of his or her behavior and inquiring about the helping process should be a regular part of the ongoing process of evaluation and helping.

Summative Evaluation

A summative evaluation usually happens at the end of the helping process. Evaluations are made of the value of the helping process relating to the client's behavior. In a summative evaluation the generalist reviews the process by asking a number of questions:

> How effective was the helping process for the clients?
>
> What different changes did the clients make?
>
> What should the worker have done differently? Why?
>
> What were the effects of theories and techniques that were used?
>
> What did the generalist learn as a result of this experience?
>
> In hindsight, was this the most effective and efficient way of helping the client?
>
> What are the implications for the generalist in terms of working more effectively in the future?

Methods of evaluation

Case Records

Evaluating the client is through monitoring case records, which contain information on the services provided to clients and the community. Each file should contain basic demographic information identifying the client, referral sources, presenting problem, worker's assessment, service contract (if any) and plan, documentation of worker–client interaction and other services offered, report of client response to interviews and functioning outside of interviews, closing summary, and evaluation. These records are a rich source of information that is utilized in day-to-day planning, supervision, training and professional development, practice and program evaluation, fiscal accountability, and research. Case records are necessary for accountability purposes and are readily available to the professionals who work with the clients as well as accrediting groups, court systems, funding organizations, and other agencies.

Depending on the agency, case recording can be brief summary recording, process or narrative recording, or problem-oriented recording. *Summary recording* involves summarizing several weeks of activity in a couple of paragraphs. This type of recording is important in situations where there is long-term contact with clients and a series of workers may have been involved in the case. These records generally provide information about what happened in the past with a specific client system.

Process or narrative recording is a comprehensive, detailed narrative account of process and progress in each session. This recording includes what happened during a client system contact, including the generalist's feelings and thoughts about what happened in a session. Narrative recording received great emphasis at one time and was used extensively in the education and supervision of workers.

Problem-oriented recording is gathered in four parts:

1. Information pertinent to the client system and the work with that client system, including demographic information such as sex, age, marital status, employment history, and results of any psychological testing of the client
2. Records of the initial complaints and the assessment by professionals

3. Plans and goals related to each client system
4. Follow-up notes on what was done and the outcome of the sessions

Problem-oriented records are generally structured to consist of checklists that can be converted into electronic data. The often-used acronym is "*SOAPing*: Subjective (the client's perspective); Objective (the generalist's perspective); Assessment (statement of the problem); and a *Plan* (LaBinca & Cubelli, 1977). In more recent years there has been a great deal of dissatisfaction with the manner in which recording is done. Kagle (1993) uses the term *new records* to indicate records that are narrowly focused on detailing the need for service, service goals, plans for service activities, and the impact of the services on the client system. Kagle found that many generalists felt that this type of recording did not provide all the information necessary for providing comprehensive services, which is important in a profession often threatened by legal action. Kagle suggests that we need to develop a new approach to in-depth recording.

When case records are to be used as part of a formal or standardized evaluation procedure, advance planning is essential to ensure that the necessary information will be included. Agency case records are a rich source of raw data for studying social work practice, community problems, and agency services. Their disadvantage or limitation in practice evaluation is that all the information is presented through the eyes of the social worker and consequently reflects that person's biases and selective memory. In recent years, additional use has been made of electronic technology to document social work practice including audio- and videotapes and, most recently, computerized records.

Videotaping or Electronic Recording

Supervision often involves listening to an audiotape or watching a videotape as these provide a complete and accurate portrayal of what really happened. Despite the hours necessary to review them, such tapes are useful for identifying events for evaluative and training purposes.

In the supervision session, a student played a segment of a videotape where she felt that she had lost control of the session. The tape was a valuable tool for learning. The student was able to look at her work more objectively, be self-critical, and learn through the process. It helped the supervisor appreciate the student's open-minded trust of her supervision, and helped the student develop better skills in dealing with clients.

Audiotaping can be effective but it is more difficult to evaluate and point out issues with only conversation and no picture. Evaluation using audiotapes is based on assessing verbal cues, such as a change in the tone of voice, and the verbal communication process taking in the session.

Use of Computers

The computer is an important tool for case recording as well as in evaluation. Computers can be used to: (1) record and analyze information in more sophisticated ways; (2) encourage the possibilities of data analysis; (3) facilitate the storing and retrieval of data; and (4) document accountability.

Although there are limitations to computer data due to confidentiality, especially if data is available to all staff members, staff should be educated about electronic filing. Generalists should know how to process information so that it can be computerized, which includes how to enter information, access existing data, and evaluate the usefulness of both hardware and software for social work purposes. If need be, a computer expert or programmer should be advised about problems with a piece of equipment or the programming itself. When putting data into the computer it is important to follow instructions carefully. All required information must be provided so that planned operations with reference to cases are carefully taken care of.

It is extremely important for generalists to know who has access to their cases and the purposes for which their case information might be used. This helps generalists to evaluate whether pertinent information is being requested and, at the same time, to protect client identification and confidentiality. If at any time the generalist believes that data are at risk, there is an ethical responsibility to inform those responsible for the operation of the programs and to ensure that the required modifications are made (Taylor, 1981).

Critical Incident Recording

Critical incident recording is a form of modified recording in which workers present an intervention or a client presents an issue which are subjected to a thorough analysis. The recording should indicate all the relevant information about the client and the worker's behavior, which helps in evaluation of a problem, an issue, or a situation.

Research–Practice Evaluation

There are many research techniques that can be used to carry out evaluations not only in research but in generalist practice as well. The following discussion will point out the relationship between practice and research when evaluating social work practice. A few research techniques that are specifically useful and suitable for the evaluation of practice are presented. They include single-subject design, goal-attainment scale, task achievement scale, use of questionnaires, interviews, and observation.

SINGLE-SUBJECT DESIGNS   In a single-subject design, the worker evaluates the impact of an intervention by using a baseline and other measurements of change. *Baseline* is a behavioral research term that denotes measurement of the frequency, intensity, and duration of a behavior and it is important in assessing the progress of a case.

Jesse, a naval officer, and Jane, his wife, seek help for their marital problems. Jane claims that her husband fights with her everyday and uses violently abusive language. Jesse responds that she does the same but that they do not fight everyday as Jane claims. Jane looks at Jesse and says angrily, "We fight a lot everyday." He responds, "We fight constantly." The generalist, Richard, has to evaluate his efforts in helping this couple, so it is important to learn whether the fights are decreasing. However, there is no

agreement about the frequency of fighting, it is impossible to know whether matters are improving between the couple. Therefore, Richard asks both Jesse and Jane to individually record the number of fights they have had in the coming week. This information provides some basis for determining whether the frequency of fights is increasing, diminishing, or remaining the same.

The term *single-subject* denotes a focus on a single individual or entity such as a family or a small group. In the single-subject design, the client becomes his or her own control group. There is also an individualized baseline that is relevant and meaningful to the client's unique problem, situation, and goals. An important characteristic feature of all single-cell designs is the "before" measure, referred to as the baseline. Establishing a baseline is important when any single-subject design is used. When intervention is used to change a particular behavior, that behavior is called the *target behavior*. The baseline is established by the frequency, the intensity, and the duration of the target behavior; for example, fighting between a couple over a period of days or weeks. It is also possible to establish a baseline by gathering information from interviews with a client on previous patterns of behavior, from interviews with the client's family and significant others, and from agency records. The term *multiple baseline* refers to the use of more than one baseline in measuring change. For example, the first problem a child faces is trouble attending school regularly, secondly he has problems in academic performance, and lastly his behavior in the classroom is disruptive. Different interventions have to be performed in order to bring about changes in each area of the child's behavior. Therefore, several baselines are established in order to evaluate effective helping.

Shaefor, Horejsi, and Horejsi (1997) and Garvin and Seabury (1997) have indentified different versions of the single-subject design using a number of initials. The letter *A* refers to the baseline and *B* refers to the intervention. Thus an AB single-subject design refers to the establishment of a baseline followed by intervention. Any change that is measured in the baseline is due to the use of the intervention. When an ABA version is used, the intervention (B) is removed after a period of time in order to test the impact of the intervention. If there is a return to the baseline, it can be assumed that the change is caused because of the intervention and not any other factor in the client's life situation (see Figure 14.2).

The ABAB design goes a step further by adding a fourth stage and restarting the intervention. For example, if there is a change from the second baseline, the worker can be quite sure that his or her intervention was responsible for the change. The BAB variation begins with an intervention, then the intervention is withdrawn to establish a baseline and restart an intervention.

Another version is called the multiple-element design or the ABCD design which is used to evaluate the impact of a series of different interventions, one following another. For instance, after the baseline (A) has been established, the first intervention (B) is tried for a few weeks, then a second intervention (C) is implemented, followed by an intervention (D). This type of design makes it possible to compare the relative effectiveness of different interventions on a target behavior.

A mother and daughter had interpersonal conflicts. One of the problems they faced was that they argued a great

deal with each other and had few calm discussions. About two weeks before the clinical sessions started, the mother and her nineteen-year-old daughter were asked to make daily records of the number of times they argued with each other over food preparation, spending money, clothes, mother's work schedule, daughter's dating patterns, and so forth, and the number of times they talked calmly to each other for at least a five-minute period. The weekly totals of their behavior was shown on a graph. The intervention consisted of a weekly joint session and a weekly group session with five other client pairs of mothers and daughters. The aim was to reduce the number of arguments and increase the degree of calm, easygoing conversations. After six weeks of intervention, the mother and daughter were asked to take a three-week break from the helping sessions. When they returned after this "vacation," they were seen for a second six-week period of intervention. A careful inspection of the graph revealed that during the first six weeks of intervention, the arguments and fighting reduced. However, when they were not in clinical sessions during the next six weeks, the arguments and fighting again increased, while calm conversations decreased dramatically. During the second period of intervention, the mother and daughter again moved in the direction of positive growth in their relationship with more calm conversations and fewer arguments (Shaefor, Horejsi, & Horejsi, 1991).

TASK ACHIEVEMENT SCALE   The purpose of the task achievement scale (TAS) is to determine the

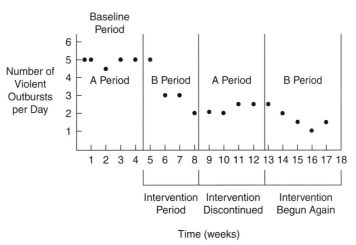

Figure 14.2 **ABAB Design**

degree to which the worker and client have completed their agreed-upon goals. The TAS is a simple and flexible evaluation tool that is used in task-centered social work and research. The client's goal is usually broken down into many small separate actions and tasks. A task is an assignment that is given to the client and is achieved in a specified amount of time. Usually the tasks are selected by mutual agreement. Each task should make sense to the client and be directly related to the client's problem or goal.

Reid (1996, 1992) and Epstein (1992) have used a four-point scale to determine a TAS rating. The progress on each task is recorded as follows: 4—completely achieved; 3—substantially achieved; 2—partially achieved; 1—minimally achieved; and 0—no progress.

A task is completely achieved when a person carries it out to its logical conclusion, such as making an appointment to go to exercise classes, writing a letter, doing the laundry, and so forth. If there is a significant amount of change, it can be said that a task is substantially achieved. Partially achieved means that there is some degree of work that remains to be done, and minimally achieved means there has been little substantive progress.

GOAL ATTAINMENT SCALE   The purpose of the goal attainment scale is to find out if clients have achieved the goals they set. By using the goal attainment scale, a worker can evaluate an intervention even when the goals and objectives of the intervention are unique to a specific client. The goal attainment scale has been used in mental health centers, drug abuse programs, correctional facilities, and other social welfare settings (Karr, 1990; Fleuridas, Leigh, Rosenthal, & Leigh, 1990). In order to be able to see the achievements, a chart is developed on which each column represents a different type of client goal. Each row in the chart represents a different level of the five levels of possible attainment. These levels are classified as: most unfavorable outcome thought likely; less than expected success; expected level of success; more than expected level of success; and most favorable outcome thought likely. An evaluator can gather valuable information about changes in clients' results based on the types of problems that were chosen as targets for intervention and their relative frequency, as well as about the types of problems in which the clients made the least or the most amount of progress.

Kiresuk, Smith, and Cardillo (1994) have worked at developing scores for measuring goal attainment for clients. Although there have been some questions with regard to the validity of the statistics, this does not preclude the use of these scales in evaluating changes that happen in individual clients (Garvin & Seabury, 1997). Figure 14.3 is an example of a modified goal attainment scale.

SELF-ANCHORED AND INDIVIDUALIZED RATING SCALES   The purpose of self-anchored and individualized rating scales is to measure the intensity of a client's emotional response to a problem. Difficulties that clients experience are often expressed in emotional terms, including sadness, anxiety, and

−3	−2	−1	0	1	2	3
Goal Given Up	Much Worse Than at Start	Little Worse Than at Start	Starting Point	Little Better Than at Start	Much Better Than at Start	Goal Attained

Figure 14.3   **Modified Goal Attainment Scaling**
SOURCE: M. McMahon (1996). *The General Method of Social Work Practice.* Englewood Cliffs, NJ: Prentice-Hall, p. 252.

even a lack of pleasure in the representation of problems. Bloom et al. (1995) describe two different types of scales: the "do it yourself" scale and the "all purpose measurement procedure" scale. Both scales are similar except the self-anchored scale is completed by the client, whereas the rating scale is completed by a person, other than the client. One way of doing this is to ask the client to imagine a scale of 0 to10, on which 10 represents the problem or emotion in a very intense manner and 0 means that the problem or emotion is practically nonexistent. This method could be used to baseline any emotion a person may feel and to determine the level of emotion that is induced by various difficulties experienced by a person.

BEHAVIORAL COUNTS This simply means counting the number of times a client acts in a specified manner. The worker normally suggests that clients maintain a chart on which they jot down the number of times a particular type of behavior occurs. A behavioral count can be used to measure changes in a problematic behavior. For example, twelve-year-old Juan realizes that every time there is a fight in the family, he gets involved by taking sides with the weaker person in the fight. During one week, he noted that this had happened at least nine times. After noting this frequency, Juan wanted to change his behavior and not take sides in fights but attempt to be an impartial arbitrator.

VALUE RATINGS Workers will sometimes seek to rate behavioral change, emotional change and also move toward complex goals such as attitude and value dimensions in understanding a person and his or her behavior. For example, a Catholic parent in an inter-religious marriage may be willing to allow her teenage children to choose the religion they wish to follow. She may not approve the religious mores for herself but she will allow her children to explore a different value system.

Many ways have been developed to measure the values that people hold (Beardslee, 1989). For example, Simon, Howe, and Kirschenbaum (1972) have devised a value grid to rate people

along the following dimensions in reference to their employment:

1. Are you proud (prize or cherish) of obtaining this job so easily?
2. Has your position as a high-ranking employee been publicly affirmed?
3. Were there other alternatives available to you but you took this position because you wanted to do so?
4. Have you given considerable thought about the pros and cons of the position you are holding and what the consequences of this position are?
5. Did you take this position because you needed to or did you do so freely?
6. Did you act on or do anything because of your belief in what you can do to improve this company?
7. Have you acted on improving the company with repetition, or consistency?

Some clients may have problems dealing with seven different scales, in which case, the worker can pick and choose the most appropriate items for the client. A worker might then evaluate the client on a three-point scale (Garvin & Seabury, 1997) to examine how often—(1) frequently; (2) occasionally; (3) seldom or never—a person does a specific behavior.

PROBLEM-SOLVING SKILLS AND EVALUATION

Generalists often have to evaluate the problem-solving skills of clients—whether clients have learned to use logical processes in solving problems. Utilizing the following rating scale, the worker can evaluate the client's problem-solving skills (Garvin, 1981):

1. Is the client seeking additional relevant information to work through the problem? For instance, if the problem is returning to school to get

a better education and improve life choices, has the client looked at the different options in fields and courses available based on skills, interests, and earlier training?

2. After understanding personal interests, has the client identified the alternatives that are available? For example, if the first college and type of course does not work out, has the client obtained sufficient information to work through alternatives?

3. Has the client evaluated the alternatives and used criteria such as:

- The alternative that the client has chosen will most likely help achieve the goal to the optimum.
- The alternative that is chosen has few disadvantages or costs.
- The alternative that is chosen is consistent with the client's values.

4. Has the client chosen the alternative that was evaluated in a favorable manner?

5. Does the client have an alternative plan that can be implemented?

All of these questions can be answered with a "yes" or a "no." Also, these questions could be evaluated on a five-point scale, from 0, meaning that the client has no plan, to 5, meaning the client has everything completely planned.

EVALUATION OF FAMILIES

Family evaluation is done in many different ways. In some cases, a family situation is evaluated on the changes made in one of the individuals in the family; in other cases, the family will use standardized approaches to offering one-on-one help. Nevertheless, it is crucial to evaluate family-level changes. There are no standards or general criteria for good outcomes for the family as an entity. Additionally, there have not been any specific criteria developed for measuring success in families.

Gurman and Kniskern (1981) agree that not much has been done in systematically studying outcomes in family work, however, there have been several excellent studies conducted that can be used as models for future investigations. Some of the noteworthy studies include the outstanding work on family management of schizophrenia by Falloon (1991). Another exemplary investigation is Epstein, Baucom, and Rankin's (1993) analysis of behavioral marital therapy in which the investigators separated therapy into specific elements for analysis of the relative contribution of each to its treatment outcome. Other examples include Sanders and Dadds's (1993) study of client resistance to parent management of training; Piercy, Trepper, and Jurich's (1993) evaluation of family therapy in decreasing HIV high-risk behaviors among adolescents; and Liddle, Dakof, and Diamond's (1992) study of young teenage drug abusers and their families in treatment.

There are several practitioners who have specifically looked at measurements to bring about family change including Strauss (1969) and Cromwell, Olson, and Fournier (1976). Others have investigated specific factors to evaluate a family change, including: marital quality (Reding, Charles, & Hoffman, 1967); marital relationship (Fanschel, 1958; Bray & Jouriles, 1995); family interaction (Postner, 1971; Campbell & Patterson, 1995); family functioning (Bowen, 1961; Henggeler, Borduin, & Mann, 1993); and communication behaviors (Cadogan, 1977; Sprenkle & Bischoff, 1995).

Instruments that are used to bring about change can also be used to evaluate progress. When the worker is restructuring the family, he or she can use diagrams of the family to look at structure. Assessment techniques like the eco-map can be used to make an evaluation of a family. Additionally, family members could create their own diagrams generating a kind of "face validity" when clients perceive that the family situation has changed. A worker making an evaluation of a family should keep in mind the growth of individual family members, as well as the gains made by the family as a whole in the helping process and the areas they need to work on (Garvin & Seabury, 1997). Videotapes and critical incident recordings can also be used for evaluation of families. Videotapes used in the beginning sessions monitoring a family's behavior could be replayed toward the end of treatment to see if there has been positive change and growth in the family members.

It should be remembered, however, that empirical investigations have generally been conducted on therapies that are more pragmatic in nature: that is, those concerned with behavior change such as behavioral, structural, and strategic therapies (Gurman & Kniskern, 1991; Colapinto, 1991; Madanes, 1991; Heneggeler et al., 1993). Very few studies have been conducted on intergenerational patterns and social construction because the data is viewed as not being empirical in nature.

Quantitative design improvements been made for evaluation purposes. Increasingly, consistency and rigor have promoted qualitative studies and evaluations as well. With regard to qualitative studies one that can serve as a model of future evaluations and future investigations is the study of family treatment of adolescent drug abusers and their families conducted by Harvey Joanning and his colleagues (Joanning, Thomas, Quinn, & Mullen, 1992).

GROUP EVALUATION

Workers have noted how individual members have progressed and evaluated their success or failure in the group. When evaluating groups Corey (1990) acknowledges the value of objectivity; however, he indicates that in spite of a number of tests and so forth, before and after a group experience, "none of these measures were adequate in detecting subtle changes in attitudes, beliefs, feelings, and behavior. Consequently, I have come to rely on subjective measures that include a variety of self-reports" (p. 138). Ways of evaluating groups include collecting information through testimonials, reports

and group histories, making direct observations, and reviewing videotapes of group meetings.

Testimonials

As Reid (1991) indicates, testimonials are usually written self-reports in which a group member is asked a number of questions about a particular phenomenon. Group members answer based on their personal observation. Questions include:

> Were you satisfied with the group?
>
> In what ways have you changed since you have been in the group?
>
> Have your changes lasted for a long time?

This is not purely an evaluation of the group, as a whole but rather of the experiences of different members of the group.

Samples from the journals of clients who have been in a self-actualization group reveal the power of testimonials.

> I am a recovering alcoholic. It took me a long time to accept and work with it[.] I felt that I was a terrible person and would never make it, but with the help of the members of my group it became clear to me that this is not true. My interactions with other group members has shown me that I am okay and others are okay too, and that I need to work at my issues just like the rest of the group and not feel I am alone. We are all in it together and the group has been a real healing for me.

Another group member writes,

> The group experience has helped me to understand myself much better[.] I realize that I can care for other people, and I feel I interacted very well with the different group members and also gave a lot to them. I have learned to understand that I enjoy giving and sharing and this has helped me in my own growth and also in my understanding of myself.

Reviews of interviews, logs or journals, and similar approaches are ways of evaluating practice.

Rogers (1970) and Martin (1993) call this a naturalistic study in which a client can use personal and subjective feelings to describe the significance of the deep insights derived from the group experience. These self-reports illuminate the process and the outcomes from the members' perspective.

Corey and Corey (1992) use a brief questionnaire after the group work has been completed that asks members to evaluate the techniques used, the impact of the group on them, and also the degree to which they think they changed because of their participation in the group.

It should be kept in mind that subjective reports have obvious limitations, but they do give some degree of information as group members evaluate their group experience. Because those participating in treatment groups are people seeking help for their own problems, most of the methods discussed above in connection with individual intervention are applicable to work with individuals in groups as well as others.

Content Analysis

Gentry (1978) and Zuckerman (1995) used an audiotape to analyze the content in group sessions. Two concepts are important in content analysis: (1) the unit of analysis or scoring, and (2) the categories for analysis. The unit of analysis refers to the portion of content that will be the standard measure used in each session's content as it is being coded. This unit also provides the boundaries and the criteria for studying a session's content. For example, a unit of analysis could be a single verbal action that is used by any group member and is bounded on either side by the speech of any other member. The categories for analysis refer to the classification scheme in which units of content are organized systematically for the purpose of coding as well as counting. A category could be, for example, a topic that is discussed by the group in a group session.

Sociometry

Sociometry is a technique used to measure the social relationships of group members with each other. It also reveals the patterns of interaction within that group which could lead to an in-depth understanding of how the group functions.

A group leader develops a questionnaire that is tailored to a specific group, including questions on age, social and emotional levels of functioning, and other typical activities, such as the type of work a person performs, and so forth. The group members are also asked questions regarding their preferences toward other group members. This information is then presented in diagrammatic form called a *sociogram*. Typical questions suggested by Reid and Hanrahan for sociometric evaluation (1982) include:

> Work: List three members you would like to work with in the group.
>
> Play: Name three members you would like to play with in a soccer game.
>
> Psychological and emotional support: Who are the different members you would go to if you had a problem or if you were sad or unhappy about something?
>
> Social activity: Who are the three people in the group you would like to be friends with?

When this type of measurement is used it shows which group members are popular, who are not, and how members pair themselves. It provides an idea about subgroupings, the isolates in the group, the indigenous leader, and so forth. This type of measurement could be used in the beginning stages of a group and again toward the end. It provides an idea about how group members feel about themselves and others and whether these feelings change over time.

Another way of studying relationship patterns in groups is through observation of such things as seating arrangements, and who talks to whom and for how long. Observing group members enhances the quality of information that is required to make interpretations and conclusions. A lot of the information that is obtained can be checked for accuracy by the group members and by repeated observations over time (Postuma, 1989).

According to Berg (1995), workers interpreting sociograms often go beyond the actual data concerning subgrouping, interpersonal attraction, and isolation within the group to make judgments about behavior outside the group. He cautions that these conclusions should be considered speculative. Additional information obtained through individual interviews outside the group sessions is needed to assess emotional content, qualitative aspects of the relationships, or causative factors.

The Group Worker as Monitor

A group worker can monitor and evaluate the behavior of group members and is thus in a unique position to measure changes that happen. Also, immediate feedback on specific changes in client behavior in response to specific interventions is available to the worker. For example, if a member's maladaptive behaviors are increasing and the adaptive ones are decreasing, the leader knows immediately that what he or she was doing is ineffective and also detrimental to the group (Rompf & Royse, 1994).

Self-Monitoring

Self-monitoring is similar to monitoring by the worker except this is done by group members. It can also be called self-observation and self-recording. These terms are part of a two-step process wherein clients identify the occurrences of a particular behavior and then systematically record their observations. These records identify the frequency with which the behavior occurs. The purpose is for the group member and the group leader to become aware of what changes have or have not occurred (Kopp, 1988).

Diaries and Logs

Group workers often encourage members to maintain a diary or a log. A log lists the type of information that the worker indicates needs to be collected. The purpose of this chart is to help clients keep track of feelings and behavior and the events that trigger undesirable responses. Another purpose is to encourage members to carry out assigned tasks between sessions.

Group Evaluation Questionnaire

The group evaluation questionnaire can help group workers determine if they have succeeded in their efforts. Some of the sample questions, as indicated by Corey and Corey (1992), that the group worker may ask are:

1. How would you evaluate the overall group experience?
2. What were the highlights of this group experience for you?
3. What new insights did you develop about your lifestyle and way of dealing with problems?
4. Did you accomplish any changes as a member of the group?
5. What were the techniques used by group leaders that had the highest degree of impact on you?
6. Did you make any changes as a result of the group experiences?
7. Were there any negative experiences that the you faced as a member of the group?
8. What contribution do you think you made to the group?
9. Would this experience help you to become involved in other groups?
10. In retrospect, would you discuss any of the questions and doubts you had about the group process itself and the motivation of different group members?
11. What other information would you care to provide in order to give us [the group leaders] a complete picture of what meaning the group had for you?

STRENGTHENING GAINS

An aim of the helping process is to help clients maintain the gains they have made through the process so that if they are faced with new problems they will have the strength and the coping skills to deal with them by themselves. Clients fail to maintain gains because they have a natural tendency to revert to habitual response patterns and because of pressures from the environment.

In evaluating what has been accomplished, the worker can assist clients to consolidate their gains by reviewing the problems for which they sought help and the steps that were used to resolve them. The worker's role is to reinforce the gains by helping clients own their effective problem solving in a particular situation or life process.

Clients should be made aware of relapse prevention services. Over the past decade, practitioners and researchers have developed relapse prevention strategies including self-management techniques and processes of cognitive, emotional, behavioral, and lifestyle components. Daley (1991) has identified various factors that lead to relapse due to addictions, identified beliefs, and so forth. Marlatt and Gordon (1985) have contributed to and edited a comprehensive book that focuses on relapse prevention.

The worker should help clients use support systems in their natural environments, particularly clients with limited skills. This could take the form of encouraging mental patients to affiliate with Recovery Incorporated, alcoholics with Alcoholics Anonymous, single parents with Parents without Partners, child-abusing parents with Parents Anonymous, and so forth. Although workers are happy to see their clients recover and leave the social work setting, it is important that clients know they can return if they need to, and the worker should demonstrate continued interest in clients. Thus even after evaluating the outcomes, irrespective of the fact that they are positive, it is best to reinforce growth by relying on constructive support systems.

THE PRACTITIONER EVALUATION

The worker must ask for feedback from clients while they are being helped in order to understand how the helping process works. Criticisms and requests must be invited. Positive feedback will make workers happy, if they have done something for the clients. Clients are also aware of that fact, and may therefore give positive feedback more readily.

The most obvious form of negative feedback happens when the client drops out of treatment. At times, clients will give negative feedback that is painful to the practitioner. However, negative feedback is extremely helpful in understanding behaviors, attitudes, and mannerisms that may be distracting. Just as clients have blind spots, so do practitioners; consequently, negative feedback as well as constructive criticism should be viewed as opportunities for growth.

Stanley had a way of frowning when listening carefully to his clients, who were school children. Often the children did not confide in him and were restrained in his presence. Stanley became very concerned when he received reports that the children were uncomfortable with him. One day a ten-year-old told Stanley that he looked angry "just like my father." When Stanley looked surprised she pulled her eyebrows together and added, "That's the way my father looks when he is angry." This input helped Stanley see how he presented himself to his clients. Although he had trouble changing this habit, he learned to explain to his clients that frowning was simply his way of concentrating.

Another type of evaluation, called the *regular formal evaluation,* is conducted by a competent senior social worker of a new social worker. There is some degree of informal supervision, but formal evaluation takes place as a periodic examination of the worker's overall activity in the agency and identifies practice performance and suggestions for improvement. Evaluating performance is an administrative tool that may have positive or negative consequences for the worker. It may lead to promotion and rewards or probation or termination. There are three aspects of formal worker evaluation: the supervisor, the criteria for evaluation, and the process of evaluation.

The Supervisor

The supervisor should be a competent person who is able to understand that a new social worker will reveal uneven abilities in the early stages of practice. It is the supervisor's role to create a trusting relationship that will help the person develop to his or her fullest potential. Supervision should focus on the new worker's competencies. Unfortunately, this may not occur in some agencies overwhelmed by other negative administrative outcomes. The new social worker may not learn to be productive in such a setting with a supervisor who is overly critical.

The Criteria

How the social worker is to be evaluated should be clear before the evaluation begins. If not, confusion and anxiety are created in the new worker. Although there have been no specific criteria for each area of worker evaluation, the following has been put forth by Kadushin and Kadushin (1997):

Sample Content Areas: Worker Evaluation

1. Ability of the new worker to maintain meaningful, effective, and objective professional relationships with client systems

   - Attitudes presented are appropriate behaviors toward clients
   - Disciplined and objective use of self in relationship to clients
   - Utilizing professional objective values in client relationships and contact

2. Utilization of social work process: knowledge and skills

   - Utilizing data-gathering skills
   - Utilizing data assessment skills
   - Utilizing treatment skills
   - Utilizing interviewing skills
   - Utilizing recording skills

3. Agency objectives, policies, and procedures and orientation to the agency administration
4. Relationship to the supervisor and the use of supervision

   - Administrative aspects
   - Interpersonal aspects

5. Relationships with the staff and the community

6. Ability to manage work requirements and workload
7. Self-evaluation in terms of professionally related attributes and attitudes

The Process

The worker's performance assessment has to be made in the form of narrative statements, translated to evaluative scales, or both. These should be viewed from the context of process and discussed by supervisor and worker. Based on the discussion of evaluation materials, the worker and supervisor should establish further goals, change or modify assignments, and plan professional developmental activities that will strengthen the supervisee for the next evaluation. The supervisor should be supportive and, if need be, help the worker carry out the modified assignments, as well as follow the progress being made and plan for new development. The agency's recorded documents on the new worker serve as part of the agency's accountability plan, to protect the worker from arbitrary personnel actions, and most importantly help the worker move toward professionalism.

OTHER TREATMENT FACTORS IN EVALUATION

There are a number of factors that need to be addressed as part of evaluation as difficult as it is to measure the helping process. These include the influence of the worker on the client and the professional relationship. A worker can engage in a great deal of persuasive communication in order to encourage the clients to speak, behave, and think differently. Also, the client usually trusts and respects the worker's power of suggestion, which greatly enhances the relationship. The worker has a reinforcing effect that motivates the client to change in some particular way.

Also, there are certain demands that workers make while helping that persuade clients to do what is considered to be necessary and important. At times, clients are given assignments to do and they are helped to complete the assignments regularly and conscientiously, which affects the degree and direction of change. Also, clients often desire to please their worker. In many ways this affects the behavior of the client from the degree of improvement to what the client invests in the relationship. Other factors that affect the results of the helping process are certain "demands" that the worker places on the client such as instructions and expectancies.

Clients' desire to change is also affected by the belief systems and instructions that bring about change. Clients who receive high-demand instructions to carry out a task or behavior may respond to counseling differently than those who receive low-demand instructions (Jacobson & Traux, 1991). Clients who receive suggestions of therapeutic improvement without any formal help may demonstrate a great deal of clinical progress. Also, clients' expectations, which vary from person to person, affect the course and outcome of the helping process (Kazdin & Krouse, 1983; Southworth & Kirch, 1988).

Part of success in the helping process is attributable to the worker's ability to mobilize the type of help a client needs. If the client sees the worker as highly credible, then the client's chances of improvement are enhanced. There is also research to indicate that helping outcomes are the result of a positive expectancy which has been established for the client.

Another factor to be considered is the reactivity to measurement. There are some procedures to which a client's change in the helping process is reactive; that is, the process of collecting data itself may contribute to client change. This happens as a consequence of observing and recording behavior, in addition to treatment intervention (Cormier & Cormier, 1997).

Thus, practically speaking, a number of factors come into play while working with clients: the influence of the worker, the demand characteristics of the helping process, the client's expectations, and the reaction of certain types of measures that can be assets for maximizing desired therapeutic changes in the client. These factors are important sources of influence and cause therapeutic change as well as the use of intervention strategies and techniques.

ORGANIZATIONS AND COMMUNITIES

Approaches used in evaluation of individuals, families, and groups can be utilized with communities and organizations as well. For instance, goal attainment, target problem scaling, and data analysis can be utilized with larger systems because we are always working with different groups of people.

Case Studies

Case studies can be done with individuals, families, groups, organizations, and communities. Case studies are qualitative measurements of a single case or a small group of cases. Case studies enable us to study problems such as need for the cleanup of a community or a lack of water supply in a community or the role of autocratic leadership in an organization on its members. Case studies allow us to review problems in depth and to identify the factors that lead to a certain outcome.

We can conduct case studies through unstructured interviews and ask questions that will be helpful in understanding needs, intervention, and evaluation. Interviews conducted with neighborhood members may indicate whether the interventions applied in a neighborhood brought about satisfaction or dissatisfaction. For example, while working in a neighborhood you could talk to some of the community members to determine the most important issues that need to be remedied. After the work has been accomplished, follow-up can lead to positive or negative evaluations, which could lead to completion of work or a reinvestment in some of the work that needs to be handled.

Quality Assurance Reviews

A quality assurance review evaluates the patterns of problems with the outcome of service delivery and then corrects the problem (Sashkin & Kiser, 1993). Quality assurance is an ongoing effort conducted to recognize and deal with problems in agency service delivery. The purpose of the quality assurance program is to evaluate whether the agency is meeting its own standards of quality. Quality assurance is done through reviewing case files, records of complaints, and letters from different clients. In quality assurance, the evaluation leads to finding defects and enhancing the quality of services to clients for agencies that have some accepted standards of performance. For instance, if your agency has a policy that requires that all suspected incest abuse cases to be investigated within forty-eight hours, records should be reviewed to note if this level of service is being attained. Quality assurance reviews focus on finding drawbacks in services and promoting a uniform quality of service.

Program Evaluation

A social program is a planned sequence of activities for bringing about desired individual or social change and it requires a systematic examination to note how it is achieving its goals and objectives. Guba and Lincoln (1989) have identified five categories of program evaluation: (1) front-end analysis including needs assessment; (2) process analysis; (3) evaluability assessment; (4) outcome analysis including cost-benefit analysis; and (5) program monitoring. The procedures used to make evaluations and the problems associated with process are essentially the same regardless of whether the evaluation is of a program or is being conducted by a practitioner and a client in a specific intervention plan (Chambers, Wedel, & Rodwell, 1992). They specify that program evaluation has three dimensions. Program *effort* includes type and quantity of activities, staffing patterns, and clientele served. Program *effective-*

ness refers to the attainment of program goals, and program *efficiency* refers to the cost of achieving the objectives.

Shaefor et al. (2000) have provided guidelines for making a program evaluation:

1. Who are the users of the evaluation data and report? These include administrators, practitioners, program planners, legislators, and also fund-raisers. What is the purpose of evaluation and what types of information are they looking for? In what way will evaluation results affect the program? Would evaluation results allow the program to be continued, modified, or terminated?

2. Is it necessary to make an evaluation? Cost and benefits become important. What amount of money, time, and skill is available for this purpose. Are the key members interested in the program evaluation? Has the program been in operation long enough to make the evaluation feasible for that purpose?

3. What are the goals and objectives of the program? Objectives have to be clearly stated in order to be measurable, which is an important criterion for program evaluation. Also, the program cannot measure anything beyond its goals and objectives, including its intervention activities.

4. What are the program interventions to be evaluated? The worker has to ask where intervention activities begin and end, and has to be clear on criteria for them. For example, if a client has attended an assertiveness training group only three out of five scheduled sessions, has the person moved successfully toward being self-assertive?

5. Are the selected indicators of change measurable? The worker has to be specific about behaviors and conditions that the program is supposed to change and clear about the type of interventions to be used to bring about these changes. Also, what are the indicators selected to detect change? Those indicators should reasonably be attributable to a program's intervention.

6. What are the appropriate and feasible data collection and measurement tools to collect, tabulate, and analyze the data? Instead of developing a valid and reliable instrument, which is extremely time-consuming, it is best to use instrument that has already been applied to similar program evaluations. Sources of useful instruments for program evaluation have been identified by Buros (1986), Feldman and Sherman (1987), Magura and Moses (1986), Hudson (1982), Chambers et al. (1992), and others.

Data that are collected should be sufficient and useable. What is the plan to gather data from case files, from computers or from former service consumers? Will the data you are looking for actually be available and accessible?

7. How will the results of your evaluation be interpreted. The results of the study should be reported so that there is appropriate recognition of the quality of services or recommended modifications of the program.

Exercises

1. A couple of students role-play the evaluation process. One is the worker, and the other is the client in their final session together. The worker asks the client about his or her satisfaction with the process of helping, the outcomes of the process, and so forth. The class observes the questions being asked and the responses of the client. They make their observations and then comment on what they think of the outcomes of treatment.

2. The students role-play a family in its ending phase of therapy, the worker can then help evaluate the outcome in the family based on the needs and requirements of the family group. How did family therapy help the family members feel more like a "we group"? What were the other outcomes in terms of communications and family issues?

3. Six or seven students role-play members of a group, and one person role-plays the group leader. The group is at the ending phase, and the group leader asks the group members to evaluate their own growth, the performance of other group members, and the significance of the group to them in terms of their own growth.

4. A group of students role-play members of a community with different concerns where the generalist has to prioritize the problems in terms of need and majority vote.

Later, all the students discuss the different evaluation processes they witnessed and the similarities and differences, as well as the pros and cons, of each client system in evaluation. They should keep in mind that all systems are interrelated and changes in one system will affect and bring about changes in other systems.

5. As a worker, which specific evaluation tools would you feel comfortable in using with (a) individuals, (b) families, (c) groups, and (d) communities and organizations. What is your rationale for these preferences?

6. As a new supervisee, what are some of the issues that you believe you and your supervisor should discuss?

CHAPTER SUMMARY

There are two types of evaluation: social treatment and program evaluation. Bloom et al. (1995) have pointed out criteria for measurement purposes and highlight that there should be specific goals and objectives of intervention. The purposes of evaluation vary from assessing therapeutic outcomes to justifying efficiency and effectiveness. There are different forms of evaluation which include formative, summative, and evaluation as a corrective process.

Methods of evaluation include videotaping or electronic recording, and critical incident recording. Other methods include single-subject designs, task achievement scale, goal attainment scale, self-anchored and individualized rating scales, behavioral counts, and value ratings. Another type of evaluation refers to the problem-solving skills of clients.

Gurman and Kniskern (1997) state that not much has been done systematically to study outcomes in family therapy. However, eco-maps, videotaping, and critical incident recording could be used to evaluate families.

Group evaluation can be done through testimonials, content analysis, and sociometry. The group worker can also monitor and evaluate the behavior of group members, clients can self-monitor and diaries and logs can be kept. There are other factors in treatment and they include the influence of the worker, the effects of the worker–client relationship, client belief systems, and client expectations. The gains made in treatment are strength-ened by evaluating and assisting clients in consolidating the same. Practitioner evaluation is based on clients' evaluation of them and also on evaluation by a supervisor.

In communities and in organizations, case studies and quality assurance reviews are helpful. Program evaluation is a planned sequence of activities that are designed to bring about change. The guidelines vary from identifying users of the evaluation data to interpreting the results of the evaluation.

15

TERMINATION

Termination is the last phase of the helping process; the ending or the disengagement phase. This is the period when the professional working relationship, whether simple or complex, comes to an end. To help the clients with termination, there are feelings, thoughts, behaviors, and services that the generalist needs to consider.

In many ways, termination is the by-product of evaluation. When evaluation reveals that clients have achieved some or all of their goals or nothing further can be done, termination follows. The whole purpose of the helping process is to empower clients to move forward in their own lives.

In this chapter, the meaning of termination, its purpose, functions, and tasks, and the different types of termination and principles of effective closure will be discussed. Termination factors in work with individuals, families, groups, communities, and organizations will also be highlighted.

WHAT IS TERMINATION?

Termination refers to the time taken and the process used by a generalist and clients to plan the ending of their contacts with one another. Ideally, termination happens when clients and a practitioner have adhered to the guidelines in their contract, and they can then review the accomplishments of the objectives and jointly agree to bring this formal professional helping process to an end. Termination also takes place when either party cuts the process short unilaterally, regardless of the reasons.

John decided after three sessions with the generalist that he had reached his goal which was to understand why he allowed his girlfriend to mistreat him. Although the generalist disagreed with this decision, John did not return. Clients may leave because they feel they have achieved their goals, even though the generalist may not agree, or because they may not be willing to bring about significant changes. In this case, the worker felt that John needed to be in treatment for a longer period of time to work on his self-esteem, but at that point John was not willing to put forth the effort.

Sometimes the generalist may feel that the goals have been accomplished, but the client may disagree and may not be willing to leave.

Tess had been in the helping process for six months to mourn the loss of her mother. She worked through the grieving process successfully but was unwilling to leave as she liked the generalist very much and wanted to be her friend.

Then there are times when workers terminate because they do not like their clients.

Garland would come for his clinical sessions week after week as mandated by law, but would not make any effort to work with the issue of his violent temper. He had beaten his girlfriend three times while in sessions but would not work at controlling his temper. He looked angry when the worker brought up his lack of self-control. Eventually, the worker got tired of his lack of response and transferred Garland to another worker.

Because termination is so important, Shulman (1999) indicates that practitioners must give their clients an opportunity to work through their reactions to this ending. Many clients have experienced painful endings with significant others in their past. Therefore, in their relationship with the generalist, they are not prepared for the separation that termination brings. They do not understand when and how this particular ending will happen, and may not be able to participate in the leave-taking. Too many painful past experiences may have left clients feeling powerless with regard to important experiences in their lives. However, when clients are informed participants, it gives them the opportunity to have mastery over an experience by allowing them to be active in the process. Although it may appear that the clients' former conflicts are being replicated by the worker-initiated endings, this need not occur. As Teyber (1997) points out, the worker can help to make this termination different from past problematic endings in the following ways:

Inform the client about the ending in advance

Invite the client to express his or her feelings, both negative or positive

Discuss the gains and the losses

Talk about the ending and the meaning it holds for both the client and the worker

Validate the client's feelings by acknowledging the ways that the ending evokes other conflicted endings

Bid good-bye to each other

When generalists have worked intensely for a long period of time with clients whose problems are not completely resolved, workers feel guilty about letting their clients down. Because of this inappropriate guilt, workers may avoid the ending and also feel the need to invalidate the client's sad, disappointed, or angry feelings. When workers take this approach, they are actually reenacting the client's past conflicted endings. One of the major goals in termination of the helping process is that it be different from other endings. At the beginning, workers may not recognize these differences, but toward the end, the worker presents and uses termination as an opportunity to resolve long-standing conflicts by helping the client differentiate the mutually shared ending from other incomplete or unsatisfying endings.

Termination is usually planned by the generalist and clients from the first day work begins. Ideally, termination occurs when clients' needs are met. There is a timeline for termination, which is part of the planned action. Termination work can enhance a client's functioning, particularly when the strengths of the client are highlighted without overlooking the weaknesses. However, the ending of a relationship that has been helpful to a client can bring on strong feelings in both clients and workers, and these feelings can be utilized by the worker for the well-being of the client.

Bruckner-Gordon, Gangi, and Wellman (1988) suggest that when clients feel ready to end a professional relationship with a worker, they should be asked to do three things: (1) assess their own progress; (2) discuss the ending with the worker; and (3) make a decision about the termination. They provide the following checklist for clients:

I am considering ending the treatment now because (check any statements that reflect your situation)

- I have gotten a lot from my clinical sessions and am satisfied
- I keep thinking about leaving
- My friends and family want me to stop
- I, or my worker, cannot continue because of outside circumstances
- Nothing much has happened in this helping process for quite a while

- My worker and I are not working well together
- I think I've gotten all that I can working with this practitioner
- I think I've gotten most of what I want, and it doesn't seem worthwhile to continue
- My worker suggested that I should think about leaving
- I don't have the time or money to continue
- or—(whatever reason the client has to offer) (pp. 171–172)

If clients have been in treatment for a long time (particularly those who pay out of their own pockets), they may become quite dependent on the worker and therefore will not bring up the subject of termination. However, the generalist who values self-responsibility will identify the dependency as an issue to be addressed in treatment.

In one case with a client who had been in treatment for over two years, the worker brought the treatment to a different type of closure. During one session the client stated, "I am tied to you emotionally. I consult you on everything I tell my wife. I cannot be without seeing you." At this point, instead of focusing on the issues that the client was presenting regarding his relationship with his wife, the worker focused on the client's dependency on the worker and helped him to believe in himself and his decisions, rather than checking with the worker at every point during the helping process. After three months of such work, the helping process was brought to closure.

Termination needs to be negotiated thoughtfully. The manner in which termination is experienced helps determine whether clients leave treatment with a greater sense of their own personal resources and ability to manage their own lives. The termination process can have far-reaching effects on clients. It can undo the growth and resolution that has come before or confirm and extend the changes that have taken place. Thus the worker should keep in mind the clients' potential when they prepare to end their relationship.

Beginning practitioners will ask when it is time to terminate. It is time to end when clients no longer have symptoms of the problems they presented, and they respond in more flexible and adaptable ways to current situations. Practitioners who have worked with clients for a period of time know that clients are ready to terminate when:

1. Clients report that they consistently feel better and can respond to old conflict situations in more adaptive ways. They have also learned to respond in new ways that were not available to them.
2. Clients can consistently respond to the worker in new and different ways and do not fall back on their old interpersonal styles, defenses, resistance, or eliciting behaviors.
3. Significant people in their lives give clients feedback that they are different or changed and make comments such as "You never used to do that before."

THE PURPOSE OF TERMINATION

The purpose of termination is to bring closure to a responsible helping relationship in a timely manner. In her classic book *Social Work with Groups*, Northen (1969) makes this statement about groups that can be applied to systems of all sizes:

The purposeful nature of social work implies that from time to time it is necessary to assess the desirability of continuing service to the members. The judgment may be that there has been progress toward the achievement of goals and there is potential for further improvement, in which case the service should be continued. Another decision may be that little, if any, progress has been made; if this is combined with little potential for changing the presenting situation, the service should be discontinued. Still another evaluation may be that progress toward the achievement of goals has been sufficient, and the service should be terminated. Social workers have undoubtedly anticipated termination from the beginning of their work with the group and have clarified to the members its possible duration, so that the goals and means towards their achievement have been related to the plans for both individuals, groups, families, organizations, and communities. Nevertheless, there comes a time when the worker and the members must face the fact of separation from each other and often, also, the end of the group itself. (p. 222)

Thus, when closing a case, the termination of services with a client should be viewed as an essential and planned component of the helping process.

PRIMARY FUNCTIONS OF TERMINATION

Ward (1982) has summarized the various functions of termination and Compton & Gallaway (1999) have discussed some of the important tasks of termination in the helping process, which includes making an assessment of the client's readiness for termination and consolidating the learning process and resolving any leftover affective issues and bringing about closure to the client–worker relationship. The latter means that:

1. Practitioners and clients should work out the conflict between the acknowledgment of improvement and goal achievement and the fact that a client is moving away from this type of help.
2. If necessary the worker needs to help the client work through the fear of loss of relationship and offer support.
3. Both the worker and client have to examine the experience and then recognize the progress they have made.
4. The worker has to consider how this experience can be transferred to other problems as they come up.
5. The worker must look at stabilizing the gains made through the helping process.
6. Generalists have to clarify their continuing position in the situation.

Ultimately, the generalist must maximize the transfer of learning and move toward helping to increase the client's self-reliance and confidence in order to maintain change after the helping process has ended.

When the relationship between the worker and the client has been long-term, termination may entail a certain degree of grief for the client at the loss of a relationship in which they have been accepted in an unconditional manner. Such grief produces many typical reactions in clients. Clients may deny that the relationship is going to end and act as though it is permanent. At times, clients are so distraught that they may return to earlier behavior patterns and problems that have been resolved may crop up again as new problems. Sometimes clients may accuse the worker of being wrong in thinking that they could work on problems without help. Finally, some clients may break contact: "You can't fire me. I quit."

THE TASKS OF TERMINATION

What are the different tasks that need to be performed in order to terminate? First, the worker and the client must select information they want to discuss most seriously, which will govern the type of data that will be reviewed.

While terminating, new information may come up that is relevant. Some of this will ensue from the discussion of the evaluative data as clients point out additional meanings to the data and generate more information (Garvin & Seabury, 1997). At this point, the worker can ask the client to offer a descriptive, analytical, and qualitative response to questions such as, "In your own words can you tell me how things are different now than they used to be when you began the helping process?" This gives the client a chance to talk about things that may have been beneficial or that might have hurt.

This type of questioning also helps clients present perceptions of causes for change. For instance, a client who constantly blamed herself for all the problems in her marriage answered that, after working with the practitioner, she concluded that her husband contributed to the problems as well, which helped her to stop blaming herself. The client acknowledged the fact that the worker had helped her to become more assertive and she had employed these assertive strategies in difficult situations with her husband.

Another important aspect of termination is the *reinforcement* of positive changes that have taken place. When clients recognize and receive affirmation for positive changes made in their attitudes and behavior, these changes are more likely to be internalized and utilized in the future.

Practitioners need to know how well they worked with clients which is best done by asking the clients to evaluate the workers. The professional growth of workers requires that they receive this type of information from clients. This need not happen at the end of the clinical sessions; it can happen throughout the helping process. It is constructive for workers to ask for information about their performance as it lays the foundation for positive ways to ask and receive evaluative information about oneself. Clients may not be ready to give such feedback, but it is best to ask for it nevertheless.

The evaluation that clients make of workers can be oral or written. Workers and clients should discuss the written evaluation so that any more additional information that clients wish to discuss is brought to light.

Following are some of the questions asked evaluating the worker before termination as discussed by Reid (1997) and Shulman (1999) with reference to groups:

1. Can you share with me some of my discussions and actions that you found most or least helpful?
2. What actions would you have liked me to take that I did not?
3. Were there some personal qualities of mine that turned you off or were there some qualities that you thought were helpful with regard to my humor, my timing, my way of speaking, and so forth?
4. Did you feel and think I was with you in your presentation of feelings and thoughts? How did you know I was with you, how did I express it?
5. How did you experience me? Did you see me as honest and trustworthy?
6. In what ways did you experience me as caring and supportive?

Not all clients may be willing to say much that could hurt the worker's feelings. In the last few sessions, there are so many feelings to be exposed and explored that often the client can come up with a blanket statement saying that they enjoyed their work with the worker. When the relationship is based on honesty and openness, the clients often do not have much to say. However, it is at least useful to ask for feedback before termination. Endings may be painful for the clients and sometimes, for the workers, too.

TYPES OF TERMINATION

The different types of termination can be classified as short-term, long-term, one-session, sporadic, transfer, referrals, and unplanned termination by the client (see Figure 15.1).

Short-Term Termination

Short-term termination refers to a situation in which the client, from the onset, has been receiving help for a planned short period of time. At the end of a certain number of sessions, the worker can end the helping process, as has been discussed from the onset. Often this is based on time-limited

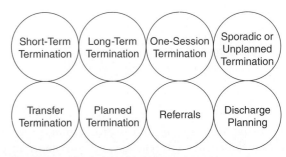

Figure 15.1   **Types of Termination**

modalities or ways of helping that strongly affect the termination process. The assumption is that when a person is aware of the ending right from the beginning, the degree of emotional attachment and dependency will be less, and the degree of loss that could be experienced by clients as a result of termination will be limited. In time-limited work, the emotional reaction to separation seems to be much less than when there is open-ended service (Hess & Hess, 1994).

Brill (1990) suggests that practitioners should initiate formal termination in the next-to-last scheduled interview and formulate a set of tasks to be addressed, which ideally should be repetitions or modest extensions of previously successful tasks. After this review the client and the worker can focus on evaluating client's accomplishments in relationship to target problems, planning for continued work on problems as needed, assisting clients to discern how they can apply the problem-solving methods they have learned to future problems, and planning for follow-up, if needed.

Brill (1990) indicates that the regular contract that is made with short-term clients is sufficient. After the clients have accomplished the specified goals, the case is terminated. If additional help is needed, a new contract with new goals and a new time frame can be negotiated if worker and client agree.

Long-Term Termination

Long-term termination occurs after the client has been in treatment for a long period of time, varying from one to three or more years (more common for clients who can pay out of their finances), and some of their problems have been worked through. The client is ready to leave, but there is a great degree of ambivalence between both the worker and the client because intense feelings, which include grieving and accepting the loss of a productive and meaningful relationship, have to be unmasked and dealt with. For some it is relatively easy, while for others it takes more time.

Long-term treatment is usually open-ended and terminating can be a major task in such situations. It is difficult to measure the amount of growth a person has made in treatment alone, because people do tend to grow with or without treatment. It is no simple task to determine when clients have achieved optimal benefit from the helping experience. Long-term service tends to foster dependency and some clients are reluctant to relinquish the gratifications they receive in the helping relationship. They often cling to the helping relationship by regressing in their behavior and failing to engage in change-oriented activities outside of the helping relationship (Hepworth, Rooney, & Larsen, 1997).

When should termination take place with such clients? Usually termination takes place when the client reaches a point of diminishing returns, and when the gains made in the sessions seem to be insignificant. In open-ended long-term cases, many clients are reluctant to bring up termination, and the worker has to introduce the idea based on impressions of the gains that clients have made in the clinical sessions. After a discussion during which the worker and clients agree that the latter have satisfactorily attained some goals, the discussion should be channeled in a natural way to the subject of ending treatment.

In an open-ended helping process, the emotional reactions to separation are of great significance (Webb, 1985). When the worker has played a significant role in the client's life over a long period of time, the client is likely to approach termination with great reluctance or ambivalence. Some clients perceive termination as traumatic and show some degree of resistance in termination. Fortune, Pearlingi, and Rochelle (1992) note that the different termination reactions which can be seen in open-ended services are present to a smaller degree in time-limited services.

At times, clients who do not wish to terminate cling to helping process and to the practitioner. Right from the beginning, the worker should take precautions to minimize dependency (except in some special cases as with children or people under trauma) by verbalizing the need for the clients to achieve independence and be able to move on with their own life.

Practitioners who are oriented to fostering maximum independence rarely perceive clients as suffering from a major trauma when termination is to occur. Even in groups, as Garvin and Seabury (1997) indicate, members who appear to be ready for termination may raise questions about the reasons the worker has decided to terminate. However, most adjust to the fact that there will be a termination.

In place of the worker, clients may attempt to locate a person on whom they can be dependent. They are attempting to find a substitute for someone whom they are afraid of losing, often at the expense of their own growth. If such a situation begins to develop just as termination starts, the worker should help the client recognize the pertinent dynamics and understand the possible consequences of such a choice (Hepworth & Larsen, 1997).

On a positive note there is also a "natural ending" in a long-term case because the client's work is completed. One of the worker's main goals is to foster natural endings and to accept both sides of the client's feelings about endings. The worker takes pleasure in clients' independence and actively supports their movement on their own. At the same time, clients feel that the worker will accept their continuing need and not be disappointed or burdened if they return at a later point. This resolution of the separateness–relatedness dialectic in the worker–client relationship is a potent corrective emotional experience. When clients are assured of the worker's support for all their feelings, clients can internalize the worker as a good introject, strengthen their own sense of self, and successfully end the relationship on an empowered note (Teyber, 1997).

One-Session Termination

One-session termination happens when the clients who have come for help decide that they do not wish to return. The termination is not planned but the client does not wish to set up appointments or breaks those that are set up. The worker has no control in this situation and must accept the fact that the client may have gained something in that one session and leave it at that.

There are also some clients who come for some specific purpose. They may come for information, advice, a referral, or a concrete service that can be provided in a single session. Even if they come for treatment and decide against it, the worker can leave the door open if the client decides to seek help at a future time.

Sporadic or Unplanned Termination

Sometimes a client may come for sessions for a certain period of time and then decide not to continue. These terminations are called premature or unilateral terminations or "dropping out of treatment." Although it is preferable in the helping process to plan the termination mutually, this does not happen in all cases for any number of reasons. Some clients lose interest in working on their problems; others continuously break appointments until the worker issues an ultimatum and the clients drop out of the helping process. Some clients may announce at the end of a session that they are not coming back and the practitioner has little opportunity to explore the reasons for their decisions. In such situations, the worker may go along with the decision, but suggest one more session, which may or may not work out.

Kanfer and Schefft (1988) offer some reasons why clients terminate prematurely:

They feel that they have accomplished their goals

They believe they do not need the worker's assistance even though the goals have not been accomplished

They fear that they may be talked into staying in treatment for a longer period

They are dissatisfied with their progress, or the manner in which the worker is helping them

They do not see a "fit" between their problems and the helping process

They view their pain as being too great compared to the outcomes that are being produced

Their lives have changed and they find that receiving help is no longer necessary.

An effective practitioner may be able to pick up on these cues and deal with them with immediacy. Ongoing monitoring and evaluation of the helping process should catch such cues early on.

When clients terminate prematurely, they are expressing feelings of unresolved discomfort in the worker–client relationship. If the client is subtly showing negative feelings it would be productive for the worker to ask the client to share the concern. If the client is willing, the practitioner should try to get the issue on the table and discuss it openly and nondefensively. If the client does not return, this issue obviously was not resolved. This type of termination could be worrisome to a worker, but in most cases it is likely that the client got as much as possible out of the helping process. However, if clients constantly and voluntarily keep dropping out of the helping process, the worker needs to discuss this in supervision. There may be a possibility that the worker is not doing something right or is presenting himself or herself in a less than positive light.

At times, clients will drop out of the helping process after two or three sessions, claiming that they have benefitted sufficiently and no longer need assistance. Research (Presley, 1987; Toseland, 1987) indicates that in such cases, it is a mistake on the part of practitioners to think that most premature terminations indicate dissatisfactions by clients and also negative outcomes. Some clients seek help in a time of crisis and see no need to continue when the emergency is past. If the worker gets an opportunity to discuss the benefits of staying in the helping process, however, it could be useful. While social workers must respect a client's right to self-determination, they also have a professional obligation to offer expert opinions if this

is acceptable to the client and the client is available for another session.

Transfer Termination

Sometimes the worker–client relationship is terminated because the worker is ending her or his employment in an agency or is being transferred to a new position. If the new position is in the same agency the worker has an ethical obligation to continue with the client if possible, because this is in the client's best interest. If the worker is leaving the agency, the worker has an ethical obligation to plan the move far enough in advance to avoid or minimize traumatic terminations or breaking contracts. In such cases the worker should give special attention to the client's needs.

Often this is the best time for the client to terminate with the worker and the agency. In other cases, this may not be the right time for the client and the client must be transferred to another worker. Clients may be angry because the worker is breaking a contract and they may have feelings of abandonment that rekindle old feelings about previous separations. The worker, too, will be experiencing feelings of guilt about leaving clients and breaking contracts. Although the worker may be preoccupied with taking on a new job, it is important, however painful, that the worker and clients deal with the issues directly.

When workers leave on their own initiative, they have to work at eliciting clients' feelings, however painful they may be. The worker should be able to accept, and try to work through, the clients' anger, resentment, and feelings of rejection. In the case of a transfer to another worker, it is useful to introduce the new worker to the client and for all three to briefly discuss the client's problems in terms of the work that is being done and the possibilities for future work. After this, the first worker and the client can have their final session at which they can appropriately say their goodbyes and terminate the relationship.

Effective termination may be blocked by the worker's own conflicts. There are some workers who have difficulty terminating a relationship in which some of their own emotional needs are being fulfilled.

Helene mentioned to a colleague, "Pam came in today as usual, but I was really disappointed because she would not cry when she saw me as she used to do for the past three months. I was really disappointed." This is a case in which the worker does not seem to have her act together and finds satisfaction in the client's tears.

Some workers have a need to control others, which can be satisfied more easily in a relationship with a dependent person. The worker is hanging on to a client because it is a "perfect case." Finally, there are workers who care too much for clients and want to compensate for their previous losses in relationships and life. When a worker is aware of these feelings, focusing on the *client's* needs and goals, should prevent the blocking of an effective termination (Johnson, 1995).

Planned Terminations Determined by Temporal Constraints

In some settings, the service provided to clients involves fixed timings and termination happens within a designated time period. This is true of school settings, in which services are concluded at the end of the academic year, and in hospital settings, in which service is offered for a duration of time determined by the length of the hospitalization or confinement. Because social work help may depend on how long the patient stays in that setting, there are time limits placed on the client and it is best that the worker make the client aware of this from the beginning of the helping process. If not, the client may interpret the time limits as being arbitrarily imposed and view the practitioner's leaving as desertion or abandonment (Kadushin, 1997).

The best way to deal with these situations is to be aware of the time limits. For instance, while working with a school-age child, the worker can tell the child, "I will see you for eight weeks,

which is the amount of time before the school year ends." Thus the client is prepared for termination even before the helping sessions begin. If the worker has to terminate early, which can create an untimely separation if the client has more problems to deal with, the worker faces the dual tasks of working through feelings associated with terminating and also referring clients for services elsewhere.

Also the way of helping in these settings is different. In many school and hospital settings, where the social workers have a large caseload, they may not have time for weekly interviews over an extended period of time. If ongoing counseling or help is needed, it may be best to refer out before the worker and client develop an intense treatment relationship. If the social worker wants to help on a long-term basis there should be a commitment on the part of the worker, and his or her employer, to have this as an official part of the workload, with adequate time allotted. This should reduce the incidence of untimely terminations.

Another area where termination happens in an untimely fashion is when students who are placed in a field practicum have to leave when their semester comes to an end. As Germain and Gitterman (1996) indicate, students have an ethical responsibility to inform the clients that they are students and will have to terminate either at the end of the year or the semester. Students need to be genuine in these situations. Concealing a student's status does not foster a trusting relationship with a client and does not help one to be totally authentic in the relationship. Sometimes the student worker and the client have made substantial gains when the external time constraints demand termination. In some cases the treatment process is only in midstream but the student worker must initiate termination before clients are ready. In these cases, termination is determined by temporal factors and constraints rather than when it might happen naturally.

However, untimely terminations can be reduced if plans are made in advance as part of the treatment contract. Time limits can also be used as important spurs to progress in the helping process. In some hospitals, there is no possibility of offering long-term help. The client who applies for service will probably need to have several interviews, sometimes daily, within a short period of time. The focus of the contract is more likely to be on practical issues related to medical problems rather than counseling per se. In such cases, an intense relationship is not likely to develop and termination is not difficult.

In some cases, termination arouses emotional responses that are far more intense and difficult than the worker or client anticipated. When both deny the reality of the impending ending and do not squarely confront it, the interpersonal process will usually replicate the client's other conflicts and prevent them from fully resolving their conflicts.

The single most important guideline for a successful termination is to *unambiguously acknowledge the reality of ending.* Clients must discuss their emotional reactions about the ending. Workers and clients must mutually agree that they need to terminate due to outside constraints, and they must set a specific date for the final session. As practitioners and clients have to work through their ending, the final session should be set several weeks hence. The worker should begin to count down to the final sessions and repeatedly invite clients to discuss their reactions to termination:

"After this session, we only have three left. How does it feel when you hear me say that?"

"We have only two sessions left and it is important that we talk about ending the sessions."

"Next week will be our last session and I would like to know what are you feeling?"

This type of countdown precludes any ambiguity that clients may feel at the end of the last session, and it is more common in micro work or work with individuals, families, and small groups. When generalists do not address the termination directly, they are often acting out their own sepa-

ration anxieties. In such cases, the workers need to discuss the problem with a supervisor.

Referrals

Termination also happens when clients have to be referred to other resources for help. There are agencies that provide time-limited services and connect clients with essential resources elsewhere. A client may come to you for help not knowing that you do not provide a particular kind of service. For example, you may be working in an adoption agency and a client who sees babies going in and out of the agency makes an assumption about the functions of the agency and comes to you as a pregnant teenager who wants an abortion. Because your agency does not provide this type of service, you should be able to refer her to an appropriate agency where she will receive the kind of help she is looking for.

Workers have to be knowledgeable about the various resources that are available in the community and also be available to act as a liaison between the client and the agency the client is referred to. Practitioners should be aware of the general policies and procedures of the different agencies. It is the worker's role to share relevant information so that clients can make informed decisions about what they wish to do.

Sometimes a practitioner may work with clients for a certain period of time and then refer them to another agency as deemed appropriate. Before this is done, the generalist must find out the feelings of the clients, who may be apprehensive about the type of service they will receive at the new agency. Clients have to recognize the need for referral. Clients who do not feel the need for more services and are referred to another agency are not unlikely to follow through.

Also, when possible options for referral are suggested, the clients' need for making their own decisions should be respected. However, when a recommendation is offered, it must be clear which one would be most beneficial to the client (Hepworth et al., 1997). To throw a decision back at a distressed client is an abrogation of professional responsibility under the guise of asking the client to participate.

The worker should avoid making false promises about what the other agency can do for the client. Unrealistic reassurances can create false hopes in the client that may never be fulfilled. This may also "set up" the client for additional disappointment and frustration, as well as create resistance to seeking professional help. Clients may be apprehensive about meeting another practitioner and the generalist should be able to reassure the clients accordingly. Practitioners can prepare clients for the referral by reminding them that the practitioner has a responsibility to share information with the new agency to the extent possible in order to get the best help that the agency can offer.

The worker should not be overly enthusiastic to the client about what the new worker will do for them. Every worker has a specific style of functioning and working with clients and this should be left to the client to explore. If not, the client is again being set up for disappointment.

Termination by Discharge Planning

The American Hospital Association (1985) defined discharge planning in hospital settings as any activity or set of activities that facilitates the transition of the patient from one environment to another. The complexity of discharge plans varies and is described by four levels of outcome:

1. Patient and family understanding of the diagnosis, anticipated level of functioning, discharge medications, and anticipated medical follow-up
2. Specialized instruction or training so that the patient or family can provide posthospital care
3. Coordination of community support systems, which enable the patient to return home
4. Relocation of the patient and coordination of support systems or transfer to another health care facility.

A great deal of discharge planning is done in hospital settings with patients who must adjust to psychological complications such as illness, and major physical changes in lifestyle and follow-up (Rossen, 1987). Social work's concern about the person–environment fit is truly effective in discharge planning.

Discharge planning involves planning by an interdisciplinary staff, which is also a part of other settings such as residential treatment, and aiding victims of abuse, rape, and domestic violence. Discharge planning is carried out with all kinds of clients including individuals, families, and groups and involves interaction with legal, medical, educational, and social welfare professionals. Starting fresh by making a physical transition from one environment to another creates special problems for the client, because a number of institutional and friendship relationships must be terminated and the client has to again adapt to a new, or old, environment. The worker must focus on this transition and the work with the client so that termination with the worker becomes a secondary matter.

When we view termination from the perspective of a disturbed teenage girl in a treatment group, the termination from the worker does not seem as painful as the other matters that may happen in this young woman's life. Termination is reached after an interdisciplinary team, which consists of a psychiatrist, nurse, cottage parents, and a social worker, meets to discuss the progress and the need to transfer the client to another setting. The final task of terminating with the client is left to the social worker. However, termination from the social worker is of less importance to these young adolescents in a residential treatment center than being separated from the place and people with whom they have spent six months or more of their lives to return to their own family or another family. Such a transition is an awesome new challenge.

Booster Sessions

Follow-up in the form of booster sessions is important. Kanfer and Schefft (1988) have suggested that booster sessions be included as part of the overall helping process, however, this would depend on the type of client. "Booster's sessions can be arranged at intervals to provide additional consultation or to recapitulate and strengthen coping techniques or other self-regulatory skills that the client . . . learned during treatment and that . . . faded" (p. 287). These sessions are usually contracted at the end of the formal helping process on an as-needed basis. However, this should not be used by the worker as an excuse to prolong the helping process because some clients need this type of support. Booster sessions may be combined with the follow-up evaluation interviews to observe the growth and progress of the client.

TIMING AND TERMINATION

When is it appropriate for you to terminate with a client without the time constraints discussed earlier? Fortune et al. (1991) asked practitioners to describe their criteria for ending. The practitioners reported that they looked for client improvements in coping skills and psychological functioning, requests for closure, and attainment of goals.

More specifically, practitioners can ask clients the following questions to determine when to terminate with them:

Has the presenting problem or symptom been reduced, eliminated, or managed?

Has the original stress been dissipated or decreased to a large degree?

Is the client coping better with all problems and concerns?

Is the client able to understand himself or herself better due to the helping process?

Has the client's self-esteem increased since he or she has been in the helping process?

Is the client functioning better relating to other people?

How is the client functioning on an everyday basis including work and other activities?

Has the client loosened up and is he or she enjoying life more and having fun?

Does the client feel that he or she can live effectively without further counseling?

PRINCIPLES OF EFFECTIVE CLOSURE AND TERMINATION

Brucker-Gordon et al. (1988) discuss four tasks that clients and workers need to be aware of in termination: exploring one's reactions to ending the helping process; planning leave-taking with the worker; completing the tasks that they wanted to accomplish in the helping process; and actually saying good-bye to the worker. How much time does this take a client? That depends on the amount of time that has been spent in working through issues. If a person has been in the helping process for a year or more, it would take a significant amount of time; if it was an even longer period, the worker and client might have to spend a few minutes each session for weeks talking about termination.

Egan (1990) offers some suggestions and guidelines about termination that can be used to bring the helping process to a close. As mentioned before, the worker should build termination into the helping process from the beginning. The treatment contract should include a time frame for achieving certain goals and tasks, which should be discussed not only at the beginning but all through the helping process.

Self-indulgent and self-destructive dependency that the client and the worker may feel toward each other should be avoided. When termination is regarded as a natural part of the helping process, it will not come as a surprise and the client will not see a practitioner's "letting go" of them as rejection.

Working and helping the client must be effective and efficient, which means the worker must move matters along as quickly as possible. Of course this may not happen in every session, but it is difficult to accept a worker's excuse, after six months of work, that "nothing happened with that client." The worker has a responsibility as well.

Do not terminate with a client because you do not like him or her. Not all clients may appeal to you, but we need to develop the ability to work with all kinds of people. If clients are presenting themselves as well as they can and you are not interested, examine your own motivation and consider transferring the case.

In some situations, the worker may take a gradual approach to termination and lengthen the time between sessions. The generalist thus becomes a consultant who works with what the client is doing. Longer periods between sessions give the client the opportunity to function on his or her own, without cutting the therapeutic cord completely. In the final session the worker can review with the client some of the gains the client has made, how these can be maintained and improved, and how they might be transferred to other situations.

When a client wishes to terminate, the worker should allow it to happen, but be aware that if the client is dangerous others should be informed. In such situations, it is best to take counsel with colleagues regarding your own legal and moral obligations.

OTHER COMPONENTS OF TERMINATION

Reminiscing (Pincus & Minahan, 1973; Germain & Gitterman, 1995) is a form of reviewing the type of work that has been done prior to termination. Reminiscing is usually a positive way of looking at different achievements and strides that the client has made in the helping process. In this process, the worker highlights how pain is a way of growing up; this in turn, minimizes the anxiety that the client has felt about the work that was done by the client and the generalist.

When clients regress, new problems may arise. Regression can be described as behaviors and thought patterns that indicate a return to an earlier level of development. In this situation, work-

ers and clients need to examine the problems and decide if there is a valid reason for them to come up or whether clients can deal with them by themselves. If some of the problems are based on the fear of termination, the worker needs to reassure the clients that they have enough strength to deal with the ongoing problems in living. The worker can also explain how only some clients work through all their problems and highlight the clients' strengths and coping skills.

The feelings that clients have about termination vary in intensity and the nature of the helping process. If the intensity or period of time the worker and the client spend together is minimal, then the feelings that the client will experience will be minimal. Clients who have faced success in their work may have different feelings than those whose experiences were not as positive. Clients who have faced losses in their lives and have not dealt with these losses will have a harder time with separation and loss. Such clients may feel abandoned and at a loss.

In a group setting, the worker can empathize with the group members and assist them to express their feelings and weigh them against the totality of the group experience. The worker can make a statement such as "I know you are feeling bad about my leaving. I want you to know that I feel bad about leaving and it would be easy to keep you here. But you have accomplished so much in these sessions and coped so well with all your issues. I am aware that it was not easy for you to confide in me but you did and you learned to cope with your difficulties. Better still, you and I know that you have the ability to deal with such issues whenever similar problems come up because you do have and have brought out your constructive problem-solving skills. I realize that you are somewhat upset about this closure; you have shared so much with me so you can tell me what you are feeling at this moment."

Termination becomes especially difficult when the client must cope with many changes and demands. The reasons for termination will affect both the client and the worker. If the worker is leaving, he or she still must highlight the positives that have occurred and also relate the reasons for his or her leaving, emphasizing that it does not have anything to do with the client but the worker's own life. This can also help reinforce to the client that all human beings must cope with life problems. This also presents the humaneness of the worker as caring and patient while helping clients deal with their emotions. If goals have more or less been achieved it may lead to a constructive happy ending.

All clients need to be reassured that the worker is not personally rejecting the client but leaving because the work has been accomplished. Clients must understand that life goes on; they must work through their negative feelings and re-experience positive feelings toward their accomplishments and the practitioner.

Nevertheless, there are terminations with unsuccessful outcomes. In some cases, the worker imposes termination on a client because the case is not moving, leaving clients hopelessly stalemated to surmount the impasse. When possible, workers should discuss the reason why the sessions were unsuccessful including factors that prevented clients from moving in the right direction and working toward achieving the appropriate goals, and the clients' feelings about what they would like to do about seeking additional help in the future. The worker has to be empathetic, warm, and genuine, but also challenge clients regarding their unwillingness to move ahead in their own life.

Not all termination is negative. Quite often, clients experience more positive than negative feelings when terminating with a worker. Although there may be a degree of sadness in the ending, this is only because the worker, as one client put it, has "been a good friend." The benefits obtained in the helping process seem to outweigh the negatives and often the clients leave the final helping sessions with the feeling of having learned a sense of mastery which both workers and the clients are able to rejoice over. Also the worker and the client have experienced a mutual enrichment from the personal but professional encounter and, in an authentic manner, each person has grown from the experience.

The type of ending a client and worker experience depends on whether the ending is natural or unnatural. As noted, in natural endings there is permission to leave; the worker enjoys a feeling of success in the client's independence and has hopes that the client will commit to other new relationships with a feeling of independence. Clients are emancipated, but they are aware that they have permission to return if they wish to do so. This offers the client support and reinforces the client's own individuation and mastery striving. It also helps clients develop and maintain their own sense of identity and empowerment in working toward personal goals.

For workers, when the ending is unnatural as in the case of school students, the finality of the sessions must be acknowledged and the worker must respond to the client's emotional reactions. This can be difficult for some workers, because the work they started with the client is unfinished. In such situations, workers have to acknowledge and accept the limitations of the relationship and help clients accept the work that has been accomplished without feeling the need to reject the worker. Even when work is incomplete the client can internalize the gains, so the relationship continues to be successful and productive.

The following case concerns a client during termination who feels disgusted and exploited by his worker and how the worker, using her interpersonal style and skills, works with this client. The case has been adapted from Teyber (1992).

Timothy has been in the helping process for a period of one year. He was an ambitious and successful businessman who overextended himself and expanded his company rapidly on borrowed money, but without very good planning. The lack of planning caught up with him and Timothy filed for bankruptcy. He lost everything including his house, his expensive cars, and most of his friends. When the whole world appeared to be crumbling around him, he came into the helping process as a lonely, scared, desperate, and suicidally depressed man.

However, in treatment Timothy realized that life does go on. His attitude improved and his depression and preoccupation with suicide disappeared. He had bragged to his only friend that he could not have made it without the worker. The treatment was winding down and Timothy was ready to quit. However, it did not appear that he was ready to acknowledge how he felt and what the helping process had done for him. In fact, he started the session by being angry with the worker, apparently because he had paid the worker so much money. Thus the treatment session started with the client being critical and angry with the worker.

Timothy asked the worker, "Why did you charge me so much money? You know you have not done much!"

Without getting into termination, which was apparently causing Timothy pain, the worker responded to Timothy's provocation by saying, "You are angry about the billing and the money you have paid me. Let's talk about it."

Timothy, still very angry, continued to attack the worker, "You are only a social worker, why are you charging me so much money. Do you think you are a medical doctor? That you are fulfilling your parents' dreams of being a real doctor by charging me like a psychiatrist who is a real doctor, unlike you!"

Timothy was used to attacking people with provocations, which had always resulted in the breaking up of relationships. However, the worker did not respond to Timothy in the manner he expected him to. Instead the worker mediated her own reflexive response and tried to maintain a neutral attitude and a middle-ground approach.

"I realize you are very angry with me. I do charge you for my time and financially this has been a difficult time for you. Also there are a large number of problems in your life that have not changed and all this has been tough on you."

The manner in which the worker responded made Timothy more angry because he had expected her to be defensive or upset, which did not happen. Consequently, he responded furiously, "I hate the way you come across as so-o-o understanding. I hate to come here, meet you, and then pay you. Why are you being nice to me, is this a strategy? When people are falling apart you make them get dependent on you and then take all their money. There must be something wrong with you. You're more sick than anyone I have ever seen!"

The worker replied, "It seems you are angry with me, because you think I am making you dependent on me and taking your money?"

Timothy, who by this time was really out of control, screamed:

"Yes, you fool. I want to leave and get out of here, but I can't. I cannot believe it, but I am dependent on you. I know I will get depressed and sad when I leave and I might kill myself. I need you to help me get out of this depression, but then you take the little money I have. I feel tied to you, and also trapped by you. You got me where you really want me to be. I hate the position I am in, and I hate you!"

It took a well-balanced and an insightful worker to understand that a central conflict in Timothy's life was being reenacted in this transference. Based on the client's earlier history, the worker reasoned that Timothy's needing someone in his life also meant that he would be used by them. The worker used that information to help Timothy and articulated what the client was experiencing in their relationship at that particular point in time.

Worker: "If you do not wish to be in the sessions, that is your choice. What you are really feeling is your own need to be helped and understood. However, you have learned through the years that when you trust someone they will take advantage of you and use you. So now you think that if you stay in the helping process with me, I will be like the others and exploit you for my own good. Therefore, the only way for you to resist me is to leave. Timothy, I want you to know that I have a different kind of relationship with you. I want to respond to your needs by offering help. I will not use your trust and vulnerability to better my position in any way."

After some time, Timothy became calm and was able to accept what the worker was saying. Timothy reacted to the worker as if she was manipulating his dependency in order to meet her own financial need. This was the crux of Timothy's generic conflict with people. As a child, Timothy lived in a foster home because his mother, a single parent, was unable to take care of her four children. Her visits were sporadic and she then lost touch with him. Timothy's foster parents who seemed to be "worthy" people to outsiders exploited him to the utmost when he was a child. Besides going to school, he had to work with his father in the donut store that his father owned. He put in long hours in the morning before he got to school and long evening hours after he returned from school. At a young age he felt exploited by them and felt that his love for them was used to exploit him. As he grew up, he left his foster home with an inability to forgive his foster parents for using him. Consequently, he decided that he would become rich and strong financially so that no one would ever exploit him or hurt him.

The incident and confrontation that took place between the worker and the client proved to be a corrective emotional experience for Timothy. Timothy's old fear of being used came up with the worker as well. The angry outburst did not bring out the reactions that he expected from her and his old defense eliciting behavior did not turn the worker away from him. She continued to be involved with Timothy and remained responsive to his concerns. When she did not respond in a manner which Timothy expected, as had happened in earlier situations and relationships, the next feeling in his affective constellation began to emerge. After experiencing anger, feelings of hurt and being deprived emerged. The worker responded to these feelings effectively and they soon receded. Timothy reexperienced with the worker the same conflicts and fears he had experienced in the past. However, her empathetic response to his problems was very different from the earlier responses he had encountered. The worker validated Timothy's perceptions that he had been taken advantage of when he was a child, but constantly stressed to him that others were not trying to take advantage of him in his current relationships. Instead of putting him down, or confronting his angry behavior, the worker observed that as a child, Timothy had made the best and only adaptation that he could make to his childhood predicament. The worker continued that there was courage and strength in Timothy's defensive attempt to rise above the conflicts in his past life experiences by adopting an aggressive and defiant interpersonal style. The worker continued to reassure him that this style of communication was no longer necessary or effective although as a child it had protected him from feelings of vulnerability. After a couple of such sessions, Timothy understood what the worker was trying to help him understand that it took as much effort and strength to confront his old conflicts and his feelings of being exploited as it did when he was a child. He reacted aggressively, compulsively striving toward success and power.

With the worker's constant, validating support, Timothy began to reexamine his old feelings of need of his foster parents and also his tremendous outrage at being used and exploited by them. Slowly Timothy began to change. He dropped the guard that he had set up against the worker and started to let go of the painful feelings of his childhood that seemed to be, as he put it, "so disgusting and weak." He started to become more friendly with the worker and also less competitive and mistrusting. Timothy's high sensitivity to needing the worker and being taken advantage of was reduced considerably.

Timothy started to apply these changes to other relationships as well. He began to establish sensible male friendships where he was no longer highly competitive. His relationships with women changed, too. Earlier his relationships with women had been short-lived, superficial, exploitative encounters, but this started to change as well. He appeared to be more genuine in all his relationships.

Timothy's business associates remarked he was less driven and more humane with them. He was no longer driven so mercilessly to achieve, due to his childhood conflicts and sense of being used. Instead, he developed a healthy work ethic in which he wanted to make a good life for himself without being so competitive. He was ready for termination when he got a job in a company for whom he had done some earlier consulting work. Not all of Timothy's problems were solved, but Timothy did not replicate his earlier conflicts as the helping process came to an end. He wanted to know if he could meet with the worker if he needed to at a later point. With a positive response to this request, Timothy terminated and never contacted the worker again.

In this case, Timothy made some changes in himself through the helping process. These changes were utilized in the helping process and also reinforced outside of it. Thus, when these changes became stabilized, the helping process came to an end.

Stabilizing Change

Positive, constructive changes, whether dramatic or not, need to be stabilized when they occur. The following section discusses stabilizing skills.

When a client and worker have decided on termination, one of the first things that the worker needs to do is to focus on the changes that have taken place in the helping process by reviewing all the work that has happened in the sessions. The different changes that have taken place in the client need to be pointed out and highlighted.

Felicia came for help she had just ended a negative but long-term relationship with her boyfriend who had left her for another woman. In sessions, Felicia constantly lamented that she was nothing without a man and refused to look at her own strengths. However, after receiving two years of help, she realized that she did not need a man to feel whole and that she could do things for herself. Felicia's earlier life pattern had been to give in to men if they liked her, but she did make choices on her own about who she wanted to be with. Through the helping process, this changed and Felicia began to see herself as capable of making a living on her own. She worked hard at building her self-esteem and her trust in herself and was ready to leave the helping process with a high degree of self-confidence. In terms of growth, she was able to tell the worker all the positive gains she had made in the helping process; the worker and Felicia also discussed the possibility of her meeting men who did not measure up to what she wanted in her life. Felicia was able to discuss how she would handle this situation in the future. Felicia felt that she had resources that would enable her to make it on her own and knew how to use these resources.

Figure 15.2   **Growth Promotion**

At termination, the worker should be able to identify the support systems and other resources in a client's environment that might be useful in coping with life situations. These include family and friends, religious organizations, women's centers, and other places to meet people. Another means of stabilizing change is to encourage continued growth. This can be done by discussing with clients where they wish to go from that point on. Possible goals for future growth and resources useful to reach those goals should be discussed.

One of the critical strategies to promote continued growth is *self-management* (Cormier & Cormier, 1998). When clients have made some gains and changes in personality, the generalist can move them toward self-management, which depends on their own motivation to change and the need to maintain change. Self-management is a process by which clients direct their own behaviors with one or more specific strategies.

There are three distinct self-management strategies (see Figure 15.2). *Self-monitoring* provides information about the social and environmental context that influences behavior. For example, Janet realized that she should not go into bars where she would inevitably get drunk. *Stimulus-control* procedures require a predetermined arrangement of environmental conditions as antecedents of a target behavior or cues to increase or decrease a particular type of behavior. For instance, Mindy decided to study in the library because she knew she would concentrate more and get better grades than if she

studied in the dorm with the distractions of her friends, the television, and music playing. *Self-reward* involves presenting oneself with a positive stimulus after engaging in a particular specific behavior. After Mindy had studied for three hours in the library and was satisfied with her performance, she rewarded herself by buying a bag of french fries that she had promised herself. Clients who learn to self-manage in the helping process have an easier time utilizing these strategies in their lives to maintain gains and incorporate new and positive changes and behaviors.

At termination, there are inevitably some unresolved conflicts that clients still have to face. By utilizing strategies of self-management, coping, and problem solving learned in the helping process, clients can take charge of their own lives. There are limitations to what a worker can do, but the different stages of the helping process point clients in the right direction.

TERMINATION FACTORS IN FAMILIES

The end of the therapeutic helping journey in family work generally seems to be less troublesome for family members and the generalist than for individuals and groups in the helping process. As Kayser (1993) observes, in relation to marital and divorce work, the couple are heavily transferred to each other, and the transferences to the practitioner are, therefore, diluted. In this form of help, regression is kept to a minimum by focusing on problem solving in the here and now, using the past mainly for understanding the present, and conducting the clinical sessions at intervals of one week. On occasion, when the going is particularly rough, a couple may be granted an extra interview.

Though termination may be less traumatic, the role of the family therapist is no less important. Zuk (1968) and Wells (1998) labeled the role of the family therapist as a celebrant role; that is, the family therapist has to join the family at appropriate times in a celebration regarding their accomplishments. Rather than seeing termination as an ending it is viewed as another celebration. Wells says that in the truest sense termination is analogous to a school graduation. Family members have acquired new skills, competencies, and insights into each other's behaviors. There is an understanding that there is much to be learned but, hopefully, the family knows how to deal with future encounters. This is an appropriate end for an effective helping process. The final outcome goal in treatment is not just remediation or crisis intervention but prevention. With exposure to the therapeutic process there are transferences of content and skills, as well as the process, to which couples and families are exposed and that they can employ on their own. This graduation process can also be related to the process of individuation from one's family of origin. A different, modified, or new system is developed and the various members of the family are now able to move into new activities.

Preparing for Termination

While in the helping process, there is a notable decrease in conflict in the family. So when does a practitioner know that it is time for a family or a couple to terminate? The family is ready to terminate when they are ready to assume more responsibility for change and when family members,

particularly the adults, have repositioned themselves in significant ways with other family members and speak of their accomplishments with a sense of ownership. The family members have become experts in dealing with their problems and do not need the worker to resolve all their problems. The family consistently discusses what they have learned and family members demonstrate increased interest and enjoyment. They have gradually stopped distancing themselves from each other as they have begun to feel safe. They rarely shift blame and disappointment over the behavior of other family members. The members become more creative and spontaneous with each other (Freeman, 1992).

As they near termination, family members report changes in other systems in their lives: They have thought through friendships, and their work situations and also have set their priorities, appropriately. Noticing positive movement in the family, the astute worker should make it a point to inquire about changes in other systems, including their own social networks. There is a general sense of being in charge of their own lives in which family members take responsibility for their own choices and are not easily defeated by other peoples' reactions to their choices (Freeman, 1992).

As the need for termination becomes clearer, sessions should be reduced in number just as with individuals. By the time the family is ready to terminate, there should be less frequent sessions. This will help family members take more responsibility for their changes, and they will be less likely to see results as being connected with the helping process itself. When a family or a couple reveals a sense of their own power, expertise, and resources, it is time to terminate.

In preparation for termination, the family is asked to reflect on the overall process, so that they can come to the final session prepared to discuss it. Before the termination session is scheduled, the worker must ensure that the family members are not ambivalent about ending the helping process. If there is any ambivalence, it should be discussed and worked through before the final session. It is important that the timing is right for the family to terminate.

Termination with families happens for three reasons:

1. The number of contracted sessions has come to an end
2. The couple or family decides that they want to stop sessions
3. The worker and family decide that it is time to terminate

Regardless of why a family wants to terminate, a process must be identified to facilitate termination. This process gives family members an opportunity for input and also offers feedback.

Elements in the Family Termination Process

Barnard and Corrales (1979), Carlson, Sperry, and Lewis (1997), and Freeman (1992) have identified nine elements in the termination process:

1. The family is asked to review what has taken place in therapy. Each family member is asked to identify two or three things that they have learned about themselves, about each other, and about the family relationship. The purpose for this review is twofold: first to find out what the family or couple regard as having been significant, at least on a conscious level, rather than taking it for granted that the practitioners know what has been meaningful to the couple. The second reason is that the lively discussion among the family or couple, when asked to search their memories for material reinforces, emphasizes, and underlines what they have learned.

2. After the family has presented their review, the worker provides the family with perceptions of the different changes they have made. Quite often, the family has thoroughly and completely identified the changes that have happened. At this point, the worker would endorse and reinforce their statements, along with additions or a different perspective that was not mentioned by the family. Also, the worker must identify pockets of anxiety that different family members present and examine how the connections between different family members have changed.

3. The family also focuses on describing to the worker the highs and lows they have experienced in the helping process. The worker asks the family, "What were some of your disappointments? What areas would you have liked me to have put more effort into or focused on in greater depth? What aspects of the helping process was most helpful?" It is extremely helpful to both the worker and the couple to identify what was especially helpful to the couple in developing an appreciation of themselves and their relationships to each other.

4. It is important criteria in termination that the family is complimented, praised, and recognized for the initiative that it has taken in creating changes that are now evident. The reasons for doing this are twofold: (1) the reinforcement of the idea that the initiative for change must come from the family, and (2) giving the family positive feedback encourages and subtly suggests changes that they can appropriately make by themselves outside of the sessions. This means that they should not only maintain the changes that have happened, but be prepared for advancing more positive changes.

5. Family members are asked about the different changes they might want in the family after the clinical sessions are over. This encourages family members to verbalize their interests and reasons for changes they expect to make, and focuses on how the family will maintain the changes that it has already made. Besides identifying what they wish to change, the family should also identify ways to facilitate changes in the future.

6. The worker in turn explores the potentials for internal change and offers suggestions for the family's consideration. A common suggestion is that family members should continue to explore their potential resources keeping in mind the needs, desires, and potentials of different family members.

7. The family should be allowed to leave without split loyalties. This is an essential aspect of the final stage of helping, is, in fact, a final reinforcement to keep the family from believing that they are letting the worker down by no longer needing him or her. As the worker presents and discloses encouragement and respect for the family's changes that are beyond the worker's office, the worker is once again reinforcing their change and independence.

8. Treatment does not end with only positives highlighted and reinforced. In fact, the worker spends some amount of time discussing the counterproductive factors in the helping process. This can include comments about the worker, the helping process itself, and the manner in which family members function or participate that was not helpful to the family. Could the family have done things differently to reach the same results more easily?

9. In the last part of termination, the worker communicates to the family that they can come back for help if they wish to, particularly if they find that they are emotionally stuck. The family members have to be reassured that returning is not an indication of failure and sometimes one session about a difficult life event can help a family move on in more creative ways. Freeman (1992) suggests that it is best to inform the family that the therapeutic process is about mastery over life's problems, not finding solutions to all problems. The goal of the family sessions is to help families become more masterful in their coping and adapting skills when dealing with life's events. Family problems should be seen as opportunities to learn about oneself and not as indications of failure.

Family treatment is different from individual treatment because the family comes in as an intact group and generally leaves as such, the exceptions being when there is a divorce or children are placed in foster care. The aim of termination is to help family members see, accept, and work with the changes they have already made. However,

there are situations where family work has to be done differently. At times, family work starts out as individual treatment, then the other family members come into the helping process. At other times, after family work is completed, one or more members may continue sessions to deal with individual problems. All the different circumstances raise different questions about the termination process.

Julie came to family sessions with her husband and their two-year-old daughter. Jack was drinking heavily and Julie had wanted him to undergo treatment for alcoholism. In the helping process, Jack was noncommittal about his drinking most of the time and always managed to turn the focus to blaming his wife as a nag who wanted to control him. Although he could finish a six-pack of beer in one sitting, he insisted that he had control over his drinking. Finally, with persuasion and encouragement from the worker, Jack agreed to join AA, which appeared to lead to better communication between husband and wife.

Julie was elated and after a couple of months started to talk about wanting to terminate. The worker felt that this was what the family wanted and started working on termination while Jack absented himself from a couple of sessions. The day of their last session, Julie came by herself to the session. Looking distressed, she cried helplessly when she saw the worker. Her mother, whom Julie loved very dearly but with whom she did not communicate well, had had a heart attack. As an only child, Julie needed to take care of her mother. She was filled with sadness and guilt and an overwhelming fear of death. Julie continued in the helping process, while she worked through some of her problems with her mother and ended as an individual client, even as her marriage continued to improve.

When some family work ends, there may be one or more members who may remain in order to receive additional services. At times, unhappy and irrevocable departures of family members such as spouses cause pain and hurt to the rest of the family and must be dealt with in the helping process. In these instances, termination would have to be dealt with differently, if at all. It could take more time, and there may be a need to hold a person's hand more than when the family leaves the clinical sessions intact.

When family relationships are intact, the worker's sense of loss at termination is minimal. Depending on the type of family work that is done, family ties may be stronger than when the family entered the helping process. When they leave, the worker can believe that they are better equipped to work with their own problems because they have understood their communication patterns and also have developed some insight into their own personalities as members of a family. Termination is associated with greater problem-solving capacity, and therefore the work performed by the worker is valued but not overrated. The kind of work after which the family walks away with positives is likely to be easier on them than when a family structure is destroyed or serious problems result with one or two persons remaining in the helping process for a longer period of time.

At times, family members come for treatment after destabilizing events like divorce, institutional placement, or removal of a family member by court order. In these situations, it is essential to remember that the family—that is, the unit of father, mother, and children—is still the same and everyone is an important member of the family. The treatment plan should include all family members, but most often one adult person like a spouse remains in the helping process and the others do not return. When family relationships end in divorce, the feelings of the family members and the worker are devastated. Feelings involved in separations are very intense and the family members may need help in coping with the whole process of grieving, healing, and starting afresh.

A husband and wife, who were constantly bickering, had been in clinical sessions for two years. When they would stop coming to the sessions for several weeks, the problems would start again. The husband was overly strict with his stepchildren and the mother was overly indulgent. They did not seem to be able to find a mutually acceptable middle ground. Added to this problem, the wife did not get along with her in-laws who lived nearby. The wife resented the fact that every time there was a problem in the family, the husband would go to his parents, who supported him and condemned their daughter-in-law. This was a pattern that he refused to break. His par-

ents would not come for the sessions, which they saw this as unnecessary.

After a great deal of hard work the wife moved toward separation, despite the protests of the husband who felt that his wife had to adjust to him and his ways. It was an extremely difficult situation for a family with three children who were experiencing a great deal of pain and anger, as was the worker who had been involved with the family for so long. The wife agreed to remain in treatment with the worker but the husband did not wish to, so the worker recommended another practitioner who would work with the husband as she felt each one of them needed tremendous support when they embarked on their new roles.

TERMINATION IN GROUPS

In group treatment, as in individual and family treatment, there is a beginning, a middle, and an ending. Endings are difficult for the group members and the leader. Smalley (1967) indicates that just as beginnings are psychologically imbued with feelings of birth, so endings are imbued in varying proportions with feelings of death and separation. While endings carry a sense of accomplishment, freedom, and moving on to new situations, they also mean having to deal with stress and discomfort. Often, group members feel ambivalent and experience a mixture of sadness and joy—sadness because they are leaving not only the worker but also each other; joy because of their newly developed confidence (Reid, 1991).

Corey (1990) indicates that the most important group-leadership skill is being able to assist group members to transfer what they have learned in the group to their outside environment. When termination begins, this consolidation of learning becomes even more profound. This is the time the group leader summarizes, pulls together loose ends, and integrates and interprets the group experience. Corey (1990) sees the engagement and the final stage of the group as crucial in terms of what the members have learned about themselves. The initial stage sets the tone for making group work effective as group members get to know each other and also establish their own identities within the group. The final stage is crucial because it is when members make decisions regarding what they have learned about themselves. If the termination phase is handled badly by the group leader, the members' ability to use what they learned in the group will be greatly reduced. Also, there is a chance that the clients' unresolved issues may not be brought to a closure because the group leader is no longer providing any direction.

Reasons for Group Termination

Work with different groups ends for many reasons (Reid, 1997). Ideally, a group ends when the individual and group members have achieved their objectives and goals. The members have learned enough in the group and are willing to work on their own, based on the progress they have made. Often, groups terminate because there is a predetermined time limit, after which the group ends on schedule. Another reason why a group may not last is due to a lack of interest and commitment to the group by its members. This might happen because the momentum required to allow the group to function adequately is not achieved. It could be that members may have dropped out of the group and no new members have replaced them. Groups also end because group coping strategies are maladaptive (Johnson, 1995) or because the group has become destructive. Some therapeutic groups do not die, old members leave and new members join regularly.

Group Reactions to Termination

The final stage of the group is critical because this is the time when group members should be consolidating their gains. It is a difficult time as members are aware that the group is going to dissolve. They begin to distance themselves in different ways, such as becoming more passive, failing to bring in new concerns, or failing to examine the learning in the group that would be of use to them in or out of the group situation.

According to Kramer (1990), the ending stage is characterized by a mixture of feelings, among them sadness, confusion, and also joy. There are tasks that are numerous and difficult including endings as a psychological experience, recapitulating the treatment experience, obtaining closure, and finally, the ultimate freedom of experiencing new beginnings. Kramer concludes no other stage of treatment challenges a group more than this particular one.

A main task is for members to discuss what transpired from the first to the final session and what they have learned from each other. If the group is different at the end than at the beginning, then the group members need to know why.

In an open group that continues to function with some members leaving and others coming in, Corey and Corey (1992) note that maintenance tasks include:

> Providing a structure in which members can review and integrate their own learning
>
> Making sure that most unfinished business is taken care of when a member is about to terminate
>
> Allowing time for the person who is leaving to prepare for termination and for the other members to say their good-byes and share their reactions and feedback
>
> Making referrals as appropriate for individual, couple, family, or group support treatment (Corey & Corey, 1992)

In time-limited groups some members may be reluctant to terminate though they may be well aware of the specific date and time. These individuals experience anxiety as well as anticipation about the separation. Reid (1997) identified different types of reactions which include: denial, that is they block out of their memory the fact that the group is ending; clustering when the group starts to become more cohesive, which is backsliding because members become angry and reveal greater dependency on each other; recapitulation of past activities and events in the group; evaluation of past events or experiences compared with the present; annihilistic flight when group members miss meetings and drop out of the group before termination; and positive flight with members developing new interests and friends outside of the group while continuing as group members.

Feelings of separation become intense in some members who feel that the trust experienced in the group cannot be replicated elsewhere. The central task for the worker is to remind group members that cohesion could not have taken place without the attendance and participation of each member of the group. They also need to be reminded that close relationships in the group did not take place without active steps by different group members.

In order to help group members express their feelings about separation, it is important for the facilitator to recognize and be able to deal with personal feelings about the ending of the group. If the group leader avoids dealing with feelings of sadness, the members will probably follow suit.

Unfinished Business

There may be some group members who have unfinished business. Some may not have all their issues resolved and should be encouraged to take advantage of this final opportunity. It is not realistic to think that all issues will be taken care of, but if there is anything crucial that a particular member wishes to discuss, this should be brought out into the open. If there is one member who wishes to discuss some personal matter with another member of the group, that too has to be raised and explored. If members are given a few more sessions, then they will have time to complete their own personal agendas. The group can also point out areas in which members can focus productively once they leave the group. Clients will often wait until the end to bring up important matters. However, in a time-limited group, it may not be possible to extend the number of sessions. If necessary, an individual session can be scheduled.

Reviewing the Experiences of the Group

At the final stage of the group, members are asked about the different lessons they have learned in the group. The group has to set aside time for evaluating the turning points in the group for each member, and what it was about the group that they liked and did not like as well as the ways in which the group might have had greater impact. Also, the entire history of the group should be in perspective. If, as Corey and Corey (1992) relate, members make general statements like "the group was fantastic, and I grew a lot from it," the worker has to ask them to be specific about how the group has been important to them and in what ways they think the group has been "fantastic."

Practicing Changes in Behavior

Group members need to be encouraged to think of ways in which they can continue their work after the group has terminated, as well as solidify and consolidate their learning within the group. In such situations, the worker must rely on role playing and rehearsals anticipating interactions and also teach group members specific skills for dealing with changes. Group members should be encouraged to try out new ways of behavior, both inside and outside of the group.

Drew mentioned that keeping his anger to himself and being "nice" to people was really destructive for him, too. It led to feelings of depression and also to many psychosomatic ailments. Practicing to express his anger constructively helped him acquire some important skills in his life. It took Drew a lot of time before he was able to convince people to take him seriously since he could easily forget his hard-earned lessons.

Group Feedback

During termination, it is important that group members get feedback from the group regarding what they have or have not achieved in terms of their own growth and how empowered they feel. This can begin by asking members for a brief report on how they have perceived themselves in the group, what the group meant to them, and what if any decisions need to be made. Others then give their own opinions and impressions to the group member. Some group members may give only positive feedback to group members to whom they feel close. In such cases, the group leader has to help them express their doubts and concerns as suggested by Corey & Corey (1992):

> My greatest fear for you is . . .
>
> My hope for you is . . .
>
> I hope that you will seriously consider . . .
>
> I see you blocking your strengths by . . .
>
> I feel empowered in . . .
>
> Some things I hope you will think about doing yourself are . . . (p. 222)

The worker should prevent group members from making global remarks such as, "Our group was fantastic," or "You were a super leader." In such cases, the worker has to ask the members to be specific. For example, a group member may say to the leader, "I like your ability to be honest and direct in giving feedback and at the same time to treat people with dignity."

Feedback should be constructive and stated in such a way that the person is not left hanging. Nevertheless, in the ending sessions it is not appropriate for group members to unload pent-up negative reactions on a person who may not have an opportunity to work through this feedback.

Learning by Action

As members participate in the group they learn about themselves. One person learns that she is very impatient, another that he allows people to walk all over him. After developing some awareness, the group members work on their own situations in the sessions. The final session is only a beginning in many ways. For example, the person who was nonassertive has become aware of it and has learned to work at it in the group; he now needs to maintain these gains outside of the group. At termination, members have new directions to follow in dealing with problems in everyday life.

Corey and Corey (1992) suggest that group members, while terminating, be asked to write

their own contracts in terms of what they can do for themselves. The goals should not be too ambitious, which might set members up for failure. If the group members wish, they can read their contracts aloud in the group and get feedback and specific suggestions. They could also make arrangements with another member of the group to whom they can report progress toward their goals. This creates a mechanism for accountability and also reinforces the need for establishing a support system outside of the group.

Transferring Group Learning to Everyday Life

When the group is about to terminate, the members have to be helped to apply their learning to everyday life. At this stage, group members are usually very receptive to considering what they have learned in the group and how to sustain in it.

Corey and Corey (1992) suggest the following principles for the worker to stress with the group:

1. Realize that the group is a means to an end
2. Realize that change may be slow and subtle
3. Do not expect one group alone to renovate your life
4. Decide what to do with what you have learned in the group
5. Last but not least, think for yourself

Realizing that the group is a means to an end is often forgotten and the group experience becomes an end in itself. For some group members, the main payoff is what happens within the group setting and the emotional closeness the members feel in it. But the main purpose is to help members look at themselves and decide whether they like what they see and how to change for the better. What have they learned, how did they learn it, and what do they intend to do with their own insights?

Emily was overly trusting in relationships and got hurt by her openness and innocence. She learned in the group that when she presented her goodness and warmth, people mistook it for weakness and hurt her. When she realized the consequences of her behavior after it happened to her repeatedly, she decided to do something about it. She learned not to be completely trusting of people until she got to know them, and not to get involved in one-way relationships.

Forgetting that change may be slow and subtle, people sometimes expect miracles and become frustrated if there are setbacks. They will learn in the group that change is slow and that old patterns do die hard.

Allen used to be bullied by his girlfriend who always complained that he was fat. She would prepare his favorite meals and feed him but ridicule him in front of her family and his. Allen wanted to be assertive with her and did not wish to leave her so he learned to tell her not to cook his favorite dishes for him. Instead, he suggested that either he would cook a simple meal or take her out for a simple dinner. Allen was very proud of himself for a few sessions. During the termination sessions, however, he started to relapse and was very unhappy with his behavior because he had reverted to the earlier pattern of allowing himself to be dominated. The group members helped him to understand that permanent change takes time—and happens in small steps with ups and downs.

Some members get into a therapeutic group with the purpose of setting everything right with a rapid dramatic change. This person has unrealistic goals and expectations. Group members have to understand that change is a process, not a product. Further, the group experience is not a shortcut to a finished product. The process of change takes time and energy, and is a product of trial and error.

People will set aside time to get themselves into "psychological shape" for instance, to write a book. It is not possible to work through family issues and problems by setting aside a certain amount of time in a weekend. This only happens gradually as people work at their problems. There are no shortcuts to being "together" as a person; it is a process of trial and error that takes time, effort, and conscious desire.

Naomi is an active ambitious twenty-five-year-old who was promoted to a manager's position in a fairly large

and sophisticated company. Her problem in treatment was how to "make" her subordinates function as effectively and efficiently as she did. In the treatment group, she wanted shortcuts to working with her subordinates assuming, "once they listen to you, they always will." Naomi was promoted over her immediate boss. She also had a large number of projects for her subordinates, including her hostile ex-boss who she thought would "get over it quickly" and listen to her orders because she was now the boss. Naomi wanted some quick tips on how to be a boss but did not realize that being a boss was itself a process. She could not be a "finished product" after a couple of group sessions. There were a number of self-growth issues that Naomi had to work through, and it would not happen in a weekend.

Members have decided what they wish to do with what they have learned in the group. While functioning as a member of a group, group members are forced to look at themselves as others see them, as well as how they present themselves to others. Group members should use this information for their own growth.

In a women's self-growth group, Erin spent her time in the ten sessions complaining how her boyfriend was causing her pain and making her miserable. As the group sessions progressed, it became clear that Erin was blaming everyone else for her problems. If the session did not go the way she wanted, she blamed a member of the group and left feeling miserable. Slowly but surely, Erin learned that if she waited for others to make her miserable or happy, she would be miserable. Erin had control over her life and had options about the decisions she made. As the group process progressed, Erin realized that she was not helpless and that everyone has a choice about how they live. The responsibility of choosing how to live was the most valuable outcome of Erin's participation in the group.

Group members have to think for themselves. Many people seek help because they have lost the ability to find their own way and look to others to lead them. They may be tuned in sensitively to the group and observe what to expect from the group.

Abigail, age twenty-five, mentioned that she wanted to leave her parents' home. Her mother made her feel guilty about this even though both her parents were in good health. The group urged her to leave home. Early on, Abigail mentioned her home situation was her only way to relate to life, but as the group members urged her on she tried to plunge into life by leaving home. The result was that Abigail felt lonely and unhappy. In retrospect, it was clear that Abigail was not ready to make the move but was yielding to group pressure.

Finally, even when the group is terminating the group members need to be reminded of confidentiality. Group members can share what happened and what they learned in the group but they should be careful not divulge the identities of other members.

TERMINATION WITH COMMUNITIES AND ORGANIZATIONS

While working with communities and organizations we are still working with people, and we still require people skills to terminate. Termination is understood in the context of an entire course of treatment. Decisions made early about focus and goals provide the potential for review during termination (Compton & Galaway, 1999). In working with larger systems additional approaches are needed when stabilization of change takes place. Kettner, Daley, and Nichols (1985) suggest the following: routine procedures and processes; clarification of policies and procedures; reducing the influence of the change agent; and addressing the needs of clients.

Routine Procedures and Processes

Acquiring needed services for different groups of clients in the community involves knowledge of how organizations function, as well as having effective communication skills and using the expertise of the agency to influence outcomes in the community. One of the goals in working with larger systems is to ensure that whatever changes are accomplished will continue indefinitely. For in-

stance, consider the creation and influence of social policies on ethnic elderly. The conditions contributing to the vulnerability and poorer status of ethnic minority individuals is magnified among the elderly. Income and retirement policies, health care policies such as Medicare and Medicaid, and even policies regarding publicly assisted housing have major ramifications for the elderly from different ethnic groups. The most comprehensive policy approach designed for the elderly is the Older Americans Act (OAA), enacted in 1965, which was to provide a variety of services to the elderly in the community. The OAA has been amended. A 1973 amendment focused on providing services for the most vulnerable of the elderly, whose needs involve language barriers and racial and cultural barriers. The 1987 amendment recognized the specific needs of elderly Native Americans and granted nations the right to request specific funding services under the OAA.

Based on community needs and community work done by social workers and others, an example of the way in which services are offered is that of nutrition programs. For instance in a city in California kitchens prepared lunches for Korean, Mexican, Portugese, Jewish, Vietnamese, Polish, and Chinese elderly. This type of sensitivity is important for increasing service participation. The aims of the group are laudable and it is important to continue their efforts. Involving the ethnic elderly and natural leaders to ensure that these programs are continued and expanded is an important aspect of work that, though started by social workers, should be carried out long after the social workers have left the scene. In such situations the torch is passed on to the natural leaders of the community who will continue to stabilize the change and take action if need be. Goals of the community are achieved consistently when policies and procedures become routine.

Clarifying Policies and Procedures

One way to clarify policies and procedures is to ensure that they are clear to the community members.

The generalist and community leaders can help by putting policies and procedures into writing, so there is always something for the community members to refer to, to follow through on, and to monitor. If you can get the support of local people in pursuing continuous support then you can ask for funding from philanthropists in the local community and create not only a money source, but local interest and concern. This is a way of formalizing informal help and fitting into the local community organization.

After the work has been accomplished the generalist has to reduce his or her influence in the organization and let the local natural and formal community leaders assume responsibility for taking care of their own. This is done by reducing your attendance at their local community meetings. In the beginning stages of termination when the generalist is reducing his or her attendance at the meetings, some community members may continue to call and consult the generalist. As time passes, the number of calls become less frequent. Finally, when the community takes over, the generalist can play the role of a consultant, if needed.

Termination in communities, organizations, and committees has long been known for its ritualized endings. These rituals include parties, ceremonies, certificates of merit, voting approval of a final committee report, and notifications of different types of funding. All of these activities affirm accomplishments, mark endings, and serve as bridges to new beginnings. Even in closure ceremonies, generalists work toward offering members opportunities to reflect on their work together and define their future relationships with each other.

As Germain and Gitterman (1996) state, "When the change in an organization's purpose, structure, and procedures of service arrangements is no longer perceived as change, but as an integral part of its ongoing activities, the innovation is institutionalized." (p. 395). By this time a number of relationships have been created between members. At closure, organizational and community workers should wholeheartedly support indigenous leadership and intrasystem alliances.

Individual Client Exercises

1. Two students role-play the worker and Bess in the following situation.

Bess has been in the clinical sessions for over two years where she has worked on self-assertiveness and self-esteem issues. She has been prepared for termination for the past three months. This is her next to last session, but she is ambivalent, angry, and is feeling rejected. The class observes and comments on how the worker helps Bess work through her problems of ambivalence, anger, and sense of rejection. After the role play, both the students should present how the role play affected them in terms of loss of a relationship and any other emotions. Why did they feel the way they did? Did they both believe that termination was handled in a constructive and professional manner in the role play? Later, the rest of the class can comment on the role play and also make appropriate suggestions.

2. Role-play an unnatural ending as you (the student) has to terminate with a client (another student) when the academic year has come to an end.

You are a social work intern in a nursing home. Emma, a sixty-five-year-old lady has moved from her natural home and been placed in this setting because her husband died a few months ago, and she fell on the kitchen floor and broke her leg. You have taken a liking to her and feel sorry that she has nobody to turn to. Her daughter visits her sporadically. You are feeling guilty about leaving her because she has become very attached to you and looks forward to your visits. You have been helping her to make friends and become sociable with other people in this setting. You start to prepare her because you are leaving the agency in three weeks. As you mention leaving, Emma pretends that she did not hear you and distracts you with other pieces of information about the nursing home. At one point she says that she wished she had not left her home. At another point she mentions that she does not like the nursing home. You assume that perhaps she has not heard you, so you mention to her again that you are leaving, and she distracts you again and talks about her sister.

How does it feel for you to be a worker in this situation and how did the student who played

Emma feel? Let the class comment on what they think was happening in this initial termination session.

Family Exercises

1. About five students can role-play an intact family with father, mother, and three school-age children, and another student can play the worker in the following case study.

The family has come for help because of marital conflict. Early family interviews reveal that there were no consistent rules in the family, and the mother was over-burdened with too many responsibilities including a part-time job, care of all the children, and cooking and cleaning as her major chores. Her husband hardly helps with the "household chores," which he calls "woman's work." However after being in clinical sessions the family moved progressively and positively toward better understanding and a fairer distribution of work. The family members blame each other less, and the children, who tended to take sides with either parent, do not do so. It seems that this family has worked out its problems fairly well and is ready for termination. The worker has asked the family members to share all the gains they have made in therapy and how they are progressing. The family members are pleased with themselves and ready to leave. The worker likes this family and is happy, but also somewhat sad, to see them go.

How is termination handled in this case by the worker and the different family members? Why is the worker ambivalent about the clients leaving, although they seemed happy to leave? How would the termination be different if when the intact family is no longer together when it terminates from the help that is being offered? Let each person who role-played present how they felt in the different roles. The class, based on observation, should comment on the role play regarding the students' observations of the termination process.

2. Let students role-play the given family scene with one student playing the generalist.

In a single-parent family, the mother controls her three teenage children by using their dead father as a model for discipline. In one situation, she tells sixteen-year-old Jodi that her [dead] father told the mother that Jodi should not date the boy she was going with because he was "bad." The real reason is that the mother does not like him. Jodi and her brother and sister resent the mother using the father as an authority figure in controlling them, since he has been dead for seven years.

How would the student playing the family therapist deal with this situation? After the role play, the students can discuss the different solutions that could be offered to this family and also the reasons why this should be done. In what way would the given solutions be helpful and beneficial to the rest of the family?

Group Exercises

1. This exercise (adapted from Day, Macy, & Jackson, 1984) could be carried out in a classroom as part of the termination process. The class could be broken into groups of six members: one observer, one social worker, and four resident members of a treatment center for disturbed and runaway girls.

Four girls had each run away from home a number of times and were committed to the residential treatment setting. Denise, fourteen, was sexually abused by her father and is seen as "incorrigible"; Dollie, thirteen, is pregnant; thirteen-year-old Dawn has been hanging around with older teens who shoplift and steal cars for kicks; and Dottie, twelve, is angry at her parents for divorcing. Now the group is at the termination stage. Dollie, Dottie, and Dawn are being released the next day from the residential setting and will go back to their parental homes, while Denise will go to a foster home. All of the girls have made substantial progress and are seen as ready to return to the community. One of the girls is fearful, another one is ambivalent and somewhat confused.

The social worker's job is to use the group process, as well as his or her clinical skills to help in the process of termination. The observer should note how the group interacts and its leadership patterns, cohesiveness, and mutual support systems. After ten minutes, each observer should report on the processes to their group. Then, the full class can discuss how useful the role play was with the termination process and how effectively the group process was used.

2. In this group termination exercise, different students can play the role of the group leader and view a small group of students role-playing a group of single parents with children that is about to terminate. The purpose is to prepare members to leave the group. After a few students have played the role of group leader, process how the group members experienced it. Respond to it accordingly. In termination, information can be presented flexibly since what applies to a group can sometimes apply to a family or to an individual and vice versa. The worker should be alert and use this termination process sensitively and appropriately.

Community and Organizational Exercises

1. You are working as a generalist in charge of a community program called Health Care for Homeless Veterans. This program was earlier known as the Homeless Chronically Mentally Ill Veterans Program, which is the most accurate description since most of the agency resources are still reserved for the mentally ill or substance abusers, not the medically needy. There are four other social workers in the agency whom you will supervise, who have worked there for many years.

Your initial role is to help the social workers and others change their approach to the community issues and help the medically deprived homeless veterans. One student can play the role of an agency administrator, and four others can play social workers. All need to resolve their conflict with the changes in the functions of the agency. How can the workers be helped to understand that the old services are terminated and the new ones are in place, without losing their support?

2. Three students role-play this scenario.

Three social workers have participated actively in bringing about some effective change by creating a center for disabled people in a small community where such services were not available. They feel that they have made lasting differences in the lives of disabled people and their families in the community. However, they quickly find out that there are other pressing problems in the community, including drug abuse by teenagers. Change is an evolutionary process in all communities. How would you go about addressing this pressing issue in this community?

CHAPTER SUMMARY

Termination is the last stage of the helping process. It is also called the ending or the disengagement stage. Termination refers to the time taken and the process used by a worker and a client system to plan the ending of their contact with each other. The purpose of termination is to bring to closure a responsible professional helping relationship in a timely fashion. The primary function of termination is to make an assessment of the client's readiness to terminate and also consolidate the learning process. The tasks of termination vary from dealing with new information clients wish to discuss to reinforcing positive changes.

The types of termination are: short-term, long-term, one session termination, sporadic or unplanned termination, transfer termination, planned termination determined by temporal constraints, referrals, discharge planning, and booster sessions. The timing of termination should be appropriate depending on whether the presenting problem has been reduced or ended and whether clients feel they can live effectively without further help. The principles of effective closure and termination include four tasks from exploring one's reactions to ending treatment to leave-taking with the worker. Other components of termination include looking at the different achievements and strides the client has made, depending on the intensity and nature of the helping process, and the nature of the ending, which can be natural or unnatural.

Positive changes in clients are not dramatic, but when they happen they should be stabilized.

Promoting self-growth is also called self-management. It includes self-monitoring, stimulus control procedures, and self-rewards.

Termination factors in families are less troublesome when the family leaves intact with positive changes. The family has to review what has taken place in treatment. In the last part of termination, the family is invited to return for treatment if necessary or for consultation. When family relations are intact, the sense of loss of the worker is minimal; but when there are destabilizing events like divorce, institutional placement, or removal of a family member by court order, the family is affected differently and, accordingly, termination must be dealt with differently.

Termination in groups carries a sense of accomplishment and freedom to move on to new situations. Reasons for group termination are based on the achievement of group goals. The group's reaction to termination is characterized by a mixture of feelings, among them sadness, confusion, and joy. In time-limited groups, members experience denial, clustering, recapitulation, evaluation, annihilistic flight, and also positive flight. The group takes care of the unfinished business they have with each other such as discussing some personal matters with another member which must be raised and explored. The group may review its experiences, practice changes in behavior, receive group members' feedback, and transfer learning to everyday life. Group members learn by action and by transferring group learning to everyday life.

In terminating with communities and organizations the generalist should aim toward ensuring that changes accomplished in larger systems are continued indefinitely. Ritualized ceremonies often are used to mark accomplishments as well as to terminate with a generalist, while new beginnings are created and maintained among community members.

REFERENCES

Abramson, J. S. (1988). Participation of elderly patients in discharge planning: Is self-determination a reality. *Social Work, 33*(5), 443–448.

Albert, J. (1994). Talking like "Real People." The "Straight Ahead" Prism group. In A. Gitterman & L. Shulman (Eds.), *Mutual aid groups: Vulnerable populations and the life cycle* (pp. 199–214). New York: Columbia University Press.

Allan, E. F. (1979). Psychoanalytic theory. In F. J. Turner, (Ed.), *Social Work Treatment* (2nd. ed., pp. 54–72). New York: Free Press.

Allport, G. W. (1954). *The Nature of Prejudice.* Reading, MA: Addison-Wesley.

Amador, X. F., Flaum, M., Andersen, N. C., Strauss, D. H., Yale, S. A., Clark, S. C., & Gorman, J. M. (1994). Awareness of illness in schizophrenia and schizoaffective and mood disorders, *Archives of General Psychiatry, 51,* 826–836.

American Hospital Association. (1985). *The role of the social worker in planning.* Chicago: Author.

American Psychological Association. (1985). *White paper on duty to protect.* Washington, DC.

American Public Welfare Association and National Association of State Units on Aging. (1988). *Adult protective services: Programs in state and social services agencies and state units on aging.* Washington, DC: Authors.

Anderson, C. M., & Stewart, S. (1983). *Mastering resistance. A practical guide to family therapy.* New York: Guilford.

Anderson, J. (1984). *Counseling through group process.* New York: Springer.

Anderson, J. (1997). *Social work with groups.* New York: Longman.

Anderson, J. D. (1990, March). *Preparing students for family-centered practice in the 1990s. A multicultural perspective.* Paper presented at the annual program meeting of the Council on Social Work Education, Chicago, IL.

Anderson, R., & Carter, I. (1990). *Human behavior in the social environment: A social systems approach.* (4th ed.). New York: Aldine de Gruyter.

Arches, J. (1991). Social structure, burnout, and job satisfaction. *Social Work, 36*(3), 202–206.

Atkinson, D. R., Morten, G., & Sue, D. W. (Eds.). (1994). *Counseling American minorities* (4th ed.). Madison, WI: Brown & Benchmark.

Atwood, J. (1999). *Family therapy: A systemic behavioral approach.* Pacific Grove, CA: Brooks/Cole.

Auslander, G. K., & Litwin, H. (1987). The parameters of network interventions: A social work application. *Social Service Review, 61,* 26–29.

Austin, D. M., & Hasenfeld, Y. (1985). A prefatory essay on the future administration of human services. *Journal of Applied Behavioral Sciences, 11,* 351–354.

Bachelor, A. (1995). Client's perception of the therapeutic alliance: A qualitative analysis. *Journal of Counseling Psychology, 42*(3), 323–337.

Badding, N. C. (1989). Client involvement in case recording. *Social Casework, 70*(9), 539–548.

Baer, B. L., & Federico, R. C. (1978). *Educating the baccalaureate social workers.* Cambridge, MA: Ballinger.

Baier, K. (1969). What is value: An analysis of the concept. In K. Baier & N. Rescher, (Eds.), *Values and the future* (pp. 33–67). New York: The Press.

Bailey, C. (1993, July 16). Program helps pregnant teens bear healthy babies. *Oakland Tribune,* p. A13.

Balcazar, F. E., Mathews, R. M., Francisco, V. T., & Fawcett, S. B. (1994). The empowerment process in four advocacy organizations of people with disabilities. *Rehabilitation Psychology, 39,* 189–203.

Bandler, R., & Grinder, J. (1975). *The structure of magic.* Palo Alto, CA: Science and Behavior Books.

Bandura, A. (1962). Social learning through imitation. In M. R. Jones (Ed.). *Nebraska symposium on maturation.* Lincoln: University of Nebraska Press.

Bandura, A. (1991). Social cognition theory of self-regulation. Special issue: Theories of cognitive self-regulation. *Organizational Behavior and Human Decision Processes, 50*(2), 248–287.

Bandura, A. (1993). Perceived self-efficacy in cognitive development and functioning. *Educational Psychologist, 28,* 117–148.

Bandura, A., & Cervone, D. (1983). Self-evaluative and self-efficacy mechanisms governing the motivational effects of goal systems. *Journal of Personality and Social Psychology, 45,* 1017–1028.

Bandura, A., Cioffi, D., Taylor, C., & Brouillard, M. E. (1988). Perceived self-efficacy in coping with cognitive stressors and opioid activation. *Journal of Personality and Social Psychology, 55,* 477–488.

Baradell, J. G., & Klein, K. (1993). Relationship of life stress and body consciousness to hypervigilent decision making. *Journal of Personality and Social Psychology, 64*(2), 267–273.

Barker, R. L. (1987). *The social work dictionary* (1st ed.). Washington, DC: NASW Press.

Barker, R. L. (1995). *The social work dictionary* (3rd ed.). Silver Spring, MD: NASW Press.

Barlow, D. H., & Durand, V. M. (1995). *Abnormal psychology.* Pacific Grove, CA: Brooks/Cole.

Barnard, C. P., & Corrales, R. G. (1979). *The theory and techniques of family therapy.* Springfield, IL: Charles C. Thomas.

Barnard, C. P., & Kuehl, B. P. (1995). Ongoing evaluations in session procedures for enhancing the working alliance and therapy effectiveness. *American Journal of Family Therapy, 23*(2), 161–172.

Bartlett, H. (1961). *Analyzing social work practice by fields.* New York: NASW.

Bartlett, H. M. (1970). *The common base of social work practice.* Silver Springs, MD: NASW Press.

Bassin, A. (1993). The reality therapy paradigm. *Journal of Reality Therapy, 12*(2), 3–13.

Beardslee, W. R. (1989). The role of self-understanding in resilient individuals: The development of a perspective. *American Journal of Orthopsychiatry, 59*(2), 266–278.

Beavers, W. R. (1982). Healthy, midrange, and severely dysfunctional families. In F. Walsh, (Ed.), *Normal Family Processes.* New York: Guilford.

Beck, B. (1977). Professional associations of social workers. In J. Turner (Ed.), *Encyclopedia of social work* (17th ed., pp. 1084–1093). Washington, DC: NASW.

Beck, J. T., & Strong, S. R. (1982). Stimulating therapeutic change with interpretations: A comparison of positive and negative connotations. *Journal of Counseling Psychology, 29,* 551–559.

Becker, H. (1963). *The outsiders: Studies in the sociology of deviance.* New York: Free Press.

Beehr, T. A., & McGrath, J. E. (1995). The methodology of research and coping: Conceptual, strategic and operational-level issues. In M. Zeidner & N. S. Endler (Eds.). *Handbook of Coping. Theory, Research, Applications.* New York: John Wiley and Sons, pp. 65–82.

Bellah, R. N., Madsen, R., Sullivan, W. M., Swidler, A., & Tipton, S. M. (1985). *Habits of the heart.* Berkeley: University of California Press.

Benjamin, A. (1987). *The helping interview; with case illustrations.* Boston: Houghton-Mifflin.

Bennis, W. G. and Shepard, H. A. (1987). A theory of group development. In G. S. Gibbard, J. J. Hartman, & R. D. Mann, *Analysis of groups* (pp. 415–437). San Francisco: Jossey Bass.

Bensley, D. A. (1998). *Critical thinking in psychology.* Pacific Grove, CA: Brooks/Cole.

Benson, H., & Stuart, E. M. (Eds.) (1992). *The wellness book: The comprehensive guide to maintaining health and treating stress-related illness.* New York: Birch Lane.

Berk, R. A., & Rossi, P. H. (1990). *Thinking about program evaluation.* Newbury Park: Sage.

Berkman, B. (1978). *Knowledge base and program needs for effective social work practice in health: A review of the literature.* Chicago: Society for Hospital Work Directors and the American Hospital Association.

Biestek, F. (1957). *The casework relationship.* Chicago: Loyola University Press.

Biggerstaff, M. A. (1995). Licensing, Regulation, and Certification. In R. L. Edwards (Ed.), *Encyclopedia of Social Work* (19th ed., pp. 1616–1624). Washington, DC: NASW Press.

Billings, A., & Moos, R. H. (1981). The role of coping responses and social resources in attenuating the stress of life events. *Journal of Behavioral Medicine, 4,* 157–189.

Bisno, H. (1988). *Managing conflict.* Newbury Park, CA: Sage.

Blades, J. (1985). *Mediate your divorce.* Englewood Cliffs, NJ: Prentice-Hall.

Blanckenhorn, W. U. (1991). Fitness consequences of food-based territoriality in water striders, Gerris remigis. *Animal Behavior, 42,* 147–149.

Bloom, M. (1978). Challenges to the helping professions and the response of scientific practice. *Social Service Review, 52,* 584–595.

Bloom, M., Fischer, J., & Orme, J. (1995). *Evaluating practice: Guidelines for the accountable professional* (2nd ed.). Boston: Allyn & Bacon.

Boehm, W. (1959, April). The nature of social work. *Social Work, 3,* 10–18.

Bohart, R. (1980). *Skills pattern book.* Lexington, MA: Lexington Books.

Boisservain, J., & Clyde, M. J. (1973). *Network analysis studies in human interaction.* Paris: Mouton.

Bolton, F., & Bolton, S. (1987). *Working with violent families.* Newbury Park, CA: Sage.

Booth, R. (1990). *Sexual orientation: Overview and implications.* Unpublished manuscript. Black Hawk College, Moline, IL.

Boscolo, L., Cecchin, G., Hoffman, L., & Penn, P. (1987). *Milan systemic family therapy.* New York: Basic Books.

Boulding, K. (1978). *Ecodynamics: A new theory of societal evolution.* Beverley Hills, CA: Sage.

Bowen, M. (1978). *Family therapy in clinical practice.* New York: Jason Aronson.

Bowen, M. (1961). The family as a unit of study and treatment. *American Journal of Orthopsychiatry, 31,* 40–60.

Bowlby, J. (1973). Affectional Bonds: Their nature and origin. In R. S. Weiss (Ed.), *Loneliness: The experience of emotional and social isolation* (pp. 38–42). Cambridge, MA: MIT Press.

Boyd-Franklin, N. (1993). Race, class, and poverty. In F. Walsh, *Normal Family Processes* (2nd ed., pp. 361–376) New York: Guilford

Brammer, L. M., Shostrom, E. L., & Abrego, P. J. (1989). *Therapeutic psychology: Fundamentals of counseling and psychotherapy* (5th ed.). Englewood Cliffs, NJ: Prentice-Hall.

Bray, J. H., & Jouriles, E. (1995). Treatment of martial conflict and prevention divorce. *Journal of Marital and Family Therapy, 21,* 461–474.

Bray, J. H., Shepard, J. N., & Hays, J. R. (1985). Legal and ethical issues in informed consent to psychotherapy. *American Journal of Family Therapy, 13*(2), 50–60.

Brehm, S. S. (1976). *The application of social psychology in clinical practice.* New York: Wiley.

Breggin, P. R. (1991). *Toxic psychiatry.* New York: St. Martin's Press.

Breton, M. (1994). On the meaning of empowerment and empowerment-oriented social work practice. *Social Work with Groups, 17*(3), 2–27.

Breton, M. (1993). Relating competence-promotion and empowerment. *Journal of Progressive Human Services, 5*(1), 27–44.

Brewer, M. B., & Campbell, D. T. (1976). *Ethnocentrism and intergroup attitudes: East African evidence.* New York: Sage.

Brilhart, J., & Galanes, G. (1995). *Effective group discussion* (8th ed.). Madison, WI: Brown & Benchmark.

Brill, A. (1972). *Freud's contribution to psychiatry.* Gloucester, MA: Peter Smith.

Brill, N. I. (1990). *Working with people.* New York: Longman.

Brill, N. I. (1995). *Working with people: The helping process* (5th ed.). White Plains, NY: Longman.

Briscoe, R. V., Hoffman, D. B., & Bailey, J. S. (1975). Behavioral community psychology: Training a community board to problem solve. *Journal of Applied Behavior Analysis, 8,* 157–168.

Broskowski, A. (1991). Current mental health care environments. Why managed care is necessary. *Professional Psychology: Research and Practice, 22*(1), 6–14.

Brower, A., & Nuruis, P. S. (1993). *Social cognition and individual change. Current theory and counseling guidelines.* Newbury Park, CA: Sage.

Brown, L. S., & Ballou, M. (1992). *Personality and Psychopathology. Feminist Reappraisal.* New York: Guilford Press.

Brown, J. H., & Christensen, D. N. (1999). *Family therapy: Theory and practice* (2nd ed.). Pacific Grove, CA: Brooks/Cole.

Brown, L. (1991). *Groups for growth and change.* New York: Longman.

Brown, R. (1995). *Prejudice.* Malden, MA: Blackwell.

Brown, R. A. (1973). Feedback in family interviewing. *Social Work, 18*(5), 52–59.

Brucker-Gordon, F., Gangi, B. K., & Wellman, G. U. (1988). *Making therapy work.* New York: Harper & Row.

Brueggemann, W. G. (1996). *The practice of macro social work.* Chicago, IL: Nelson-Hall.

Burghardt, S. (1982). *Organizing for community action.* Beverly Hills, CA: Sage.

Buros, O. K. (1986). *Mental measures yearbook* (8th ed., Vols. 1 & 2). Lincoln: University of Nebraska Press.

Cadogen, D. A. (1977). Marital group therapy in the treatment of alcoholism. *Quarterly Journal of Studies in Alcoholism,* 1187–1194.

Cameron, G. (1990). The potential of informal support strategies in child welfare. In M. Rothery & G. Cameron (Eds.), *Child maltreatment: Expanding our concept of helping* (pp. 15–168). Hillsdale, NJ: Erlbaum.

Campbell, T., & Patterson, J. (1995). The effectiveness of family interventions in the treatment of physical illness. *Journal of Marital and Family Therapy, 21,* 545–584.

Carkhuff, R. (1985). *Helping and human relations. Practice and research.* New York: Holt, Rinehart & Winston.

Carlson, J, Sperry, L., & Lewis, J. A. (1997). *Family therapy: Ensuring treatment efficacy.* Pacific Grove, CA: Brooks/Cole.

Carlton, T. (1984). *Clinical social work in health settings.* New York: Springer.

Carroll, L. (1978). *Hacks, blacks, and cons: Race relations in a maximum security prison.* Lexington, MA: Lexington.

Carter, E. A., & McGoldrick, M. (1988). Overview: The changing family life cycle: A framework for family therapy. In B. Carter & M. McGoldrick (Eds.), *The changing family life cycle: A framework for family therapy* (2nd ed., pp. 1–26). New York: Allyn & Bacon.

Carver, C. S. (1996). Forward. In M. Zeidner & N. S. Endler (Eds.), *Handbook of Coping* (p. xi). New York: Wiley.

Carver, C. S., Coleman, E. A., & Glass, D. C. (1976). The coronary-prone behavior pattern and the suppression of fatigue on a treadmill test. *Psychosomatic Medicine, 33,* 460–466.

Casey, K., & Vanceburg, M. (1985). *The promise of a new day: A book of daily meditations.* New York: Harper/Hazelden.

Castex, G. (1994). The function of stereotyping processes: A challenge for practice. In L. G. Gardella, R. Daniel, M. C. Joyner, N. Mokuau, & J. M. Shriver (Eds.), *In memory of Ronald C. Federico: A BPD Festschrift* (pp. 8–16). Springfield, MO: BPD.

Cautela, J. R. (1977). *Behavior analysis forms for clinical intervention* (Vol. 2). Champaign, IL: Research Press.

Chaffee, J. (1998). *The thinker's way.* Boston: Little, Brown.

Chambers, D. E. (1993). *Social policy and social programs: A method for the practical public policy analyst* (2nd ed). New York: Macmillan.

Chambers, D. E., Wedel, K. R., & Rodwell, M. K. (1992). *Evaluating social programs.* Boston: Allyn & Bacon.

Chan, V. C. (1989). Issues of identity development among Asian-American lesbians and gay men. *Journal of Counseling and Development, 68,* 16–20.

Chandler, S. (1985). Mediator: Confronting problem solving. *Social Work, 30,* 346–349.

Chang, V. N., & Scott, S. T. (1999). *Basic interviewing skills. A Workbook for Practitioners.* Pacific Grove, CA: Brooks/Cole.

Chavis, D., & Wandersman, A. (1990). Sense of community in the urban environment: A catalyst for participation and community development. *American Journal of Community Psychology, 14,* 24–40.

Christianson, J., & Gray, D. Z. (1994). What CMHC's can learn from two states' efforts to capitate Medicaid benefits. *Hospital and Community Psychiatry, 48*(8), 777–781.

Claiborn, C. D., Ward, S. R., & Strong, S. R. (1981). Effects of congruence between counselor interpretations and client beliefs. *Journal of Counseling Psychology, 28,* 101–109.

Claiborn, D. (1982). Interpretation and change in counseling. *Journal of Counseling Psychology, 29,* 439–453.

Clow, D. R., & Vogler, D. E. (1990). Treatment for spouse abusive model. In S. M. Stith, M. B. Williams, & K. Rosen (eds), *Violence hits home.* New York: Springer.

Coady, N. E. (1993). The worker–client relationship revisited. *Families in Society. The Journal of Contemporary Human Services, 74*(5), 291–300.

Colapinto, J. (1991). Structural family therapy. In A. S. Gurman & D. P. Kniskern (Eds). *Handbook of family therapy* (Vol. 2, pp. 310–360). New York: Brunner/Mazel.

Cole, C. L., & Cole, A. L. (1993). Family therapy theory: Implications for marriage and family enrichment. In P. G. Boss, W. J. Doherty, R. LaRossa, W. R. Schumm, & S. K. Steinmetz. (Eds.), *Sourcebook of family theories and methods. A contextual approach* (pp. 525–530). New York: Plenum.

Coley, S. M., & Scheinberg, C. A. (1990). *Proposal writing.* Newbury Park, CA: Sage.

Collins, B. G. (1993). Reconstruing codependency using self-in-relation theory: A feminist perspective. *Social Work, 38,* 470–476.

Compton, B. R., & Galaway, B. (1989). *Social work processes.* Belmont, CA: Wadsworth.

Compton, B. R., & Galaway, B. (1994). *Social work processes* (5th ed.). Pacific Grove, CA: Brooks/Cole.

Compton, B. R., & Galaway, B. (1999). *Social work processes* (6th ed.). Pacific Grove, CA: Brooks/Cole.

Connaway, R. S., & Gentry, M. E. (1988). *Social work practice.* Engelwood Cliffs, NJ: Prentice-Hall.

Connor-Greene, P. (1993). The therapeutic context: Preconditions for change in psychotherapy. *Psychotherapy, 30,* 375–382.

Conrad, P., & Schneider, J. W. (1992). *Deviance and medicalization: From badness to sickness.* Philadelphia: Temple University Press.

Cooley, E. (1994). Training and interdisciplinary team in communication and decision-making skills. *Small Group Research, 25,* 5–25.

Cooper, S. (1973). A look at the effect of racism on clinical work. *Social Casework, 54,* 76–84.

Corcoran, K., & Vandiver, V. (1996). *Maneuvering the maze of managed care.* New York: Free Press.

Corcoran, M. (1985). Myth and reality: The causes and persistence of poverty. *Journal of Policy Analysis and Management, 4,* 516–537.

Corey, G. (1990). *Theory and practice of counseling* (3rd. ed.). Pacific Grove, CA: Brooks/Cole.

Corey, G. (1995). *Theory and practice of counseling and psychotherapy* (5th ed.). Pacific Grove, CA: Brooks/Cole.

Corey, G., Corey, M. S., & Callahan, P. (1993). *Issues and ethics in the helping professions* (3rd ed.). Pacific Grove, CA: Brooks/Cole.

Corey, G., Corey, M. S., Callahan, P., & Russell, J. M. (1992). *Group Techniques* (2nd ed.). Pacific Grove, CA: Brooks/Cole.

Corey, G., Corey, M., & Callahan, P. (1993). *Issues and ethics in the helping professions* (4th ed.). Pacific Grove, CA: Brooks/Cole.

Corey, M. S., & Corey, G. (1998). *Becoming a helper* (3rd ed.). Pacific Grove, CA: Brooks/Cole.

Corey, M., & Corey, G. (1992). *Groups: Process and practice* (4th ed.). Pacific Grove, CA: Brooks/Cole.

Cormier, S., & Cormier, B. (1998). *Interviewing strategies for helpers. Fundamental skills and cognitive behavioral interventions.* Pacific Grove, CA: Brooks/Cole.

Cormier, W. H., & Cormier, L. S. (1990). *Interviewing strategies for helpers* (3rd ed.). Pacific Grove, CA: Brooks/Cole.

Cormier, W., & Cormier, J. L. (1996). *Interviewing strategies for helpers. Fundamental skills and cognitive behavioral interventions* (2nd ed.). Pacific Grove, CA: Brooks/Cole.

Costa, P. T., Somerfield, M. R., & R. R. McCrae (1996). Personality and Coping: A Reconceptualization. In M. Zeidner & N. S. Endler (Eds.), *Handbook of Coping* (pp. 24–43). New York: Wiley.

Council on Social Work Education. (1992). *Curriculum policy statement for the baccalaureate degree programs in social work education.* Alexandria, VA: Author.

Council on Social Work Education. (1992). *Curriculum policy statement for the master's degree programs in social work education.* Alexandria, VA: Author.

Cournoyer, B. (1991). *The social work skills workbook.* Belmont, CA: Wadsworth.

Cournoyer, B. R. (1996). *The social work skills workbook* (2nd ed.). Pacific Grove: Brooks/Cole.

Cournoyer, B. R. (2000). *The social work skills workbook* (3rd ed.). Pacific Grove, CA: Brooks/Cole.

Cournoyer, B. R., & Byers, K. V. (1999). Basic communications skills for work with groups. In B. R. Compton & B. Galaway (Eds.), *Social Work Processes* (6th ed., pp. 221–232). Pacific Grove, CA: Brooks/Cole.

Cowger, C. D. (1994). Assessing client strengths: Clinical assessment for client empowerment. *Social Work, 39*(3), 262–267.

Cox, E. O., & Parsons, R. (1993). *Empowerment-oriented social work practice with the elderly.* Pacific Grove, CA: Brooks/Cole.

Cox, T. (1979). *Stress.* Baltimore: University Park Press.

Coyle, G. (1958). *Social science knowledge in the education of social workers.* NY: Council on Social Work Education.

Crandall, R. C. (1969). *Gerontology: A behavioral science approach.* Boston: Addison-Wesley.

Crohn, J. (1995). *Mixed matches: How to create successful interracial, interethnic, and interfaith relationships.* New York: Fawcett, Columbia.

Cromwell, R., Olson, D. M., & Fournier, D. (1976). Diagnosis and evaluation in marital and family counseling. In D. H. L. Olson (Ed.), *Treating Relationships* (pp. 41–47). Lake Mills, IA: Graphic.

Cross, C. P. (Ed.). (1974). *Interviewing and communication in social work.* Boston: Routledge and Kegan Paul.

Cross, T. L., Bazron, B. J., Dennis, K. W., & Isaacs, M. R. (1989). *Towards a culturally competent system of care.* Washington, DC: Georgetown University Child Development Center.

Crowfoot, J., Chesler, M. A., & Boulet, J. (1983). Organizing for social justice. In E. Seidman (Ed.), *Handbook of social interaction* (pp. 253–255). Newbury Park, CA: Sage.

Cuesta, M. J., & Peralta, V. (1994). Lack of insight in schizophrenia. *Schizophrenia Bulletin, 20,* 359–366.

Cyrus, V. (1997). *Experiencing race, class, and gender in the United States* (2nd ed.). Mountain View, CA: Mayfield.

Daft, R. L. (1992). *Organization theory and design.* New York: West.

Daley, D. C. (1991). *Kicking addictive habits once and for all. A relapse prevention guide.* New York: Lexington.

Daley, D. C. Relapse prevention with substance abusers: Clinical issues and myths. *Social Work, 32,* 138–142

Davis, I. (1975). Advice giving in parent counseling. *Social Casework. The Journal of Contemporary Social Work, 56,* 343–347.

Day, J. (1995). Obligation and motivation: Obstacles and resources for counselor well-being and effectiveness. *Journal of Counseling and Development, 73,* 108–110.

Day, P. J. (1989). *A new history of social welfare.* Englewood Cliffs, NJ: Prentice-Hall.

De Bono, E. (1992). *Serious creativity.* New York: Harper-Collins.

Deffenbacher, J. L. (1985). A cognitive-behavioral response and a modest proposal. *Counseling Psychologist, 13,* 261–269.

De Jong, P., & Miller, S. D. (1995). How to interview for client strengths. *Social Work, 40*(6), 729–736.

de Shazer, S. (1988). *Clues: Investigating solutions in brief therapy.* New York: Norton.

de Waal, F. (1989). *Peacemaking among primates.* Cambridge, MA: Harvard University Press, 1989.

de Waal, F., & Ren, F. (1988). Comparison of the reconciliation behavior of stumptail and rhesus monkeys. *Ethology, 78,* 129–142.

Dean, R. G. (1989). Ways of knowing in clinical practice. *Clinical Social Work Journal, 17*(20), 116–127.

Deavers, K. (1992). What is rural? *Policy Studies Journal, 20*(2), 183–189.

Deegan, P. (1992). The independent living movement and people with psychiatric disabilities: Taking back control over our own lives. *Psychological Rehabilitation Journal, 15*(3), 3–19.

Delaney, R., Brownlee, K., Sellick, M., & Tranter, D. (1997). Ethical problems facing northern social workers. *The Social Worker/Le Travailleur, 65*(3), 55–65.

Delbecq, A., & Van de Ven, A. (1971, July–August). A group process model for problem identification and program planning. *Journal of Applied Behavorial Science.*

Denzin, N. K. (1992). *Symbolic interactionism and cultural studies: The politics of interpretation.* Cambridge, MA: Blackwell.

Deutch, C. J. (1984). Self-reported sources of stress among psychotherapists. *Professional Psychology: Research and Practice, 15*(6), 833–845.

Devore, W., & Schiesinger, F. G. (1981). *Ethnic-sensitive social work practice.* St. Louis: Mosby.

Dewey, J., & Bentley, A. (1949). *Knowing and the known.* Boston: Beacon.

Dickerson, M. (1981). *Social work practice with the mentally retarded.* New York: Free Press.

DiClemente, C. C., Prochaska, J. O., Fairhurst, S. K., & Velicer, W. F. (1991). The process of smoking cessation: An analysis of precontemplation, contemplation, and preparation stages of change. *Journal of Consulting and Clinical Psychology, 59*(2), 295–304.

Dies, R. R. (1983). Clinical implications of research on leadership in short-term group psychotherapy. In R. R. Dies and R. MacKenzie (Eds.), *Advances in group psychotherapy: Integrating research and practice* (American group psychotherapy association monograph series, pp. 27–28). New York: International University Press.

Diller, J. V. (1999). *Cultural diversity. A primer for the human services.* Pacific Grove, CA: Brooks/Cole.

Dixon, D. N., & Glover, J. A. (1984). *Counseling: A problem-solving approach.* New York: Wiley.

Doel, M., & Lawson, B. (1986). Open records: the client's right to partnership. *British Journal of Social Work, 16*(4), 407–430.

Dollard, J., & Miller, N. E. (1950). *Personality and psychotherapy: An analysis in terms of learning, thinking, and culture.* New York: McGraw Hill.

Donigian, J., & Hulse-Killacky. (1999). *Critical incidents in group therapy* (2nd ed.). Pacific Grove, CA: Brooks/Cole.

Dorn, F. I. (1984). The social influence model: A social psychological approach to counseling. *Personal and Guidance Journal, 62,* 342–345.

Doyle, R. E. (1998). *Essential skills and strategies in the helping process* (2nd ed.). Pacific Grove, CA: Brooks/Cole.

Drake, B. (1994). Relationship competencies in child welfare services. *Social Work 39*, 595–602.

Draper, B. J. (1979). Black language as a adaptive response to a hostile environment. In C. Germain (Ed.), *Social work practice: People and environments*. New York: Columbia University Press.

Driscoll, R. (1984). *Pragmatic psychotherapy*. New York: Van Nostrand Reinhold.

Dubois, B., & Miley, K. K. (1996). *Social work: An empowering profession* (2nd ed.). Boston: Allyn & Bacon.

Dubos, R. (1978). Health and creative adaptation. *Human Nature, 1*, 78–82.

Dudley, J. R. (1987). Speaking for themselves: People who are labeled as developmentally disabled. *Social Work, 32*, 80–82.

Duffy, T. (1994). The check-in and other go-rounds in group work: Guidelines for use. *Social work with Groups, 17*(1/2), 163–175.

Dulaney, D. D., & Kelly, J. (1982). Improving services to gay and lesbian clients. *Social Work, 27*, 178–183.

Dumont, M. (1968). *The absurd healer*. New York: Viking.

Dupree, D., Spencer, M. B., & Bell, S. (1997). African American children. In G. Johnson-Powell & J. Yamamoto (Eds.), *Transcultural child development: Psychological assessment and treatment* (pp. 237–268). New York: Wiley.

Duvall, E. M. (1977). *Marriage and family development* (5th ed.). New York: Lippincott.

Eckert, P. A., Abeles, N., & Graham, R. N. (1988). Symptom, severity, psychotherapy process and outcome. *Professional Psychology, Research, and Practice, 18*, 353–359.

Edinburg, G. M., & Cottler, J. M. (1995). Managed Care. In L. Edwards (Ed.). *Encyclopedia of social work* (19th ed., pp. 1635–1642). Washington, DC: NASW Press.

Edwards, E. (1983). Native-American elders. Current issues and social policy implications. In R. McNeely & J. Colen (Eds.), *Aging in minority groups*. Beverly Hills, CA: Sage.

Edwards, M., & Steinglass, P. (1995). Family therapy treatment outcomes for alcoholism. *Journal of Marriage and Family Therapy, 21*, 475–510.

Edwards, R. L., & Minotti, T. (1989). Mandated case recordings: Rural and urban perspectives. *Journal of Applied Social Sciences, 13*(2), 317–342.

Egan, G. (1990). *The skilled helper* (4th ed.). Pacific Grove, CA: Brooks/Cole.

Egan, G. (1994). *The skilled helper: A problem-management approach in helping* (5th ed.). Pacific Grove, CA: Brooks/Cole.

Egan, G. (1998). *The skilled helper: A problem-management approach to helping* (6th ed.). Pacific Grove, CA: Brooks/Cole.

Egan, G. (1999). *The skilled helper* (4th ed.). Pacific Grove, CA: Brooks/Cole.

Elder, G. H., Jr. (1984). Families, kin, and the life course: A sociological perspective. In R. D. Parke (Ed.), *Review of child development research* (Vol. 7, pp. 80–136). Chicago: University of Chicago Press.

Elliot, D. S., Wilson, W. J., Huizinga, D., Sampson, R. J., Elliot, A., & Rankin, H. (1996). The effects of neighborhood disadvantage on adolescent development. *Journal of Research in Crime and Delinquency, 33*(4), 339–426.

Elliott, R. (1985). Helpful and nonhelpful events in brief counseling interviews: An empirical taxonomy. *Journal of Counseling Psychology, 32*, 307–322.

Ellis, A. (1973). *Humanistic psychotherapy. The rational-emotive approach*. New York: McGraw-Hill.

Ellis, A. (1984). *Rational-emotive therapy and cognitive behavior therapy*. New York: Springer.

Ellis, A., & Dryden, W. (1987). *The practice of rational-emotive therapy*. New York: Springer.

Ely, A. (1985). Long-term group treatment for young male schizophrenic youths. *Social Work, 30*, pp. 5–10.

Emery, G. (1981). *A new beginning*. New York: Simon and Schuster.

Emment, D. (1972). Ethics of the social worker. *British Journal of Psychiatric Social Work, 6*(6), 165–172.

Endler, N. S., & Parker, J. D. (1990). Multidimensional assessment of coping: A critical evaluation. *Journal of Personality and Social Psychology, 58*, 844–854.

Engel, K., & Rothman, S. (1984). The parades of prison reform: Rehabilitation, prisoners' rights, and violence. *Harvard Journal of Law and Public Policy, 7*, 414.

Ennis, R. H. (1987). A taxonomy of critical thinking dispositions and abilities. In J. Baron & R. Sternberg (Eds.), *Teaching thinking skills: Theory and practice* (pp. 27–38). New York: Freeman.

Ephros, P. H., & Vasil, T. V. (1988). *Groups that work*. New York: Columbia University Press.

Epstein, L. (1988). *The task-centered approach*. Columbus, OH: Merrill.

Epstein, L. (1992). *Brief treatment and a new look at the task-centered approach* (3rd ed.). New York: Macmillan.

Epstein, N., Baucom, D. H., & Rankin, L. A. (1993). Treatment of marital conflict. A cognitive-behavioral approach. *Clinical Psychology Review, 13,* 45–57.

Erickson, M. H., Rossi, F., & Rossi, S. (1976). *Resolving sexual abuse: Solution-focused therapy and Ericksonian hypnosis for adult survivors.* New York: Norton.

Erikson, E. H. (1963). *Childhood and society* (2nd. ed). New York: Norton.

Erikson, E. H. (1982). *The life cycle completed. A review.* New York: Norton.

Esten, G., & Wilmont, L. (1993). Double bind messages: The effects of attitude toward disability and therapy. *Women and Therapy, 14*(3/4), 29–41.

Etcheverry, R., Siporin, M., & Toseland, R. (1986). The uses and abuses of role-playing. In P. Glasser & N. Mayadas (Eds.), *Group workers at work: Theory and practice in the 80s* (pp. 116–130). Totowa, NJ: Rowman & Littlefield.

Evans, D., Hearn, M., & Uhlemann, M. & Ivey, A. (1993). *Essential Interviewing: A programmed approach to effective communication* (4th ed.). Pacific Grove, CA: Brooks/Cole.

Fairchild, H. H. Yee, A. H., Wyatt, G. E., & Weizman, F. (1995). Readdressing psychology problems with race. *American Psychologist, 50,* 46–47.

Falloon, I. R. H. (1991). Behavioral family therapy. In A. S. Gurman & D. P. Kniskern (Eds.), *Handbook of family therapy* (Vol. 2, pp. 556–591). New York: Brunner/Mazel.

Falsck, H. (1988). *Social work: The membership perspective.* New York: Springer.

Fanschel, D. (1958). *An overview of one agency's casework operations.* Pittsburgh: Family and Children's Service.

Fanshel, D., & Shinn, E. B. (1978). *Children in foster care. A longitudinal investigation.* New York: Columbia University Press.

Farber, B. A. (1983). *Stress and burnout in human service professionals.* New York: Pergamon.

Farber, B. A., & Heitjetz, L. J. (1982). The process and of burnout in psychotherapists. *Professional Psychology, 13*(2), 293–301.

Fawcett, S. B., Paine-Andrews, A., Fransico, V. T., Schultz, J. A., Richter, K. P., Lewis, R. K., Harris, K. J., Williams, E. L., Berkeley, J. Y., Lopez, C. M., & Fisher, J. L. (1996). Empowering community help: Initiatives to evaluation. In D. M. Fetterman, S. J. Kaftarian, & A. Wandersman (Eds.), *Empowerment evaluation: Knowledge and tools for self-assessment and accountability* (pp. 161–187). Thousand Oaks, CA: Sage.

Feld, S., & Radin, N. (1982). *Social Psychology: For social work and metal health profession.* New York: Columbia University Press.

Feldman, N., & Sherman, R. (1987). *Handbook of measurement for marriage and family therapy.* New York: Brunner/Mazel.

Fellin, P. (1987). *Community and the social worker.* Itasca, IL: Peacock.

Fellin, P. (1995). *Community and the social worker* (2nd ed.). Itasca, IL: Peacock.

Fensterheim, H. (1983). Basic paradigms, behavioral formulation and basic procedures. In H. Fensterheim & H. Glazer (Eds.), *Behavioral psychotherapy. Basic principles and case studies in an integrative clinical model* (pp. 40–87). New York: Brunner/Mazel.

Ferguson, M. (1987). *The aquarian conspiracy: Personal and social transformation in the 1980s.* Los Angeles: Tarcher.

Field, L. K., & Steinhardt, M. A. (1992). The relationship of internally directed behavior to self-reinforcement, self-esteem, and expectancy values for exercise. *American Journal of Health, Promotion, 7,* 21–27.

Finn, J., & Rose, S. (1982). Development and validation of the interview skills role-play test. *Social Work Research and Abstracts, 18,* 21–27.

Fisch, R. (1990). The broader implications of Milton H. Erickson's work. *Ericksonian Monographs, 7,* 1–5.

Fisch, R., Weakland, J., & Segal, L. (1985). *The tactics of change. Doing therapy briefly.* San Francisco: Jossey-Bass.

Fischer, J., & Corcoran, K. (1994). *Measures for clinical practice* (2nd ed.). New York: Free Press.

Fisher, R. (1984). *Let the people decide: Neighborhood organizations in America.* Boston: Twayne.

Fisher, R., & Ury, W. (1983). *Getting to yes: Negotiating agreement without giving in.* New York: Penguin.

Fishman, S. T., & Lubetkin, B. S. (1983). Office practice of behavior therapy. In M. Hersen (Ed.), *Outpatient behavior therapy: A clinical guide* (pp. 27–35). New York: Grune & Stratton.

Fleming, R., Baum, A., & Singer, J. E. (1985). Social support and the physical environment. In S. Cohen and S. L. Syme (Eds.), *Social support and health* (pp. 327–345). New York: Academic.

Fleuridas, C., Leigh, G. K., Rosenthal, D. M., & Leigh, T. E. (1990). Family goal recording: An adaptation of goal attainment scaling for enhancing family therapy and assessment. *Journal of Marital and Family Therapy, 16*(4), 389–406.

Fong, M. L., & Cox, B. G. (1983). Trust as an underlying dynamic in a counseling process: How clients test trust. *Personal and Guidance Journal, 62,* 163–166.

Ford, F. R. (1983). Rules: The invisible family. *Family Process, 22*(2), 135–145.

Forsyth, D. R. (1990). *Group dynamics* (3rd ed.). Pacific Grove, CA: Brooks/Cole.

Fortune, A., Pearlingi, B., & Rochelle, C. (1992). Reactions to termination of individual treatment. *Social Work, 37*(2), 159–171.

Franklin, C., & Jordon, C. (1999). *Family practice: Brief systems methods for social work.* Pacific Grove, CA: Brooks/Cole.

Freeman, D. S. (1992). *Family therapy with couples. The family-of-origin approach.* Northvale, NJ: Jason Aronson.

Freidson, E. (1970). *Professional dominancy.* New York: Atherton.

Freire, P. (1972). *Pedagogy of the oppressed.* New York: Seabury.

Freud, S. (1974). *The ego and the id.* London: Hogarth. (Original work published 1923).

Friedman, J. (1971). One social worker's fight for mental patients rights. *Social Work, 16*(4), 92–95.

Friesen, B. J. (1987). Administration: Interaction Aspects. *Encyclopedia of social work* (18th ed., pp. 17–27). Silver Spring, MD: NASW Press.

Gallant, C. (1982). *Mediation in special education disputes.* New York: NASW Press.

Gambrill, E. (1983). *Casework: A competency-based approach.* Englewood Cliffs, NJ: Prentice-Hall.

Gambrill, E. (1990). *Critical thinking in clinical practice: Improving the accuracy of judgement and decisions about clients.* San Francisco: Jossey-Bass.

Gambrill, E. (1997). *Social work practice. A critical thinker's guide.* New York: Oxford University Press.

Garvin, C. (1987). *Contemporary group work* (2nd ed.). Englewood Cliffs, NJ: Prentice-Hall.

Garvin, C. D. (1981). *Contemporary group work.* Englewood Cliffs, NJ: Prentice-Hall.

Garvin, C. D. (1997). *Contemporary group work* (3rd ed.). Boston: Allyn & Bacon.

Garvin, C. D., & Seabury, B. A. (1984). *Interpersonal practice in social work. Processes and procedures.* Englewood, NJ: Prentice-Hall.

Garvin, C. D., & Seabury, B. A. (1997). *Interpersonal practice in social work. Promoting competence and social justice* (2nd ed.). Boston: Allyn & Bacon.

Gazda, G. M., Asbury, F. S., Balzer, F., Childerss, W. C., Phelps, R. E., & Walters, R. P. (1995). *Human relations development: A Manual for educators* (5th ed.). Boston, MA: Allyn & Bacon.

Geertz, C. (1988). *Works and lives.* Stanford, CA: Stanford University Press.

Gelso, C. J., & Carter, J. A. (1985). The relationship in counseling and psychotherapy: Components, consequences, and theoretical antecedents. *The Counseling Psychologist, 13,* 155–243.

Gelso, C. J., & Carter, J. A. (1994). Components of the psychotherapy relationship: Their interaction and unfolding during treatment. *Journal of Counseling Psychology, 41,* 296–306.

Gelso, C. J., & Fretz, B. R. (1992). *Counseling psychology.* New York: Harcourt Brace Jovanovich.

Gentry, M. (1978). Tape recording group sessions: A practical research strategy. *Social Work with Groups, 1*(1), 95–102.

Gerber, P. J., Ginsberg, R., & Reiff, H. B. (1992). Identifying alterable patterns in employment success for highly successful adults with learning disabilities. *Journal of Learning Disabilities, 25,* 475–487.

Germain, C. (1976, July). Time as a variable in social work practice. *Social Casework,* 419–426.

Germain, C. B. (1978, November). Space, an ecological variable in social work practice. *Social Casework,* 512–522.

Germain, C. B. (1983). Using social and physical environments. In A. Rosenblatt & D. Waldfogel (Eds.), *Handbook of clinical social work* (pp. 110–133). San Francisco: Jossey-Bass.

Germain, C. B. (1984). *Social work practice in health care. People and environment.* New York: Columbia University Press.

Germain, C. B. (1985). The place of community work within an ecological approach to social work practice. In S. H. Taylor & R. W. Roberts (Eds.), *Theory and practice of community social work* (pp. 50–55). New York: Columbia University Press.

Germain, C. B. (1991). *Human Behavior in the social environment. An ecological view.* New York: Columbia University Press.

Germain, C. B., & Gitterman, A. (1995). Ecological Perspective. In R. Edwards (Ed.), *Encyclopedia of Social Work* (19th ed., Vol. 1, pp. 816–824). Washington, DC: NASW.

Germain, C. B., & Gitterman, A. (1996). *The life model of social work practice.* New York: Columbia University Press.

Gest, T. (1992, May 4). The Prison Boom Bust. *U.S. News & World Report,* p. 28.

Gewirtz, J. L., & Pelaez-Nogueras, M. (1992). Skinner, B. F.: Legacy to human infant behavior and development. *American Psychologist, 47,* 1411–1422.

Gibbs, L., & Gambrill, E. (1996). *Critical thinking for social workers.* Thousand Oaks, CA: Pine Forge.

Gibelman, M., & Schervish, P. H. (1993). *Who we are: The social work labor force as reflected in the NASW membership.* Washington, DC: NASW Press.

Giele, J. Z. (1980). Adulthood as transcendence of age and sex. In N. J. Smelser & E. Erikson (Eds.), *Themes of work and love in adulthood* (pp. 151–173). Cambridge, MA: Harvard University Press.

Gil, D. G. (1994). Confronting social injustice and oppression. In F. G. Reamer (Ed.), *The foundations of social work knowledge* (pp. 231–263). New York: Columbia University Press.

Gilbert, N., & Specht, H. (1986). *Dimensions of social welfare policy.* Englewood Cliffs, NJ: Prentice-Hall.

Gilliland, B. E., & James, R. K. (1997). *Crisis intervention strategies* (3rd ed.). Pacific Grove, CA: Brooks/Cole.

Ginsberg, L. H. (1995). *Social work Almanac* (2nd ed). Washington, D.C.: NASW Press.

Gitterman, A. (1983). Uses of resistance: A transactional view. *Social Work, 28,* 127–130.

Gitterman, A., & Shulman, L. (1985/86). The legacy of William Schwartz: Group practice as shared intervention (Special issue). *Social Work with Groups, 8*(4).

Gladstein, G. (1983). Understanding empathy: Integrating counseling development and social psychology perspectives. *Journal of Counseling Psychology, 30,* 467–482.

Glaser, B., & Strauss, A. (1967). *The discovery of grounded theory.* Chicago: Aldine.

Glaser, B., & Strauss, A. (1978). *The discovery of grounded theory* (2nd ed.). Newbury Park, CA: Sage.

Glassman, U., & Gates, L. (1990). *Group work. A humanistic approach.* Newbury, CA: Sage.

Gochros, H. L., Gochros, J. S., & Fischer, J. (1986). *Counseling the sexually oppressed.* Englewood Cliffs, NJ: Prentice-Hall.

Gochros, J. S., & Ricketts, W. (1986). Women. In H. L. Gochros, J. S. Gochros, & J. Fischer (Eds.), *Counseling the sexually oppressed* (pp. 52–65). Englewood Cliffs, NJ: Prentice-Hall.

Gold, N. (1990). Motivation: The crucial but unexplored component of social work practice. *Social Work, 35*(1), 49–56.

Goldenberg, I., & Goldenberg, H. (2000). *Family therapy: An overview* (5th ed.). Pacific Grove, CA: Brooks/Cole.

Goldstein, E. G. (1984). *Ego psychology and social work practice.* New York: Free Press.

Goldstein, H. (1973). *Social work practice: A unitary approach.* Columbia: University of South Carolina. Press.

Goldstein, H. (1983). Starting where the client is. *Social Casework, 64,* 267–275.

Goldstein, H. (1990). The knowledge base of social work practice, wisdom and analogue, or art? *Families in Society 71,* 41.

Goleman, D. (1985, August 2nd). Switching therapists may be the best. *Indianapolis News,* p. 9.

Goodall, J. (1971). *In the shadow of man.* New York: Dell.

Goode, W. J. (1969). The theoretical limits of professionalization. In A. Etizioni (ed.), *The semi-professions and their organizations.* New York: Free Press.

Goodyear, R. K., & Sennett, E. R. (1984). Current and emerging ethical issues for counseling psychologists. *The Counseling Psychologist, 12*(3), 87–98

Gordon, R. (1992). *Basic interviewing skills.* Itasca, IL: Peacock.

Gordon, W. E. (1964). Notes on the nature of knowledge. *Building social work knowledge.* New York: NASW Press.

Gordon, W. E. (1969). Basic concepts for an integrative and generative conception of social work. In Gordon Hearn (Ed.), *The general symptoms approach: Contributions towards a holistic conception of social work* (pp. 5–12). New York: Council on Social Work Education.

Gothard, S. (1989). Power in court. The social worker as an expert witness. *Social Work, 34,* 65–67.

Gothard, S. (1990). Legal issues: Confidentiality and privileged communication. In R. Edwards (Ed.), *Encyclopedia of social work* (19th ed., 1579–1584). Washington, DC: NASW Press.

Gottlieb, N. (1987). Sex discrimination and inequality. In A. Minahan (Ed.), *Encyclopedia of social work* (18th ed., 561–569). Silver Spring, MD: NASW Press.

Gottlieb, N. (1995). Women Overview. In R. Edwards (Ed.), *Encyclopedia of social work* (19th ed., 2518–2528). Washington, DC: NASW Press.

Goulding, M. M. (1990). Getting the important work done fast: Contract plus redecision. In J. Zeig & S. Gilligan (Eds.), *Brief therapy: Myths, methods and metaphors* (pp. 303–317). New York: Brunner/Mazel.

Graber, L., & Nice, J. (1991). The family unity model. The advanced skill of looking for and building on strengths. *The Prevention Report, 3–4.*

Green, J. (1982). *Cultural awareness in the human services.* Englewood Cliffs, NJ: Prentice-Hall.

Green, J. (1989). *Cultural awareness in the human services* (2nd ed.). Englewood Cliffs, NJ: Prentice-Hall.

Green, J. W. (1995). *Cultural awareness in human services: A multi-ethnic approach* (2nd ed.). Boston: Allyn & Bacon.

Green, J. W., & Leigh, J. W. (1985). The ethnographic interview: A contribution to the skill of ethnic competent practice. Paper presented at the NASW Professional Symposium, Chicago: Il.

Greenberg, L. S., & Safran, J. D. (1989). Emotions in psychotherapy. *American Psychologist, 44,* 19–29.

Greeno, J. G. (1989). A perspective of thinking. *American Psychologist, 2,* 131–141.

Greif, G. L., & Lynch, A. A. (1983). The eco-systems perspective. In Meyer, C. H. (Ed.), *Clinical social work in the eco-systems perspective.* New York: Columbia University Press.

Grieger, R., & Boyd, J. (1980). *Rational-emotive therapy: A skills based approach.* New York: Van Nostrand Reinhold.

Grinnell, R. M., Kyle, N. S., Bostwick, G. J. (1981). Environmental modification. In A. N. Maluccio (Ed.), *Promoting competence in clients: A newfold approach to social work practice* (pp. 152–184). New York: Free Press.

Grinter, R. (1992). Multicultural of antiracist education? The need to choose. In J. Lynch, C. Modgil, & S. Modgil (Eds.), *Cultural diversity in the schools* (Vol. 1, pp. 95–111). London: Falmer.

Gross, E. (1995). Deconstructing politically correct practice literature: The American Indian case. *Social Work, 40*(2), 206–213.

Grusec, J. E. (1992). Social learning theory and developmental psychology: The legacies of Robert Sears and Albert Bandura. *Developmental Psychology, 28,* 776–786.

Guba, E. G., & Lincoln, Y. S. (1989). *Fourth generation evaluation.* Newbury Park, CA: Sage.

Gunderson, J. G. (1999). Personality Disorders. In A. M. Nicholi (Ed.), *The Harvard Guide to Psychiatry* (pp. 308–327). Cambridge, MA: Belknap Press of Harvard University Press.

Gurman, A. S., & Kniskern, D. P. (1981). Family therapy outcome research: Knowns and unknowns. In A. S. Gurman & D. P. Kniskern (Ed.). *Handbook of family therapy* (pp. 742–775). New York: Brunner/Mazel.

Gutheil, I. A. (1992). Considering the physical environment: An essential component of practice. *Social Work, 37*(5), 391–396.

Gutierrez, L. M. (1989). *Empowerment in social work practice: Considerations for practice and education.* Paper presented at the annual program meeting of the Council on Social Work Education, Chicago, IL.

Gutierrez, L. M. (1990). Working with women of color: An empowerment perspective. *Social Work, 35,* 149–153.

Gutierrez, L. M. (1994). Beyond coping: An empowerment perspective in stressful life events. *Journal of Sociology and Social Welfare, 21*(3), 201–220.

Gutierrez, L. M., & Lewis, E. A. (1999). *Empowering women of color.* New York: Columbia University Press.

Gutierrez, L. M., Parsons, R. J., & Cox, E. O. (1998). *Empowerment in social work practice. A source book.* Pacific Grove, CA: Brooks/Cole.

Gutman, D. (1982). Neighborhood as a support system for Euro-American elderly. In D. E. Biegell and A. Naparstek (Eds.), *Community support systems and mental health: Practice and policy and research* (pp. 73–85). New York: Springer.

Haase, R., & Tepper, D. (1972). Nonverbal components of empathetic communication. *Journal of Counseling Psychology, 19,* 417–424.

Hackney, H., & Cormier, L. S. (1994). *Counseling strategies and interventions* (4th ed.). Boston: Allyn and Bacon.

Hahn, H. (1991). Alternative views on empowerment. Social services and civil rights. *The Journal of Rehabilitation, 57*(4), 17–30.

Haley, J. (1973). *Uncommon therapy. The psychiatric techniques of Milton H. Erickson, M. D.* New York: Norton.

Haley, J. (1984). *Ordeal therapy: Unusual ways to change behavior.* San Francisco: Jossey-Bass.

Hall, E. (1966). *The hidden dimension.* New York: Doubleday.

Halpern, D. E. (1996). *Thought and knowledge: An introduction to critical thinking* (3rd ed.). Hillsdale, NJ: Erlbaum.

Hamilton, G. (1940). *Theory and practice of social case work.* New York: Columbia University Press.

Hamilton, G. (1951). *Theory and practice of social casework* (2nd. ed.). New York: Columbia University Press.

Hamilton, G. (1958). Foreword. In Stein and Cloward (Eds.), *Social perspectives on behavior* (pp. xi). Glencoe, IL: Fress Press.

Handelsman, M. M., Kemper, M. B., Kesson-Craig, P., McCain, P., & Johnsrud, C. (1986). Use, content, and readability of written informed consent forms of treatment. *Professional Psychology, Research, and Practice, 17*(6) 514–518.

Handler, P. (Ed.). (1970). *Biology of the future of many.* New York: Oxford University Press.

Hardman, D. G. (1960). *Authority in my job. Authority in casework, a bread and butter theory; the constructive use of authority.* New York: National Council on Crime and Delinquency.

Hare-Mustin, R. T., Marecek, J., Kaplan, A. G., & Lisslevinson, N. (1979). Rights of clients, responsibilities of therapists. *American Psychologist, 34*(1), 3–16.

Hareven, T. K. (1982). Preface. In T. K. Hareven and K. J. Adams (Eds.), *Aging and life course transitions: An interdisciplinary perspective* (pp. xiii–xvi). New York: Guilford Press.

Hartman, A. (1981). The family: A central focus on practice. *Social Work, 26,* 7–13.

Hartman, A. (1990, January). Many ways of knowing. *Social Work, 35,* 3–4.

Hartman, A. (1993). The professional is political. *Social Work, 38,* 365–366.

Hartman, A. (1994). Diagrammatic assessment of family relationships. In B. R. Compton & B. Galaway (Eds.), *Social work processes* (5th ed., pp. 153–165). Pacific Grove, CA: Brooks/Cole.

Hartman, B. L., & Wickey, J. M. (1978). The person-oriented record in treatment. *Social Work, 23*(4), 269–299.

Hartmann, H. (1964). *Essays on ego psychology: selected problems in psychoanalytic theory.* New York: International University Press.

Harvey, D. F., & Brown, D. R. (1991). *An experiential approach to organization development.* Englewood Cliffs, NJ: Prentice-Hall.

Hasenfeld, Y. (1987). Program development. In F. M. Cox, J. L. Erlich, J. Rothman, & J. E. Tropman (Eds.), *Strategies of community organization: Macro practice* (4th ed., pp. 142–145). Itasca, IL: Peacock.

Health Letter (1992). Only 750 restrictions on doctor's hospital privileges reported in the first year of data bank operation. *Health Letter, 8*(3). Published by Public Citizen Research Group, Washington, DC.

Heap, K. (1977). *Group therapy for social workers: An introduction.* New York: Pergamon.

Hearn, G. (1958). *Theory building in social work.* Toronto: University of Toronto Press.

Heineman, M. B. (1981). The absolute scientific imperative in social work research. *Social Service Review, 55,* 371–397.

Heller, K., & Swindle, R. W. (1983). Social networks, perceived social support and coping with stress. In R. D. Felner, L. A. Jason, J. Moritsugu, & S. S. Farber (Eds.), *Preventive psychology, theory, research, and practice* (pp. 87–103). New York: Pergamon.

Henggeler, S., Borduin, C., & Mann, B. (1993). Advances in family therapy. Empirical foundations. In T. Ollendick & R. Prinz (Eds.), *Advances in clinical child psychology* (Vol. 15, pp. 35–71). New York: Plenum.

Henri, P., & Saul, L. J. (1971). *Dependence in man. A psychoanalytic study.* New York: International University Press.

Henry, S. (1992). *Group skills in four-dimensional approach* (2nd ed.). Pacific Grove, CA: Brooks/Cole.

Hepworth, D. H. (1993). Managing manipulative behavior in the helping relationship. *Social Work, 38*(6), 674–684.

Hepworth, D. H., & Larsen, J. A. (1990). *Direct social work practice* (3rd ed.). Belmont, CA: Wadsworth.

Hepworth, D. H., & Larsen, J. A. (1993). *Direct social work practice* (4th ed.) Belmont, CA: Wadsworth.

Hepworth, D. H., Rooney, R. H., & Larsen, J. A. (1997). *Direct social work practice. Theory and skills* (5th ed.). Pacific Grove, CA: Brooks/Cole.

Hersen, M., & Hassett, V. B. (Eds.), (1998). *Basic interviewing: A practical guide for counselors and clinicians.* Mahwah, NJ: Erlbaum.

Hess, H., & Hess, P. M. (1994). Termination in context. In B. R. Compton & B. Galaway (Eds.), *Social work processes* (pp. 529–539). Pacific Grove, CA: Brooks/Cole.

Hidalgo, H., Peterson, T. L., & Woodman, N. J. (1985). *Lesbian and gay issues: A resource for social workers.* Silver Spring, MD: NASW Press.

Hoff, L. A. (1995). *People in crisis. Understanding and helping* (4th ed.), San Francisco: Jossey-Bass.

Hogan-Garcia, M. (1999). *The four skills of cultural diversity competence: A process for understanding and practice.* Belmont, CA: Wadsworth.

Hoge, M. A., Davidson, L., Griffith, E. E., Sledge, W. H., & Howenstine, R. A. (1994). Defining managed care in public-sector psychiatry. *Hospital and Community Psychiatry, 45*(11) 1085–1089.

Holahan, C. J., Moos, R. H., & Schaefer, J. A. (1996). Coping: Stress resistance and growth: Conceptualizing adaptive functioning. In M. Zeidner & N. S. Endler (Eds.), *Handbook of coping, theory, research, and applications* (pp. 24–43). New York: Wiley.

Holland, T. P., & Petchers, M. K. (1987). Organizations: Context for social service delivery. In A. Minahan (Ed.), *Encyclopedia of social work* (18th ed., Vol. 2, pp. 204–217). Silver Spring, MD: NASW Press.

Hollis, F. (1967). Principles and assumptions underlying casework principles. In E. Younghusband (Ed.), *Social work and social values* (pp. 22–38). London: Allen & Unwin.

Hollis, F. (1968, June). What shall we teach? The social work educator and knowledge. *Social Service Review, 42,* 184–196.

Hollis, F. (1979). *Casework: A psychosocial theory* (2nd ed.). New York: Random House.

Hollis, F., & Woods, M. E. (1981). *Social casework: A psychosocial therapy* (3rd ed). New York: Random House.

Holmbeck-Grayson, N., & Lavigne, J. V. (1992). Combining self-modeling and stimulus fading in the treatment of an electively mute child. *Psychotherapy, 29,* 661–667.

Holmes, J. A., & Stevenson, C. A. (1990). Differential effects of avoidant and attentional coping strategies on adaptation to chronic and recent-onset pain. *Health Psychology, 9,* 577–584.

Homan, M. (1999). *Promoting community change: Making it happen in the real world* (2nd ed.), Pacific Grove, CA: Brooks/Cole.

Homan, M. (1999). *Rules of the game: Lessons from the field of community change.* Pacific Grove, CA: Brooks/Cole.

Hook, S. (1967). Does philosophy have a future? *Saturday Review, 11,* 12–23.

Hopps, J. G., Pinderhughes, E., & Shankar, R. (1995). *The power to care: Clinical effectiveness with overwhelmed clients.* New York: Free Press.

Horowitz, M. (1986). *Stress response syndromes.* London: Jason Aronson.

Hoyt, M. F. Introduction: Competency-based future-oriented therapy. In M. F. Hoyt (Ed.), *Constructive Therapies 1* (pp. 1–10). New York: Guilford.

Hudson, J., & Grinnell, R. M. (1989). Program Evaluation. In B. R. Compton, & B. Galaway, (Eds.), *Social work processes* (pp. 691–711). Belmont, CA: Wadsworth.

Hudson, W. (1982). *The clinical measurement package.* Homewood, IL: Dorsey.

Hudson, W. W. (1978). First axioms of treatment. *Social Work, 23,* 65–66.

Hull, C. L. (1943). *Principles of behavior.* New York: Appleton-Century-Crofts.

Hull, G., Jr. (1982). Child welfare services to Native Americans. *Social Casework, 63,* 340–347.

Hutchins, D. E., & Cole, C. G. (1992). *Helping relationships and strategies* (2nd ed.). Pacific Grove, CA: Brooks/Cole.

Hutchins, D. E., & Vaught, C. C. (1997). *Helping relationships and strategies* (3rd ed.). Pacific Grove: Brooks/Cole.

Ilgen, D. R., & Klein, H. J. (1988). Organizational behavior. *Annual Review of Psychology, 40,* 327–351.

Irving H. (1981). *Divorce mediator: The rational alternative.* Toronto: Personal Library.

Itzhaky, H., & York, A. S. (1991). Client participation and the effectiveness of community social work intervention. *Research and Social Work Practice, 1,* 387–398.

Ivanoff, A., Blythe, B., & Tripodi, T. (1994). *Involuntary clients in social work practice: A research-based approach.* Hawthorne, NY: Aldine & Gruyter.

Ivey, A. E. (1988). *Intentional interviewing and counseling* (2nd ed.). Pacific Grove, CA: Brooks/Cole.

Ivey, A. E. (1994). *Intentional interviewing and counseling* (3rd ed.). Pacific Grove, CA: Brooks/Cole.

Ivey, A. E., & Authier, J. (1978). *Microcounseling* (2nd ed.). Springfield, IL: Charles C. Thomas.

Ivey, A. E., & Gluckstern, N. (1984). *Basic interviewing skills: Participant manual.* Amherst, MA: Micro-Training Associates.

Ivey, A. E., & Ivey, M. B. (1999). *Intentional interviewing and counseling: Facilitating client development in a multicultural society* (4th ed.). Pacific Grove, CA: Brooks/Cole.

Ivey, A. E., Gluckstern, N. B., & Ivey, M. B. (1993). *Basic attending skills* (3rd ed.). North Amherst, MA: Microtraining Associates.

Ivey, A. E., Ivey, M. B., & Simek-Downing, L. (1987). *Counseling and psychotherapy: Skills, theory and practice* (2nd ed.). Englewood Cliffs, NJ: Prentice-Hall.

Ivey, A. E., Ivey, M. B., & Simek-Morgan, L. (1993). *Counseling and psychotherapy: A multicultural perspective* (3rd ed). Boston, MA: Allyn & Bacon.

Jacobs, E., Harvill, R., & Masson, R. (1994). *Group counseling: Strategies and skills*. Pacific Grove, CA: Brooks/Cole.

Jacobs, E., Masson, R. L., & Harvill, R. L. (1998). *Group counseling: Strategies and skills* (3rd ed.). Pacific Grove, CA: Brooks/Cole.

Jacobson, N. S., & Traux, P. (1991). Clinical significance: A statistical approach in defining meaningful change in psychotherapy research. *Journal of Consulting and Clinical Psychology, 59,* 12–19.

Jaffe, D. T. (1986). The inner strains of healing work: Therapy for self-renewal for health professionals. In C. D. Scott & J. Hawk (Eds.), *Heal thyself: The health of health care professionals.* New York: Brunner/Mazel.

James, P. (1991). Effects of a communication training component added to an emotionally focused couples therapy. *Jounral of Marital and Family Therapy, 17*(3), 263–275.

Janchill, Sister Mary Paul. (1969, February). Systems concepts in casework theory and practice. *Social Casework, 77.*

Jansson, B. S. (1993). *The reluctant welfare state* (2nd ed.). Belmont, CA: Wadsworth.

Janzen, C., & Harris, O. (1997). *Family treatment in social work practice* (3rd ed.). Itasca, IL: Peacock.

Jenkins, Y. M. (1993). Diversity and social esteem. In J. L. Chin, V. De La Cancela, & Y. M. Jenkins (Eds.), *Diversity in psychotherapy: The politics of race, ethnicity and gender* (pp. 45–63). Westport, CT: Praeger.

Joanning, H., Thomas, F., Quinn, W., & Mullen, R. (1992). Treating adolescent drug abuse: A comparison of family systems therapy, group therapy and family drug education. *Journal of Marital and Family Therapy, 18,* 345–356.

Johnson, C. (1974). Planning for termination of the group. In P. Glasser, R. Sarri, & R. Vinter (Eds.), *Individual change through small groups* (pp. 258–265). New York: Free Press.

Johnson, D. W., & Johnson, F. P. (1994). *Joining together: Group theory and group skills* (4th ed.). Englewood Cliffs, NJ: Prentice-Hall.

Johnson, L. C. (1983). *Social work practice. A generalist approach.* Boston: Allyn & Bacon.

Johnson, L. C. (1984). *Social work practice.* Boston: Allyn & Bacon.

Johnson, L. C. (1995). *Social work practice: Generalist approach.* (5th ed.). Boston: Allyn & Bacon.

Johnson, L. C., & Schwartz, C. L. (1997). *Social welfare. A response to human need* (4th ed.). Boston: Allyn & Bacon.

Johnson, L. C., & Schwartz, C. L., & Tate, D. S. (1997) *Social Welfare* (4th ed.). Boston: Allyn & Bacon.

Jones, A. S., & Gelso, C. (1988). Differential effects of style of interpretation: Another look. *Journal of Counseling Psychology, 35,* 363–369.

Jones, J. M. (1990). Who is training our ethnic minority psychologists and are they doing it right? In G. Stricker (Ed.), *Toward ethnic diversification in psychology education and training* (pp. 41–49). Washington DC: APA.

Jourard, S. (1968). *Man disclosing to himself.* New York: Van Nostrand Reinhold.

Kadushin, A. (1959). The knowledge base of social work. In A. J. Kahn (Ed.), *Issues in American Social Work* (p. 67). New York: Columbia University Press.

Kadushin, A. (1985). *Supervision in social work.* New York: Columbia University Press.

Kadushin, A. (1990). *The social work interview: A guide for human professionals* (3rd ed.). New York: Columbia University Press.

Kadushin, A. (1995). Interviewing. In Richard L. Edwards (Ed.), *Encyclopedia of Social Work,* (19th ed., Vol. 1, pp. 1527–1538). Washington, DC: NASW Press.

Kadushin, A. (1997). *The social work interview.* New York: Columbia University Press.

Kadushin, A., & Kadushin, G. (1997). *The social work interview. A guide for human service professionals.* New York: Columbia University Press.

Kagle, J. (1991). *Social work records.* Belmont, CA: Wadsworth.

Kagle, J. D. (1993). Record keeping: Directions for the 1990s. *Social Work, 38,* 190–196.

Kagle, J. D. Recording. In R. L. Edwards (Ed.), *Encyclopedia of social work* (19th ed., pp. 2027–2033). Washington, DC: NASW Press.

Kahn, A. (1966). *Neighborhood information centers. A study and some proposals.* New York: Columbia University Press.

Kahn, A. J. (1965). New policies and service models: The next phase. *American Journal of Orthopsychiatry* (July).

Kahn, A. J. (1979). *Social policy and social services.* New York: Random House.

Kahn, M. (1991). *Between therapist and client.* New York: Freeman.

Kahn, R. L., & Cannell, C. F. (1957). *The dynamics of interviewing theory, technique and cases.* New York: Wiley.

Kamerman, S. B. (1983). The new mixed economy of welfare: Public and private. *Social Work, 28,* 5–9.

Kanfer, F. H., & Saslow, G. (1969). Behavioral diagnosis. In C. M. Franks (Ed.), *Behavior therapy: Appraisal and status* (pp. 417–444). New York: McGraw-Hill.

Kanfer, F. H., & Schefft, B. K. (1988). *Guiding therapeutic change.* Champaign, IL: Research Press.

Kantor, D., & Lehr, W. (1975). *Inside the family.* San Francisco: Jossey-Bass.

Karger, H. J., & Stoesz, D. (1994). *American social welfare policy: A pluralistic approach.* New York: Longman.

Karr, J. (1990). Goal attainment in the treatment of children with behavioral disorders. *School Social Work Journal, 15*(1), 14–20.

Katz, D. (1979). Laboratory training to enhance interviewing skills. In F. Clark, M. Arkava, and Associates (Eds.), *The pursuit of competence in social work* (pp. 205–226). San Francisco: Jossey-Bass.

Katz, R. L. (1963). *Empathy.* New York: Free Press.

Kaus, M. (1992). *The end of equality.* New York: Basic.

Kayser, K. (1993). *When love dies. The process of marital disaffection.* New York: Guilford.

Kazdin, A. E. (1973). Methodological and assessment considerations in evaluating reinforcement programs in applied settings. *Journal of Applied Behavior Analysis, 6,* 517–531.

Kazdin, A. E., & Krouse, R. (1983). The impact of variables in treatment rationales on expectancies for therapeutic change. *Behavior Therapy, 14,* 657–671.

Keeney, B. P. (1979). Ecosystemic epistemology: An alternative paradigm for diagnosis. *Family Process.*

Kelman, H. C., & Warwick, D. P. (1978). The ethics of social intervention: Goals, means and consequences. In G. G. Bermant, H. C. Kelman, & D. P. Warwick (Eds.), *The ethics of social intervention* (p. 4). Washington, DC: Hemisphere.

Kemp, S. (1995). Practice with communities. In C. H. Meyer & M. A. Mattaini (Eds.), *The foundations of social work practice* (pp. 176–204). New York: Columbia University Press.

Kemp, S. P., Whittaker, J. K., & Tracy, E. M. (1997). *Person-environment practice. The social ecology of interpersonal helping.* New York: Aldine De Gruyter.

Kettner, P. M., Daley, J. M., & Nichols, A. W. (1985). *Initiating change in organizations and communities: A macro practice model.* Monterey, CA: Brooks/Cole.

Khinduka, S. K., & Coughin, B. J. (1975). A conceptualization of social action. *Social Service Review, 49*(1), 1–14.

Kieffer, C. (1984). Citizen empowerment. A developmental perspective. In J. Rappaport, C. Swift, & R. Hess (Eds.), *Studies in empowerment: Toward understanding and action* (pp. 9–36). New York: Haworth.

Kiresuk, T., Smith, A., & Cardillo, J. E. (1994). *Goal attainment scaling: Applications, theory, and measurement.* Hillsdale, NJ: Erlbaum.

Kirschenbaum, D. S. (1985). Proximity and specificity of planning. *Cognitive therapy and Research, 9,* 489–506.

Kirst-Ashman, K. K., & Hull, G. H. (1997). *Generalist practice with communities and organizations.* Chicago, IL: Nelson-Hall.

Kishardt, W. E. (1992). A strengths model of case management. The principles and functions of a helping relationship with persons with persistent mental illness. In D. Saleeby (Ed.), *The Strengths Perspective in Social Work Practice* (9th ed., pp. 50–830). New York: Longman.

Kishardt, W., & Rapp, C. (1992). Bridging the gap between principles and practice: Implementing a strengths perspective in case management. In S. Rose (Ed.), *Case management and social work practice* (pp. 112–123). New York: Longman.

Kitchener, K. S. (1986). The reflective judgment model: Characteristics, evidence, and measurement. In R. A. Mines & K. S. Kitchener. *Adult cognitive development: Methods and models* (pp. 76–910). New York: Praeger.

Klier, J., Fein, E., & Genero, C. (1984). Are written or verbal contracts more effective in family therapy? *Social Work, 29,* 298–299.

Kluckholn, F. (1958). Variations in the basic values of the family systems. *Social Casework, 39*(2), 63–72.

Knapp, M. L., & Hall, J. (1992). *Nonverbal communication in human interaction* (3rd ed.). Orlando, FL: Holt, Rinehart & Winston.

Koeske, G. E., & Kelly, T. (1995). The impact of over-involvement on burnout and job satisfaction. *American Journal of Orthopsychiatry, 65*(2), 282–292.

Kohn, P. M. (1996). On coping adaptively with daily hassles. In M. Zeidner & N. S. Endler (Eds.), *Handbook of coping. Theory, research, applications* (pp. 181–201). New York: Wiley.

Kokotovic, A. M., & Tracey, T. J. (1990). Working alliance in the early phase of counseling. *Journal of Counseling Psychology, 37*(1), 16–21.

Kopp, J. (1988). Self-monitoring. A literature review of research and practice. *Social Research and Abstracts, 24*(4), 8–15.

Kottler, J. A. (1986). *On being a therapist.* San Francisco: Jossey-Bass.

Kottler, J. (1995). *Growing a therapist.* San Francisco: Jossey-Bass.

Kramer, S. A. (1990). *Positive endings in psychotherapy. Bringing meaningful closure to therapeutic relationships.* San Francisco: Jossey-Bass.

Kuhn, D. (1993). Connecting scientific and informal reasoning. *Merrill-Palmer Quarterly, 39,* 74–103.

Kumabe, K., Nishida, C., & Hepworth, D. (1985). *Bridging ethnocultural diversity in social work and health.* Honolulu: University of Hawaii Press.

Kutchins, A., & Kutchins, S. (1978). Advocacy and social work. In G. W. Weber & G. J. McCall (Eds.), *Social scientists as advocates* (pp. 13–48). Beverly Hills, CA: Sage.

LaBinca, O. S., & Cubelli, G. E. (1976–1977, Winter). A new approach to building social work knowledge. *Social Work in Health Care,* 139–152.

LaFromboise, T., & Dixon, D. N. (1981). American Indian perception of trustworthiness in a counseling interview. *Journal of Counseling Psychology, 28,* 135–139.

LaFromboise, T., Coleman, H. L. K., & Gerton, J. (1993). Psychological impact of biculturalism. Evidence and theory. *Psychological Bulletin, 114,* 395–412.

Laing, R. D., & Esterson, A. (1970). *Sanity, madness, and the family.* Baltimore, MD: Penguin.

Laird, J. (1989). Women and stories: Restorying women's reconstructions. In M. McGoldrick, S. M. Anderson, & F. Walsh (Eds.), *Women in families* (pp. 427–450). New York: W. W. Norton.

Landon, P. S. (1995). Generalist and advanced generalist practice. In R. Edwards (Ed.), *Encyclopedia of social work* (19th ed., Vol. 2, pp. 1101–1108). Washington DC: NASW Press.

Lane, H. (1991). *The mask of benevolence: Disabling the deaf community.* New York: Random House.

LaVigna, G. W., Willis, T. J., Schaull, J. F., Abedi, M., & Sweitzer, M. (1994). *The periodic service review: Total quality assurance for human services in education.* Baltimore, MD: Paul H. Brookes.

Lawton, M. P. (1980). *Environment and aging.* Monterey, CA: Brooks/Cole.

Lazarus, A. A. (1976). *Multimodel behavior therapy.* New York: Springer.

Lazarus, A. A. (1989). *The practice of multimodel therapy.* Baltimore, MD: John Hopkins University Press.

Lazarus, R. S., & Folkman, S. (1984). *Stress, appraisal, and coping.* New York: Springer.

Lee, J. A. B. (1994). *The empowering approach to social work practice.* New York: Columbia University Press.

Lee, P. R. (1930). Social work: Cause and function. In *Proceedings of the National Conference of Social Work.* Chicago, IL: University of Chicago Press.

Levinson, H. (1977). Termination of psychotherapy. Some salient issues. *Social Casework, 58,* 480–489.

Levy, C. S. (1976). *Social work ethics.* New York: Human Services Press.

Lewis, E. (1988). Role strengths and strains of African-American mothers. *Journal of Primary Prevention, 9,* 77–91.

Lewis, E. (1991). Social change and citizen action: A philosophical exploration for modern social group work. *Social Work with Groups, 14*(3/4), 23–24.

Lewis, E. A., & Suarez, Z. E. (1995). Natural helping networks. In R. Edwards (Ed.), *Encyclopedia of social work* (19th ed., pp. 1765–1771). Washington, DC: NASW Press.

Lewis, E., & Ford, B. (1990). The network utilization project: Incorporating traditional strengths of African-Americans into group work practice. *Social Work with Groups, 13,* 7–22.

Lewis, J. A. (1992). Gender sensitivity and family empowerment. *Topics in Family Psychology and Counseling, 1*(4), 1–7.

Lewis, J. A., Lewis, M. D., & D'Andrea, M. J. (1998). *Community counseling: Empowerment strategies for a diverse society* (2nd ed.). Pacific Grove, CA: Brooks/Cole.

Lewis, J. M., Beavers, W. R., Gossett, J. T., & Philips, V. A. (1976). *No single thread: Psychological health in family systems.* New York: Brunner/Mazel.

Lewis, R. G., & Ho, M. K. (1975) Social work with native Americans. In B. R. Compton, & B. Galaway, (Eds.), *Social work processes* (4th ed., pp. 155–161). Belmont, CA: Wadsworth.

Liddle, H. A., Dakof, G. A., & Diamond, G. (1992). Adolescent substance abuse: Multidimensional family therapy in action. In E. Kaufman and P. Kaufman (Eds.), *Family therapy of drug and alcohol abuse.* Boston: Allyn & Bacon.

Liddle, N., Breunlin, D., & Schwartz, R. (Eds.). (1988). *The handbook of family therapy and supervision.* New York: Guilford.

Lipman, M. (1991). *Thinking in education.* Cambridge, Eng.: Cambridge University Press.

Lippmann, W. (1922). *Public Opinion.* New York: Harcourt Brace.

Lister, L. (1987). Contemporary direct practice roles. *Social Work 32,* 384–391.

Lloyd, G. A. (1995). HIV/AIDS overview. In R. Edwards (Ed.), *Encyclopedia of social work* (19th ed., pp. 1257–1290). Washington, DC: NASW Press.

Lloyd, J. E. (1975). Aggressive mimicry in Photuris fireflies: Signal repertoires be femme fatales. *Science, 197,* 452–453.

Locke, B., Garrison, R., & Winship, J. (1998). *Generalist social work practice. Context, story, and partnerships.* Pacific Grove, CA: Brooks/Cole.

Loewenberg, F. M. (1983). *Fundamentals of social intervention* (2nd ed.). New York: Columbia University Press.

Loewenberg, F. M., & Dolgoff, R. (1982). *Ethical decisions for social work practice* (3rd ed.) Itasca: IL: Peacock.

Loewenberg, F. M., & Dolgoff, R. (1992). *Ethical decisions for social work practice* (4th ed.). Itasca, IL: Peacock.

Long, L., & Prophit, P. (1981). *Understanding/responding: A communication manual for nurses.* Monterey, CA: Wadsworth Health Sciences.

Long, L., Paradise, L. V., & Long, T. J. (1981). *Questioning: Skills for the helping process.* Pacific Grove, CA: Brooks/Cole.

Long, V. O. (1996). *Communications skills in helping relationships: A framework for facilitating personal growth.* Pacific Grove, CA: Brooks/Cole.

Lorenz, J. (1981). *The foundations of ethology.* New York: Simon & Schuster.

Lorenz, K. (1963). *On aggression.* New York: Bantam.

Luborsky, L., McLellan, T., Woody, G. E., O'Brien, C. P., & Auerbach, A. (1985). Therapist success and its determinants. *Archives of General Psychiatry, 42,* 602–611.

Lum, D. (1986). *Social work practice and people of color. A process-stage approach.* Monterey, CA: Brooks/Cole.

Lum, D. (1992). *Social work practice and people of color. A process-stage approach* (2nd ed.). Pacific Grove, CA: Brooks/Cole.

Lum, D. (1996). *Social work practice and people of color: A process-stage approach* (3rd ed.). Pacific Grove, CA: Brooks/Cole.

Lum, D. (1999). *Culturally competent practice. A framework for growth and action.* Pacific Grove, CA: Brooks/Cole.

Lutz, W. (1956). Concepts and principles underlying social work practice. *Social Work in medical care and rehabilitation setting.* Monograph. No. 3. New York: NASW Press.

Mackelprang, R. W. (1986). *Social and emotional adjustment following spinal injury.* Unpublished doctoral dissertation. Salt Lake City, University of Utah.

Mackelprang, R. W., & Salsgiver, R. O. (1999). *Disability: A diversity model approach in human service practice.* Pacific Grove, CA: Brooks/Cole.

Madanes, C. (1981). *Strategic family therapy.* San Francisco: Jossey-Bass.

Madanes, C. (1991). *Strategic family therapy.* In A. S. Gurman & D. P. Kniskern (Eds.). *Handbook of family therapy* (Vol. 2). New York: Brunner/Mazel.

Maeder, T. (1989, December). Wounded healers. *Atlantic Monthly,* 37–47.

Maes, S., Leventhal, H., & de Ridder, D. T. D. (1996). Coping with chronic illness. In M. Zeidner & N. S. Endler (Eds.), *Handbook of Coping* (pp. 221–251). New York: Wiley.

Maguire, L. (1991). *Social support systems in practice: A generalist approach.* Silver Spring, MD: NASW Press.

Magura, S., & Moses, B. (1986). *Outcome measures for child welfare services.* Washington, DC: Child Welfare League of America.

Maholick, L. T., & Turner, D. W. (1979). Termination: That difficult farewell. *American Journal of Psychotherapy, 33,* 583–591.

Mahoney, M. J. (1977). Some applied issues in self-monitoring. In J. Cone & R. Hawkins (Eds.), *Behavior assessment: New directions in clinical psychology* (pp. 241–254). New York: Brunner/Mazel.

Mallinckrodt, B., Gantt, D., & Coble, H. (1995). Attachment patterns in the psychotherapy relationship: Development of client attachment to therapist scale. *Journal of Counseling Psychology, 42,* 307–317.

Maluccio, A. N. (1979). *Learning from clients: Interpersonal helping as viewed by clients and social workers.* New York: Free Press.

Markowitz, L. M. (1991). Homosexuality: Are we still in the dark? *The Family Therapy Networker, 15*(1), 27–35.

Marks I. (1994). Behavior therapy as an aid to self-care. *Current Directions in Psychological Science, 3,* 19–22.

Marlett, G. A., & Gordon, J. R. (1985). *Relapse prevention: maintenance strategies in the treatment of addictive behaviors.* New York: Guilford.

Marten, P., & Heimberg, R. (1995). Toward an integration of independent practice and clinical research. *Professional Psychology, 26,* 48–53.

Martin, G. T. (1990). *Social policy in the welfare state.* Englewood Cliffs, NJ: Prentice-Hall.

Martin, L. L. (1993). *Total quality management in human service organizations.* Newbury, CA: Sage.

Martin, P. Y., & O'Connor, G. G. (1989). *The social environment.* New York: Longman.

Martinez, C. (1988). Mexican-Americans. In L. Comas-Dias & E. E. H. Griffith (Eds.), *Clinical guidelines in cross-cultural mental health* (pp. 182–203). New York: John Wiley.

Marziali, E., & Alexander, L. (1991). The power of the therapeutic relationship. *American Journal of Orthopsychiatry, 61*(3), 383–391.

Maslow, A. H. (1968). *Toward a psychology of being.* (2nd ed.). New York: Van Nostrand & Reinhold.

Mathews, R. M., & Fawcett, S. B. (1981). *Matching clients and services: Information and referral.* Beverly Hills, CA: Sage.

Matsumoto, D. (1997). *Culture and modern life.* Pacific Grove, CA: Brooks/Cole.

Mattaini, M. A. (1993). *More than a thousand words: Graphics for clinical practice.* Washington, DC: NASW Press.

Mattaini, M. A. (1995). Knowledge for practice. In C. H. Meyer & M. A. Mattaini (Eds.), *The foundations of social work practice* (pp. 59–85). Washington, DC: NASW Press.

Mayer, J. E., & Timms, S. N. (1970). *The client speaks.* Chicago: Aldine.

Mayeroff, M. (1971). *On caring.* New York: Harper & Row.

McClam, T., & Woodside, M. (1994). *Problem solving in the helping professions.* Pacific Grove, CA: Brooks/Cole.

McConnaughy, E., Prochaska, J., & Velicer, W. (1983). Stages of change in psychotherapy: Measurement and sample profiles. *Psychotherapy, 20,* 368–375.

McCreath, J. M. (1984). The new generation of chronic psychiatric patients. *Social Work, 29,* 436–441.

McDaniel, S. H., Hepworth, J., & Doherty, W. J. (1993). A new prescription for family health care. *Family Networker, 17*(2) 18–29, 62–63.

McGoldrick, M., Anderson, C., & Walsh, F. (1989). Women in families and family therapy. In M. McGoldrick, C. A. Anderson, & F. Walsh (Eds.), *Women in families. A framework for family therapy.* New York: Norton.

McGoldrick, M., & Gerson, R. (1985). *Genogram in family assessment.* New York: Norton.

McGoldrick, M., Garcia-Preto, N., Hines, P. M., & Lee, E. (1989). Ethnicity and women. In M. McGoldrick, C. M. Anderson, & F. Walsh (Eds.), *Women in families: A framework for family therapy* (pp. 169–189). New York: Norton.

McGowan, B. G. (1995). Values and Ethics. In C. H. Meyer & M. A. Mattaini (Eds.), *The foundations of social work practice* (pp. 28–41). Washington, DC: NASW Press.

McGrath, T., Tsui, E., Humphries, S., & Yule, W. (1990). Successful treatment of a noise phobia in a nine-year-old girl with systematic desensitization in vivo. *Educational Psychology, 10,* 79–83.

McKee, J. O. (1985). Humanity on the move. In J. O. McKee (Ed.), *Ethnicity in contemporary America* (pp. 1–30). Dubuque, IA: Kendall Hunt.

McMohan, M. O. (1990). *The general method of social work practice. A problem solving approach.* Englewood Cliffs, NJ: Prentice-Hall.

Mcmullen, R. (1986). *Handbook of cognitive therapy techniques.* New York: Norton.

Mead, G. H. (1934). *Mind, self, and society.* Chicago: University of Chicago Press.

Mechanic, D. (1974). Social structure and personal adaptation: Some neglected dimensions. In G.

Coelho, D. Hamburg, & J. Adams (Eds.), *Coping and adaptation* (pp. 32–46). New York: Basic.

Mechanic, D., Schlesinger, M., & McAlpine, D. D. (1995). Management of mental health and substance abuse services: State of the art and early results. *Milbank Quarterly, 73*(1), 19–55.

Meenaghan, T. M., Washington, R. O., & Ryan, R. M. (1987). *Macro practice in the human services.* New York: Free Press.

Meier, S. T. (1989). *The elements of counseling.* Pacific Grove, CA: Brooks/Cole.

Menaghan, E. (1982). Measuring coping effectiveness: A panel analysis of marital problems and coping efforts. *Journal of Health and Social Behavior, 23,* 230–234.

Merriam-Webster's Tenth New Collegiate Dictionary. (1996). Springfield, MA: Merriam-Webster.

Merton, R. (1961). *Social theory and social structure.* Glencoe, IL: The Free Press.

Messner, M. (1995). Masculinities and athletic careers. In M. L. Andersen & P. H. Collins, (Eds.), *Race, Class, and Gender* (2nd ed., pp. 165–181). Belmont, CA: Wadsworth.

Meyer, C. (1976). *Social work practice: The changing landscape.* New York: Free Press.

Meyer, C. H. (1970). *Social work practice.* New York: Columbia University Press.

Meyer, C. H. (1983a). *Beginning again. Clinical social work in eco-systems perspective.* New York: Columbia University Press, pp. 5–34.

Meyer, C. H. (1983b). Selecting appropriate practice models. In A. Rosenblatt & D. Waldfogel (Eds.), *Handbook of clinical social work* (pp. 731–749). San Francisco: Jossey-Bass.

Meyer, C. H. (1983c). The search for coherence. In Meyer, C. H. (Ed.), *Clinical Social Work in Eco-systems Perspective.* New York: Columbia University Press.

Meyer, C. H., & Mattaini, M. (Eds.). (1995). *The foundations of social work practice.* Washington, DC: NASW Press.

Meyer, J. W., & Rowan, B. (1977). Institutional Organizations: Formal structures as myth and ceremony. *American Journal of Sociology, 83,* 440–463.

Mickelson, J. (1995). Advocacy. In R. Edwards (Ed.), *Encyclopedia of social work* (19th ed., pp. 95–100). Washington, DC: NASW Press.

Middleman, R. R., & Wood, G. G. (1990). *Skills for direct practice in social work.* New York: Columbia University Press.

Miles, A. (1965). The utility of case recording in probation and parole. *Journal of Criminal Law, Criminology and Police Science, 56,* 285–293.

Miley, K. K., O'Melia, M., & DuBois, B. L. (1998). *Generalist social work practice* (2nd ed.). Boston: Allyn & Bacon.

Miley, K., O'Melia, M., & DuBois, B. (1995). *Generalist social work: An empowering approach.* Boston: Allyn & Bacon.

Milgram, D., & Rubin, J. S. (1992). Resisting resistance: Involuntary substance abuse group therapy. *Social Work with Groups, 15*(1), 95–110.

Milne, C. R., & Dowd, E. T. (1983). Effect of interpretation style on counselor social influence. *Journal of Counseling Psychology, 51,* 603–606.

Minuchin, S. (1974). *Families and family therapy.* Cambridge, MA: Harvard University Press.

Minuchin, S., & Fishman, H. C. (1981). *Family therapy techniques.* Cambridge, MA: Harvard University Press.

Minuchin, S., & Nichols, M. P. (1993). *Family healing. Strategies for hope and understanding.* New York: Free Press.

Minuchin, S., Lee, W., & Simon, G. M. (1996). *Mastering family therapy. Journeys of growth and transformation.* New York: John Wiley & Sons.

Minuchin, S., Rosman, B. L., & Baker, L. (1978). *Psychosomatic families. Anorexia nervosa in context.* Cambridge MA: Harvard University Press.

Mischel, W. (1973). *Personality and assessment* (2nd ed.). New York: Wiley.

Mitchell, R. E., Cronkite, R. C., & Moos, R. H. (1983). Stress, coping, and depression among married couples. *Journal of Abnormal Psychology, 92,* 433–448.

Mokuau, N. (1985). Counseling Pacific-Islander-Americans. In P. Pedersen (ed.). *Handbook of cross-cultural counseling and therapy.* Westport, CT: Greenwood.

Mondros, J. B., & Berman-Rossi, T. (1991). The relevance of stages of group development to community organization practice, *Social Work with Groups, 14*(3–4), 203–221.

Mondros, J. B., & Wilson, S. M. (1994). *Organizing for power and empowerment.* New York: Columbia University Press.

Monkman, M. M. (1991). Outcome objectives in social work practice: Person and environment. *Social Work, 36,* 253–258.

Moon, S., Dillon, D., & Sprenkle, D. (1990). Family therapy and qualitative research. *Journal of Marital and Family Therapy, 16,* 357–373.

Moore, C. W. (1986). *The mediation process.* San Francisco: Jossey-Bass.

Moore, S. T. (1990). A social work practice model of case management: The case management grid. *Social Work, 35*(5), 444–448.

Moos, R. H., & Schaefer, J. A. (1993). Coping resources and processes: Current concepts and measures. In L. Goldberger & S. Breznitz (Eds.), *Handbook of stress: Theories and clinical aspects* (2nd ed., pp. 234–257). New York: Free Press.

Moran, D. K., Kurpius, D. J., Brack, G., & Rozecki, T. G. (1994). Relationship between counselors' clinical hypothesis and client ratings of counselor effectiveness. *Journal of Counseling and Development, 72,* 655–660.

Morgan, R. (1962). Role performance in a bureaucracy. In National Conference on Social Welfare (ed.) *Social Work Practice* (pp. 111–126). New York: Columbia University Press.

Morgan, R. F. (1983). *The iatrogenics handbook. A critical look at research and practice in the helping professions.* Toronto: IPI.

Moroney, R. (1986). *Shared responsibility.* New York: Aldine.

Morris, R. (1977, September). Caring versus caring about people. *Social Work.*

Morrison, J. (1995). *The first interview: A guide for clinicians.* New York: Guilford.

Munz, P. (1985). *Our knowledge of the growth of knowledge: Popper or Wittgenstein.* London: Routledge & Kegan Paul.

Murphy, L. (1974). Coping, vulnerabilities and resilience in childhood. In G. Coelho, D. Hamburg, & J. Adams (Eds.), *Coping and Adaptation* (pp. 69–100). New York: Basic.

Napier, R. W., & Gershenfeld, M. K. (1993). *Groups: Theory and experience* (5th ed.). Boston: Houghton Mifflin.

National Association of Social Workers. (1973). *Legal regulation of social work practice.* Washington, DC: Author.

National Association of Social Workers. (1981). *Standards for social work practice in child protection.* Silver Spring, MD: Author.

National Association of Social Workers. (1990). *Standards for social work professional practice.* Silver Spring, MD: Author.

National Association of Social Workers. (1992). Case management in health, education and human service settings. In S. Rose (Ed.), *Case management and social work practice.* White Plains, NY: Longman.

National Association of Social Workers. (1995). *Code of Ethics.* Silver Spring, MD: Author.

National Association of Social Workers. (1996). *Code of Ethics of the National Association of Social Workers.* Washington, DC: Author.

National Association of Social Workers. (1981). Report of a task force on labor force classification. *NASW News, 26*(19), 7.

National Clearing House on Licensure, Enforcement, and Regulation, and Council on State Governments. (1986). *State credentialing of the behavioral science professions: Counselors, psychologists, and social workers.* Lexington, KY: Council of State Governments.

Nelson, J. (1981). Issues in single subject research for non-behaviorists. *Social Work Research and Abstracts, 17*(2), 31–37.

Neugarten, B. L. (1979). Time, age, and the life cycle. *American Journal of Psychiatry, 136,* 887–894.

Newsome, M., Jr., & Pillari, V. (1991). Job satisfaction and the worker-supervisor relationship. *Clinical Supervisor, 9*(2), pp. 14–21.

Nichols, M. P. (1995). *The lost art of listening.* New York: Guilford.

Nichols, M. P., & Schwartz, R. C. (1995). *Family therapy. Concepts and methods* (3rd ed.). Boston, MA: Allyn & Bacon.

Nickerson, R. S. (1986). *Reflections on reasoning.* Hillsdale, NJ: Erlbaum.

Nickerson, R. S. (1988). On improving thinking through instruction. In E. Z. Rothkopf (Ed.). *Review of education in research* (pp. 3–57). Washington, DC: American Educational Research Association.

Nickerson, R. S., Perkins, D. N., & Smith, E. E. (1985). *The teaching of thinking.* Hillsdale, NJ: Erlbaum.

Norman, P. (1981). *Shout!* New York: Simon & Schuster.

Northen, H. (1969). *Social work with groups.* New York: Columbia University Press.

Northen, H. (1982). *Clinical social work.* New York: Columbia University Press.

O'Connor, K., & Schaefer, C. (1990). *Handbook of play therapy,* Vol. 2. New York: Wiley.

O'Connor, K., & Schaefer, C. (1994). *Handbook of play therapy.* New York: John Wiley.

O'Hanlon, W. H., & Weiner-Davis, M. (1989). *In search of solutions: A new dimension in psychotherapy.* New York: Norton.

O'Looney, J. (1993). Beyond privatization and service integration: Organizational models for service delivery. *Social Service Review, 67*(4), 501–534.

Okun, B. F. (1976). *Effective helping: Interviewing and counseling techniques.* North Scituate, MA: Duxbury.

Okun, B. F. (1987). *Effective helping: Interviewing and counseling techniques* (3rd ed.). Pacific Grove, CA: Brooks/Cole.

Okun, B. F. (1992). *Effective helping: Interviewing and counseling techniques* (4th ed.). Pacific Grove, CA: Brooks/Cole.

Okun, B. F. (1997). *Effective helping: Interviewing and counseling techniques* (5th ed.). Pacific Grove, CA: Brooks/Cole.

Okun, B. F., Fried, J., & Okun, M. L. (1999). *Understanding diversity. A learning-as-practice primer.* Pacific Grove, CA: Brooks/Cole.

Okun, B. K., & Rappaport, L. J. (1980). *Working with Families. An introduction to family therapy.* North Scituate, MA: Duxbury.

Oliver, J., & Brown, L. B. (1987). Introduction. In J. Oliver & L. B. Brown (Eds.), *A resource guide for human service professionals: Socio-cultural service issues in working with gay and lesbian clients* (pp. ix–xv). Albany, NY: Rockefeller College Press.

Onken, S. J., & Mackelprang, R. W. (1997). Building on shared experiences: Teaching disability and sexual minority content and practice. Presented at the Annual Program Meeting. Council on Social Work Education. Chicago, IL.

Otani, A. (1989). Client resistance in counseling: Its theoretical rationale and taxonomic classification. *Journal of Counseling and Development, 67,* 458–462.

Oxley, G. B. (1966). The caseworker's expectations in client motivation. *Social Casework, 47*(7), 432–437.

Oz, S. (1995). A modified balance-sheet procedure for decision making in therapy. Cost-cost comparison. *Professional Psychology, 25,* 78–81.

Padilla, A. M., & De Synder, N. S. (1985). Counseling Hispanics: Strategies for effective intervention. In P. Pedersen (Ed.), *Handbook of cross-cultural counseling and therapy* (pp. 157–164). Westport, CT: Greenwood.

Parloff, M. B., Waskow, I. E., & Wolfe, B. E. (1978). Research on therapist variables in relation to process and outcomes. In S. L. Garfield and A. E. Bergin (Eds.) *Handbook of psychotherapy and behavior change* (2nd ed.). New York: Wiley.

Parsons, R. J. (1991). Empowerment: purpose and practice principle in social work. *Social Work with Groups, 14*(2), 7–21.

Parsons, T. (1960). *Structure and process in modern society.* New York: Free Press.

Patterson, L. E., & Eisenberg, S. (1983). *The counseling process* (3rd ed.). Boston: Houghton Mifflin.

Patterson, L. E., & Welgel, E. R. (1994). *The counseling process* (4th ed.). Pacific Grove, CA: Brooks/Cole.

Patti, R. (1983). *Social welfare administration.* Englewood Cliffs, NJ: Prentice-Hall.

Patton, M. Q. (1990). *Qualitative evaluation and research methods* (2nd ed.). Newbury Park, CA: Sage.

Patton, M. Q. (1991). *Family sexual abuse: Frontline research and evaluations.* Newbury Park: CA: Sage.

Paul, R. (1993). *Critical thinking: What every person needs to know to survive in a rapidly changing world.* Santa Rosa, CA: Foundation for Critical Thinking.

Peal, E. (1975, September). "Normal" sex roles: An historical analysis. *Family Process, 14,* 389–409.

Pearlin, L. I., & Schooler, C. (1978). The structure of coping. *Journal of Health and Social Behavior, 19,* 2–21.

Pedersen, P. B. (1986). *Are APA ethical principles culturally encapsulated?* Unpublished manuscript. Syracuse University.

Perlman, B., & Pablo, S. (1978). Community development possibilities for effective Indian reservation child abuse and neglect efforts. In M. Lauderdale, R. Anderson and S. Cremer (Eds.), *Child abuse and neglect: Issues on innovation and implementation* (pp. 98–116). Washington, DC: U.S. Department of Health, Education and Welfare.

Perlman, H. (1975). In quest of coping. *Social Casework, 56*(4) 213–225.

Perlman, H. (1986). The problem solving model. In F. Turner (Ed.), *Social work treatment* (3rd ed., pp. 242–261). New York: Free Press.

Perlman, H. H. (1971). *Perspectives on social casework.* Philadelphia Temple University Press.

Peterson, C., Patrick, S., & Rissmeyer, D. (1990). Social work's contribution to psychosocial rehabilitation. *Social Work, 35*(5), 468–472.

Piaget, J. (1950). *The psychology of intelligence.* San Diego, CA: Harcourt Brace Jovanovich.

Pierce, D. (1984). *Policy for the social work practitioner. Model and method.* Itasca, IL: Peacock.

Piercy, F., Trepper, T., & Jurich, J. (1993). The role of family therapy in decreasing HIV high-risk behaviors among adolescents. *AIDS education and prevention 5*(1), 71–86.

Pillai, R. (1996). Crisis and the emergence of charismatic leadership in groups. An experimental investigation. *Journal of Applied Social Psychology, 26,* 543–562.

Pillari, V. (1986). *Pathways to family myths.* New York: Brunner/Mazel.

Pillari, V. (1991). *Scapegoating in families. Intergenerational patterns of physical and emotional abuse.* New York: Brunner/Mazel.

Pillari, V. (1991). *Scapegoating in families. Intergenerational patterns of abuse.* New York: Brunner/ Mazel.

Pillari, V. (1997). *Shadows of Pain.* Northvale, NJ: Jason Aronson.

Pillari, V., & Newsome, Jr., M. (1998). *Human behavior in the social environment. Families, Groups, Organizations, and Communities.* Pacific Grove, CA: Brooks/Cole.

Pincus, A., & Minahan, A. (1973). *Social work practice. Model and method.* Itasca, IL: Peacock.

Pinderhughes, E. B. (1983). Empowerment for our clients and for ourselves. *Social Casework, 64,* 331–338.

Pinderhughes, E. B. (1989). *Understanding race, ethnicity, and power.* New York: Free Press.

Platt, A. (1977). *The child savers: The intention of delinquency* (2nd ed.). Chicago: University of Chicago Press.

Polanyi, M. (1958). *Personal knowledge.* Chicago: University of Chicago Press.

Pollak, O. (1956). *Integrating social science and psychoanalytic concepts.* New York: Sage.

Pollak, O. (1972). *Social science and psychology of children.* New York: Russell Sage.

Polsky, H. (1962). *Cottage six.* New York: Russell Sage.

Pope, K. S., & Singer, B. L. (Eds.). (1978). *The stream of consciousness: Scientific investigations into the flow of human experience.* New York: Plenum.

Popper, K. R. (1992). *In search of a better world: Lectures and essays from thirty years.* London: Routledge & Kegan Paul.

Popple, P. R. (1983). Contexts of practice. In A. Rosenblatt, & D. Waldfogel, (Eds.), *Handbook of clinical social work* (pp. 70–96). San Francisco: Jossey-Bass.

Porter, L. S., & Stone, A. A. (1996). As approach to assessing daily coping. In M. Zeidner & N. S. Endler (Ed.), *Handbook of coping. Theory research and application* (pp. 133–150). New York: Wiley.

Postner, R. (1971). Process and outcome in conjoint family therapy. *Family Process, 19,* pp. 451–473.

Postuma, B. (1989). *Small groups in therapy settings: Process and leadership.* Boston: College-Hill.

Poulin, J. E., & Walter, C. A. (1993). Social workers' burnout: A longitudinal study. *Social Work Research and Abstracts, 29*(4), 5–11.

Pray, J. (1991). Respecting the uniqueness of the individual: Social work practice within a reflective model. *Social Work, 36,* 80–85.

Presley, J. H. (1987). The clinical dropout: A viewpoint from the clients' perspective. *Social Casework, 68,* 603–608

Prestby, J., Wandersman, A., Florin, P., Rich, R., & Chavis, D. (1990). Benefits, costs, incentive management, and participation in voluntary organizations: A means to understanding and promoting empowerment. *American Journal of Community Psychology, 18,* 117–150.

Preston-Shoot, M. (1989). Using contracts in groupwork. *Groupwork, 2*(1), 36–47.

Proshansky, H., Ittelson, W., & Rivlin, L. (1976). *Environmental psychology. People and their setting.* New York: Holt, Rinehart & Winston.

Pyszcznski, T., & Greenberg, J. (1987). Self-regulatory preservation and the depressive self-focusing style: A self-awareness theory of depression. *Psychological Bulletin, 102,* 122–138.

Queralt, M. (1984). Understanding Cuban immigrants. A cultural perspective. *Social Work, 29,* 115–121.

Rappaport, J. (1987). Terms of empowerment/exemplars of prevention: Toward a theory for community psychology. *American Journal of Community Psychology, 15*(2), 121–144.

Reamer, F. G. (1987). Values and ethics. In A. Minahan (Ed.), *Encyclopedia of social work: Vol. 2* (18th ed., pp. 801–809). Silver Spring, MD: NASW Press.

Reding, G. R., Charles, L. A., & Hoffman, M. B. (1967). Treatment of couples by a couple: Conceptual framework, case presentation, and follow-up study. *British Journal of Medical Psychology, 40,* 243–251.

Rees, S. (1991). *Achieving power: Practice and policy in social welfare.* North Sydney, Australia: Allen & Unwin.

Reid, K. (1991). *Social work practice with groups. A clinical perspective.* Belmont, CA: Wadsworth.

Reid, K. (1997). *Social work practice with groups: A clinical perspective* (2nd ed.). Pacific Grove, CA: Brooks/Cole.

Reid, K. E. (1991). *Social work practice with groups. A Clinical Perspective.* Pacific Grove, CA: Brooks/Cole.

Reid, K. E. (1998). *Social work practice with groups* (6th ed.). Pacific Grove, CA: Brooks/Cole.

Reid, P. N., & Popple, P. (1992). *The moral purpose of social work.* Chicago: Nelson-Hall.

Reid, W. (1978). *The task-centered system.* New York: Columbia University Press.

Reid, W. (1985). *Family problem solving.* New York: Columbia University Press.

Reid, W. (1992). *Task strategies: An empirical approach to clinical social work.* New York: Columbia University Press.

Reid, W. (1996). Task-centered social work. In F. J. Turner (Ed.), *Social work treatment: interlocking theoretical approaches* (4th ed., pp. 69–93). New York: Free Press.

Reid, W. J., & Hanrahan, P. (1982). Recent evaluation of social work: Grounds for optimism. *Social Work, 27*(4), 328–340.

Resnick, H. (1980a). Effecting internal change in service organizations. In H. Resnick & R. J. Patti (Eds.), *Change from within: Humanizing social welfare organizations.* Philadelphia: Temple University Press.

Resnick, H. (1980b). Tasks in changing the organization from within: In H. Resnick & R. J. Patti (Eds.). *Change from within. Humanizing social welfare organizations.* Philadelphia: Temple University Press.

Resnick, H. B. (1982). Facilitating productive staff meetings. I. M. Austin & W. E. Hershey (Eds.), *Handbook of mental health administration* (pp. 196–197). San Francisco: Jossey-Bass.

Resnick, R. J. (1995). How come outcome? *The American Psychological Association Monitor, 26*(6), 2.

Reynolds, P. D. (1975). *A primer in theory construction.* Indianapolis: Bobbs Merrill.

Rhodes, S. (1977). Contract negotiation in the initial stage of casework. *Social Service Review, 51,* 125–140.

Richmond, M. (1917). *Social diagnosis.* New York: Russell Sage.

Riley, M. W. (1985). Women, men and the lengthening life course. A. S. Rossi (Ed.), *Aging the life course* (pp. 333–347). New York: Aldine.

Rioch, M. (1978). The work of Wilfred Bion on groups. In G. S. Gibbard, J. J. Hartman & R. D. Mann (Ed.). *Analysis of groups.* San Francisco: Jossey-Bass.

Rivier, C. (1991). Role of interleukins in the stress response. In G. Jasmin & M. Cantin (Eds.), *Stress Revisited 1. Neuroendocrinology of stress* (pp. 63–79). New York: Karger.

Robertson, I. (1987). *Sociology* (3rd ed.). New York: Worth.

Rogers, C. (1951). *Client-centered therapy.* Boston, MA: Houghton-Mifflin.

Rogers, C. R. (1961). *On becoming a person.* Boston: Houghton Mifflin.

Rogers, C. (1970). *Carl Rogers on encounter groups.* New York: Harper & Row.

Rohde, P., Lewinsohn, P. M., Tilson, M., & Seeley, J. R. (1990). Dimensionality of coping and its relation to depression. *Journal of Personality and Social Psychology, 58,* 499–511.

Rompf, E. L., & Royse, D. (1994). Choice of social work as a career: Possible influences. *Journal of Social Work Education, 30*(2), 163–171.

Ronaldson, S. (1986). *The chimpanzees of Gombe.* Cambridge, MA: Beakan Press and the Harvard University Press.

Rooney, R. (1988). Socialization strategies for involuntary clients. *Social Casework: Journal of Contemporary Social Work, 69*(3), 131–140.

Rooney, R. (1991). *Strategies for work with involuntary clients.* New York: Columbia University Press.

Rooney, R. H. (1992). *Strategies for work with involuntary clients.* New York: Columbia University Press.

Rose, S. (1972). *Treating children in groups.* San Francisco: Jossey-Bass.

Rose, S. (1992). Case Management: An advocacy/empowerment design. In S. Rose (Ed.), *Case management and social work practice* (pp. 271–297). New York: Longman.

Rose, S. D. (1995). Goal setting and Intervention Planning. In R. Edwards (Ed.), *Encyclopedia of Social Work* (19th ed., pp. 1124–1129). Washington, DC: NASW Press.

Ross, K., & Goss, J. (1989). *Domestic violence statistics.* Washington, DC: U.S. Department of Justice, Bureau of Justice Statistics.

Ross, S. D. (1981). Assessment in groups. *Social Work Research and Abstracts, 17*(1), 29–37.

Rossen, S. (1987). Hospital Social Work. In R. Edwards (Ed.), *Encyclopedia of Social Work* (18th ed., pp. 816–821). Silver Springs, MD: NASW Press.

Rossi, P. H., Wright, J. D., Fisher, G. A., & Willis, G. (1987, March 13). The urban homeless: estimating composition and size. *Science, 235,* 1336–1434.

Rounds, K. A., Weil, M., & Bishop, K. K. (1994). Practice with culturally diverse families of young children with disabilities. *Families in Society, 75*(1), 3–14.

Rupp, G. (1991). Communities of collaboration: Shared commitments and common tasks. In L. S. Rouner (Ed.), *On community* (pp. 192–208). Notre Dame, IN: University of Notre Dame Press.

Sabatelli, R. M., & Sheehan, C. L. (1993). Exchange and resource theories. In P. G. Boss, W. J. Doherty, R. LaRossa, W. R. Schumm, & S. K. Steinmetz (Eds.), *Sourcebook of family theories and methods: A contextual approach* (pp. 395–411). New York: Plenum.

Saleeby, D. (1979). The tension between research and practice: Assumptions of the experimental paradigm. *Clinical Social Work Journal, 7,* 267–284.

Saleeby, D. (1992). Conclusion: Possibilities and problems with the strengths perspective. In D. Saleeby (Ed.), *The strengths perspective in social work practice* (pp. 169–179), New York: Longman.

Sanders, M. R., & Dadds, M. R. (1993). *Behavioral family intervention.* Boston: Allyn & Bacon.

Sarri, R. (1987). Administration in social welfare. In A. Minahan (Ed.), *Encyclopedia of social work* (18th ed., Vol. 1., pp. 27–40). Silver Spring, MD: NASW.

Sashkin, M., & Kiser, K. J. (1993). *Putting total quality management to work: What TQM means, how to use it and how to sustain it over the long run.* San Francisco: Berrett-Koehler.

Satir, V. (1983). *Conjoint family therapy* (3rd ed.). Palo Alto, CA: Science and Behavior Books.

Satir, V. M., & Baldwin, M. (1983). *Satir: Step by step.* Palo Alto, CA: Science and Behavior Books.

Satir, V., Banmen, J., Gerber, J., & Gomori, M. (1991). *The Satir model. Family therapy and beyond.* Palo Alto, CA: Science and Behavior Books.

Schaefer, M. (1987). *Implementing change in service programs: Project planning and management.* Newbury, CA: Sage.

Schaefer, R. (1993). *Racial and ethnic groups* (5th ed.). New York: HarperCollins.

Schatz, M., Jenkins, L., & Shaefor, B. (1990). Milford redefined: A model of initial and advanced generalist social work. *Journal of Education in Social Work, 26*(3), 217–231.

Scheffler, I. (1965). *Conditions of knowledge.* Glenview, IL: Scott & Foresman.

Scheflen, A., & Ashcraft, N. (1976). *Human territories: How we behave in space and time.* Englewood, NJ. Prentice-Hall.

Schein, E. (1992). *Organizational culture and leadership* (2nd ed.). San Francisco: Jossey-Bass.

Schiff, J. L. (1975). *Cathexis reader. Transactional analysis treatment of psychosis.* New York: Harper & Row.

Schinke, S., Blythe, B., Gilchrist, L., & Smith, E. (1980). Developing intake-interviewing skills. *Social Work Research and Abstracts, 16,* 29–34.

Schlesinger, E. G., & Devore, W. (1995). Ethnic sensitive social work practice: The state of the art. *Journal of Sociology and Social Welfare, XXII*(1), 29–58.

Schon, D. A. (1983). *The reflective practitioner: How professionals think in action.* London: Temple Smith.

Schopler, J. H., & Galinsky, M. J. (1995). Group Practice Overview. In R. Edwards (Ed.), *Encyclopedia of Social Work* (19th ed., pp. 1120–1142). Washington, DC: NASW Press.

Schriner, K. F., & Fawcett, S. B. (1988). Development and validation of a community concerns report method. *Journal of Community Psychology, 16,* 306–316.

Schubert, M. (Ed.). (1991). *Interviewing in social work practice* (rev. ed.). Alexandria, VA: Council on Social Work Education.

Schulman, E. D. (1991). *Intervention in human services: A guide to skills and knowledge* (4th ed.). New York: Merrill.

Schur, E. (1973). *Radical non-intervention: Rethinking the delinquency problem.* Englewood Cliffs, NJ: Prentice-Hall.

Schwab, G. J. (1996). Working with Raskal gangs in the Highlands of Papua New Guinea. In L. M. Grobman (Ed.), *Days in the lives of social workers* (pp. 225–230). Harrisburg, PA: White Hat Communications.

Schwartz, I. M. (1989). *(In) justice for juveniles: Rethinking the best interests of the child.* Lexington, MA: Heath.

Schwartz, I. S., & Baer, D. M. (1991). Social validity assessments: Is current practice state of art? *Journal of Applied Behavior Analysis, 24,* 189–204.

Schwartz, W. (1961). The social worker in the group. In *New Perspectives on Services to Groups: Theory,*

Organization, and Practice, National Association of Social Workers, p. 7–34; and the Social Welfare Forum, New York: Columbia University Press, 1961, pp. 146–77.

Schwartz, W. (1976). Between client and system: The mediating function. In R. Roberts & H. Northen (Eds.). *Theories of social work with groups.* New York: Columbia University Press.

Schwartz, W. (1977). Social group work: The interactionist approach. In *Encyclopedia of social work* (Vol. II, pp. 980–990). New York: NASW.

Schwarz, R. M. (1994). *The skilled facilitator: Practice wisdom for developing effective groups.* San Francisco: Jossey-Bass.

Scott, D. (1989). Meaning, construction and social work practice. *Social Service Review, 63,* 39–51.

Scott, R., & Meyer, J. (Eds.). (1994). *Institutional environments and organizations.* Newbury Park, CA: Sage.

Searles, H. E. (1960). *The Non-human environment.* New York: International University Press.

Searles, H. E. (1994). *My work with borderline patients.* Northvale, NJ: Jason Aronson.

Sederer, L. I., & Bennet, M. J. (1996). Managed mental health care in the United States: A status report. *Administration and Policy in Mental Health, 23*(4), 289–306.

Sedney, M., Baker, J., & Gross, E. (1990). The "story" of a death: therapeutic considerations with bereaved families. *Journal of Marital and Family Therapy, 20,* 287–296.

Seekins, T., & Fawcett, S. B. (1987). Effects of poverty-clients' agenda on resource allocations by community decision makers. *American Journal of Community Psychology, 15*(3), 305–320.

Seilgman, M. E. P. (1975). *Helplessness: On depression, development, and death.* San Francisco: W. H. Freeman.

Selby, J. W., & Calhoun, L. G. (1980). Psychodidactics: An undervalued and underdeveloped treatment tool of psychological intervention. *Professional Psychology, 11,* 236–241.

Senge, P. (1994). *The fifth discipline: The art and practice of the learning organization.* New York: Doubleday.

Shainberg, D. (1993). *Healing in psychotherapy.* Langhorne, PA: Gordon & Breach Science.

Sheafor, B. W., Horejsi, C. R., & Horejsi, G. A. (1991). *Techniques and guidelines for social work practice* (2nd ed.). Boston: Allyn & Bacon.

Sheafor, B. W., Horejsi, C. R., & Horejsi, G. A. (1997). *Techniques and guidelines for social work practice* (4th ed.). Boston: Allyn & Bacon.

Shaefor, B. W., Horejsi, C. R., & Horejsi, G. A. (2000). *Techniques and guidelines for social work practice* (5th ed.). Boston: Allyn & Bacon.

Shera, W. (1993). *Assessing the efficacy of a partnership model of case management.* Paper presented at the Education and Research for Empowerment Conference, Seattle, WA.

Sherman, E., & Reid, W. J. (1994). Introduction: Coming of age in social work—The emergence of qualitative research. In E. Sherman & B. Reid (Eds.), (pp. 1–15). *Qualitative Research in Social Work* New York: Columbia University Press.

Shulman, L. (1979). *The skills of helping.* Itasca, IL: Peacock.

Shulman, L. (1981). *Identifying, measuring, and teaching helping skills.* New York: CSWE.

Shulman, L. (1984). *The skills of helping individuals and groups* (2nd ed.). Itasca, IL: Peacock.

Shulman, L. (1991). *Interactional social work. Toward an empirical theory.* Itasca, IL: Peacock.

Shulman, L. (1992). *The skills of helping individuals, families, and groups* (3rd ed.). Itasca, IL: Peacock.

Shulman, L. (1999). *The skill of helping individuals, families, groups, and communities* (4th ed.). Itasca, IL: Peacock.

Siegal, M. (1979). Privacy, ethics and confidentiality. *Professional Psychologist, 37*(7), 802–809.

Silverman, C., Segal, S., & Anello, E. (1992). *Community and the homeless disabled: The structure of self-help groups.* Berkeley, CA: Center for Self-Help Research.

Simmons, R. L., & Aiger, S. M. (1979, April). Facilitating an eclectic use of practice theory. *Social Casework, 60,* 201–208.

Simmons, R. L. (1985). Inducement as an approach to exercising influences. *Social Work, 30*(1), 56–62.

Simon, A. D., Lustman, P. J., Wetzel, R. D., & Murphy, G. E. (1985). Predicting response to cognitive therapy of depression: The role of learned resourcefulness. *Cognitive Therapy and Research, 9,* 79–89.

Simon, B. L. (1990). Rethinking empowerment. *Journal of Progressive Human Services, 1,* 27–39.

Simon, B. L. (1994). *The empowerment tradition in American social work: A history.* New York: Columbia University Press.

Simon, S. B., Howe, L. W., & Kirschenbaum, H. (1972). *Value clarification: A handbook of practical strategies for students and teachers.* New York: Hart.

Simons, R. L., & Aigner, S. M. (1985). *Practice principles: A problem-solving approach in social work.* New York: Macmillan.

Siporin, M. (1975). *Introduction to social work practice.* New York: Macmillan.

Siporin, M. (1980). Ecological systems theory in social work. *Journal of Sociology and Social Welfare, 7,* 507–532.

Siporin, M. (1983 fall). Morality and immorality in working with clients. *Social Thought 9:*10–28.

Siporin, M. (1985). Current social work perspectives on clinical practice. *Clinical Social Work Journal, 13,* 198–217.

Siporin, M. (1989). Metamodels, models and basics: An essay review. *Social Service Review, 63,* 474–480.

Siporin, M. (1989). Morality and immorality in working with clients. *Social Thought, 15(3/4)* 52–54.

Skidmore, R. A., Thackeray, M. G., & Farley, O. W. (1997). *Introduction to social work* (7th ed.). Boston, MA: Allyn & Bacon.

Skinner, B. F. (1935). Two types of conditional reflex and pseudo type. *General Psychology, 12,* 66–77.

Slester, B. J., & Miller, D. E. (1993). *Homeless families: The struggle for dignity.* Urbana: University of Illinois Press.

Sluzki, C. (1978). Marital therapy from a systems theory perspective. In T. J. Paolino, & B. S. McCrady (Eds.), *Marriage and Marital Therapy: Psychoanalytic behavioral and systems theory perspective* (p. 201). New York: Brunner/Mazel.

Smalley, R. (1967). *Theory for social work practice.* New York: Columbia University Press.

Smith, E. W. (1985). *The body in psychotherapy.* Jefferson, NC: McFarland.

Smith, L. W., Patterson, T. L., & Grant, I. (1990). Avoidant coping predicts psychological disturbances in the elderly. *Journal of Nervous and Mental Disease, 178,* 525–530.

Smith, P. C., Kendall, L. M., & Hulin, C. L. (1969). *The measurement of satisfaction in work and retirement.* Chicago: Rand McNally.

Solomon, B. (1976). *Black empowerment: Social work in oppressed communities.* New York: Columbia University Press.

Sommers-Flanagan, J., & Sommers-Flanagan, S. (1995). Intake interviewing with suicidal patients: A systematic approach. *Professional Psychology, 26,* 41–47.

Southworth, S., & Kirch, I. (1988). The role of expectancy in exposure—Generated fear reduction in agoraphobia. *Behavior Research and Therapy, 26,* 113–120.

Speight, S. L., Myers, L. J., Cox, C. I., & Highlen, P. S. (1991). A redefinition of multicultural counseling. *Journal of Counseling and Development, 70,* 29–36.

Spence, D. P. (1982). *Narrative truth and historical truth: Meaning and interpretation in psychoanalysis.* New York: W. W. Norton.

Spence, K. W. (1956). *Behavior theory and conditioning.* New Haven, CT: Yale University Press.

Spiegel, S. B., & Hill, C. E. (1989). Guidelines for research on therapist interpretation: Toward greater methodological rigor and relevance in practice. *Journal of Counseling Psychology, 36,* 121–129.

Sprafkin, R., Gershaw, J., & Goldstein, A. (1993). *Social skills for mental health.* Boston: Allyn & Bacon.

Sprenkle, D., & Bischoff, R. (1995). Research in family therapy: trends, issues and recommendations. In M. Nichols & R. Schwartz (Eds.), *Family Therapy: Concepts and methods* (3rd ed., pp. 554–573). Boston: Allyn & Bacon.

Stack, C. (1974). *All our kin. Strategies for survival in a black community.* New York: Harper Colophon Books.

Strean, H. S. (1975). *Personality theory and social work practice.* Metuchen, NJ: Scarecrow.

Staples, L. (1984). *Roots to power: A manual for grassroots organizing.* New York: Praeger.

Stea, D. (1970). Home range and the use of space. In L. Pastalav & D. Carson (Eds.), *Spatial behavior of older people.* Ann Arbor: University of Michigan.

Stein, H. (1960). The concept of the social environment in social work practice. *Smith College Studies in Social Work, 30,* 187–210.

Stein, H., & Cloward, R. (Eds). (1959). *Social Behavior.* New York: Free Press.

Stern, D. (1985). *The interpersonal world of the infant.* New York: Basic Books.

Stierlin, H., Rucker-Embden, I., Wetzel, N., & Wirsching, M. (1980). *The first interview with the family.* New York: Brunner/Mazel.

Stevenson, H. C., & Renard, G. (1993). Trusting ole wise ones: Therapeutic use of cultural strengths in African-American families. *Professional Psychology, 24,* 433–442.

Stierlin, H., Rucker-Embden, I., Wetzel, N., & Wirsching, M. (1980). *The first interview with the family.* New York: Brunner/Mazel.

Strauss, A. (1969). Coaching. In B. Biddle & E. Thomas (Eds.), *Role theory, concepts, and research* (pp. 350–353). New York: Wiley.

Strauss, A., & Corbin, J. (1990). *Basics of qualitative research. Grounded theory and techniques.* Newbury, CA: Sage.

Strean, H. S. (1975). *Personality theory and social work practice.* Metuchen, NJ: Scarecrow.

Strong, S. R. (1968). Counseling. An interpersonal influence process. *Journal of Counseling Psychology, 15,* 215–224.

Strong, S. R., & Claiborn, C. (1982). *Change through interaction: Social psychological processes of counseling and psychotherapy.* New York: Wiley-Interscience.

Studt, E. (1968). Social work theory and implications in practice methods. *Social Work Education Reporter, 16(2),* 22–24, 42–46.

Sue, D. W. (1981). *Counseling the culturally different: Theory and practice.* New York: Wiley.

Sue, D. W. (1992). Culture-specific strategies in counseling: A conceptual framework. *Professional Psychology, 21,* 424–433.

Sue, D. W., and Sue, D. (1990). *Counseling the culturally different. Theory and practice* (2nd ed.). New York: Wiley.

Sue, H. (1992). *Group skills in social work* (2nd ed.). Pacific Grove, CA: Brooks/Cole.

Sue, S., & Zane, N. (1987). The role of culture and cultural techniques in psychotherapy: A critique of reformulation. *American Psychologist, 42(1),* 37–45.

Suls, J., & Fletcher, B. (1985). The relative efficacy of avoidant and non avoidant coping strategies: A meta-analysis. *Health Psychology, 4,* 249–288.

Swenson, C. R. (1998). Clinical social work's contribution to a social justice perspective. *Social Work, 43(6),* 527–537.

Swift, C., & Lewis, G. (1987). Empowerment: An emerging mental health technology. *Journal of Primary Prevention, 8,* 71–94.

Szasz, T. (1994). *Cruel compassion: Psychiatric control of society's unwanted.* New York: Wiley.

Tarasoff v. The Regents of the University of California, 551, p. 2d 334 (California, 1976).

Targum, S. S., Capedanno, A. E., Hoffman, H. A., & Foundraine, C. (1982). Interventions to reduce the rate of hospital discharge against medical advice. *American Journal of Psychiatry, 139(5),* 657–659.

Tatara, T. (1993). *Summaries of the statistical data on elder abuse in domestic settings in FY 90 and FY 91.* Washington, DC: National Aging Resource Center on Elder Abuse.

Tatara, T. (1995). Elder Abuse. In R. Edwards (Ed.), *Encyclopedia of Social Work* (pp. 834–842). Washington, DC: NASW Press.

Taussig, I. M. (1987). Comparative responses of Mexican-Americans and Anglo-Americans to early goal setting in a public mental health clinic. *Journal of Counseling Psychology, 34,* 214–217.

Taylor, J. (1992). *Paved with good intention. The failure of race relations in Continental America.* New York: Carroll & Graf.

Taylor, J. B. (1981). *Using microcomputers in social agencies.* Beverly Hills, CA: Sage.

Taylor, J., & Schneider, B. (1992). The sport-clinical intake protocol: A comprehensive interviewing instrument for applied sport psychology. *Professional Psychology, 23,* 318–325.

Teyber, E. (1992). *Interpersonal process in psychotherapy* (2nd ed.). Pacific Grove, CA: Brooks/Cole.

Teyber, E. (1997). *Interpersonal process in psychotherapy* (3rd ed.). Pacific Grove, CA: Brooks/Cole.

Teyber, E. (2000). *Interpersonal process in psychotherapy: A relational approach* (4th ed.). Pacific Grove, CA: Brooks/Cole.

Thomas, A. P. (1994). *Crime and the sacking of America. The roots of Chaos.* Washington, DC: Brassey's.

Thomas, E. J., & Feldman, R. A. (1967). Concepts of role theory. In E. J. Thomas (Ed.), *Behavioral science for social workers.* New York: Free Press.

Thompson, M. S., & Peebles-Wilkins, W. (1992). The impact of formal, informal and societal support networks on psychological well-being of black adolescent mothers. *Social Work, 37,* 322–329.

Thorndike, E. L. (1911). *Animal intelligence: Experimental studies.* New York: Macmillan.

Thornton, S., & Garrett, K. J. (1995). Ethnography as a bridge to multicultural practice. *Journal of Social Work Education, 31,* 67–74.

Thyer, B. A. (1994). Social learning theory. Empirical applications to culturally diverse practice. In R. R. Greene (Ed.), *Human behavior theory: Diversity applications.* New York: Aldine de Gruyter.

Thyer, B., & Wodarski, J. (1998). *Handbook of empirical social work practice.* New York: Wiley.

Tieman, A. R. (1991). *Group treatment of female incest survivors using TFA systems.* Unpublished doctoral dissertation, Virginia Polytechnic Institute and State University of Blacksburg, Virginia.

Tillich, I. (1962). The philosophy of social work. *Social Service Review, 36*(1), 12–16.

Timms, N. (1972). *Recording in social work.* Boston: Routledge & Kegan Paul.

Tolman, E. C. (1949). There is more than one kind of learning. *Psychology Revised, 56,* 144–155.

Toseland, R. (1987). Treatment discontinuance: Grounds for optimism. *Social Casework, 68,* 195–204.

Toseland, R. W., & Rivas, R. F. (1995). *An introduction to group work practice* (2nd ed.). Boston, MA: Allyn & Bacon.

Tower, K. D. (1994). Consumer-centered social work practice: Restoring client self-determination. *Social Work, 39,* 292–296.

Towle, C. (1945). *Common human needs.* Washington, DC: NASW Press.

Towle, C. (1954). *The learner in education for the profession.* Chicago: University of Chicago Press.

Tracy, B., & DuBois, B. (1987, September). *Information model for generalist social work practice.* Paper presented at the meeting of the Baccalaureate Program Directors of social work programs, Kansas City, KS.

Tracy, E. M., & Whitaker, J. K. (1990). The social network map: Assessing social support in clinical practice. *Families in Society, 72*(8), 461–470.

Trader, H. (1977). Survival strategies for oppressed minorities. *Social Work, 22*(1), 10–13, 30.

Traux, C. B., & Mitchell, K. M. (1971). Research on certain therapist interpersonal skills in relation to process and outcome. In A. Bergin & S. Garfield (Eds.), *Handbook of psychotherapy and behavior change: An empirical analysis* (pp. 299–344). New York: Wiley.

Trickett, E. J., Watts, R., & Birman, D. (1993). Human diversity and community psychology: Still hazy after all these years. *Journal of Community Psychology, 21,* 264–279.

Tripodi, T., Felin, P., & Epstein, I. (1978). *Differential social program evaluation.* Itasca, IL: Peacock.

Troiden, R. R. (1993). The formation of homosexual identities. In L. D. Garnes & D. C. Kimmel (Eds.), *Psychosocial perspectives on lesbian and gay male experiences* (pp. 191–217). New York: Columbia University Press.

Tsui, P., & Schultz, G. L. (1985). Failure of rapport: Why psychotherapeutic engagement fails in the treatment of Asian clients. *American Journal of Orthopsychiatry, 55,* 561–569.

Turner, K. D. (1994). Consumer-centered social work practice: Restoring client self-determination. *Social Work, 39,* 191–196.

Turquet, P. M. (1978). Leadership: The individual in the group. In G. S. Gibbard, J. J. Hartman, & R. D. Mann (Eds.), *Analysis of groups.* San Francisco: Jossey-Bass.

U.S. Bureau of the Census. (1992). Nation's population more urban. *The Census and You, 27*(1), 1–2.

U.S. Bureau of the Census (1995). *Poverty in the United States.* (Current Population Reports, Series P-60, N. 175). Washington, DC: U.S. Government Printing Office.

U.S. Bureau of the Census (1995). *Statistical abstract of the United States: 1995* (115th ed.). Washington, DC: U.S. Government Printing Office.

Uba, L. (1994) *Asian Americans: Personality patterns, identity, and mental health.* New York: Guilford.

Uhlemann, M. R., & Koehn, C. V. (1989). Effects of covert and overt modeling on the communication of empathy. *Canadian Journal of Counseling, 23,* 372–381.

Uhlemann, M., Lee, Y. D., & Martin, J. (1994). Client cognitive responses as a function of quality of counselor verbal responses. *Journal of Counseling and Development, 73,* 198–203.

Vaillant, G. (1999). The alcohol-dependent and drug-dependent person. In A. M. Armand, (Ed.), *The Harvard Guide to Psychiatry* (3rd ed., pp. 672–683). Cambridge, Mass: Belknap Press of Harvard University Press.

Valentine, B. (1978). *Hustling and other hard work.* New York: Free Press.

Van Den Bergh, N. (1995). Employee assistance programs. In *Encyclopedia of Social Work* (Vol. 1, pp. 842–849). Washington, DC: NASW Press.

Van Den Bergh, N., & Cooper, L. B. (1987). Feminist Social Work. In *Encyclopedia of Social Work* (Vol. 1, pp. 610–618). Silver Spring, MD: NASW Press.

Van Den Bergh, N., & Cooper, L. B. (1986). Introduction. In N. Van Den Bergh & L. B. Cooper (Eds.), *Feminist visions for social work* (pp. 1–28). Silver Spring, MD: NASW Press.

Vigilante, J. (1974). Between values and sciences: Education for the profession during a moral crisis or is proof truth? *Journal of Education for Social Work, 10,* 107–115.

Vinter, R. D. (Ed.). (1967). *Readings in group work practice.* Ann Arbor, MI: Campus Publishers.

Von Bertalantfy, Ludwig. (1967). General systems theory. In N. I. Demerath III & R. A. Paterson (Eds.), *Systems changes and conflict* (p. 115). New York: Free Press.

Vonda, O. L. (1996). *Communication skills in helping relationships: A framework for facilitating personal growth.* Pacific Grove, CA: Brooks/Cole.

Vondracek, F., & Corneal, S. (1995). *Strategies for resolving individual and family problems.* Pacific Grove, CA: Brooks/Cole.

Wall, M. D., Kleckner, T., Amendt, J. H., & Bryant, R. D. (1989). Therapeutic compliments: Setting the stage for successful therapy. *Journal of Marriage and Family Therapy, 15,* 159–167.

Walter, J. L., & Peller, J. E. (1992). *Becoming solution-focused in brief therapy.* New York: Brunner/Mazel.

Waltz, T. H., & Blum, N. S. (1987). *Sexual health in later life.* Lexington, MA: Lexington Books.

Ward, D. E. (1982). A model for the more effective use of theory in group work. *Journal for Specialists in Group Work, 7,* 224–230.

Warren, D. (1981). *Helping networks.* Notre Dame, IN: University of Notre Dame Press.

Wartel, S. (1991). Clinical considerations for adults abused as children. *Families in Society, 72*(3) 157–163.

Wasik, B. (1990). *Home visiting procedures for helping families.* Newbury, CA: Sage.

Wasserman, S. L. (1979). Ego psychology. In F. J. Turner, (Ed.), *Social Work Treatment* (2nd ed., pp. 33–68). New York: Free Press.

Watkins, C. E. (1985). Countertransference: Its impact on the counseling situation. *Journal of Counseling and Development, 63*(6), 356–359.

Watkins, C. E. (1990). The effects of counselor self-disclosure. A research review. *The Counseling Psychologist, 18,* 477–500.

Watson, J. B. (1916). Psychology as the behaviorist views it. *Psychological Review, 20,* 158–177.

Watson, J. B. (1925). *Behaviorism.* New York: Norton.

Webb, N. B. (1985). A crisis intervention perspective on termination process. *Clinical Social Work Journal, 13,* 329–340.

Webster's New Universal Unabridged Dictionary. (1996). New York: Random House.

Wehrly, B. (1999). *Pathways to multicultural counseling and competence.* Pacific Grove, CA: Brooks/Cole.

Weiner, M. (1986). *Practical psychotherapy.* New York: Brunner/Mazel.

Weiner, M. E. (1990). *Human services management: Analysis and applications* (2nd ed.). Belmont, CA: Wadsworth.

Weiner-Davis, M., & de Shazer, S., & Gingerich, W. J. (1987). Building on pretreatment change to construct the therapeutic solution: An exploratory study. *Journal of Marital and Family Therapy, 13,* 359–363.

Weisberg, R. (1986). *Creativity, genius, and other myths.* New York: Freeman.

Weiss, M. (1990). Using house calls in psychotherapy practice. In P. Keller & S. Heyman (Eds.), *Innovations in clinical practice. A source book* (Vol. 9, pp. 229–238). Sarasota, FL: Professional Resource Exchange.

Weissman, A. (1976). Industrial social services. Linkage technology. *Social Casework, 57,* 50–54.

Welch, I. D. (1998). *The path of psychotherapy matters of the heart.* Pacific Grove, CA: Brooks/Cole.

Wells, C. C. (1998). *Stepping to the dance: The training of a family therapist.* Pacific Grove, CA: Brooks/Cole.

Werner, H. D. (1967, May). Adler, Freud, and American social work. *Journal of Individual Psychology,* xxiii.

Wernet, S. P. (1999). An introduction to managed care in human services. In S. P. Wernet (Ed.), *Managed care in human services* (pp. 1–18). Chicago, IL: Lyceum.

Westra, M. (1996). *Active communication.* Pacific Grove, CA: Brooks/Cole.

Whiston, S., & Sexton, T. (1993). An overview of psychotherapy outcome research: Implications for practice. *Professional Psychology, 24,* 43–51.

Whitaker, C. A., & Keith, D. V. (1981). Symbolic-experiential family therapy. In A. S. Gurman & D. P. Kniskern (Eds.), *Handbook of family therapy* (pp. 187–225). New York: Brunner/Mazel.

White, M. (1995). *Re-authoring lives: Interviews and essays.* Adelaide, Australia: Dulwich Center Publications.

White, M., & Epston, P. (1990). *Narrative means to therapeutic ends.* New York: Norton.

White, R. (1960). Competence and the psychosexual stages of development. In R. Jones Marshall (Ed.), *Nebraska symposium on maturation* (Vol. 6, pp. 97–141). Lincoln: University of Nebraska Press.

White, R. (1974). Strategies of adaptation: An attempt at systematic description. In G. Coelho, D. Hamburg & J. Adams (Eds.), *Coping and adaptation* (pp. 47–68). New York: Basic.

White, R. W. (1963). Ego and reality in psychoanalytical theory: A proposal regarding independent ego energies. *Psychological Issues, 3*(3), 1–210.

Whitman, D. (1988, February 29). Hope for the homeless. *U.S. News and World Report,* pp. 24–35. Shapiro, J. P., Kalb, D., Golden, S. F., & Dzik, E., in New York, and Ellis-Simons, P., in Los Angeles, contributed to this report.

Whittaker, J. K., & Tracy, E. M. (1991). Social network interventions in intensive family-based preventive services. *Prevention in Human Services, 9*(1), 175–192.

Wickhan, E. (1993). *Group treatment in social work.* Toronto: Thompson.

Wilensky, H., & Lebeaux, C. (1965). *Industrial society and social welfare.* New York: Free Press.

Will, O. (1959). Human relatedness and the schizophrenic reaction. *Psychiatry, 22*(3), 205–223.

Williams, G. C. (1996). *Adaptation and natural selection.* Princeton, NJ: Princeton Science Library.

Wills, T. A. (1985). Supportive functions of interpersonal relationships. In S. Cohen & S. L. Syme (Eds.), *Social support and health* (pp. 61–82). New York: Academic.

Wilshere, P. J. (1996). Mucho Gusto A Conocerie. It has been my pleasure to meet you. Working with migrant farm families. In L. M. Grobman (Ed.), *Days in the lives of social workers.* (pp. 245–249). Harrisburg, PA: White Hat.

Wilson, W. J. (1996). *When work disappears. The world of the new urban poor.* New York: Vintage.

Wingate, P. (1972). *The Penguin medical encyclopedia.* Harmondsworth; Eng.: Penguin.

Wichita Eagle. (1998, August 7). p. 11a.

Wolin, S. J., & Wolin, S. (1993). *The resilient self: How survivors of troubled families rise above adversity.* New York: Villard.

Woltersdorf, M. A. (1992). Videotaping, self-modeling in the treatment of attention-deficit hyperactivity disorder. *Child and Family Behavior Therapy, 14,* 53–73.

Wood, K. (1978). Casework effectiveness: A new look at the research evidence. *Social Work, 23,* 437–458.

Woods, M. E., & Hollis, F. (1990). *Social casework: A psychosocial therapy* (4th ed.). New York: Random House.

Worchel, S., Cooper, J., & Goethals, G. R. (1988). *Understanding social psychology* (4th ed.). Chicago: Dorsey.

Worden, M. (1999). *Family therapy basics* (2nd ed.). Pacific Grove, CA: Brooks/Cole.

Worthington, E. (1989). Matching family treatment in family stressors. In C. Figley (Ed.), *Treating stress in families* (pp. 44–63). New York: Brunner/Mazel.

Woy, J. R., & Efran, J. S. (1972). Systematic desensitization and expectancy in the treatment of speaking anxiety. *Behavior Research and Therapy, 10,* 43–49.

Wynne, L. C. (1961). The study of intrafamilial alignments and splits in exploratory family therapy. In N. W. Ackerman, F. L. Beatman, & N. Sherman (Eds.), *Exploring the base for family therapy.*

Yalom, I. (1983). *Inpatient group psychotherapy.* New York: Basic Books.

Yalom, I. (1985). *The theory and practice of group psychotherapy.* New York: Basic Books.

Yessian, M. R., & Broskowski, A. (1983). Generalists in human service systems: Their problems and prospects. In R. M. Kramer & H. Specht (Eds.), *Readings in community organization practice* (pp. 180–198). Englewood Cliffs, NJ: Prentice-Hall.

Zastrow, C. (1989). *The practice of social work* (3rd ed.). Chicago, IL: Dorsey.

Zastrow, C. (1992). *The practice of social work* (4th ed.). Belmont: Wadsworth.

Zastrow, C. (1995). *The practice of social work practice* (5th ed.). Belmont, CA: Wadsworth.

Zastrow, C. (1997). *Social work with groups.* Pacific Grove, CA: Brooks/Cole.

Zastrow, C., & Kirst-Ashman, K. (1990). *Understanding human behavior and the social environment* (2nd ed.). Chicago: Nelson-Hall.

Zuckerman, E. (1995). *The clinician's thesaurus: The guide for working psychological reports* (4th ed.). Sarasota, FL: Professional Resource Press.

Zuk, G. (1968). The side-tracking function in family therapy. *American Journal of Orthopsychiatry, 38,* 553–559.

INDEX